PROPORTION

Of the many arguments for proportion systems in architecture the most ancient and compelling is that the natural world is an intelligible, mathematically ordered whole, and the artifacts we place in it, as extensions of nature, should obey the same laws. Although this was still the argument of Le Corbusier – as earlier of Alberti – it was profoundly shaken by post-Renaissance science and the empiricist philosophy which flowed from it.

In *Proportion*, Richard Padovan looks at the problem from a new angle, taking empiricism as a starting-point. In order to know anything about the world, we have to discover regularities in it. These regularities can be explained not by assuming that they are inherent in nature and that nature impresses them on the mind but that they are inherent in the mind and the mind impresses them on nature. Our perception of the world, our scientific hypotheses, are therefore artifacts, no less than our buildings and other works of art. Both science and art are ways of making the world intelligible; that is to say, of making an intelligible world. And in art as in science the key to intelligibility is mathematical order.

Richard Padovan lectures at the University of Bath. He has worked as an architect in various European countries and published extensively. He is the author of *Dom Hans van der Laan: Modern Primitive* (1994) and his translation of Van der Laan's *Architectonic Space* appeared in 1983.

Without waiting, passively, for repetitions to impress or impose regularities upon us, we actively try to impose regularities upon the world.

(Karl Popper, Conjectures and Refutations)

PROPORTION

SCIENCE, PHILOSOPHY, ARCHITECTURE

RICHARD PADOVAN

LONDON AND NEW YORK

First published 1999 by E & FN Spon

Reprinted 2001, 2003

by Spon Press

2 Park Square, Milton Park, Abingdon, Oxon OX14 4RN

Simultaneously published in the USA and Canada

by Routledge

270 Madison Ave, New York, NY 10016

Transferred to Digital Printing 2008

Routledge is an imprint of the Taylor & Francis Group, an Informa business

Typeset in Bembo by Solidus (Bristol) Limited

Printed and bound in Great Britain by

TJI Digital, Padstow, Cornwall

British Library Cataloguing in Publication Data

A catalogue record for this book is available from the British Library

Library of Congress Cataloguing in Publication Data

Padovan, Richard

Proportion : science, philosophy, architecture / Richard Padovan.

p. cm.

Includes bibliographical references and index.

ISBN 0-419-22780-8 (pbk.)

1. Architecture—Composition, proportion, etc. I. Title.

NA2760.P34 1999

720′.1—dc21 98-49274

CIP

ISBN 10: 0-419-22780-6
ISBN 13: 978-0-41922780-9

CONTENTS

LIST OF FIGURES

PREFACE

In my schooldays, mathematics was for me a nightmare. What made this worse was that from an early age I wanted to be an architect, and my elders warned me that mathematics was essential for architecture. It seemed that my inveterate inability to get a sum right would for ever bar me from my chosen profession.

Nevertheless, I somehow got to architecture school, where a number of things helped to cure me of my phobia. First, I was relieved to find that most of my fellow students were no better at mathematics than I was (or alas, still am). But above all I began to discover what my previous teachers had never suggested: that numbers and geometrical constructions are beautiful in themselves, and moreover that they are a source of beauty in the things around us, such as crystals, plants, animals and buildings.

In the preface to my earlier book, *Dom Hans van der Laan: Modern Primitive*, I tell the story of my early captivation with Le Corbusier's *modulor*, followed by a virtual loss of faith in proportion systems until a chain of happy accidents brought me into contact with Van der Laan and his work, and revived the old fascination. In that book, however, only one chapter is devoted to proportion, and then almost exclusively to Van der Laan's own proportion system, the *plastic number*.

My original intention in writing the present study was to broaden the scope of that single chapter, bringing together everything I had learnt about architectural proportion in the nearly fifty years since I first became aware of it. I described it to my publisher as 'both a handbook and a polemic'. The book was to have two aspects: on the one hand, it would be a comparative guide to the known proportion systems, and on the other it would set out various arguments for and against the use of mathematical rules of proportion in art. In the end, although the text has become much longer, its scope has become narrower. I concluded that it must be either a handbook or a polemic; it could not be both, and I chose the latter. Furthermore, a polemic could not present all the arguments and counter-arguments, but must focus on one.

Paradoxically, the argument that finally took over the whole book was the one that initially I had planned to mention briefly only to reject it as no longer relevant: the ancient idea that the world is a harmonious mathematical creation, and that, in order to participate in that harmony, the things we make must obey the same mathematical laws. When I began to write, I accepted unquestioningly Rudolf Wittkower's conclusion that the scientific revolution of the seventeenth century and the empiricist philosophy that flowed from it had shaken, 'perhaps for all time', the universal values that had formerly provided the objective foundation of proportion systems, and that in the absence of such values art was bound to fall back on individual subjective judgement.[1] In the process of writing, I have become convinced that the quarrel between what I shall call 'empathy' and 'abstraction' is not yet over, nor did it begin only in the seventeenth century. Moreover, it seems to me that neither side in the debate removes the philosophical ground for using mathematical ordering systems in art. On the one hand it is still possible for a twentieth century architect like Le Corbusier to write that 'nature is ruled by mathematics, and the masterpieces of art. . . express the laws of nature and themselves proceed from those laws;'[2] on the other, one can equally justify systems of measure as empirical frameworks that we do not derive from, but impose upon, nature.

The debate between these two points of view has become the backbone of this book. It would be strange, however, if a work on architectural proportion contained no examples of the use of systems in architecture; and the underlying mathematics of the systems must be outlined if these examples are to be understandable. Therefore the more or less chronological history of ideas breaks off from time to time to describe the systems as such, or to give proportional analyses of single buildings.

I am indebted to all those people, far too many to name individually, who have helped or encouraged my investigation of proportion over the years, and especially to those who have contributed directly to the existence and the final form of this book.

1. R. Wittkower, 'The changing concept of proportion', in *Idea and Image*, Thames & Hudson, 1978, pp. 117, 122.
2. Le Corbusier, *The Modulor*, Faber & Faber, 1961, pp. 29–30.

Chapter one

THE HARMONY OF THE WORLD MADE MANIFEST IN FORM AND NUMBER

Language analysts believe that there are no genuine philosophical problems, or that the problems of philosophy, if any, are problems of linguistic usage, or of the meaning of words. I, however, believe that there is at least one philosophical problem in which all thinking men are interested. It is the problem of cosmology: the problem of understanding the world – including ourselves, and our knowledge, as part of the world.[1]

1.1 NOT WITH A BANG, BUT A WHIMPER

On 18 June 1957 the motion 'that Systems of Proportion make good design easier and bad design more difficult' was defeated, by 60 votes to 48, in a debate at the Royal Institute of British Architects in London. The debate is remarkable less for the arguments put forward than for its timing: just ten years after the appearance in 1947 of Colin Rowe's *The Mathematics of the Ideal Villa*.[2] Rowe's essay coincided with the start of a period during which the theory of proportion and the application of mathematical systems to design became a burning issue in architecture. It was followed, a few years later, by a trio of more substantial publications: *Architectural Principles in the Age of Humanism*, in which Rowe's tutor Rudolf Wittkower presented Renaissance architecture in a new light, as an abstract art of mathematical harmonies;[3] *Le Modulor*, Le Corbusier's exposition of a new system of proportions derived from the golden section and the human body;[4] and *Symmetry*,[5] an account by the eminent

1. K.R. Popper, *The Logic of Scientific Discovery*, Hutchinson, 1959, p. 15.
2. C. Rowe, 'The mathematics of the ideal villa', first publ. in *Architectural Review*, 1947; and in C. Rowe, *The Mathematics of the Ideal Villa and Other Essays*, MIT Press, 1976, pp. 1–27.
3. R. Wittkower, *Architectural Principles in the Age of Humanism*, Warburg Institute, 1949; Alec Tiranti, 1952.
4. Le Corbusier, *Le Modulor*, Editions de l'Architecture d'aujourd'hui, 1950; *The Modulor*, Faber & Faber, 1954, paperback edition 1961.
5. H. Weyl, *Symmetry*, Princeton University Press, 1952.

mathematician Hermann Weyl of the laws governing symmetry and proportional harmony in art and nature. The summit of this wave of enthusiasm, but also the first signs of its decline, can be identified with the holding, in 1951, of the First International Congress on Proportion in the Arts at the Ninth Triennale in Milan.

According to Rudolf Wittkower the Milan congress fizzled out 'without making an appreciable impact on the younger generation'.[6] By 1957, the year of the RIBA debate, the focus of architectural thought was already shifting in other directions – to the question of space,[7] and about a decade later to semiotics.[8] One of the opposers of the motion, Peter Smithson, declared that

> Proportion was important to architects, as a matter of tooth and claw debate, in 1948 and 1949. Then one could have had a debate in which people's actual beliefs were tested against other people's strident disbeliefs, rather than this somewhat polite exchange of qualified attitudes... If one went to look at the Palladian buildings in 1948, one could not step an inch without tripping over an architect, and what were they all there for? They were looking for something to believe in.[9]

Ten years later, that quest for a faith was ending with half-hearted apologies and lame excuses.

The motion itself betrayed the narrowing of vision since the heady days of the 1940s. As Misha Black, leading the opposition, put it: 'The conviction is diluted to something which makes good design easier (as though design were a safe which could be cracked with the help of a system of numbers)...'[10] The wording of the motion was borrowed from Albert Einstein's comment on the *modulor,* when Le Corbusier presented it to him at Princeton in 1946, that it 'makes the bad difficult and the good easy.'[11] Note that Einstein did not say 'bad design' and 'good design': simply '*the* bad' and '*the* good'. He had in mind something wider and more all-embracing than aesthetics: a moral goodness, or even a cosmological one, of which the visual appearance of a work of art was no more than the outward sign. In contrast, by 1957, at least for the proposers of the motion (E. Maxwell Fry and W.E. Tatton Brown), proportion had come to be regarded as entirely an aesthetic matter, and proportion systems simply as devices or prescriptions for avoiding

6. R. Wittkower. 'The changing concept of proportion', in *Architects' Year Book V*, 1953; reprinted in *Idea and Image*, Thames & Hudson, 1978, p. 121.
7. See for example B. Zevi, *Architecture as Space*, Horizon Press, 1957.
8. See for example U. Eco, *La struttura assente: Introduzione alla ricerca semiologica*, Bompiani, 1968; reprinted as 'Function and sign: the semiotics of architecture', in G. Broadbent, R. Bunt and C. Jencks (eds), *Signs, Symbols, and Architecture*, John Wiley & Sons, 1980, pp. 11–69.
9. P. Smithson, quoted in report on debate, *RIBA Journal*, Sept. 1957, p. 461.
10. M. Black, quoted in report on debate, *RIBA Journal*, Sept. 1957, p. 459.
11. Le Corbusier, *The Modulor*, 1961, p. 58.

shapes that were ugly and for making shapes that were pleasing.

The difficulty with the aesthetic argument for proportion is that it quickly becomes entangled in a mesh of contradictions. Are certain shapes or relations inherently more pleasing than others? If so, how can one explain the fact that the buildings of both Palladio and Le Corbusier are regarded as beautifully proportioned, although they are based on quite different mathematical principles?[12] In any case, is not the aesthetic impact of a work more or less instantaneous, whereas to appreciate the underlying mathematical relations – leaving aside the problem of their distortion by perspective – requires patient study, measurement and calculation? And again: do the rules constitute fundamental principles to be followed at the start of the design process, or are they to be applied only as correctives at the end? If the former, and if the recipes are effective, do taste and talent become superfluous? But if the latter, must not the adjustment of forms conceived in the white heat of creativity, to fit a rigid set of mathematical formulae, lead inevitably to a watering down or a deadening of the original inspiration?

For Le Corbusier, and apparently also for Einstein, the *modulor's* proportions were 'good' because they were in harmony with nature's laws, which however subtle are ultimately consistent and graspable by human reason. Einstein's comment on the *modulor*, interpreted in the light of his general attitude to science, accords entirely with the view of architectural proportion held up to and during the Renaissance. 'God', as he famously remarked, 'does not play dice with the world.' And: 'Without the belief that it is possible to grasp the reality with our theoretical constructions, without the belief in the inner harmony of our world, there could be no science.'[13]

Mathematical systems of order in art have always been connected, of course, with visual beauty, but beauty in art was formerly regarded not just as an optical phenomenon but as the outward sign of something more profound: an accord with the general harmony of the world. It was from this deeper harmony that it derived its 'goodness' or its 'truth'. Alberti called such order *concinnitas* (mutual agreement or harmony), and he saw it as the underlying law of nature. In the ninth of his ten books *On the Art of Building* he writes that 'Everything that Nature produces is regulated

12. P.H. Scholfield, *The Theory of Proportion in Architecture*, Cambridge University Press, 1958, p. 5.

13. A. Einstein and L. Infeld, *The Evolution of Physics*, Simon & Schuster, 1938, p. 296.

by the law of *concinnitas*, and her chief concern is that whatever she produces should be absolutely perfect.' And since 'It is in our nature to desire the best, and to cling to it with pleasure,' it follows that

> When you make judgements on beauty, you do not follow mere fancy, but the workings of a reasoning faculty that is inborn in the mind. . . For within the form and figure of a building there resides some natural excellence and perfection that excites the mind and is immediately recognized by it.[14]

In the opening pages of his *Architectural Principles*, Wittkower attributes the practice of mathematical harmony by Alberti and others to an underlying *spirituality* of aim, contradicting the then customary interpretation of Renaissance architecture as the expression of a new worldliness.[15] The term 'Humanism' should not, he implies, be misinterpreted as meaning that the Renaissance valued only, or even chiefly, the human as opposed to the divine, or that the age sought in art only that which was pleasing to the human eye. In the RIBA debate, Smithson quoted with approval Wittkower's remark that

> It is obvious that. . . mathematical relations between plan and section cannot be correctly perceived when one walks about in a building. Alberti knew that, of course, quite as well as we do. We must therefore conclude that the harmonic perfection of the geometrical scheme represents an absolute value, independent of our subjective and transitory perception. And. . . for Alberti – as for other Renaissance architects – this man-created harmony was a visible echo of a celestial and universally valid harmony.[16]

Le Corbusier, like Einstein, had a breadth of vision that makes him an heir to that Renaissance mentality. No other Modern Movement architect has given so central a role to mathematical proportion in architecture. Mathematical law is, for him, not just a prescription for beauty, nor even a means by which human beings are somehow able to comprehend their world, but the axis or ruling principle of the universe itself, and the source of the unity and harmony of nature and of art. Near the start of *Le Modulor* he quotes

14. L.B. Alberti, *On the Art of Building in Ten Books*, MIT Press, 1988, pp. 302–3.
15. R. Wittkower, *Architectural Principles in the Age of Humanism*, 1952, p. 1.
16. *Ibid.*, p. 7.

his own statement to the Swiss mathematician Andreas Speiser that

> Nature is ruled by mathematics, and the masterpieces of art are in consonance with nature; they express the laws of nature and themselves proceed from those laws. Consequently, they too are governed by mathematics, and the scholar's implacable reasoning and unerring formulae may be applied to art.[17]

The argument demands, if not a religious faith, at least a mystical attitude to nature, such as is expressed by the biologist Sir D'Arcy Thompson in the epilogue of his book *On Growth and Form*, from which I have taken the title of this chapter: 'For the harmony of the world is made manifest in Form and Number, and the heart and soul and all the poetry of Natural Philosophy are embodied in the concept of mathematical beauty.'[18] Underlying Le Corbusier's approach is the implication that a guiding intelligence or will governs the universe:

> This axis leads us to assume a unity of conduct in the universe and to admit a single will behind it. . . and if we recognize (and love) science and its works, it is because both one and the other force us to admit that they are prescribed by this primal will. If the results of mathematical calculation appear satisfying and harmonious to us, it is because they proceed from the axis. If, through calculation, the airplane takes on the aspect of a fish or some object of nature, it is because it has recovered the axis.[19]

Thus (even if only by a side door) God the Geometer enters the scene, armed with a gigantic pair of dividers, much as he was pictured in Medieval manuscripts. Just as the Medieval architect, according to Otto von Simson, felt that by submitting to geometry he was imitating the work of the Creator, who had composed the world according to geometrical laws,[20] so Le Corbusier believed that the artist 'feels and discerns nature and translates it in his own works', and that the key to this process lay in 'the spirit of geometry which is in man as it is also in the very law of nature'.[21]

If Le Corbusier's, Alberti's and Einstein's belief in the mathematical rationality of nature can be sustained, it

---

17. Le Corbusier, *The Modulor*, pp. 29–30.
18. D'A.W. Thompson, *On Growth and Form*, abridged edn, Cambridge University Press, 1961, pp. 326–7.
19. Le Corbusier, *Towards a New Architecture*, Architectural Press, 1946, pp.192–3.
20. O. von Simson, *The Gothic Cathedral*, Harper & Row, 1964, p. 35.
21. Le Corbusier, *The Modulor*, p. 30.

provides the strongest and deepest possible foundation for the use of mathematical rules of proportion in art – a foundation compared with which the arguments put forward at the RIBA in 1957 are revealed in all their shallowness. If the universe and everything it contains, including our own bodies, are governed by mathematical harmony, what could be more reasonable than to apply a parallel – though not necessarily identical – harmony to the things we add to that universe? The question whether the mathematical relations can be perceived by the eye when one walks about in a building then becomes a secondary, even a trivial one: they are intended, as it were, for the eye of God. On the other hand, if no such universal harmony can be shown to exist, what other justification, if any, can be found for using proportion systems in art?

1.2 CRITIQUE OF WITTKOWER

The search for answers to these questions is the main subject of this book – the child of a love affair with proportion that began for me almost fifty years ago. I became a student of architecture in 1952, when *Le Modulor* was only two years old, and the first widely available edition of *Architectural Principles* had just been published by Tiranti. I was captivated immediately, and the spell has never worn off. But by 1957, when I finished my studies, general interest in the subject was petering out. It has remained unfashionable ever since, confined to a fringe of more or less mystically inclined researchers,[22] or surviving as a marginal aspect of the study of architectural geometry.[23]

Wittkower, who attended the ill-fated RIBA debate, concluded that faith in mathematical rules of proportion was necessarily a thing of the past: 'We are in a particularly bad position as regards proportion. . . We cannot find a position of belief as individuals because a broader foundation is lacking. . .'[24] The aim of the present book is to investigate the validity of this assessment. I have no quarrel with Wittkower's essential thesis – set out at the start of his brilliantly lucid and concise summary of the history of mathematical systems in art, 'The changing concept of proportion' – that the same order was formerly expressed in science, art and architecture; and that the present age, in which artistic proportion tends to be regarded as a matter of

22. See for example K. Critchlow, *Order in Space*, Thames & Hudson, 1969; G. Doczi, *The Power of Limits*, Shambhala Publications, 1981; R. Lawlor, *Sacred Geometry*, Thames & Hudson, 1982; J. Michell, *The Dimensions of Paradise*, Thames & Hudson, 1988.
23. See for example R. Evans, *The Projective Cast*, MIT Press, 1995; A. Pérez-Gómez and L. Pelletier, *Architectural Representation and the Perspective Hinge*, MIT Press, 1997.
24. R. Wittkower, quoted in report on debate, *RIBA Journal*, Sept. 1957, p. 462.

individual subjective judgement, is in this respect untypical. Wittkower's aim, he writes, will be to try to explain the causes of this change.

He attributes them to the collapse of the broad cosmological foundation of proportion as a result of the Galilean and Newtonian scientific revolution:

> In the new era which dawned, beauty and proportion were no longer regarded as being universal, but were turned into psychological phenomena originating and existing in the mind of the artist. Thus beauty and proportion became dependent on what was believed to be an irrational creative urge. This was the answer of the artist to the new conception of the universe which emerged from the 17th century onwards – a universe of mechanical laws, of iron necessity with no ulterior plan, a universe in which the artist had to find his bearings by substituting purely subjective standards for the old super-personal ones.[25]

I differ from Wittkower's conclusions in three main respects:

(1) The decline of numerical systems of proportion began in architecture more than a century before Newton published his laws; this decline was associated with the rise of Mannerism in the mid-sixteenth century, and continued with the Baroque. The impact of Newtonian science did not lead to a turning away from these systems, but coincided with their *revival*, in the work of English neo-Palladians like Robert Morris, and in the treatises of C.-E. Briseux and Bernardo Vittone.[26] And there is no obvious reason why the universe revealed by seventeenth-century science should have undermined the cosmological basis of proportion systems in art. That universe was certainly governed by 'mechanical laws', but it was far from being without an 'ulterior plan'. No conception of nature has been more perfectly harmonious and unified – the whole reducible, essentially, to a single mathematical proportion: Newton's famous equation for gravity. And this perfectly functioning machine was conceived and constantly maintained in working order by a divine Creator, of Whose existence it constituted the strongest proof. As Newton argues, 'This most beautiful system of the sun, planets, and comets could

25. R. Wittkower, 'The changing concept of proportion', p. 117.
26. A. Pérez-Gómez, *Architecture and the Crisis of Modern Science*, MIT Press, 1983, p. 77.

only proceed from the counsel and domination of an intelligent and powerful Being.' Oddly enough, in the opening paragraph of the essay, Wittkower seems to undermine his own theory. He argues – citing Galileo's study of the laws of accelerated motion – that the fact that modern science interprets nature in predominantly mathematical terms is not something that *distinguishes* our civilization from those of the past, but that on the contrary,

> All higher civilizations believed in an order based on numbers and relations of numbers, and. . . sought and established a harmony, often a fanciful and mystical one, between universal and cosmic concepts and the life of man.[27]

It is true that he goes on to connect the expression of this order and harmony in art and architecture with the fact that these 'were devoted to religious, ritual, cosmological and magical purposes.'[28] But this implies that it was the increasingly secular function of buildings, rather than developments in science, that destroyed the mathematical basis of proportion in modern Western art. That, of course, would be an entirely different argument; and it is not the one that Wittkower chooses to pursue.

(2) Although there has always been a relation between cosmological ideas and architecture – a relation that it is one of the aims of this book to illustrate – documented examples of the direct impact on architecture of discoveries in mathematics or science are scarce. The influence of the Pythagorean numerical harmonies expounded in Plato's *Timaeus* on the Italian Renaissance architecture studied by Wittkower in his *Architectural Principles* is the exception rather than the rule; and it is significant that Alberti's *On the Art of Building* was written around 1450, eighteen centuries after Plato's dialogue. Conversely, the many attempts to prove that the same mathematics influenced ancient Greek architecture – for instance, the proportions of the Parthenon (*c.* 468–432 BC) – remain inconclusive. It seems that the mathematics of architectural proportion has generally developed alongside, but independently of, changing ideas about the mathematics of the universe. The relation was based on analogy, not on direct equivalence. A building was designed in accordance with mathematical laws, *just as* the universe was believed to be. But there was no need for these laws to be identical in both. The mathematics of architectural proportion has always

27. R. Wittkower, 'The changing concept of proportion', p. 109.
28. *Ibid.*

been of a kind suited to the forms and techniques of building, and these have changed little in their essentials, even today.
(3) What finally placed a gulf between the human mind and the external world, and therefore between the works of man and of nature, was not a development in science but the doubts raised about half a century later – as Wittkower himself recognizes in the closing pages of *Architectural Principles*[29] – by David Hume and other empiricist philosophers about the possibility of any certain knowledge of the external world. Hume drew a sharp distinction between 'relations of ideas' and 'matters of fact'. The first – exemplified by mathematics, and presumably also by its offspring, systems of proportion – were certain, and discoverable by pure thought. But they had no necessary relation to the external world: 'Though there never were a circle or a triangle in nature, the truths demonstrated by Euclid would for ever retain their certainty and evidence.'[30] On the other hand, our knowledge of matters of fact was uncertain, being based only on induction from repeated experience: '*That the sun will not rise tomorrow* is no less intelligible a proposition. . . than the affirmation, *that it will rise*.'[31] Or as Einstein would remark nearly two hundred years later, 'As far as the propositions of mathematics refer to reality, they are not certain; and as far as they are certain, they do not refer to reality.'[32] Applied to the sphere of art, the effect of Hume's criticism is to reduce decisions to what Wittkower calls 'psychological phenomena operating. . . in the mind of the artist'. Like empirical judgements of 'matters of fact', they are based only on repeated observation – in this case, observation of that which is generally found pleasing – coupled with the artist's individual 'genius'.[33] Artistic choices become a question of taste.

Bertrand Russell writes in his *History of Western Philosophy* that by making empiricism self-consistent, Hume made it incredible:

> The growth of unreason throughout the nineteenth century and what has passed of the twentieth is a natural sequel to Hume's destruction of empiricism. It is therefore important to discover whether there is any answer to be found to Hume within the framework of a philosophy that is wholly or mainly empirical. If not, there is no intellectual difference between sanity and insanity.[34]

29. R. Wittkower, *Architectural Principles in the Age of Humanism*, 1952, pp. 131–4.
30. D. Hume, *Enquiry Concerning Human Understanding*, Oxford University Press, 1975, p. 25.
31. *Ibid.*, pp. 25–6.
32. A. Einstein, 'Geometry and experience', lecture to the Prussian Academy of Sciences, 1921, in *Ideas and Opinions*, Dell Publishing Co., 1954, p. 228.
33. D. Hume, 'Of the standard of taste', in *Essays: Moral, Political and Literary*, Oxford University Press, 1963, pp. 235–6.
34. B. Russell, *History of Western Philosophy*, George Allen & Unwin, 1961, p. 646.

Among the side effects of Hume's undermining of all certainty in human knowledge was the 'growth of unreason' that has characterized much of the architecture of the past two centuries: the abandonment by the artist of 'objective standards of proportion'[35] and the reliance instead on what Wittkower calls 'an irrational creative urge'.[36]

In philosophy, however, a bridgehead beyond the dead end left by Hume was in fact quickly established by Immanuel Kant. Nor has nineteenth- and twentieth-century thought been so largely given over to unreason as Russell suggests. Among recent philosophers who have strenghened the bridgehead, Karl Popper strikes me as having a particular resonance for architecture. His answer to Hume's scepticism is to turn it on its head:

> Instead of explaining our propensity to expect regularities as the result of repetition, I proposed to explain repetition-for-us as the result of our propensity to expect regularities and to search for them. . . Without waiting, passively, for repetitions to impress or impose regularities upon us, we actively try to impose regularities on the world.[37]

That statement might stand as the *leitmotiv* of the present book, in which I claim to have done little more than apply Popper's solution of the problem of scientific discovery to that of architectural proportion. I shall argue that architectural proportion can be re-founded on the basis, no longer of the unity of nature and art, but of their duality. It need no longer be derived from the order of nature, but imposed upon it. In the words of Kant: 'The order and regularity in objects, which we entitle *nature*, we ourselves introduce.'[38]

1.3 BUILDING AND KNOWING

An alternative title for this book might have been 'Architecture and Epistemology'. Its argument can be summarized as follows.

The primary reason why systems of proportion have been and continue to be important for architecture is that they enable our buildings to embody a mathematical order that we either *distil out of* or *impose upon* nature. Besides this, the other reasons commonly put forward – that these systems bring about a pleasing visual harmony, or that through

35. R. Wittkower, 'The changing concept of proportion', p. 117.
36. *Ibid.*
37. K.R. Popper, *Conjectures and Refutations*, Routledge & Kegan Paul, 1965, p. 46.
38. I. Kant, quoted in A. Flew (ed.) *A Dictionary of Philosophy*, Pan Books, 1979, p. 176.

modular coordination they enable building components to fit together neatly and without waste – are relatively trivial. To investigate the parallels between measure in architecture and the mathematics of nature is therefore the basic aim of this study.

The question whether mathematics is inherent in nature and distilled out of it by human reason, or is a construction of the human mind that we impose upon nature in order to measure it, has been debated by mathematicians and philosophers at least since Pythagoras (*c.* 530 BC). According to the first view the mathematical order that we discover more or less imperfectly manifested in phenomena constitutes their true or essential nature. The primary purpose of studying mathematics is to penetrate beyond the shifting appearances of things and lay bare this essence. Hermann Weyl, whose book *Symmetry* is mentioned above as one of the high points of the heyday of proportion in the early 1950s, has said that

> There is inherent in nature a hidden harmony that reflects itself in our minds under the image of simple mathematical laws. That then is the reason why events in nature are predictable by a combination of observation and mathematical analysis.[39]

Mathematics is not just the instrument of knowledge, but its object: not only the way, but the goal.

At the opposite extreme, mathematics can be regarded as a purely artifical construction, a system of conventional signs and the rules for manipulating them. All assertions about the ultimate nature of the universe, whether mathematical or not, are rejected as 'metaphysical'. No knowledge is possible, unless it come first through the senses; but such knowledge is at best uncertain. The certainty of mathematics is due precisely to the fact that it is man-made, the uncertainty of nature to the fact that it is not. For the only way to know something is to make it oneself. Truth is literally *fact*: that which is made (*factum*). If natural phenomena, when we investigate them, appear to conform remarkably well to mathematical laws, it is because that investigation involves first sieving them through a mathematical mesh of our own devising. In the words of Sir Arthur Eddington, who in 1919 conducted the tests that confirmed Einstein's general theory of relativity:

39. H. Weyl, lecture, quoted in M. Kline, *Mathematics: The Loss of Certainty*, Oxford University Press, 1980, p. 347.

> The mind has by its selective power fitted the processes of Nature into a frame of law or a pattern largely of his own choosing; and in the discovery of this system of law the mind may be regarded as regaining from Nature that which the mind has put into Nature.[40]

Historians of philosophy generally denote these two opposed viewpoints by such terms as 'realism' or 'rationalism' on the one hand, and 'nominalism', 'empiricism' or 'positivism' on the other. The problem with these terms is that they tend to be attached to particular historical periods, or have different meanings according to which century is being referred to. Moreover, since my real goal is architecture and not philosophy, it seems more appropriate if possible to employ art-historical labels, and the terms 'empathy' and 'abstraction', first used as contraries by Wilhelm Worringer in 1909, suggest themselves. I shall describe as 'empathy' the tendency to hold that, being ourselves part of nature, we have a natural affinity with it and an innate ability to know and understand it. Le Corbusier calls this affinity 'an indefinable trace of the Absolute which lies in the depths of our being'.[41] I shall describe as 'abstraction' the contrary tendency to regard nature as elusive and perhaps ultimately unfathomable, and science and art as abstractions, artificial constructions that we hold up against nature in order in some sense to grasp it and command it. The first approach leads to a 'naturalistic' art – and in the case of architecture, to a metaphorical representation of natural forms, for instance by imitating the proportions of the human body. The second leads to an 'abstract' art and architecture in which no reference to natural forms is made.

One would expect both arguments to be reflected in the literature of architectural proportion, just as they are in philosophy. In fact, however, the former view has predominated to the virtual exclusion of the latter. Even today, empirically minded architects are inclined to reject the use of mathematical systems altogether, while the champions of proportion, like Le Corbusier, belong almost universally to the empathic tradition. Architecture is for Le Corbusier

> the first manifestation of man creating his own universe, creating it in the image of nature, submitting to the laws which govern our own nature, our universe. . . A supreme

40. A.S. Eddington, *The Nature of the Physical World*, Everyman's Library, 1935, p. 238.
41. Le Corbusier, *Towards a New Architecture*, p. 187.

> determinism illuminates for us the creations of nature and gives us the security of something poised and reasonably made, of something modulated, evolved, varied and unified.[42]

The outstanding exception to this rule is the Dutch Benedictine monk-architect Dom Hans van der Laan, the only architectural writer I can think of who proposed an unequivocally empirical theory of proportion. 'Our understanding,' he writes, 'is wholly based on our sensory perception. No intellectual knowledge is possible, unless it has first been passed through the senses.'[43] And he asserts that the system of proportion he discovered, the *plastic number*, was not derived from nature and applied to architecture but, on the contrary, manifested in architecture and imposed upon nature.[44] He completely rejects Le Corbusier's naturalistic determinism:

> The form of the house. . . is not determined by nature, like the nest of a bird. . . Wherever the human intellect intervenes as the formative principle, there immediately appears a breach with the homogeneous world of natural forms.[45]

The main aim of this book is to put the case for the epistemological approach to architectural proportion as such, irrespective of whether that approach is based on 'abstraction' or 'empathy'. As a disciple of Van der Laan, however, I am perhaps inevitably drawn more to the abstractionist side of the argument. In view of the vast imbalance in favour of the opposite tendency in the existing literature, that seems to be no bad thing.

1.4. THE REBUILDING OF CONVICTION

Although the structure of this book is roughly chronological, it does not aim to provide a complete history of architectural proportion, still less of science and philosophy. In Le Corbusier's words, it is 'the outcome of a passion'.[46] I have written it out of a need to sort out my own ideas; to complete a gradual rebuilding of conviction that, following an almost total loss of faith in the 1960s, has continued

42. *Ibid.*, pp. 69–70.
43. H. van der Laan, lecture, Breda, 11 June 1946, p. 3.
44. H. van der Laan, in an unpublished letter to W. Lockefeer, 6 April 1983, p. 3.
45. H. van der Laan, *Het plastische getal*, E.J. Brill, 1967, p. 6.
46. Le Corbusier, *The Modulor*, p. 80.

through the 1970s, 1980s and 1990s. That rebuilding was made possible by my encounter with the work and thought of Van der Laan, who will appear here as the companion figure to Le Corbusier, and at the same time as his antithesis. I have chosen these two architects as representatives of the two contrasting philosophical currents that run through the book.

My goal is to throw light not on the past, but on the immediate future. I do not aspire to set the historical record straight – as Wittkower sought to do by uncovering, in *Architectural Principles*, the symbolic mathematical and spiritual harmonies that underlay the classical forms of Renaissance architecture, or as Lionel March, digging still deeper and over a wider terrain, has in turn recently exposed vast tracts unexplored by Wittkower.[47] In this respect my intention is closer to that of Van der Laan in *Architectonic Space*[48] or Le Corbusier in *Le Modulor*, and closer still, perhaps, to that of Jay Hambidge in *The Elements of Dynamic Symmetry*. None of these last three writers was interested in history for its own sake; what interested them was the light it could throw on the relevance of proportion for an architect working today. They used and misused history to that end. Van der Laan's analysis of Stonehenge in *Architectonic Space* is at variance with the probable order of its construction; but its real purpose is to show how we, *today*, might 'gain an insight into the disposition of the human habitat',[49] and to demonstrate the working of the plastic number.[50] Le Corbusier claims to find confirmation of the *modulor* at Hagia Sophia and elsewhere,[51] but writes that the system 'would only be worth something if it is applied on a mass scale in the dimensioning of manufactured articles'.[52] Both men put forward their systems as 'necessary instruments'[53] whose usefulness was perennial. Similarly, one does not have to accept Hambidge's dubious claim to have rediscovered the forgotten source from which the Ancient Egyptians and Classical Greeks drew the unique grace and vitality of their art; what matters is his vision of the promise that dynamic symmetry holds for the art of his own time. 'The present need,' he writes, 'is for an exposition of the application of dynamic symmetry to the problems of today.'[54] These writers believed that their words were, and must be, relevant to things yet to be made, not just to things made in the past. I share that belief.

That is not to say, however, that proportion systems are to be regarded merely as devices that can be 'used' or 'applied'

47. L. March, *Architectonics of Humanism: Essays on Number in Architecture*, Academy Editions, 1998.
48. H. van der Laan, *De architectonische ruimte*, E.J. Brill, 1977; Engl. trans. *Architectonic Space*, E.J. Brill, 1983.
49. *Ibid.*, p. 185.
50. *Ibid.*, pp. 185–204.
51. Le Corbusier, *The Modulor*, pp. 191–205.
52. *Ibid.*, p. 62.
53. Le Corbusier, *Towards a New Architecture*, p. 69.
54. J. Hambidge, *The Elements of Dynamic Symmetry*, Dover Publications, 1967, p. xvii.

in order to fulfil some ulterior purpose, as the debaters of 1957 assumed. Van der Laan encouraged me to see a proportion system not as a tool or a recipe that makes good design 'easier', but as something vastly more important. The role of the system he discovered, the 'plastic number', is not to help make a better architecture, but rather, the role of architecture is to embody the plastic number. 'For me,' he said, 'the plastic number is not a means, but the end, of making architecture.'[55]

The purpose of architectural proportion is for Van der Laan certainly aesthetic, but only if 'aesthetic' is understood in the pristine meaning of the word. 'Aesthetic' derives from *aesthetikos*, perception; the Greek word for beauty is *kallos*. In fact the word 'beauty' never occurs in Van der Laan's writings. In his view architecture, and in particular architectural proportion, serve not just to please the eye, but to enable us to survive in the world, both physically and mentally. The natural world presents itself to us not as a limited, measured, and therefore comprehensible cosmos, but as a measureless continuity in which we find ourselves, as it were, 'out of our depth'. Although buildings, as shelter, serve our physical survival in nature (and this may be why we build in the first place), they provide the occasion for – and demand – the satisfaction of a higher existential need: to perceive and to know the world and to make it our own by giving it measure. It is not a question of measuring space in general by some arbitrary unit like the metre, but of transforming a delimited piece of space into a measured whole. The proportions between measures bring to light the relations between the building's masses, between these and its spaces, and ultimately between the architectonic space and the space of nature. In the same way, through the measured relations between sounds, music gives measure to a portion of time – a kind of measure quite different, for instance, from that provided by a clock.

Van der Laan rejected outright an interviewer's suggestion that this concept implied something esoteric or mystical: 'No, above all, no mysticism; in this context that is the worst word I know.'[56] Much like Hume, he confined his thought to what can be experienced directly, by walking in a field or staying within the four walls of a room. It is Le Corbusier, the agnostic, whose standpoint is mystical:

> Mathematics. . . holds both the absolute and the infinite, the understandable and the forever elusive. It has walls

55. H. van der Laan, unpublished letter to the author, 26 October 1983, p. 2.
56. H. de Haan and I. Haagsma, 'Dom H. van der Laan: speuren naar de grondbeginselen van architectuur', *intermediair*, 13 February 1981, p. 5.

> before which one may pace up and down without result; sometimes there is a door: one opens it – enters – one is in another realm, the realm of the gods, the room which holds the key to the great systems. These doors are the doors of the miracles. Having gone though one, man is no longer the operative force, but rather it is his contact with the universe.[57]

It is customary to write introductory chapters after a book is more or less complete, and this is no exception. Looking back, therefore, over what follows, I see a danger that it may be misinterpreted as an attempt to magnify Van der Laan at the expense of Le Corbusier. I have no such intention. Naturally, a sense of fair play (or of mischief) may lead one to wish to topple idols and to rescue others from undeserved obscurity. But the two men were so opposite in most respects, their strengths lay in such different fields, that it is nonsensical to weigh one against the other.

Both made proportion the pivot of their architecture; but whereas Le Corbusier believed in the intrinsic unity of man's thinking and building with the natural world, Van der Laan insisted on their separateness. Le Corbusier was incomparably the 'greater' artist, if greatness is measured in terms of prolific creativity, uniqueness and inventiveness. Almost everything he built opened up a new path for architecture. By contrast, Van der Laan built little, and he consciously turned his back on any striving for novelty. He did not set out to be 'original' unless by originality is understood 'a return to the origins'. For him, the more 'ordinary', the less 'unique' the work, the better. Consequently his example is 'normative' in a way that Le Corbusier's could never be, despite all the latter's championship of standardization and the *objet type.* As Van der Laan and his brother Nico wrote about one of their early buildings: 'We have deliberately not avoided the old forms, but on the contrary chosen forms so ancient that they have never been new.'[58] He was delighted by the comment of the artist Théodore Stravinsky on a visit to his abbey church at Vaals, that it was the first time he had experienced in a modern building the feeling that one gets in an ancient one.

The focus of this book is not buildings, however, but ideas about buildings; and on this level my two protagonists are more evenly matched. Le Corbusier was one of those rare architects who was also a gifted writer (Adolf Loos is

57. Le Corbusier, *The Modulor*, p. 71.
58. H. and N. van der Laan, 'Kapel te Helmond', *Bouwkundig Weekblad*, 35/36, 1951, pp. 319–21.

another example). His writings are full of brilliant insights. However, these insights are loosely strung together, given an apparent unity by the flow of rhetoric rather than by reasoned argument. Not surprisingly, they are riddled with contradictions. Van der Laan is a more rigorous, penetrating and consistent thinker. He builds up his theory gradually, step by patient step, in a series of deductions drawn from a few elementary observations. This is not to say that his conclusions are unerringly correct or unassailable. I find myself in disagreement with him on a number of fundamental issues – notably his dogmatic insistence that the plastic number is the 'only' system that fits our human interpretation of space, and that it therefore supersedes and invalidates all others.

However, the real difference between Le Corbusier and Van der Laan, from the point of view of the present book, lies not so much in the relative value of their achievement as in the contrasting philosophical traditions that they represent. Wittkower concluded that somewhere around 1700 the connections between science and art, rationality and creativity, were fatally severed. If he was right, the practice of architectural proportion reached a dead end at that time. Le Corbusier simply ignores the disconnection, forging ahead as if it did not exist. Van der Laan points to a way around the impasse; proportion is for him a regularity imposed by the mind upon the world - an intellectual abstraction - and not something latent in and derived from that world. That is what makes him, for me, a more *modern* thinker than Le Corbusier. And the fact that his thought was deeply rooted in early Greek philosophy makes him also, paradoxically, a more ancient one.

Chapter two

ABSTRACTION AND EMPATHY

*If, in considering the various systems of proportions known to us, we try to understand their meaning rather than their appearance. . . they will reveal themselves as expressions of the same 'artistic intention' (*Kunstwollen*) that was realized in the buildings, sculptures and paintings of a given period or a given artist. The history of the theory of proportion is the reflection of the history of style; furthermore, since we may understand each other unequivocally when dealing with mathematical formulations, it may even be looked upon as a reflection which often surpasses its original in clarity. One might assert that the theory of proportions expresses the frequently perplexing concept of the* Kunstwollen *in clearer or, at least, more definable fashion than art itself.*[1]

2.1 WILHELM WORRINGER

As Erwin Panofsky writes in the essay quoted at the head of this chapter, proportion systems reflect, in a precise mathematical form, the *Kunstwollen* of an epoch or an individual. I propose to extend this hypothesis: to speculate that they condense, not only a *Kunstwollen*, but a *Weltanschauung* – a complete outlook on the world. More specifically, I shall try to show how the belief in architectural proportion has been affected by the two broad schools of thought about human knowledge, which in the last chapter I classified as 'empathy' and 'abstraction'. From the viewpoint of empathy, to know something is to belong to it: we can know and understand nature because we are of it; and mathematics is the key to this understanding because nature is essentially mathematical. But from the viewpoint of abstraction, to know something

1. E. Panofsky, 'The history of the theory of human proportions as a reflection of the history of styles', in *Meaning in the Visual Arts*, Peregrine Books, 1970, p. 83.

is to have made it oneself: we cannot know nature because we have not made it; but we can interpret it through mathematics because mathematics is our own creation.

In 1907 a young German art historian, Wilhelm Worringer, wrote a dissertation entitled *Abstraction and Empathy: A Contribution to the Psychology of Style.* It sets up two absolutely clear categories of art, corresponding to two opposed human attitudes to the external world. The one regards it as intrinsically ordered, comprehensible and benign, the other as chaotic, unpredictable and threatening. Worringer's thesis provides an ideal starting-point from which to launch our contending arguments: the 'old certainty', which I have identified with Le Corbusier, and the post-Humian scepticism, which I have linked with Van der Laan.

Although Worringer's portrayal of cultural history, with its stereotypical characterizations of 'Primitive', 'Classical' and 'Oriental' man, is over-simplified, he was gifted with an extraordinary sense that something momentous was about to happen in the world of art. In the year he wrote, 1907, an important retrospective of the work of Paul Cézanne was held in Paris, and Pablo Picasso painted *Les Demoiselles d'Avignon*, setting modern art on the road towards abstraction. The derisive name 'Cubism' was given to the new tendency by Henri Matisse in response to an exhibition of the landscapes Georges Braque brought back from an expedition to L'Estaque in 1908; and in 1909, the year that Worringer's thesis was published, Picasso made his first fully Cubist paintings during a summer spent at Horta del Ebro. In 1911 Wassily Kandinsky published his own abstractionist manifesto, *Concerning the Spiritual in Art.*[2] And by 1913 Piet Mondrian was producing completely abstract compositions derived from seascapes and cityscapes. These works demanded theoretical justification, and Worringer's book supplied it. He attributed its immediate success to the coincidence of his scholarly art-historical speculations with an actual revolution in art that both demonstrated and required them. 'Thus at the time, without knowing it, I was the medium of the necessities of the period.'[3]

By setting up abstraction (from *abstrahere*, 'to draw away from') and empathy (*Einfühlung*, literally 'in-feeling') as opposite poles of artistic intention, corresponding to the two possible relations between human beings and the external

2. W. Kandinsky, *Concerning the Spiritual in Art*, Dover Publications, 1977.
3. W. Worringer, *Abstraction and Empathy*, Routledge & Kegan Paul, 1963, p. vii.

world – the first a relation of duality, the second of unity – and by identifying naturalism with the latter, Worringer overthrows the centuries-long tradition that since the Renaissance had held naturalism alone to be the goal of art. Art is now polarized between two contrary tendencies. The art of primitives, of Egypt or of Byzantium is no longer to be explained as the result of an inferior capacity to represent nature, but as the expression of an attitude to nature fundamentally different from that of the Classical Greeks or Renaissance Italians. Moreover, Worringer implies that it is the abstract attitude of estrangement or *withdrawal from* nature, and not the Classical attitude of empathy or *feeling into* nature, that constitutes the original or primitive human state.

He reduces the Classical or naturalistic attitude to 'the simplest formula': 'Aesthetic enjoyment is objectified self-enjoyment. To enjoy aesthetically means to enjoy myself in a sensuous object diverse from myself, to empathise myself into it.'[4] Such an attitude to the external world, he says, can emerge only where men feel completely at home in it, as the result of 'innate disposition, evolution, climatic and other propitious circumstances'.[5]

With regard to the primitive state of man, Worringer turns on its head the conventional picture of a paradisal golden age, and of primitive man as a noble savage, living in close and harmonious intimacy with nature. Instead, he portrays the world-view of primitive cultures as one of alienation and fear. Whereas empathy starts out from the premiss that nature is ordered and comprehensible, abstraction is a response to a world that is seen as chaotic, unpredictable and dangerous. The function of the artefact, for the primitive, is that of intermediary, protector, or refuge:

> Tormented by the entangled interrelationship and flux of the phenomena of the outer world, such peoples were dominated by an immense need for tranquillity. The happiness they sought from art did not consist in the possibility of projecting themselves into the things of the outer world, of enjoying themselves in them, but in the possibility of taking the individual thing of the external world out of its arbitrariness and seeming fortuitousness, of eternalising it by approximation to abstract forms and, in this manner, of finding a point of tranquillity and a refuge from appearances.[6]

4. *Ibid.*, p. 5.
5. *Ibid.*, p. 45.
6. *Ibid.*, pp. 16–17.

Picasso, when he first encountered primitive works of art, immediately recognized and identified with this feeling of being a stranger in the midst of nature, and the need to make art works as a defence against it. In 1907, the very year in which Worringer wrote his thesis, and while he was working on *Les Demoiselles d'Avignon*, the painter paid his first visit to the Ethnographical Museum (now Musée de l'Homme) in the old building of the Trocadéro. As he later told André Malraux:

> The masks weren't just like any other pieces of sculpture. Not at all. They were magic things. . . The Negro pieces were *intercesseurs*, mediators. . . They were against everything – against unknown, threatening spirits. . . I understood; I too am against everything. I too believe that everything is unknown, that everything is an enemy! Everything. I understood what the Negroes used their sculpture for. . . The fetishes were weapons.[7]

But Worringer also describes a second kind of abstract culture, more evolved and permanent than the 'primitive': this is the 'Oriental'. If his picture of the 'primitive' is meant to portray the first stages of man's adaptation to external reality, the abstraction of the Oriental represents its third and most mature phase:

> The Oriental is far nearer to primeval man than is Classical man, and yet a whole cycle, an entire world of development, lies between them. . . The same fear of the world, the same need for liberation lives in him. . . But with this difference, that in Oriental man all this is not something preliminary which recedes before growing intellectual knowledge. . . but a stable phenomenon, superior to all development, which is not *before* all knowledge but *beyond* it. . . The art of the East, like that of primitive man, is strictly abstract and bound to the rigid, expressionless line and its correlate, the plane surface. But. . . [the] elementary creation has become a complicated artistic form: primitiveness has become culture and the higher, more matured quality of world-sensibility reveals itself in an unmistakable manner, in spite of the outward sameness of the medium of expression.[8]

Despite Picasso's complete self-identification with

7. P. Picasso, conversation with A. Malraux, in J. Richardson, *A Life of Picasso*, Jonathan Cape, 1996, vol. II, p. 24.
8. W. Worringer, *Form in Gothic*, G.P. Putman, 1927, pp. 35–7.

Worringer's vision of the 'primitive', Worringer's concept of the 'Oriental' is in general more relevant to the outlook of the modern artist. Although Picasso and other modernists were inspired, at about the time he wrote, by the art of Africa and the New Hebrides, no twentieth-century European artist, trained in the Classical academic tradition, can be primitive in the same sense. Leaving aside the vexed question whether even so-called native cultures can legitimately be described as primitive,[9] one must, if one is not to dismiss the whole business of imitating tribal masks and figures as mere cultural tourism, look deeper, to the common urge to abstraction that modern abstract artists shared with artists of the past. To describe Mondrian, for instance, as primitive makes little sense; but in view of the important part played by Theosophy in his art and life the description 'Oriental' fits him reasonably well. Cubism and De Stijl did not precede naturalism, but succeeded it, just as, according to Worringer, the Oriental represents a third stage of development, more mature than the Classical: 'not *before* all knowledge, but *beyond* it'.

2.2 PARADOXICAL NATURE OF THE TWO CATEGORIES

The commonplace view of naturalistic art is that it holds up a mirror to nature, and hence that like a mirror it plays an entirely *passive* role in the relationship. Art takes its lead from and merely reflects the external world. But in his later book *Form in Gothic* (1912) Worringer points out that the opposite is in fact the case. He describes empathy as

> another name for the unity of man and the world, that is to say, for the completely accomplished subjugation of the world by mind and sense which annihilates the original dualism. . . And. . . the artistic development runs strictly parallel to this religious development. Art. . . becomes, like the Greek world of gods, an idealization of nature.[10]

The same observation is made by the psychologist Carl Jung in the chapter on 'The type problem in aesthetics' in his *Psychological Types* (1921). He links empathy with extroversion and abstraction with introversion, and points out that empathy presupposes an initial emptiness of the object,

9. P.S. Wingert, *Primitive Art*, New American Library, 1962, pp. 3–11.
10. W. Worringer, *Form in Gothic*, pp. 28–9.

in order that the subject (the artist) can fill it with his own vitality, his own creative will.[11] Like the easy sociability of the extrovert, the Classical vision of nature involves a degree of overlooking or overriding of the identity of the object (the other), its transformation into what the subject ideally wishes or believes it to be. The order and harmony that Classical man (or Le Corbusier) perceives in the external world he himself projects into it.

This self-projection is largely unconscious. The artist really believes that he is merely interpreting the nature of the object, unaware that by identifying himself with the object, submerging himself in it, he is at the same time transforming it in his own image. Looking at the object, he does not notice that he is seeing his own reflection. Worringer derived this concept of the subjection of natural forms to the human will from Alois Riegl's principle of *Kunstwollen* or 'artistic volition':

> Since we recognize as only secondary the role played by the natural model in the work of art, and assume an absolute artistic volition, which makes itself the master of external things as mere objects to be made use of, as the primary factor in the process that gives birth to the work of art, it stands to reason that we cannot accept the popular interpretation of the concept style... [that] involves, as the primary and crucial factor, the endeavor to render the natural model.[12]

Thus empathy implies an outward projection of the human mind *into* nature before it means an absorption of nature into the mind. It is subjective before it is objective. Worringer writes that

> The value of a line, of a form consists for us in the value of the life that it holds for us. It holds its beauty only through our own vital feeling, which, in some mysterious manner, we project into it.[13]

In this he follows Theodor Lipps' statement, which he quotes, that

> The form of an object is always its being-formed by me, by my inner activity. It is a fundamental fact of all psychology, and most certainly of all aesthetics, that a

11. C.G. Jung, *Psychological Types*, Kegan Paul, Trench, Trubner & Co., 1946, pp. 362–3.
12. *Ibid.*, pp. 33–4.
13. W. Worringer, *Form in Gothic*, p. 14.

> 'sensuously given object', properly understood, is an unreality, something that does not, and cannot, exist. In that it exists for me – and such objects alone come into question – it is permeated by my activity, by my inner life.[14]

Therefore empathy turns out to be not so much the naturalization of the human as the humanization of nature. This ambiguity was inherent in Classical art theory, both in Graeco-Roman antiquity and in the Italian Renaissance. In *Idea*, his study of the Ideal as a concept in art theory, Erwin Panofsky observes that it combined, and never fully reconciled, two conflicting ideas:

> There was the notion that the work of art is inferior to nature, insofar as it merely imitates nature, at best to the point of deception; and there was the notion that the work of art is superior to nature because, improving on the deficiencies of nature's individual products, art independently confronts nature with a newly created image of beauty. Side by side with the endlessly varied anecdotes about painted grapes that attract sparrows, painted horses that real ones neigh at, a painted curtain that fools even the artist's eye. . . there is the admission that the works of Polycletus had lent the human figure 'a grace surpassing truth'. . .[15]

The two great subjects of naturalistic art – the human body and the landscape – each provide an outstanding example of empathy's projection of the human into the natural. During the Renaissance and the centuries that followed it the human body was held up as the most perfect manifestation of natural form and proportion. Man was made in God's image; the proportions of his body manifested the divine harmony of His creation, and were the model for proportion in art and architecture. And the ideal setting of this body – the paradisal landscape – was not the wild or desolate landcape of untamed nature but a humanized and pastoral one.

The paradox of empathy – that it is the humanization of nature rather than the imitation of it – is matched by a similar paradox within abstraction. Abstraction begins, as Jung points out, with our awareness of the powerful presence of nature, and at the same time of its separateness from us. It

14. Quoted, *ibid.*, pp. 6–7.
15. E. Panofsky, *Idea*, Icon Editions, p. 14.

> . . .presupposes a certain living and operating force on the part of the object; hence it seeks to remove itself from the object's influence. Thus, the abstracting attitude is centripetal, i.e. introverted. . . It is significant that Worringer describes the influence of the object in terms of fear or dread.[16]

If empathy is a self-confident faith in man's ability to conquer nature and subjugate it, then abstraction is an awed respect for nature as an unknown and indomitable force. Again, the commonplace view – that abstraction is the denial of nature – is mistaken. True abstraction is a meditation on and a distillation from nature. It begins with an overpowering sense of the *terribilità* of the natural world.

The work and thought of Mondrian is an illustration of this complex relation of abstraction to nature. Despite the apparent contrast between his early landscapes of the years 1900–8 and his most uncompromising abstractions of around 1930, they are in fact connected by an unbroken evolutionary development. For all the stories about how he screened the windows of his Paris studio to filter out the natural light, how he painted white the green leaf of the artificial tulip that was the only vestigially 'natural' object permitted there, and how, dining in a restaurant, he would position himself to avoid a view of the trees outside, nature remained of the greatest importance as a source of his art.

He expresses this in a series of 'trialogues' published in *De Stijl* in 1919–20. The conversations take place between a naturalistic painter, X, a layman, Y, and an 'abstract-real' painter, Z, who represents Mondrian himself. They occur during and after a country walk by moonlight, Mondrian's preferred light for landscape painting. After the three friends have returned to Z's studio, which in the description resembles Mondrian's own, Y expresses his regret that such a beautiful walk had to end, but Z replies:

> The evening is over *but the beauty remains.* We haven't just 'beheld' with our eyes: an *interaction* has taken place between us and the perceived object. This interaction must have produced something; it has given rise to certain images. For us these images do not merely remain in existence, but gain in strength now that we are alone with them, now that we are away from nature. *These images*, and not the things themselves that we saw, *are now for us the true*

16. *Ibid.*

> *manifestations of the beautiful*. . . So in the artist's work we see the image of beauty develop and as it were break loose from things. *By freeing itself from the object, the image grows from individual to universal beauty*.[17]

So both empathy and abstraction turn out to be virtually the opposite of our naive preconceptions of them. The naturalistic art of empathy proves to owe far more to the human, and abstract art far more to nature, than the associations of 'naturalism' and 'abstraction' lead us to assume. Inside every empathist there is an abstractionist fighting to get out, and vice versa.

These paradoxes lie at the root of the problem, not just of art, but of our knowledge of the world. They have preoccupied philosophy since the early Greeks. In the seventeenth and eighteenth centuries they showed themselves in the contrast between rationalists like Descartes and Leibniz, and empiricists such as Locke, Berkeley and Hume. Like empathy, rationalism approaches nature as it were 'centrifugally', from the inside outwards, starting from the reasoning mind (*cogito ergo sum*). But empiricism, like abstraction, is 'centripetal'. It starts from the experience of things through the senses, and ends by concluding that we can ultimately have no certain knowledge of nature, but only of our own sensations and the things we make ourselves.

2.3 EMPATHY AND ABSTRACTION IN ARCHITECTURAL PROPORTION

The same division that Worringer makes between empathy and abstraction in representational art applies equally to the relation of architectural proportion to nature's laws. The presumption that proportion in art proceeds from, and is validated by, the mathematical harmony of nature is characteristic of empathy, and can be described as essentially naturalistic. It is founded on an attitude to the external world that assumes and relies on the possibility of a perfect accord between the human mind and the perceived world.

The regularity that is sought by the 'primitive' and the 'Oriental' is of a quite different order from the mathematical harmony envisaged by Worringer's 'Classical man'. It is no longer a serene reflection or elucidation of the underlying harmony of nature, but a protest or reaction against nature's

17. P. Mondrian, 'Natuurlijke en abstracte realiteit', in *De Stijl*, III (5), 1920, p. 41 (author's translation).

overwhelming formlessness and unfathomability. The regularity and clear delimitation of man's own products are a defence against nature's caprice and obscurity:

> He begins with the rigid line, which is essentially abstract and alien to life. . . He seeks further geometrical possibilities of line, creates triangles, squares, circles, places similarities together, discovers the advantages of regularity, in short, creates a primitive ornament which provides him not only with a mere delight in decoration and play, but with a table of symbolic absolute values, and therefore with the appeasement of his condition of deep spiritual distress.[18]

On the one hand, therefore, we have the image of nature and man as a harmonious unity, and on the other, the essentially *abstract* concept of their duality. From the point of view of abstraction, architectural proportion is an artificial and abstract mathematical ordering, an ordering that is our response to a universe that confronts us as mysterious or unknowable. It is useless to enquire whether nature is founded on mathematical principles. Even if it were, it would not follow that nature's proportions can be grasped by the human mind, or that they can or should be manifested in art.

Nevertheless, proportion is essential to art, and the more abstract the art, the more clearly proportions are revealed in it. Again, the example of Mondrian is illuminating. All the evidence suggests that with the exception of the series of paintings based on regular grids made in 1918 and 1919 (for example, *Lozenge with grey lines*, 1918), Mondrian did not use numerical or geometrical methods of composition, but arrived at the proportions of his paintings by a painstaking process of intuitive reflection and trial and error. His friend the American painter and critic Charmion von Wiegand reports that even after exhibiting a work he would return to it to make almost imperceptible changes of proportion:

> He explained that when he saw this canvas in the exhibition he felt that two lines near the edge of the canvas needed widening; he intends to repaint them half a centimetre broader. To my eyes, this made only the slightest difference; but he is so extraordinarily sensitive to the laws of proportion that, to him, it seemed of the highest importance.[19]

18. W. Worringer, *Form in Gothic*, p. 17.
19. C. von Wiegand, 'The meaning of Mondrian', in *The Journal of Aesthetics*, II (8), 1943, pp. 62–70; quoted in F. Elgar, *Mondrian*, Thames & Hudson, 1968, p. 180.

Strictly speaking, therefore, Mondrian falls outside the scope of the discussion of proportion as a rational *mathematical* discipline. Nevertheless, his observations on proportion throw light on the relation between proportion, abstract art, and nature. In the first of the series of trialogues quoted above, Z remarks that whereas the naturalistic painter lays the stress on tone and colour, he himself places the emphasis

> on the *representation of proportion*. . . We both make our pictures by means of the contrast of colour and line, and this contrast is *proportion*. . . the more the natural is abstracted, the more the proportion comes out. The new painting shows this; it finally arrives at representation through *pure proportion*.[20]

2.4 LE CORBUSIER, CLASSICAL ARCHITECT

In modern architecture empathy and abstraction, as polarities representing two opposed attitudes to the artist's relation to the external world, are personified by two outstanding personalities who made proportion the pivot of their work: Le Corbusier and Van der Laan. Le Corbusier's is the way of empathy: a denial of the duality of nature and humanity. As Worringer says, 'With the coming of Classical man the absolute dualism of man and the outer world ceases to exist.'[21] The other approach – Van der Laan's – is the way of abstraction, which takes the fact of the duality as its starting point.

In Chapter 1 I compared Le Corbusier's belief in a mathematical harmony underlying and sustaining nature to Alberti's concept of *concinnitas*. Among modern architects he is the outstanding representative of this Classical tradition of looking to the cosmos for the ultimate justification of mathematical proportions in art. He exemplifies the attitude of empathy with the external world, but also the ambiguity towards nature inherent in that attitude. Le Corbusier's 'nature' is a nature in accord with his humanistic vision of an ideal, harmonious, and mathematically ordered universe. If this universe is in harmony with man, it is because man has previously emptied it of everything that could threaten his own vision. As he writes in *Towards a New Architecture*, 'Architecture is the first manifestation of man *creating his own*

20. P. Mondrian, 'Natuurlijke en abstracte realiteit', *De Stijl*, II (8), 1919, pp. 85–6.
21. W. Worringer, *Form in Gothic*, p. 28.

universe, creating it in the image of nature, the laws which govern our own nature, our universe.'[22] If man creates his universe 'in the image of nature', it is only because Le Corbusier never doubts that the laws of nature are the laws of '*our* nature'.

These Classical affinities did not show themselves immediately or without a fight. They emerged through what H. Allen Brooks, in his fascinating study of Le Corbusier's early years, describes as an 'agonizing conversion to classicism that required overthrowing most of the values that he previously held dear'[23] – the Medievalist and ornamentalist values, that is, of Ruskin and of his teacher Charles L'Eplattenier. According to Brooks, the crucial factor in this conversion was the sojourn in Germany, 1910–11, and particularly the five months spent working in Peter Behrens' office in Berlin. In his own accounts, typically, Le Corbusier (then still calling himself Charles-Edouard Jeanneret) went out of his way to conceal these sources and to stress the heroism and loneliness of his struggle. If he did his utmost to denigrate Behrens and to diminish the importance of the whole German experience, it was precisely because these were in fact decisive for him: 'His debt was so great, indeed so profound, that Le Corbusier thought it best that it should be left unknown.'[24]

The conversion was complete by 1918, when Jeanneret and the painter Amedée Ozenfant launched Purism as a counterblast to an already tired and decaying Cubism. As an answer to Cubism's abstraction, which in their view had degenerated into a decorative formalism, Purism would bring back the Classical representation of recognizable objects. In their manifesto *Après le Cubisme*, and in the journal *L'Esprit Nouveau*, which the two men founded in 1920, they held up as models antique Classical monuments like the Parthenon and the Pont du Gard, and advocated a return to mathematical methods of composition based on the golden section.

Once made, the conversion was decisive and permanent – or at least he chose to make it appear so. Outwardly, Le Corbusier now had eyes only for 'Egyptian, Greek or Roman architecture', which are made up of 'cubes and cylinders, pyramids and spheres'.[25] Lacking this elementary geometry, Gothic architecture, his former obsession, was now dismissed as 'not very beautiful', so that 'We search in it for compensations of a subjective kind outside plastic art.'[26]

22. Le Corbusier, *Towards a New Architecture*, Architectural Press, 1946, pp. 69–70 (author's italics).
23. H.A. Brooks, *Le Corbusier's Formative Years*, University of Chicago Press, 1997, p. 245.
24. *Ibid.*, p. 247.
25. Le Corbusier, *Towards a New Architecture*, p. 31.
26. *Ibid.*, p. 32.

The marvellous tension that characterizes all Le Corbusier's work is the result of a series of such violent resolutions of deep inner conflicts. Each solution is a precariously achieved balance between opposites, but he prefers to present it in his writings as the unconditional and decisive victory of one side over the other. He often portrays the conflict in the form of a dialogue, in which he clearly intends the reader to identify him with one side only, while in fact both sides represent the debate within himself. Thus in *The Decorative Art of Today* he contrasts the 'iconolater' who demands that useful objects should have souls, and therefore be decorated, with the 'iconoclast' who insists that they are only 'slaves, menials, servants',[27] and as such must be stripped bare and, when worn out, discarded. But the first view, which is that of Ruskin, L'Eplattenier and Jeanneret himself before 1910, he never fully abandoned, merely submerged. In *Towards a New Architecture*, a compilation of articles written at different times and presumably in different moods, the contradictions are nearer the surface. He defines the house at one point as 'a machine for living in', comprising 'baths, sun, hot-water, cold-water, warmth at will, conservation of food, hygiene, beauty in the sense of good proportion',[28] while at another he demands that the house be not merely 'practical', but that its walls must 'rise towards heaven in such a way that I am moved. . .This is Architecture'.[29]

Where, then, is the 'real' Le Corbusier? A Classicist, or at heart a Romantic and even a Gothicist? Does the latent Medievalist in him resurface in later works like the chapel at Ronchamp? It is never allowed to do so entirely. The conversion to Classicism was permanent and profound. It was not an adopted attitude, but innate. Even in the later years, as at Chandigarh, the dominant characteristics of his work were grand horizontal perspectives, plain surfaces, and calculated proportional harmonies, while the masterly *design* of every notebook sketch and art school exercise done before 1910 reveals, inside the young Jeanneret, the Classicist Le Corbusier fighting to get out. He was aware of Worringer's book, incidentally, at the time of his conversion to Classicism; his travelling companion on the Oriental Journey in 1911, August Klipstein, was 'a Worringer protégé',[30] and Jeanneret mentions Worringer in his notebook and letters.

Empathic art, as defined by Worringer, relies on a similar balance between opposites. By denying the gulf between the

27. Le Corbusier, *The Decorative Art of Today*, Architectural Press, 1987, p. xxi.
28. Le Corbusier, *Towards a New Architecture*, p. 89.
29. *Ibid.*, p. 187.
30. H.A. Brooks, *Le Corbusier's Formative Years*, p. 256.

human and the natural, it seems to make possible an art that is simply the reflection or extension of nature. But before this can happen, nature itself must be recast in the human mould, so that (to adapt Sir Arthur Eddington's phrase to a slightly different context) *the mind regains from nature that which the mind has put into nature.*[31] The visible world is metrically organized according to *man's* mathematical scheme, not vice versa. Le Corbusier himself was well aware of this polarity. The united front he presented to the world concealed a precarious balance between opposite forces within himself, and he recognized the same opposition in man's relation to nature. Sometimes both sides of the struggle come to the surface in his writings. In *Urbanisme* (1924) he writes that

> Man, created by the universe, is the sum of that universe, as far as he himself is concerned; he proceeds according to its laws and believes he can read them; *he has formulated them and made of them a coherent scheme*, a rational body of knowledge on which he can act, adapt and produce. . . *Nature presents itself to us as a chaos*. . . The actual scene which lies before our eyes, with its kaleidoscopic fragments and its vague distances, is a confusion. There is nothing there which resembles the objects with which we surround ourselves, and which we have created. . . But the spirit which animates Nature is a spirit of order; we come to *know* it. We differentiate between what we see and what we learn or know. *We therefore reject appearance and attach ourselves to substance.*[32]

The passage is full of contradictions: that is its greatness. Le Corbusier allows both sides of nature, both sides of *our* nature, to appear side by side. On the one hand man is created by nature, and acts according to its laws. But on the other hand, he is himself the formulator of those laws. Nature appears to us as a chaos; but nature is animated by a spirit of order. The conflict is resolved much as Plato resolved it: by distinguishing between appearances and knowledge. The world of appearances is no more than the confused reflection of the underlying order of nature, the real world of substances and intelligible principles, manifested in geometry. These can be distilled out of phenomena by careful observation and thought:

31. A.S. Eddington, *The Nature of the Physical World*, Everyman's Library, 1935, p. 238.
32. Le Corbusier, *The City of Tomorrow* (translation of *Urbanisme*, 1924), The Architectural Press, 1971, pp. 23–5 (author's italics).

> The laws of gravity seem to resolve for us the conflict of forces and to maintain the universe in equilibrium; as a result of this we have the vertical. The horizon gives us the horizontal, the line of the transcendental plane of immobility. . . The right angle is as it were the sum of the forces which keep the world in equilibrium. . . it is unique and constant. In order to work, man has need of constants. . . The right angle is lawful, it is part of our determinism, it is obligatory. . . Culture is an orthogonal state of mind.[33]

Not surprisingly, the ambiguities and contradictions inherent in empathy and highlighted by Worringer and Jung re-emerge in Le Corbusier's attitude to landscape. He freely acknowledges his selective appreciation of nature. Although a Swiss, he admits to an almost eighteenth-century dislike of mountain scenery:

> I am a man of space, not only mentally but physically: I love airplanes and ships. I love the sea, the flat coasts and the plains more than the mountains. The foothills of the Alps, the Alps themselves crush me. Higher up, near the summits, on the last pasture meadows and on the peaks, space is born again, but the materials employed there bear witness to the savagery of unleashed elements, the catastrophe of geological upheavals. How much deeper is my feeling for the admirable clock of the sea, with its tides, its equinoxes, its daily variations according to the most implacable of laws, but also the most imperceptible, the most hidden law that exists.[34]

His preferred landscape was the Virgilian Mediterranean pastoral vision evoked by Poussin and Claude, which he identified with that of his own Suisse Romande: 'Je me sens ici comme en terre classique.'[35] This Classical landscape appears in innumerable sketches, and he envisaged it as the setting of the Villa Savoye.[36] The natural world upon which he believed his *modulor* to be founded was a human landscape projected horizontally from the body, determined by the cone of Albertian perspective: 'In order to establish contact with the universe, man uses his eyes, which are at a distance of about 1.60 metres from the ground. His eyes look forward (obviously!).'[37]

His Classical viewpoint is equally expressed by Le

33. *Ibid.*, pp. 26–7, 43.
34. Le Corbusier, *Modulor 2*, Faber & Faber, 1958, p. 27.
35. Le Corbusier, 'La Maison Suisse', in *Etrennes Helvétiques*, 1914, pp. 33–9.
36. *Le Corbusier & Pierre Jeanneret, Oeuvre Complète de 1910–1929*, Editions Girsberger, 1956, pp. 90, 187.
37. *Ibid.*, p. 19.

Corbusier's worship of the human body, which he holds up as a paradigm of natural order and specifically as the key to his system of proportions, the *modulor*. For the *modulor* is founded on the measures of the body as the literal *embodiment* of nature's fundamental proportion (as Le Corbusier believes): the golden section (see Chapter 15, Figure 15.13). This places him firmly in the company of nineteenth- and early twentieth-century writers like D.R. Hay, Adolf Zeising, Jay Hambidge and Matila Ghyka – and goes back, through Leonardo, to Vitruvius.

2.5 DOM HANS VAN DER LAAN, MODERN PRIMITIVE

Since Van der Laan is still not widely known, it is necessary to preface this account with a brief sketch of his life. He was born in Leiden in 1904, the son of an architect, and architecture was an early choice of career. Leaving school at seventeen, he took a course in higher mathematics before beginning his own formal architectural studies at Delft in 1923. He was quickly disillusioned by the academic nature of the architectural teaching, however, and abandoned his studies at the end of his third year to become a Benedictine monk. He later said that by thus distancing himself from the problem of architecture he created a favourable condition for looking at it in a new light.[38] He discovered the plastic number, the system of proportions that plays so important a role in his theory of architecture, in 1928, two years after entering the monastery. His abbey church at Vaals, the first building that fully realized his ideals, was designed in 1956–57 and completed in 1968. He published his first book, *Le nombre plastique*, in 1960,[39] and this was followed by two more general treatises on architecture and art: *De architectonische ruimte* (1977)[40] and *Het vormenspel der liturgie* (1985).[41] He died in 1991.

Architecture is for Van der Laan an abstraction imposed upon nature: a frame projected onto the natural continuum in order to make it measurable and intelligible. But this does not mean that architecture has no *relation* to nature; on the contrary, for him as for the eighteenth-century British empiricists, our initial encounter with nature through the senses is the starting point of all making and thought:

38. H. van der Laan, 'Het menselijk verblijf: grootte, vorm, ruimte', *Plan*, April 1977.
39. H. van der Laan, *Le nombre plastique*, E.J. Brill, 1960; Dutch edition, *Het plastische getal*, E.J. Brill, 1967.
40. H. van der Laan, *De architectonische ruimte*, E.J. Brill 1977; 2nd edn, 1992; English edn, *Architectonic Space*, E.J. Brill, 1983; French edn, *L'espace architectonique*, E.J. Brill, 1989; German edn, *Der architektonische Raum*, E.J. Brill, 1992.
41. Publ. E.J. Brill.

> We derive our knowledge in the first instance from material things, by way of the senses. . . From these sensory images the intellect abstracts its ideas. . . Once in possession of these ideas, we can bring them into relation with each other by thinking.[42]

Van der Laan – unlike Hume – regards the abstracted, internalized, intellectual image of nature not as a fainter copy of the original sensory impression, but as even stronger and more definite. Without that initial impression, however, it would be as it were false, rootless, and sterile; to this extent he agrees with Hume and differs markedly from Plato, for whom the world perceived by the senses is intrinsically inferior and less real: 'the thing that becomes and passes away, but never has real being'.[43] The plastic number does not belong, therefore, to a Platonic world of pure mathematics, but constitutes a bridge between the abstracting mind and the world of concrete phenomena.

The first chapter of *Architectonic Space* is significantly entitled 'Nature and Architecture'. In his early years he felt a strong empathy with the world of nature. Although he grew up in a family of architects, and himself intended from an early age to follow the same profession, his childhood ambition was to be not an architect but a biologist. As a boy, his favourite occupation was the study of nature: 'This intense discovery of nature at an impressionable age has determined the direction of my whole life.'[44] Nevertheless, his attitude to nature was founded on an awareness of a duality, even a conflict, between the mind and its natural objects. As he wrote in his first book, *Le nombre plastique*:

> The intellect is not, like animal instinct, determined by nature, but directs itself freely towards its goal and itself chooses the means of reaching it. The form of a house brought into being in this way is likewise not determined by nature, like the nest of a bird. Of necessity it contrasts with all naturally produced forms.[45]

The conflict between our human desire for precise measure and the immeasurable continuity of nature, which was as we shall see a crucial problem in Greek philosophy, is an example of a wider conflict between the human and the natural that in Van der Laan's view it is the function of art to resolve:

42. H. van der Laan, *Het vormenspel der liturgie*, E.J. Brill, 1985, p. 13.
43. Plato, *Timaeus*, in F.M. Cornford, *Plato's Cosmology*, Routledge & Kegan Paul, 1937, p. 22.
44. H. van der Laan, unpublished letter to the author, 5 November 1987, p. 4.
45. H. van der Laan, *Het plastische getal*, E.J. Brill, 1967, p. 6.

> The space of nature has three aspects that leave us at a loss. . . The sheer fact that we refer to natural space using negative terms like 'immeasurable', 'invisible', and 'boundless' indicates that it lacks something for us. We do not feel altogether in our element within it. Architecture, then, is nothing else but that which must be added to natural space to make it habitable, visible and measurable.[46]

He distinguishes between the initial *impression* we receive of the external world through the senses, and the *expression* we project outwards into the world in the form of works of art. The work of art is necessarily quite different in appearance from the impression of nature from which it has been distilled. The most obvious aspect of this abstraction is the straight-edged geometry of human artefacts and, in Van der Laan's case, the strict rectilinearity he sought in his work. It recalls the forms that Socrates, in Plato's *Philebus*, commends as those that give pure, absolute, and therefore true pleasure:

> By 'beauty of figures' I mean. . . a straight line, a curve and the plane and solid figures that lathes, rulers and squares can make from them. . . I mean that, unlike other things, they are not *relatively* beautiful: their nature is to be beautiful in *any* situation, just as they are. . .[47]

Van der Laan would point out that the Dutch word for civilization, *beschaving*, means literally planing, as in the squaring and smoothing of a piece of wood. One is reminded of Le Corbusier's epigram: 'Culture is an orthogonal state of mind.'[48] But for Van der Laan artistic form is not derived from nature, but imposed upon it; and this applies also to proportion. He makes it clear that the plastic number is a strictly human creation, projected onto the external world. He regards this imposition of measure through architecture as so important that one can say that we build *in order* to manifest proportion, if for no other reason.

As a student of theology in his early years in the monastery, Van der Laan was taught a version of the Aristotelian and Thomistic theory of knowledge summed up in the saying *nihil est in intellectu quod non prius fuerit in sensu* (nothing in the intellect unless first though the senses). In its uncompromising empiricism this outdoes Locke's statement that 'Our observation, employed either about *external sensible objects, or about the internal operations of our minds. . . is that*

46. H. van der Laan, unpublished lecture, 28 May 1985, pp. 3–5.
47. Plato, *Philebus*, Penguin Books, 1982, p. 121.
48. Le Corbusier, *The City of Tomorrow*, p. 43.

which supplies our understandings with all the materials of thinking.'[49] Van der Laan recalls:

> I learnt from philosophy that the intellect is originally a *tabula rasa* which must be written upon by perception; but from my familiarity with the study of nature I knew that the acquisition of knowledge is a living process.[50]

He was aware, in other words, that the mind is not just a passive recipient of whatever happens to fall into it, through the senses, from the external world, but actively elicits information from that world.

Nevertheless, it is very far from being like Kant's inquisitorial mind, which 'compels nature to reply to its questions'.[51] The acquisition of knowledge is a two-way process, a cooperation between the mind and its object, close to St Thomas Aquinas' formulation (which Mies van der Rohe adopted as his architectural maxim[52]): '*Veritas est adaequatio rei et intellectus*', or 'truth is the concordance of thing and intellect'.[53] For Van der Laan the intellect is not Locke's 'white paper void of all characters',[54] waiting to be written on *by* the world, but on the other hand nor can it know anything except what it gleans *from* that world. In this process the work of art plays a special role. It acts as an intermediary in the work of abstracting the initial sensory impression into a pure object of thought.

Thus for Van der Laan our encounter with the external world is necessarily an alternating process, like breathing. The question is, which comes first: breathing in or breathing out? The problem is analogous to Worringer's contrast between empathy and abstraction: empathy begins with a projection outwards *into* nature, abstraction with a drawing inwards *from* nature. Another parallel might be drawn with the opposition between philosophical rationalism and empiricism: for the rationalist, reason unaided can discover the nature of what exists, while for the empiricist the first stage must be an impression received through the senses. For Van der Laan, art – like life – must start with a drawing in, not a giving out:

> Breathing begins at birth with an inspiration and ends at death with an expiration; so too when we make something we must conceive the influence of forms upon our mind as the initial life-giving movement.[55]

49. J. Locke, *An Essay Concerning Human Understanding*, Everyman's Library, 1961, vol. 1, p. 77.
50. H. van der Laan, unpublished letter to the author, 5 November 1987, p. 4.
51. I. Kant, *Critique of Pure Reason*, Everyman's Library, 1934, p. 10.
52. F. Schulze, *Mies van der Rohe*, University of Chicago Press, 1985, p. 173.
53. Aquinas, *Quaestiones disputatae*, S.P. Lethielleux, Paris, 1925, vol. I, p. 4.
54. J. Locke, *An Essay Concerning Human Understanding*, p. 77.
55. H. van der Laan, *Het vormenspel der liturgie*, p. 63.

Like the eighteenth-century empiricists, he believes that the first stage, whether of science or art, must be an intake of information, an *impression*:

> In the first instance our mind is activated by the perception of natural things. Later, the stimulus comes also from the things we ourselves make, but the forms of nature remain always the objective starting point of our making: here art connects with and completes the natural creation.[56]

In contrast to empathy's direct projection of the self into the natural object, Van der Laan's abstract vision involves the projection of an intellectual perception of that object into a work of art, which may in turn give rise to further abstraction and intellectualization. In other words, the work of art – be it a painting, a house or a saucepan – becomes itself a source of knowledge, something like a scientific experiment. Art and science are not separate activities, but mutually necessary. This process of 'learning by doing', of making and testing, is the indispensable role of art in the process of cognition:

> The ascending and descending movement between the intellect and its products begins with the products and not with the intellect. That is why our making must always proceed by trial and error. . . We must learn *how* to make from the things *that* we make.[57]

Unlike Worringer, Van der Laan identifies empathy, 'the idea that all our doing and making begins from within', with a Romantic rather than a Classical view of the world:

> Nowadays we are mistakenly inclined to lay the emphasis on a so-called expression, by which the individual feelings of the maker are projected outwards, through the medium of the made object. . . However, this is contrary to the opinion of all the great civilizations, which have always striven towards that objective expression which proceeds from the work itself.[58]

Romanticism (which in Van der Laan's view still dominates our civilization) prizes above all the technical imperfections that reveal the individual hand of the artist, interpreting and valuing these as evidence of his personal genius. Typical of

56. *Ibid.*, p. 62.
57. *Ibid.*, pp. 62–3.
58. *Ibid.*, pp. 63–4.

this Romantic view is John Ruskin's plea 'that any degree of unskillfulness should be admitted, so only the labourer's mind had room for expression. . . and *the demand for perfection is always a sign of a misunderstanding of the ends of art*'.[59] But for Van der Laan the true artist aims not at the expression of his own mind but at the expression of the object he is making, as an example of its type. The more developed his skill the more typical and universal the work will be, and the fewer traces will remain of the individual maker.

In both the cases just highlighted – that of Le Corbusier and that of Van der Laan – the order that is discovered in nature is in reality a human construction. Mathematical order in our creations is equally justified by both. Le Corbusier stresses the unity of man and nature, Van der Laan their duality; but the need for a system of proportions can be deduced just as logically from either viewpoint. It is made necessary just as much by a conviction of our inability to discover with certainty any order in nature, as by the belief that such an order exists and that we can know it. In either case, it is a question of trying to reconcile what Theodore Cook describes as our 'hunger for finality and definite conceptions' with the 'constantly changing and bewilderingly varied phenomena of organic life'.[60] It is our never-ending struggle to bridge the gulf between what Plato calls 'that which is always real and has no becoming, and. . . that which is always becoming and is never real'.[61]

Furthermore, the battle between abstraction and empathy must end in a truce: the realization that each contains an intimation of its opposite. Le Corbusier is forced to admit that before man can act according to the laws of nature, he himself has to formulate them; he must first make a coherent scheme out of nature's apparent chaos. Conversely Van der Laan, starting out from man's need to construct his own artificial, delimited world within the limitless world of nature, comes to the conclusion that this little man-made world is a necessary conclusion of the natural process as such. In *Architectonic Space* he writes that 'It is as if nature awaited the work of our hands to be wholly complete.'[62] In a lecture given ten years before, he had developed the idea in more detail, and with a more specifically religious slant than he permits himself in his published writings.

> If I compare a house with a human body or a tree or the universe with all its stars and planets, I can only say that

59. J. Ruskin, *The Stones of Venice*, Everyman's Library, 1907, vol. II, p. 156.
60. T.A. Cook, *The Curves of Life*, Dover Publications, 1979, p. 24.
61. Plato, *Timaeus*, Everyman's Library, 1965, p. 13.
62. H. van der Laan, *Architectonic Space*, p. 60.

> the house is like the work of a child. But when I consider our artefacts from another point of view, they appear as the glory of creation, for here something has happened within creation, towards which the whole creation leads.[63]

God, he observes, makes things infinitely small, infinitely large, infinitely many; but He has not allowed us to discover the limits of the universe, or to find out how small things can be. All we can do is to distil, out of this chaos of measures with which nature confronts us, a yardstick of our own. And with this yardstick – the seven measures of the plastic number – we can measure the things that we make, imitating the way God has measured out His own creation.

> Architecture then appears to be a game in which we replay, under the eyes of God, the whole system of the natural creation. We do with seven measures what He has done with infinitely many.[64]

63. H. van der Laan, lecture, Den Bosch, 9 December 1967, pp. 9–10.
64. Ibid., p. 13.

Chapter three

UNIT AND MULTIPLIER

For measuring and counting, two things are indispensable: a unit and a system. That is to say, one needs both a static principle and a dynamic multiplication-system.[1]

3.1 ORDER AND COMPLEXITY

Before we explore further the historical relation between science, philosophy and systems of architectural proportion, we must first try to get a clear idea of what these systems are. I shall define them as methods of ordering the relations between the measures of a building, and thereby also between the two- and three-dimensional shapes to which these measures give rise. However, it is not just a matter of reducing the number of sizes and shapes to a minimum, but of achieving unity within a multiplicity of different elements.

In his book *Aesthetic Measure*[2] the American mathematician George D. Birkhoff (1884–1944) treats order and complexity as contraries. The gist of his theory is contained in the formula $M = O/C$: that is, (aesthetic) Measure equals Order divided by Complexity. The aesthetic value of an object increases, therefore, in direct proportion to its degree of order, and in inverse proportion to its complexity. And since he holds that the order and complexity of a two-dimensional figure can be exactly calculated – its order, by determining the degree of vertical or rotational symmetry, perpendicularity, etc., its complexity by counting the number of straight lines needed to delineate it – it is possible to quantify the aesthetic merit of any geometrically definable object. At the top of Birkhoff's order of merit are the square and the square grid.

Against this, I would argue that the elimination of complexity tends towards disorder, or rather non-order. Uniformity – the repetition of a single element, for instance an uninflected grid of square panels of standard size – is, paradoxically, the antithesis of order. Where uniformity is absolute and complexity approaches zero, as happens with a

1. H. van der Laan, *Het plastische getal*, E.J. Brill, 1967, p. 3.
2. G.D. Birkhoff, *Aesthetic Measure*, Harvard University Press, 1933.

blank sheet or a vacuum, there is nothing to which order can be given. The works of Minimalist artists like Donald Judd or Agnes Martin rely precisely on this principle. Like tightrope walkers, they explore just how far one can approach absolute simplicity without excluding the possibility of order. The fact that this exploration involves risk is what makes such work exciting rather than boring.

Conversely, the absence of order is not complexity but confusion. Just as order needs complexity to become manifest, complexity needs order to become intelligible. E.H. Gombrich, drawing on ideas derived from both Karl Popper and the naturalist Konrad Lorenz, suggests that the mechanism by which the sense of order is activated has deep biological roots. In order to be able to interpret and survive in a hazardous environment, every organism has a built-in 'expectation of regularity'. It continually seeks out regularities or patterns of order within its surroundings, which it can absorb into its own activity: 'The organism must probe the environment and must, as it were, plot the message it receives against that elementary expectation of regularity which underlies what I call the sense of order.'[3] When the environment lacks all complexity or variety, so that the expectation of regularity is continually fulfilled, the perceptual mechanism switches off, and we experience boredom: 'When the expected happens in our field of vision we cease to attend and the arrangement sinks below the threshold of our awareness.'[4] There is an obvious connection between Gombrich's theory and Popper's statement that

> We are born with expectations; with 'knowledge' which, although not *valid a priori*, is *psychologically or genetically a priori*, i.e. prior to all observational experience. One of the most important of these expectations is the expectation of finding a regularity. It is connected with an inborn propensity to look out for regularities, or with a *need* to *find* regularities. . .[5]

Delight lies, therefore, as Gombrich writes,

> somewhere between boredom and confusion. If monotony makes it difficult to attend, a surfeit of novelty will overload the system and cause us to give up; we are not tempted to analyse the crazy pavement.[6]

3. E.H. Gombrich, *The Sense of Order*, Phaidon, 1984, p. 3.
4. *Ibid.*, p. 9.
5. K.R. Popper, *Conjectures and Refutations*, Routledge & Kegan Paul, 1965, p. 47.
6. E.H. Gombrich, *The Sense of Order*, p. 9.

The aim of proportion systems can be described as the creation of an *ordered complexity*. Order and complexity are twin poles of the same phenomenon. Neither can exist without the other, and aesthetic value is the measure of both. Birkhoff's equation must be reformulated, as the psychologist H.J. Eysenck has proposed, as $M = OC$.[7]

3.2 MEASURING AND COUNTING

The first words of Van der Laan's book *Le Nombre plastique* are: 'An architect is someone who is continually occupied with measuring and counting.'[8] And the history of proportion in architecture – and of a great part of mathematics – could be told in terms of solutions of the problem of resolving the conflict between these two operations. When we count, we count individual things: indivisible units. The words 'individual' and 'indivisible' have a common origin. We shall see in the next chapter that the Pythagoreans taught that the world was actually composed of such indivisible units, and that visible objects were made up of very large numbers of these atomic particles arranged in various ways: as cubes, pyramids, and so on (see Chapter 4, Figures 4.9 and 4.10). Space was intrinsically 'countable', and therefore measurable. But the discovery that the diagonal of a square was incommensurable with its sides shattered for ever this beautifully simple picture of the world. Counting and measuring, number and geometry, no longer fitted perfectly together.

Much of Aristotle's *Physics* and his *Metaphysics* are concerned with the problems that arise from the continuity of space and time and the difficulty of defining units and unity within this continuity. While rejecting the Pythagoreans' doctrine that 'Numbers are the primary elements of the whole of nature',[9] he proposes that in practice we imitate nevertheless the indivisibility of numerical units in order to quantify our surroundings:

> An accurate measure is something which cannot be taken from or added to; hence the measure of number is most accurate, for the unit is in every way indivisible. We adopt a similar standard of measurement in all other cases.[10]

In place of the Pythagorean notion of physical units underlying the universe, Aristotle gives us the more

7. H.J. Eysenck, *Sense and Nonsense in Psychology*, Penguin Books, 1958, pp. 326–31.
8. H. van der Laan, *Het plastische getal*, p. 1.
9. Aristotle, *Metaphysics*, Everyman's Library, 1956, p. 64.
10. *Ibid.*, p. 306.

pragmatic idea of nominal units that we ourselves devise and impose on the external world in order to grasp and deal with its measureless continuity.

Irrespective of what may be the current scientific view of this matter, this is still a fairly accurate picture of our everyday experience, and – since everyday experience is what matters for architecture – of the relationship between measure and architectural proportion. The unit is conceived as something *chosen* – but not chosen at random. It must be large enough to count with respect to the thing to be measured, while on the other hand, if the unit is to be of any use as a measure, it naturally cannot be of a similar size to the thing to be measured. In relation to the thing, the unit must be 'not too little, and not too big'.

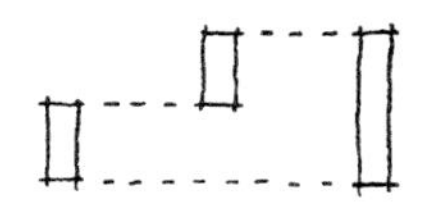

Figure 3.1 The beginning of counting: 1 + 1 = 2.

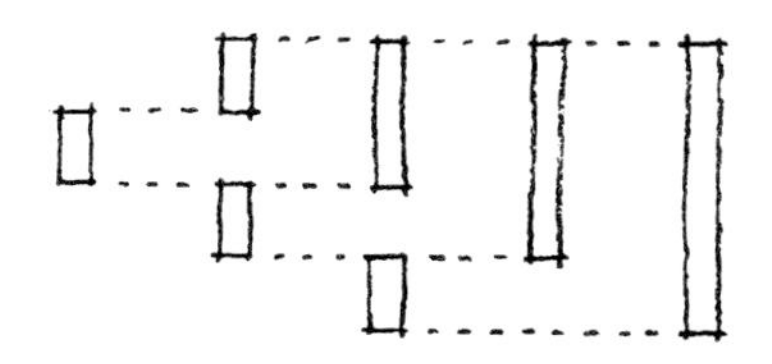

Figure 3.2 Arithmetic progression.

3.3 BETWEEN ONE AND TWO

The beginning of proportion, like the beginning of counting and of all mathematics, is the passage from one to two: the equation $1 + 1 = 2$. When we count, we must begin by adding the unit to itself; for, since the unit is by definition indivisible, nothing smaller is available to be added to it. We add one to itself, and get two (see Figure 3.1). Having taken this first step, there are three ways of proceeding.

(1) The first and most obvious method is the process of addition. We continue to add the unit to the number last formed, and so generate the simple arithmetic progression used in counting: 1, 2, 3, 4, 5. . . (see Figure 3.2). This sort of progression, formed by repeatedly adding a constant increment, is infinitely flexible, since the series contains all possible sums of its terms. But it does not yet constitute a satisfactory system of proportion. As the numbers get larger, the unit, being constant, evanesces in relation to them. The ratios between consecutive measures diminish at each stage, becoming ever less perceptible, ever less significant in relation to the whole. No two are the same; they dissolve in meaningless profusion. Conversely, at the bottom of the scale, the choices are too few. What is needed is a scale in which the constant is not the size of the interval between measures but the ratio between each measure and its successor.

(2) Instead of adding the unit constantly to the last number

formed, we can multiply each number by a constant to produce the next. If, for example, the constant multiplier is 2, we form the geometric progression 1, 2, 4, 8, 16, etc. This method has the effect of thinning out the permissible numbers as the series advances, maintaining a constant relation between the number of choices and the size of the measures. If the numbers below the unit are at the same time progressively halved, forming the descending progression 1, 1/2, 1/4, 1/8, etc., a very simple and recognizable kind of order is created (see Figure 3.3). The series constitutes an embryonic system of proportion.

It is not yet an adequate one, however. The series 1, 2, 4, 8, . . . offers only a single additive combination, $1 + 1 = 2$, repeated at every stage: $2 + 2 = 4$, $4 + 4 = 8$, and so on. No other sums formed between the terms produce members of the series: for example, $1 + 2 = 3$, $1 + 4 = 5$, $1 + 8 = 9$. Therefore any combination of two different elements in a design based on such a series must produce a third element that is not a member of it. The composition is liable to degenerate through increasing complexity into total disorder. Conversely, if one attempts to preserve order by the repetition of a uniform element, the result, as we have seen, is merely another kind of disorder. True order being a balanced combination of unity and complexity, an effective system of proportions must combine the multiplicativeness of the geometric progression with the additiveness of the arithmetic progression.

A second defect of the geometric progression based on doubling is that the jump from one to two is simply too great. In practice, the builder or architect needs to be able to employ ratios that are greater than 1 : 1 but less than 2 : 1. For instance, he must be able to make a room longer than a square but shorter than two squares (see Figure 3.4). So our second requirement for designing an effective system is that the multiplier between consecutive measures must lie somewhere between one and two.

(3) A first step towards overcoming these problems is to reduce the constant multiplier, and most systems of proportion do in fact have multipliers smaller than two. Table 3.1 shows the decimal values of the basic ratios used in architecture.

However, except in the case of the golden section and Van der Laan's plastic number, the geometric series based on these constants are not truly additive. As we have seen in the

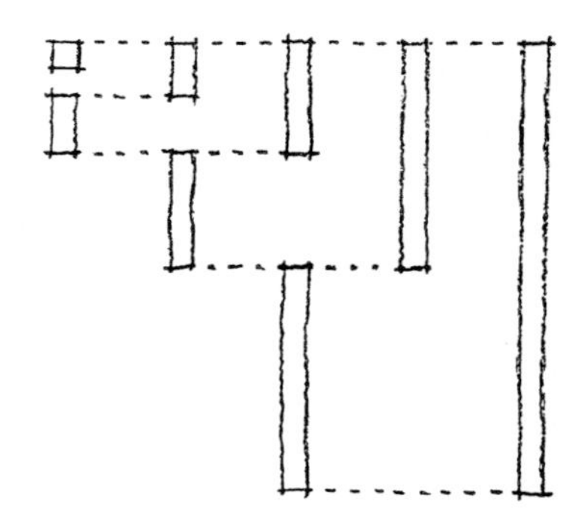

Figure 3.3 Geometric progression.

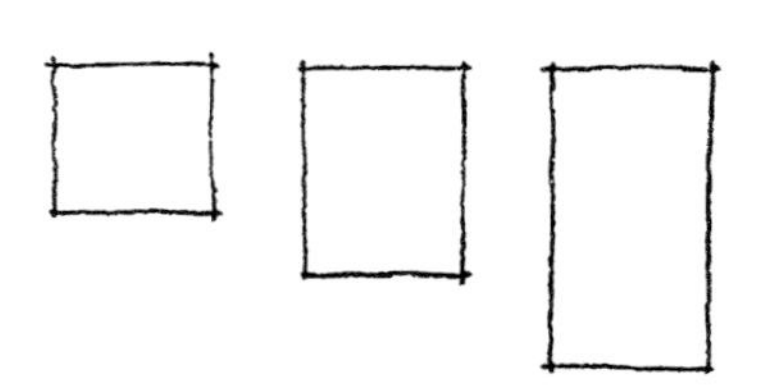

Figure 3.4 Mediation between the square and double square.

TABLE 3.1

BASIC RATIO	DECIMAL
square root of two ($\sqrt{2}$)	1.4142. . .
square root of three ($\sqrt{3}$)	1.732. . .
square root of four ($\sqrt{4}$)	2.0
square root of five ($\sqrt{5}$)	2.236. . .
golden section (ϕ)	1.618. . .
plastic number ratio (ψ)	1.325. . .

case of the doubling or $\sqrt{4}$ progression, only the addition of one term to itself produces a sum that belongs to the series. The solution is to *interweave* two geometric progressions, rather as the warp and weft are interwoven in a piece of cloth. The warp series might still be the doubling progression 1, 2, 4, . . ., but the multiplier of the weft series will be the sum of two terms of the warp series: for example, 1 + 2 = 3. In this way the grid of measures shown in Table 3.2 is generated.

By combining the various warp and weft measures one obtains new ratios such as 3/2, 4/3, 9/4, 9/8 and 16/9. The number of available additive combinations is greatly increased:

1 + 1 = 2, 3 + 3 = 6, etc.
1 + 2 = 3, 3 + 6 = 9, etc.
1 + 3 = 4, 3 + 9 = 12, etc.
1 + 8 = 9, 3 + 24 = 27, etc.

This is in effect the 'Renaissance' or 'Pythagorean–Platonic' system. In practice, all systems of proportion are based on such interwoven grids. The nucleus of every proportion system can be reduced to Table 3.3, where x and y represent any multipliers whatsoever.

If we let $x = 2$ and $y = x + 1$, we get the 'Renaissance' measures shown in Table 3.2. In fact, this is simply the special case where $x^2 = 4$, a perfect square, so that its square root, x, is a rational number. Other systems are produced by supplying different values for x^2, such as 2, 3 or 5, none of which are perfect squares. In each case, the interweaving brings about a high degree of additiveness among the measures. A most interesting case is where $x = \sqrt{5}$ or approximately 2.236, and $y = (x + 1)/2$. The system that arises combines the square root of five with the golden section, since $(\sqrt{5} + 1)/2 = \phi$, the golden section ratio or about 1.618.

TABLE 3.2

1	3	9	27
2	6	18	54
4	12	36	108
8	24	72	216

TABLE 3.3

1	y	y^2	y^3
x	xy	xy^2	xy^3
x^2	x^2y	x^2y^2	x^2y^3
x^3	x^3y	x^3y^2	x^3y^3

3.4 PROPORTION SYSTEMS AS A UNIFIED FIELD: GEOMETRY OR NUMBER?

Both Jay Hambidge[11] and Rudolf Wittkower[12] make a fundamental distinction between two families of proportion systems, which Hambidge calls 'dynamic' and 'static'

11. J. Hambidge, *The Elements of Dynamic Symmetry*, first published in *The Diagonal*, Yale University Press, 1919–20; republished by Dover Publications, 1967.
12. R. Wittkower, 'The changing concept of proportion', first published in *Architects' Year Book V*, 1953; republished in *Idea and Image*, Thames & Hudson, 1978.

symmetry, and Wittkower the 'geometrical' and the 'arithmetical' classes of proportion. Although these two classifications are broadly similar, Hambidge complicates the issue by saying that 'Static symmetry. . . was based upon the pattern properties of the regular two-dimensional figures such as the square and the equilateral triangle.'[13] These figures are precisely those that give rise to the irrational square roots of two and three, which later in the same book Hambidge discusses, along with $\sqrt{5}$ and the golden section, in connection with *dynamic* symmetry.[14] In the first instance, however, he looks upon the square and triangle as modular elements within a repeated pattern, whereas in the second he considers their internal geometry: that is, the ratios that arise between the diagonal of a square and its side, or the height of an equilateral triangle and half its base.

Both Hambidge's and Wittkower's classifications are misleading. The significant distinction is not between two *classes* of systems, some of which are intrinsically geometrical and others numerical, but between two *ways* – by geometry or by number – in which *all* systems can be generated. The important exception to this is the plastic number. Neither Hambidge nor Wittkower was aware of it, however, since Van der Laan's book *Le nombre plastique* was not published until 1960.

Hambidge bases his argument for the superiority of dynamic symmetry on the Euclidian principle of 'commensurability in the square': that is, that the areas of the squares on the sides of a shape (of, for instance, a $\sqrt{2}$ rectangle) are mutually commensurable, although the lengths of these sides are not (see Figure 3.5). He connects this with the phenomenon of phyllotaxis in nature, which he takes as a confirmation of his argument for 'dynamic' irrational ratios:

> The dynamic rectangles, which are obtained from the growth phenomena, are distinguished by this property of area measurableness. . . Because of the persistence of the normal ratios of phyllotaxis the conclusion is inevitable that the measurable area themes possess life and all the qualities that go with it, while areas which do not have this peculiar quality do not have life. They are 'static' or dead areas, at least as far as design is concerned. . . We know that one characteristic of Greek design is just this life-suggesting quality. . . We know also that Roman art,

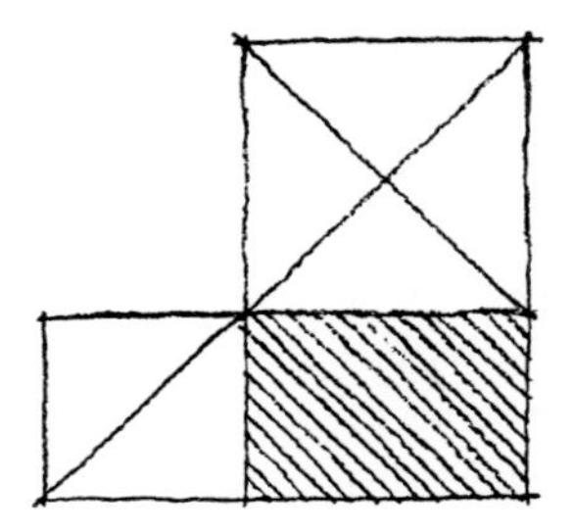

Figure 3.5 Commensurability in the square: the hatched area is a $\sqrt{2}$ rectangle; the square on the long side is twice the square on the short side.

13. J. Hambidge, *The Elements of Dynamic Symmetry*, p. xiii.
14. *Ibid.*, pp. 17–24, 33–50.

> by comparison, is lifeless.[15]

But as P.H. Scholfield points out, the commensurability of areas applies only to the root rectangles themselves. The golden or 'whirling square' rectangle that Hambidge advocates most strongly is commensurable neither in length nor in square.[16]

And nature itself seems to prefer whole numbers. In the example that Hambidge cites – phyllotaxis – it is not the irrational number ϕ, approximately 1.618, but the whole-number Fibonacci series 1, 1, 2, 3, 5, . . .,[17] that plants actually exhibit. Hambidge attempts to explain away this embarrassing fact by the rather unconvincing argument that 'The fractions necessary to make the ratio 1.618 complete for the system are so small that their presence in a system could not be noted.'[18] This implies that if a botanist possessed instruments accurate enough, he would discover these small increments. Clearly that is nonsense. Nature employs whole numbers because she is counting, not measuring. It is a matter of the number of seeds in a sunflower, or of branches from a stem. One seed is possible, or two, but not an irrational number of seeds.

Hambidge argues that

> A much closer representation [than the Fibonacci series] would be obtained by a substitute series such as 118, 191, 309, 500, 809, 1309, 2118, 3427, 5545, 8972, 14 517, etc. One term of this series divided into the other equals 1.6180, which is the ratio necessary to explain the symmetry of the plant design system.[19]

In fact, any sequence in which each number is the sum of its two preceding numbers will converge towards ϕ in exactly the same way as the Fibonacci series, but a little more *slowly*. No matter which two numbers one starts with, the ratio between the ninth and tenth terms of the series will be a fairly good approximation of ϕ. Hambidge's 'substitute series' merely begins 1, 5, 6, 11, . . . instead of 1, 1, 2, 3, . . . It continues as follows: 17, 28, 45, 73, 118, 191, etc. The ratio between the ninth and tenth terms of the sequence (191/118 = 1.618 644) is slightly less close to ϕ (1.618 033 9. . .) than that between the corresponding terms of the Fibonacci series (55/34 = 1.617 647).

In any case, the Fibonacci numbers that occur in plants

15. *Ibid.*, pp. 10-11.
16. P.H. Scholfield, *The Theory of Proportion in Architecture*, Cambridge University Press, p. 118.
17. Named after Leonardo of Pisa, 'filius Bonacci', who published it in his *Liber abici* in 1202.
18. J. Hambidge, *The Elements of Dynamic Symmetry*, p. 11.
19. *Ibid.*, p. 3.

tend to be only the first few terms of the series. As Christopher Alexander has commented,

> It is true that we find pentagons, five-petalled flowers, equiangular spirals, serial arrangements of leaves on branches. But all these patterns are governed by the way in which they have been made. . . Yet. . . we still find people writing as though nature uses the golden section in order to be harmonious. The numbers actually found in nature (ratios like 5/8, 3/5, 2/3, 1/2), are not at all close to ϕ. . . ϕ itself plays no part in natural growth; but the first few members of the Fibonacci series, and the structure of the series, do picture the serial growth of certain forms.[20]

Whole-number additive progressions such as the Fibonacci series are at least as significant manifestations of the golden section and other theoretically incommensurable ratios as are the irrational limits towards which these progressions converge. And in architecture, just as in nature, whole numbers reflect the reality of building. Even when a building is not constructed of individual units like bricks, it is still necessary to measure it out in units: inches or centimetres. Although it would be easy, as Van der Laan points out, to express the basic ratio of the plastic number as the decimal solution of the equation $1 + x = x^3$ (that is, 1.3247. . .),

> From an architectonic point of view the result of this cubic equation would tell us very little. . . A mathematical calculation gives us only abstract numbers with many decimals, and we then lose contact with the concrete reality of the plastic datum.[21]

In other words, in order to be architectonically expressive, number must be experienced in a very concrete way. It must be something like counting pebbles on a beach. This is how Van der Laan treats mathematics throughout his book and also, as we shall see in the next chapter, how the ancient mathematicians understood it. The word 'calculate' derives, incidentally, from the Latin *calculus*, meaning a small stone.

With the exception of the plastic number, all the systems listed in Table 3.1 can be generated by simple geometry. And all the systems, *including* the plastic number, can be generated

20. C. Alexander, 'Perception and modular coordination', *RIBA Journal*, October 1959, p. 426.
21. H. van der Laan, *Architectonic Space*, E.J. Brill, 1983, p. 99.

as additive series of whole numbers like the 'Renaissance' system shown in Table 3.2. The intention of the following two sections is to show how these twin sources give the known systems a fundamental unity. In reality they are not six separate systems but variations on a common pattern. This pattern can manifest itself either as geometry or as number. We shall look first at geometry.

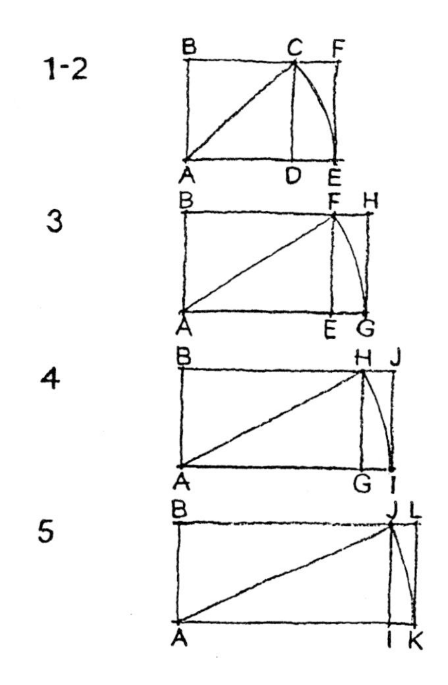

Figure 3.6 Construction of $\sqrt{2}$, $\sqrt{3}$, $\sqrt{4}$ and $\sqrt{5}$ rectangles.

3.5 THE SOURCE IN GEOMETRY

All five of the square root ratios listed in Table 3.1 – those based on the square roots of 2, 3, 4 and 5, together with the golden section – are revealed by the same very simple and familiar geometrical construction, which Hambidge himself illustrates in Lesson 1 of *The Elements of Dynamic Symmetry* (see Figure 3.6).[22]

(1) Draw a unit square, ABCD.
(2) With centre A draw an arc through C to cut the extended baseline AD at E. The sides of the square being of unit length, AE = $\sqrt{2}$. Draw a perpendicular from E to cut BC extended at F, completing the rectangle ABFE.
(3–5) Repeat the process, drawing successive arcs with centre A, to construct rectangles ABHG, ABJI and ABLK. The lengths AG, AI and AK are respectively $\sqrt{3}$, $\sqrt{4}$ and $\sqrt{5}$. Consequently ABFE, ABHG, ABJI and ABLK are a 'root two rectangle', a 'root three rectangle', a 'root four rectangle' (i.e. double square) and a 'root five rectangle'.

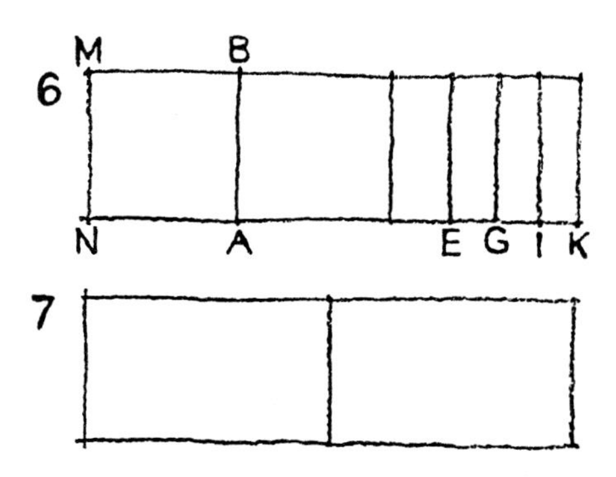

Figure 3.7 Square added to the root rectangles (6). Division into two ϕ rectangles (7).

Hambidge's construction can be taken further, however, and must be, if the four ratios are to reveal their full potential, and become systems in the sense defined in section 3.2: i.e. interwoven grids. For by themselves, as has been said, the geometric progressions based on $\sqrt{2}$, $\sqrt{3}$, $\sqrt{4}$ and $\sqrt{5}$ have negligible additive properties, and are of limited use as systems of proportion. But the progressions produced by adding the *unit* to the square roots of 2, 3, 4 and 5 – that is, $1 + \sqrt{2}$, $1 + \sqrt{3}$, $1 + \sqrt{4}$ and $1 + \sqrt{5}$ – are additive, and their additive potential is further increased when they are interwoven with their parent square root progressions.

So we must finally construct (6) a second unit square ABMN adjacent to the first (see Figure 3.7). The purpose of this is to reveal the additional lengths EN, GN, IN and KN,

22. J. Hambidge, *The Elements of Dynamic Symmetry*, p. 18.

and thus the proportionally all-important complementary numbers $1 + \sqrt{2}$, $1 + \sqrt{3}$, $1 + \sqrt{4}$ and $1 + \sqrt{5}$, or approximately 2.414, 2.732, 3.0 and 3.236. In this way we provide each of the four systems with the weft series it needs to become completely effective. Moreover, bisecting the $1 + \sqrt{5}$ rectangle (7), we obtain two ϕ rectangles, since $\phi = (1 + \sqrt{5})/2$.

The fact that the construction produces both the irrational numbers $\sqrt{2}$, $\sqrt{3}$ and $\sqrt{5}$ and the rational number $\sqrt{4}$ shows that the gulf that is commonly supposed to exist between the commensurable or arithmetical 'Renaissance' system derived from the square root of 4, and the incommensurable, geometrical or 'dynamic' systems derived from the square roots of 2, 3 and 5, is relatively shallow. Other geometrical sources of these proportions are the following.

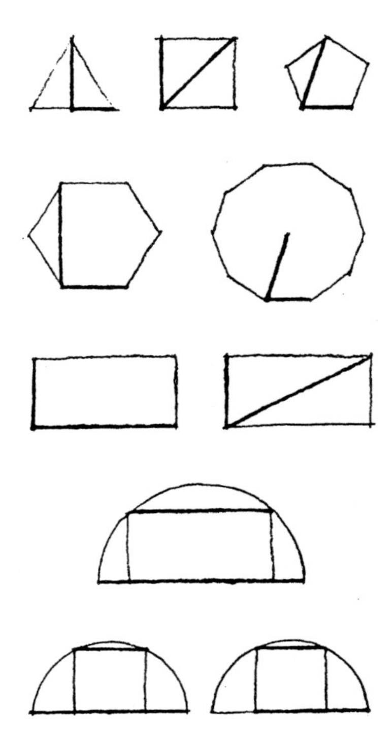

Figure 3.8 Series of regular polygons.

(1) *The series of regular polygons.* The *equilateral triangle* embodies the square root of 3, as the ratio of the height to half the base. The *square*, as we have seen, embodies the square root of 2, as the ratio of the diagonal to the side. The *regular pentagon* embodies the golden section, as the ratio of the diagonal to the side. The *regular hexagon* embodies the square root of 3, as the ratio of the height to the side. The *regular decagon* embodies the golden section, as the ratio of the radius to the side. Furthermore, the *double square* embodies the square root of 4, as the ratio of the longer to the shorter side, and also the square root of 5, as the ratio of the diagonal to the shorter side. The *double square inscribed in a semicircle* embodies the square root of 2, as the ratio of the diameter of the semicircle to the long side of the double square. And the *square inscribed in a semicircle* embodies the square root of 5, as the ratio of the diameter of the semicircle to the side of the square; this construction also embodies the golden section (see Figure 3.8).

(2) *The five regular polyhedra.* The *regular tetrahedron* embodies the square roots of 2 and 3, the first being the ratio of the edge to the diameter of the *midsphere* (that is, the sphere that touches the midpoints of the edges) and the second that of the ratio of the diameter of the *circumsphere* or circumscribing sphere to the diameter of the midsphere. The *cube* embodies the same two square roots, the first being the ratio of the diameter of the midsphere to the edge, and the second that of the diameter of the circumsphere to the edge. The *regular octahedron* embodies the square root of 2, as the ratio

of the diameter of the circumsphere to the edge. The *regular icosahedron* embodies the golden section, as the ratio of the diameter of the midsphere to the edge. Finally, the *regular dodecahedron* embodies ϕ^2, as the ratio of the diameter of the midsphere to the edge (see Figure 3.9 and Table 8.1).

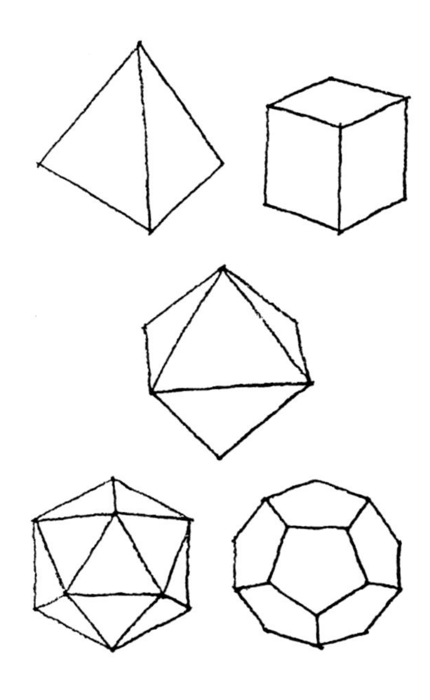

Figure 3.9 The five regular polyhedra: tetrahedron, cube, octahedron, icosahedron, dodecahedron.

3.6 THE SOURCE IN NUMBER

However, it is at least as important to explore how the same systems can be generated by as it were 'counting pebbles', as to consider their source in geometry. It is no less valid to regard them as additive progressions of whole numbers that happen to converge towards irrational values, than as progressions of irrational numbers that arise from geometrical constructions such as the diagonal of a square. We can start by looking once more at Table 3.3. If we substitute $y = x + 1$, this becomes Table 3.4. Multiplying out, we get the summations shown in Table 3.5.

The general warp multiplier x must next be replaced by the separate values $\sqrt{2}$, $\sqrt{3}$, $\sqrt{4}$ and $\sqrt{5}$. These will henceforth be designated, on the analogy of ϕ, by the Greek symbols α, β, γ and δ, and consequently the weft multipliers $(\sqrt{2} + 1)$, $(\sqrt{3} + 1)$, $(\sqrt{4} + 1)$ and $(\sqrt{5} + 1)$ become $(\alpha + 1)$, $(\beta + 1)$, $(\gamma + 1)$ and $(\delta + 1)$ respectively. If at the same time we consider that $\alpha^2 = 2, \beta^2 = 3, \gamma^2 = 4$ and $\delta^2 = 5$, we obtain the four distinct systems shown in Tables 3.6–3.9. The distinctive additive principle of each system now begins to show itself. The upper cases of the same Greek symbols will henceforth be use to designate the four *systems* derived from these ratios: that is, A, B, Γ and Δ. For simplicity, the last two rows in each table, which comprise respectively the doubles, triples, quadruples and quintuples of the first two rows, will henceforth be omitted.

Study of the top rows of the algebraic sums in Tables 3.6–3.9 reveals that in each case characteristic pairs of integers emerge as multipliers. These are shown in Table 3.10. All four sequences start with 1, 1. The first integer in each succeeding column is the sum of the two integers in the preceding column. For example:

$$5 = 3 + 2 \qquad 6 = 4 + 2 \qquad 7 = 5 + 2 \qquad 8 = 6 + 2$$

TABLE 3.4

1	$x + 1$	$(x + 1)^2$	$(x + 1)^3$
x	$x(x + 1)$	$x(x + 1)^2$	$x(x + 1)^3$
x^2	$x^2(x + 1)$	$x^2(x + 1)^2$	$x^2(x + 1)^3$
x^3	$x^3(x + 1)$	$x^3(x + 1)^2$	$x^3(x + 1)^3$

TABLE 3.5

1	$x + 1$	$x^2 + 2x + 1$	$x^3 + 3x^2 + 3x + 1$
x	$x^2 + x$	$x^3 + 2x^2 + x$	$x^4 + 3x^3 + 3x^2 + x$
x^2	$x^3 + x^2$	$x^4 + 2x^3 + x^2$	$x^5 + 3x^4 + 3x^3 + x^2$
x^3	$x^4 + x^3$	$x^5 + 2x^4 + x^3$	$x^6 + 3x^5 + 3x^4 + x^3$

TABLE 3.6 System A

1	$\alpha + 1$	$2\alpha + 3$	$5\alpha + 7$
α	$\alpha + 2$	$3\alpha + 4$	$7\alpha + 10$

The second integer in each succeeding column is formed by adding the second integer in the preceding column to respectively two, three, four and five times the first integer in that column. For example:

$7 = 3 + (2 \times 2)$ $10 = 4 + (3 \times 2)$ $13 = 5 + (4 \times 2)$
$16 = 6 + (5 \times 2)$

These whole-number summations form sequences of convergent ratios that approach as limits the irrational values $\sqrt{2}$, $\sqrt{3}$ and $\sqrt{5}$ and the rational value $\sqrt{4}$. This means that even when the differences between the separate values α, β, γ and δ are disregarded, the whole-number multipliers are by themselves sufficient to define the unique character of each system as a convergent series. It is therefore possible to replace all four systems by convergent series that consist entirely of rational whole numbers. Table 3.13 will be recognized as identical with the first two rows of Table 3.2, for system Γ is essentially the Renaissance system. It differs from the other three in that it is the only one that does not converge towards an irrational value, but reaches directly the rational values $\sqrt{4}$ and $(\sqrt{4} + 1)$: that is, 2 and 3. Thus γ can have only one numerical value, 2. On the other hand it is relatively unimportant what numbers are used to replace α, β and δ. Any numbers chosen will generate series that eventually converge towards these irrational limits. In Tables 3.11–3.14, α and β have been replaced by 1, γ and δ by 2.

The numbers in all four tables obey the additive rule that each number is the sum of the number to its left and the one below that (for example, in Table 3.11, 12 = 5 + 7). This follows inevitably from the fact that all warp series (columns) are x progressions and all weft series (rows) are $(x + 1)$ progressions. Besides this common pattern, each measure is twice the measure to its left in the same row, plus a particular multiple of the measure to the left of that. For system A this multiple is 1, for system B it is 2, for system Γ, 3 and for system Δ, 4. For example:

$12 = (5 \times 2) + (2 \times 1)$
$16 = (6 \times 2) + (2 \times 2)$
$27 = (9 \times 2) + (3 \times 3)$
$32 = (10 \times 2) + (3 \times 4)$.

Greater overall simplicity can be achieved in Table 3.14 by

TABLE 3.7 System B

1	$\beta + 1$	$2\beta + 4$	$6\beta + 10$
β	$\beta + 3$	$4\beta + 6$	$10\beta + 18$

TABLE 3.8 System Γ

1	$\gamma + 1$	$2\gamma + 5$	$7\gamma + 13$
γ	$\gamma + 4$	$5\gamma + 8$	$13\gamma + 28$

TABLE 3.9 System Δ

1	$\delta + 1$	$2\delta + 6$	$8\delta + 16$
δ	$\delta + 5$	$6\delta + 10$	$16\delta + 40$

TABLE 3.10

System A	1, 1	2, 3	5, 7
System B	1, 1	2, 4	6, 10
System Γ	1, 1	2, 5	7, 13
System Δ	1, 1	2, 6	8, 16

TABLE 3.11 System A

1	2	5	12
1	3	7	17

TABLE 3.12 System B

1	2	6	16
1	4	10	28

TABLE 3.13 System Γ

1	3	9	27
2	6	18	54

TABLE 3.14 System Δ

1	3	10	32
2	7	22	72

halving the horizontal multiplier between consective terms in each row. The effect of this is to reduce the irrational limit towards which the horizontal pairs of numbers converge from $(\sqrt{5} + 1)$ to $(1 + \sqrt{5})/2$. But $(1 + \sqrt{5})/2 = \phi$, so we now have a system that converges towards the golden section. In Table 3.15 the system has been extended by two rows to the left in order to show the origin of both rows in unity. The numbers in the top row now constitute the Fibonacci series and those in the second row the closely related Lucas series.[23] Both series are convergents for ϕ, while the relations between successive Lucas numbers and their corresponding Fibonacci numbers converge towards $\sqrt{5}$. In addition, successive Lucas numbers converge towards corresponding powers of ϕ: that is, L_n converges towards ϕ^n. For instance $\phi^9 = 76.012\ldots$, and 76 is the ninth Lucas number. We have, in effect, a new system, and we can rename it system **Φ**.

The horizontal additive rule is now much simpler: each number is the sum of the two numbers to its left. Vertically, each Lucas number is also the sum of four consecutive, or two alternate, Fibonacci numbers, while conversely the sum of four consecutive, or two alternate, *Lucas* numbers equals a quintuple *Fibonacci* number. Moreover, the product of corresponding Fibonacci and Lucas numbers equals a Fibonacci number. Examples of these additive combinations are given in Table 3.16.

A similar simplification can be achieved with system B, but here, if fractions are to be avoided, the horizontal multiplier must be halved only between *alternate* pairs of columns. The result is shown in Table 3.17, where this time the system is extended by two columns to the right to show the alternating rhythm of the weft series. The resulting additive rule alternates between those for systems A and **Φ**. If a given number is the sum of the two preceding numbers in the same row, e.g. 4 = 1 + 3, then the next number is *twice* its preceding number in the same row plus once the number before that, e.g. 11 = (4 × 2) + 3. Alternatively it can be regarded as the sum of two adjacent numbers in the previous column, e.g. 11 = 4 + 7.

System **Φ** can be looked at in two ways. While it belongs to the family of square root proportions through its relationship to $\sqrt{5}$, it is at the same time a member of a quite different family, which has its source in number alone. For it is the simplest of infinitely many additive systems that might be constructed, in which each number is the sum of two

TABLE 3.15 System **Φ**

1	1	2	3	5	8
1	3	4	7	11	18

TABLE 3.16

8	= 3 + 5
	= 2 × 4
5 × 5	= 3 + 4 + 7 + 11
	= 7 + 18
11	= 1 + 2 + 3 + 5
	= 3 + 8
55	= 5 × 11

TABLE 3.17 System **B** revised

1	1	3	4	11	15
1	2	5	7	19	26

23. Lucas published the series named after him in the *American Journal of Mathematics*, I, 1878.

previous numbers of the series. To explain this in more general terms it is necessary to return to algebra. The general formula for all such systems is $1 + x^n = x^{(n+p)}$, where n and p can be any numbers.

If $n = p = 1$, then $1 + x = x^2$, so $x = \phi$, and we have the golden section/$\sqrt{5}$ system Φ. If $n = 1$ and $p = 2$, then $1 + x = x^3$, and x equals the basic multiplier of the plastic number system, approximately 1.325. As we have so far denoted each system by a Greek letter, it will be useful to follow the precedent set by Gérard Cordonnier, who discovered the plastic number independently of Van der Laan and apparently about four years earlier, by calling this number ψ. We shall designate the system as a whole by the upper case of the same letter, Ψ.

Table 3.18 shows some of the more obvious series that might be constructed on the basis of the formula $1 + x^n = x^{(n+p)}$. They are arranged in two groups according to whether n is constant while p varies, or vice versa. None, however, seems so useful for architecture as systems Φ and Ψ. As can be seen from the table both ϕ and ψ occur in both sets, but whereas ϕ is the solution of the one equation $1 + x^1 = x^2$, ψ is the solution of two distinct equations, $1 + x = x^3$ and $1 + x^4 = x^5$.

We have already seen how the irrational ϕ series translates into the whole-number Fibonacci and Lucas series. The two equivalent series for ψ are given in Table 3.19. Because of the relatively slow growth rate of the system, it needs to be extended to twelve columns in order to show its additive potential. The series shown in the second row is not mentioned by Van der Laan, but it is logical to include it since the relation between the two series mirrors that between the Fibonacci and Lucas series. Each number in the second row is the sum of four consecutive or two alternate terms of the first: for example, 8 = 1 + 2 + 2 + 3 = 3 + 5. As with system Φ, the combination of the two series possesses far richer additive properties than either series alone. The relation between corresponding terms of the two rows converges towards $1 : (\psi^4 - 1)$ or about 1 : 2.08.

Although the golden section is generally regarded as the most flexible of all systems,[24] the additive properties of system Ψ are richer still. Every measure of either series of system Ψ is the sum of two, three or five consecutive measures of its own series, while every measure of the second series is the sum of four and of eight consecutive

TABLE 3.18

VALUE OF n	VALUE OF p	FORMULA	RATIO	SYMBOL ADOPTED
1	1	$1 + x^1 = x^2$	1.618	ϕ
1	2	$1 + x^1 = x^3$	1.325	ψ
1	3	$1 + x^1 = x^4$	1.221	–
1	4	$1 + x^1 = x^5$	1.167	–
1	5	$1 + x^1 = x^6$	1.135	–
1	1	$1 + x^1 = x^2$	1.618	ϕ
2	1	$1 + x^2 = x^3$	1.465	–
3	1	$1 + x^3 = x^4$	1.380	–
4	1	$1 + x^4 = x^5$	1.325	ψ
5	1	$1 + x^5 = x^6$	1.285	–

TABLE 3.19 System Ψ

1	1	1	2	2	3	4	5	7	9	12	16
1	2	3	3	5	6	8	11	14	19	25	33

24. P.H. Scholfield, *The Theory of Proportion in Architecture*, p. 11.

measures, as well as of two or four *alternate* measures, of the first. Examples of these sums are given in Table 3.20.

The additive richness of systems like the plastic number and the golden section has a direct impact on their capacity to generate designs that are at once ordered and complex. Broadly speaking, one can say that the potential complexity of a system is directly proportional to its wealth of additive properties, whereas its ordering capacity is inversely proportional to the density of measures. In other words, the more additive permutations a system offers, the greater the potential complexity, while the larger the basic multiplier, the greater the order. Thus the plastic number, with its more varied additiveness, favours complexity, and the golden section, with its larger multiplier (1.618 against the plastic number's 1.325) has a stronger ordering potential. However, since order and complexity are not mutually antagonistic, but tend on the contrary to enhance each other, the effectiveness of a proportion should be regarded as the product of both factors.

TABLE 3.20

16	= 7 + 9
	= 4 + 5 + 7
	= 2 + 2 + 3 + 4 + 5
25	= 11 + 14
	= 9 + 16
	= 6 + 8 + 11
	= 4 + 5 + 7 + 9
	= 3 + 3 + 5 + 6 + 8
	= 1 + 1 + 2 + 2 + 3 + 4 + 5 + 7
	= 2 + 4 + 7 + 12

3.7 ARCHITECTURAL PROPORTION AND PROGRESS IN MATHEMATICS

All known systems of proportion are solutions to the problem of how to punctuate the interval between 1 and 2 in such a way that the resulting series of measures is both additive and multiplicative, and consequently productive of both order and complexity. The golden section and the plastic number are merely particular cases of this general principle. With the exception of the plastic number, all the systems mentioned employ mathematical principles that were well known to the ancient Greeks. The great advances in mathematics made in the last four centuries have thus left architectural proportion virtually unchanged. This fact has been remarked upon by several writers. P.H. Scholfield comments in *The Theory of Proportion in Architecture* that developments in this field have not been comparable to the continuous progress made in the physical sciences: 'It is not simply that progress has been slower than in in some other fields of human thought, but it has been intermittent and at times almost completely interrupted.'[25] Robin Evans, in *The Projective Cast*, observes that proportion has traditionally been regarded as the foundation of architecture, and

25. *Ibid.*, p. 2.

> The job of a foundation is to be as firm as a rock. It is supposed to be inert. . . From the point of view of the architect seeking firmness and stability, the best geometry is surely a dead geometry, and perhaps that, by and large, is what architecture is made with.[26]

This is not to say, however, that the practice of architectural proportion is unaffected by our changing ideas about the connection between mathematics and the existence of order in nature, or that it does not need to be sustained by these ideas. It is the purpose of the present book to argue that it was both sustained and affected. But it does mean that, as I observed in Chapter 1, the relation between the two spheres is based on analogy, not identity. Architectural proportion has always needed to suit the forms and techniques of building, and despite technical advances these do not change fundamentally, nor do they require great mathematical sophistication. Triangles, rectangles and circles may be, as Evans points out, 'pretty well exhausted as subjects of geometrical enquiry',[27] but this does not reduce their value for architecture.

The same is true of the strictly practical kinds of measurement used in building and engineering. The mathematician Tobias Dantzig points out that

> Some modern interpreters of mathematical thought have been inclined to dismiss the ideas of the early Pythagoreans as naive notions of a bygone age. And yet in the eyes of the individual who uses mathematical tools in his daily work. . . these notions are neither obsolete nor naive. For such numbers as are of significance to him result either from *counting* or from *measuring*, and are, therefore, either *integers* or *rational fractions*. To be sure, he may have learned to use with comparative facility symbols and terms which allude to the existence of non-rational entities, but this phraseology is to him but a useful turn of speech. In the end, the rational number emerges as the only magnitude that can be put to practical use.[28]

It is true that the golden section and the plastic number are based theoretically on irrational numbers, but this is ignored in practice. Both systems use either rounded-off decimal approximations like 1.618 and 1.325, or whole-number

26. R. Evans, *The Projective Cast*, MIT Press, 1995, p. xxvii.
27. *Ibid.*
28. T. Dantzig, *Number*, George Allen & Unwin, 1962, pp. 325–6.

progressions like the Fibonacci and Lucas series, which obey the same additive rule and therefore converge towards the same irrational limit.

Chapter four

THE HOUSE AS MODEL FOR THE UNIVERSE

I believe that the Milesians, like their oriental predecessors who took the world for a tent, envisaged the world as a kind of house, the home of all creatures – our home . . . There was movement, there was change in this home, there was hot and cold, fire and moisture. There was a fire in the hearth, and on it a kettle with water. The house was exposed to the winds, and a bit draughty, to be sure; but it was home, and it meant security and stability of a sort. But for Heraclitus the house was on fire.[1]

4.1 CIRCLE AND SQUARE

The last chapter concluded with the observation that the mathematics of architectural proportion has remained more or less that of the ancient Greeks – even of the first, almost legendary Greek mathematician, Pythagoras – and that this is because measures and forms in architecture have to conform to the forms and techniques of building, not to developments in mathematics. The argument can be turned the other way around, however: the reason why early mathematics conforms so well to the nature of architecture is that in the beginning ideas about the world were based on the experience of building. The house was the first model of the universe. If the mathematics of science and architecture have since diverged, it is because this is no longer the case.

W.R. Lethaby speculates in his books *Architecture, Mysticism and Myth* (1891) and *Architecture, Nature and Magic* (1928) that the earliest palaces and temples were intended as representations of the 'world fabric' as it was conceived at the time; the earthly building was meant

1. K.R. Popper, *Conjectures and Refutations*, Routledge & Kegan Paul, 1965, pp. 141, 144.

> to set up a local reduplication of the temple not made with hands, the World Temple itself – a sort of model to scale, its form governed by the science of the time; it was a heaven, an observatory, and an almanack.[2]

But the reverse is at least equally true: that the cosmos was conceived as an enlarged model of the earthly construction. The sky was a flat or domed ceiling, a wall of mountains enclosed the earth and supported the sky at its edges, and the ground plan, like that of the earliest dwellings, was either a circle or a square.

Moreover, it seems that where houses were round, so was the universe conceived to be, and where they were square, the earth became four-cornered. In the later book Lethaby acknowledges that forms originating in building furnished the prototypes for cosmology. In the earlier work he supposes that 'a square formed universe preceded the hemispherical'.[3] In the later one he reverses this:

> The earliest constructive works of man – holes for shelter, pits for burial, and clay vessels – would obviously have been more or less round in general like a child's sand pit or a bird's nest. At some time an observant man must have noticed that the sun in the heavens was a perfectly true example of the same shape.[4]

He supposes rectangular geometry to have been a later development, but equally one that began with the process of making and was later projected onto the universe as a whole:

> The discovery of the square as a general geometrical idea was a great advance of mind. The form was probably, I think, first recognized in weaving and in folding and dividing woven things. . . In settled agricultural ages, dividing up land was done in rectangles. . . The square, when discovered, became a rival, and more than a rival, of a circle, in representing the foundational conception of building, and general adoption of the square type of building was soon reflected back on the world structure.[5]

Whether round houses and a circular universe preceded the square ones, or whether they evolved separately in different places, need not concern us here. Very possibly both forms evolved concurrently, out of different techniques.

2. W.R. Lethaby, *Architecture, Mysticism and Myth*, Architectural Press, 1974, p. 5.
3. *Ibid.*, p. 12.
4. W.R. Lethaby, *Architecture, Nature and Magic*, Duckworth, 1956, p. 18.
5. *Ibid.*, p. 20.

Pottery tends to produce rounded forms; weaving gives rise to rectangular ones. The combination of the two geometries is the source of most proportion systems: those based on the square roots of 2, 3, 4 and 5, and the golden section. A classic example is provided by the traditional granaries and baskets of the Dogon people: the squarish mud-walled granaries are capped with round thatched roofs; the baskets have square bases and circular rims. Both shapes together represent the Dogon universe. As Paul Parin comments, the Dogon

> see even the most commonplace object as part of an all-embracing system. The beautiful woven basket which the Dogon woman uses to carry grain and onions on her head, and as a unit of measure, has a square bottom and a round rim; the cosmos is represented by the basket inverted: the sun is round and the heaven above it is square. The heavenly granary in which the Nommo brought to earth all the animals, plants, and kinds of grain has the form of the inverted basket, as do the granaries in which the Dogon store up their food through the long months between harvests. The use of a granary or basket of some other form would disturb the relationship of sun and heaven and affect the annual rains. The granaries would remain empty, and the continuity of the creation with the present generation would be upset.[6]

Early conceptions of the universe were more like the forms that arise in making dwellings, clay pots, baskets, woven mats and carpentry than these things were like the world as it actually appears. Apart from the sun and the moon, perfect circles in nature appear seldom to the unaided human eye, and the square is more exceptional still. Man had to construct the universe, just as he had to build his houses, in order to make it intelligible for himself. To know something, one must have made it oneself. And he used the same geometry in both building and cosmology: the circle and the square. The relation between these two figures provides the starting point of both architectural proportion and the mathematical investigation of nature.

A circle can easily be drawn on the ground with a stick tied to one end of a cord, the other end of which is anchored by a peg. In order to measure out their rectangular fields (the source of the word *geometry*), the Egyptians had an almost equally simple method of constructing a right angle. A rope

6. P. Parin, *The Dogon People*, in C. Jencks and G. Baird (eds), *Meaning in Architecture*, Barrie & Rockliff: The Cresset Press, 1969, pp. 178–9.

was accurately divided by knots into twelve equal lengths, and the two ends joined. It was then stretched into a triangle with sides of three, four and five lengths. The angle between the two shorter sides is then a right angle (see Figure 4.1). The father of Greek science, Thales of Miletus, was reputed to have learnt this method in Egypt. Later, the theorem of Pythagoras established the general rule for right-angled triangles: that the square on the hypotenuse (the side opposite the right angle) equals the sum of the squares on the other two sides.[7] In the case of the 3 : 4 : 5 triangle the squares are respectively 9, 16 and 25, and since 9 + 16 = 25, the triangle is right angled (see Figure 4.2). The next three 'Pythagorean' triangles – that is, right-angled triangles with mutually commensurable sides – have the proportions 5 : 12 : 13, 9 : 12 : 15 and 8 : 15 : 17. These are the exception, however. In most cases the theorem results in an incommensurability of one or all of the sides. For instance, the hypotenuse of a right-angled isosceles triangle whose two equal sides are one unit long equals the square root of 2 (see Figure 4.3), and the height of a right-angled scalene triangle with a shortest side of one unit and a hypotenuse of two units equals the square root of 3 (see Figure 4.4). In these cases, however great the number of equal lengths marked out on a rope, they will not measure out all three sides of the triangle, because the square roots of 2 and 3 are irrational numbers. The discovery that irrational numbers arise from these primary geometrical figures had important consequences for both architectural proportion and pure mathematics.

Any triangle drawn within a semicircle, with the diameter as its base and its apex touching the circumference, will be right angled.[8] A perpendicular dropped from the apex to the base will divide the first triangle into two similar triangles (that is, triangles of identical shape with the first), and its length will be the *geometric mean* of the two segments into which it divides the base (see Figure 4.5). The geometric mean is that middle term between two others – called the *extremes* – that stands to the first extreme as the second stands to the mean. Thus, A and C being the extremes and B their geometric mean, $A : B = B : C$. The geometric mean between any two lengths can be determined geometrically by constructing a semicircle with their combined length as diameter and erecting a perpendicular at their meeting point to cut the semicircle.

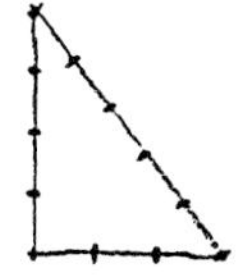

Figure 4.1 Construction of a right angle with knotted rope.

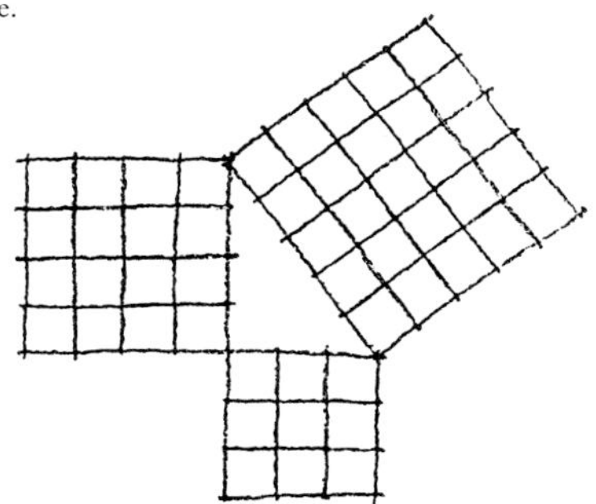

Figure 4.2 Areas of squares on the sides of the knotted rope triangle: 9 + 16 = 25.

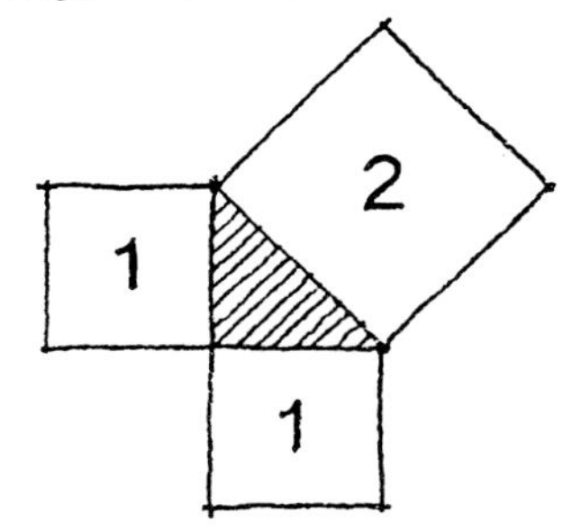

Figure 4.3 Squares on the sides of an isosceles right-angled triangle: 1 + 1 = 2.

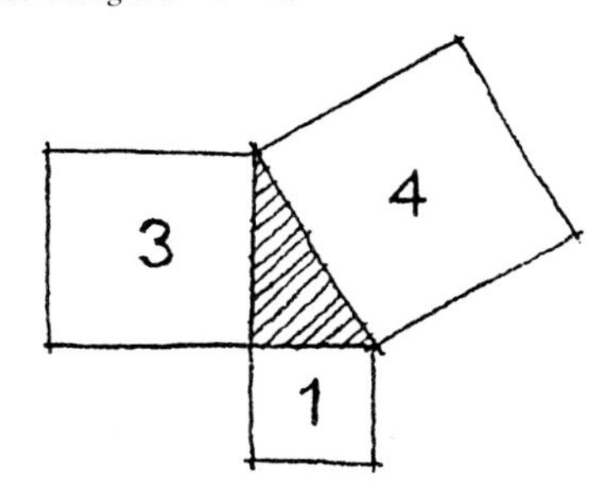

Figure 4.4 Squares on the sides of a half equilateral triangle: 1 + 3 = 4.

7. Euclid, *Elements*, Book I, proposition 47, Dover, 1956, vol. 1, p. 349.
8. *Ibid.*, Book III, proposition 31, vol. 2, p. 61.

A square inscribed in the half circle divides the diameter into three parts related by the golden section, i.e. in the ratio $1 : \phi : 1$.[9] The ratio of a side of the square to the diameter is then $1 : \sqrt{5}$; that is, 1 to the square root of 5 (see Figure 4.6). A rectangle equal in height to the square and in width to the diameter is therefore a $\sqrt{5}$ rectangle. It is composed of two overlapping golden rectangles, or two smaller golden rectangles plus the square. Thus almost all the irrational numbers important for architectural proportion are generated by simple constructions involving the circle, square and right-angled triangle. The exception is the plastic number, which cannot be constructed geometrically.

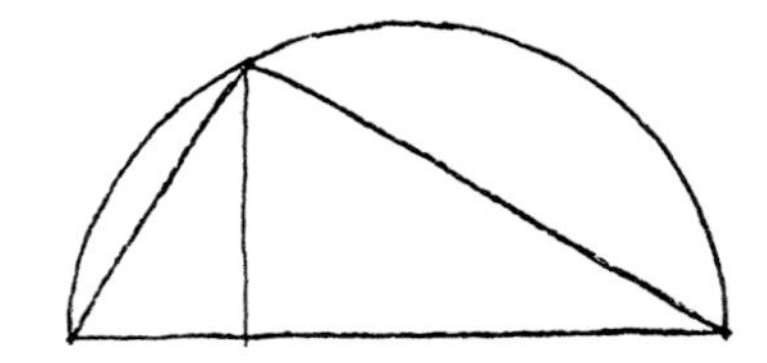

Figure 4.5 The perpendicular divides the triangle inscribed in a semicircle into two similar triangles.

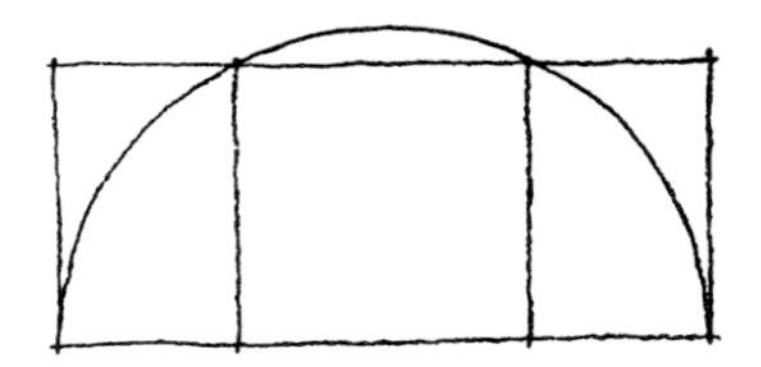

Figure 4.6 Square inscribed in a semicircle.

4.2 THE HOUSE BUILT OF NUMBERS

Karl Popper's observation, quoted at the head of this chapter, that the Milesian thinkers looked upon the world as a kind of house, can be applied more widely: to the Presocratics as a whole, and even to the cosmology of Plato's *Timaeus*. Approaching the world as a house, the Greeks based its architecture on the way a building is built. The questions they asked themselves concerned its structure, its ground plan, and its building material, and, in the case of the mathematical schools of Plato and Pythagoras, above all its measures and proportions. Earlier philosophers, like Thales (fl. *c.* 585 BC) and his fellow Milesians Anaximander (*c.* 610–546 BC) and Anaximenes (fl. *c.* 555–525 BC), emphasized the material: the world was composed of water, or air, or of a fundamental, unformed element, the 'boundless'. But for Pythagoras (fl. *c.* 532 BC), what mattered was not so much the material of which the building blocks of the house were made, as their size and shape. And since our present concern is not with the structure, planning or materials of buildings but with architectural proportion, it is this aspect that is relevant.

Pythagoras taught that the essence of nature lies in number – indeed, that numbers constitute as it were the building blocks of the world. Aristotle – not a sympathetic witness – wrote later that the Pythagoreans

> thought they saw in numbers, rather than in fire or earth or water, many resemblances to things which exist and which come into being. . . Hence they considered the

9. See Chapter 8, p. 141.

> principles of numbers as the principles of all things, and the whole universe as a harmony and a number.[10]

Numbers were conceived as molecular arrangements of atomic units (like dots or pebbles), and were represented as such. The number of units determined their arrangement, and thus the shape of the block, and ultimately the form of the whole house.

Therefore, in contrast to the more materialistic approach of the Milesians, the outlook of the Pythagoreans tended to be mystical and mathematical. They sought a key not in the material world that could be seen or felt, but rather in the ideas or principles that underlay these appearances. By this means they hoped to discover the underlying secrets of nature. They studied mathematics not just for its own sake, or for practical purposes like commerce and technology, but as the essential principle of nature. Their mathematics, like that of Plato, which it largely inspired, was *ontological*: its concern was the nature of being. Therefore Pythagoras is the first representative of one of the two schools of thought that I have identified, namely 'empathy'. This school recognizes no gulf between the human intellect, exemplified by mathematics, and the real nature of the world. If differences appear, they must be illusory, because the mind has the power to penetrate and grasp the reality underlying appearances. In other words, it has a complete *empathy* with nature itself. If there is a conflict between reason and appearances, so much the worse for appearances. As Aristotle goes on to say:

> They collected and systematized all the instances they could find of correspondences between numbers or harmonies and properties and relations of the heavens and the whole universal order. If anything was lacking to complete their theories, they quickly supplied it. They held, for instance, that 10 is a perfect number and embraces all the powers of number. On this view they asserted that there must be ten heavenly bodies; and as only nine were visible they invented the 'counter-earth' to make a tenth.[11]

Legend credits Pythagoras with the discovery of the correspondence between the first natural numbers – 1, 2, 3 and 4, the sum of which is 10 – and the basic harmonies of

10. Aristotle, *Metaphysics*, trans. J. Warrington, Everyman's Library, 1956, p. 64.
11. *Ibid.*

Greek music. He is supposed to have found that a string, shortened to three quarters of its length, sounds a fourth higher; shortened again, to two thirds of the remaining or half the original length, it sounds a fifth higher still, and an octave higher than the first note. The octave can be composed as a fourth followed by a fifth ($4/3 \times 3/2 = 2/1$), or as a fifth followed by a fourth ($3/2 \times 4/3 = 2/1$), or as *two* fourths separated by a tone ($4/3 \times 9/8 \times 4/3 = 2/1$) (see Figure 4.7). The mathematics is simple, but no principle has had a greater impact on the theory of proportion. The harmonious relationships of sounds were shown to correspond to simple numerical proportions in space – 4 : 3, 3 : 2 and 2 : 1 – and seemed to provide clear evidence of the underlying mathematical unity of natural phenomena. During the Italian Renaissance these ratios became the basis of architectural proportion. The musical consonances were audible evidence, it was thought, of the universal cosmological significance of the simplest numerical ratios.[12]

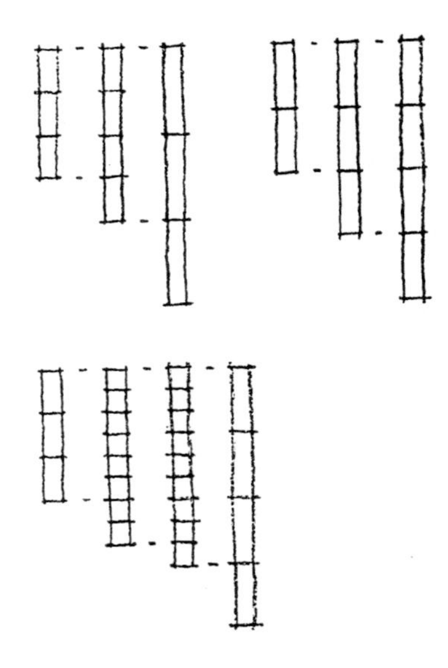

Figure 4.7 Divisions of the octave.

The implications of the discovery extend beyond either music or architecture: they concern the whole conception of space. For it implies that space is *granular*: that is, not continuous but made up of discrete segments. These segments correspond exactly to the units of the natural numbers 1, 2, 3, 4, etc. This is why, as we shall see, the discovery that the square root of 2, the length of the diagonal of a unit square, is irrational, posed such a problem for the Pythagorean mathematicians.

The first four numbers were regarded by the Pythagoreans as constituting a spatial hierarchy: 1 corresponded to the point, 2 to the line, 3 to the plane and 4 to the solid. This arrangement is arguably more illuminating than the modern attribution of one dimension to the line, two to the plane and three to the solid, since a line can be defined by two points, a plane by three and a solid by four (see Figure 4.8).

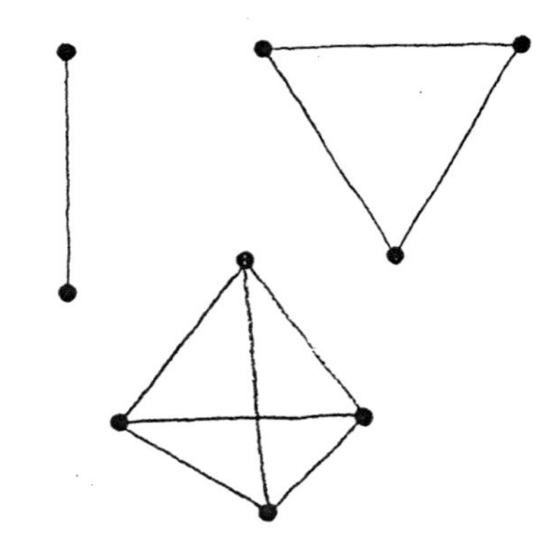

Figure 4.8 Line, plane and volume.

The unit was conceived as having a dimension, however small: it was a discrete quantity, a *smallest indivisible whole*. It followed from this that combinations of units formed characteristic space-filling shapes, depending on their arrangement. They could form series of plane figures or solid forms: triangular, square, oblong, cubic, etc. Matter was believed to consist of combinations of such shapes.

Each series of planar numbers is thus the summation of a particular arithmetical progression (see Figure 4.9). The general rule for the series of *polygonal* numbers – triangular,

12. For the Renaissance, see R. Wittkower, *Architectural Principles in the Age of Humanism*, Alec Tiranti, 1952, pp. 89–124; for Pythagoras, see J. Burnet, *Greek Philosophy*, Macmillan, 1964, pp. 35–9.

square, etc. – is that if n is the number of sides of the polygon, then the series is the summation of the arithmetical progression $1, 1 + (n-2), 1 + 2(n-2), 1 + 3(n-2)$, etc. Thus the triangular number $10 = 1 + (1 + 1) + (1 + 2) + (1 + 3)$, since for the triangle $n - 2 = 1$. The *oblong* numbers are twice their corresponding triangular numbers, and also the summations of the series of even numbers. The formation of the first four polygonal number series and the oblong series is shown in Table 4.1.

Besides these there are 'solid' numbers (see Figure 4.10). These can be tetrahedral – the summations of triangular numbers, for example $1 + 3 + 6 = 10$; pyramidal – summations of square numbers, for example $1 + 4 + 9 = 14$; or cubic – more complicatedly, summations of *the sums of alternate pairs of triangular numbers with four times their intervening number*, for example $27 = [0 + (4 \times 0) + 1] + [0 + (4 \times 1) + 3] + [1 + (4 \times 3) + 6] = 1 + 7 + 19$. These formations are shown in Table 4.2.

At first, the Pythagoreans appeared to have unified arithmetic and geometry: to have reduced space to arrangements of numbers. However, one of their outstanding discoveries, the theorem of Pythagoras, revealed the existence of irrational numbers. It thus undermined the fundamental principle of Pythagorean mathematics: the concrete reality of the unit as an indivisible whole. The most elementary geometrical relations – those of the sides to the diagonal of a square or double square, and of the sides to the height of an equilateral triangle – were shown to be irrational. For suppose a line AB is drawn, of unit length. Then the positive integers can be marked off on the line by extending the line and marking off a series of intervals equal to AB, and conversely by dividing AB into any number of aliquot parts we can represent all rational fractions. But if we draw a square on AB, and describe an arc equal to the diagonal AC, cutting AB extended at D, then AD corresponds to no rational number (see Figure 4.11). As Tobias Dantzig observes,

> It is true that if *all* rational numbers were *mapped* on the axis we would obtain a compact set; yet these points would by no means fill the line: there would be left an infinite number of gaps which would admit of no such representation. And. . . *the irrational gaps far exceed the rational points.*[13]

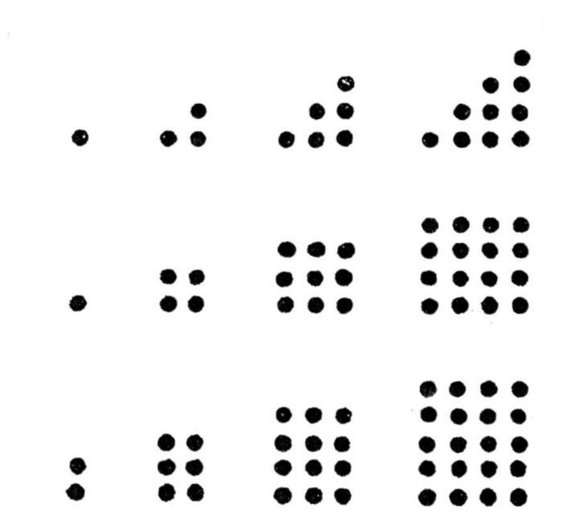

Figure 4.9 Planar numbers: triangular, square, oblong.

TABLE 4.1

FIGURE	N	N − 2	SUMMATION	SERIES
Triangle	3	1	1 + 2 + 3 + 4 + 5,. . .	1, 3, 6, 10, 15,. . .
Square	4	2	1 + 3 + 5 + 7 + 9,. . .	1, 4, 9, 16, 25,. . .
Pentagon	5	3	1 + 4 + 7 + 10 + 13,. . .	1, 5, 12, 22,35,. . .
Hexagon	6	4	1 + 5 + 9 + 13 + 17,. . .	1, 6, 15, 28,45,. . .
Oblong	4	2	2 + 4 + 6 + 8 + 10,. . .	2, 6, 12, 20,30,. . .

TABLE 4.2

FORM	SUMMATION	SERIES
Tetrahedron	1 + 3 + 6 + 10 + 15,. . .	1, 4, 10, 20, 35,. . .
Pyramid	1 + 4 + 9 + 16 + 25,. . .	1, 5, 14, 30, 55,. . .
Cube	1 + 7 + 19 + 37 + 61,. . .	1, 8, 27, 64, 125,. . .

13. T. Dantzig, *Number*, George Allen & Unwin, 1962, p. 107.

The idea that everything in nature could be reduced to countable monads or particles was threatened with collapse. Karl Popper writes that

> The discovery of the irrationality of the square root of two. . . destroyed the Pythagorean programme of 'arithmetizing' geometry. . . The tradition that this discovery was at first kept secret is, it seems, supported by the fact that Plato still calls the irrational at first '*arrhetos*', i.e. the secret, unmentionable mystery. . .[14]

Later, the Pythagorean notion of the discrete unit, and of space as composed of a multiplicity of discrete points or 'units having position', was attacked at a still more fundamental level by the Eleatic philosophers Parmenides and Zeno. The doctrine of Parmenides (born *c.* 510 BC) was an extreme example of the tendency to place reason and logical deduction above the evidence of the senses. The result was a complete monism. He taught that all change, all movement, all infinity, all coming into being or ceasing to be, all creation and destruction, must be an illusion. Since non-being cannot be thought of, it cannot be:

> It needs be that what can be spoken of and thought *is*; for it is possible for it to be, and it is not possible for what is nothing to be.[15]

Consequently nothing can come into being or cease to be: there can be no change and no movement, no past and no future:

> One path only is left for us to speak of, namely that *it is*. In this path are very many tokens that what is is uncreated and indestructible; for it is complete, immovable, and without end. Nor was it ever, nor will it be; for now *it is*, all at once, a continuous one.[16]

Because there can thus be no empty space separating one thing from another, the Pythagorean concept of a multiplicity of separate units is an impossibility. So, contrary to appearances, the real world must be everywhere uniformly dense, uncreated and timeless. It comprises a solid sphere, single, complete, finite, homogeneous, indivisible, eternal, unchanging and motionless:

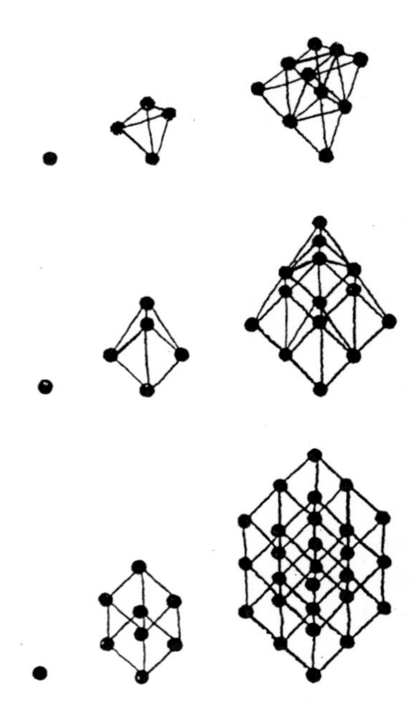

Figure 4.10 Solid numbers: tetrahedral, pyramidal, cubic.

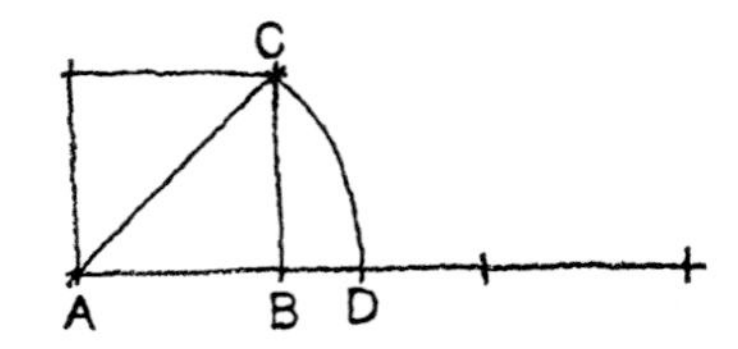

Figure 4.11 Rational and irrational number.

14. K.R. Popper, *The Open Society and its Enemies*, Routledge & Kegan Paul, 1962, vol. I, p. 249.
15. Parmenides, 'The way of truth', in J. Burnet, *Early Greek Philosophy*, A & C Black, 1930, p. 174.
16. *Ibid*., pp. 174–5.

> It is the same, and rests in the self-same place, abiding in itself. . . Wherefore it is not permitted to what is to be infinite; for it is in need of nothing; while, if it were infinite, it would stand in need of everything.[17]

Parmenides' follower Zeno defended this thesis by exposing the contradictions inherent in Pythagoreanism. He argued that since a line can be bisected, and that what can be done once can always be repeated, it follows that if the line is made up of indivisible points they must be infinitely many. Let us consider again the line AB, which can be divided into any number of fractions, 1/2, 1/4, 1/8, 1/16 and so on. Since the denominator can be increased indefinitely it follows that the size of the segments reduces *ad infinitum*. But if the size of the segments – the indivisible points or 'grains' out of which the Pythagoreans believed space to be composed – is zero, then the sum of any number of these points must also be zero. Conversely, if the points have magnitude, and are infinitely many, the line must be infinitely long. There is an unbridgeable gulf between Pythagorean arithmetic with its discrete units – the series of integers, starting with 1 – and geometry with its continuous space.

Nor, as we have just seen, does the infinity of the series of integers solve the problem of continuity. For although the domain of rational numbers is conceived as *everywhere dense* – a '*compact, continuous mass, seemingly without gaps*',[18] – and although it is possible in theory to map the infinitely many rational numbers as points on the line AB, there will remain between them an infinite number of points to which no rational number can be assigned: points that correspond to the infinite domain of irrational numbers, of which the square roots of 2, 3 and 5 are only the most obvious examples.

4.3 PYTHAGOREAN MATHEMATICS AND ARCHITECTURAL PROPORTION

The irrational square roots of 2, 3 and 5, together with the offspring of $\sqrt{5}$, the golden section, provide one of the two constituent principles on which architectural proportion is based. The other principle is founded on the harmonic division of the octave, which as we have seen was also a Pythagorean discovery. These two schools can be traced through history, up to our own day. Rudolf Wittkower

17. *Ibid.*, p. 175.
18. T. Dantzig, *Number*, p. 106.

writes in 'The changing concept of proportion' that

> two different classes of proportion, both derived from the Pythagorean–Platonic world of ideas, were used during the long history of European art. . . the Middle Ages favoured Pythagorean–Platonic geometry, while the Renaissance and Classical periods preferred the numerical, i.e. the arithmetical side of that tradition.[19]

However, as we saw in the last chapter, the basic ratios of the 'arithmetical' principle, 2:1, 3:2 and 4:3, and those of the irrational square root systems originating in geometry, are generated by the same *xy* grid of interwoven warps and wefts. The only difference – admittedly a significant one – is that in the first case $x^2 = 4$, which happens to be a perfect square, so $x = 2$, a rational number. Furthermore, as we shall see in later chapters, documentary evidence does not suggest that the predominance of one tradition during the Middle Ages and the other during the Renaissance was as absolute as Wittkower seems to imply. In architecture, in any case, the distinction between irrational and rational numbers must be overcome in practice, since only whole-number dimensions can be measured out on a building site. The theory that Medieval buildings were set out geometrically, using arcs of circles, rather than by taking linear measurements, remains unproven.

Although irrational numbers can never be calculated exactly, there are various ways by which they can be 'trapped' between rational limits, to any desired degree of accuracy. A particularly elegant method, which enables one as it were to see the process of entrapment unfold, is the *continued fraction*, which approaches the irrational value *as limit* – in other words, as the goal that it would reach if it were continued to infinity. Some historians of mathematics believe that this method was known to the Greeks, but according to Tobias Dantzig the first surviving record of it dates from as late as 1572.[20] The fractions which converge towards $\sqrt{2}$ and $\sqrt{3}$ are:

$$\sqrt{2} = 1 + \cfrac{1}{2 + \cfrac{1}{2 + \cfrac{1}{2 + \cfrac{1}{2}}}} \qquad \sqrt{3} = 1 + \cfrac{1}{1 + \cfrac{1}{2 + \cfrac{1}{1 + \cfrac{1}{2}}}}$$

$$\sqrt{2} = \frac{1}{1}\ \frac{3}{2}\ \frac{7}{5}\ \frac{17}{12}\ \frac{41}{29} \qquad \sqrt{3} = \frac{1}{1}\ \frac{2}{1}\ \frac{5}{3}\ \frac{7}{4}\ \frac{19}{11}$$

19. R. Wittkower, 'The changing concept of proportion', in *Idea and Image*, Thames & Hudson, 1978, p. 116.
20. T. Dantzig, *Number*, p. 155.

The successive approximations for each stage are, for $\sqrt{2}$, 1.0, 1.5, 1.4, 1.4166. . ., 1.4138. . ., and for $\sqrt{3}$, 1.0, 2.0. 1.6666. . ., 1.75, 1.7273. . ., 1.7333. . . They are alternately below or above the actual value of the elusive square root: calculated to seven decimal places, $\sqrt{2}$ = 1.414 213 5 and $\sqrt{3}$ = 1.732 050 8.

The following two alternative fractions both converge towards $\sqrt{5}$:

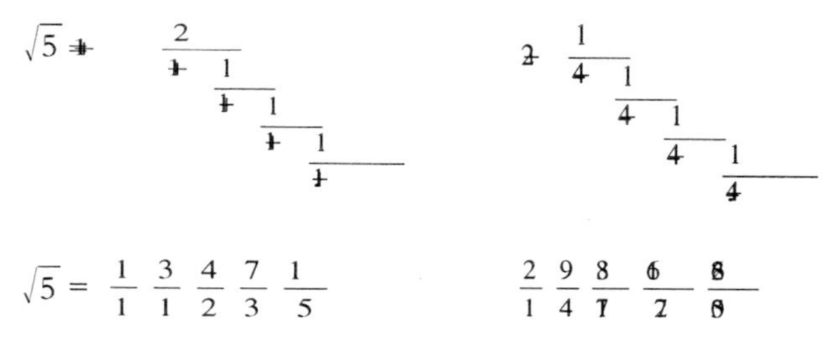

The first gives successive decimal approximations of $\sqrt{5}$ = 1.0, 3.0, 2.0, 2.3333. . . and 2.2, and the second, 2.0, 2.25, 2.2353. . ., 2.2361. . . and 2.2361. Calculated to seven decimals, $\sqrt{5}$ = 2.236 067 9. Thus the second fraction approaches the limit more rapidly, but the first has the advantage of exposing more clearly the close connection between root five, the golden section, and the Fibonacci and Lucas series. The denominators of the successive fractions constitute the Fibonacci series and their numerators the Lucas series, and both series converge towards the golden section number ϕ as limit. However, when the fractions 2/1, 9/4, 38/17,. . . are doubled, they too are found to contain the same series, but only every third term: that is, 4/2, 18/8, 76/34, etc.

The series of convergents for the number ϕ itself is produced by a still simpler and more beautiful continued fraction:

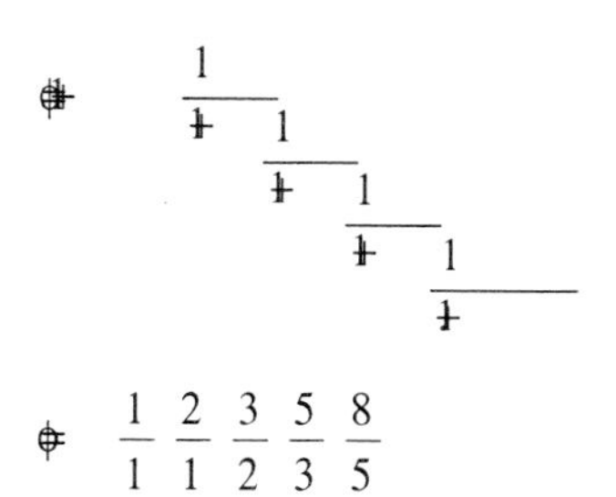

Here both numerators and denominators form the Fibonacci series 1, 1, 2, 3, 5, 8,. . .

Thus with the exception of the plastic number value 1.325, rational convergents for all the irrational numbers that we have mentioned as important for architectural proportion – $\sqrt{2}$, $\sqrt{3}$, $\sqrt{5}$ and ϕ – are obtained from these four continued fractions. Note that the successive numerators and denominators are identical with the numbers in Tables 3.11, 3.17 and 3.15 in Chapter 3.

4.4 THE HOUSE ON FIRE

Henri Bergson (1859–1941) argues, in *Creative Evolution*, that the whole of Western science and philosophy since the Greeks has been under the spell of the 'cinematographic mechanism of thought' – the illusion that the real is the static, and the tendency to conceive time and motion as a series of frozen instants. This is our 'natural' way of thinking, sustained by language and the practical business of living:

> The Greeks trusted to nature, trusted the natural propensity of the mind, trusted language above all, in so far as it naturally externalizes thought. . . As becoming shocks the habits of thought and fits ill into the moulds of language, they declared it unreal. In spatial movement and change in general they saw only illusion. . . Experience confronts us with becoming: that is the *sensible* reality. But the *intelligible* reality, that which *ought* to be, is more real still, and that reality does not change. . . Such was the fundamental principle of the philosophy which developed throughout the classic age, the philosophy of Forms, or to use a term more akin to the Greek, the philosophy of Ideas.[21]

Even today, Bergson observes, 'We shall philosophize in the manner of the Greeks. . . in the exact proportion that we trust in the cinematographical instinct of our thought.'[22] But this is not the way to a true understanding of reality:

> In order to advance with the moving reality, you must replace yourself within it. Install yourself within change, and you will grasp at once both change itself and the successive states in which *it might* at any instant be immobilized.[23]

21. H. Bergson, *Creative Evolution*, Macmillan & Co., 1928, pp. 331–2.
22. *Ibid.*, p. 333.
23. *Ibid.*, pp. 324–5.

Being can be grasped properly only as becoming.

However, the need to 'install oneself within change' is precisely the message of Heraclitus (fl. *c.* 500 BC), for whom reality is a perpetual flux, things continually in motion. Strangely, Bergson does not mention him. By overlooking Heraclitus, he ignores the fact that there have always been two opposed schools of thought, the one built on discrete states and the other on continuous change. Just as Pythagoras represents the rationalist or 'empathic' belief that the essential nature of the universe is directly accessible to human reason through mathematics, Heraclitus can be regarded as the representative of its opposite: the abstractionist recognition of the gulf between the mind and the external world.

Like David Hume, Heraclitus demands an empirical approach to nature: 'The things that can be seen, heard and learned,' he writes, 'are what I prize the most.'[24] Surprised by visitors while warming himself at the kitchen stove, he welcomed them in, saying that 'There also there were gods.'[25] Similarly, Hume draws nearly all the examples in his *Treatise* from the things he can see around him in the room in which he writes: his table, the room itself, the fire burning in the grate.[26] And both philosophers are sceptical about the possibility of certain knowledge: 'Nature loves to hide',[27] writes Heraclitus. He specifically attacks Pythagoras and others:

> The learning of many things teacheth not understanding. . . Pythagoras, son of Mnesarchos, practised scientific inquiry beyond all other men, and. . . claimed for his own wisdom what was merely a knowledge of many things and an imposture.[28]

The conflict between Heraclitus and Pythagoras shows up with particular clarity the perennial struggle between our intellectual tendency to reduce reality to discrete, calculable quantities and regular patterns, and the fluidity, continuity and unpredictability of the actual experience. We are faced with a duality: on the one hand the world of exact, intelligible ideas, and on the other, the world of appearances – ever changing, boundless, formless and immeasurable. For Heraclitus, the wise man recognizes that the world is a perpetual flux, a continual strife between opposites. Things cannot be isolated and defined but are continuously being

24. Heraclitus, 'Fragments', in J. Burnet, *Early Greek Philosophy*, p. 134.
25. Aristotle, *On the Parts of Animals*, quoted in F.M. Cornford, *Before and After Socrates*, Cambridge University Press, 1960, p. 93.
26. D. Hume, *A Treatise on Human Nature*, Everyman's Library, 1911.
27. Heraclitus, 'Fragments', p. 132.
28. *Ibid.*, p. 134.

transformed, coming into being and passing away. He singles out fire as the fundamental element, but not in the literal sense that Thales thought the world was composed of water; it is a metaphor for continual transformation and change:

> This world, which is the same for all, no one of gods or men has made; but it was ever, is now, and ever shall be an ever-living Fire, with measures of it kindling, and measures going out. . . All things are an exchange for Fire, and Fire for all things. . .[29]

Heraclitus had hit on an explanation of the world that seems extraordinarily *modern*, in the sense that it conflicts hardly at all with our current cosmologies. His statement that 'He who does not expect the unexpected will not detect it; for him it will remain undetectable, and unapproachable'[30] seems, for instance, to foreshadow Popper's principle that the role of observation and experiment in scientific discovery is not to confirm theories, but to refute them, for 'It is easy to obtain confirmations, or verifications, for nearly every theory – if we look for confirmations.'[31] Popper's commentary on Heraclitus in *Conjectures and Refutations* stresses his contemporary relevance, and repeats the architectural metaphor of the house as image of the world:

> There is no stability left in the world of Heraclitus. 'Everything is in flux, and nothing is at rest.' *Everything* is in flux, even the beams, the timber, the building material of which the world is made. . . The beams are rotting, the earth is washed away and blown away, the very rocks split and wither, the bronze cauldron turns into green patina. . . But the decisive point is, of course, that this inspired philosophy is *true*, for all we know. With his uncanny intuition Heraclitus saw that things are processes, that our bodies are flames. . .[32]

So ahead of its time was this idea that the philosophy of Heraclitus and his school would be dismissed by Plato, Aristotle and others as a refusal to think clearly or say anything definite. Plato writes in the *Theaetetus* that

> There is no discussing these principles of Heraclitus. . .; you might as well talk to a maniac. Faithful to their own

29. *Ibid.*, pp. 134–5.
30. *Ibid.*, quoted in K.R. Popper, *Conjectures and Refutations*, p. 147.
31 K.R. Popper, *Conjectures and Refutations*, p. 36.
32 *Ibid.*, pp. 144, 148.

> treatises they [his followers] are literally in perpetual motion. . .You will never get anywhere with any of them; for that matter they never get anywhere with one another, but take very good care to leave nothing settled either in discourse or in their own minds. . .[33]

Aristotle says in the *Metaphysics* that

> They. . . observed that the whole sensible world of nature is constantly changing, and they concluded that no true statement can be made about something that is always and everywhere in a state of flux. . . Cratylus, for example, ended by refusing to commit himself to any statement whatever, and would only move his finger.[34]

It is only in the nineteenth and twentieth centuries that the philosophy of the Presocratics, and of Heraclitus in particular, has finally came into its own. If they now seem to us more modern than their successors it is because in the past two hundred years the order of nature has become increasingly *abstract* and elusive; or rather, it appears to reveal itself only where one would least expect it, out of chaos and indeterminacy. Order emerges suddenly out of randomness:

> Men do not know how what is at variance agrees with itself. It is an attunement of opposite tensions, like that of the bow and the lyre. It is the opposite which is good for us. The hidden attunement is better than the open.[35]

And:

> Couples are things whole and things not whole, what is drawn together and what is drawn asunder, the harmonious and the discordant.[36]

Modern, too, is Heraclitus' relativism:

> To God all things are fair and right, but men hold some things wrong and some right. We must know that war is common to all things and strife is justice, and that all things come into being and pass away through strife. . . The way up and the way down is one and the same.[37]

One is reminded of William Blake's *Marriage of Heaven and*

33. Plato, 'Theaetetus', in F. Cornford, *Plato's Theory of Knowledge*, Routledge & Kegan Paul, 1935, p. 93.
34. Aristotle, *Metaphysics*, Everyman's Library, 1956, p. 136.
35. Heraclitus, 'Fragments', p. 136.
36. *Ibid.*, p. 137.
37. *Ibid.*, pp. 137–8.

Hell (*c*.1790–93):

> Without Contraries is no progression. Attraction and Repulsion, Reason and Energy, Love and Hate, are necessary to human existence. From these contraries spring what the religions call Good & Evil.[38]

But what has all this to do – the reader may be asking at this point – with the problem of architecture? At first sight, Heraclitus' teaching seems antithetical to all notions of mathematical order. When the house is on fire, who stops to think about its proportions? What can this negative-sounding doctrine contribute to the quest for a foundation for architectural proportion, except to say that no such foundation exists and the search is in vain? Only this: that if architectural proportion has a basis in nature, the first step towards its discovery is to realize that 'nature loves to hide'. If Pythagoras can be regarded as the ancestor of Leibniz's *Monadology* (1714) and Le Corbusier's *modulor*, Heraclitus is the precursor of Hume and Van der Laan, whose plastic number is founded on the principle that we must learn 'to know by not knowing' – that is, by recognizing the narrow limits of our knowledge.

4.5 ATTEMPTS TO REBUILD THE HOUSE

More specifically, the limitations of our knowledge manifest themselves in the conflict between the sensible and the intelligible, between what we can experience and what we can understand: the paradox of continuity and discreteness. For Van der Laan, whose thought is steeped in that of the ancient Greeks, the plastic number functions as a 'bridge'; its purpose is to bring about 'the meeting together of the continuous quantity of concrete size and the discrete quantity of abstract number'.[39] Similarly, one might without too much exaggeration describe the efforts of the fifth- and fourth-century Greek thinkers as attempts to 'rebuild the house'; or to build a bridge between the continuously changing world of Heraclitus and the discrete, finite universe of Parmenides. Plato describes these opposed viewpoints that have to be reconciled as on the one hand the ancient tradition 'that Ocean and Tethys, the source of all things, are

38. W. Blake, 'The Marriage of Heaven & Hell', in *Blake: Complete Writings*, Oxford University Press, 1969, p. 149.
39. H. van der Laan, *Architectonic Space*, E.J. Brill, 1983, p. 69.

flowing streams and nothing at rest', and on the other the doctrine 'that all things are a Unity which stays still within itself, having no room to move in'. Somehow or other, he says, philosophy must find a middle way between these extremes:

> For, little by little, our advance has brought us, without our knowing it, between the two lines; and, unless we can somehow fend them off and slip through, we shall suffer for it, as in that game they play in the wrestling schools, where the players are caught by both sides and dragged both ways at once across the line.[40]

Among the first to try to find a middle way was Empedocles of Acragas (*c.* 493–433 BC). He introduced the idea that the universe was composed of four elements, thus bringing together the earlier theories about its basic material – that it was composed of water (Thales), air (Anaximenes), or fire (Heraclitus) – and adding a fourth, earth. In themselves these four elements are, like the unitary sphere of Parmenides, permanent and unchanging. The variety and mutability of the perceived world is caused by their continual mixing and separating, brought about by the mutually opposing influences of love and strife. The Heraclitean idea that the world is ruled by strife is balanced by the contrary notion that it is held together by love. The elements are alternately united and divided, as first love and then strife win dominance over the world: 'At one time it grew to be one only out of many; at another, it divided up to be many instead of one.'[41] The world thus oscillates cyclically between a state in which the four elements are completely united by love, through stages of partial separation like the present, to a state in which under the influence of strife everything has broken down into its elementary components.

Anaxagoras of Clazomenae (*c.* 500–428 BC) continued the scientific tradition of his Ionian predecessors Thales, Anaximander and Anaximenes. He taught that there is an infinity of different substances, originally equally mixed together. The present state of the world came about through the separating out of the mixture, but this process is only partial. Each thing still contains something of everything, mixed in varying proportions. There is always a certain balance between opposites, such as hot and cold, white and black.

---

40. Plato, 'Theaetetus', pp. 94–5.
41. Empedocles, 'Poem on Nature', in J. Burnet, *Early Greek Philosophy*, p. 207.

Another attempt to reconcile the mutability of the perceived world with the Parmenidean concept of permanence was made by the atomists, Leucippus of Miletus (fl. *c.* 450–420 BC) and Democritus of Abdera (*c.* 460–370 BC), and later by Epicurus (341–270 BC) and the Latin poet Lucretius (*c.* 99–51 BC). Atomism substituted for the unitary, static universe of Parmenides an infinity of minute particles, constantly moving, combining and separating in an infinite empty space. Each atom resembles a tiny Parmenidean world, being solid, homogeneous, uncreated, unchanging, indestructible and physically (though not geometrically) indivisible. And all atoms have the same composition – unlike the four distinct elements of Empedocles – but they differ in size and shape. The appearance of continual change in the world around us (the Heraclitean flux) arises from the constant rearrangement and collision of these elementary bodies. Thus there is constant change, but an eternal changelessness of the fundamental particles.

Atomism overcame the problem posed by Zeno, that the Pythagorean concept of the point as a discrete, indivisible, space-filling unit conflicted with that of the line as infinitely divisible. By positing the indivisible atom as the basic component of matter, Democritus presented the later Pythagoreans, as Benjamin Farrington observes, 'with a solid little brick with which to build their mathematical world'.[42] The mathematical works of Democritus are lost; but according to Archimedes (287–212 BC) he correctly calculated that the volume of a cone equals that of a cylinder of the same diameter and one third of its height. The solution requires the cone to be considered as composed of an infinite number of parallel layers or discs. As the number of layers increases towards infinity, the difference between the actual and calculated volumes becomes vanishingly small. But as Democritus asks in a surviving fragment:

> If a cone is cut by a plane parallel to its base, what are we to think of the surfaces of the two sections? Are they equal or unequal? If they are unequal, they will make the cone uneven; for it will have many step-like incisions and roughnesses. If they are equal, then the sections will be equal, and the cone will have the properties of a cylinder, which is composed of equal, not unequal, circles. Which is most absurd.[43]

42. B. Farrington, *Greek Science*, Penguin Books, 1944, vol. I, p. 61.
43. Democritus, 'Fragment', in J. Burnet, *Early Greek Philosophy*, pp. 161–2.

H.W. Turnbull writes that 'This quotation is striking; for it foreshadows the great constructive work of Archimedes, and, centuries later, that of Cavalieri and Newton. It exhibits the infinitesimal calculus in its infancy.'[44]

The concept of limits, which is the basis of Democritus' calculation of the volume of a cone, provides the solution of the first two paradoxes of Zeno (fl. *c.* 450 BC), which are basically similar: that since one must first reach the halfway point of any given distance, and so on indefinitely, one will never reach the goal; and that Achilles can never overtake the tortoise because at each stage he must reach a point that the tortoise has already left, so the tortoise is always ahead. Both paradoxes rest on the assumption that series such as 1/2 + 1/4 + 1/8 + 1/16 +. . . or 1/2 + 1/6 + 1/12 + 1/20 +. . . can be extended indefinitely without ever adding up to a complete whole; but that is precisely what, for modern mathematics (and supposedly for Democritus), such a series does. We say that both these series, which can be rewritten 1/2, 3/4, 7/8, 15/16,. . . and 1/2, 2/3, 3/4, 4/5,. . . respectively, are *asymptotic to one another*, and that they *converge towards 1 as limit.*[45]

Democritus was a contemporary of Socrates, and belonged to a generation of philosophers that was beginning to ask no longer *what* we can we know about the world, but *if* and *how* we can know anything. Epistemology, the theory of knowledge, became and would remain a pressing concern. The objects of our perception are not, according to Democritus, the things themselves, but 'images' given off by surrounding bodies in the form of atoms, and projected onto the sense organs. The image seen by the eye is not an exact likeness of the thing itself, but distorted by the intervening air. Here Democritus anticipates not only Plato's fundamental distinction between appearance and reality and his concept of the image or copy (see Chapter 6), but also a major concern of seventeenth- and eighteenth-century science and philosophy: the distinction between the 'primary' qualities inherent in external objects and the 'secondary' ones that come about through the process of perception itself. For Democritus the atoms possess only solidity, extension and shape. All other perceptible qualities, such as colour, taste, sound and heat, are not intrinsic to them, but result from their interaction with our senses:

By use there is sweet, by use there is bitter; by use there is

44. H.W. Turnbull, *The Great Mathematicians*, Methuen & Co., 1962, pp. 25–6.
45. T. Dantzig, *Number*, pp. 139–62.

> warm and by use there is cold; by use there is colour. But in sooth there are atoms and the void. . . By the senses we in truth know nothing sure, but only something that changes according to the disposition of the body and of the things that enter into it or resist it.[46]

Two thousand years later Galileo and Locke would make similar points. 'To excite in us tastes, odors and sounds,' writes Galileo, 'I believe that nothing is required in external bodies except shapes, numbers, and slow or rapid movement.'[47] And Locke: 'Take away the sensation of them. . . and all colours, tastes, odours, and sounds. . . vanish and cease, and are reduced to their causes, i.e. bulk, figure, and motion of parts.'[48]

Democritus' theory of knowledge, together with his anticipation of the calculus and of the atomic theory itself, with its concomitant the concept of an infinite space, make him seem an extraordinarily accurate forerunner of the scientific revolution of 1600–1900. Milic Capek writes:

> The only difference between Greek atomism and nineteenth-century physics was that the latter had incomparably more efficient technical and conceptual tools at its disposal than Democritus and Leucippus. . . Fundamentally, however, the basic conceptions were the same. This was the deep historical reason why the birth of modern science occurred simultaneously with the revival of atomism by Bruno, Bacon, Gassendi and others.[49]

Yet as Bertrand Russell points out, the approach of the early Greek thinkers was not scientific in the modern sense:

> The atomic theory was revived in modern times to explain the facts of chemistry, but these facts were not known to the Greeks. There was no very sharp distinction, in ancient times, between empirical observation and logical argument. . . By good luck, the atomists hit on a hypothesis for which, more than two thousand years later, some evidence was found, but their belief, in their day, was none the less destitute of any solid foundation.[50]

On the other hand, he comments that Democritus

> is the last of the Greek philosophers to be free from a

46. Democritus, 'Fragments', in J. Burnet, *Early Greek Philosophy*, p. 160.
47. G. Galilei, 'The Assayer', in S. Drake, *Discoveries and Opinions of Galileo*, Doubleday Anchor Books, 1957, p. 276.
48. J. Locke, *An Essay Concerning Human Understanding*, Everyman's Library, 1961, vol. I, p. 107.
49. M. Capek, *The Philosophical Impact of Contemporary Physics*, D. Van Nostrand Company, 1961, p. 123.
50. B. Russell, *History of Western Philosophy*, George Allen & Unwin, 1961, p. 85.

certain fault which vitiated all later ancient and medieval thought. All the philosophers we have been considering so far [i.e. the Presocratics] were engaged in a disinterested effort to understand the world. They thought it easier to understand than it is, but without this optimism they would not have had the courage to make a beginning. . . From this point onwards, there are first certain seeds of decay. . . and then a gradual decadence. What is amiss, even in the best philosophy after Democritus, is an undue emphasis on man as compared to the universe.[51]

51. *Ibid.*, pp. 89–90.

Chapter five

THE PROPORTIONS OF THE PARTHENON

If one takes the trouble to delve into some of the proportional analysis of the 'poor old Parthenon'. . . it will be seen that almost anything under the sun can be proved. . . Can one blame sceptics if they brush aside the whole quest for proportion as a silly pastime, unrecorded in J. Huizinga's Homo Ludens*?*[1]

5.1 NUMERICAL AND GEOMETRICAL INTERPRETATIONS

Pythagoras was active around 530 BC. Plato, the subject of the next chapter, died in 347 BC. Between these two dates, virtually the whole of the mathematics necessary for the subsequent history of architectural proportion was worked out by the Greeks. During the same period, they also built a series of buildings that many regard as among the most perfectly proportioned structures ever designed: the temple of Apollo, Corinth (*c.* 540 BC); the temple of Aphaia, Aegina (*c.* 500–475 BC); the temple of Zeus, Olympia (*c.* 460 BC); and in Athens the Hephaisteion (449–444 BC), the Parthenon (447–432 BC), the Propylaea (437–432 BC), the temple of Athena Nike (*c.* 425 BC) and the Erechtheum (421–405 BC). The conclusion that the two developments were connected is an obvious one. John Pennethorne, whose *Elements and Mathematical Principles of the Greek Architects and Artists* appeared in 1844, believed that among the ancient Greeks not only were art and mathematics regarded as a unity, but it was art that led the way for mathematical studies, just as the physical sciences were stimulating them in modern Europe. He writes that:

> A very superficial investigation of the remaining works of Athenian architecture is, I think, sufficient to prove the

1. R. Wittkower, 'The changing concept of proportion', in *Idea and Image*, Thames & Hudson, 1978, p. 121.

> close and inseparable union that existed between the geometry and the arts of ancient Greece. When we consider the state of the Greek astronomy at the time when both the arts and the geometry had attained their highest point, it appears natural to conclude. . . that the division of ancient art, at the head of which Plato has placed architecture, was the practical science of the Greeks, and the one that chiefly excited them to the study and cultivation of the several branches of the mathematics; for it is now ascertained that all the branches of the Greek geometry were applied in the designing of the Greek works of architecture.[2]

If Pennethorne's opinion is correct, it extends the speculation in the last chapter that the circle-and-square geometry that arose in building, pottery and weaving may have been the source of early cosmological ideas; but is such a conclusion justified, as Pennethorne asserts, by the architectural evidence?

In the almost total absence of written documents that could help to determine the issue, the most varied speculations have been built up upon the conjectural analysis of measurements of buildings. The problem with this is that when one already has a theory one tends to find confirmation of it wherever one looks. Determined researchers, if they have the patience, can 'prove' almost anything they want about the proportions of a building, though this sometimes means basing the analysis on lines and shapes invisible in the building itself and existing only in the researcher's mind or on paper. No building has been subjected to so many and such conflicting interpretations of its proportions as the Parthenon.

The temple has been explained in terms of both of Wittkower's 'two different classes of proportion' – that based on whole numbers as well as that based on geometry and the irrational geometrical square root ratios and the golden section. The earliest researchers, like F.C. Penrose and W.W. Lloyd, tended to conclude that the key measures of Greek Doric temples were mutually related by simple whole-number ratios.[3] The opposite approach, the geometrical, was taken by numerous other interpreters in the late nineteenth and early twentieth centuries – Adolf Zeising,[4] D.R. Hay,[5] E.E. Viollet-le-Duc,[6] August Thiersch,[7] Heinrich Wölfflin,[8] Frederik Macody Lund,[9] Jay Hambidge[10] and Ernst

2. J. Pennethorne, *The Elements and Mathematical Principles of the Greek Architects and Artists*, William Clowes & Sons, London, 1844, p. 9.

3. F.C. Penrose, *An Investigation of the Principles of Athenian Architecture* (1851), and W.W. Lloyd, *Memoir of the systems of proportion employed in the design of the Doric temples at Phigaleia and Aegina* (1860), both quoted in P.H. Scholfield, *The Theory of Proportion in Achitecture*, Cambridge University Press, 1958, p. 93.

4. A. Zeising, *Neue Lehre von den Proportionen des menschlichen Koerper*, Leipzig, 1854.

5. D.R. Hay, *The Science of Beauty as developed in Nature and applied to Art*, Edinburgh, 1856.

6. E.E. Viollet-le-Duc, *Discourses on Architecture*, 1860.

7. A. Thiersch, in *Handbuch der Architektur*, vol. IV, Darmstadt, 1883.

8. H. Woelfflin, *Zur Lehre von den Proportionen*, 1889.

9. F.M. Lund, *Ad Quadratum: A Study of the Gemetrical Bases of Classic & Medieval Religious Architecture*, Batsford, 1921.

10. J. Hambidge, *The Parthenon and other Greek Temples*, Yale University Press, 1924.

Moessel[11] – while Auguste Choisy adopts both the numerical method (*méthode modulaire*) and the geometrical method (*méthode graphique*).[12]

Viollet-le-Duc and Lund exemplify the shortcomings of such conjectural analysis. In the ninth of his *Discourses on Architecture*, Viollet-le-Duc speculates on the proportional principles underlying Egyptian, Greek, Roman, Gothic, Renaissance and Islamic architecture.[13] Common to all he finds the use of the equilateral and certain isosceles triangles. In particular, he favours what he calls the 'Egyptian' triangle – one formed of two back-to-back right-angled triangles, each with a base of four and a height of five units – and another, based on the diagonal cross-section of a pyramid of which the orthogonal cross-section is an equilateral triangle. He discovers the Egyptian triangle, which has a total base measuring eight units, a height of five units, and sides measuring $\sqrt{41}$ or just over 6.4 units, in the proportions of the Basilica of Constantine in Rome, Notre Dame in Paris, and the Cathedral of Amiens. There is in fact no real need to regard this figure as a geometrical construction, and to do so merely confuses the issue, because it can be more simply described as an eight by five rectangle, and therefore one that breaks down into a simple numerical arrangement of squares (see Figure 5.1).

The second triangle, derived from the diagonal of a pyramid, is the one that Viollet-le-Duc applies to the Parthenon. It too comprises two right-angled triangles, each with a base of $\sqrt{2}$, a height of $\sqrt{3}$ and a hypotenuse of $\sqrt{5}$ units, so the total width of the base is $2 \times \sqrt{2}$ units (see Figure 5.2). Because all its sides are incommensurable, this figure can only be constructed geometrically, and not by measurement. He claims that if the apex of the triangle coincides with that of the pediment of the temple, the points where its sloping sides intersect the plane of the stylobate or topmost step of the platform are the same at which it is intersected by the plumb line of the architrave. The centre lines of the third and sixth columns are determined by the intersections of the sides of the triangle with the underside of the entablature, and by dividing these centre lines into three equal parts one locates the second, fourth, fifth and seventh columns (see Figure 5.3). The crucial question, of course, is what determines the height of the pediment-plus-entablature, on which the height and spacing of the columns depend. The actual ratio of this height to the total height including the

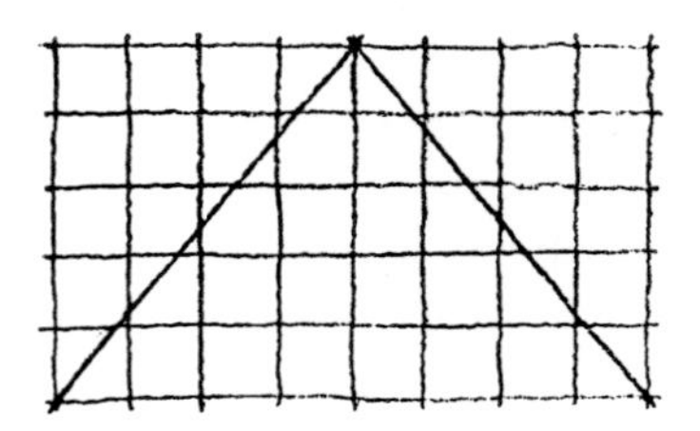

Figure 5.1 E.E. Viollet-le-Duc, Egyptian triangle.

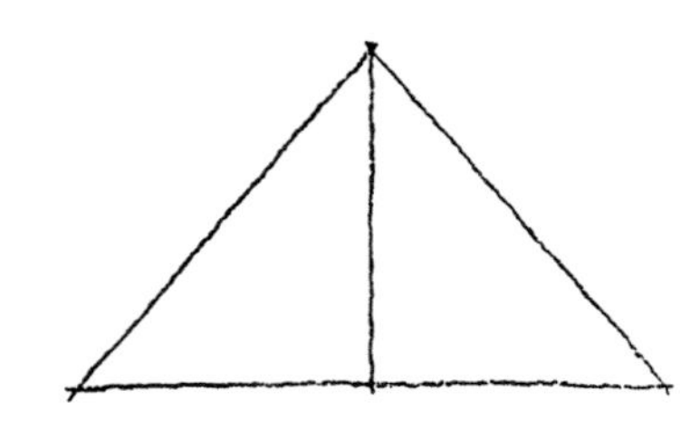

Figure 5.2 Viollet-le-Duc, diagonal cross-section of pyramid.

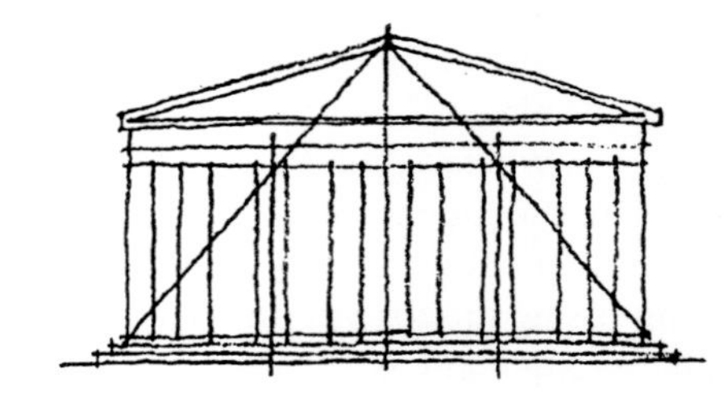

Figure 5.3 Viollet-le-Duc, analysis of the Parthenon.

11. E. Moessel, *Die Proportionen in Antike und Mittelalter*, Munich, 1926.
12. A. Choisy, *Histoire de l'architecture*, Bibliothèque de l'Image, 1996, vol. I, pp. 384–402.
13. E.E. Viollet-le-Duc, *Discourses on Architecture*, Allen and Unwin, 1959, pp. 389–429.

columns is about 1 : 2.37 or approximately 3 : 7. Since this has no simple numerical or geometrical relation to any construction that can be derived from Viollet's triangle, the correspondences that he does find appear to be purely coincidental.

Lund's book *Ad Quadratum* is a more extreme example of the dangers of imposing a preconceived geometrical construction on the plan or elevation of a building. He interprets both Medieval churches and Greek temples by means of star diagrams derived from polygonal figures such as the regular hexagon, octagon and decagon. His analysis of the Parthenon employs no less than three sets of pentagons, decagons and star pentagons – the first constructed within a circle circumscribed around the extreme limits of the building (the corners of the *euthynteria* or lowest step), the second within a circle whose diameter equals the length of the stylobate, and the third within one whose diameter equals its breadth. The problem is that there is no geometrical relation between the three sets of polygons, and that despite this and the extreme complication of the diagram almost none of the important lines or intersections seems to correspond to significant points in the building. Lund's diagram of the elevation is even less convincing than the plan. The whole analysis appears to be entirely arbitrary.

Even the best conjectural 'solutions' tend to assume that all the proportions of the building were worked out in advance down to the smallest detail, and executed with minute accuracy. But if the conclusion of Rhys Carpenter is correct – that the Parthenon in its final form is the result of a *rebuilding* on a much enlarged scale by Ictinus of a half-finished earlier structure of quite different proportions designed by Callicrates, and that the columns and much other material from the previous building were reused – then any interpretation that assumes an absolute and total perfection must be thrown into serious doubt. Carpenter writes that as a consequence of the rebuilding

> A considerable element of empirical improvisation entered into the creation of the building which, on uninformed inspection of its makeshift anomalies, has been thought to depend on the most carefully calculated mathematical relationships and the most delicately and minutely adjusted proportions.[14]

14. R. Carpenter, *The Architects of the Parthenon*, Penguin Books, 1970, p. 16.

On the other hand, the improvisatory method by which the Greeks executed their designs can also be taken as a strong argument for the necessity of a clear overall proportional scheme, however roughly it may have been carried out. According to J.J. Coulton the Greeks – unlike the Egyptians and Babylonians –

> developed a technique of design which did not involve scale drawing. Certainly no plans or elevations of Greek architecture have survived, and there is no clear mention of them in Greek literature or building inscriptions before the Hellenistic period; nor have any instruments for technical drawing been found.[15]

Instead, they employed a kind of technical description or written specification, the *synographai*, in which the general lines of the building were described in words. Without a clearly worked out scheme of proportions to ensure that things fitted together, this method would have been unworkable. A basic frame of reference was essential to the architect, not only to enable him to give clear instructions to the builders on site, but even in order to visualize and manipulate the forms of the building in his own mind.

5.2 HAMBIDGE AND DYNAMIC SYMMETRY

The work of the American Jay Hambidge is more convincing than most attempts to analyse the proportions of the Parthenon, and no writer has had a greater impact on the general theory of architectural proportion in our century. As Wittkower points out:

> He bridged the gap between Greek art – still the ideal of the older generation of modern artists (Picasso, Le Corbusier) – and modern aspirations. . . What could be more appealing than the discovery that the Greeks had worked according to the law of dynamic growth found in nature? Moreover, Hambidge has the simple and strong diction of a man with strong convictions. . . He was biased, and in this lay his strength.[16]

Although he devoted so much attention to the study of

15. J.J. Coulton, *Ancient Greek Architects at Work*, Cornell University Press, 1977, p. 53.
16. R. Wittkower, 'The changing concept of proportion', p. 120.

ancient art, Hambidge was no dry museum scholar, nor did he advocate the imitation of historical prototypes. His theory of 'dynamic symmetry' was directed towards the present and the future. He wrote in 1919 that

> The present need is for an exposition of the application of dynamic symmetry to the problems of today. The indications are that we stand on the threshold of a design reawakening. . .When it is realized that symmetry provides the means of ordering and correlating our design ideas, to the end that intelligent expression can be given to our dreams, we shall no longer tolerate pilfering. Instead of period furniture and antique junk we shall demand design expressive of ourselves and our time.[17]

As I have said, Hambidge's fundamental distinction between 'static' and 'dynamic' symmetries is similar to – though not identical with – Wittkower's between the numerical and geometrical principles. The first difference is that, as Wittkower writes, Hambidge is biased. For him the two principles are not just alternatives, or, as with Wittkower, the expressions of different but equally valid cultural approaches to proportion. The numerical or commensurable systems are intrinsically 'static' and therefore inferior to incommensurable or 'dynamic' ones like the golden section. They lack the vitality and refinement characteristic of living organisms and of the highest levels of artistic production, which he identifies exclusively with ancient Egypt and Greece of the Classical period. He writes that

> There is no question of the superiority of the dynamic over the static. . . Static symmetry, as the name implies, is a symmetry which has a sort of fixed entity or state. . . The dynamic is a symmetry suggestive of life and movement. . . Its great value to design lies in its power of transition or movement from one form to another in the system. It produces the only perfect modulating process in any of the arts. . . It is the symmetry of man and of plants, and the phenomenon of our reaction to classic Greek art and to certain fine forms of other art is probably due to our unconscious feeling of the presence of the beautiful shapes of this symmetry.[18]

The distinction between static and dynamic symmetry, as

17. J. Hambidge, *The Elements of Dynamic Symmetry*, Dover Publications, 1967, p. xvii.
18. *Ibid.*, pp. xii–xvi.

understood by Hambidge, is best illustrated by Lesson 9 of his *Elements of Dynamic Symmetry*, which deals with the $\sqrt{4}$ rectangle or double square. This shape, he says, can be treated either dynamically or statically. It can be treated statically by superposing upon it its reciprocal, which is likewise a double square, and exactly one quarter of the whole area. Therefore four such smaller rectangles make up the whole (see Figure 5.4). The entire construction is perfectly commensurable.

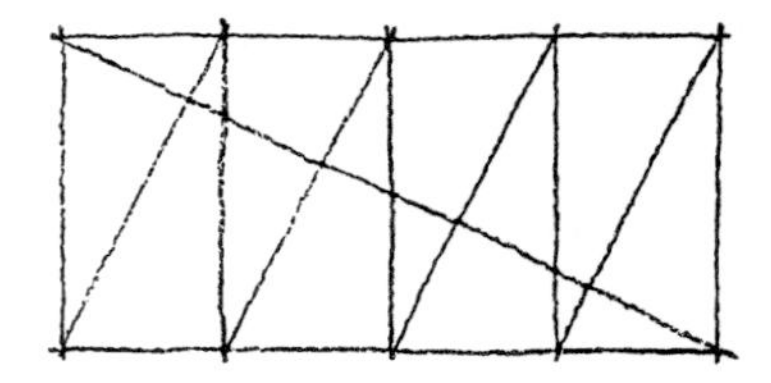

Figure 5.4 Jay Hambidge, 'static' subdivision of a double square.

When treated dynamically, however, 'it is divided either by root-five or the whirling square [i.e. golden section] rectangle.'[19] Division by the $\sqrt{5}$ rectangle is as follows:

(1) Draw four diagonals joining the midpoints of the four sides of the rectangle.
(2) Draw two semicircles with the short sides as diameters and the midpoints of these sides as centres.
(3) Draw perpendiculars through the intersections of the semicircles with the four diagonals.

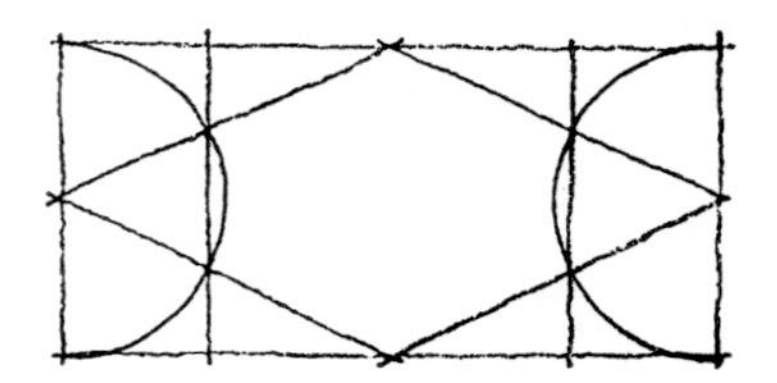

Figure 5.5 Hambidge, 'dynamic' subdivision of a double square generating $\sqrt{5}$ rectangles.

The perpendiculars divide the whole rectangle into two $\sqrt{5}$ rectangles and a central area with the irrational proportion 1 : 1.1055. This shape can be further broken down into two squares and four golden rectangles, and each of the $\sqrt{5}$ rectangles into a square and two golden rectangles (see Figure 5.5).

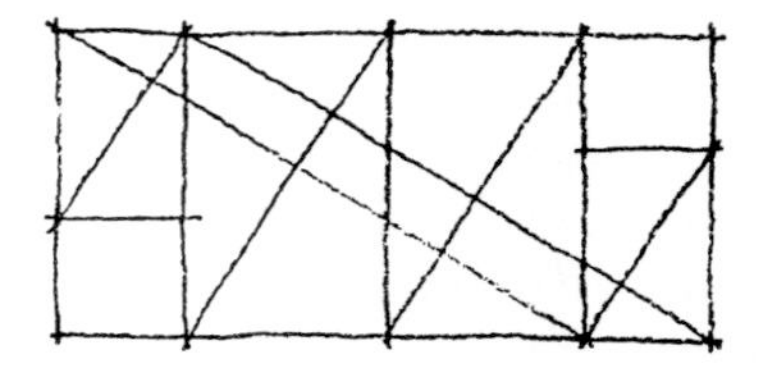

Figure 5.6 Hambidge, 'dynamic' subdivision of a double square into ϕ rectangles.

Alternatively, golden rectangles can be inscribed at each end of the original double square so that they overlap, dividing it into two areas with the ratio $1 : \phi^{-2}$, approximately 1 : 0.382, and a central area with the ratio $1 : 2\phi^{-1}$, approximately 1 : 1.236. The former areas each comprise a golden rectangle lengthened by a square, and the central area comprises two golden rectangles (see Figure 5.6).

The dynamic subdivision of the rectangle, which gives rise to $\sqrt{5}$ and the golden section, is exactly the kind of construction that Hambidge claims to discover in the Parthenon. It involves unequal and incommensurable ratios constructed geometrically, whereas the static subdivision produces shapes that are commensurable, measurable and modular. He attaches great importance, in arguing the superiority of dynamic symmetry, to 'the application of areas'.[20] This is an extension of Euclid's principle of 'commensurability in the square'.[21] Thus a figure whose sides are incommensurable as lengths (for instance, a $\sqrt{2}$ rectangle) is nevertheless commensurable in terms of the squares

19. *Ibid.*, p. 52.
20. *Ibid.*, pp. 28–9.
21. Euclid, *Elements*, Dover Publications, 1956, vol. III, pp. 10–11.

on its sides. Hambidge extends this principle to his preferred figure, the 'rectangle of the whirling squares' or ϕ rectangle, arguing that if a square is constructed inside the shorter side of such a golden rectangle, an area equal to this square, and therefore commensurable with it in area, can be constructed inside the longer side by drawing a parallel through the intersection of the square with the diagonal of the original figure (see Figure 5.7). Although he mentions in passing that the same principle holds if the square is replaced by 'any rectangular area whatever',[22] he ignores the fact that the original figure, too, can be *any rectangle one cares to choose*. It can therefore equally well be one of the shapes he condemns as 'static', such as the 3 : 2 and 4 : 3 rectangles. This seems to undermine completely the argument that only certain rectangles possess this 'natural property'[23] of area measurableness, which for Hambidge is 'really the great secret of Greek design'.[24]

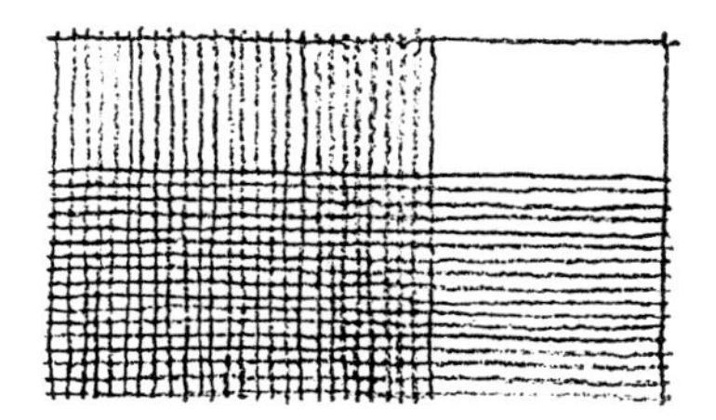

Figure 5.7 Hambidge, 'application of areas'.

Whereas he thus speculates that the Greek artists used geometry to generate the dynamic proportions of their works, Hambidge proceeds, rather illogically, to adopt an analytical arithmetical method that the Greeks themselves, lacking a decimal notation, could not have employed. He substitutes decimal approximations like 1.4142 and 1.618 for the irrational numbers on which dynamic symmetry relies. His reason is ease of exposition to a modern lay readership. He writes:

> Mathematicians have frequently asked the writer why he doesn't use algebraic symbols. The answer is simple. . . the average designer or the average layman is not sufficiently familiar with the processes of either algebra or geometry and to use mathematical formulae would result in placing design knowledge beyond the reach of those most interested in the subject.[25]

In the following description of Hambidge's analysis of the Parthenon I shall use both the decimal approximations and powers of the algebraic symbol ϕ.

5.3 HAMBIDGE'S PARTHENON

Hambidge succeeds in reducing the temple to arrangements of three geometrically interrelated figures:

22. J. Hambidge, *The Elements of Dynamic Symmetry*, p. 29.
23. *Ibid.*, p. 18.
24. *Ibid.*
25. *Ibid.*, p. 101.

(1) the $\sqrt{5}$ or 2.236 rectangle;
(2) the golden or 1.618 rectangle; and
(3) a composite figure, slightly wider than the $\sqrt{5}$ rectangle; this has the ratio 1 : 2.138, and is made up of two $\sqrt{5}$ rectangles and two squares (see Figure 5.9).

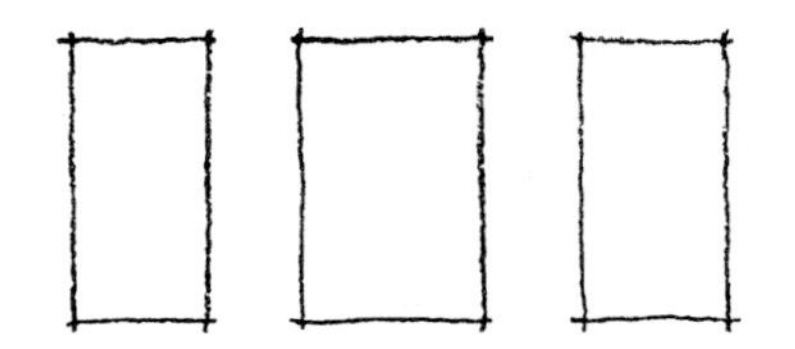

Figure 5.8 Hambidge, analysis of the Parthenon: three key rectangles.

It is possible that the combination of $\sqrt{5}$ with the golden section may correspond to mathematical knowledge developed by the Pythagoreans before the Parthenon was designed, but this cannot be taken for granted. When discussing the five regular polyhedra in the *Timaeus* even Plato avoided any detailed treatment of the dodecahedron, and therefore of the regular pentagon, which could have led him to the golden section. Euclid handles both, but his *Elements* date from about 300 BC, a century and a half after the Parthenon was completed. If Ictinus, the architect of the Parthenon, was as familiar with them as Hambidge assumes, then architecture was ahead of, and may – as Pennethorne believed – have stimulated development in pure mathematics, and not the other way around.

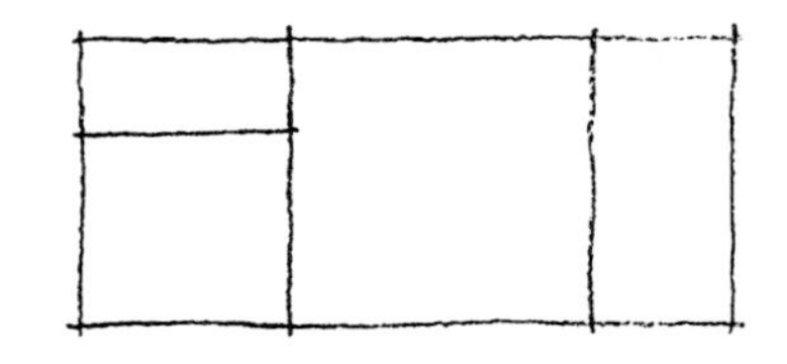

Figure 5.9 Hambidge, analysis of the Parthenon: ground plan.

Hambidge's analysis of the plan takes the *euthynteria* or lowest step as the determining figure. Although to the eye this figure suggests a $\sqrt{5}$ or 2.236 rectangle it is in fact a slightly broader shape, which he defines as composed of two figures with the more complex ratio 1 : 1.447 or $\sqrt{5} : 2\phi$. One of these figures is placed perpendicular to the other. Each is in turn composed of two relatively simple shapes: a square and a $\sqrt{5}$ rectangle. The combination of the two squares and two rectangles gives a total ground plan with the complex ratio 1 : 2.138 or $1 : (4\phi^2 + 5)/2\phi\sqrt{5}$ (see Figure 5.9). Hambidge compares this with the measured dimensions, 238.003 × 111.31 English feet, or 1 : 2.138 199 6.

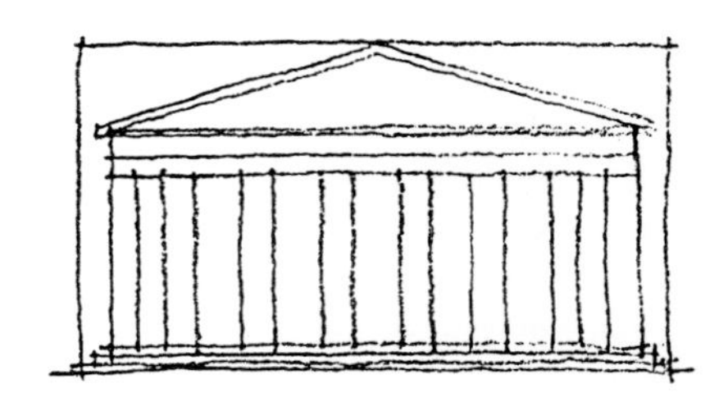

Figure 5.10 Hambidge, analysis of the Parthenon: temple front (1).

The second most important shape is that of the temple front. Hambidge concentrates on the rectangle that contains the whole facade, including the pediment and the three steps. This is of course an entirely abstract figure, which has no concrete embodiment in the building, since its sides are imaginary vertical lines projected upwards from the face of the lowest step, and its upper edge is an imaginary horizontal drawn through the apex of the pediment (see Figure 5.10). At first sight this figure resembles a 1.618 or ϕ rectangle, but like the plan shape it is in fact a composite figure built up of ϕ rectangles and squares. It can be composed most simply as two vertical ϕ rectangles with between them a more complex figure comprising a vertical ϕ rectangle plus a horizontal double square (see Figure 5.11). The ratio of this central figure is 1 : 2.118 or 2 : ϕ^3. The ratio of the whole rectangle containing the facade is 1 : 1.708 or $\phi^2 : 2\sqrt{5}$.

Hambidge finds that the whole rectangle is divided horizontally in the golden section ratio by a line AB corresponding to the underside of the entablature. The area above AB comprises two horizontal $\sqrt{5}$ rectangles: that is, its ratio is 1 : 4.472. The area below AB comprises two rectangles with the composite ratio 1 : 1.382 or $\phi : \sqrt{5}$. This area can also be regarded as made up of two overlapping ϕ rectangles. The area of overlap is composed of two 4.236 or ϕ^3 rectangles, each comprising two ϕ rectangles and a square (see Figure 5.12).

The diagonals of the two overlapping ϕ rectangles intersect on the centre line of the facade at a point that determines the height of the stylobate. This defines a horizontal line that I shall call CD. The rectangle ABCD containing the columns has the relatively simple overall ratio of 1 : 3.236 or 1 : 2ϕ; in other words, it comprises two horizontal ϕ rectangles (see Figure 5.13). Each of these ϕ rectangles can be further broken down into two vertical ϕ rectangles plus a ϕ^2 area; this means that the whole width of the temple front is made up of six lengths with the ratios 1 : ϕ : ϕ : ϕ : ϕ : 1 (see Figure 5.14). The two ϕ^2 areas are now further subdivided vertically by the golden section, into a ϕ^3 and a ϕ^4 area. The dividing line determines the centre line of the corner columns. If the four central ϕ rectangles are each broken down into nine smaller ones, alternate verticals determine the centre lines of the six central columns (see Figure 5.15).

Finally, the dividing line between the pediment and the top of the entablature is established by the intersection of two diagonals: that of the whole rectangle of the facade and that of one of the two $\sqrt{5}$ rectangles composing the area above the line AB. This line divides the combined height of the pediment and entablature in the ratio 1 : 1.309 or 2 : ϕ^2 (see Figure 5.16).

All the dimensions involved can be traced to two interwoven ϕ progressions, with a mutual ratio of 1 : 1.171 or $\sqrt{5} : \phi^2$. This ratio occurs, for instance, between corresponding measures of the two ϕ rectangles that make up ABCD and the larger overlapping ϕ rectangles that comprise the whole area below AB.

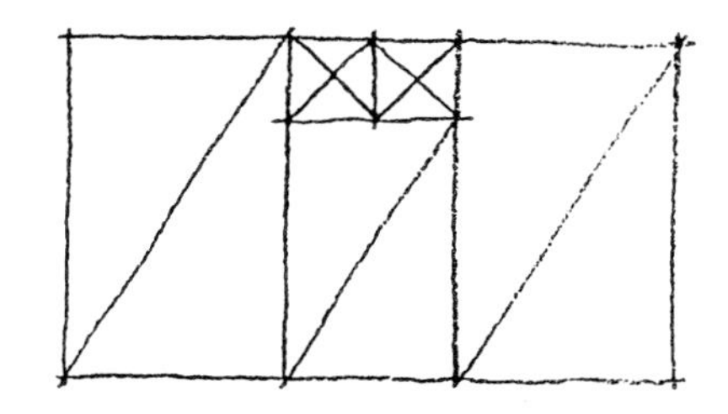

Figure 5.11 Hambidge, analysis of the Parthenon: temple front (2).

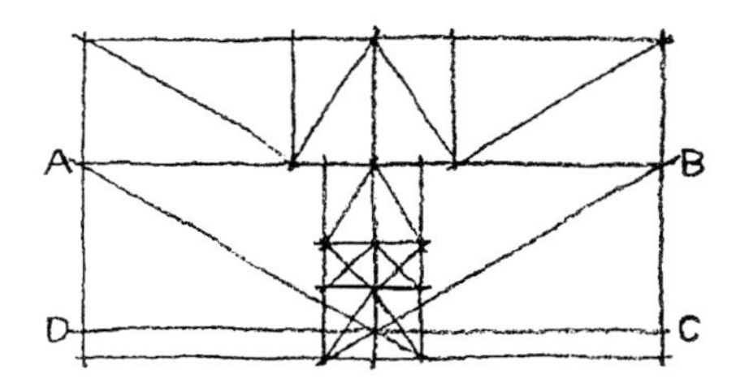

Figure 5.12 Hambidge, analysis of the Parthenon: temple front (3).

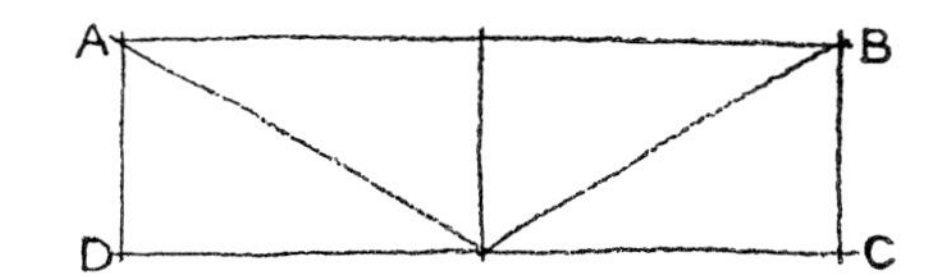

Figure 5.13 Hambidge, analysis of the Parthenon: temple front (4).

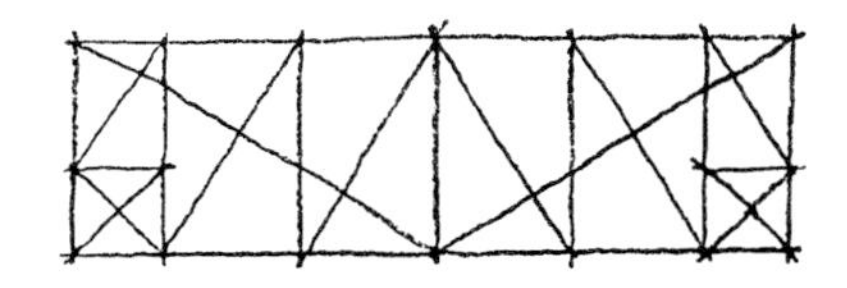

Figure 5.14 Hambidge, analysis of the Parthenon: temple front (5).

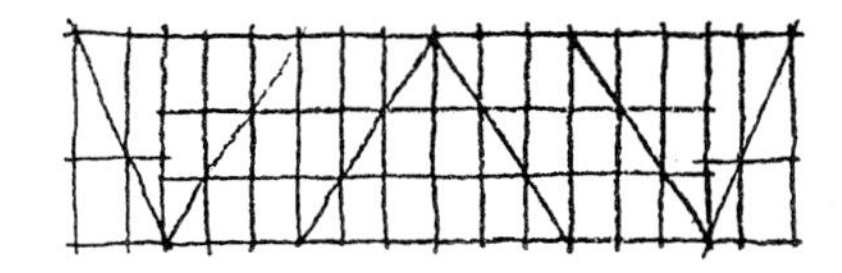

Figure 5.15 Hambidge, analysis of the Parthenon: temple front (6).

The very exact correspondence of Hambidge's mathematics to the actual measurements says much for his ingenuity and his rigorous refusal to accept an easier solution that does not fit the facts. However, although his exposition has here been greatly simplified, the reader who has patiently followed the analysis must still be impressed by its complexity, and by the fact that of the visually significant shapes only one – the rectangle ABCD – is a simple figure composed of two ϕ rectangles. Walter Dorwin Teague, a supporter of Hambidge's theory, argues in his book *Design this Day* that if the designer of the Parthenon had started with a simple golden section or $\sqrt{5}$ rectangle for the elevation or the plan 'neither of these areas would have had the amazing versatility of the area he chose.'[26] I find it hard to believe, however, that if as Teague claims the aim was 'to preserve the golden section principle, and to apply it with an easy fluency',[27] the builders would have chosen to arrive at their goal by such a circuitous route. If abstract geometrical purity was their aim, it is not credible that they would have been content with a series of additions and subtractions of the key rectangles by which the final scheme is pieced together like a patchwork quilt.

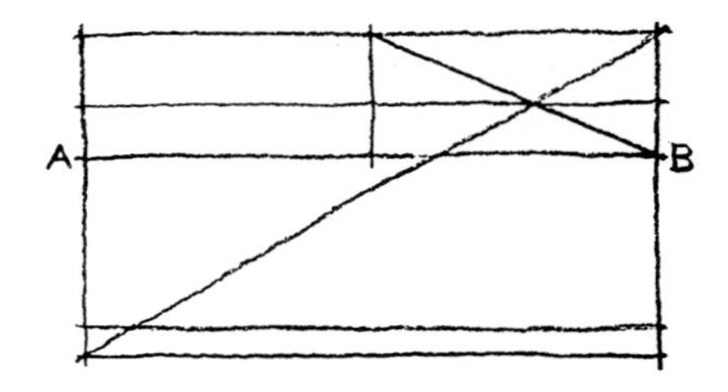

Figure 5.16 Hambidge, analysis of the Parthenon: temple front (7).

The whole exercise depends, moreover, on lines that can be drawn on paper but are not visible in the building. The one geometrically simple figure, the rectangle ABCD, is a complete abstraction, since its vertical edges are delineated by imaginary lines projected upwards from the base of the *euthynteria*. The shapes of all the physically embodied elements – for example, the rectangles defined by the plane of the stylobate and the top of the entablature, or the ratio of the column diameter to the center to centre column interval – are arrived at only indirectly, by way of a complex series of calculations.

All this becomes even less plausible if Rhys Carpenter's theory about the reuse of the columns and other parts from the half-finished earlier temple is correct. In such circumstances it is hardly probable that the architects would have used so complex and perfectionist a process of design. One must question whether Hambidge's great principle, an absolute conformity of the calculated dimensions with the actual measurements, is really the main issue. The evidence suggests that the Greek builders of the classical period not only tolerated departures from mathematical exactitude, but even welcomed them. For nowhere are the shapes in the Parthenon so simple or the dimensions so regular as they at

26. W.D. Teague, *Design this Day*, The Studio, 1946, p. 218.
27. *Ibid.*

first appear. Many of the deviations from uniformity are clearly intentional and minutely calculated: the slight upward curves towards the centre of the steps, of the entablature, and of the plane of the stylobate; the inward inclination of the columns and the outer faces of the cella walls; and the barely perceptible convex curvature of the column shafts and capitals. Others, however, such as the irregular spacing of the columns and the uneven widths of the metopes and cornice blocks, seem arbitrary. The column intervals vary by up to 43 mm, about 1% of the average measure. Builders who took such extreme care in calculating barely discernible visual refinements would not have allowed such relatively large variations to occur through sheer carelessness. Rhys Carpenter concludes that

> While the deviations from exact uniformity must have been intentional, at the same time they were deliberately casual and designedly unsystematic, having been taken at random for a purely aesthetic purpose, in order to temper lifeless mathematical rigidity with those minute irregularities which distinguish the living organism from its abstract generic pattern. . .[28]

In Carpenter's view, these variations resulted from the influence on architecture of the movement among contemporary sculptors – notably Polycleitus and Pheidias – towards more lifelike, less strictly canonical measurements.[29] Now, if such imperceptible deviations from mathematical regularity were introduced on purpose, what would be the point of starting out from perfectly exact dimensions in the first place? Is it not more reasonable to regard the mathematical scheme as a generic 'law of growth', like that which makes all the leaves of a tree follow the same general pattern, although no two leaves are identical and the mathematically perfect shape is manifested in no single individual?

5.4 THE PIRAEUS ARSENAL

A further objection to Hambidge's interpretation of the Parthenon's proportions is that it is entirely based on deduction from the measurements, unsupported by textual evidence about the methods actually followed by the Greek architects. Although at the start of this chapter I spoke of

28. R. Carpenter, *The Architects of the Parthenon*, pp. 14–15.
29. *Ibid.*, pp. 126–8.

'the absence of written documents', such evidence does in fact exist, although dating from about a century later than the Parthenon. An inscribed marble stele has survived that contains the technical specification or *synographai* giving the principal measures and proportions of the naval arsenal of the Piraeus, built in 340–330 BC by the architect Philon of Eleusis.[30] Even though the arsenal was a secular building and not a temple, this inscription provides an invaluable clue to the principles on which the proportions of temples may have been based. It may well teach us something, therefore, about how we should approach the proportions of the Parthenon.

Two things strike one as remarkable about the Piraeus inscription: on the one hand, the proportions are based on simple commensurable ratios like 1 : 2 and 2 : 3; and on the other, these ideal ratios are rounded up or down where necessary in order to retain whole-number measures in feet. Were the ideal ratios sacrificed to a practical consideration – to make the measuring process easy for the builders? This seems hardly likely, in view of the Greeks' ability, when they wanted, to make minute adjustments of measure. A more probable explanation is that in ancient times the appointed unit of measure was regarded as in some way sacrosanct, and one went to great lengths to avoid mutilating it, even at the cost of distorting the geometry. We shall find the same tendency in Gothic architecture when we come to consider the proportions of Chartres Cathedral in Chapter 10.

The ideal or theoretical measures of the arsenal, as fractions of the whole width of the facade, are given in Table 5.1 (see Figure 5.17). The internal width of the building is specified as 50 ft, with a central hall of 20 and bays of 15 on either side; the wall thicknesses add a further 5 ft to the external width, making a total of 55 Greek feet. Since 55 is not divisible by 2 or 3, fractions of a foot would arise if the ideal proportions shown in Table 5.1 were maintained exactly. Table 5.2 shows these fractions alongside the actual measures rounded to give whole numbers of feet.

It is also noteworthy that perfect squares and odd numbers tend to predominate among the ratios. In Choisy's opinion

> The Greeks, guided by the Pythagorean doctrines... classified numbers in the following order of preference: first, the square numbers or 'powers', and in the second rank the odd numbers.[31]

TABLE 5.1

A	Whole width	1/1
B	Whole height	2/3
C	Height to entablature	1/2
D	Width of cornice over doors	1/2
E	Height of same	1/3
F	Width of each door	1/6
G	Height of doors	1/4

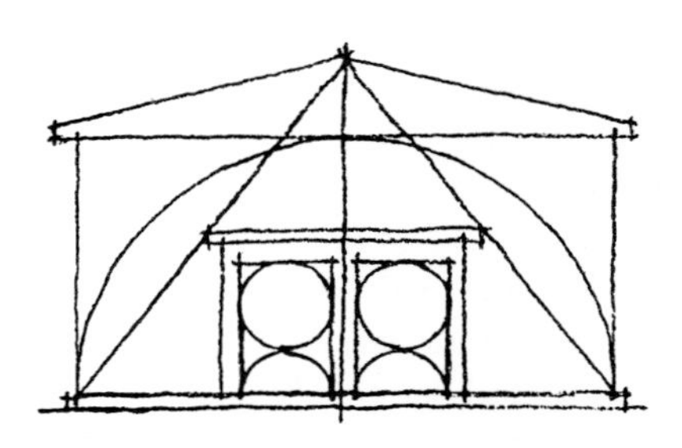

Figure 5.17 Piraeus arsenal, facade proportions; from A. Choisy, *Histoire de l'architecture*.

TABLE 5.2

A	55	55
B	$36\frac{2}{3}$	36
C	$27\frac{1}{2}$	27
D	$27\frac{1}{2}$	27
E	$18\frac{1}{3}$	18
F	$9\frac{1}{6}$	9
G	$13\frac{3}{4}$	14

30. A. Choisy, *Histoire de l'architecture*, pp. 388–90, and J.J. Coulton, *Ancient Greek Architects at Work*, pp. 53–5.

Even numbers other than squares were, he says, avoided wherever possible.

5.5 INTERPRETATIONS OF THE PARTHENON BASED ON WHOLE-NUMBER RATIOS

A much simpler explanation than Hambidge's of the proportions of the Parthenon is given by A.W. Lawrence,[32] and also by Carpenter.[33] Admittedly this demands slightly larger tolerances than Hambidge is willing to allow, but it has the advantage of being based on mathematical principles that were certainly known at the time: the Pythagorean numerical division of the octave, and the relations between square numbers. It also conforms in principle with the preference for commensurable ratios and whole-number measures that we have seen in the Piraeus arsenal. Furthermore, these simple relations are directly embodied in the most important visible elements of the design. They are:

(1) the ratio of the plane of the stylobate, which directly determines the placing of the columns, the outer face of which is flush with the top step;
(2) the ratio of the temple front, defined by the width of the stylobate and the height of the order, comprising column plus entablature;
(3) the ratio of the column interval to the lower diameter of the column.

All of these ratios are very nearly the same: 9 : 4, i.e. the relation between the squares of 3 and 2. The stylobate measures 69.51 × 30.88 m, an actual ratio of 2.250 971 5 : 1. The rectangle containing the front columns and entablature measures 30.88 × 13.728 m, giving a ratio of 2.249 417 2 : 1. And the normal intercolumniation being 4.295 m and the lower column diameter 1.91 m, the ratio between them is 2.248 691 : 1. The same ratio of nearly 9 : 4 recurs between the column diameter and the width of the triglyph. Although it is not impossible that architecture led the way for mathematical studies, as Pennethorne concluded, this scheme, making use of known mathematical techniques, is more plausible than Hambidge's assumption that the architects were already familiar with the golden section a century or so

31. A. Choisy, *Histoire de l'architecture*, p. 390.
32. A.W. Lawrence, *Greek Architecture*, Penguin Books, 1957; revised by R.A. Tomlinson, 1983, pp. 195–202.
33. R. Carpenter, *The Architects of the Parthenon*, p. 125.

before it was discussed in the works of mathematicians (such as Eudoxus of Cnidus, fl. *c.* 360).[34]

Two other visually important relations remain unaccounted for, however: (1) the ratio of the total height of the order to the column interval, measured centre to centre, which determines the shape of the typical structural bay; and (2) the ratio of the column height to that of the entablature. At first sight neither ratio lends itself to simple expression in whole numbers, although both are close to 16 : 5 or 3.2 : 1: the first is about 3.196 : 1 and the second 3.166 : 1. The problem is that unless these relations can be shown to have a necessary connection to the key ratio of 9 : 4, the latter's significance is weakened. For what we have so far are two sets of relations: on the one hand those uniting the measures of the stylobate with the visually most important vertical dimension of the facade, and on the other those connecting the column interval, column thickness, and triglyph width. Even though these smaller elements repeat the same ratio as the building as a whole, there is no continuity of relations between the two sets of measures.

What is significant, when one experiences the proportions of a building, is not a particular, precise ratio that happens to recur in a few isolated instances, but a system of ordered relations connecting each part to the whole. It is less important that these relations be precise, than that they be continuous. The test of a *system* of proportions is thus whether it generates a sequence of different but related ratios. Then the choice of a particular ratio ceases to be an arbitrary matter, because as we saw in Chapter 3 only certain sets of mathematical relations have the necessary mutual affinity.

5.6 FURTHER DEVELOPMENT OF THE WHOLE-NUMBER INTERPRETATION

What relation can be found, then, between the column interval and the larger set of dimensions? Compare the proportion of the stylobate, 9 : 4, with that of the number of columns in the length and breadth of the building, 17 : 8. Unless these two different proportions can somehow be reconciled, the column spacing along the flanks of the building will differ slightly from that of the temple front, in a ratio of about 18 : 17. Two peculiarities of the Greek Doric

34. F. Lasserre, *The Birth of Mathematics in the Age of Plato*, Hutchinson, 1964, p. 102.

order help to make such a reconciliation possible: the column intervals at the corners are reduced, as mentioned above; and the outer faces of the columns are flush with the edge of the platform. Consequently the plan does not consist of a uniform grid of squares, with a column in the centre of each, but of a core rectangle composed of 15 by 6 standard column spaces (that is, spaces measured to the centre lines of the normal intercolumniations), surrounded by a narrower band of constant width, containing the colonnade itself. This perimeter zone is the stylobate proper – literally the 'column-walk'.[35] The two ratios that still have to be reconciled are now 9 : 4 and 15 : 6 or 5 : 2.

The overall dimensions of the stylobate and the height of the order can be expressed as a continued proportion, 81 : 36 : 16. If the length and breadth of the stylobate are regarded as 81 and 36 units, it will be found that the dimension that must be subtracted from both of these to arrive at a core shape of 5 : 2 is 6 units, i.e. 81 – 6 = 75, 36 – 6 = 30, and 75 : 30 = 5 : 2. There is thus a core rectangle measuring 75 × 30, surrounded by a perimeter band three units wide (see Figure 5.18). Now, if the 75 unit dimension contains 15 normal column intervals and the 30 unit dimension contains 6, the standard interval must equal 5 units. Therefore the ratio of the height of the order to the column interval can only be 16 : 5.

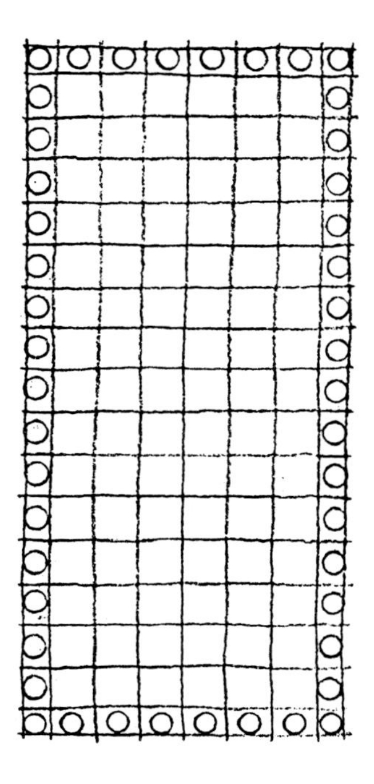

Figure 5.18 The Parthenon: 9 : 4 stylobate and 15 : 6 core rectangle.

An obvious assumption is that 16 : 5 is also the intended ratio between the heights of the column and entablature, actually 3.166 or $3^1/_6$: 1. However, the height of the order, comprising 16 of our hypothetical units, must then also be divided into 21 parts, in order that 16 parts can be given to the column and 5 to the entablature. The resulting division of the whole height into 16 × 21 = 336 parts produces very awkward ratios between the column and entablature and all other elements. But if instead we assume an intended ratio of 3 : 1, then the 16 units of the order divide easily into 12 parts for the column and 4 for the entablature, and all other relationships remain simply commensurable. Furthermore, the same ratio, 3 : 1, is then echoed by that of the width of the stylobate to the column height (36 : 12 units).

There is now a continuous sequence of commensurable ratios, based on 9:4, 3:1 and 16:5, connecting all the building's key dimensions, from the length of the stylobate to the column diameter. These are explored more fully in

35. R. Carpenter, *The Architects of the Parthenon*, p. 115.

Tables 5.5 and 5.6 below. It is also noteworthy that, as at the Piraeus arsenal, perfect squares and odd numbers tend to predominate among the ratios.

We are still presented with a problem, however. The unit I have so far adopted, 1/16 of the height of the order, or 858 mm, has no obvious basis in any known Greek system of measures, while conversely none of the standard measures cited by various authorities corresponds even approximately to the actual measurements of the Parthenon. However one looks at it, the unit of measure remains a puzzle. Carpenter, for instance, cites at one point an 'Olympic' foot of 326 mm, exactly 32 of which compose the column height;[36] and at another a minimally larger 'Periclean' foot of 328 mm.[37] Presumably these are variations of the same measure. He also mentions an 'older' foot of 295.7 mm.[38] D.S. Robertson reverses the chronology, stating that what he calls an 'Attic' foot of 328 mm was 'used in all Athenian buildings till Roman times',[39] whereas 'the so-called "Attic" and Roman foot of 0.295 or 0.296 metres'[40] makes its first appearance in Hellenistic buildings like the fourth-century temple of Athena Polias at Priene. But the same measure, 296 mm, is referred to by Choisy as the 'Italic' foot and described as a standard measure at Greek sites in Italy like Paestum, but not in Greece itself.[41]

It is widely stated – by Choisy among others – that the standard measure in Athens of the classical period was neither 328 nor 296 mm but a foot of about 308.3 mm,[42] equal to 25/24 Roman feet. It has been conjectured that the width of the stylobate, 30.88 m, is intended to be exactly 100 of these units. In support of this it is claimed that the Parthenon is referred to in Greek texts as the *hekatompedon* or 'hundred foot temple'.[43] It may also be argued that in Greek measures 100 ft equal 1 *plethron*, 6 of which units equal 1 stadium. A preference for such 'perfect' measures appears widely in history; we shall encounter it again in Gothic cathedrals. However, when we try to express the other dimensions in terms of a 308 or 308.8 mm foot, all except the length of the stylobate (= 225 ft) give rise to awkward fractions of the unit, since 100 is not exactly divisible by 9. Yet another measure that has been put forward as 'much used in classical Greece and elsewhere'[44] is 6/10 of an Egyptian cubit: that is, 315 mm. This gives 220 ft for the length and 98 ft for the width of the stylobate, but fits none of the other key dimensions.

---

36. *Ibid.*, p. 117.
37. *Ibid.*, p. 175.
38. *Ibid.*
39. D.S. Robertson, *A Handbook of Greek and Roman Architecture*, 1945, p. 82 n.
40. *Ibid.*, p. 149.
41. A. Choisy, *Histoire de l'architecture*, pp. 385–8.
42. *Ibid.*; also H. Plomer, *Ancient and Classical Architecture*, Longmans, 1956, p. 174; J. James, *The Contractors of Chartres*, Mandorla Publications, 1981, p. 60; L.C. Stecchini, 'Notes on the relation of the ancient measures to the Great Pyramid', in P. Tompkins, *Secrets of the Great Pyramid*, Penguin Books, 1978, pp. 350–2.
43. L.C. Stecchini, 'Notes', p. 359.
44. N. Feather, *Mass, Length and Time*, Edinburgh University Press, 1959, p. 11.

Must we conclude, then, that the Parthenon's measures are not exact multiples of a standard unit like that of the Piraeus arsenal? Or are we forced to abandon the whole search for an underlying scheme based on whole-number ratios? Happily some order is still discoverable amongst the apparent confusion. The Greek foot – whether of 308.3 or 328 mm – is generally assumed to have been divided into 16 digits. If we consider the larger of these measures, and divide it into 16 digits of 20.43 mm, we find that 42 such digits equal our measure of 858 mm almost exactly. There are thus two almost equally promising alternatives. We can consider the proportional scheme as being based on either (1) a unit of 858 mm or 42 digits, or (2) an Attic or Periclean foot of 328 mm. These solutions are compared in Tables 5.3 and 5.4. In each case the 'ideal' dimension, calculated in round numbers of units, is compared with the actual measurement. The margin of error is expressed as a percentage of the respective ideal measure.

With the exception of the dimensions of the columns and entablature, most of the ideal measures based on either the 42- or the 16-digit unit are accurate to within a few thousandths of the total dimension concerned. The discrepancies that arise with these two elements may be accounted for by Rhys Carpenter's theory that Ictinus reused columns and parts of the entablature from the earlier design by Callicrates.

Besides being in most cases very accurate, the analysis based on 42 digits or 858 mm has the advantage, as mentioned above, of producing an unbroken chain of commensurable ratios, which unite the length of the stylobate with the column diameter. The more significant of these ratios are shown in Table 5.5. Note the preponderance of odd numbers (5, 3) and of squares or cubes (81, 36, 27, 16, 9, 4, 1).

The mutual affinities of the ratios are revealed with greater clarity when they are expressed as powers or multiples of the first four prime numbers, 1, 2, 3 and 5, as in Table 5.6.

Nevertheless, the proportions of the Parthenon, like those of other Greek temples, leave us with a number of unanswered questions – including the most basic one: whether apparent correspondences to one or another mathematical formula, however plausible, may not be entirely fortuitous. Only contemporary documentary evidence about the Greek theory of architectural proportion could finally solve

TABLE 5.3

	ELEMENT	UNITS OF 858 mm = 42 DIGITS	ACTUAL DITTO	MARGIN (%)
A	Length of stylobate	81	81.002	0.0025
B	Width of stylobate	36	35.991	0.025
C	Height of order	16	16	0.0
D	Height of column	12	12.16	1.333
E	Depth of entablature	4	3.84	4.0
F	Column interval	5	5.006	0.12
G	Column diameter	20/9 = 2.222	2.222	0.0

TABLE 5.4

	ELEMENT	UNITS OF 328 mm = 16 DIGITS	ACTUAL DITTO	MARGIN (%)
A	Length of stylobate	212	211.92	0.038
B	Width of stylobate	94	94.146	0.155
C	Height of order	42	41.854	0.348
D	Height of column	32	31.808	0.6
E	Depth of entablature	10	10.046	0.46
F	Column interval	13	13.08	0.615
G	Column diameter	6	5.823	2.95

the riddle, and that is lacking, despite the valuable clues provided by the later Piraeus inscription. The nearest thing we have to a written account of Greek architectural theory is later still. It is provided by the only surviving treatise from the ancient world: the *Ten Books* by the Roman architect Vitruvius, which will be discussed in Chapter 9.

It would therefore be rash to put forward either Hambidge's or the rational number scheme as a final answer to the problem of the Parthenon's proportions. Nevertheless, such investigations are not without value. A system of proportion need not be regarded as something that is necessarily *prescriptive* (that is, as a recipe followed by the architect – or in the case of plants and animals, by nature itself). It may also be *descriptive* (a means of interpreting phenomena in general). As Theodore Cook warns us about his studies of the spiral in nature,

> Because we can draw a spiral line through a series of developing members, it does not follow that a plant or a shell is attempting to make a spiral, or that a spiral would be of any advantage to it. . . Geometrical constructions do not, in fact, give any clue to the causes which produce them, but only *express* what is seen. . .[45]

That expression is essential, however, both in science and in art, if we are to interpret anything at all.

TABLE 5.5

B : E=	9 : 1	B : D = D : E =	3 : 1
B : F = C : G = 36 : 5		D : F =	12 : 5
A : D=	27 : 4	A : B = B : C = F : G =	9 : 4
A : C=	81 : 16	E : G =	9 : 5
C : E =	4 : 1	C : D=	4 : 3
C : F =	16 : 5	F: E =	5 : 4

TABLE 5.6

B : E =	$3^2 : 1^2$	B : D = D : E =	3 : 1
B : F = C : G =	$(2 \times 3)^2 : 5$	D : F =	$(2^2 \times 3) : 5$
A : D=	$3^3 : 2^2$	A : B = B : C = F : G =	$3^2 : 2^2$
A : C=	$3^4 : 2^4$	E : G =	$3^2 : 5$
C : E =	$2^2 : 1^2$	C : D =	$2^2 : 3$
C : F =	$2^4 : 5$	F : E =	$5 : 2^2$

45. T.A. Cook, *The Curves of Life*, Dover Publications, 1979, p. 23.

Chapter six

PLATO: ORDER OUT OF CHAOS

Desiring, then, that all things should be good and, so far as it might be, nothing imperfect, the god took over all that is visible – not at rest, but in discordant and unordered motion – and brought it from disorder into order, since he judged that order was in every way the better.[1]

6.1 THE ORIGINAL AND THE COPY

I have presented the later Presocratics, Empedocles, Anaxagoras, Leucippus and Democritus, as builders of bridges across the gulf that had opened up between the extreme positions of Parmenides and Heraclitus. They tried to reconcile the view that the world, however complex and changing it appears, must in reality be completely intelligible, with the doctrine that reality is ever moving, ever evading the grasp of the human mind, and that its order, if it exists, is a hidden one. The two great thinkers who are the subject of this and the following chapter, Plato (427–347 BC) and Aristotle (384–322 BC), forged more powerful and more comprehensive syntheses of these opposed views, but their solutions differed radically from each other. Both recognized that neither the intellectual nor the sensible aspects of our experience can be denied, and that they must be brought into some kind of relation with each other. Plato gave pre-eminence to the intellectual, mathematical side of this relationship (the world of pure *Forms* or *Ideas*) whereas Aristotle identified what he called *substances*, that is the basic realities, with individual, perceptible things: animals and plants, heavenly bodies, and human artefacts. Plato's philosophy, being more mathematical, has had the more direct impact on architectural proportion. He is a pivotal figure in this story, connecting Pythagoras with Alberti and Palladio,

1. Plato, 'Timaeus', in F.M. Cornford, *Plato's Cosmology*, Routledge & Kegan Paul, 1937, p. 33.

and indeed with Le Corbusier. In the view of Karl Popper it was also Plato

> who chose geometry as the new basis, and the geometrical method of proportion as the new method; who drew up a programme for a *geometrization of mathematics*, including arithmetic, astronomy, and cosmology; and who became the founder of the geometrical picture of the world, and thereby also the founder of modern science – of the science of Copernicus, Galileo, Kepler, and Newton.[2]

Plato's cosmology, set out principally in the *Timaeus*, weaves together strands inherited from the previous Greek thinkers – the mathematics of Pythagoras, the finite, spherical universe of Parmenides, the flux and the tuning of opposites of Heraclitus, the four elements of Empedocles, the primeval mixture of Anaxagoras, the atoms of Leucippus and Democritus, and the latter's distinction between the image and the thing itself – as well as, inherited from his own teacher Socrates (*c.* 470–399 BC) and the sophist Protagoras (*c.* 485–20 BC), the new emphasis on the human. The basis of Plato's synthesis is the notion of the *image*. The world perceived by the senses is an image or *eikon*, a copy or representation of the real world comprising the eternal Ideas or Forms. The *Timaeus* opens with a question that draws a clear distinction between the world of Forms and its image:

> We must, then, in my judgement, first make this distinction: what is that which is always real and has no becoming, and what is that which is always becoming and is never real? That which is apprehensible by thought with a rational account is the thing that is always unchangeably real; whereas that which is the object of belief together with unreasoning sensation is the thing that becomes and passes away, but never has real being.[3]

Thus for Plato ultimate reality resides in the universal Forms – including the eternal truths of mathematics – of which the sensible world is only the changing shadow, the reflection, or the representation. The universe, however, is not confined to the Forms alone, but involves both Forms and images. At least in the later dialogues – the *Sophist*, *Statesman*, *Timaeus*, *Critias*, *Philebus* and *Laws* – it appears that

2. K.R. Popper, *The Open Society and its Enemies*, Routledge, 1966, vol. I, p. 319.
3. Plato, 'Timaeus', in op. cit., p. 22.

the world of phenomena cannot simply be discounted, as it was by Parmenides. In the *Sophist* Plato's mouthpiece, 'the stranger from Elea', concludes that

> only one course is open to the philosopher who values knowledge and the rest above all else. He must refuse to accept from the champions either of the One or of the many Forms the doctrine that all Reality is changeless; and he must turn a deaf ear to the other party who represents Reality as everywhere changing. Like a child begging for 'both', he must declare that Reality or the sum of things is both at once – all that is unchangeable and all that is in change.[4]

Plato thus resolves the dilemma that had faced the earlier thinkers: the conflict between Being and Becoming, the One and the Many, thought and experience. In a rather cryptic passage in the *Timaeus* he tells us that the 'World-Soul' is composed by compounding together 'the indivisible Existence that is ever in the same state and the divisible Existence that becomes in bodies', so as to form 'a third form of Existence composed of both', and that this in turn is then blended into a unity with Sameness and Difference.[5] In Chapter 3 I pointed to a similar blending of opposites in the case of architectural proportion, with its fusion of order and complexity.

Further descriptions of the relation between the changing and unchanging worlds can be found in the *Republic*. Human beings are there compared to prisoners chained in a cave from birth, in such a way that they cannot turn to look towards its mouth. They see only the shadows of objects projected on the back wall by the light of a fire behind them, and take these shadows for the reality. If one of them were set free and shown the real objects, and still more if he came out of the cave into the daylight, he would at first be dazzled and confused. And if, having at last become accustomed to the bright light of reality, he were to return and try to tell his former companions what he had seen, and to convince them that what they saw were merely shadows, they would ridicule him and probably try to kill him. That is how society treats anyone who, like Socrates, has had a glimpse of the truth.[6]

This sounds as if the world of appearances is indeed purely illusory. Just before describing the cave, however,

4. Plato, *The Sophist*, in F.M. Cornford, *Plato's Theory of Knowledge*, Routledge & Kegan Paul, 1960, p. 242.
5. Plato, 'Timaeus', pp. 59-60.
6. Plato, *Republic*, trans. F.M. Cornford, Oxford University Press, 1941, pp. 222–6 .

Plato talks about the possibility of making representations that, though they can only be copies or imitations of reality, neverthless come as close as possible to the intelligible world of Forms. He compares the degrees of reality, or rather 'clarity and obscurity', to the parts of a line divided in a certain proportion, one part representing the visible world and the other the intelligible world. Both parts are then further subdivided in the same proportion (see Figure 6.1):

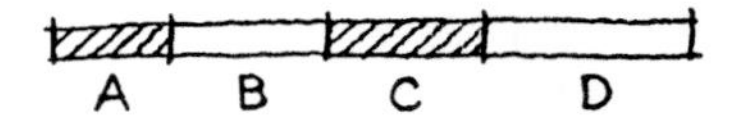

Figure 6.1 Plato: shadow and reality in the visible and intelligible worlds.

> Then (A) one of the two sections in the visible world will stand for images. By images I mean first shadows, and then reflections in water or. . . polished surfaces, and everything of that kind. . . Let the second section (B) stand for the actual things of which the first are likenesses, the living creatures all about us and all the works of nature or of human hands.[7]

The part that represents the intelligible world is divided similarly into two parts:

> In the first (C) the mind uses as images those actual things which themselves had images in the visible world; and it is compelled to pursue its inquiry by starting from assumptions and travelling. . . down to a conclusion. In the second (D) the mind moves in the other direction, from an assumption up towards a principle which is not hypothetical; and it makes no use of the images employed in the other section, but only of Forms, and conducts its inquiry only by their means.[8]

He instances the diagrams that students of geometry make in order to represent mathematical concepts:

> They make use of visible figures and discourse about them, though what they really have in mind is the originals of which these figures are images: they are not reasoning, for instance, about this particular square and diagonal which they have drawn, but about *the* Square and *the* Diagonal; and so in all cases. The diagrams they draw and the models they make are actual things, which have their shadows or images in water; but now they serve in their turn as images, while the student is seeking to apprehend those realities which only thought can apprehend.[9]

7. *Ibid.*, p. 219.
8. *Ibid.*, pp. 219–20.
9. *Ibid.*, p. 220.

Thus proportional relations enter into Plato's picture of reality in two different ways. The relation of the Forms to their sensible images is likened to a proportion, and this proportion is echoed in the relation between those sensible images themselves and their reflections or shadows. And geometrical constructions like the square and its diagonal – that is, proportional diagrams – are seen as images of the higher realities that only thought can apprehend.

Later in the same dialogue Plato gives another example. He compares three levels of representation: (1) the 'ideal or essential Bed', which exists in the world of Forms; (2) the bed made by a carpenter, which is a copy of (1); and (3) the painting of a bed made by an artist, which is a copy of (2), described as being 'at the third remove from the essential nature of the thing',[10] and in consequence inferior to the carpenter's bed, which is in turn inferior to the ideal Bed.

The difficulty of giving an account of the real nature of the universe, as Plato sets out to do in the *Timaeus*, is of a similar kind to that faced by the painter. The physical universe is itself a copy. Only a description of the eternal model can hope to be eternal and irrefutable, like the truths of mathematics, but a description of the likeness can be at best only 'a likely story'.[11] Indeed, being a copy of the copy, it risks being, like the painter's representation of a bed, still further removed from the truth than the world of semblances. No exact description of nature is therefore possible. Instead of attempting to analyse nature as we experience it, beginning with how it appears and then taking it apart, Plato tries as far as possible to penetrate beyond appearances to their underlying mathematical principles. Again, the *Republic* gives a clue to what he has in mind. There are two possible methods:

> In the first the mind uses as images those actual things which themselves had images [i.e. shadows or reflections] in the visible world; and is compelled to pursue its enquiry by starting from assumptions and travelling, not up to a principle, but down to a conclusion. In the second the mind moves in the other direction, from an assumption up towards a principle which is not hypothetical; and it makes no use of the images. . . but only of the Forms, and conducts its enquiry solely by their means.[12]

10. *Ibid.*, p. 320.
11. F.M. Cornford, *Plato's Cosmology*, pp. 28–32.
12. Plato, *Republic*, pp. 219–20.

The second is the method that Plato proposes to adopt in the *Timaeus*. His description of the cosmos resembles those geometrical figures that refer, not 'downwards' to things as they appear, but 'upwards' to the original Forms of which appearances are the shadows or reflections. When in the dialogue he describes the body of the world as spherical, he does not base this assumption on the existence of spherical forms in the world around us – such as the sun, the moon, or certain plant and animal forms – but on geometry. The sphere is perfect, he says, because it is 'the figure that comprehends in itself all the figures there are', and is 'equidistant every way from centre to extremity'.[13]

Mathematics, rather than observation, is therefore the way to truth. With Plato, however, there comes a shift from the position of Pythagoras, for whom the visible world was itself composed of numbers: material particles arranged as pyramids, cubes, and so on. Plato regards them, on the contrary, as *intelligible objects*, inaccessible to the senses. Without arriving at the conclusion reached by modern mathematicians, that these objects also reside in the intellect – that they are wholly or partially a creation of the human mind – he nevertheless posits the existence of an abstract mathematical universe. In so far as he sees the mathematical realities not as a human projection onto nature, but as an essential property of nature itself, the study of which leads to a knowledge of ultimate reality, Plato's thought is empathic; but to the extent that it embodies a synthesis, it also contains an element of abstraction.[14]

However, the crucial test, which decides on which side of the dividing line he must be placed, is the question: 'Do we know because we belong to what we know, or because we have made it?' For Plato, we know because we belong. The human soul has access to knowledge because it originates from the same source. Knowledge is recollection, *anamnesis*. In the *Meno* Socrates says that

> The soul then being immortal, having been often born, having beheld. . . all things, there is nothing of which she has not gained the knowledge. No wonder, therefore, that she is able to recollect, with regard to virtue as well as to other things, what formerly she knew.[15]

He proceeds to demonstrate this by showing that an uneducated slave-boy, with a little coaching, can 'recollect'

13. Plato, 'Timaeus', in op. cit., pp. 34–7.
14. F. Lasserre, *The Birth of Mathematics in the Age of Plato*, Hutchinson, 1964, p. 28.
15. Plato, 'Meno', in *Five Dialogues of Plato on Poetic Inspiration*, Everyman's Library, 1910, p. 90.

that the side of a square twice as large in area as another must equal the diagonal of the smaller square.[16]

6.2 GOD AS ARRANGER

Plato presents his cosmology in the form of a cosmogony – a creation myth – starting out, as has been said, not from the evidence of the visible world but from reasoning about how the world must have been put together according to first principles. For the first time in Greek philosophy, the world is described as being made like a work of art, by a 'Demiurge' – literally a craftsman – out of raw material already present, like the clay used by a potter or the wood and stone used by the builder of a house.

Plato posits the Demiurge as a rhetorical device or metaphor, in order to present the construction of the world as a process. In his analysis of the *Timaeus* Francis Cornford writes that

> The whole subsequent account of the world is cast in a mould which this figure dictates. What is really an analysis of the elements of rational order in the visible universe and of those other elements on which order is imposed, is presented in mythical form as the story of a creation in time.[17]

Unlike the God of Genesis the Demiurge is not an object of worship, and does not create the world out of nothing, but like a human designer or architect he merely rearranges it so as to bring it 'from disorder into order'. Neither the formless matter ('Necessity') nor the rational Forms he imposes on it ('Reason') originate with him; he merely brings them together. Nor is he all-powerful; he cannot make a perfect work, but only one that is 'as good as possible' in the circumstances, given the imperfect and changing nature of his raw material. That the result falls short of perfection is not the fault of the god, but due to the primordial flux of matter or Necessity.[18] This concept brings together the boundless primal matter of Anaximander, the perpetual strife and flux of Heraclitus, the original mixture of opposites posited by Anaxagoras, and the Necessity that is the prime mover of the atoms of Leucippus. It is a first component of the Platonic synthesis.

16. *Ibid.*, pp. 91–100.
17. F.M. Cornford, *Plato's Cosmology*, p. 27.
18. *Ibid.*, pp. 34–7.

In the first part of the dialogue, 'The Works of Reason', Plato approaches the world as it were from above, from the direction of the ideal Forms that the creator or Demiurge takes as his model. In the second, 'What comes about of Necessity', he approaches it from below, beginning with the uncreated, unformed matter and space with which the Demiurge had to work, and, moving upwards, shows how he imposed rational form upon it. The third and final part, 'The Cooperation of Reason and Necessity', deals with the human constitution.

In order that the world should be as perfect as possible, the god sees that it must have intelligence, and therefore be equipped with a soul as well as a body. It is a living being like ourselves. Its model can be no particular species, however, because then it would be a copy of what is already a copy and thus incomplete. Instead, the Demiurge makes it in the likeness of 'that Living Creature of which all other living creatures, severally and in their families, are parts'[19] – in other words, as like as possible to the Form of all living creatures, an archetypal animal, 'containing within itself all living things whose nature is of the same order'.[20] So that it will be as close as possible to the original, he also makes it one and complete, 'nothing being left over'. Were something left outside the world, or were there more than one, the resulting plurality would have to be absorbed into a higher unity, a yet higher world.

6.3 THE PROPORTIONAL MEAN

The first step in making the body of the world is the separating out of the elements from the undefined primal chaos. First, fire (in order that the world be visible) and earth (in order that it be tangible). 'But two things cannot be satisfactorily united without a third: for there must be some bond between them tying them together.'[21] Here for the first time Plato introduces the mathematical theory of proportion: two things, called the *extremes*, are united by a third, the *mean*. The important point here is the function of proportion in *binding things together*. It binds together the parts of Plato's world just as it binds together the parts of a building. In both cases, it is a matter of *construction*: of uniting separate elements to make an integrated whole. This looks forward to Alberti's concept of *concinnitas*, 'that reasoned harmony of all

19. Plato, 'Timaeus', in op. cit., p. 40.
20. *Ibid.*
21. *Ibid.*, p. 44.

the parts within a body, so that nothing can be added, taken away, or altered, but for the worse'.[22] The kind of mean that Plato selects as being the best is the *geometric*.

Since they play such an important part in the theory of architectural proportion, and also in Plato's description, it is necessary to break off at this point in order to discuss the nature of proportional means. The ancient mathematicians Nicomachus (fl. *c*. AD 150) and Pappus (fl. *c*. AD 300) each list 10 kinds of mean, of which 9 are common to both, making 11 altogether.[23] Of these, we need here consider four: the *geometric*, the *arithmetic*, the *harmonic*, and the *contraharmonic*.

The *geometric* mean, which Plato favours, is that middle term between a higher and a lower term that stands to the lower term as the higher stands to the mean. In other words, A and C being two terms and B their geometric mean, then $A : B = B : C$ (see Figure 6.2). The geometric mean of two numbers also equals the square root of their product: that is, the two numbers being again A and C, their geometric mean is given by the formula $B = \sqrt{AC}$. For instance, let $A = 1$ and $C = 4$; then

$$B = \sqrt{1 \times 4} = \sqrt{4} = 2$$

The *arithmetic* mean is that middle term between two other terms that divides both their sum and their difference into two equal parts. If B is the arithmetic mean between two terms A and C, then $B = (A + C)/2$ (see Figure 6.3). Suppose $A = 1$ and $C = 3$; then

$$B = \frac{1+3}{2} = \frac{4}{2} = 2$$

The *harmonic* mean is that middle term between two others that divides their difference in the same ratio as the two terms have to each other. B is the harmonic mean between A and C when $B = 2AC/(A + C)$ (see Figure 6.4). For example, if $A = 3$ and $C = 6$, then

$$B = \frac{2 \times 3 \times 6}{3 + 6} = \frac{36}{9} = 4$$

Finally, there is a fourth mean, usually ignored, that it is important to mention: the *contraharmonic* mean. As its name suggests, this divides the difference between two extremes in

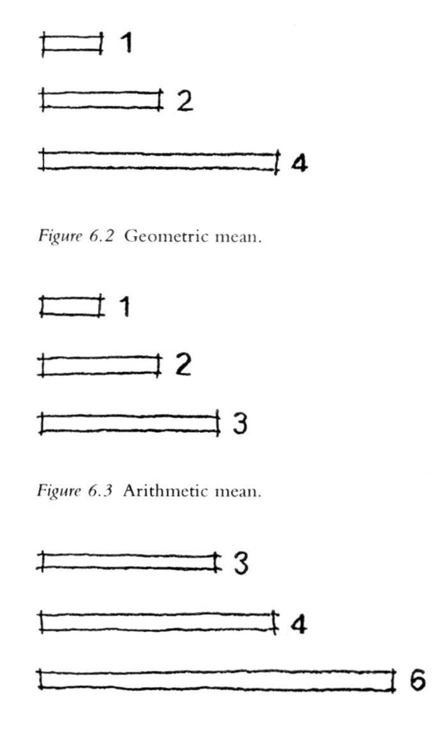

Figure 6.2 Geometric mean.

Figure 6.3 Arithmetic mean.

Figure 6.4 Harmonic mean.

22. L.B. Alberti, *On the Art of Building in Ten Books*, MIT Press, 1988, p. 156.
23. M. Ghyka, *The Geometry of Art and Life*, Dover Publications, 1977, pp. 4–5; and L. March, *Architectonics of Humanism*, Academy Editions, 1998, pp. 72–7.

the opposite way to the harmonic mean: that is, in the inverse of the ratio that they have to each other. Here B is the contraharmonic mean of A and C when $B = (A^2 + C^2)/(A + C)$. Let $A = 3$ and $C = 6$, then

$$B = \frac{9 + 36}{3 + 6} = \frac{45}{9} = 5$$

(see Figure 6.5).

The first three means can all be illustrated by the 'Renaissance' system of proportion shown in Chapter 3, Table 3.2. This is repeated in Table 6.1, but extended by one row and reduced by one column. If the table is imagined as indefinitely extended vertically and laterally, each number exhibits the first three kinds of mean in its relations to its close neighbours:

(1) It is the geometric mean between its predecessor and its successor in the same column or the same row: for example, 12 is the geometric mean of 6 and 24, and also of 4 and 36.
(2) It is the arithmetic mean between two numbers in the column to its left, or in the row above: for example, 12 is the arithmetic mean of 8 and 16, and also of 6 and 18.
(3) It is the harmonic mean between two numbers in the column to its right, or in the row below: for example, 12 is the harmonic mean of 9 and 18, and also of 8 and 24.

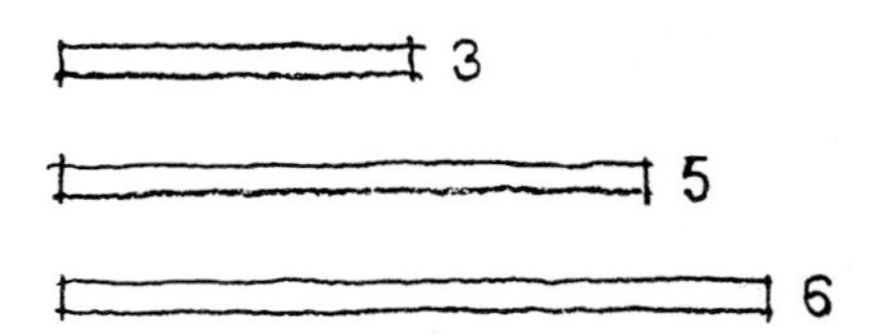

Figure 6.5 Contraharmonic mean.

TABLE 6.1

1	3	9
2	6	18
4	12	36
8	24	72
16	48	144

The four elements, earth, water, air and fire, had already been propounded by Empedocles. By applying the concept of means, however, Plato deduces the necessity of there being neither more nor less than four elements by a mathematical reasoning derived from Pythagoras. If the world were two-dimensional, he argues, a single mean would be enough to unite the two extremes, fire and earth; similarly the two square numbers 1 and 4 are united by a single geometric mean, 2. But in fact the world is to be three-dimensional – that is, solid; and to unite two solid or cubic numbers two means are required. Suppose the two cubic numbers are 1 and 8, then the two means are 2 and 4; thus $1 : 2 = 2 : 4 = 4 : 8$.

> Accordingly the god set water and air between fire and earth, and made them, so far as possible, proportional to one another, so that as fire is to air, air is to water, and as air

is to water, so is water to earth, and thus he bound together the frame of the world visible and tangible.[24]

In form, the world's body is a perfect Parmenidean sphere: 'For the living creature that was to embrace all living creatures within itself, the fitting shape would be the figure that comprehends in itself all the figures there are. . .'[25] Later, in the second part, these other figures will make their appearance: the five regular solids, tetrahedron, cube, octahedron, icosahedron and dodecahedron. The sphere 'contains them all' because each of them can be inscribed exactly within a sphere. So the world is made perfectly round, smooth, and without external features: no eyes or ears, because there is nothing outside to see or hear; no other openings, because the world is self-sufficient, neither breathing nor eating nor excreting but living off its own waste; and no limbs, because there is nothing outside to grasp and no ground to stand upon. It merely revolves uniformly on its own axis. The argument recalls Parmenides' description of the world as 'complete on every side, like the mass of a rounded sphere, equally poised from the centre in every direction'.[26]

TABLE 6.2

Natural numbers	1	2	3
Square numbers	1	4	9
Cubic numbers	1	8	27

TABLE 6.3

			1			
		2		3		
	4				9	
8						27

6.4 MAKING THE WORLD'S SOUL

Pythagorean mathematics again comes to the fore in the making of the world's soul. This passage is one of two that had a crucial impact on the later development of architectural proportion, the other being the already mentioned theory of the five regular solids, to which we shall return. The Demiurge compounds the soul-stuff into a mixture, which he rolls out in a long strip and proceeds to divide into lengths that correspond to the first three natural numbers with their squares and cubes, as in Table 6.2.

It helps to arrange these in the form of the Greek letter Λ (lambda), as in Table 6.3. This reveals that the seven numbers comprise two geometric progressions, both starting with the unit: the one formed by multiplying by 2 and the other by 3. Plato next proceeds to subdivide the intervals between the numbers in accordance with the Pythagorean theory of musical harmony; until he does so, however, they have in themselves, unlike the first four natural numbers 1, 2, 3, 4, no obvious connection with music. The range from 1 to 27,

24. Plato, 'Timaeus', in op. cit., p. 44.
25. *Ibid.*, p. 54.
26. Parmenides, *The Way of Truth*, in J. Burnet, *Early Greek Philosophy*, A & C Black Ltd, 1920, p. 176.

encompassing four octaves plus a major sixth, is musically arbitrary. Other reasons for the choice of numbers must be put forward: that the two series stop at the cubes because the world is to be 'cubic'; that the seven numbers correspond to the seven planets, which Plato is shortly to introduce; or perhaps that 1 + 2 + 3 + 4 + 9 + 8 = 27, so that 27, being the sum of the other six numbers, makes the series complete.

Now comes the harmonic subdivision. Cutting off more pieces from the mixture, the Demiurge places within each interval two means: the harmonic and the arithmetic. The extended lambda, with the original seven numbers printed in bold, is shown in Table 6.4.

TABLE 6.4

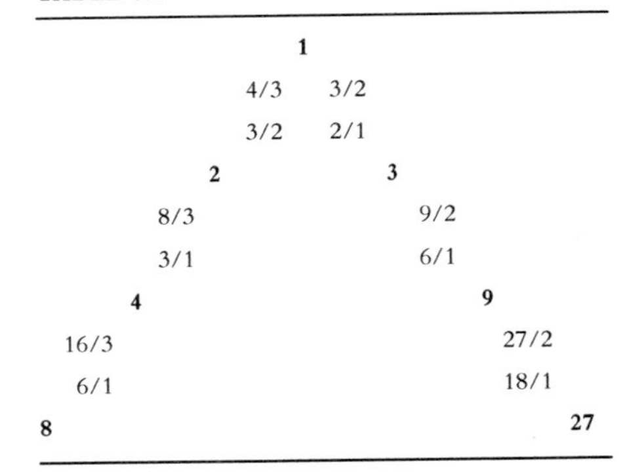

1	
4/3	3/2
3/2	2/1
2	**3**
8/3	9/2
3/1	6/1
4	**9**
16/3	27/2
6/1	18/1
8	**27**

The interval between each mean and its nearest extreme is now, in the double series, 4/3 (in music, a fourth), and in the triple series, 3/2 (a fifth). The interval between the harmonic and arithmetic means, in the double series, is 3/2 × 3/4 = 9/8 (a tone) and in the triple series 2/1 × 2/3 = 4/3. Each fifth is further divisible into a fourth plus a tone (3/2 = 4/3 × 9/8), so the whole system reduces to a sequence of fourths and tones. The Demiurge now tries to equalize the intervals still further, by dividing each fourth into two tones. But two consecutive tones make 9/8 × 9/8 = 81/64, which is short of 4/3 by 256/243 (i.e. 81/64 × 256/243 = 4/3). Therefore each interval of 2/1 (octave) is finally made up of five intervals of 9/8 (tones) and two of 256/243 (hemitones) (see Figure 6.6).

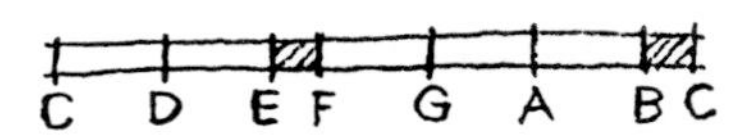

Figure 6.6 Platonic division of the octave into five tones and two semitones.

Two thousand years later the series of numbers shown in Table 6.4 would form the principal basis of what we have called the 'Renaissance' system of proportion, set out by Alberti in the ninth of his ten books *On the Art of Building*.[27] Since the *Timaeus* survived in Latin translation through the Dark and Middle Ages, and its proportion theory is also contained in the writings of Augustine and Boethius,[28] there are grounds for speculating that it may also have been used as a proportioning system by Medieval architects, but there is a lack of documentary confirmation for this. Applied to architecture, it produces mutually commensurable dimensions, and shapes in plan and elevation composed of arrangements of squares. Plato, however, uses it for quite different purposes, making it the basis of his planetary system.

Meanwhile the Demiurge has apparently joined all the pieces together again in a long strip, because he now splits it lengthwise into two bands. These he arranges as a cross and curls round into two rings, one inside the other. The outer

27. L.B. Alberti, *On the Art of Building*, pp. 305–7.
28. Augustine, *De Ordine* and *De Musica*, and Boethius, *De Istitutione Arithmetica*, trans. M Masi, Rodopi, Amsterdam, 1983.

ring, corresponding to the sphere of fixed stars, he leaves undivided, but the inner one he splits again into seven unequal circles, corresponding presumably to the seven planetary orbits, spaced out in accordance with the six intervals between the numbers 1, 2, 3, 4, 9, 8 and 27. The exact meaning is unclear. Perhaps these numbers are the respective diameters of the orbits; this is speculation, however, for Plato has yet to mention the planets by name.

TABLE 6.5

FORM	*A*	*E*	*F*	FACE FIGURE
Tetrahedron	4	6	4	Equilateral triangle
Cube	8	12	6	Square
Octahedron	6	12	8	Equilateral triangle
Icosahedron	12	30	20	Equilateral triangle
Dodecahedron	20	30	12	Pentagon

6.5 MAKING THE WORLD'S BODY

Since this is not intended as a full account of the *Timaeus*, but only of the parts of it relevant to architectural proportion, we can move on rapidly to the second part, where Plato discusses the forms of matter, and specifically the four primary elements of which the world's body is made up. In the primeval chaos, fire, air, water and earth already existed as inchoate 'powers', swirling about like grains in a winnowing basket, and without any defined shapes or proportions between them. So 'the god then began by giving them a distinct configuration by means of shapes and numbers'.[29] To each of the four elements the Demiurge assigns one of the five regular polyhedra: those solids whose surfaces are composed of identical regular, that is equilateral and equiangular, polygons (see Figure 3.9 in Chapter 3). The fifth, the dodecahedron, with twelve pentagonal faces, he reserves for the 'whole' – the sphere of the fixed stars, which he decorates with the figures of the constellations – and Plato says no more about it. This is too obvious an evasion of the problem that there were five regular solids and only four elements to fill them, and it failed to satisfy even Plato's followers. A fifth element, 'ether', was therefore posited, making its appearance in an apocryphal dialogue, the *Epinomis*.[30] Plato's pupil Xenocrates claims in his biography that Plato 'divided up living things into categories and parts. . . until he reached the five elements of all beings, which he called *five figures* and *five bodies:* ether, fire, water, earth and air'.[31]

By including the dodecahedron with its pentagonal faces, two further irrational numbers are obtained – $\sqrt{5}$ and ϕ – which are of still greater significance in both nature and art. These will be discussed in connection with Euclid's *Elements* in Chapter 8. The more obvious properties of the five regular polyhedra are described in Table 6.5. The general rule

29. Plato, 'Timaeus', in op. cit., p. 198.
30. F. Lasserre, *The Birth of Mathematics*, pp. 80–4.
31. Xenocrates, *Life of Plato*, in F. Lasserre, *The Birth of Mathematics*, p. 83.

illustrated by the table would be established much later by René Descartes: that if a polyhedron has A apices, E edges and F faces, then $A - E + F = 2$.[32]

A general theory of irrational square roots, the construction of the regular polyhedra based on them, and the proof that there can be no more than five such regular solids, are contained in the *Elements* of Euclid (*c.* 330–275). They are traditionally thought to have been first worked out earlier, however, either within or close to Plato's circle by his contemporary, the mathematician Theaetetus (*c.* 414–369), of whom François Lasserre says that the originality of his discoveries 'marks him out as one of the greatest of all time'.[33] The significance of his contribution is disputed, however, by Arpád Szabó and others.[34]

Plato makes Theaetetus the interlocutor of three of the dialogues: the *Sophist*, the *Statesman*, and the eponymous *Theaetetus*. In a passage in the last-named dialogue Theaetetus tells Socrates how his own teacher Theodorus of Cyrene had discovered the irrational square roots up to $\sqrt{17}$, at which point

> For some reason he stopped. The idea occurred to us, seeing that these square roots were evidently infinite in number, to try to arrive at a single collective term by which we could designate all these roots.[35]

He concludes that the square roots of all numbers that are not square numbers (that is, perfect squares, like 1, 4, 9, 16,. . .) will be irrational or incommensurable *as lengths*; they are, however, commensurable *as areas* – that is, in terms of the squares constructed on these lengths. This seems to be the origin of Jay Hambidge's principle of 'area measurableness', mentioned in Chapter 3, section 3.4 and Chapter 5, section 5.2.

Theaetetus is also traditionally regarded as the discoverer of the octahedron and icosahedron, which make up, with the tetrahedron, cube and dodecahedron, which were already known to the Pythagoreans, the full complement of five regular polyhedra.[36] T.L. Heath argues, however, that all five were Pythagorean discoveries, and that Theaetetus may have been only the first to write at length about the two attributed to him.[37] The proof that no others are possible is presented as follows by Euclid[38] (see Figure 6.7).

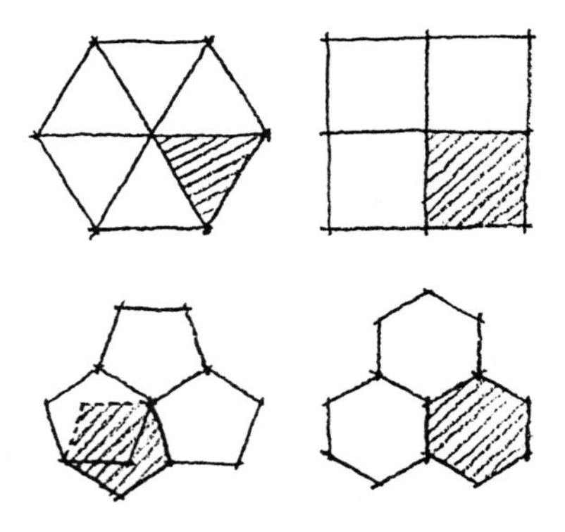

Figure 6.7 Proof that there can be no more than five regular polyhedra.

32. R. Descartes, *Geometry*, 1637.
33. F. Lasserre, *The Birth of Mathematics*, p. 65; cf. pp. 65–78 passim.
34. A. Szabó, *The Beginnings of Greek Mathematics*, D. Reidel Publishing Co., 1978, pp. 55–85.
35. Plato, 'Theaetetus', in F.M. Cornford, *Plato's Theory of Knowledge*, p. 23.
36. See scholium 1 to Euclid, book XIII, quoted by T.L. Heath in a note to the *Elements*, Dover Publications, 1956, vol. III, p. 438.
37. T.L. Heath, *ibid.*
38. Euclid, *Elements*, vol. III, pp. 507–8.

(1) To construct a solid angle at least three planes must meet at a point.
(2) Three equilateral triangles make the apex of the regular tetrahedron; four, that of the octahedron; five, that of the icosahedron; but six meeting at a point make a plane figure, the regular hexagon, since their meeting angles add up to four right angles or 360°.
(3) Three squares meeting at a point make the apex of the cube, but four squares make a plane figure, in fact a larger square, since they again complete four right angles.
(4) Three regular pentagons meeting at a point make the apex of the dodecahedron, but the meeting angles of four pentagons add up to more than four right angles, so again no solid angle can be formed.
(5) Finally, three hexagons meeting at a point already complete four right angles, and therefore make a plane figure.

Consequently no regular polyhedron can have faces with more than five edges.

Two thousand years later two more, equilateral but not equiangular, polyhedra – the twelve-sided rhombic dodecahedron and the thirty-sided rhombic triacontahedron – were discovered by Johannes Kepler;[39] but these are excluded from the number of the regular solids, strictly defined, by the unequal angles of their faces.

Plato assigns one of the four forms to each element: the cube, the most stable, to earth; the tetrahedron, the lightest body with the sharpest points, to fire; the next lightest, the octahedron, to air; and finally the icosahedron to water. This attribution of the first four solids to the four elements combines the element theory of Empedocles with the atomic theory of Leucippus and Democritus. But where the atomists allowed an innumerable variety of shapes, Plato limits them to four, and gives them a precise geometry.

He concerns himself almost exclusively with the plane figures that form their surfaces, however, rather than their at least equally important stereometry. He moves in one sentence from the solidity of the four forms to the fact that (1) every solid has a surface, (2) every surface that has straight edges can be reduced to triangles, and (3) every triangle can be reduced to two right-angled triangles. All right-angled triangles, he says, are of one of two kinds: they are either isosceles – that is, with angles of 45°, 90° and 45° – or scalene (that is, with the two smaller angles unequal). 'Now,' says Plato,

39. J.V. Field, *Kepler's Geometrical Cosmology*, Athlone Press, 1988, pp. 201–19.

> the isosceles is of one type only; the scalene, of an endless number. . . For ourselves, however, we postulate as the best. . . one kind, passing over all the rest; that, namely, a pair of which compose the equilateral triangle,[40]

that is, with angles of 30°, 60° and 90°. Had Plato been interested in the dodecahedron and the pentagon, and consequently in the golden section, he would certainly have instanced, besides these two right-angled triangles, the isosceles triangle with angles of 72°, 36° and 72°, which embodies the ratio $\phi : 1$ between its long and short sides. This triangle plays an important part in Euclid's geometry, as we shall see in Chapter 8 (Figures 8.10, 8.11).

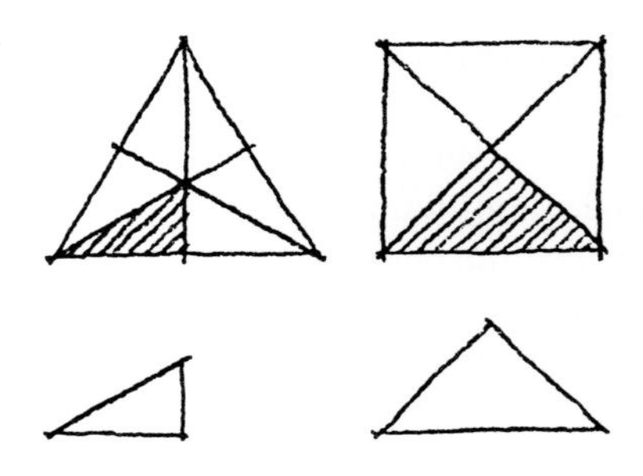

Figure 6.8 Equilateral triangle and square: component right-angled triangles according to Plato.

Two, or four, isosceles right-angled triangles make up a square, the face of a cube; two, or six, of Plato's preferred scalene triangles compose an equilateral triangle, the face of a tetrahedron, octahedron or icosahedron (see Figure 6.8). He in fact stipulates division into four and six respectively, rather than the more obvious two and two. The tetrahedron is thus bounded by 24 of these smaller scalene triangles, the octahedron by 48 and the icosahedon by 120, while the cube is bounded by 24 of the smaller isosceles triangles.

Plato's aim in choosing these particular shapes seems to have been to break the impasse that the discovery of the irrationality of the square roots of 2 and 3 presented for Pythagorean mathematics. He attempts to confront it head-on, placing these very irrationals at the heart of the construction of matter. If the basic monads or units of matter themselves embody irrational proportions, they can measure out lengths that are mutually incommensurable. In other words, the side and the diagonal of a square are each commensurable with either the short sides or the hypotenuse of Plato's isosceles unit-triangle, and the same holds for the side and height of an equilateral triangle with respect to his scalene unit. According to Karl Popper, Plato had at that time every reason to presume that all other irrationals could be composed of various combinations of $\sqrt{2}$, $\sqrt{3}$ and the unit. Particularly striking is the coincidence that $\sqrt{2} + \sqrt{3}$ is a very close approximation for π, the excess over π being less than fifteen parts in ten thousand.[41]

Plato neglects, however, to consider the awkward fact that only one of the five completely regular solids – the cube – is capable of complete space-filling. All others, when close packed, leave interstitial spaces between them. It is true that

40. Plato, 'Timaeus', in op. cit., p. 214.
41. K.R. Popper, *The Open Society and its Enemies*, pp. 251-3.

close-packed octahedra give rise to tetrahedral interstices, so these two shapes do in fact fill space completely when combined; presumably, however, this combination would require that water and fire be always mixed together in equal portions, which is clearly not the case. It might be argued that the cubic element, earth, is the only one that is completely solid and stable, the other three – water, air and fire – being in varying degrees mobile, and that this mobility is made possible by the interstitial voids separating their atoms. But this explanation, though perhaps plausible in itself, conflicts with the fact that Plato's description of the world's body implies that like Parmenides' it is everywhere full and fills the whole of space, nothing being left over. For 'He who put it together made it consist of all the fire and water and air and earth, leaving no part or power of any one of them outside'.[42] The god intended that it be 'whole and complete', and also 'single, nothing being left over, out of which such another might come into being'.[43] This does not seem to allow for unfilled voids within or between the elements, such as the atomist theory assumed. Plato's failure to consider the polyhedra as stereometric forms – his exclusive concentration on the figures of their surfaces – shows that his approach is not rigorously mathematical – like those of his contemporaries Theaetetus and Eudoxus of Cnidus (391–338 BC) – but poetic, metaphorical and mythical.

The remaining parts of the *Timaeus* throw no further light on the theory of architectural proportion. To sum up, therefore: the dialogue presents two contrasting aspects of early Greek mathematics, and suggests two possible approaches to the problem of architectural proportion. The first, contained in the description of the composition of the world's soul, employs whole-number ratios derived from the Pythagorean theories of musical harmony and of numbers as finite monads arranged in various patterns to constitute the visible world. In the second, the analysis of the first four regular polyhedra as the primary atomic constituents of fire, earth, air and water, Plato attempts to resolve the paradox presented by the Pythagorean discovery of irrational numbers, and in so doing opens up the way to the geometrization of mathematics, developed further by Euclid, Archimedes, Apollonius and others. Both aspects of the *Timaeus* had a more or less direct influence on the theory of architectural proportion during the Renaissance, and very possibly the Middle Ages.

42. Plato, 'Timaeus', in op. cit., p. 52.
43. *Ibid.*

Chapter seven

ARISTOTLE: CHANGE, CONTINUITY, AND THE UNIT

According to Plato the forms physical matter takes on exist on their own account outside matter as actual objects of understanding called Ideas. . . *But according to Aristotle the forms of physical things exist only in matter and not as actually understandable. Since we can only understand what is actually understandable. . . our minds need to make things actually understandable by abstracting their forms from their material conditions. Our ability to do this we call our* agent mind.[1]

7.1 'SIGHT IS THE PRINCIPAL SOURCE OF KNOWLEDGE'

Bertrand Russell says of Aristotle that his metaphysics 'may be described as Plato diluted by common sense. He is difficult because Plato and common sense do not mix easily.'[2] Born at Stagira on the northern shores of the Aegean in 384 BC, Aristotle spent two important periods of his life in Athens and in the proximity of Plato and the Academy. For twenty years, from 367 until Plato's death in 347, he was first a student and then a teacher and independent researcher at the Academy. Returning to Athens in 335, he taught at his own rival school, the Lyceum, until twelve years later, having been indicted like Socrates for impiety, he fled to Chalcis in order not to suffer the same fate. He died the following year, in 322 BC. Inevitably, therefore, his name is linked with that of Plato, as the two giants of ancient Greek – and all European – philosophy, and his thought tends first of all to be compared or contrasted with that of his teacher.

Aristotle was a prolific writer; his surviving works, which

1. T. Aquinas, *Summa Theologiae*, Methuen, 1989, I.79.3, p. 122.
2. B. Russell, *History of Western Philosophy*, George Allen & Unwin, 1961, p. 175.

even now fill twelve volumes, represent only a fifth of his total output. The early dialogues written for publication are all lost, and what we have are collections put together later either from his lecture notes or from textbooks intended for his students. His scope was encyclopedic. He wrote on metaphysics and the theory of knowledge; on astronomy, physics, mechanics, chemistry and mathematics; on history, politics and law; on ethics and psychology; and on language, art and poetry. But it was above all in biology and zoology that he made his greatest and most lasting contribution; his researches in these fields are something quite new in Greek science, and contrast dramatically with the increasingly cerebral and mathematical direction taken by Plato and his successors at the Academy. In the treatise *On the Parts of Animals* he urges his students not to confine their attention only to the 'celestial things', which may seem more attractive precisely because they are remote and inaccessible to knowledge, but to study 'perishable plants and animals' about which 'we have abundant information, living as we do in their midst'. He writes:

> There is a story that, when some strangers who wished to meet Heracleitus stopped short on finding him warming himself at the kitchen stove, he told them to come boldly in, for 'there also there were gods'. In the same spirit we should approach the study of every form of life without disgust, knowing that in every one there is something of Nature and beauty. For it is in the works of Nature above all that design, in contrast with random chance, is manifest; and the perfect form which anything born or made is designed to realise, holds the rank of beauty.[3]

The link Aristotle makes between beauty and order in nature, particularly in biology, is interesting in the light of the later history of the theory of proportion. It was precisely biology that provided nineteenth- and twentieth-century writers such as Adolf Zeising,[4] Theodore Cook,[5] D'Arcy Wentworth Thompson,[6] Jay Hambidge,[7] Matila Ghyka[8] and eventually Le Corbusier[9] with the basis for a mathematical approach to proportion in nature and art. At present, however, it is the treatises most relevant to pure mathematics, and particularly to the concept of space, that mainly concern us: the *Physics* and the *Metaphysics*. Both titles are misleading. *Physics* is not a translation but a transliteration of the Greek

3. Aristotle, *On the Parts of Animals*, quoted in F.M. Cornford, *Before and After Socrates*, Cambridge University Press, 1960, pp. 93–4.
4. A. Zeising, *Neue Lehre von den Proportionen des menschlichen Körpers*, Leipzig, 1854.
5. T.A. Cook, *The Curves of Life*, Constable & Co., 1914.
6. D.W. Thompson, *On Growth and Form*, Cambridge University Press, 1917.
7. J. Hambidge, *The Elements of Dynamic Symmetry*, Yale University Press, 1919–20.
8. M. Ghyka, *Esthétique des proportions dans la nature et dans les arts*, 1927.
9. Le Corbusier, *Le Modulor*, Editions de l'Architecture d'aujourd'hui, 1950.

word for *Nature*. The *Metaphysics* probably consists of a number of separate papers first brought together and given a title that simply means 'After the Physics' by its first editor, Andronicus of Rhodes, two centuries after they were written; a more appropriate title would be *First Philosophy*.

Aristotle was, like Plato, a synthesizer. Both philosophers attempted to reconcile that which could be clearly understood – the world of permanent rational concepts and discrete Pythagorean numbers – with the flowing, changing world experienced by the senses. Neither believed that reality is restricted to ideas or to experience alone. But the synthesis that Aristotle sought was the opposite of Plato's. Of the two approaches to truth that Plato defines in the *Republic* – that by which 'the mind uses as images those actual things which themselves had images in the visible world', or that by which 'it makes no use of the images. . . but only of the Forms'[10] – Aristotle adopts the first. He follows the very path that Plato has warned against on the grounds that it compels the mind 'to pursue its inquiry by starting from assumptions and travelling, not up to a principle, but down to a conclusion'.[11]

Although both Plato and Aristotle seek a mean between the two extremes of empathy and abstraction, Plato is closer to empathy, in the special 'Worringerian' sense in which I have defined the term. Knowing is for him a matter of belonging, and therefore essentially passive; to know the Forms we have only to recollect them from our former incorporeal existence. If by abstraction, on the other hand, we mean the attitude that we first have to make something in order to know it, Aristotle is closer to abstraction. He places the emphasis on knowledge as an activity, a kind of making, an *art*. In the treatise *On the Soul* the mind is portrayed as having two aspects: it is both passive and active. In its first aspect it is analogous to matter, in that it is capable of 'becoming all things': that is, of imagining any object. In its second aspect it is like the artist who imposes a form on the formless matter; it gives form to the thing that is thought, in order to make it intelligible. Thus:

> Since in every class of things, as in nature as a whole, we find two factors involved, (1) a matter which is potentially all the particulars included in the class, (2) a cause which is productive in the sense that it makes them all (the latter standing to the former, as e.g. an art to its material), these

10. Plato, *Republic*, trans. & ed. F.M. Cornford, Oxford University Press, 1941, pp. 219–20.
11. *Ibid*.

> distinct elements must likewise be found in the soul. And in fact mind as we have described it [so far] is what it is by virtue of becoming all things, while there is another which is what it is by virtue of making all things: this is a sort of positive state like light; for in a sense light makes potential colours into actual colours.[12]

St Thomas Aquinas puts this more succinctly. He quotes Aristotle as saying: 'In the mind, just as in the rest of nature, besides what is receptive of existence there is what makes things exist.'[13] Thus both Plato and Aristotle use the image of the artist as the maker of forms. But where in the *Timaeus* Plato portrays the god as the artist who shapes the cosmos out of the primeval chaos, Aristotle employs the same image to describe the mind's activity in *reshaping* the sensible world into intelligible concepts.

Nevertheless, in every area of research, according to Aristotle, we must begin with appearances, and having reflected upon them, to appearances we must return, bringing to them the clearer insight we have gained through thought. They constitute the datum against which we must test our speculations. The search for knowledge begins with the senses, and is developed through memory and thought. The opening words of the *Metaphysics* are:

> All men by their very nature feel the urge to know. That is clear from the pleasure we take in our senses, for their own sake, irrespective of their utility. Above all, we value sight;. . . we prefer it, I believe, to every other sense, even when we have no material end in view. Why? Because sight is the principal source of knowledge and reveals many differences between one object and another. . . Brute beasts live by sense-impression and memory with but a small share in connected experience, whereas the human race lives by art and science. Man derives experience through memory; his several acts of memory give rise to a single effect which we call experience. The latter is easily confused with art and science, which are, however, its results. . . You have art where from many notions of experience there proceeds one universal judgement applying in all similar cases.[14]

Knowledge begins, therefore, not with recollection but with observation – which for Aristotle includes the observing of

12. Aristotle, 'On the Soul', in *The Works of Aristotle*, Encyclopaedia Britannica, 1952, vol. I, p. 662.
13. T. Aquinas, *Summa Theologiae*, p. 122.
14. Aristotle, *Metaphysics*, Everyman's Library, 1956, p. 51.

men's common beliefs and the way they ordinarily use language.

Aristotle's reliance on appearances, and on common-sense opinions and the collective experience of ordinary men, is a strength in fields such as biology, where, as he says, 'we have abundant information, living as we do in [its] midst'. It becomes a source of weakness, from a modern viewpoint, the more he turns his attention to the 'celestial things' that are 'remote and inaccessible to knowledge'. It severely limits his ability to deal even with things nearer to hand, like velocity and acceleration, which require the evidence of the senses to be backed up by accurate measuring instruments and corrected by an adequate conceptual apparatus. In contrast to the rigorously quantitative method that has characterized Western science since the seventeenth century, he approaches things chiefly in terms of their qualities; that is, their essential natures. Unlike the Pythagoreans, who had already posited the centrality of the sun, he takes the earth to be the stationary centre about which the whole universe revolves, and towards which all heavy objects are drawn 'as their natural place'. He explains the acceleration of falling bodies by their growing eagerness as they draw close to home. Heavier objects, he thinks, fall faster than light ones, and the distance, D, covered by a moving object in a given time, T, is directly proportional to the force, F, applied to it and inversely proportional to the density of the resisting medium, R. Today we might express this by the equation $D/T = F/R$, but this misrepresents Aristotle's viewpoint: for a magnitude, according to the Greek way of thinking, could only result from a proportion between quantities *of the same kind*. A ratio between things of different kinds, like distance and time, or force and density, was no true proportion, so the Greeks could have no clear concept of velocity as a quantity. Aristotle describes motion only in terms of distances and times.[15] The formula is useful, nevertheless, because it highlights two conclusions that Aristotle does in fact draw. First, as soon as the force ceases the object will instantly come to a stop (that is, if $F = 0$, then $F/R = 0$, so $D/T = 0$). He is forced to explain the continued motion of projectiles as resulting from the commotion of the disturbed air, the object being pushed along by the displaced air rushing to fill the vacuum at the back. Second, he concludes that speed in a vacuum must be infinite. For this and other reasons he concludes that there

15. A.C. Crombie, *Augustine to Galileo*, Mercury Books, 1961, vol. II, p. 48; D.C. Lindberg, *The Beginnings of Western Science*, University of Chicago Press, 1992, p. 60.

can be no empty space in the universe.

With the advantage of hindsight we may now be inclined to regard such conclusions as absurd. They are due, however, not to Aristotle's over-reliance on observation, but to the inappropriateness of the conceptual framework of his time for analysing its results. But the questions that the seventeenth century would ask are not the same ones that mattered to the Greeks. The measure of a philosophy is not the degree to which it anticipates modern thought, but how far it deals with the philosophical problems of its time. Moreover, Aristotle's philosophical empiricism, precisely *because* of its contradictions, would lead in the later Middle Ages to a critical process that became the basis of the experimental tradition of modern science.

Observation, for Aristotle, must be developed by the active search for causes: in other words, by interpretation or analysis. He compares the development of understanding to the learning of an art or a trade. For

> He who has only experience knows that a thing *is* so, but not *why* it is so, whereas an artist knows the why and the wherefore. This is why a master craftsman in any trade is more highly esteemed, is considered to know more, and therefore to be wiser than an artisan, because he understands the reason for what is done.[16]

So perception is inescapably an interpretative and selective process, and we become more skilled in it through practice. Our picture of the world is the representation we ourselves make of it.

7.2 THE REAL IS THE INDIVIDUAL

The place of the Platonic Forms is taken, in Aristotle's philosophy, by the concept of substance. 'Substance' translates the Greek word *ousia*; a less confusing translation would be 'reality'. For by substance he does not mean what today we tend to understand by the word, or what the *Oxford Dictionary* gives as its first meaning: 'a particular kind of material having more or less uniform properties'. Primary substances, for Aristotle, are individual beings – like you and me – or those things that define us as this or that individual. The chapter 'Substance' in the 'Philosophical Lexicon' that

16. Aristotle, *Metaphysics*, p. 52.

forms book Δ of the *Metaphysics* is so short that it can be quoted in full:

> 'Substance' means (1) The simple bodies (earth, fire, water, and all such things), and bodies generally and the things composed of them – living creatures as well as the stars and their parts. All these are called 'substances' because they are not predicated of a subject while everything else is predicated of them. (2) The immanent cause of being in the foregoing class of things, as the soul is of the being of animals. (3) The parts immanent in such things, defining them and marking them out as individuals, and by the destruction of which the whole is destroyed. (4) The essence, whose formula is a definition. Hence 'substance' has two senses: (a) the ultimate substratum which cannot be further predicated of anything else, and (b) that which is individual and separable, i.e. the shape or form.[17]

The individual things that are primary substances also belong, however, to a series of increasingly general classes, which are defined as secondary substances. For instance Socrates as an individual constitutes a primary substance; but he also belongs to the species *man* and still more generally to the genus *animal*. These general classifications are *predicated* on the individual substance. In the *Categories* Aristotle writes that

> Substance, in the truest and primary and most definite sense of the word, is that which is neither predicable of a subject nor present in a subject; for instance, the individual man or horse. But in a secondary sense those things are called substances within which, as species, the primary substances are included; also those which, as genera, include the species. . . Of secondary substances, the species is more truly substance than the genus, being more nearly related to the primary substance.[18]

The reason why individual things, for Aristotle, are the primary realities, is that without them the secondary ones would have nothing to support them: for

> Primary substances are most properly called substances in virtue of the fact that they are the entities which underlie everything else, and that everything else is either predicated of or present in them.[19]

---

17. ***Ibid.*, p. 18.**
18. Aristotle, 'Categories', in *The Works of Aristotle*, vol. I, p. 6.
19. ***Ibid.***

In other words, secondary substances are dependent for their existence on the primary ones; in so far as they have any reality, it is by virtue of their being embodied in a primary substance.

This view – that particular individuals, existing in the world of appearances, are the primary realities, and not mere shadows or reflections of a higher, universal reality, while conversely it is precisely the universals that have a more tenuous claim to real existence, being dependent on individuals – is clearly a complete reversal of Plato's doctrine. The consequence is that mathematical objects, which in Plato's universe have the highest place, the highest degree of reality, are reduced by Aristotle to pure abstractions: things constructed by the human mind. The number ten depends for its reality on the fact that we can say there are ten men or ten horses, but the converse is not true: 'humanity' or 'horsiness' cannot be predicated on the number ten. Similarly, a geometrical figure like a square or a circle exists primarily as an actual square or circle that we can cut out or mark out on the ground. As a geometrical concept it is merely what is left after the mind has abstracted the purely spatial attributes from all the other properties of the real figure, such as its being made of stone or scratched in the sand. As we shall see in a later chapter, this sort of argument will be made much of by the seventeenth- and eighteenth-century empiricists Locke, Berkeley and Hume.

It is important to note, however, that unlike these later philosophers Aristotle does not deny the reality of universals altogether; it is as though he still retains from his student years a residue of Plato's teaching. Species and genera remain 'substances', even if secondary and dependent ones. His fence-sitting on this point sowed the seeds of the disputes between nominalists and realists that rocked Medieval Scholasticism.

7.3 CHANGE AND ITS CAUSES

The individual being is subject to change: it moves, it is born and grows, it decays and dies. For this very reason, Plato considers it less real than the unchanging Forms: as 'the thing that becomes and passes away, but never has real being'.[20] Since for Aristotle, however, it is precisely the individual that is substantial and real, it follows that he is faced with the fact

20. Plato, 'Timaeus', in F.M. Cornford, *Plato's Cosmology*, Routledge & Kegan Paul, 1937, p. 33.

of change as a characteristic of this primary reality. Nature, he says, 'is a principle of change, so if we do not understand the process of change, we will not understand nature either'.[21]

To this extent he seems allied to Heraclitus, although, as we saw in Chapter 4, he criticizes the followers of Heraclitus for concluding that since everything is in flux, no true statement can be made about it.[22] Furthermore he denies that change is universal: 'The sensible world immediately around us is indeed subject to generation and decay; but this is a practically negligible part of the whole. . .'[23] By this he clearly does not mean that there is no *motion* in the universe as a whole, since he regards not only the planets but even the 'fixed stars' as eternally revolving, but he is making a distinction between constant, unchanging motion of this kind and the varied and changing motion of the things around us on the earth. Aristotle's universe comprises two separate regions subject to completely different laws. The whole of space is a great sphere, divided into an inner zone within the transparent spherical shell containing the moon, and the upper or celestial zone containing the stars and planets. The sublunar or terrestrial zone is composed of the four Platonic elements, and subject to change of all kinds: birth and death, increase and decrease, alteration of quality, and change of place. The celestial region is composed of the fifth element, ether, and comprises a series of transparent concentric spheres containing the planets and stars, eternally moving inside each other without friction or any void space between them. From Aristotle's point of view this celestial motion is constant and therefore changeless.

From a mathematical standpoint, however, even constant motion raises many of the same problems as other forms of change, in particular those of continuity and infinity, space and time. Aristotle says as much at the very start of his discussion of change in the *Physics*:

> The process of change appears to be continuous, and continuity seems to be the primary context of infinity. That is why in defining continuity one is almost bound to rely on the notion of infinity: it is because the continuous is what is infinitely divisible. Moreover, change seems to be impossible without place and void and time. . .[24]

Later, however, he will deny that change of place requires the existence of a void:

21. Aristotle, *Physics*, Oxford University Press, 1996, p. 56.
22. Aristotle, *Metaphysics*, p. 136.
23. *Ibid.*, p. 137.
24. Aristotle, *Physics*, p. 56.

> The fact of movement and change supports both those who say that place is something distinct from the bodies that come to occupy it, and those who say that void exists. . . But the reality of change does not mean that there has to be a void. . . since it is possible for things to make way for one another without there being any separate extension besides the moving bodies. It is as easy to see this in the case of the rotation of continuous objects as it is in the rotation of liquids.[25]

He goes on indeed to argue that a void space, far from being necessary for motion, would make it impossible, and that therefore no void can exist. For

> How can there be such a thing as natural movement if there are no distinctions within that which is void and infinite?. . . But there *are* differences between the various natural movements, and so there must be natural distinctions.[26]

Aristotle's concept of space is the opposite of the uniform, infinite, directionless, absolute void space imagined by the seventeenth-century physicists. Today, however, since Einstein's discovery that momentum, mass and energy are aspects of a finite but unbounded space–time continuum, his intuitions no longer seem so wide of the mark.

Aristotle overcomes the Heraclitean contention that nothing definite can be said about a world that is constantly changing, in a way that applies equally to the problem of motion. He investigates the conditions or *causes* of change; for as we have already seen, true skill in any field is for him the knowledge of causes. Just as 'a master craftsman in any trade is. . . considered to know more. . . because he understands the reason for what is done', so the key to the understanding of nature is to find out why things are as they are and how they came to be so. The chapter on 'Cause' in the 'Philosophical Lexicon' identifies four kinds of cause:

(1) the material out of which a thing comes into being, such as the bronze of a statue (this is traditionally called the *material cause*);
(2) the form or pattern of a thing (the *formal cause*);
(3) the person or thing that sets the change in motion – for

25. *Ibid.*, pp. 93–4.
26. *Ibid.*, p. 95.

example, the maker is the cause of the thing made (the *efficient cause*);
(4) the end or goal – that is, the purpose for which a thing exists or is made (the *final cause*).[27]

Only the efficient cause corresponds to our current notion of 'cause', because we habitually think of a cause as something external that acts on a thing to change it, and also as something that precedes its effect. But for Aristotle most causes are inherent in the thing itself; and the final cause, the goal that as it were draws the thing towards its realization, is crucially important. In the *Physics* he begins with the argument of those who maintain that things are caused only by blind necessity. For such thinkers, Zeus does not send rain *in order* that crops shall grow, but

> The vapour drawn up from the earth is bound to cool down; once it has cooled down it is bound to turn to rain and fall back to earth; and it is sheer coincidence that crops grow when this happens.[28]

But, he argues, things like rainfall 'turn out as they do either always or usually, and so does every other natural object, whereas no chance or spontaneous event ever does'.[29] The evidence of design is more striking still in the case of animals and plants: 'Some people are puzzled by how spiders, ants, and so on make what they make – do they use intelligence, or what?'[30] Human actions are purposeful; so too, therefore, are the processes of nature: 'For example, a naturally occurring house – supposing such a thing were possible – would happen in exactly the same way that a skilfully made house does.'[31] Aristotle's argument still underlies much of what has been written in the last hundred years to justify theories of proportion in art on the analogy of design in nature.[32]

He introduces two further principles that are basic to his conception of change: *actuality* and *potentiality*. By means of these he overcomes the problem of identity – of explaining how something can remain itself throughout all its changes. An oak tree is *actually* an oak tree, but an acorn is *potentially* an oak tree. Change, he writes, 'is the actuality of that which exists potentially, in so far as it is potentially this actuality'.[33] Francis Cornford's beautifully lucid description of this concept cuts through the prolixity and obscurity of Aristotle's own account:

27. Aristotle, *Metaphysics*, p. 4.
28. Aristotle, *Physics*, p. 50.
29. *Ibid.*, p. 51.
30. *Ibid.*
31. *Ibid.*
32. See notes 4–9 above.
33. Aristotle, *Physics*, p. 57.

> The end will be implicit in the beginning, and it will flower into actuality. We shall cease to think of 'matter' as an inert and passive body, awaiting the imposition of form from without, or as like the atoms of Democritus, lumps of impenetrable solidity, only to be moved by the shock of collision. Matter is not simply like the steel of which the spring is made; it is like the coiled spring in which the latent power of movement is stored.[34]

Everything in nature has a characteristic source of motion stored within it. Each of the four elements has its inherent potential to move in one direction or another: fire moves upwards, earth downwards.[35] And in living things, Cornford continues,

> This inherent power of motion can be attributed to the Form itself. . . In the process of reproduction the 'moving cause' is commonly identified by Aristotle with the specific Form actually realized in the fully developed parent; but in the act of generation this Form is communicated to the new individual, and, with it, is transmitted the force or power that will carry the process of development once more from the potential phase to the actual. Thus the specific Form travels through an unending series of individuals. . . In this way the Platonic Form of the species is brought down from its heaven of unchanging reality, and plunged in the flow of time and sensible existence.[36]

By this means Aristotle gives a certain permanence to form, while accepting the reality of change. Like Plato he rejects Heraclitus' doctrine that 'You cannot step twice into the same river.'[37] True, there is never the same water in the river at any one time, but *all* the water that flows down the river is 'potentially this actuality', namely this actual river. In the same way, a living organism remains 'itself' even though its constituent matter is constantly being renewed by the absorption of nutrients and the elimination of waste products.

7.4 CONTINUITY AND INFINITY

Change implies continuity and infinity; here Aristotle's teaching becomes directly relevant to the question of

34. F.M. Cornford, *Before and After Socrates*, pp. 97–8.
35. Aristotle, 'On the Heavens', in *The Works of Aristotle*, vol. I, pp. 403–4.
36. F.M. Cornford, *Before and After Socrates*, pp. 98–9.
37. Heraclitus, 'Fragments', in J. Burnet, *Early Greek Philosophy*, A & C Black, 1930, p. 136.

architectural proportion, for the division in mathematics between the discrete, indivisible unit used in counting and the continuous, infinitely divisible line corresponds to the division between the two 'families' of proportion systems: those that stem from the Pythagorean subdivision of the octave (such as the 'Renaissance' systems of Alberti and Palladio), and those based on square roots and other irrational numbers, like ϕ, that arise from geometry.

It is impossible, Aristotle says, for a continuum (such as a line) to consist of indivisible things (like the numerical unit or the Pythagorean concept of a point).[38] This principle applies equally to spatial quantities, to time and to movement. For

> If a magnitude consists of indivisible components, movement over that magnitude will consist of the same number of indivisible movements. . . The same would necessarily go for time as for distance and movement: time too would be indivisible and its components would be indivisible nows.[39]

He does not entertain the possibility that this might indeed be the case: that is, that there exist indivisible minima of space and time, and that motion consequently comprises a series of tiny jumps – or imperceptibly differing instants of rest – something like the sequence of images on a cinema screen. A theory of this sort was in fact proposed in the early decades of our century by a number of mathematicians and scientists including Henri Poincaré[40] and A.N. Whitehead.[41] The terms 'hodon' and 'chronon' were coined to describe the atoms of space and time, their dimensions being of the order of 10^{-13} cm and 10^{-21} seconds respectively.[42] Such a hypothesis would have pleased the Pythagoreans.

Aristotle distinguishes between two kinds of infinity: 'A thing may be infinite either by addition or by division.'[43] Thus a finite line can theoretically be divided an infinite number of times. Had Aristotle not insisted that space, unlike time, is finite (a conclusion that happens to accord, though for quite different reasons, with the curved geometry of Einstein's general theory of relativity[44]), it would have followed that the same finite line could also potentially be infinitely extended by repeated addition, just as the arithmetical progression 1, 2, 3, 4,. . . can be infinitely extended by the repeated addition of 1.

38. Aristotle, *Physics*, p. 138.
39. *Ibid.*, pp. 139–40.
40. H. Poincaré, *Dernières Pensées*, Paris, 1913, p. 188.
41. A.N. Whitehead, *The Concept of Nature*, Cambridge University Press, 1950, p. 162.
42. M. Capek, *The Philosophical Impact of Classical Physics*, D. Van Nostrand Co., 1961, pp. 230–1.
43. Aristotle, *Physics*, p. 71.
44. A. Einstein, *Relativity: The Special and General Theory*, Methuen & Co., 1960, pp. 83–96, 135–57.

But a more interesting aspect of his argument is the idea that only *processes* can be infinite, not actualities. He holds that 'No actual magnitude can be infinite, but it can still be infinitely divisible. . ., and so we are left with things being infinite potentially.'[45] Considered as a process, the division of a length can in theory be continued indefinitely; but like any infinite process that cannot be completed this remains always at the level of potentiality. Any *actual* division must be finite, because in order to be actualized the process must be terminated: one must be able as it were to point to the division and say 'That is it.' So infinity must be conceived as a process that is always *in progress*. As Aristotle puts it,

> Infinity turns out to be the opposite of what people say it is. It is not 'that which has nothing beyond itself' that is infinite, but 'that which always has something beyond itself'.[46]

The same applies to numbers: the series of natural numbers is potentially infinite, but any actual number, however large, must be counted or manifested as the number of a collection of actually existing objects, and is therefore necessarily finite.

Aristotle's distinction between actuality and potentiality provides a solution to the paradoxes concerning infinity that had been put forward about a century earlier by Zeno. Of these, the most relevant to the present argument are the 'dichotomy' and the 'Achilles'. The first states, essentially, that since one must reach the midpoint of the distance before reaching the end, and then the midpoint of what remains, and so on *ad infinitum*, the journey comprises an infinite number of stages, which would take an infinite time to complete. The second paradox is that Achilles can never overtake the tortoise if the tortoise has a start, because each time he reaches the tortoise's starting point it has moved on a little further. Experience tells us that Achilles will win the race; but it is not so easy to see how this happens. Suppose (to keep the arithmetic simple) he jogs a leisurely 100 m in the time an energetic tortoise gallops 10 m, and that the latter has a 100 m start. Then since the ratio of their speeds is 10 : 1 Achilles will overtake the tortoise when it has advanced from its starting point by one ninth of the 100 m handicap and he has covered ten ninths of the same distance, i.e. 1000/9 or 111.111 metres. We do not grasp this at first because the way the problem is framed lures us into thinking

45. Aristotle, *Physics*, p. 71.
46. *Ibid.*, p. 73.

of each separate increment instead of their totality. Aristotle makes two arguments. First,

> Although it is impossible to make contact in a finite time with things which are infinite in quantity, it is possible to do so with things which are infinitely divisible, since the time itself is also divisible in this way.[47]

Later, however, he says that this 'will not do as a response',[48] and puts forward a second argument: that

> Although there are infinitely many halves in any continuum, they are potential, not actual. Any actual division puts an end to continuous movement and creates a standstill.[49]

In other words, in order to actualize any given point Achilles must mark it in some way – for example, stop at it and start again. Instead of one continuous race there is an infinite succession of increasingly short races, each with the same proportional handicap and each brought to a stop just short of the distance Achilles needs to win. Such a series would indeed take an infinite length of time if continued indefinitely; but of course the race is in fact continuous, and not made up of discrete parts.

7.5 THE UNIT

The difficulty we experience in handling continuous quantities like distances illustrates the importance of establishing units suitable for measuring such continua. Aristotle addresses this problem in the *Metaphysics*.

He begins by enumerating various forms that unity can take. To be 'one' is

> (1) to be essentially a 'this' and separate either in place or form or in thought; (2) to be a whole and indivisible; but above all it is (3) to be the first measure of a class – especially of quantity, from which it has been extended to the other categories.[50]

A unit of measure is the means by which we can know a quantity. Once a measure is chosen, it acts somewhat like a numerical unit, which is

47. *Ibid.*, p. 143.
48. *Ibid.*, p. 219.
49. *Ibid.*, p. 220.
50. Aristotle, *Metaphysics*, p. 306.

> the starting point of number as such. Hence, in other classes too, that by which a thing is primarily known is a measure, and the measure of everything is a unit, e.g. of length, breadth, depth, weight, speed. In all these cases there is a measure and starting point which is something one and indivisible, since even among lines we treat as indivisible that which is a foot long.[51]

It is not immediately evident what Aristotle means by this; he surely cannot mean that no unit of linear measure exists smaller than a foot? It soon becomes apparent that what he intends is that the unit must be meaningful in relation to the thing that is to be measured; it must be neither so small that it does not 'count' in relation to what it measures, nor so large as to be visibly affected by small additions or subtractions from itself. For

> An accurate measure is one which cannot be taken from or added to; hence the measure of number is most accurate, for the unit is in every way indivisible. We adopt a similar standard of measurement in all other cases. In the case of a furlong, of a talent, or of anything large, any addition or subtraction is more likely to attract our notice than in the case of something smaller. We therefore choose as our measure (whether of liquids or solids, of weight or size) the first thing that cannot be added to or taken away from without detection; and we claim to know a thing's quantity when we have compared it with that measure.[52]

Again, Aristotle's distinction between actuality and potentiality comes to our help. Having selected an appropriate unit of measure, we treat it as if it were *actually* indivisible – by decree, as it were – even though we know that it is *potentially* divisible. What we do is to imitate, when dealing with continuous quantities such as size or weight, the absolute indivisibility of the unit of number.

> The unit is indivisible precisely because the first of each class of things is indivisible, but not every unit is indivisible in the same way. Thus the numerical unit is indivisible in every respect, but the foot to sense only.[53]

Such an artificial unit sets a limit, as it were, to the potentially

51. *Ibid.*
52. *Ibid.*, pp. 306–7.
53. *Ibid.*, p. 307.

infinite divisibility of the continuous quantity, enabling it to be measured.

The unit of measure must be appropriate not only to the quantity of the thing to be measured – it must be neither too big nor too small – but also to its quality. For

> The measure is always akin to the measured. Thus the measure of spatial magnitudes is itself a spatial magnitude; e.g. that of length is a length, that of breadth a breadth, that of articulate sounds an articulate sound, that of weight a weight, and that of units a unit.[54]

7.6 ARCHITECTURAL PROPORTION AND ARISTOTLE'S CONCEPT OF MEASURE

The influence of the mathematics of Plato's *Timaeus* upon architectural proportion was direct and obvious. By comparison, the relevance to architecture of Aristotle's teaching concerning the problems of continuity, infinity and the unit is neither direct nor self-evident. The inclusion of a chapter on Aristotle in this book is made necessary chiefly by his importance for two developments that will be discussed later: the rise of Medieval science and particularly, as regards architecture, the thought of Dom Van der Laan. Without waiting for these, it seems appropriate to conclude this chapter with a speculation about how Aristotle's concept of measure might generate particular kinds of proportion.

According to Aristotle the unit of measure for a continuous spatial quantity – that is, for a line, plane or volume – imitates the discreteness of the numerical unit. For the purposes of the measurement in hand we regard it 'as if' it were indivisible, even though we know that in reality it can be divided. Second, the unit of measure is of the same kind as the thing to be measured: we measure lines with a linear unit, surfaces with a planar unit, and volumes with a volumetric unit. Let us start by considering the case of the one-dimensional line.

Following Aristotle's prescription, we must choose as our 'measure and starting point. . . something one and indivisible', and 'among lines we treat as indivisible that which is a foot long'.[55] Then since the chosen unit is treated as an indivisible whole it follows that nothing less than a foot is

54. *Ibid.*
55. *Ibid.*

available to compose the first greater length; thus this length can only be 2 ft, the next length must be 3 ft, and so on.

We, however, are concerned not just with measurement but with proportion; and quantities are proportional to each other, as Euclid states at the start of the fifth book of the *Elements*, when they have a constant ratio: 'Let magnitudes which have the same ratio be called *proportional*.'[56] If we accept Euclid's definition, it follows that in order to obtain a proportional sequence the initial ratio of 1 : 2 between the unit and the first larger measure must be repeated each time, producing the geometric progression 1, 2, 4, 8,. . . If instead we make each increment *double* the preceding measure we get the complementary series 1, 3, 9, 27,. . . (see Figure 7.1). These two series are of course the basis of the proportions of the World's Soul in the *Timaeus*, and of what we have called the 'Renaissance' system of proportion (see Chapter 3, section 3.3).

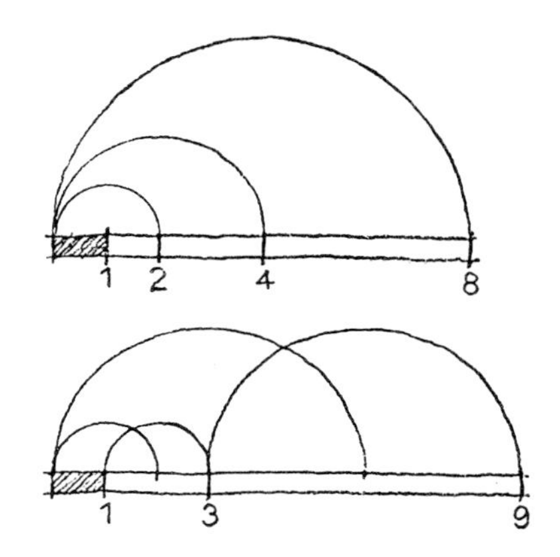

Figure 7.1 Linear measure: geometric progressions produced by doubling and trebling.

Now let us apply the same principle to two dimensions: to a series of planes. The unit of measure is now a 1 ft square. The first larger area can again only be formed by adding the unit to itself, so it consists of two squares. But since both dimensions are now available to us, we should not continue to add increasing numbers of squares in a linear sequence, as we did when considering one dimension, to produce the same series 1, 2, 4, 8,. . . Instead, we can let the larger dimension of the third plane equal the *sum* of the two dimensions of the preceding one: that is, 1 + 2 = 3. Applying this rule as a constant, we get the sequence 1, 2, 3, 5, 8,. . . In other words, we obtain the Fibonacci series, which converges towards the golden section. The diagram is formed by adding a series of squares to the longer side of each preceding figure, generating a spiral. By starting off from a ϕ rectangle as core figure in place of a square we obtain a true golden section sequence (see Figure 7.2). This is the diagram that leads Jay Hambidge to call the ϕ rectangle the 'rectangle of the whirling squares'.[57]

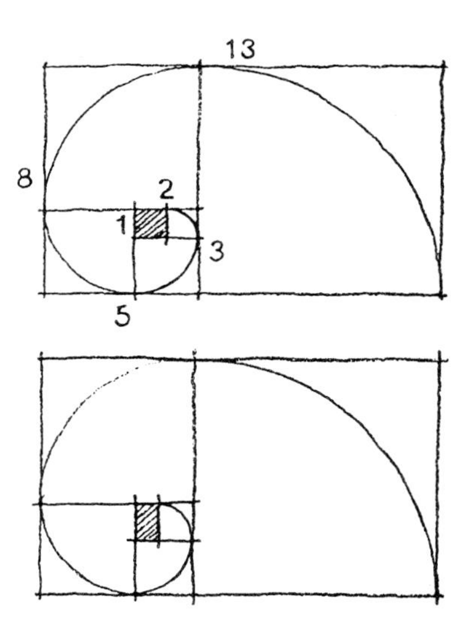

Figure 7.2 Planar measure: generation of the Fibonacci series and ϕ progression.

If instead of squares we form a series of double squares in the same way we get the sequence known as Pell's series, 1, 2, 5, 12, 29,. . ., which comprises the numerators of the continued fractions 1/1, 2/3, 5/7, 12/17,. . . that we encountered in Chapter 4, section 4.3 as convergents for the irrational square root of two ($\sqrt{2}$), approximately 1.4142. By starting the same sequence with a triple square the denominators of the same fractions are obtained: 1, 3, 7, 17, 41,. . .

56. Euclid, *The Thirteen Books of the Elements*, Dover Publications, 1956, vol. II, p. 114.
57. J. Hambidge, *The Elements of Dynamic Symmetry*, Dover Publications, 1967, pp. 10, 30.

An equivalent spiral sequence, composed of alternating double and single squares, generates the two series 1, 1, 3, 4, 11, 15,. . . and 1, 2, 5, 7, 19, 26,. . ., according to whether the series starts off with one or two single squares (see Figure 7.3). These form respectively the numerators and denominators of the continued fractions 1/1, 1/2, 3/5, 4/7,. . . which converge towards the square root of three ($\sqrt{3}$), approximately 1.732.

Thus by applying the Aristotelian concept of the unit to various sequences of lines and planes we have generated all the principal proportion systems known to have been used in historical architecture: the whole-number Renaissance system, the Fibonacci and ϕ series, and the so-called *ad quadratum* and *ad triangulum* systems based on the square roots of two and three.

It remains to consider a series of volumes. Here the unit of measure is of course a cube, and the first larger volume must be the cube added to itself: that is, a double cube. The three dimensions of the unit are thus 1, 1, 1, and those of the second volume 1, 1, 2; but it is not easy to determine what proportional rule must be followed in order to measure out the succeeding volumes. All three dimensions of the unit are of course equal, and the largest dimension of the second volume is clearly the sum of two of them, but which? If the three unit dimensions are denoted by 1_1, 1_2 and 1_3, then 2 can equal either $1_1 + 1_2$ or $1_1 + 1_3$ or $1_2 + 1_3$. Suppose it is the last of these. Then the sequence of volumes will begin:

Unit	1	1	1				
2nd volume		1	1	2			
3rd volume			1	2	3		
4th volume				2	3	5	
5th volume					3	5	8

The sequence is again the Fibonacci series: 1, 1, 2, 3, 5, 8,. . ., and the series of volumes will be as in Figure 7.4.

If instead we assume $2 = 1_1 + 1_3$, then the sequence will instead be:

Unit	1	1	1				
2nd volume		1	1	2			
3rd volume			1	2	3		
4th volume				2	3	4	
5th volume					3	4	6

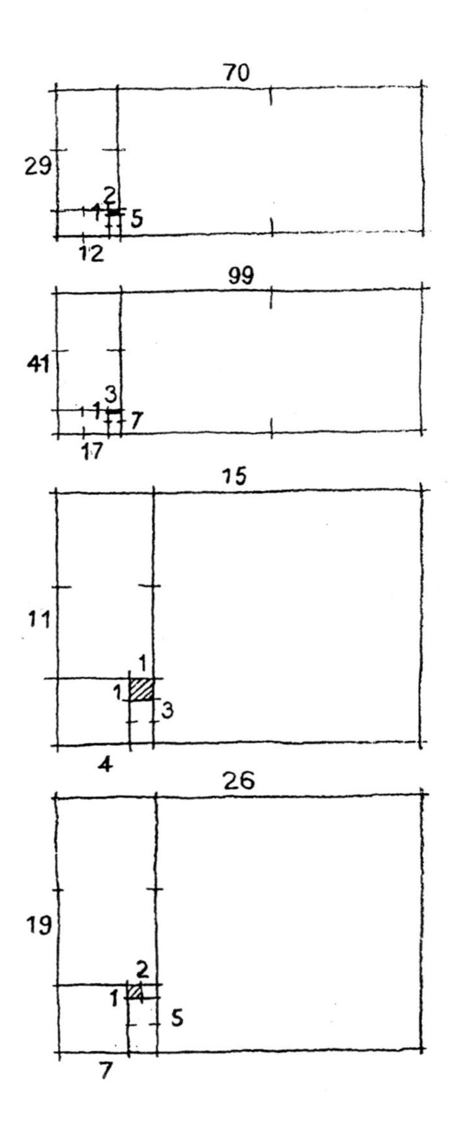

Figure 7.3 Planar measure: generation of Pell's series and $\sqrt{3}$ series.

In this case the series generated is 1, 1, 1, 2, 3, 4, 6, 9, 13, 19, 28,. . . So far as I am aware this series has never been discussed in the context of architectural proportion; it seems to constitute a completely new and untried system, and one certainly worthy of investigation. The series converges to the irrational value x, where x is the solution of the cubic equation $x^2 + 1 = x^3$. The approximate value of x is 1.465. We already encountered but did not discuss this number in Chapter 3, where it appears in Table 3.18. The series of volumes produced is shown in Figure 7.5.

Finally, 2 can equal $1_1 + 1_2$. The sequence of volumes is then:

Unit	1	1	1				
2nd volume		1	1	2			
3rd volume			1	2	2		
4th volume				2	2	3	
5th volume					2	3	4

Here the series generated is that of the plastic number: 1, 1, 1, 2, 2, 3, 4, 5, 7, 9, 12, 16,. . . The series converges to the irrational value x, where x is the solution of the cubic equation $x + 1 = x^3$, and its approximate numerical value is 1.325. The resulting series of volumes is shown in Figure 7.6. Comparison of the three sets of volumes shows that the plastic number sequence, being based on the smallest ratio, gives the slowest rate of growth. Since the series of volumes increases by the cube of the ratio, it can be argued that the smaller ratio provides a more suitable system of measures, and also that since we are seeking the *first* size that is distinctly larger than the unit, the smallest possible increment is the correct one. For these and other reasons the plastic number's discoverer, Dom Van der Laan, held it to be the only one of the three sequences that truly conforms to the nature of three-dimensional quantity, and therefore – since the space that we inhabit and express through our architecture is by definition three-dimensional – the only system of proportion appropriate to architecture or indeed to any of the plastic arts. Even if one does not accept this claim, however, the series is of great practical and theoretical interest. It will be discussed in more detail in Chapter 16.

Aristotle's concept of measure, applied in turn to series of lines, planes and volumes, thus proves to be a source not only of the four 'historical' proportion systems but also of two

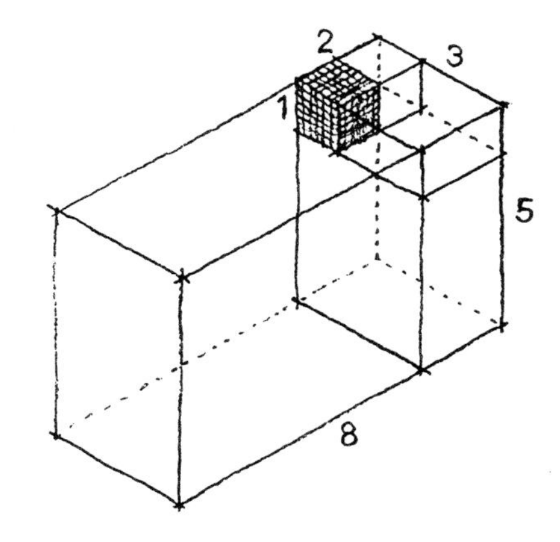

Figure 7.4 Volumetric measure: generation of the Fibonacci series.

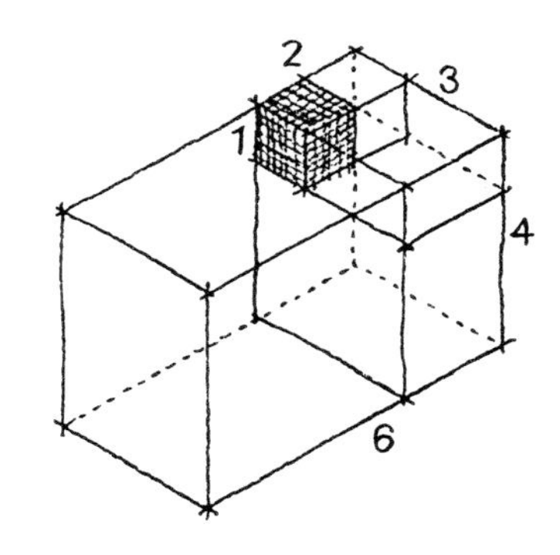

Figure 7.5 Volumetric measure: generation of the 1.465 series.

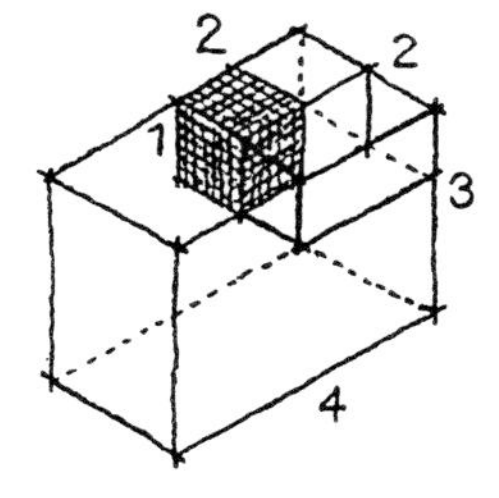

Figure 7.6 Volumetric measure: generation of the plastic number series.

new ones: what we may call the '1.465 system', and the plastic number. That is not to suggest that my hypothetical investigation of lines, planes and cubes has any historical basis in Aristotle's own thinking. It clearly goes far beyond what he intended when he wrote about the unit. Its value is rather that it illustrates the great fecundity of his thought, and demonstrates once more the fundamental *unity* of all systems of proportion, and their common grounding in reflections upon the nature of the world and our human relation to it.

Chapter eight

EUCLID: THE GOLDEN SECTION AND THE FIVE REGULAR SOLIDS

[The] discovery of the irrationality of the square root of two which led to the breakdown of the Pythagorean programme of reducing geometry and cosmology (and presumably all knowledge) to arithmetic, produced a crisis in Greek mathematics;. . . Euclid's Elements *are not a textbook of geometry, but rather the final attempt of the Platonic School to resolve this crisis by reconstructing the whole of mathematics and cosmology* on a geometrical basis, *in order to deal with the problem of irrationality systematically rather than* ad hoc, *thus inverting the Pythagorean programme of arithmetization.*[1]

8.1 THE ARCHITECTURAL RATIOS INHERENT IN EUCLIDEAN SPACE

The climax of Euclid's *Elements*, for which the whole work has been described as a preparation, is contained in the thirteenth and final book. This is devoted to two great areas of mathematical knowledge: the golden section, called by Euclid 'division in extreme and mean ratio', and the geometry of the five regular solids,[2] which involves ϕ together with the square roots $\sqrt{2}$, $\sqrt{3}$, $\sqrt{4}$ and $\sqrt{5}$. The ratios traditional in architectural proportion are thus implicit in the very nature of Euclidean space: an infinite and uniform space in which parallel straight lines never meet. For over two thousand years this concept remained unchallenged as the definitive picture of the space of nature. In the seventeenth century it formed the basis of Newton's physics. And in our own century, despite the discovery that non-Euclidean geometries are not only logically possible but

1. K.R. Popper, *The Open Society and its Enemies*, Routledge & Kegan Paul, 1966, vol. I, p. 319.
2. H.W. Turnbull, *The Great Mathematicians*, Methuen & Co., 1962, p. 36.

correspond better to observed phenomena, these ratios were still the ones adopted by Le Corbusier and other modern architects. This is not necessarily an anachronism. Euclid's space, and the proportions inherent in it, have not lost their validity at the terrestrial scale of the world we inhabit: the world as we see it with the naked eye, the world in which we construct our buildings. As Sir Edmund Whittaker observes:

> It is not to be expected that a single mathematical system of geometry, such as Euclid's, should furnish relations covering the whole extensional aspect of physical reality. However, Euclidean geometry undoubtedly describes with close approximation a large class of properties of the actual world, and embodies our most fundamental notions of it.[3]

The chronology of the exploration of the golden section and the five solids is a matter of debate among historians of mathematics. B.L. van der Waerden has traced much of Euclid to the ancient civilizations of India, China and Babylon, and even further back, to the Neolithic period between 3000 and 2500 BC.[4] T.L. Heath writes in his *History of Greek Mathematics* that

> There is probably little in the whole compass of the *Elements* of Euclid. . . which was not in substance included in the recognized content of the geometry and arithmetic by Plato's time. . .[5]

In his edition of the *Elements* the same author says of the construction of the five solids that:

> Some of them, the cube, the tetrahedron (which is nothing but a pyramid), and the octahedron (which is only a double pyramid with a square base), cannot but have been known to the Egyptians. And it appears that dodecahedra have been found. . . which belong to periods earlier than Pythagoras' time by some centuries. . .[6]

Others prefer a later date, at some time beween the foundation of Plato's Academy and the composition of the *Elements*: that is, between about 400 and 300 BC. In his *Mathematical History of Division in Extreme and Mean Ratio* Roger Herz-Fischler sees the *Elements* as the result of a

3. E. Whittaker, *From Euclid to Eddington*, Cambridge University Press, 1949, pp. 8–9.
4. B.L. van der Waerden, *Science Awakening*, Noordhoff, 1954, and *Geometry and Algebra in Ancient Civilizations*, Springer-Verlag, 1983.
5. T.L. Heath, *A History of Greek Mathematics*, Oxford University Press, 1921, vol. I, p. 217.
6. T.L. Heath, *Euclid: The Elements*, vol. III, Dover Publications, 1926 p. 438.

concerted programme to establish mathematics on a more rigorous, geometrical basis:

> About the time the Academy opened, *c.* –386, a mathematician or group of mathematicians not directly attached to the Academy, embarked on a 'programme' to rigorously construct the regular polygons. . .The inscription of the pentagon led. . . to the area definition of DEMR. . .[7]

– that is, to a precise mathematical knowledge of the golden section. Only if the architects were well ahead of the mathematicians in this field is it likely that knowledge of the golden section could have developed in time for it to be the basis of the proportions of the Parthenon, as Jay Hambidge and others have speculated.

The present chapter will concentrate mainly on that crucial thirteenth book of Euclid. It will prepare the ground by first outlining briefly certain earlier definitions and propositions that either bear directly on the conclusions of the final book or are relevant to the architectural theory of proportion in general, and to the golden section in particular. It will not keep strictly to Euclid's method of presentation, however. In order to bring out more clearly the architectural relevance of the constructions, only the results of his rigorous geometrical proofs will be given. To show the underlying unity of the propositions concerning division in extreme and mean ratio, these will all be related to two universal diagrams that incorporate all the separate diagrams that illustrate the *Elements*. The first of these universal diagrams is derived from the square inscribed in a semicircle, the second from the regular decagon and the star-pentagon (see Figure 8.1). The force of the proofs will, I hope, be immediately apparent from the diagrams, without lengthy verbal descriptions. This method accords fairly well, moreover, with the ancient Greek tendency, which still underlies Euclid's method, to think of geometrical figures as tangible shapes that can be displaced physically or laid over each other. As William M. Ivins writes in *Art and Geometry*:

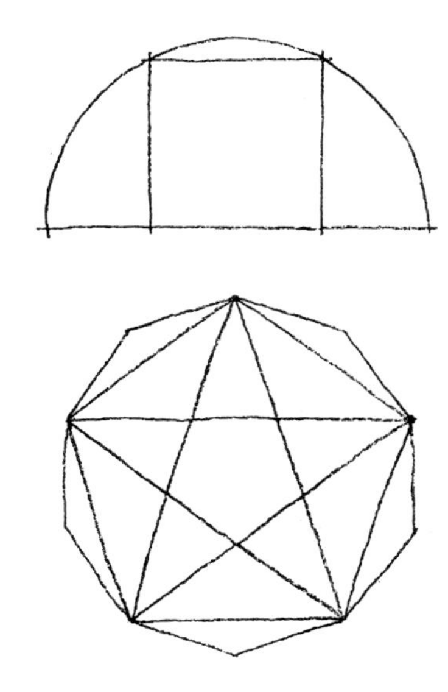

Figure 8.1 Key diagrams used to describe Euclid's propositions concerning the golden section.

> The way Euclid proved his basic theorem (I, 4) – that two triangles, having two sides and the angle between them equal, are equal to each other – was by picking one triangle up and superimposing it on the other.[8]

7. R. Herz-Fischler, *A Mathematical History of Division in Extreme and Mean Ratio*, Wilfred Laurier University Press, 1987, p. 98.
8. W.M. Ivins, *Art and Geometry: A Study in Space Intuitions*, Dover Publications, 1964, p. 40.

8.2 THE THEOREM OF PYTHAGORAS AND THE PRINCIPAL RATIOS USED IN ARCHITECTURAL PROPORTION

Book I, proposition 47 demonstrates the theorem of Pythagoras: that 'In right-angled triangles, the square on the side subtending the right angle is equal to the squares on the sides containing the right angle.'[9] Since Euclid's version of the proof is rather complicated, it is here replaced by a visual demonstration, which may or may not be the one that suggested the theorem to its original discoverer (see Figure 8.2). Besides being one of the most fundamental of mathematical proofs, the theorem is central to the theory of architectural proportion. It proves the irrationality of the key ratios $\sqrt{2}$, $\sqrt{3}$, $\sqrt{5}$ and ϕ, and also the rationality of the Pythagorean triangles with all three sides commensurable, the simplest of which is that with its sides in the proportion 3 : 4 : 5. Before discussing the relevant parts of Euclid's text, I shall begin by considering the four key incommensurable ratios as a group, in the light of their derivation from Pythagoras' theorem. The following account extends the brief description in Chapter 3, section 3.5.

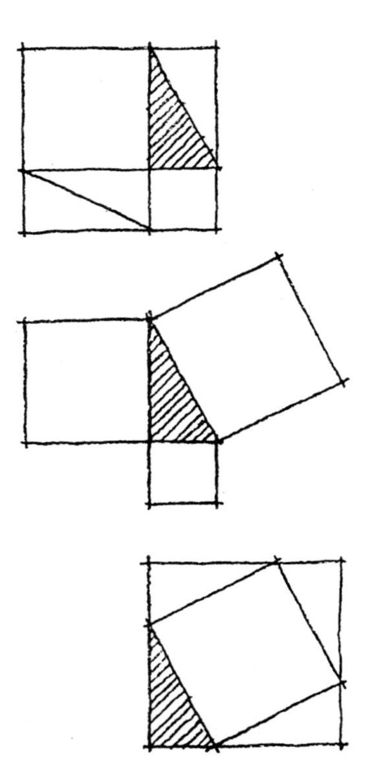

Figure 8.2 Demonstration of the theorem of Pythagoras.

The square root of 2

This is the ratio of the base of a right-angled isosceles triangle to its two perpendicular sides, and therefore of the diagonal of a square to its side, or of the diameter of a circle to the side of a square inscribed within it (see Figure 8.3).

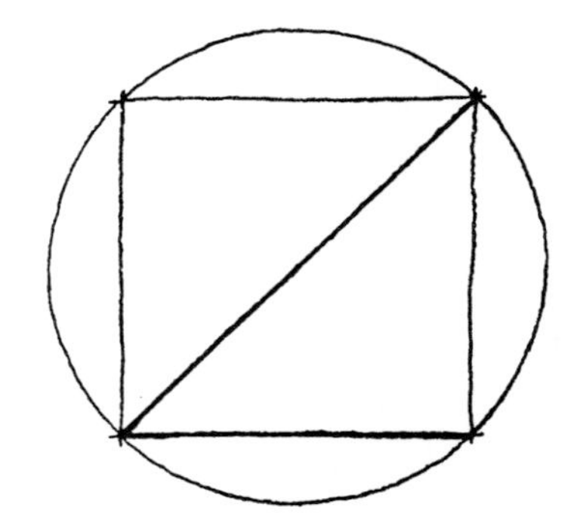

Figure 8.3 Square root of 2.

The square root of 3

This is the ratio between the perpendicular sides of a 30°–60°–90° triangle, and therefore also of the height to the base of a regular hexagon. It is also the ratio of the diameter to the edge of a cube (see Figure 8.4).

The square root of 5

This is the ratio of the hypotenuse to the shorter side of a right-angled triangle whose perpendicular sides are in the

9. Euclid, *Elements*, Dover Publications, 1956, vol. I, p. 349.

ratio 2 : 1, or of the diagonal of a double square to its shorter side (see Figure 8.5). Now consider this double square as one half of a complete square ABCD, bisected by EF. Construct a semicircle with the diagonal DE of this half square as radius and E, the midpoint of AB, as centre. Let the semicircle cut AB extended at GH. Complete the rectangle GHLK (see Figure 8.6). Then the ratio $\sqrt{5}$: 1 occurs as DE : AE and as GH : GK. Thus GHLK is a $\sqrt{5}$ rectangle.

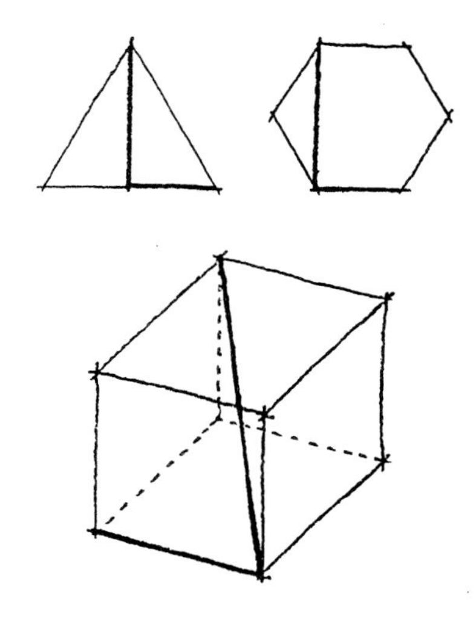

Figure 8.4 Square root of 3.

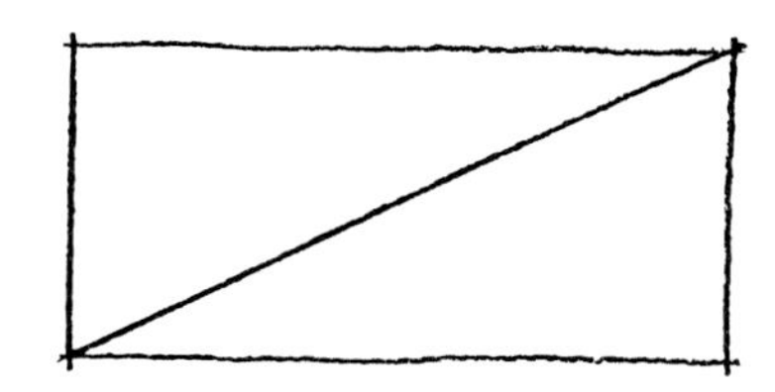

Figure 8.5 Square root of 5.

The golden section

As mentioned above, there are two basic geometrical sources of the ratio $\phi : 1$, the square inscribed in a semicircle, which is incorporated in Figure 8.6, and the star-pentagon. Let us start with the first source.

In Figure 8.6, let AD = 1, therefore AE = 1/2.
By the theorem of Pythagoras,

$$DE^2 = AD^2 + AE^2 = 1 + \frac{1}{4} = \frac{5}{4}$$

Therefore

$$DE = EG = EH = \frac{\sqrt{5}}{2}$$

Therefore

$$BG = AH = \frac{\sqrt{5}+1}{2}, \text{ which we know equals } \phi.$$

Therefore

$$AG = BH = \phi - 1 = \phi^{-1}.$$

Repeating Figure 8.6, draw the diagonal AC, and construct a square on AG by drawing a diagonal perpendicular to AC, cutting GK at M. Draw MQ parallel to GH, cutting AD, AC, BC and HL at N, O, P and Q. Through O, draw ROS perpendicular to MQ, cutting GH at R and CD at S. This completes our first universal diagram for division in extreme and mean ratio or the golden section (see Figure 8.7). We now have:

$BG = AH = \phi$
$AB = AD = 1$

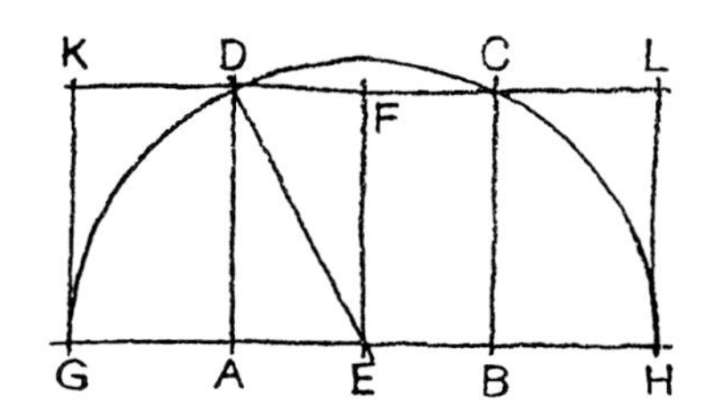

Figure 8.6 Semicircle, square, $\sqrt{5}$ rectangle and golden section.

$AG = AR = \phi^{-1}$
$BR = KM = \phi^{-2}$.

And as a general conclusion it is apparent that

$1 = \phi^{-1} + \phi^{-2}$
$\phi = 1 + \phi^{-1}$
$\phi^2 = \phi + 1$, etc.

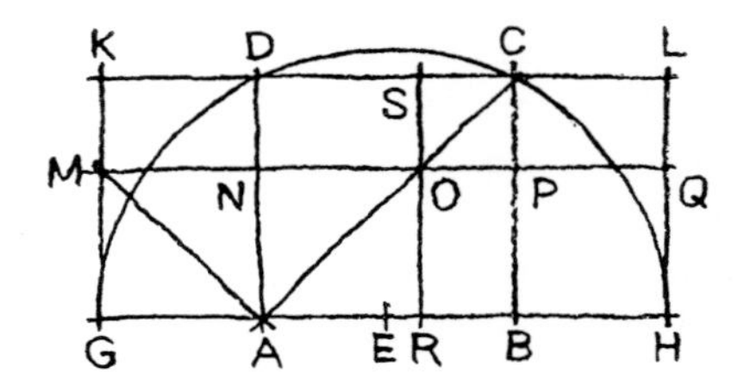

Figure 8.7 Further development of Figure 8.6.

The second source of the golden section is found in the regular decagon and star-pentagon. These can be constructed as follows.

Draw a circle with centre O and diameter MN. Erect a perpendicular at O, cutting the circumference at A. Bisect MO at P, and with centre P and radius AP, describe an arc to cut NO at Q.

Let MO, the radius of the circle, equal 1. Then $OP = \frac{1}{2}$.

Therefore AP, the radius of the first arc, $= \frac{\sqrt{5}}{2}$.

Therefore $MQ = \frac{\sqrt{5}+1}{2} = \phi$ and $OQ = \phi^{-1}$.

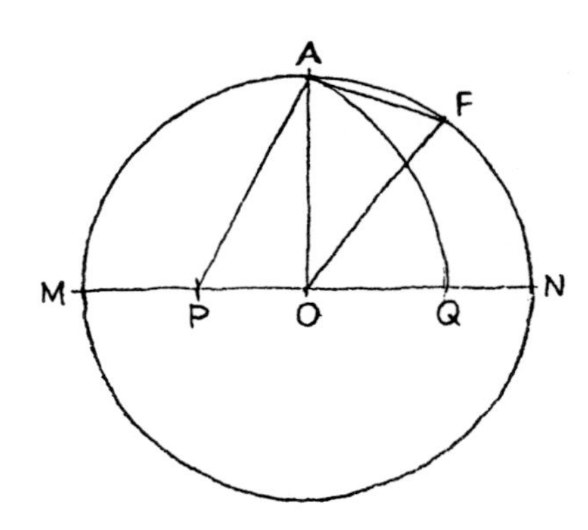

Figure 8.8 Construction of a regular decagon.

Now, OQ equals the side of the regular decagon, which is completed by drawing chords equal to OQ, dividing the circumference of the circle into 10 equal parts. Call the first of these chords AF, and join FO. Then in the isosceles triangle AFO the base $AF = OQ = \phi^{-1}$ and the two equal sides AO and FO equal 1. Thus the ratio of the radius of the circle to the side of the inscribed decagon is $\phi : 1$ (Figure 8.8). Euclid demonstrates in book IV, proposition 10, that each of the angles at the base of this triangle is double the remaining angle.[10] That is, since the three angles of any triangle compose 180°, each of the base angles is 72° and the third angle is 36°.

The regular pentagon can be inscribed in the same circle, as follows. Starting with Figure 8.8, with centre A and radius AQ describe a second arc to cut the circumference at B. Then AB equals the side of the inscribed regular pentagon, which is completed by drawing the chords BC, CD, DE equal to AB (Figure 8.9).

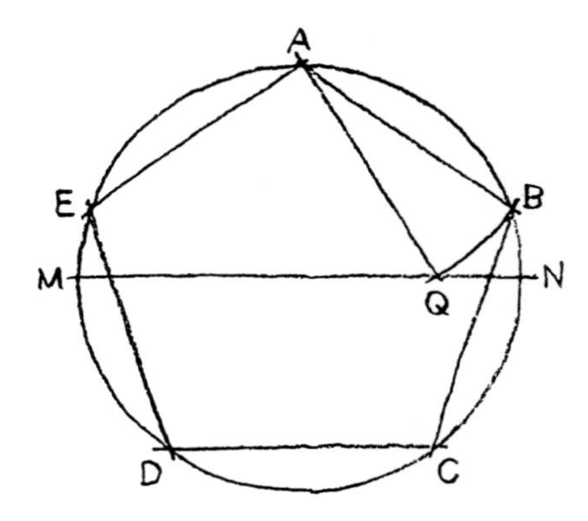

Figure 8.9 Construction of a regular pentagon.

Now, from the theorem of Pythagoras, in the right-angled triangle AOQ,

10. *Ibid.*, vol. II, pp. 96–100.

$AQ^2 = AO^2 + OQ^2$

But

$AO = 1$ and $OQ = \phi^{-1}$.

Therefore

$AQ^2 = 1 + (\phi^{-1})^2 = 1 + \phi^{-2} = \phi\sqrt{5}\ ^{-1}$.

Therefore the side of the pentagon, $AB = AQ = \sqrt{1+\phi^{-2}}$ $= \sqrt{\sqrt{5}\ \phi^{-1}} = 1.1755$ approx.

To inscribe the five-pointed star within the pentagon, join the diagonals AC, AD, BD, BE and CE (see Figure 8.10). This is the second of our universal diagrams. The star inscribed in the pentagon (or 'star-pentagon') comprises five superimposed 72°, 72°, 36° triangles. From this we can deduce that the ratio of the diagonal to the side of the pentagon is $\phi : 1$. The diagonals intersect each other so as to divide each diagonal into three segments with the ratio $\phi : 1 : \phi$.

Let us consider now one of the component isosceles triangles by itself. Bisection of one of the base angles divides the opposite side AD in the ratio $\phi : 1$, thus dividing the original triangle into a smaller similar triangle plus a 108°, 36°, 36° isosceles triangle. The process can be continued indefinitely, generating a logarithmic spiral (see Figure 8.11).

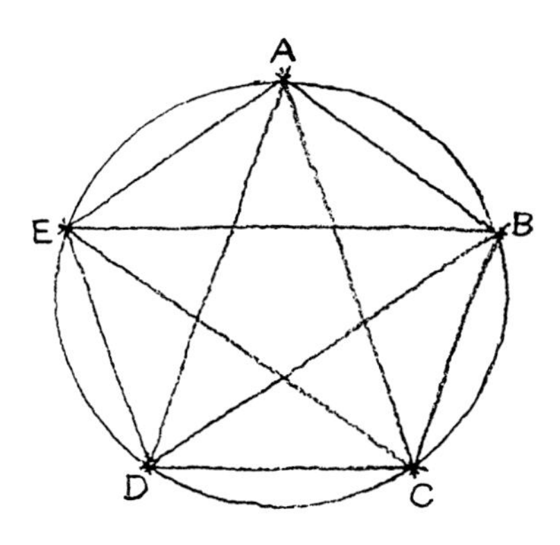

Figure 8.10 Five-pointed star inscribed within the regular pentagon.

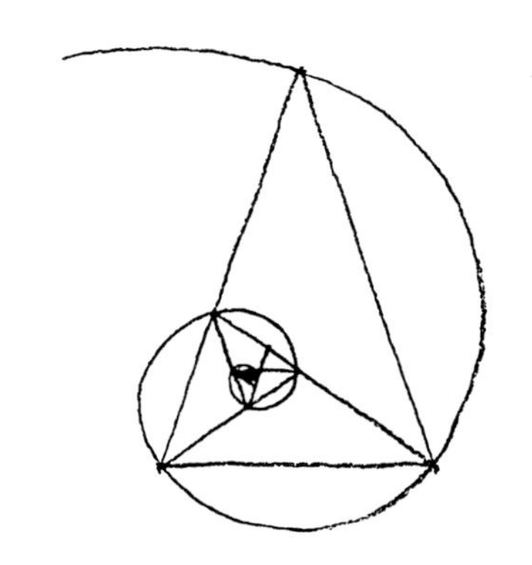
Figure 8.11 Spiral generated by the ϕ triangle.

8.3 THE GOLDEN SECTION: EUCLID'S PROOFS FROM THE SQUARE

A selection from the thirteen books of the *Elements* of propositions that have a more or less direct bearing on division in extreme and mean ratio will now be briefly described, using as illustration the two universal diagrams: the first (Figure 8.7) derived from the square inscribed in a semicircle, and the second (Figures 8.8 and 8.10) derived from the regular decagon and star-pentagon. (At this point the non-mathematical reader is advised to skip sections 8.3 and 8.4, and move straight on to section 8.5.)

In book II, 11, without as yet calling it 'division in extreme and mean ratio', Euclid gives what is essentially the classic construction of a golden section and of a root five rectangle. He defines it thus: 'To cut a given straight line so that the rectangle contained by the whole and one of the segments is equal to the square on the remaining segment.'[11] Referring to Figure 8.7, this means that if AB is the given straight line, then AB × BR = AR^2.

Euclid starts out, as in Figure 8.6, by constructing the square ABCD, dividing it into two halves, and using the diagonal DE of one of the half squares to establish the length of AG. He does not mention, however, that a semicircle of radius DE will contain ABCD. Strange as it may seem, the method of inscribing the square in a semicircle does not occur anywhere in the thirteen books, although it is inherent in the final and culminating proposition XIII, 18, in which all five regular solids are brought together in a single construction.

Having added the smaller square AGMN to the original square ABCD, Euclid shows by purely geometrical means that the rectangle CDNP is equal to AB × BR, and the square AGMN is equal to AR^2. The proof can be greatly abbreviated by using algebraic formulae not available to the ancient Greek mathematician. In section 8.2 we already established that

$$AB = 1$$
$$AG = AR = \phi^{-1}$$
$$BR = KM = \phi^{-2}$$

Therefore the rectangle CDNP = $1 \times \phi^{-2} = \phi^{-2}$, and the square AGMN = $\phi^{-1} \times \phi^{-1} = \phi^{-2}$. The two areas are thus equal.

Book VI, 13 shows how 'to find a mean proportional' to two given straight lines.[12] Euclid's proposition has a general application irrespective of the ratio of the two given lines. It has a particular relevance to division in extreme and mean ratio, however, which he does not mention at this stage. We shall therefore discuss it in connection with our universal diagram (Figure 8.7).

Let BG, BH be the given lines, placed end to end, and the whole line GH be the base of a semicircle (see Figure 8.12). Since GCH is an angle inscribed in a semicircle, it is a right angle (this has previously been proved in III, 31). And since BC is drawn from this right angle and perpendicular to the base GH, the two smaller triangles BCG and BCH are similar to each other and to the whole triangle CGH; this has already been proved in book VI, 8.[13] Consequently

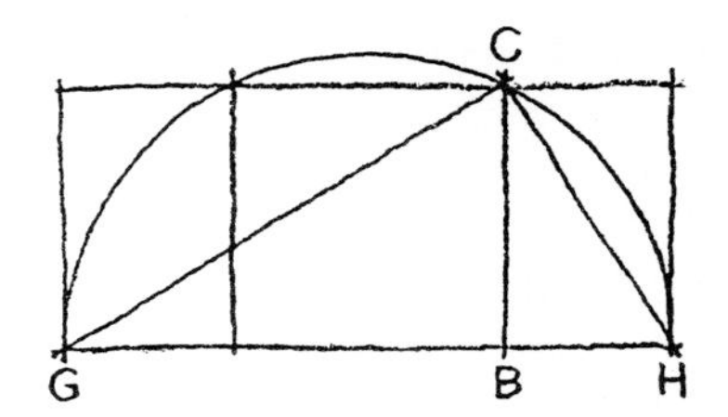

Figure 8.12 Construction of the 'mean proportional' of two given straight lines.

11. *Ibid.*, vol. I, p. 402.
12. *Ibid.*, vol. II, p. 216.
13. *Ibid.*, vol. II, pp. 209–11.

GB : BC = BC : BH, so BC is the proportional (i.e. geometric) mean of BG and BH. Using algebra, and letting BG = ϕ and BH = ϕ^{-1}, then their proportional mean BC = 1.

Proposition 17 in the same book is again a general one, not necessarily involving division in extreme and mean ratio. It is closely related to proposition 13. It states that 'If three straight lines be proportional, the rectangle contained by the extremes is equal to the square on the mean. . . [and conversely]'.[14] Taking Euclid's proof as read, let us apply it to Figure 8.7. We know that the three lines BG, BC and BH are proportional. If BC is made the side of a square, then according to the proof a rectangle whose sides equal BG and BH is equal to the square on BC. That is, the area BGMP = ABCD.

The proposition applies to the golden section on condition that the square on BC is exactly inscribed in the semicircle, as in our diagram. Euclid does not make this a condition, and his proposition has a more general application. In our particular example, however, BG = ϕ, AB = 1 and BH = GM = ϕ^{-1}. Consequently BG × GM = $\phi \times \phi^{-1} = 1$, and AB × BC = 1 × 1 = 1, so BGMP = ABCD.

The result of VI, 17 has a direct application in VI, 30, in which Euclid finally uses the phrase 'To cut a given finite straight line in extreme and mean ratio.'[15] The proof demonstrates that as the given line is to the larger segment, so is the larger segment to the smaller. Applied to Figure 8.7, this means that AB being the given line, AB : AR = AR : BR. Using algebra, therefore, $1 : \phi^{-1} = \phi^{-1} : \phi^{-2}$.

The first six propositions of the concluding book XIII all deal with aspects of division in extreme and mean ratio related to the square. The first states that 'If a straight line be cut in extreme and mean ratio, the square on the greater segment added to the half of the whole is five times the square on the half.'[16] Applied to Figure 8.7, this means that if AB is cut at R in extreme and mean ratio, $(AR + AE)^2 = 5 \times AE^2$. But AR = AG. Therefore the proposition can be restated as $EG^2 = 5 \times AE^2$. But EG = DE, and as we saw from the first stage of our universal diagram (Figure 8.6), DE = $\sqrt{5}/2$, therefore if $DE^2 = 5 \times AE^2$, it follows that $(\sqrt{5}/2)^2 = 5 \times (1/2)^2$. That is to say, 5/4 = 5 × 1/4, which is obviously the case.

The proposition is thus seen to be in effect the same as proposition II, 11, with which we began. There, we started out from the diagonal of the half square and concluded with a division of the given line in extreme and mean ratio; here,

14. *Ibid.*, vol. II, p. 228.
15. *Ibid.*, vol. II, pp. 287–9.
16. *Ibid.*, vol. III, p. 440.

we have begun with a division in extreme and mean ratio, and concluded with the diagonal of the half square.

The second proposition of book XIII is merely the converse of the first, and the third is a further variation on it, which states that 'If a straight line be divided in extreme and mean ratio, the square on the lesser segment added to the half of the greater segment is five times the square on the half of the greater segment.'[17] Referring to Figure 8.7, this means that $(BR + BH/2)^2 = 5 \times (BH/2)^2$. All the lengths are $1/\phi$ of the corresponding lengths in XIII, 1. That is, $BR = AR/\phi$, $BH = AB/\phi$ and $BH/2 = AE/\phi$. Therefore what holds for XIII, 1 holds equally for XIII, 3.

Proposition XIII, 4 states that 'If a straight line be cut in extreme and mean ratio, the square on the whole and the square on the lesser segment together are triple of the square on the greater segment.'[18] Let the given line be again AB (Figure 8.7), and the two segments AR and BR. Again, we can use algebra. The square on the whole is thus 1, that on the larger segment ϕ^{-2}, and that on the smaller segment ϕ^{-4}. The proposition states, in effect, that $1 + \phi^{-4} = 3\phi^{-2}$.

Now we know that

$$\phi^{-1} + \phi^{-2} = 1 \qquad (1)$$

consequently

$$1 - \phi^{-2} = \phi^{-1} \qquad (2)$$

and

$$\phi^{-1} = 1 - \phi^{-2} \qquad (3)$$

Dividing (2) throughout by ϕ we get

$$\phi^{-1} - \phi^{-3} = \phi^{-2}$$

And dividing (3) throughout by ϕ^2 we get

$$\phi^{-3} = \phi^{-2} - \phi^{-4}$$

Therefore

$$\phi^{-1} - \phi^{-2} + \phi^{-4} = \phi^{-2}$$

17. *Ibid.*, vol. III, p. 445.
18. *Ibid.*, vol. III, p. 447.

Add $2\phi^{-2}$ to both sides of the equation: thus

$$\phi^{-1} + \phi^{-2} + \phi^{-4} = 3\phi^{-2}$$

But from (1)

$$\phi^{-1} + \phi^{-2} = 1$$

Therefore

$$1 + \phi^{-4} = 3\phi^{-2}$$

which is what we set out to prove.

The fifth proposition states that

> If a straight line be cut in extreme and mean ratio, and there be added to it a straight line equal to the greater segment, the whole straight line has been cut in extreme and mean ratio, and the original straight line is the greater segment.[19]

The proof is essentially similar to that of proposition VI, 30.

8.4 THE GOLDEN SECTION: EUCLID'S PROOFS FROM THE DECAGON AND STAR-PENTAGON

Book IV, 11 demonstrates how 'In a given circle to inscribe an equilateral and equiangular pentagon'.[20] The construction of the 72°–36°–72° triangle, defined as having 'each of the angles at the base double of the remaining one',[21] has been shown in the previous proposition (IV, 10). Starting from the triangle ACD in Figure 8.10, bisect the two base angles ACD and ADC and extend the bisecting lines to cut the circle at E and B respectively. Join AB, BC, DE, EA to complete the pentagon ABCDE. Euclid goes on to prove that the pentagon is in fact equilateral and equiangular. All that is needed to complete the star-pentagon is to connect the remaining diagonal, BE. Euclid does not do this, however, since it is not needed for his construction of the pentagon.

Propositions 7 to 11, book XIII, return to the regular pentagon, sometimes combining it with the hexagon and decagon. Proposition 8 states that

19. *Ibid.*, vol. III, p. 448.
20. *Ibid.*, vol. II, p. 100.
21. *Ibid.*, vol. II, p. 96.

> If in an equilateral and equiangular pentagon straight lines subtend two angles taken in order, they cut one another in extreme and mean ratio, and their greater segments are equal to the side of the pentagon.[22]

This is essentially what was shown in section 8.2 (Figure 8.10), which stated that 'The diagonals intersect each other so as to divide each diagonal into three segments with the ratio $\phi : 1 : \phi$.' Where a given diagonal is intersected only by one other, therefore, the ratio is $(\phi + 1) : \phi$, or $\phi^2 : \phi = \phi : 1$.

Proposition 9 states that

> If the side of the hexagon and that of the decagon inscribed in the same circle be added together, the whole straight line has been cut in extreme and mean ratio, and its greater segment is the side of the hexagon.[23]

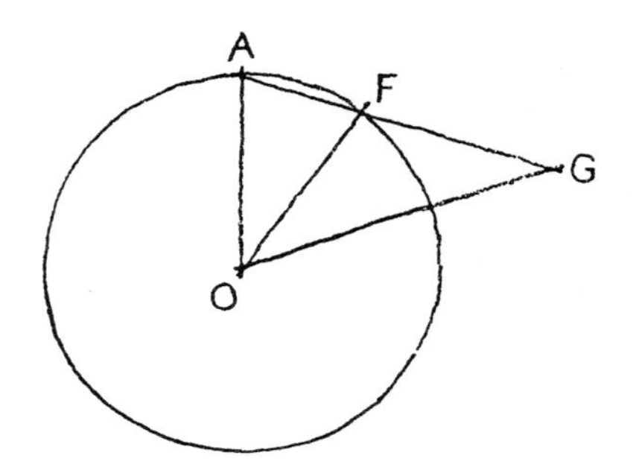

Figure 8.13 Ratio of the sides of regular hexagon and decagon inscribed in same circle if $\phi : 1$.

Here we must look again at Figure 8.8. The side AF of the decagon is extended in a straight line to G, so that FG is equal to the radius of the circle, OA, and therefore – since the side of a regular hexagon equals the radius of the circle that circumscribes it – FG also equals the side of the hexagon (see Figure 8.13). The sides of the two figures, added together, therefore equal AG. Abbreviating the proof, it is demonstrated that the two triangles AFO and AGO are similar (both being in fact 72°–36°–72° isosceles triangles). Therefore AG : AO = AO : AF. But AO = FG; therefore AG : FG = FG : AF. Therefore the whole line AG has been cut at F in extreme and mean ratio.

Proposition 10 states that

> If an equilateral pentagon be inscribed in a circle, the square on the side of the pentagon is equal to the squares on the side of the hexagon and on that of the decagon inscribed in the same circle.[24]

Euclid's demonstration being too long to summarize, I shall give only the result. Suppose the radius of the circle, and therefore the side of the hexagon, is 1, then as we have seen the side of the decagon will be ϕ^{-1}. If the square on the side of the pentagon equals the sum of the squares on these two sides it must equal $1 + \phi^{-2}$. This confirms what we found in section 8.2: that the side of the pentagon is $\sqrt{1 + \phi^{-2}}$ or approximately 1.1755.

22. *Ibid.*, vol. III, p. 453.
23. *Ibid.*, vol. III, p. 455.
24. *Ibid.*, vol. III, p. 457.

The proposition suggests two simple constructions, neither of which is mentioned by Euclid, which relate together the sides of all the principal polygons.

If the side of the pentagon is again AB as in Figure 8.9, the side of the decagon is AF and the side of the hexagon FG, the proposition states that $AB^2 = FG^2 + AF^2$. Applying the theorem of Pythagoras, the three lengths can thus be redrawn as the three sides of a right-angled triangle ABF, with the side of the pentagon AB as hypotenuse and AFB as the right angle. Let AF be again the side of the decagon and rename the side of the hexagon BF.

Then

$$AB^2 = BF^2 + AF^2, \text{ i.e. } (1 + \phi^{-2}) = (1) + (\phi^{-2})$$

Therefore

$$AB = \sqrt{1 + \phi^{-2}}, BF = 1, \text{ and } AF = \phi^{-1}$$

Construct the three regular polygons on these sides, each circumscribed within a circle (see Figure 8.14). The three circles are equal, each having a radius equal to 1.

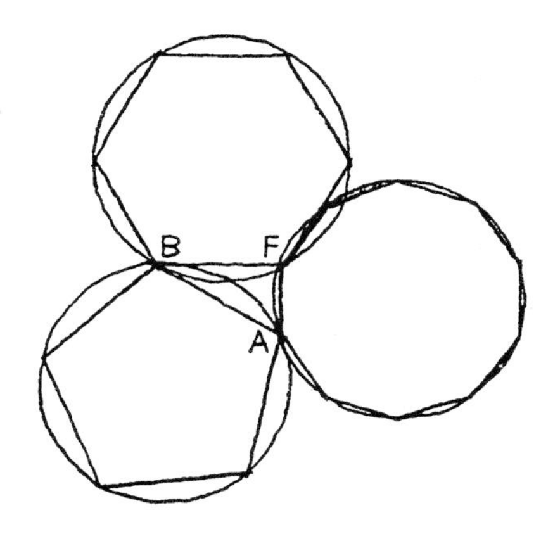

Figure 8.14 Relation between the regular pentagon, hexagon and decagon.

A similar figure can be constructed to integrate the regular hexagon with the equilateral triangle and the square. Construct the right-angled triangle LMN, with LM as hypotenuse and LNM as the right angle. Let the square on the side of the hexagon = $MN^2 = 1$, the square on LN = $LN^2 = 2$, and the square on the side of the triangle = $LM^2 = 3$.

Thus

$$LM^2 = LN^2 + MN^2, \text{ i.e. } 3 = 2 + 1$$

Therefore

$$LM = \sqrt{3}, LN = \sqrt{2}, MN = 1$$

Construct the three figures on their respective sides, each circumscribed within a circle (see Figure 8.15). The three circles are equal, each having a radius equal to 1.

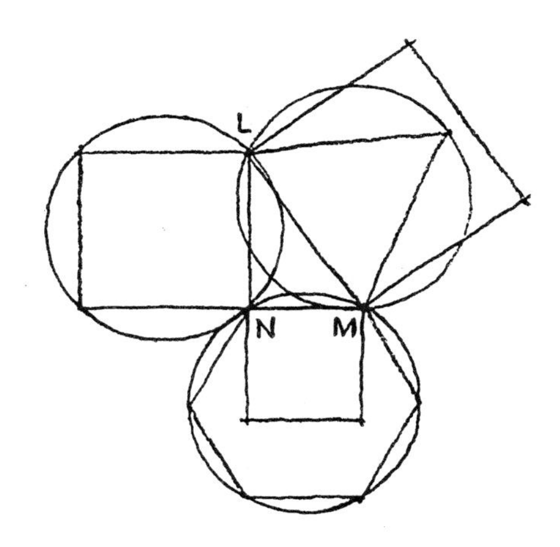

Figure 8.15 Relation between the equilateral triangle, square and regular pentagon.

8.5 THE FIVE REGULAR SOLIDS

Propositions 13–18 of book XIII all deal with the solid geometry of the five regular polyhedra, or – more exactly –

with the problem of inscribing each of them within a sphere. These results are combined in a single diagram in the final proposition 18, which thus brings the thirteen books to a conclusion. Most of the propositions for inscribing the polyhedra within spheres are too long and complicated to transcribe here, even in abbreviated form. I shall therefore only sketch out the simplest case, the circumscribing of the cube, set out in proposition XIII, 15: 'To construct a cube and comprehend it in a sphere. . . and to prove that the square on the diameter of the sphere is triple of the square on the side of the cube.'[25]

Describe a semicircle on base AG. If the semicircle were rotated through 360° about AG, it would generate the given sphere. Divide AG at O, such that

$$AG : GO = 3 : 1$$

Erect OC perpendicular to AG, cutting the circumference at C. Join AC and CG (lower Figure 8.16).

Construct a cube ABCDEFGH with edges equal to CG (upper Figure 8.16). Join the diagonals AC and AG. The triangle ABC being right angled, it follows from the theorem of Pythagoras that

$$AC^2 = AB^2 + BC^2 = 1 + 1 = 2$$

Therefore AC^2 is twice the square on the side of the cube, and $AC = \sqrt{2}$.

Similarly, in the right-angled triangle ACG

$$AG^2 = AC^2 + CG^2 = 2 + 1 = 3$$

Therefore AG^2 is three times the square on the side of the cube, and $AG = \sqrt{3}$.

It remains to show that the triangle ACG inscribed in the semicircle is the same as the triangle ACG contained in the cube.

In the semicircle, ACG and COG being similar triangles,

$$AG/CG = CG/GO$$

Multiplying by AG/CG,

$$AG^2/CG^2 = AG/GO$$

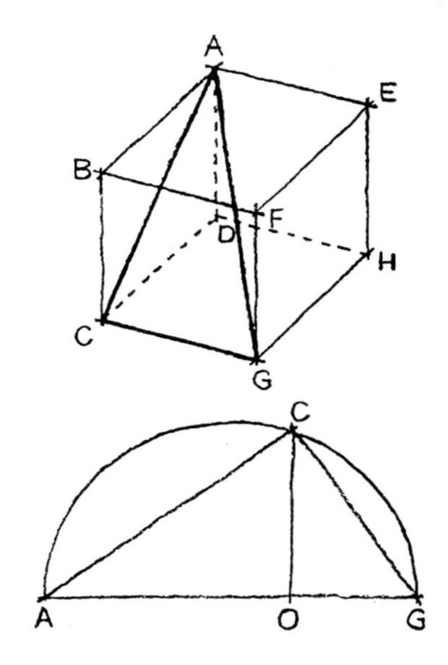

Figure 8.16 Proof that the square on the diameter of a sphere is triple the face of the inscribed cube.

25. *Ibid.*, vol. III, p. 478.

But AG/GO = 3/1, so AG^2 is three times CG^2, the square on the side of the cube. Similarly,

$$AG^2/AC^2 = AG/AO$$

But AG/AO = 3/2, so $AG^2 = 3/2\ AC^2$, and

$$AG^2 : AC^2 : CG^2 = 3 : 2 : 1$$

as in the cube. Therefore the triangle ACG inscribed in the semicircle is the same as the triangle ACG contained in the cube, and AG is the diameter of the circumscribing sphere of the cube.

Before addressing the final proposition, I shall first discuss the five forms in more general terms. Of the key irrationals that I have ennumerated as central to architectural proportion, $\sqrt{2}$ arises in the relation of the diagonal to the side of the square face of the cube, $\sqrt{3}$ as the ratio of the height to half the base of the equilateral triangle that forms the faces of the tetrahedron, octahedron and icosahedron, and ϕ as the ratio of the diagonals of each pentagonal face of the dodecahedron to its edges (see Figure 3.9 in Chapter 3).

All four irrationals – $\sqrt{2}$, $\sqrt{3}$, $\sqrt{5}$ and ϕ – also occur as ratios between edges of the regular polyhedra and the diameters of the spheres that touch either the centres of these edges (*midspheres*) or the apices (*circumspheres*), as in Table 8.1.

Moreover, ϕ is generated in another way by the interior geometry of both the dodecahedron and icosahedron. The fifteen pairs of opposite edges of the icosahedron, which correspond to lines joining the centres of adjacent faces of the dodecahedron, form the shorter sides of golden or ϕ rectangles (see Figure 8.17). Only three of the fifteen intersecting rectangles are shown in the figure.

All five regular polyhedra are united geometrically by the fact that they can be inscribed more or less simply within each other. The degree of simplicity depends on the numerical relations between the apices, edges and faces of the forms. It will help to remind ourselves of these relations by looking once more at Table 6.6, Chapter 6. It is here repeated as Table 8.2.

The table shows that the icosahedron and dodecahedron have a close reciprocity because the twelve apices

TABLE 8.1

FORM	EDGE	M/S	C/S
Tetrahedron	1	$1/\sqrt{2}$	$\sqrt{3}/\sqrt{2}$
Cube	1	$\sqrt{2}$	$\sqrt{3}$
Octahedron	1	1	$\sqrt{2}$
Icosahedron	1	ϕ	$\sqrt{\phi\sqrt{5}}$
Dodecahedron	1	ϕ^2	$\phi\sqrt{3}$

TABLE 8.2

FORM	*A*	*E*	*F*	FACE FIGURE
Tetrahedron	4	6	4	Equilateral triangle
Cube	8	12	6	Square
Octahedron	6	12	8	Equilateral triangle
Icosahedron	12	30	20	Equilateral triangle
Dodecahedron	20	30	12	Pentagon

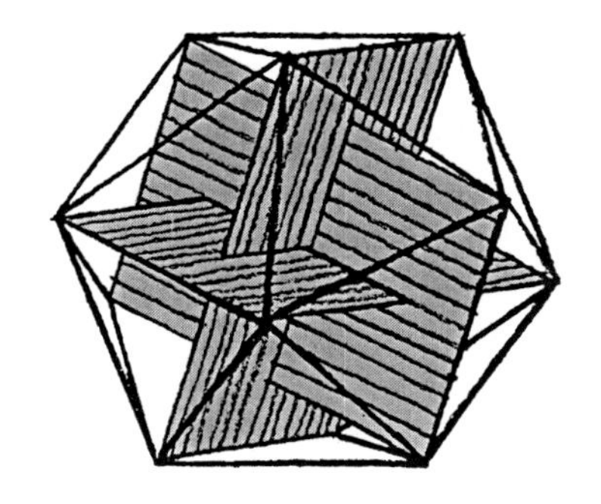

Figure 8.17 ϕ rectangles inscribed within a regular icosahedron.

of the icosahedron correspond to the twelve faces of the dodecahedron, and conversely the twenty apices of the latter correspond to the twenty faces of the former. They can thus be mutually inscribed or circumscribed, the apices of the one occupying the face-centres of the other (Figure 8.18).

A similar mutual affinity unites the cube and the octahedron: the octahedron has six apices and the cube has six faces. Conversely, the cube has eight apices and the octahedron eight faces (see Figure 8.19). The cube also relates interestingly to the dodecahedron. Six of the dodecahedron's thirty edges fit the six faces of the cube, while each of the cube's eight apices corresponds to one of the twenty apices of the dodecahedron (see Figure 8.20).

On the other hand the tetrahedron, having an equal number of apices and faces, fits neatly into itself. It also has mutual affinities with the cube and the octahedron. The tetrahedron's four apices correspond to four of the eight apices of the cube and also to four of the eight *faces* of the octahedron. Conversely, four of the eight apices of the cube correspond to the four faces of the tetrahedron, while each of the octahedron's six apices corresponds to one of the six *edges* of the tetrahedron (see Figure 8.21). In fact, all five polyhedra can be inscribed and circumscribed with respect to each other, the examples illustrated being merely the simplest and most elegant cases.

Euclid combines the five forms in a single elegant construction. In XIII, 18 it is proposed 'To set out the sides of the five figures and to compare them with one another'.[26] The construction starts out with the drawing of a semicircle, just like our construction for $\sqrt{5}$ and ϕ in section 8.2. To bring out the affinity with our universal diagram, Euclid's description and diagram will be rearranged slightly; we begin again, therefore, by inscribing a square in the semicircle (see Figure 8.22). As before, the square is ABCD, and AB coincides with the base of the semicircle, GH. GH represents the diameter of the circumsphere of all five forms: that is, if the semicircle were rotated through 360° about GH, it would generate the sphere.

Let GH equal 1. Cut GH at its midpoint, E, so

$$EG = EH = \frac{1}{2}$$

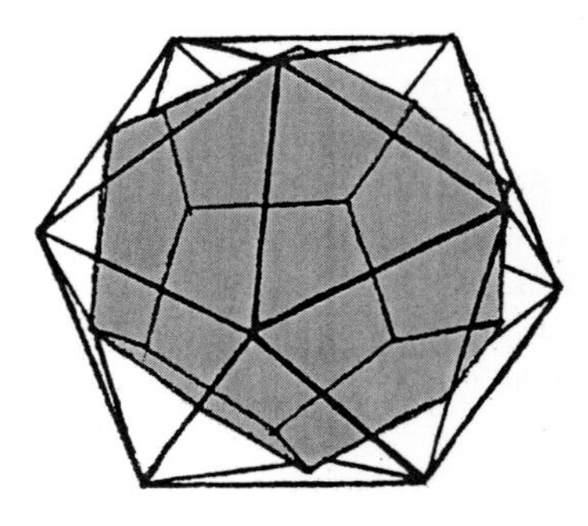

Figure 8.18 Regular dodecahedron inscribed within a regular icosahedron.

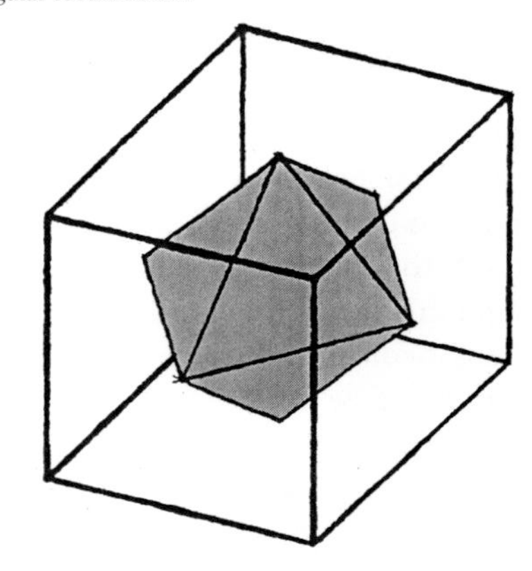

Figure 8.19 Regular octahedron inscribed within a cube.

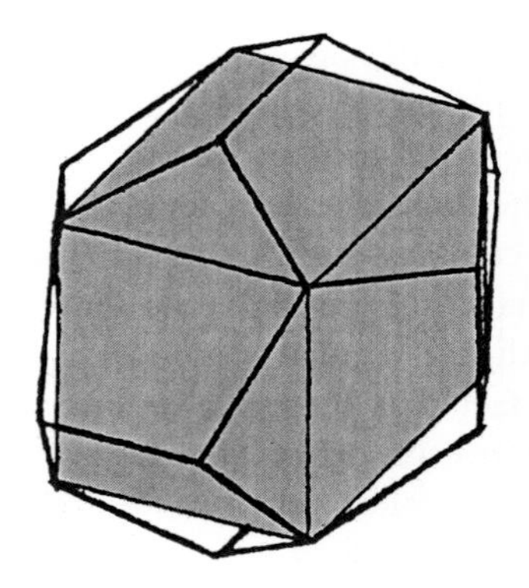

Figure 8.20 Cube inscribed within a regular dodecahedron.

26. *Ibid.*, vol. III, p. 503.

From E, erect EK perpendicular to GH, cutting the circumference of the semicircle at K, and join GK, HK. Then

$GK^2 = EG^2 + EK^2 =$

(theorem of Pythagoras), so

$$GK = \frac{1}{\sqrt{2}} = \text{the edge of the inscribed octahedron}$$

(approximately 0.7071).

Cut GH again at F, such that FG = 2 × FH and GH = 3 × FH. From F, erect FL perpendicular to GH, cutting the circumference of the semicircle at L, and join GL and HL. FL, the geometric mean of FG and FH = $\sqrt{2/3 \times 1/3}$ = $\sqrt{2/9}$.

FGL is a right-angled triangle. Therefore

$$GL^2 = GF^2 + FL^2 = \frac{4}{9} + \frac{2}{9} = \frac{2}{3}$$

(theorem of Pythagoras). Therefore

$$GL = \sqrt{\frac{2}{3}} = \frac{\sqrt{2}}{\sqrt{3}} = \text{the edge of the inscribed tetrahedeon}$$

(approximately 0.8165).

Similarly,

$$HL^2 = HF^2 + FL^2 = \frac{1}{9} + \frac{2}{9} = \frac{1}{3}$$

Therefore

$$HL = \sqrt{\frac{1}{3}} = \frac{1}{\sqrt{3}} = \text{the edge of the inscribed cube}$$

(approximately 0.5773).

Now join CH. We already know, from section 8.2, that

$GH^2 : BC^2 = 5 : 1$

and that

$BC : BH = \phi : 1$

From the theorem of Pythagoras

$$CH^2 = BC^2 + BH^2$$
$$= \frac{1}{5} + \frac{\phi^2}{5}$$

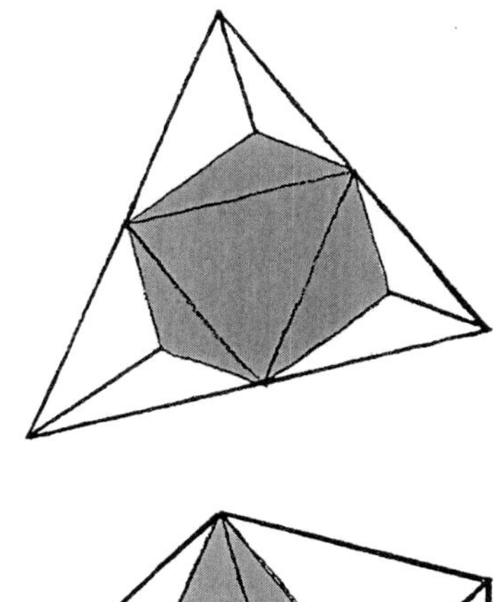

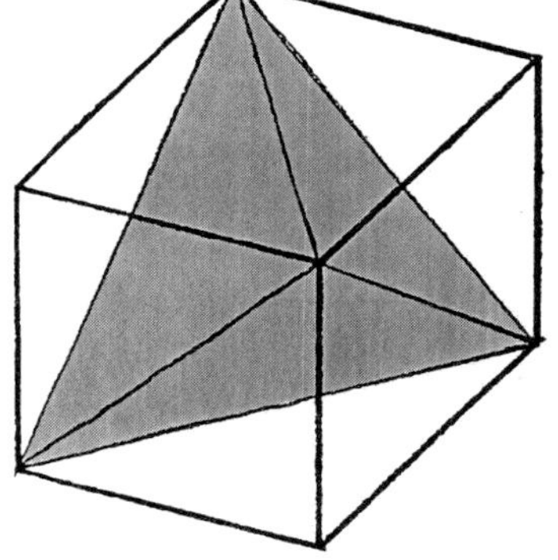

Figure 8.21 Regular octahedron inscribed within a tetrahedron, and tetrahedron within a cube.

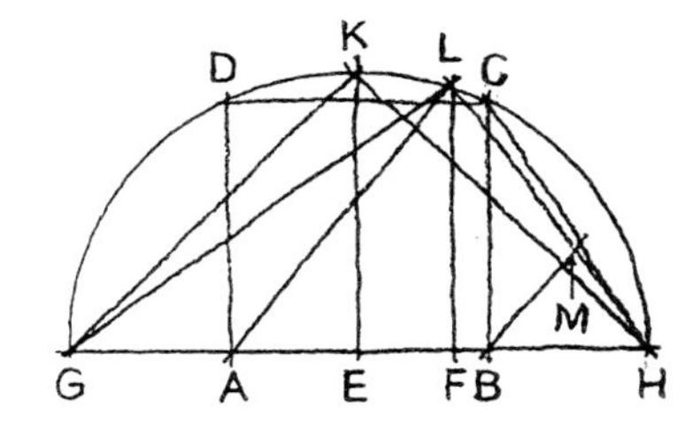

Figure 8.22 Euclid's construction for the edges of the five regular polyhedra inscribed within a circle.

$$= \frac{\phi \quad 2}{5}$$

$$= \frac{\sqrt{5}}{5\phi}$$

$$= \frac{1}{\phi\sqrt{5}}$$

Therefore

CH $\frac{1}{\sqrt{\phi\sqrt{5}}}$ = the edge of the inscribed icosahedron

(approximately 0.5257).

Finally, join AL, and from B draw BM parallel to AL, cutting HL at M. HL is thereby divided in extreme and mean ratio, since

$$LM : HM = AB : BH = \phi : 1$$

Now,

HL = $\frac{1}{\sqrt{3}}$ = the edge of the inscribed cube.

Therefore

LM $\frac{1}{\phi\sqrt{3}}$ = the edge of the inscribed dodecahedron

(approximately 0.357).

In Table 8.3 the summary of the relations given in Table 8.1 is repeated, but this time with the diameter of the circumscribing sphere as constant, as in the diagram, rather than the edges of the faces.

Proposition 18 concludes with the proof that no more than five regular polyhedra can exist, already given in Chapter 6. Thus Euclid brings his great work to a close. It remained unassailable as the definitive description of the nature of space for more than two thousand years – at no time more than towards the end of that period, when it provided the essential spatial foundation for Newton's *Mathematical Principles of Natural Philosophy* (1687). A century later Kant would regard Euclid's geometry and Newton's physics as unquestionably and eternally true, pure intuitions of the mind; indeed, the *Critique of Pure Reason* (1781) was written precisely in order to answer the question, How is such absolutely certain knowledge possible?[27]

TABLE 8.3

FORM	EDGE	M/S	C/S
Tetrahedron	$\sqrt{2}/\sqrt{3}$	$1/\sqrt{3}$	1
Cube	$1/\sqrt{3}$	$\sqrt{2}/\sqrt{3}$	1
Octahedron	$1/\sqrt{2}$	$1/\sqrt{2}$	1
Icosahedron	$1/\sqrt{\phi\sqrt{5}}$	$\phi/\sqrt{\phi\sqrt{5}}$	1
Dodecahedron	$1/\phi\sqrt{3}$	$\phi/\sqrt{3}$	1

Fifty years before Kant wrote, however, the first descriptions of geometries other than Euclid's were put forward by Girolamo Saccheri.[28] His aim was to reinforce Euclid by removing doubts about the parallel axiom on which his geometry rests. Saccheri identified three possible geometries, depending on whether the sum of the angles of a triangle equals, or is greater or less than, two right angles. He showed that only the first geometry, Euclid's, did not lead to what he considered absurd conclusions: that an infinite straight line was either impossible, or could approach another straight line indefinitely without intersecting it. But these were precisely the possibilities that in the nineteenth century would be entertained by Nikolai Lobachevskii (1793–1856), Johann Bolyai (1802–60) and Georg Riemann (1826–66). In the twentieth century Einstein would show that the actual space of the universe appears to fit Riemann's 'elliptical' geometry (1915).

The absolute supremacy of Euclidean geometry has been replaced by the possibility of inventing separate self-consistent geometries appropriate to particular purposes and different scales. Where does this leave architecture? Much modern architecture – from Sigfried Giedion's space–time hypothesis (1941)[29] to today's fashionably twisted geometries – reflects a naive desire to keep up to date with (or, by running very fast, to remain only a few decades behind) the latest discoveries in physics and mathematics. But the real lesson of these new geometries is a different one: that all geometries, including Euclid's, are not something found in nature, once and for all, but man-made frames of reference, valid for certain purposes and unsuited to others. There is no reason why the geometry needed to describe space on a scale of many light years should be appropriate to the scale of buildings that measure a few tens of metres. Euclidean space and Euclidean proportions are still relevant to architecture, therefore, but they have their place within a repertoire of spaces and proportions appropriate for other scales.

27. I. Kant, *Prologomena*, Open Court Publishing Company, 1902, pp. 32, 50.
28. G. Saccheri, *Euclides ab omni naevo vindicatus*, Milan, 1733.
29. S. Giedion, *Space, Time and Architecture*, Harvard University Press, 1941.

Chapter nine

VITRUVIUS

Vitruvius wanted to raise architecture to the level of scientia *or knowledge, and the best way to achieve this was by showing that it was a fundamentally mathematical art.*[1]

9.1 DISPUTED VALUE OF THE *TEN BOOKS ON ARCHITECTURE*

The Roman architect Marcus Vitruvius Pollio lived in the first century BC, and is thought to have dedicated his treatise *De Architectura* to the emperor Augustus in about 25 BC.[2] According to J.J. Coulton numerous earlier works, now all lost, were written during the centuries before and after the building of the Parthenon, the first of them being among the earliest Greek prose works.[3] In the absence of these, Vitruvius provides us with the nearest thing we have to an account, however second-hand, of ancient Greek architectural theory. For although he was a Roman, and writing mainly about the Italian architecture of his time, he describes the late republican phase of that architecture, in which the old Etrusco-Italic tradition had succumbed overwhelmingly to Greek influence, and had not yet developed the distinctively 'Roman' character of imperial buildings like the Colosseum or the thermae of Titus (both AD 80). Axel Boëthius and J.B. Ward-Perkins write that

> Vitruvius thus discloses to us on the one hand the legacy of old Rome. . . and on the other hand the hellenistic influence which pervaded Roman architecture of the previous centuries. Further, he describes Greek buildings with no Italic tradition,. . . which none the less were imported into this new Rome.[4]

It seems probable that what Vitruvius has to say about

1. J. Onians, *Bearers of Meaning*, Princeton University Press, 1988, p. 33.
2. W.J. Anderson, R. Phené Spiers and T. Ashby, *The Architecture of Ancient Rome*, B.T. Batsford, 1927, p. 26.
3. J.J. Coulton, *Ancient Greek Architects at Work*, Cornell University Press, 1977, p. 24.
4. A. Boëthius and J.B. Ward-Perkins, *Etruscan and Roman Architecture*, Penguin Books, 1970, p. 116.

proportion, being the most theoretical part of his treatise, is that which is closest to the imported Greek tradition.

There is much disagreement about how reliable Vitruvius' account really is, and whether it represents an advance on the earlier treatises – some of which he mentions, so presumably he had access to them – or gives only a distorted reflection of the lost Greek theory. In the opinion of John Onians,

> It was Vitruvius who composed the first study of architecture which in its scale and systematic comprehensiveness matched the elaborate texts which had already brought consistency and order to the better-recognized arts such as music and rhetoric. In the Greek world, writings on architecture had been restricted to commentaries on individual temples. . . and handbooks on individual orders such as that of Silenus on Doric symmetries.[5]

On the other hand Van der Laan, although a partisan of the *Ten Books*, comments on the frequent obscurity of the text that 'One might well ask oneself whether the author himself properly understood the data which he had presumably derived from earlier sources.'[6] Nevertheless, he concludes, in Vitruvius we have 'a late echo of the quintessential Greek theory of architecture'.[7]

The obscurity of Vitruvius' terminology has presented a problem for all his interpreters. His eighteenth-century translator W. Newton writes that 'All the commentators of Vitruvius allow this explanation of architecture to be very dark and unintelligible, and all differ in their interpretation thereof.'[8] Vitruvius' use of a number of vaguely defined terms to describe supposedly distinct aspects of proportion is particularly confusing for us; how is one to distinguish between ordonnance (*ordinatio* or *taxis*), eurhythmy (*eurythmia*), symmetry (*symmetria*), proportion (*proportio* or *analogía*) and correspondence (*commensus*)? In his book *The Theory of Proportion in Architecture* P.H. Scholfield speculates that *proportio* may denote the size of the parts as fractions of the whole, *symmetria* their size as a multiple of a module or smallest part, and *eurythmia* as 'gracefulness caused by the "rhythmic recurrence of the same ratios"'.[9] Van der Laan gives a different but remarkably consistent interpretation, described in the next section, while Wittkower concludes despairingly that 'Vitruvius' work contains no real theory of proportion.'[10]

5. J. Onians, *Bearers of Meaning*, p. 33.
6. H. van der Laan, *Het plastische getal*, E.J. Brill, 1967, p. 9.
7. *Ibid.*
8. W. Newton, translation of *De Architectura*, London, 1791, quoted in P.H. Scholfield, *The Theory of Proportion in Architecture*, Cambridge University Press, 1958, p. 16.
9. P.H. Scholfield, *The Theory of Proportion in Architecture*, p. 20.
10. R. Wittkower, *Architectural Principles in the Age of Humanism*, Tiranti, 1952, p. 120.

9.2 VAN DER LAAN'S INTERPRETATION OF THE FUNDAMENTAL PRINCIPLES

In the second chapter of the first book Vitruvius identifies six 'fundamental principles' of architecture:

(1) *ordinatio, taxis* or ordonnance;
(2) *dispositio, diathesis* or disposition;
(3) *eurythmia*;
(4) *symmetria*;
(5) *decor* or decorum; and
(6) *distributio, oikonomia* or economy.

In his book *Le Nombre plastique* (*The Plastic Number*, 1960) Van der Laan sets out to tackle head-on the baffling obscurity of Vitruvian terminology. He believes that this is caused not by confusion or ignorance on the part of the author, but by the looseness and imprecision of our own ideas about architectural proportion:

> Nowadays the words ordonnance, symmetry, rhythm, etc. are used more or less indiscriminately to express a vague and rudimentary concept of proportion that has come down to us from the ancient world. But it is certain that for the ancient mind all these terms referred to clearly defined and mutually distinct concepts.[11]

He finds a clue to the original meaning in an apparent incongruity in the list of principles. The definition of the fourth principle, *symmetria*, seems to be already included in that of the first. Vitruvius defines *ordinatio* as

> The balanced agreement of the measures of the building's members in each part separately; and the relation of the proportions of the whole building with a view to symmetry. This is achieved through quantity. Quantity is determined by the taking of units of measure, derived from the building itself in the form of elementary parts of its members, and brought into relation to the building as a whole.[12]

Compare this with the definition of symmetry:

---

11. H. van der Laan, *Het plastische getal*, p. 17.
12. Author's translation.

> Symmetry is the proper mutual agreement between the members of the building, and the relation, in accordance with a certain part selected as standard, of the separate parts to the figure of the building as a whole.[13]

How can two separate principles be so similar?

Van der Laan concludes that for Vitruvius symmetry is not something separate from ordonnance, but an aspect of it, eurhythmy being the other. By the same argument, decorum and economy are the twin aspects of disposition, which Vitruvius defines as 'the fit mutual placing of things and the judicious execution of the work in terms of the composition of measures, in accordance with the quality of things'.[14] In other words, in Van der Laan's view we are really dealing here not with six separate principles, but with two main principles – ordonnance and disposition – of which the other four are subdivisions, as shown in Table 9.1.

TABLE 9.1

ORDONNANCE		DISPOSITION	
Symmetry	Eurhythmy	Decorum	Economy

This arrangement resolves Vitruvius' (at first sight) confusing and disjointed string of definitions into a logical and coherent structure. Ordonnance now embraces two distinct aspects of proportion in building: eurythmy and symmetry. Van der Laan again gives these a fresh interpretation. In lesson IX of his book *Architectonic Space* he defines them as follows: 'Eurhythmy denotes the ratios between the different measures of the same thing, symmetry those between corresponding measures of different things.'[15] The following lesson amplifies this definition:

> Symmetry involves the comparison of corresponding measures of different forms: length is compared with length, breadth with breadth, and height with height. But the form of the squared mass as such is determined by the mutual proportions between its three dimensions, which are not symmetrical but eurhythmic: length is compared with breadth, breadth with height, and height with length. Symmetrical proportions enable us to determine the size of forms, by relating them to a form that acts as a unit of size; but eurhythmic proportions give us an insight, not into the quantity of form, but into its qualitative properties.[16]

By 'the form of the squared mass' Van der Laan has in mind the form of the whole building, or of some component of it, such as a column. In other words, eurhythmy determines the

13. *Ibid.*
14. *Ibid.*
15. H. van der Laan, *Architectonic Space*, E.J. Brill, 1983, p. 104.
16. *Ibid.*, p. 114.

shape of an individual thing, and symmetry its *scale* relative to other things.

How does this compare with what Vitruvius actually says? His definition of symmetry, given above, as 'the relation, in accordance with a certain part selected as standard, of the separate parts to the figure of the building as a whole', certainly seems to tally with Van der Laan's interpretation. Vitruvius defines eurhythmy as 'graceful appearance and good proportion in the composition of the parts. This is achieved when the members of the building are of a height suited to their breadth, and of a breadth suited to their length'.[17] Here again, the text seems to support Van der Laan's hypothesis – certainly better than it fits P.H. Scholfield's explanation.

Thus far, Van der Laan is on strong ground; but how about the two aspects of disposition? Vitruvius defines decorum as 'the correct style of the work, which comes about when the customary elements are composed in the proper manner'.[18] Among the several examples he cites are the convention that temples to Mars, Hercules, or – since she is a warrior goddess – Minerva (Athene) should be Doric, 'since the virile strength of these gods makes daintiness entirely inappropriate to their houses'.[19] Corinthian, on the other hand, is appropriate for temples to Venus, Flora, Proserpine etc., and Ionic for Juno, Diana and Bacchus. Decorum also dictates such things as the provision of adequately grand entrance courts to buildings with magnificent interiors. In other words, decorum ranges from what we might now call 'appropriate expression' to conventional associations of style with meaning – rather as, in the nineteenth century, a church might be built in the Gothic style and a bank or club in that of the Italian Renaissance. Vitruvius defines economy as

> the appropriate utilization of materials and of the site, and the sensible balancing of economy and common sense in the carrying out of the work. This is only achieved if in the first place the architect does not demand things that cannot be obtained or manufactured without great cost.[20]

It also includes the convenient planning of dwellings to suit the needs of different classes. Van der Laan sums up the fifth and sixth principles as follows: 'Decorum concerns what we would now call the style of the building, and economy its practical arrangement.'[21] Both aspects deal with the specific

17. Author's translation.
18. Author's translation.
19. M.H. Morgan's translation, Dover Publications, 1960, p. 15.
20. Vitruvius, *The Ten Books on Archiecture*, author's translation.
21. H. van der Laan, *Het plastische getal*, p. 16.

requirements – aesthetic or practical – of particular buildings, whereas the two aspects included under ordonnance, symmetry and eurhythmy, are universal. In section 9.6 of this chapter I shall argue that Vitruvius intends that these universal requirements should be addressed first, and the resulting proportions adjusted later if need be in response to the particular demands of disposition in the individual case. Thus whereas three of the six principles concern separate aspects of proportion, only one – economy – combines together all the practical and technical aspects of building (that is, of siting, selection of materials, construction, planning and economy) that today occupy most of an architect's energy and thought. If this is a true reflection of the relative importance given to proportion in ancient architecture, it should give us food for thought.

The structure of Van der Laan's analysis provides a beautiful illustration of his general philosophy of art – which, if he is correct, was also that of the ancient world. At each of the two levels there is a polarity. Ordonnance in general is the more abstract or intellectual aspect of architecture, disposition the more concrete or material one. And within each main category the same polarity is echoed by the subdivisions: symmetry is more abstract than eurhythmy – the latter being manifested in the visible and material form of the various building components, whereas the former is a more intellectual matter of relations between abstract measures – and economy is obviously more material than decorum.

Thus on one side there is quantity, measure, abstract intellectual concepts: things that can be exactly grasped by the mind. On the other, we have qualities: the world of the senses, of practical needs, social convention and religious custom. It is characteristic of Van der Laan that in direct contrast to our modern habit – but in conformity, he maintains, with the thought of Vitruvius' time – he places quantity above quality. He associates quantity with the spiritual and mental aspects, and quality with the material and sensual ones. The fundamental aim of art, for Van der Laan, is to connect these two poles: to bring the material world within the grasp of the intellect, and conversely to provide a concrete, material support for the spiritual world of abstract thought.

9.3 THE SYMMETRY OF TEMPLES AND OF THE HUMAN BODY

The part of Vitruvius' discussion of proportion that has attracted most attention is contained in the first chapter of Book III, called 'On symmetry in temples and the human body'. He begins by giving much the same definition of *proportio* or *analogía* as he has previously given of symmetry in defining the six principles:

> Proportion is a correspondence among the measures of the members of an entire work, and of the whole to a certain part selected as standard. From this result the principles of symmetry.[22]

Compare this with the definition of symmetry quoted above:

> Symmetry is the proper mutual agreement between the members of the building, and the relation, in accordance with a certain part selected as standard, of the separate parts to the figure of the building as a whole.

One definition reads like a paraphrase of the other. Whether this indicates that proportion is synonymous with symmetry, or merely that it includes it, is hard to determine. In the next sentence he refers to symmetry *and* proportion: 'Without symmetry and proportion there can be no principles in the design of any temple; that is, if there is no precise relation between its members, as in the case of those of a well shaped man.'[23] What is clear from both definitions, however, is that symmetry/proportion has three requirements:

(1) The measures of all the parts and of the whole must agree or correspond with each other.
(2) There must be a direct relation between the whole or largest measure and an elementary part or module.
(3) It follows from (1) and (2) that the measures of all other parts must likewise relate both to the whole and to the module.

From the immediately following passage it seems that he does not intend the ratio of the whole to the elementary part to be infinitely variable, but to have a fixed limit of

22. Vitruvius, *The Ten Books on Architecture*, M.H. Morgan trans., Dover Publications, 1960, p. 72.
23. *Ibid.*

1 : 10. Vitruvius applies the definition of symmetry to the proportions of the 'well shaped man', whom he assumes to be six feet tall, like Le Corbusier's *modulor* man. He writes that

> The human body is so designed by nature that the face, from the chin to the top of the forehead and the lowest roots of the hair, is a tenth part of the whole height; the open hand from the wrist to the tip of the middle finger is just the same. . .[24]

All larger members are likewise quoted as aliquot parts of the whole height: eighth, sixth, quarter, third, and so on. But smaller measures are not treated in the same way, but as sub-multiples of a tenth. Thus the face is divided into three equal thirds: chin to nostrils, nostrils to eyebrow, and forehead. The limit of 1 : 10 seems therefore to be regarded as an 'order of size', the smallest measure or unit of which constitutes in turn a whole with respect to measures belonging to a lower order. Logically, this order too should have one tenth as its lower limit – that is, one hundredth part of the total body height, or about 18.3 mm – but Vitruvius' description does not extend that far. However, the Roman foot was divided into sixteen fingers or 'digits' of about 19 mm, making 96 digits in six feet, so the digit was in fact very close to one hundredth of the total height.

The conflict between the decimal division used by Vitruvius in analysing the body, and the sextodecimal system of Roman measures, would later cause confusion amongst his Renaissance interpreters – Leonardo da Vinci (*c.* 1500), Cesare Cesariano (1521) and Daniele Barbaro (1556). Ten cannot be divided by eight or six without resorting to fractions, while ninety-six, the number of digits in six feet, is divisible by eight and by six but not by ten. Leonardo divides the man's height into ninety-six parts, Cesariano, keeping close to Vitruvius' description, into thirty, and Barbaro into one hundred and eighty, which is divisible by four, six and ten but not eight. Vitruvius touches the problem obliquely a few lines further on, in discussing the 'perfect number'. He writes that the Greeks, notably Plato, generally regarded ten as the perfect number, but that 'The mathematicians, maintaining a different view, have said that the perfect number is six. . .'[25] (on the grounds that it is the sum of its factors: 1 + 2 + 3 = 6). He also points out that the foot is one sixth of a man's height. But the Romans, 'observing that six

24. *Ibid.*
25. *Ibid.*, pp. 73–4.

and ten were both of them perfect numbers, . . . combined the two, and thus made the most perfect number, sixteen'.[26] Hence the Roman foot comprised four palms and sixteen digits or finger-breadths.

A further problem that arises from the Vitruvian description of the body is the question whether it is intended as an accurate account of actual human proportions, *derived from* average measurements, or rather as a convenient way of illustrating a mathematical scheme by *imposing it upon* the body. The second seems more likely. For no system can fail to fit the body reasonably well, provided it is rich enough in measures and one is free to choose which features of the body are significant and which among the wide variations of proportion among actual human beings are taken as normal. As P.H. Scholfield observes, Vitruvius' remarks

> make much more sense if we treat his human figure as a vivid diagram, so familiar that it does not need to be drawn, which he uses to illustrate the sort of proportions which he advocated for design in general. The stress then falls, not on the human figure itself, but on the actual proportions given to it.[27]

The choice of the body as a model for architectural proportion also had a practical aspect. Vitruvius observes that

> It was from the members of the body that they [our forefathers] derived the fundamental idea of the measures which are obviously necessary in all works, as the finger, palm, foot, and cubit.[28]

A relief has been discovered at Salamis, engraved with the outlines of precisely the body parts that were the basis of these measures: arm, foot, hand, and fingers.[29] Scholfield comments perceptively that common measures would have been necessary in order that different craftsmen could work together – so that the window frame made by a joiner would fit the opening made by a bricklayer. The next steps were to standardize the measures – so that tall and short craftsmen could work together without confusion – and to make the larger measures simple multiples of the smaller ones, while conversely the smaller were aliquot parts of the larger. And as Scholfield points out, this would automatically lead to the recurrence of certain small numbers, and thus to 'the

26. *Ibid.*, p. 74.
27. P.H. Scholfield, *The Theory of Proportion in Architecture*, p. 21.
28. Vitruvius, *The Ten Books on Architecture*, p. 73.
29. J. van de Waele, 'Vitruvius en de klassieke dorische tempel', in R. Rolf (ed.), *Vitruviuscongres 1995*, Vitruvianum Publicaties, Heerlen, 1997, p. 33.

establishment in some degree of a pattern of proportional relationships between the measures'.[30] Here we have one of the least deniable, because most practical, explanations of the need for proportion in architecture: it is demanded by the basic necessity of putting buildings together out of a number of separate bits, and of these bits fitting each other.

The second and more pressing problem is that the description satisfies only one of the requirements implied by the foregoing definitions of symmetry and proportion. There is a clear relation of 'the whole to a certain part selected as standard', that is, of the total height to the face- or hand-unit. This relation is 10 : 1. Assuming that all the intermediary measures are also expressed as aliquot parts of the total height, we get the following harmonic progression: 1/1, 1/2, 1/3, 1/4, 1/5, 1/6, 1/7, 1/8, 1/9, 1/10 (see Figure 9.1). But as multiples of the unit the same series becomes: 10, 5, 10/3, 5/2, 2, 5/3, 10/7, 5/4, 10/9, 1. Only 10, 5, 2 and 1 are simple integers, so only 1/1, 1/2, 1/5 and 1/10 of the whole are expressible as integral multiples of the unit or 'part selected as standard'. Conversely, had Vitruvius required all larger members and the whole to be multiples of the face- or hand-unit, so that the measures formed the arithmetical progression 1, 2, 3, 4, 5, 6, 7, 8, 9, 10, few of these would have been integral fractions of the whole: 1/10, 1/5, 1/2 and 1/1, but not 3/10, 2/5, 3/5, 7/10, 4/5 or 9/10. Whether the progression is harmonic or arithmetical, the ratio between consecutive terms varies between 2 : 1, 3 : 2, 4 : 3, 5 : 4, 6 : 5, 7 : 6, 8 : 7, 9 : 8 and 10 : 9. Can one speak of a 'correspondence among the measures' when there is no constant relation between them?

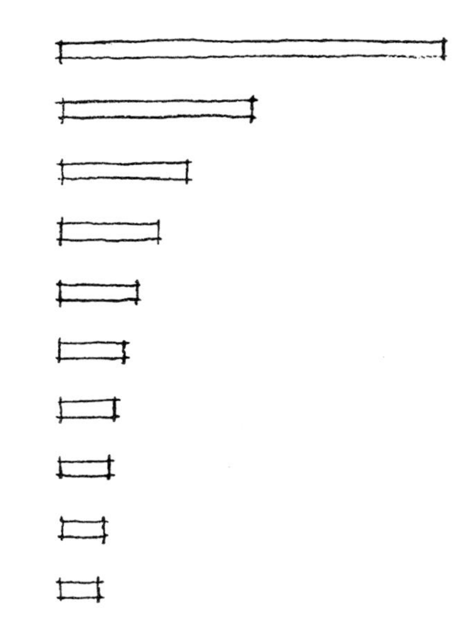

Figure 9.1 Harmonic progression.

The only way to achieve such a constant mutual relation would be to substitute a geometrical progression for the harmonic one. For instance, one might take as a constant multiplier the irrational number $10^{1/8}$, about 1.3335 or very nearly 4/3. If this multiplier is denoted by m, the series can be expressed either as parts of the whole – $10, 10/m, 10/m^2, 10/m^3, 10/m^4, 10/m^5, 10/m^6, 10/m^7, 10/m^8$ – or as multiples of the unit – $m^8, m^7, m^6, m^5, m^4, m^3, m^2, m, 1$. The ratio between any pair of consecutive measures is now constant, $m : 1$ (see Figure 9.2). But this solution requires a facility in dealing with powers and square roots and with irrational numbers that depends on the possession of a positional system of numeration and a method of algebraic notation. This Vitruvius and his contemporaries lacked.

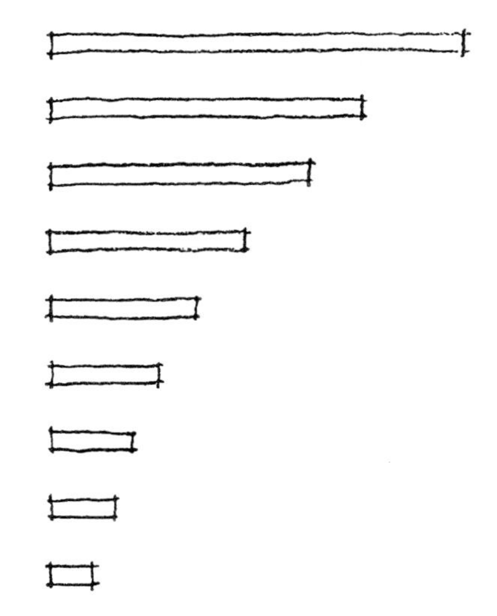

Figure 9.2 Geometric progression.

30. P.H. Scholfield, *The Theory of Proportion in Architecture*, p. 28.

Scholfield devotes almost a chapter of his book to his attempt to distil a coherent system out of Vitruvius' analysis of human measure. But in order to give the system any clarity, he is forced to abandon Vitruvius' division of the body into ten parts, each further subdivided into three, and instead adopts an initial division into four, each subdivided into four. Taking the whole body-height as *M*, he thus derives the table of measures shown in Table 9.2. Eliminating the repetitions, he obtains the simplified Table 9.3.

In effect, what Scholfield has done is to adapt the Vitruvian system to make it fit the double and triple progressions of Plato's subdivision of the World's Soul. In Chapter 11 we shall see that this is very close to the proportions prescribed by Alberti. However, in order to include Vitruvius' $M/10$ division, Scholfield then further adjusts this table, eliminating $M/9$ and $M/16$ but adding two rows of fifths and fifteenths. This effectively transforms it from the system of Alberti to that of Palladio. In Table 9.4 the divisions that Vitruvius actually uses in his analysis of the body are printed in bold.

Scholfield proposes that the remaining measures could 'be used for determining the proportions of those parts of the body which he leaves unspecified', and he concludes that the study has given rise to 'a flexible system of proportion which may perhaps be of more than historical interest'.[31] But what grounds are there for thinking that this is the system Vitruvius had in mind? As Scholfield admits, it may be objected that

> In practice Vitruvius' examples seldom have the simplicity of this system... [and] that if this is what Vitruvius meant, there was nothing to stop him from saying so in general terms, instead of giving us a vague practical example and leaving us to draw our own conclusions.[32]

He defends his hypothesis on the grounds that Vitruvius' examples were derived from traditionally evolved norms, and that since the great theoretical advances in mathematics had been made only a few centuries earlier, they had not had time to spread beyond the writings of rigorous mathematicians into the sphere of art and technology.[33] But in his ninth book Vitruvius shows that he was at least aware of the works of the Greek mathematicians of the golden age, naming Plato, Pythagoras, Archimedes, Archytas of Tarentum, Eratosthenes of Cyrene and Democritus.[34] To name is not necessarily to

TABLE 9.2

$\frac{M}{1}$	$\frac{M}{2}$	$\frac{M}{3}$	$\frac{M}{4}$
$\frac{M}{2}$	$\frac{M}{4}$	$\frac{M}{6}$	$\frac{M}{8}$
$\frac{M}{3}$	$\frac{M}{6}$	$\frac{M}{9}$	$\frac{M}{12}$
$\frac{M}{4}$	$\frac{M}{8}$	$\frac{M}{12}$	$\frac{M}{16}$

TABLE 9.3

$\frac{M}{1}$	$\frac{M}{2}$	$\frac{M}{4}$	$\frac{M}{8}$	$\frac{M}{16}$
$\frac{M}{3}$	$\frac{M}{6}$	$\frac{M}{12}$		
$\frac{M}{9}$				

TABLE 9.4

$\mathbf{\frac{M}{1}}$	$\frac{M}{2}$	$\mathbf{\frac{M}{4}}$	$\mathbf{\frac{M}{8}}$
$\frac{M}{3}$	$\mathbf{\frac{M}{6}}$	$\frac{M}{12}$	$\frac{M}{24}$
$\frac{M}{5}$	$\mathbf{\frac{M}{10}}$	$\frac{M}{20}$	$\frac{M}{40}$
$\frac{M}{15}$	$\mathbf{\frac{M}{30}}$	$\frac{M}{60}$	$\frac{M}{120}$

31. *Ibid.* p. 26.
32. *Ibid.*, pp. 26, 23.
33. *Ibid.*
34. Vitruvius, *The Ten Books on Architecture*, pp. 252–5.

understand, but it does indicate that the knowledge was available. Three centuries was more than long enough to allow the spread of information, even in those days. The truth is not that mathematical advances had not yet had time to filter through to architecture, but rather that there had been no significant progress in the field for a long time. Vitruvius lived in the middle of the long fallow period between the deaths of Archimedes and Apollonius of Perga (212–200 BC) and the flowering of the second Alexandrian school, with Hero, Pappus and Diophantus, in the third century AD. It was not that the relevant mathematics was too new, but rather that it was 'too old'. Mathematical exploration had ceased to be a burning intellectual issue.

Other, less fundamental but more immediate objections to Scholfield's conjectural reconstruction of the Vitruvian system of proportions are, first, that by reducing the basic unit to 1/120 of the whole, i.e. 1/20 of a foot or about 15 mm, he has completely abandoned the principle of an 'order of size' determined by an extreme ratio of 1 : 10, and secondly that Scholfield's unit does not correspond to the Roman digit measuring 1/16 of a foot.

9.4 BODY, CIRCLE AND SQUARE

The elementary geometry of circle and square, discussed at the start of Chapter 4, reappears in the *Ten Books* immediately after the discussion of the body's symmetry. The body's centre, Vitruvius writes, is the navel:

> For if a man be placed flat on his back, with his hands and feet extended, and a pair of compasses centred at his navel, the fingers and toes of his two hands and feet will touch the circumference of a circle described therefrom. And just as the human body yields a circular outline, so too a square figure may be found from it. For if we measure the distance from the soles of the feet to the top of the head, and then apply that measure to the outstretched arms, the breadth will be found to be the same as the height. . .[35]

No passage in Vitruvius has been more influential for architecture than these three sentences. They inspired the famous diagram by Leonardo (see Figure 11.1 in Chapter 11), and rather less compelling ones by Francesco di Giorgio,

35. *Ibid.*, p. 73.

Fra Giocondo (1511), and Cesariano. The three last named all fall into the trap of either inscribing the circle in the square, so that its diameter equals the side of the square, or circumscribing it, so that they are related in the ratio of: $\sqrt{2}$ 1. In the first case the man is too large for the circle – Fra Giocondo simply draws a larger man in one than in the other – while in the second (Cesariano) he must be stretched as on a rack to reach it. Less directly derived from Vitruvius' description are the vast number of Renaissance church plans based on circles and squares – notably, again, those sketched by Leonardo in his notebooks.

Only Leonardo seems to interpret the text accurately. His six foot square is divided into twenty-four Roman palms and ninety-six digits. Because of this, however, it cannot be reconciled exactly with Vitruvius' division by tenths. For instance, in his written notes Leonardo, like Vitruvius, gives the face and hand as 1/10 of the whole height. But he also states that the hand is one quarter of the length of the arm, measured from the shoulder, and that the length of the arm is 3/8 of the man's height, making the length of the hand 3/32 of the height, or nine digits.[36] Similarly, because the diameter of Leonardo's circle accords with anatomical reality, it can have no simple arithmetical or geometrical relation to the side of the square. By measurement, it seems to be about 116.87 digits, and 116.87/96 = 1.2174. There is no way in which, without anatomical distortion, the circle and square concept can be combined with the earlier breakdown of the body measures into aliquot parts.

A last, and mathematically most successful, descendant of the Vitruvian figure is Le Corbusier's *modulor* man, to be discussed more fully in Chapter 15 (Figure 15.13). Although he does not actually draw his man in a circle, Le Corbusier compares the height to the top of the head – again exactly six feet – with that to the navel and to the fingertips of the raised hand. This comes to virtually the same thing. One could draw a circle centred at the navel and it would touch the soles of the feet and the extended fingertips. The relation of the radius of this circle to the height of the man is a golden section: that is, 1 : ϕ or 1 : 1.618. Because the height is six feet, the radius is 6/ϕ or 3.708 ft, and the height to extended hand (equivalent to the diameter of Leonardo's circle) is 12/ϕ or 7.416 ft. The ratio of the diameter of the circle to the side of the square is thus 7.416 : 6 or 1.236 : 1, not far from Leonardo's ratio of 1.2174 : 1.

36. E. MacCurdy (ed.), *The Notebooks of Leonardo da Vinci*, Jonathan Cape, 1938, p. 200.

9.5 OTHER PROPORTIONS PRESCRIBED IN THE *TEN BOOKS*, INCLUDING THE SQUARE ROOT OF TWO

Throughout the *Ten Books*, the forms of buildings are described mathematically, in terms of numerical relationships. Vitruvius even describes catapults, *ballistae*, and other war machines in terms of their mathematical proportions.[37] Thanks to this, one can reconstruct the descriptions from the text, even though the original illustrations are lost. The descriptions of architectural details – column bases, capitals and mouldings – are too many and too elaborate for inclusion here, and the following discussion is confined to the larger elements. In the third chapter of Book III, which concerns the spacing of columns in temples, Vitruvius specifies five types, with specific ratios of column thickness to intercolumniation (measured here between faces of columns, not centre to centre) and to column height.[38] They are set out in Table 9.5. The proportion of the araeostyle spacing is not given; the columns are described merely as 'farther apart than they ought to be'.[39]

TABLE 9.5

TYPE	RATIO OF DIAMETER TO INTER-COMMUNICATION	RATIO OF DIAMETER TO COLUMN HEIGHT
Pycnostyle	2 : 3	1 : 10
Systyle	1 : 2	2 : 19
Eustyle	4 : 9	2 : 19
Diastyle	1 : 3	2 : 17
Araeostyle	1 : 4 (?)	1 : 8

The lengths of temples, as well as those of the walled sanctuaries within the peristyle, should always according to Vitruvius be twice their widths.[40] The latter are divided into two parts, the *cella* and the *pronaos*, whose lengths are respectively 5/8 and 3/8 of the whole. In Doric and Ionic temples the height of the door opening should be 5/7 of the ceiling height, and its width at the bottom 11/24 of its height: that is, 55/168 or practically 1/3 of the ceiling height.[41] Further specifications, too complicated to describe here, relate to the width of the door at the top, of the architraves, and their mouldings.

In Book V Vitruvius describes his design for the basilica at Fano. The main hall, measuring 120 by 60 ft, is surrounded by a two-storeyed gallery 20 ft wide. The large columns around the hall are 50 ft high and 5 ft thick, and the pillasters supporting the two levels of the gallery respectively 20 and 18 ft high and $2^1/_2$ and 2 ft wide. The key ratios are thus 10 : 1, 9 : 1, 8 : 1, 6 : 1, 3 : 1, 2 : 1, 6 : 5 and 10 : 9 – all proportions that correspond to the analysis of human measure in Book III.

Lastly, the prescriptions for the *atrium*, the principal room of Pompeian houses, are given in Book VI. The proportions

37. Vitruvius, *The Ten Books on Architecture*, pp. 303–8.
38. *Ibid.*, pp. 78–86.
39. *Ibid.*, p. 78.
40. *Ibid.*, p. 114.
41. *Ibid.*, pp. 117–18.

of the minor spaces – *alae* and *tablinum* – are derived from the length of the *atrium*, and will be ignored. Vitruvius specifies three proportions for *atria*, which are set out in Table 9.6 (see Figure 9.3). The width is each time taken as the unit. The remarkable thing is that the ratio of width to height is constant, 4 : 3, instead of being related to the ratio of length to width. To be consistent, one might expect that the height of the first type would be 3/5, and that of the third type $\sqrt{2}/2$ (about 5/7), with respect to the width.

The inclusion of an incommensurable ratio, $\sqrt{2} : 1$, is an apparent anomaly among the exclusively rational proportions used elsewhere. The same proportion reappears among otherwise generally commensurable ones – presumably following the example of Vitruvius – in Renaissance treatises on architecture such as those of Alberti, Cesariano, Serlio and Palladio. There is no question of the $\sqrt{2}$ proportion having been somehow slipped in, as it were, inadvertently, because in the introduction to the ninth book Vitruvius goes out of his way to illustrate Plato's account in the *Meno* of Socrates' geometrical demonstration to a servant boy that the relation of the sides of two squares, the area of one being double that of the other, is determined by the square root of two.[42] Vitruvius' version is as follows:

> A square place ten feet long and ten feet wide gives an area of one hundred feet. Now if it is required to double the square, and to make one of two hundred feet, we must ask how long will be the side of that square. . . Nobody can find this by means of arithmetic. For if we take fourteen, multiplication will give one hundred and ninety-six feet; if fifteen, two hundred and twenty-five feet. Therefore. . . let a diagonal line be drawn from angle to angle of that square of ten feet in length and width, dividing it into two triangles of equal size, each fifty feet in area. Taking this diagonal line as length, describe another square. Thus we shall have in the larger square four triangles of the same size and the same number of feet as the two of fifty feet each. . . In this way Plato demonstrated the doubling by means of lines. . .[43] [see Figure 9.4].

TABLE 9.6

LENGTH	WIDTH	HEIGHT
5/3	1	3/4
3/2	1	3/4
$\sqrt{2}$	1	3/4

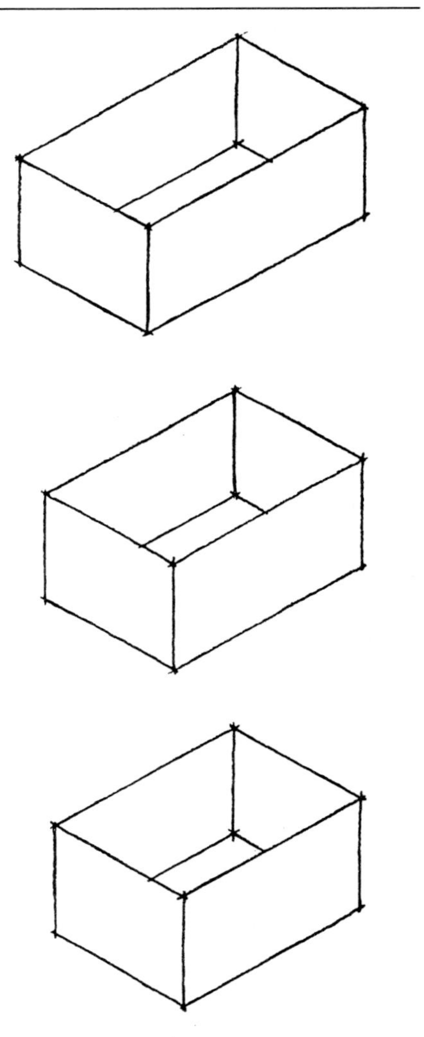

Figure 9.3 Proportions of *atria* recommended by Vitruvius.

42. Plato, *Five Dialogues on Poetic Inspiration*, Everyman's Library, 1910, pp. 91–8.
43. Vitruvius, *The Ten Books on Architecture*, p. 252.

9.6 THE SYSTEM OF PROPORTIONS AS A LAW OF GROWTH

In some ways the most interesting of all Vitruvius' observations, from the point of view of our modern attitudes to and doubts about proportion systems, is contained in the second chapter of Book VI. He writes that

> There is nothing to which an architect should devote more thought than to the exact proportions of his building with reference to a certain part selected as standard. After the standard of symmetry has been determined, and the proportionate dimensions determined by calculation, it is next the part of wisdom to consider the nature of the site, or questions of use or beauty, and modify the plan by diminutions or additions in such a manner that these diminutions or additions in the symmetrical relations may be seen to be made on correct principles, and without detracting at all from the effect.[44]

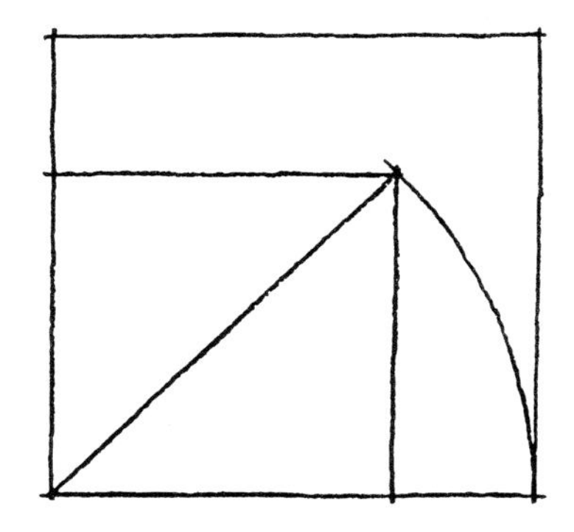

Figure 9.4 Construction of two squares, the second twice as large as the first, from Plato's *Meno*.

What makes this so significant is that, quite contrary to modern assumptions, the calculation of mathematical proportions comes at the very start of the design process, even before consideration of a particular site, particular functional demands or particular aesthetic refinements. Today, if mathematical proportions are invoked at all it tends to be towards the *end* of the process, as a final polish. The modern view is well represented by a remark in the diaries of the Bauhaus artist Oskar Schlemmer:

> It is utterly fatal to. . . invoke [laws of proportion] before the picture itself has been visualized; instead of 'freedom under law' one ends up with inspiration in handcuffs. No! The initial impulse should be emotion, the stream of unconscious, free, unfettered creation. . . If mathematical proportions and measurements are called in, they should function as a regulative.[45]

But the ancient opinion, represented by Vitruvius and revived in our time by Van der Laan, is in my view more organic and more free. It is precisely when mathematical rule is merely 'called in as a regulative' – imposed at a late stage in the process in order to bring under control something already conceived on the basis of 'the stream of unconscious

44. *Ibid.*, p. 174.
45. O. Schlemmer, *Letters and Diaries*, Northwestern University Press, 1990, pp. 271–2.

creation' – that one is apt to end up with 'inspiration in handcuffs'. Handcuffs are put on after the crime has been committed. And most modern architects apply systems of proportion – if they apply them at all – as one might put on handcuffs, a corset or a straitjacket: as a last resort, when it is already too late. The best that can be hoped for is to impose some semblance of order on a body that has become unruly or shapeless. In contrast, the ancient principle acts something like a genetic code that determines the body's general form. This form may develop variously in particular circumstances, as the final form of a tree may respond to the climatic conditions of its site.

Chapter ten

GOTHIC PROPORTIONS

The masters of Chartres, like the Platonists and Pythagoreans of all ages, were obsessed with mathematics; it was considered the link between God and the world, the magical tool that would unlock the secrets of both.[1]

10.1 THE CONTINUITY OF CLASSICAL CULTURE AND THE LEGACY OF PLATO AND VITRUVIUS

The traditional division of history into 'Ancient', 'Medieval' and 'Modern' periods is to a large extent an invention of the Renaissance, an historical *chiaroscuro* intended to highlight its own achievement as a rebirth of Classical civilization by throwing the intervening thousand years into shadow as an age of darkness and ignorance. Giorgio Vasari, for instance, writes that Brunelleschi

> was sent by heaven to renew the art of architecture. For hundreds of years men had neglected this art and squandered their wealth on buildings without order, badly executed and poorly designed, which were full of strange inventions, shamefully devoid of grace and execrably ornamented.[2]

As Erwin Panofsky observes,

> It is only on the assumption of an interval between a past supposed to have been submerged and a present supposed to have rescued this past from submersion, that such terms as *media aetas* or *medium aevum* could have come into being.[3]

Another aspect of this traditional view is that Imperial Roman civilization is seen as a continuation of that of Classical Greece, and as entirely separate from the Dark Ages

1. O. von Simson, *The Gothic Cathedral*, Harper Torchbooks, 1964, p. 27.
2. G. Vasari, *The Lives of the Artists*, Penguin Books, 1965, p. 133.
3. E. Panofsky, *Renaissance and Renascences in Western Art*, Paladin, 1970, p. 8.

that commenced with the end of the Western Empire in AD 476. But there is at least equal reason to reverse this opinion, and to regard the continuity between the Empire and the Middle Ages as more significant than its continuity with Greece. Imperial Rome initiated much that would come to fruition in the following centuries, not least in the field of art and architecture. Early fourth-century works like Diocletian's palace at Split, the Basilica at Trier or the relief sculptures on the Arch of Constantine are closer in spirit to the Romanesque of the eleventh and twelfth centuries than to Classical Greece or the Rome of Augustus. Sigfried Giedion, looking at the history of architecture chiefly as the history of concepts of space, sees the important break between the first and second 'space conceptions' as occurring around AD 100:

> The first stage embraced both the archaic high civilizations and also the Greek development. Sculptural objects – volumes – were placed in limitless space. The second stage of architectural development opened in the midst of the Roman period. Interior space, and with it the whole vaulting problem, became the highest aim of architecture. . . The Roman Pantheon, with its partial forerunners, marks the beginning. The second space conception encompasses the period between the building of the great Roman vaults, such as the thermae, and the end of the eighteenth century.[4]

Although Rome also inherited and passed on the legacy of ancient Classical culture, there remained a gap, throughout the Roman period, between the levels of discourse in Greek and Latin. Relatively few Greek writings, and still fewer works of Greek philosophy, were translated into Latin in ancient times. Latin writers tended to transmit only those parts of Greek scholarship that were most easily assimilable or had more obvious practical relevance or the widest appeal. They condensed, collected, commented and popularized. Vitruvius himself is an example of this. There was a dearth of original research in the Greek spirit. In the eastern half of the Empire original inquiry continued for some centuries, notably at the School of Alexandria, up to the time of Hero, Pappus and Diophantus around AD 250. But the result of the Roman tendency to summarize and anthologize was that after the final separation of the Western

4. S. Giedion, *The Beginnings of Architecture*, Princeton University Press, 1964, p. 521.

and Eastern empires in 395 the West was increasingly cut off from a large part of Greek science. Full contact did not begin to be restored for at least seven hundred years – first indirectly, through the mediation of Arabic translations after about 1100, and eventually by the influx of Greek scholars and the acquisition of original Greek texts that followed the fall of Constantinople in 1453.

Thus although the thread of Classical learning was never completely broken during the Dark Ages it became extremely attenuated. Since few texts were available to scholars they passed them through ever finer interpretative sieves, seeking as it were to extract every last drop of the wisdom they contained. Included in the legacy were the Greek architectural tradition embodied in the *Ten Books* of Vitruvius, and above all the mathematical science of proportion contained in the *Timaeus*. This was among the few of Plato's dialogues that survived in the West throughout the Medieval period. But it survived in a fragmentary form, and of this fragment, Otto von Simson points out:

> not the Greek original but only a garbled translation along with two commentaries, by Chalcidius and Macrobius, that viewed Plato's cosmology through the lenses of an eclectic and confused Neoplatonic mysticism.'[5]

Nevertheless, in this form it was studied in the West throughout the Middle Ages – most notably at the twelfth-century School of Chartres.

Of the two aspects of Timaean proportion – the one based on whole number ratios like 2 : 1, 3 : 2 and 4 : 3, associated with musical harmony, and the other based on the geometry of the regular solids and the incommensurable square roots of 2, 3 and 5 – it is the former that exercised the greatest fascination for the late Empire and the early Middle Ages. For many centuries after the fall of Rome the study of mathematics was largely confined to arithmetic. The only work of geometry available, the pseudonymous *Geometry of Boethius* containing fragments of Euclid, was not earlier than the ninth century.[6] Thus it was increasingly the Pythagorean – that is, the numerical and mystical – aspects of Plato's dialogue that drew most attention. Numbers were seen less as measures of quantity than as symbols for ethical concepts. The founder of Neoplatonism, Plotinus (*c.* 205–70) writes in the chapter *On Numbers* in his sixth *Ennead* that

5. O. von Simson, *The Gothic Cathedral*, p. 26.
6. A.C. Crombie, *Augustine to Galileo*, Heinemann Mercury, 1961, p. 11.

> multiplicity is a falling away from The Unity . . . A thing. . . flows outward and by that dissipation takes extension: utterly losing unity it becomes a manifold since there is nothing to bind part to part . . . broken into so many independent items, it is now those several parts and not the thing it was; if that original is to persist, the members must stand collected to their total; in other words, a thing is itself not by being extended but by remaining, in its degree, a unity . . .[7]

It is not hard to see how such meditations might derive from Platonic passages like that in which Timaeus speaks of unity being achieved by means of a bond that draws things together;[8] nor how it might have a relevance to architectural proportion. The building, by being extended in space and composed of a multiplicity of parts, risks losing its original identity and unity. If it is to retain this unity, the measures of the building's members must be 'collected to their total', bound together in numerical proportion, like the tones that make up a musical octave. Recall also Vitruvius' statement that 'Without symmetry and proportion there can be no principles in the design of any temple; that is, if there is no precise relation between its members.'[9]

Pythagorean and Neoplatonist mathematics dominate the mathematical and musical treatises of the two great thinkers whose lives spanned the slow disintegration of the Roman empire, and whose writings shaped the philosophy of Western Christendom until the rise of Aristotelianism in the thirteenth century: the *De Ordine* and *De Musica* of St Augustine (354–430), and the *De Musica* and *De Arithmetica* of Boethius (*c.* 480–524). The following example of the way Augustine, particularly in his later writings, puts Pythagorean and Neoplatonist number mysticism to the service of Christian doctrine is taken from *The City of God*:

> The works of Creation are described as being completed in six days. . . The reason for this is that six is the number of perfection. . . For six is the first number that is the sum of its parts, that is of its fractions, the sixth, the third and the half; for one, two and three make six. . . Hence the theory of number is not to be lightly regarded, since it is made quite clear, in many passages of the holy Scriptures, how highly it is to be valued. It is not for nothing that it

7. Plotinus, *The Enneads*, Faber & Faber, 1956, pp. 541-2.
8. Plato, 'Timaeus', in F.M. Cornford, *Plato's Cosmology*, Routledge & Kegan Paul, 1937, p. 44.
9. Vitruvius, *The Ten Books on Architecture*, Dover Publications, 1960, p. 72.

> was said in praise of God, 'You have ordered all things in measure, number and weight'.[10]

For Augustine, Plato's account of the creation in the *Timaeus* was a wonderful anticipation of Christian teaching. With its doctrine that ultimate reality lies in the immaterial world of spiritual ideas, and that the sensible world is its imperfect shadow, Platonism was for him supreme among pagan philosophies: 'There are none who come nearer to us than the Platonists.'[11] Although Augustine's successor Boethius sought to reconcile the teachings of Plato with those of Aristotle, intending, had he lived, to translate all their works into Latin, Western European thought was for many centuries dominated by Platonism. Of Boethius' translations from Aristotle – in the opinion of an historian of Medieval science, Alistair Crombie – 'only the *Categories* and the *De Interpretatione* were widely known before the twelfth century'.[12]

Umberto Eco stresses the symbolic importance in twelfth-century thought of the Vitruvian idea of the *homo quadratus* – the squared man, as described in the third of Vitruvius' *Ten Books*.[13]

> According to the theory of *homo quadratus*, number is the principle of the universe, and numbers possess symbolical meanings which are grounded in correspondences at once numerical and aesthetic. . . Vitruvius taught that four was the number of man, because the distance between his extended arms was the same as his height. . . Four was the number of moral perfection, and men experienced in the struggle for moral perfection were called 'tetragonal'. However, *homo quadratus* was also pentagonal, for five was another number of arcane significance. . . The number five was found in man, for if the extremities of his body were joined by straight lines they formed a pentagon (an image found in Villard de Honnecourt, and also in the much better known drawing by Leonardo). The mysticism of St Hildegard was based upon the symbolism of proportion and the mysterious fascination of the pentad.[14]

Here again we have an example of the direct translation of numbers into mystical symbols. The interest of the idea is that it introduces, well before the Renaissance, what would

10. Augustine, *The City of God*, Penguin Books, 1972, p. 465.
11. *Ibid.*, p. 304.
12. A.C. Crombie, *Augustine to Galileo*, p. 11.
13. Vitruvius, *The Ten Books on Architecture*, pp. 72-3.
14. U. Eco, *Art and Beauty in the Middle Ages*, Yale University Press, 1986, pp. 35-6.

be one of its central conceptions: the interrelation of *microcosmos* and *macrocosmos* and the centrality of man in God's universe. But the way the Renaissance treats the image of the square and circular (or pentagonal) man, exemplified by the drawings of Leonardo and others mentioned in the last chapter, is very different from the Medieval one. This is shown by a comparison of Leonardo's drawing (Figure 11.1) with the geometrized human and animal figures in the notebooks of the French master builder Villard de Honnecourt (*c.* 1235). Villard's geometry is as it were 'geometry by numbers'. It has nothing to do with relations of *measures*, in the sense that these were understood by Euclid, or as they would be understood again by Alberti or Leonardo: that is, the lengths of lines in proportion to each other, and the interdependence of these and the relative sizes of angles. When Villard imposes a five-pointed star on the figure of a man (see Figure 10.1) he so distorts the pentagonal geometry to fit the image that it is barely recognizable. The upper vertex is vestigial, and the line AB across the shoulders is about a third of, instead of equal to, the corresponding line AH that joins the shoulder to the foot. The star is five-pointed, but no more; it has no other connection with the regular star-pentagon, and bears not a trace of the golden section. Number, not geometry, rules the Gothic world.

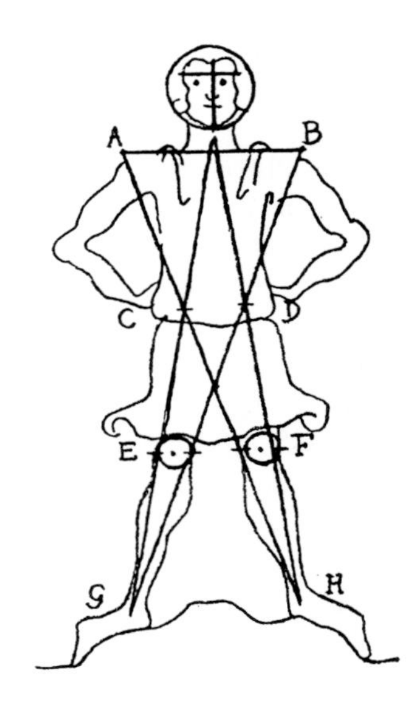

Figure 10.1 Construction of human figure, from Villard de Honnecourt, *c.* 1235.

We shall meet with a similar phenomenon when we come to discuss the proportions of Chartres Cathedral, where there are seven compartments in the nave. The fact that some of these are longer than others by as much as a fifth seems to have bothered the builders far less than the embodiment of the number seven. What mattered was not measuring *how much* but counting *how many*. This judgement is diametrically opposed, of course, to Rudolf Wittkower's conclusion that 'The Middle Ages favoured Pythagorean-Platonic geometry, while the Renaissance and Classical periods favoured the numerical, i.e. the arithmetical side of the tradition.'[15]

Although the historical break between the Imperial Age of Rome and the Middle Ages is largely unreal, and the fifteen centuries that separate the *De architectura* of Vitruvius (*c.* 25 BC) from the *De re aedificatoria* of Alberti (*c.* AD 1450) can be regarded from many points of view as a continuous philosophical and artistic development, it is too long and too complex to discuss here in its entirety. I shall concentrate,

15. R. Wittkower, 'The changing concept of proportion', in *Idea and Image*, Thames & Hudson, 1978, p. 116.

therefore, on a small portion of it, extending over little more than a century, which includes the building of the classic Gothic cathedrals of northern France and ends with the death of the great Scholastic philosopher St Thomas Aquinas in 1274.

10.2 THE PRACTICAL GEOMETRY OF THE MASTER MASONS

It is extremely doubtful that twelfth- and thirteenth-century Medieval architects had at their disposal the elaborate geometrical constructions ascribed to them by some modern interpreters and by propagandists of 'sacred geometry'. Euclid's *Elements* were translated into Latin around the middle of the twelfth century,[16] but there is no evidence that this filtered through to the lodges of the master masons. Nevertheless, despite the probable limitations of their theoretical knowledge, there are purely technical reasons why the Medieval builders may have employed some simple form of geometrical or numerical proportioning. Mathematical rules and diagrams, which could be carried in the head or sketched out roughly, were a necessary means of overcoming the absence of scale drawings and the primitiveness of measuring instruments. The proportional *schema* provided a sort of shorthand notation, as can be seen in Villard de Honnecourt's notebooks. The problem is that it is virtually impossible to ascertain what these *schemata* were. The very same factors that made a system necessary in the first place led to wide divergences among the measures realized in the finished building. And where there are many measures to choose from, none of which may be exactly the one intended, all interpretation of the proportions is subject to doubt.[17]

There has been extensive speculation that methods based on the irrational square roots of two and three (called respectively *ad quadratum* and *ad triangulum*), and less certainly the golden section, were practised by Medieval architects.[18] It is also argued that the use of these incommensurable ratios arose naturally from the Gothic builders' reliance on geometrical means of setting out rather than measurement to scale: for instance, that if the builders were using only cords and pegs to measure out on site the plan of a compartment of structure, a rectangle whose long

16. D.C. Lindberg, *The Beginnings of Western Science*, University of Chicago Press, 1992, p. 205.
17. N. Luning Prak, 'Measurements of Amiens Cathedral', *Journal of the Society of Architectural Historians*, XXV (3), Oct. 1966, pp. 209-12.
18. See for example F.M. Lund, *Ad Quadratum*, Batsford, 1921; E. Moessel, *Die Proportionen in Antike und Mittelalter*, Munich, 1926; G. Lesser, *Gothic Cathedrals and Sacred Geometry*, Alec Tiranti, 1957; N. Pennick, *Sacred Geometry: Symbolism and Purpose in Religious Structures*, Turnstone Press, 1980.

side equalled the diagonal of the square on the short side would inevitably suggest itself. Kenneth J. Conant cites Vitruvius' statement that 'A groundplan is made by the proper successive use of compasses and rule'[19] to support his conclusion that these plans would have been set out on the site

> with tapes and stretched cords. Both in the study and in the field the square with its diagonals was obviously, under these conditions, the most useful geometrical figure. . . and the diagonals (necessary for exactitude in setting out the square) would be available to determine supplementary dimensions.[20]

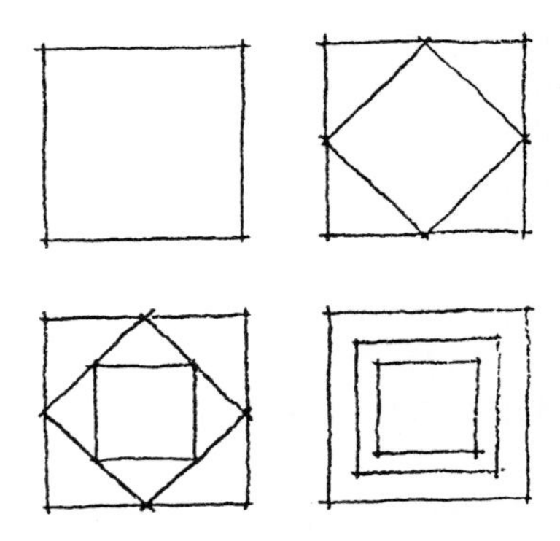

Figure 10.2 Construction of pinnacle, from Mathes Roriczer, 1486.

The argument is plausible; what is needed to make it certain, however, is documentary evidence. Unfortunately such firm evidence as there is belongs to the very end of the Gothic period. It comes from two main sources: the records of the arguments about how to complete Milan Cathedral (1389–92), and the handbooks of the German master builder Mathes Roriczer (*c.* 1435–95). The latter include the *Booklet on Pinnacles* (1486) and the *German Geometry* (1498).[21] The first of Roriczer's handbooks was published, therefore, in the same year as the first printed edition of Alberti's *On the Art of Building*, and nearly four decades after Alberti's original manuscript. It is thus by no means certain that it gives an accurate picture of the proportioning methods used by the builders of Chartres three centuries earlier.

I shall start with these later texts since they throw specific light on the question of the square and its diagonal, and then go on to consider the Milanese documents before examining the speculative theories put forward about the proportions of Chartres. The first stages of Roriczer's method for designing pinnacles certainly confirm the use of the $\sqrt{2}$ proportion:[22]

(1) Draw a square.
(2) Inscribe within it a smaller square, the corners of which are the midpoints of the first.
(3) Repeat the operation.
(4) Rotate the second square 45° so that all three are parallel and concentric, and have a constant $\sqrt{2}$ ratio between their widths (see Figure 10.2).

19. Vitruvius, *The Ten Books on Architecture*, p. 14.
20. K.J. Conant, 'The after-life of Vitruvius in the Middle Ages', *Journal of the Society of Architectural Historians*, XXVII (1), March 1968, p. 34.
21. L.R. Shelby, *Gothic Design Techniques*, Southern Illinois University Press, 1977.
22. *Ibid.*, pp. 84-6.

The elevations are then derived by extrapolation from the plan.

The *German Geometry* offers methods for constructing the regular pentagon, heptagon and octagon, for calculating the circumference of a circle of given diameter, and for drawing a square and equilateral triangle of equal area. Since most of these are only approximate they were presumably discovered by trial and error rather than by geometrical deduction. Although the *Elements* of Euclid had been available in Latin for about three centuries, it does not seem that Roriczer was familiar with them. Had he been, he would surely have made use of Euclid's simpler and exact construction for the pentagon (see Chapter eight, section 8.2) instead of the cumbersome and approximate one he describes. As his modern commentator writes, 'It is obvious that Roriczer was a long way from the mathematical science of geometry as it was understood by Euclid and Archimedes in antiquity.'[23] There is no evidence that Roriczer knew of the golden section, which is the basis of the correct – and incidentally simpler – construction for the regular decagon and pentagon that Alberti[24] and Serlio (1475–1554)[25] derived from the late Alexandrian mathematician Pappus (*c.* AD 300). Surprisingly, in view of the importance of the square root of three (*ad triangulum*) in Gothic architecture – and despite the fact that his approximation for the pentagon incidentally involves it – Roriczer makes no specific mention of this proportion. Thus his works provide us with very few and insubstantial clues on which to base a search for Gothic proportioning methods.

10.3 THE MILAN CATHEDRAL CONTROVERSY

In contrast, the records of the conflicting arguments put forward by the various architects invited to advise on the problems posed by the design of Milan Cathedral offer the most complete documentary evidence we have concerning Medieval proportion theory. The Milan documents are discussed briefly by Rudolf Wittkower in *Gothic versus Classic* (1974),[26] but James Ackerman gives a more detailed account of them in his essay *Ars Sine Scientia Nihil Est* (1949).[27] The cathedral was begun in 1386 in the Lombard

23. *Ibid.*, p. 63.
24. L.B. Alberti, *On the Art of Building in Ten Books*, MIT Press, 1988, p. 196.
25. S. Serlio, *On Architecture*, trans. V. Hart and P. Hicks, Yale University Press, 1996, vol. I, p. 29.
26. R. Wittkower, *Gothic versus Classic*, Thames & Hudson, 1974, pp. 21-4.
27. J.S. Ackerman, 'Ars sine scientia nihil est: Gothic theory of architecture at the Cathedral of Milan', in *Distance Points*, MIT Press, 1991, pp. 211-63.

Gothic manner, but it soon became apparent that this local tradition was inadequate to deal with so large a construction. The building council therefore called in a succession of advisers from northern France and Germany, and it is largely to the records of the debates between these and the local masters that we owe the documentation.

The plan, already determined by foundations laid before the foreign experts were called in, established an overall width of ninety-six *braccia* or arm-lengths. The length of the *braccio* varied fairly widely from place to place in Italy; the Milanese *braccio* measured about 595 mm, a little less than two English feet. The total width was divided into six units of sixteen *braccia*, two for the central nave and one each for the four aisles. The crucial problem was to decide the heights of these bays and of the whole building; it therefore turned essentially on a question of proportion, which the Medieval master masons seem to have regarded as a sure guide to structural stability. If the proportions were sound, so would be the structure: proportion was seen literally as (in Plato's words) 'the bond that holds things together'.

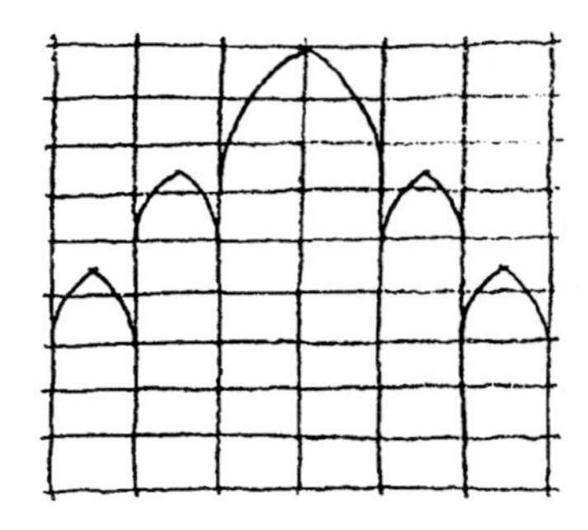

Figure 10.3 Section of Milan Cathedral, proposal of Nicolas de Bonaventure, 1389.

In 1389 the first adviser, Nicolas de Bonaventure, proposed a total height of ninety *braccia*, divided into nine units of ten. The rectangle containing the cross-section therefore comprised fifty-four unit rectangles of sixteen by ten, a proportion of 8 : 5 (see Figure 10.3). Enthusiasts for the golden section might seize on this Fibonacci ratio as evidence that the golden rectangle was the key to the intended proportional scheme. What is more striking, however, is that all the dimensions are perfectly commensurable, and suited to measurement rather than geometrical setting-out. As Ackerman comments:

> Such a unit has a sound utilitarian purpose, for it is calculated to provide measurements which might be followed readily by a mason equipped only with a measuring stick (in this case, probably 5 braccia in length).[28]

The numbers ten and sixteen correspond, moreover, to Vitruvius' statement that the Italians, 'observing that six and ten were both of them perfect numbers,. . . combined the two, and thus made the most perfect number, sixteen'.[29]

Nicolas' advice was rejected, however, and in 1391 his successor, Annas de Firimburg, proposed a scheme based on

28. *Ibid.*, p. 218.
29. Vitruvius, *The Ten Books on Architecture*, p. 74.

the equilateral triangle, the ratio of the total height to half the width being therefore $\sqrt{3} : 1$. Here, at last, is evidence of geometry and the use of an irrational square root proportion: *ad triangulum*. But it was precisely the incommensurability of the square root of three that led the building council to seek the advice of a mathematician, Gabriele Stornaloco, who substituted a rational approximation, 7 : 4, for the irrational ratio. The total height, now eighty-four *braccia*, was divided into six units of fourteen. The heights of the vaults, which had not fitted Nicolas' ten *braccia* module, were now defined exactly by the 8 : 7 rectangular grid (see Figure 10.4). Again, all the evidence suggests the use of a metrical rather than a geometical method of setting-out, and consequently the *avoidance* of irrational numbers.

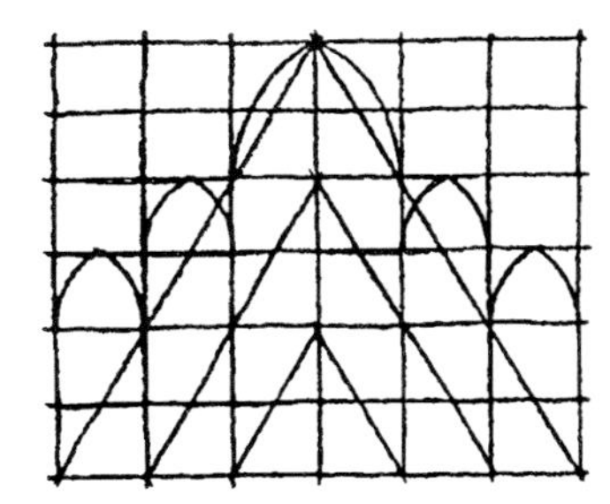

Figure 10.4 Section of Milan Cathedral, proposal of Annas de Firimburg, 1391.

This proposal, too, was rejected, and the following year a third foreign expert was called in, Heinrich Parler of Gmünd. He put forward an *ad quadratum* scheme, by which the containing rectangle was now an exact square of ninety-six *braccia*, subdivided in both directions into units of sixteen by sixteen. The diagonal of the square, the irrational square root of two, played no part in the proportions, however; the mathematical scheme was as rational and commensurable, and thus as 'perfect', as could be (see Figure 10.5). But this was likewise rejected, and the final proposal, made in 1392, was a compromise. The lower two segments of Stornaloco's scheme, totalling twenty-eight *braccia* in height, were retained, but thereafter the vertical module was reduced, from fourteen to twelve *braccia*. The defining figure for this upper part was a Pythagorean triangle, with sides in the rational proportion 3 : 4 : 5. The whole height was thereby reduced to seventy-six *braccia* (see Figure 10.6).

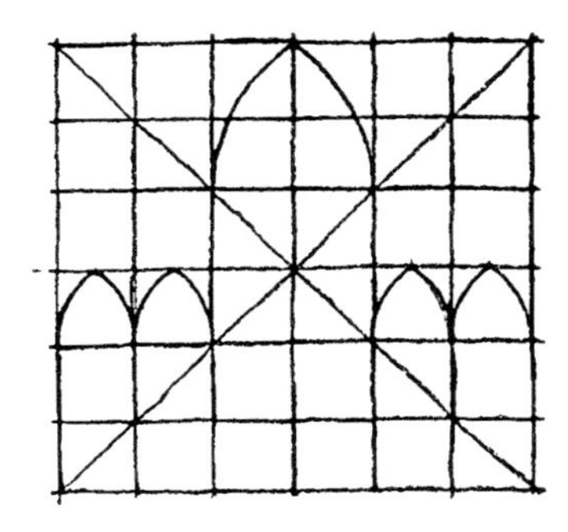

Figure 10.5 Section of Milan Cathedral, proposal of Heinrich Parler, 1392.

The entire episode undermines the assumption that Gothic proportion was the result of geometrical rather than metrical setting-out methods – that is, the doctrine that not only ground plans but even elevations were established by stretched cords and pegs instead of being measured out with yardsticks. The neat division, made by Wittkower,[30] Scholfield[31] and others, according to which Renaissance proportion was wholly metrical and rational, and Medieval proportion geometrical and irrational, proves to be greatly exaggerated, if not completely unfounded. The Milanese records give little or no support to the theory that the *ad quadratum* and *ad triangulum* principles were the sole key to

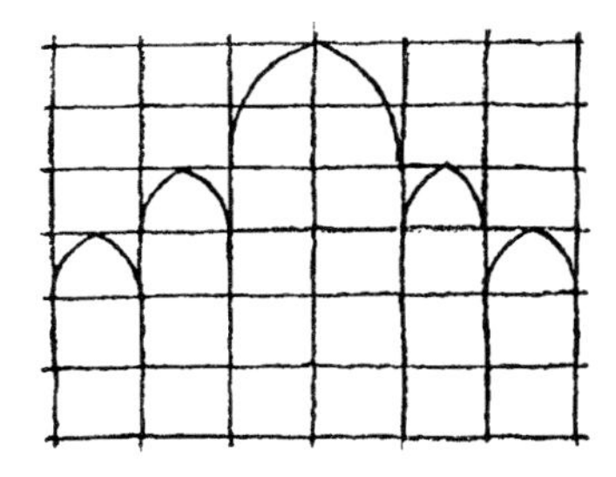

Figure 10.6 Section of Milan Cathedral, final proposal, 1392.

30. R. Wittkower, 'The changing concept of proportion', pp. 116–7.
31. P.H. Scholfield, *The Theory of Proportion in Architecture*, Cambridge University Press, 1958.

Gothic proportion, still less that there was a preference for incommensurable square root ratios derived from geometrical setting-out. Conversely, as regards the Renaissance, while as we shall see in the next chapter the whole-number ratios certainly had a particular impact, there is ample evidence in the works of Alberti, Leonardo, Pacioli and Palladio of continued interest in the irrational proportions connected with the regular polygons and polyhedra. In short, no one principle of proportion can be attributed with any confidence to any particular period.

10.4 THE PROPORTIONS OF CHARTRES CATHEDRAL

Of all Medieval buildings, the one that most obviously stands out with a pre-eminence comparable to that enjoyed by the Parthenon among Greek temples is the cathedral of Chartres. Both buildings replaced earlier structures that had perished in a disaster: the earlier Parthenon had been demolished by the Persians in the sack of Athens in 480–479 BC, while most of the Romanesque cathedral of Chartres was destroyed by fire in 1194. Both were rebuilt relatively quickly – the rebuilding of Chartres was substantially completed between 1194 and 1224 – and each was partly the fruit of a political power struggle. Just as Pericles sponsored the rebuilding of the Parthenon – and, according to Rhys Carpenter, ordered and financed the dismantling and reconstruction on a grander scale of the already partly completed new temple in order to outshine his rival Kimon[32] – so too 'The munificence of the Capetian kings toward Notre Dame of Chartres was designed to underscore and enhance the importance of the basilica as a royal cathedral.'[33] The royal house had recently made an alliance with its former local rivals, the counts of Chartres; 'It was fortunate,' writes Otto von Simson,

> that this political constellation coincided with the reconstruction of the cathedral. . . The great sanctuary. . . bears eloquent testimony to the fact that the rulers of France and Chartres vied with one another in embellishing it.[34]

32. R. Carpenter, *The Architects of the Parthenon*, Penguin Books, 1970, pp. 69–81.
33. O. von Simson, *The Gothic Cathedral*, p. 174.
34. *Ibid.*, p. 175.

The proportions of Chartres, like those of the Parthenon, have been repeatedly analysed, and explained in terms of both the two classes that Wittkower identifies: that based on geometry and incommensurable ratios such as the golden section, and that based on Pythagorean number theory. I shall consider only two of the many interpretations: the one sketched out by von Simson in *The Gothic Cathedral*,[35] and the extremely thorough investigation published by John James in *The Contractors of Chartres*.[36]

10.5 OTTO VON SIMSON

Von Simson's main thesis is that the Gothic cathedral was designed as a model or image of the mathematical structure of the universe, conceived, as in Plato's *Timaeus*, as a divine creation: a harmonious ordering of chaotic matter 'by measure, number and weight'.[37] According to him, however, the underlying geometry of the building, rather than its numerical ordering, played the major part in this: he discovers the cathedral's proportions to be dominated by the golden section. This is an odd conclusion, in view of von Simson's account, in the chapter on *Measure and Light*, of the predominantly Augustinian – and therefore musical and numerical rather than geometrical – philosophies of the two schools of thought that he posits as the two major influences on the design of Chartres. In that earlier chapter he writes that

> According to Augustinian aesthetics, the musical consonances in visual proportions created by man partake of a sacred concord that transcends them. . . In the second quarter of the twelfth century. . . Augustine's philosophy of beauty was seized upon by two powerful intellectual movements in France. The first of these centered in the group of eminent Platonists assembled at the Cathedral School of Chartres; the second movement, antispeculative and ascetic, emanated from the great monastic houses of Citeaux and Clairvaux; its personification was St Bernard.[38]

Von Simson bases his proportional analysis on two principal givens:

35. *Ibid.*, pp. 207–15.
36. J.R.H. James, *The Contractors of Chartres*, Mandorla Publications, 1981.
37. *Wisdom of Solomon*, quoted in O. von Simson, *The Gothic Cathedral*, p. 22.
38. O. von Simson, *The Gothic Cathedral*, pp. 24–5.

(1) The cross-section of the building comprises an exact square, 32.9 m in height from the keystone of the vault to the plinth, and 32.9 m in width between the outer walls of the nave and aisles. The crossing occupies half this total width, or 16.44 m. Von Simson assumes that the whole width was divided into one hundred feet of 329 mm each, making the crossing width fifty and each aisle twenty-five feet (see Figure 10.7).
(2) The longitudinal dimensions are all less than the lateral ones, however. Thus the crossing is not square, but measures only 13.99 m in length.

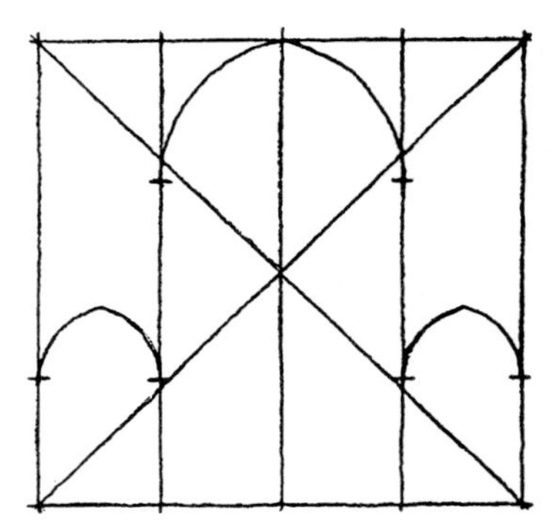

Figure 10.7 Chartres: cross-section contained in square, according to O. von Simson.

Just as the width of the nave is twice that of the aisles, so too, in the longitudinal direction, the length of two average bays of the nave arcade equals that of the crossing, that is, 13.99 m. Moreover, the bays are subtly paired to make up a unit equal to the crossing:

> The master has employed alternation without sacrificing the principle of homogeneity. His piers consist, alternatively, of a cylindrical core surrounded by octagonal colonnetes, and an octagonal core surrounded by cylindrical colonnettes.'[39]

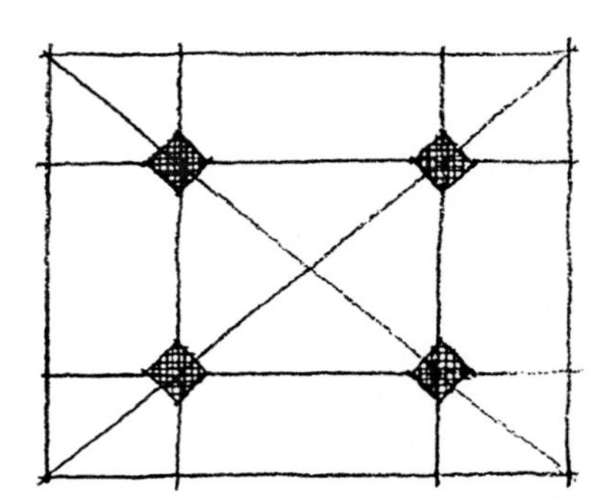

Figure 10.8 Chartres: plan of crossing.

Thus one can say that the fundamental component of the plan is a rectangle 32.9 m wide and 27.98 m long (see Figure 10.8). So if the first datum for the proportions is the squareness of the cross-section, the second is the *non*-squareness of the crossing and of the typical plan bay. Von Simson asks: 'What calculation led the architect to determine the length of the crossing – and that of the bays of the nave and choir – after this fashion?'[40]

He asserts that the Medieval architect determined all dimensions geometrically on site, using cords and pegs to set them out on the basis of a chosen key dimension – in this case 16.44 m. (This assumption conflicts, as we have seen, with the evidence of the Milan documents.) He observes that the geometrical figure that would yield a ratio of 16.44 : 13.99 is the regular pentagon. We know from Chapter 8, section 8.2, that the ratio of the side of the pentagon to the radius of its circumscribing circle is $\sqrt{1 + \phi^{-2}}$ or approximately 1.1755 : 1 (see Figure 10.9). So if 16.44 m is the side of the pentagon, the radius will be 16.44/1.1755 = 13.985:

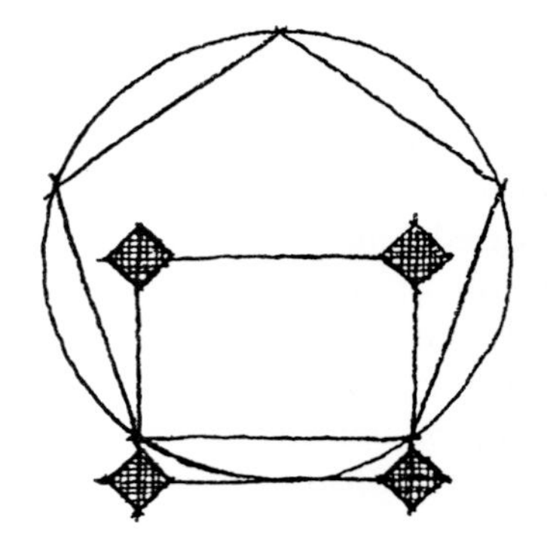

Figure 10.9 Chartres: crossing shape derived from the regular pentagon, according to O. von Simson.

39. ***Ibid.*, p. 206.**
40. ***Ibid.*, p. 207.**
41. ***Ibid.*, p. 208.**

> The correspondence between this figure and 13.99 is far too close to be accidental. . . The use of the pentagon by the master of Chartres is of great interest. The Gothic artist knew the golden section. . . .[41]

If the golden section was indeed used at Chartres, not only indirectly in the layout of the crossing but directly, as von Simson goes on to speculate, in the elevations, this would certainly be 'of great interest'. The golden section becomes the key to the spirit of the whole design. But did the Gothic builders really know of it? Their knowledge of the pentagon and its approximate construction is confirmed, as we have seen, by Mathes Roriczer's *German Geometry*. However, Roriczer's construction is not only inaccurate but, more importantly in this context, makes no use of the golden section, nor is any golden section or $\sqrt{5}$ construction, such as the square-in-semicircle, included in his book.

Moreover, the construction is extremely cumbersome. It would require seventeen separate operations, a vast diagram marked out with seventeen pegs and cords, spread out over an area measuring about fifty metres in each direction on the presumably uneven and obstructed building site. What is surprising is not that an error of five millimetres arose, but that it was not far larger. Is it credible that a builder, needing to establish the proportions of the crossing, would set about it in this laborious and indirect way, rather than simply measuring it out with a rod? A further objection is that by this operation the integrity of the foot measure, embodied in the hundred-foot dimension of the height and width of the church, has been completely lost sight of. The length of the crossing, being based on an irrational number, ϕ, is incommensurable with its width: 13.99 m is not divisible by 329 mm.

These problems are compounded when von Simson transfers his pentagonal construction to the interior elevation. First, in order to obtain the key vertical dimension for the elevation, thus integrating it with the plan, he requires a regular decagon to be inscribed within the same circle that contains the pentagon, and that the side of this decagon, $13.99/\phi$ or 8.646 m, be applied to the elevation as the height from the top of the plinth of the nave piers to the springing of the nave arcade. By multiplying or dividing this dimension by ϕ he obtains larger and smaller measures: the height of the shafts, from the top of the nave piers to the springing of the vault (which he gives as 13.85 m), and the distance from the top of the nave piers to the lower string course (5.345 m). But why is it necessary to arrive at these dimensions by such a roundabout route, via the side of a decagon inscribed in a circle that is itself circumscribed around a pentagon, the side of which corresponds in turn to the width of the crossing? And then to have to reconstruct these dimensions, still using stretched cords and pegs, somehow suspended in the air (since the elevation has not yet, of course, been built)?

Von Simson admits 'the difficulties of taking vertical measurements by means of cords',[42] but only to explain a small inaccuracy of 3 cm in the measurements, not to suggest how the apparently insoluble technical problem might have been overcome. He does not distinguish, in fact, between the relative ease of measuring out *known* lengths with tapes or rods, and the more difficult geometrical construction, on site, of new, *unknown* dimensions, such as the irrational golden section measures he quotes. Measurement by rods, as Ackerman says was envisaged at Milan, is by far the more practical method; but this requires reasonably simple whole-number measures. And it so happens that 13.85, 8.646 and 5.345 m translate into 329 mm foot-units reasonably well, as respectively 42 ft 0 in, 26 ft 3 in and 16 ft 3 in. Von Simson overlooks this, however.

Nevertheless, he concludes that

> In Chartres, proportion is experienced as the harmonious articulation of a comprehensive whole; it determines the ground plan as well as the elevation; and it 'chains', by the single ratio of the golden section, the individual parts not only to one another but also to the whole that encompasses them all. The same desire for unification that induced the architect to treat piers and superimposed shafts not as independent units but rather as articulations of a continuous vertical rhythm suggested to him the choice of the proportion that might indeed be called the mathematical equivalent of that unifying design.'[43]

42. *Ibid.*, p. 209.
43. *Ibid.*, p. 214.

10.6 JOHN JAMES

Between von Simson and John James there is a fundamental difference of approach. Where von Simson sits in his library studying the writings of Augustine and Boethius, which underly the Platonic philosophy of the School of Chartres, and looks at the measurements of the cathedral within the parameters of this mathematico-metaphysical framework, one imagines James with a tape-measure, crouched on hands and knees in the dusty spaces over the vaults or in the triforium, measuring the height of every stone course and the profile of each moulding with extreme accuracy. He bases his speculation on these painstaking measurements, made to a tolerance of 20–50 mm for the larger dimensions involving the building as a whole or its main elements, such as bay widths, and only 2 mm for details. As a result of this patient detective work he discovers two things of great significance for the general theory of Gothic proportion.

(1) The cathedral was built – like one assumes most others at the time – in a succession of short 'campaigns' by a series of different masters and their teams of craftsmen. This staccato work pattern was made necessary, not only by the running out of overstretched funds, but also by technology: the fatty lime mortars used needed time to gain full strength before work could proceed further. James estimates that each team would have comprised a core of about a hundred skilled men, who followed their master from job to job: 'The crew would have been no larger than a fair sized circus of today – and indeed, this is a not unfair comparison.'[44] He has traced the work of the same teams who worked at Chartres to other centres: Reims, Le Mans, Laon and so on. Each newly arrived architect was forced to adapt to the geometry and the measure-system established by his predecessors:

> Once one understands that there is no reason why great architecture cannot be created in this additive way... then the apparent chaos in the organization of these giant structures begins to reveal an underlying order. Nine contracting teams built the bulk of the cathedral, returning again and again in a disorderly and little super-vised annual sequence for over thirty years. Beyond

44. J.R.H. James, *The Contractors of Chartres*, p. 12.

Chartres, from Tours to Reims there seem to have been less than thirty crews who between them worked on all the greatest buildings that survive to us.[45]

(2) An almost sacred importance was attached by the Medieval architects to standard measures and to the use of whole units. Each succeeding team at Chartres had its own preferred measure, and used it consistently throughout the period of its involvement. Since each master kept to his own foot measure, which was regarded with a reverence quite alien to our casual attitude to the impersonal and infinitely divisible metre, the study of the proportioning system must begin by identifying these measures – and in particular the foot used by the first master – whom James dubs 'Scarlet' – in laying out the plan. Scarlet's successors were constrained by this choice, and would have had to relate their own measures to his by some simple rule of conversion. James concludes from his measurements that this original master adopted a Roman foot of 294.45 mm. He lists thirteen standard feet, however, many descended from remote antiquity, and ranging in length from 277 to 370 mm. None corresponds exactly to von Simson's 329 mm unit, although the Teuton foot of 332 mm is fairly close. These are set out in Table 10.1.

TABLE 10.1 Standard feet in mm

Megalithic	277
Punic	280.5
Roman	294–296
Egyptian	299.6
English	303–305
Olympic	308
Cretan – small	316
Cretan – large (*pied du roi*)	321–325
Teuton	332–335
Royal	346–349
pes manualis	354
Black	360
Sumerian	366–370

Since these foot measures were the basis of all dimensioning, it follows that if incommensurable measures derived from geometrical figures were used they would have had to be adjusted to exact foot multiples. Exact geometry must give way to exact arithmetic; nevertheless, the arithmetic, according to James, is first derived from geometry. In other words, the numbers chosen are always convergents for irrational geometrical relationships derived from simple figures such as the square, pentagon and hexagon.

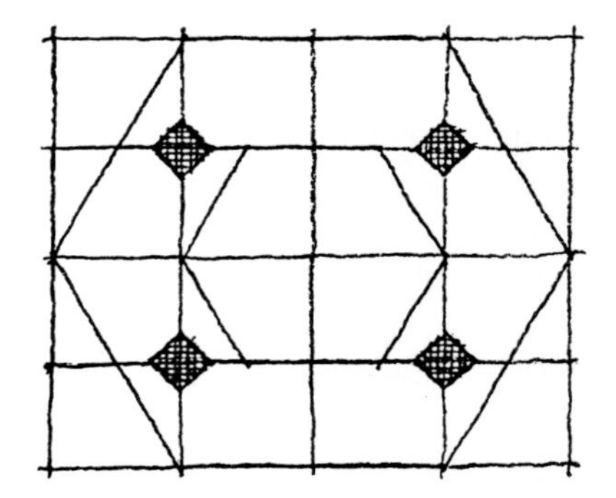

Figure 10.10 Chartres: crossing shape derived from the regular hexagon, according to J. James.

Thus whereas he interprets the geometry of the crossing and its surrounding bays in terms of the hexagon – in contrast to von Simson's pentagon – it is a hexagon whose perfect regularity is sacrificed to whole-number arithmetic. The spatial unit comprises the crossing itself as core, surrounded by an outer ring composed of the first bays of the nave, choir and transepts. James regards the crossing as measuring 56 × 48 RF (a Roman foot measuring 294.45 mm), and the overall dimensions of the whole spatial unit as 112 × 97 RF. The ratio 97 : 112 or 0.866 : 1 is a very good approximation for $\sqrt{3}:2$, the relation between the height

45. *Ibid.*, pp. 14–5.

and base of an equilateral triangle, or between the inscribed and circumscribed circles of a regular hexagon (see Figure 10.10). The ratio 48 : 56, that is, 6 : 7 or 0.857 : 1, is a slightly less good one. The numbers 3, 7, 56 and 97 appear, incidentally, as numerators and denominators in the continued fraction, which converges towards $\sqrt{3}$: 1/1, 2/1, 5/3, 7/4, 19/11, 26/15, 71/41, 97/56,. . . (see Chapter 4, section 4.3). The resulting foot measures are given in Table 10.2, together with their metric equivalents and James' average real measurements.

Assuming James' measurements to be correct, and the results of taking averages to be meaningful, his ideal proportion of the crossing, 56/48 or 1.1666. . ., gives a perfect match to the actual ratio. It fits far better than von Simson's 1.1756 derived from the pentagon, and has the added advantage of being more simply and more easily constructed. However, despite his painstaking measurements and his insistence on the hallowed character of the master's foot unit, there is a fairly wide disparity between his assumed foot measures and the individual dimensions. His nominal measures are merely mathematical averages of actual dimensions that vary widely between themselves. The lengths of the nave and choir bays range between 6.09 and 7.58 m, and those of the transepts between 7.17 and 8.24 m, while within the crossing itself there is a difference of 145 mm from east to west, and 100 mm from north to south. Moreover, few actual bay dimensions are even nearly approximate multiples of the 294.45 mm foot. One is forced to agree with Choisy's judgement, that the irregularity of the construction encountered in Medieval buildings makes it virtually impossible to determine the proportional scheme from measurements, and that only the simplest relations, apparent to the eye, give any basis for judgement.[46]

The most significant relation in the whole plan is the grandest. It is the distance from the centre of the crossing, the midpoint of the whole scheme, to the two other foci: the centre of the altar, which is also the rond-point of the apse, and the centre of the circular labyrinth that coincides with the axis of the fourth pier of the nave. It cannot be accidental that these distances are very nearly equal: James gives them as 35.592 and 35.37 m: that is, 120.878 and 120.122 RF, or 241 RF together. He sees this total measure as the diameter of the circumscribing circle of yet another hexagonal figure. The opposite sides of the figure, whose distance apart he

TABLE 10.2

ELEMENT	RF	METRES (RF × 0.29445)	METRES (ACTUAL)
Length of average nave/choir bay	24	7.07	7.08
Length of crossing	48	14.13	14.01
Total width of transept and aisles	97	28.56	28.26
Width of crossing	56	16.49	16.35
Total width of nave and aisles	112	32.98	32.54

46. A. Choisy, *Histoire de l'architecture*, Bibliothèque de l'Image, 1996, vol. II, p. 403.

gives as 208.7 ft, determine the end walls of the transepts (see Figure 10.11). The ratio of 208.7 to the half of 241 is again a good approximation for $\sqrt{3}$ (1.731 95 instead of 1.732 05).

James' analysis of the elevations lacks the unity of von Simson's, and fails to integrate the vertical proportions with the shapes in plan. For the elevations he brings into play the whole armoury of known proportion systems, mixing together whole number ratios such as 5 : 2, 5 : 6 and 3 : 4 with the square roots of two and three, these with the golden section, and composing yet further, more complicated ratios, by multipication and division of these irrational numbers. Even von Simson's pentagon makes a reappearance. The more different and mutually conflicting the solutions he introduces, the more his interpretation loses credibility. One has the impression that in his patient research he became so closely involved with every nook and cranny of the building that he could no longer see it as a whole: he saw each individual stone, but lost sight of the cathedral.

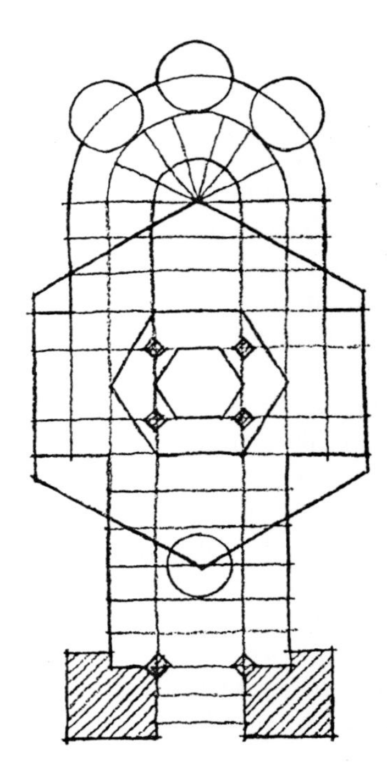

Figure 10.11 Chartres: ground plan derived from the regular hexagon, according to J. James.

10.7 TOWARDS A SIMPLER AND MORE COMPREHENSIVE SOLUTION

Let us try to look, therefore, at the cathedral's proportions in very broad terms, considering only what Auguste Choisy, in his *Histoire de l'architecture*, calls *les rapports simples*: those 'simple relations' that reveal themselves to the eye at first sight, without measurement or calculation.[47] As examples, Choisy cites not Chartres but Notre Dame and Amiens (see Figure 10.12):

> At Notre-Dame the evident intention has been to give the body of the facade the figure of a square, above which the towers rise to a height equal to half the side of this square; at Amiens the architect based the composition [of the interior elevation] on two large equal divisions, separated at mid height by a string course.[48]

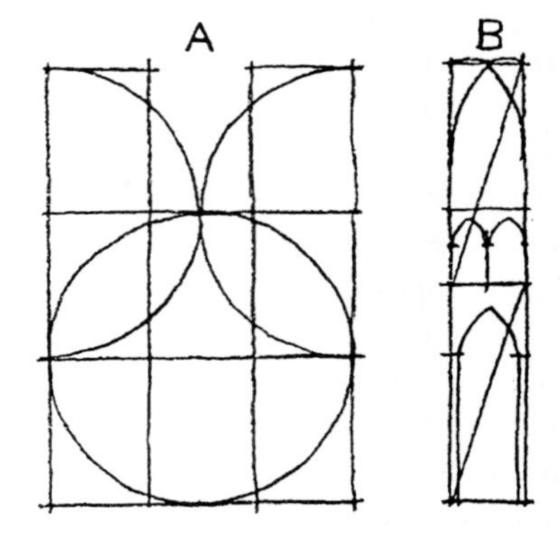

Figure 10.12 Notre Dame and Amiens: proportion diagrams after A. Choisy.

The case of Chartres is more complicated than either of these examples, however. Not only do the separate dimensions fluctuate wildly around any possible standard measure, but the central axis of the whole cathedral is violently skewed. As John James remarks,

47. *Ibid.*
48. *Ibid.*, p. 404.

> The plan sways and pulses like a living thing. . . Until I understood the way the axes had been bent I was unable to uncover the first geometry, for it was all too chaotic with each side swinging past the other, and with intermediate parts like chapels squeezed or stretched to fit. . . The master's formal design lies hidden below his surface irregularities. As with a flower, the mathematics has to be sought beyond the individuality of each plant.[49]

The best one can hope to do, consequently, is to suggest the broad lines of this underlying 'formal design'. In the difficult business of reconstructing the proportions of such a building what matters is not so much mathematical accuracy as

(1) the *spirit* in which the whole structure appears to have been designed,
(2) the mathematical knowledge available to the builders, and
(3) the technical feasibility and rationality of the setting-out operation demanded.

I shall consider only the proportions of the plan and the interior elevations. The most striking feature of the plan is that it is governed by three major foci: the centres of the crossing, of the labyrinth and of the apse. The crossing is twice as long as a typical nave or choir bay. There are altogether five crossing-lengths or double bay-lengths between the centre of the labyrinth and that of the apse. James gives the total length from centre to centre as a little over seventy metres, making the average double bay-length about fourteen metres. His corresponding lateral dimension averages about 32.5 m.

When we turn to the interior elevations, James' dimensions roughly (but not exactly) confirm von Simson's assumption that the cross-section of the main body of the church fits into a square. The overall height, measured from the plinth, is in fact about 2% more than the width. This does not invalidate von Simson's interpretation, however; no one would seriously suggest that a proportion of 51 : 50 was intended instead of 1 : 1. The small discrepancy is hardly surprising, given the thirty-year interval between the setting-out of the plan and the vaulting of the nave, and the succession of masters who followed each other over this period, each with his preferred foot measure. The most likely

49. J.R.H. James, *The Contractors of Chartres*, pp. 144, 146.

candidate for the dominant foot measure used, at least for the elevations, is what James calls the commercial or large Cretan foot (CF), in this case 320 mm. Taking James' measurement for the height from the plinth to the keystone of the vault, 33.63 m, as a datum, we get a total of 105 CF. If the elevation of the nave were laid flat across the floor, it would fit over the plan (see Figure 10.13).

Second, we find that the dimension of the crossing or of two typical nave bays, about 14.4 m or 45 CF, is repeated three times as a vertical measure: as the height from the floor to the lower string course, as the height of the shafts above the piers, measured from the pier capitals to springing of the vault, and finally as the distance from the upper string course to the keystone of the vault. The elevation of a double nave bay thus comprises three overlapping 45 CF squares. The triforium, contained between the two string courses, forms an intermediary zone of 15 CF between the lower and upper squares, and these are overlapped by the third 45 CF square, which has the effect of binding the whole composition together (see Figure 10.14). The height of the triforium being exactly a third of that of one of the squares, the proportion of the double bay is 7 : 3.

The vertical measures of the elevation are all sums composed of three basic dimensions, which we can call A, B and C. The smallest, A, is the distance from the upper string course to the springing of the vault; the second, B, is the height of the triforium; and the largest, C, is the distance between the top of the nave piers and the lower string course – that is, the zone containing the nave arches. The ratio $A : B : C$ is 4 : 5 : 6. Since $B = 15$ CF, it follows that $A = 12$ and $C = 18$ CF. The three together make up the dimension of the intermediate overlapping square, 45 CF.

The full range of dimensions is set out in Table 10.3, where it is compared with John James' survey measurements (see Figure 10.15). His horizontal measures (in italics) are augmented by 2% to compensate for the slight increase of the vertical dimensions. The dimensions of the crossing, G and F, given here as 52.5 and 45 CF, make the proportion of the typical plan compartment 7 : 6. This complies with James' finding. However, the dimensions are not only slightly too large but introduce fractional units: the overall width is 105 CF, the nave width is $52^1/_2$ CF and the width of each aisle is $26^1/_4$ CF. Was the standard measure changed between the laying-out of the plan and the building of the walls? If

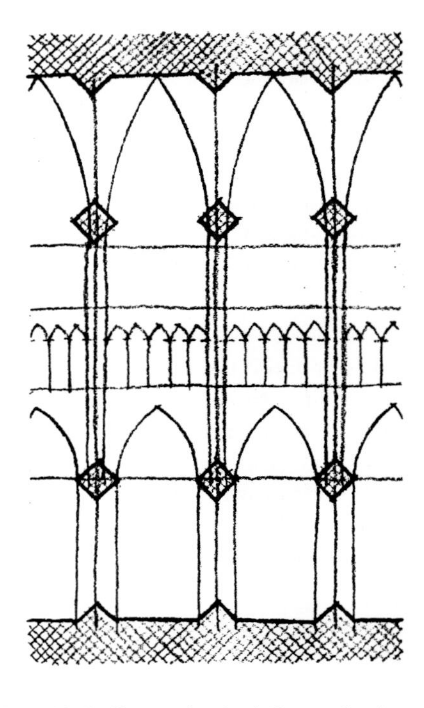

Figure 10.13 Chartres: elevation laid across the plan, according to J. James.

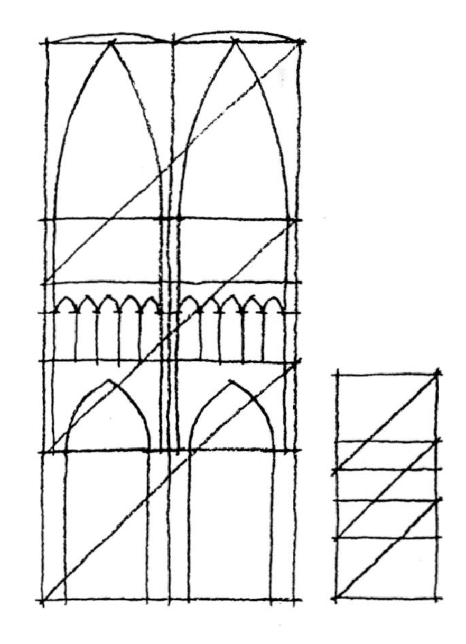

Figure 10.14 Chartres: analysis of interior elevation based on overlapping squares.

the planning unit is James' 294.45 mm Roman foot, and the 320 mm Cretan foot applies only to the elevations, then the two sets of dimensions nearly coincide at 112 RF = 105 CF. The discrepancy is almost exactly 2%, since 112 × 0.294 45 = 32.98 m, 105 × 0.32 = 33.6 m, and 33.6/32.98 = 1.0188 = nearly 2% more than 1. The 2% difference between the horizontal and vertical dimensions is thus explained. The widths of nave and aisles can now be measured in whole units: 56 and 28 RF.

Both 105 and 112 are multiples of seven. Is this significant? The number seven has always had strong symbolic associations. In the case of Chartres it had particular meaning, together with nine, as a symbol connected with the Virgin Mary, of whose cult and pilgrimage Chartres was the centre. In view of this symbolic importance the recurrence of the number seven, often in association with six, nine or twelve, merits consideration as a factor in the proportional scheme.

We have already encountered two examples. The height of the triforium, which forms the central band of the elevation and the intermediary between the two 45 CF squares above and below it, is one seventh of the whole height; and the proportion of the typical plan compartment is 7 : 6. There are also seven bays in the apse, and it is surrounded by seven chapels. But there is another, still more obvious example: there are seven bays in the nave. In order to achieve this number the architects went to the trouble of cutting back the existing west towers to a depth of over 2 m; even then the last three bays of the nave are squeezed into a space about 2.5 m too short. John James comments that

> It is as if the master had been instructed by the clergy to incorporate both seven and nine. . . for in doing so he had to reconcile this instruction with his geometry, and the three squashed bays at the west represent the unavoidable compromise that resulted. These conflicting ideas on number and geometry had to be fitted within the solid boundaries formed by the remains of the old building.[50]

There is little doubt that all this was intentional, because the seventh bay is terminated by two extra-large, many-shafted piers matching those of the crossing. These are clearly meant to mark off the nave proper from the two bays between the towers, which function as a narthex (see Figure 10.11).

TABLE 10.3

	COMPOSITION (PERMUTATIONS OF *A*, *B*, *C*)	CF	METRES (CF × 0.32)	METRES (ACTUAL)
A	1*A*	12	3.84	4.05
B	1B	15	4.8	4.74
C	1C	18	5.76	5.73
D	*A* + *B*	27	8.64	(1) 8.52 (2) 8.79
E	*B* + *C*	33	10.56	10.58
F	*A* + *B* + *C* = 3*B*	45	14.4	(1) *14.4* (2) 14.25 (3) 14.53 (4) 14.63
G	$\frac{2A + 3B + 2C}{2}$	52.5	16.8	*16.89*
H	2*A* + 2*B* + *C* = 4*C*	72	23.04	23.05
I	2*A* + 3*B* + 2*C*	105	33.6	(1) *33.58* (2) 33.63

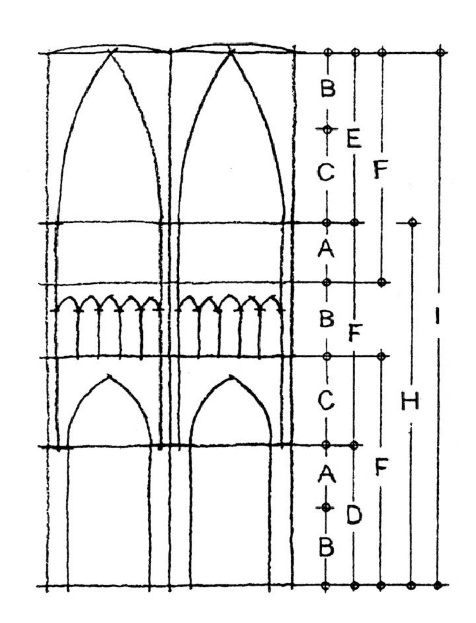

Figure 10.15 Chartres: analysis of interior elevation; key to Table 10.3.

50. *Ibid.*, p. 160.

A further example relates to the plan as a whole. The total length of the nave and choir, from the just-mentioned twin piers to the farthest point of the apse, comprises seven double bay units, marked out by the alternation of round and octagonal piers. These units are divided by the central axis of the crossing into a group of four and a group of three – numbers likewise charged with symbolism (see Figure 10.16). Allowing 48 RF for each unit, the total length would be 336 RF, and it is actually very close to this figure, because the extra depth of the apse makes up for the contraction of the last three bays of the nave. Taking it as exactly 336 RF, the main space composing the nave with its aisles and the chancel, 112 RF wide and 105 CF high, is contained within three cubes (see Figure 10.17).

These speculations go beyond our main purpose, however, which was to seek out what Choisy calls *les rapports simples*, relations apparent to the eye, and methods of setting out the dimensions of a building that would have made sense to the people on the ground. We have found a series of whole-number foot dimensions that would have allowed the work to be measured out with a yardstick – perhaps literally a three foot measure, since all the vertical dimensions are multiples of three feet. Cords and pegs would still have been needed, of course, as they are today, to determine right angles. Apart from this, measuring with rods is more feasible, particularly where elevations are concerned, than the exclusive use of geometry and the incommensurable square root dimensions that arise from diagonals of squares or double squares, pentagons or hexagons.

It is not suggested, however, that we have here finally 'solved' the mystery of the proportions of Chartres. The analysis can be more reasonably regarded as a way of 'scanning' the proportions – that is, making them intelligible for ourselves – than as a reconstruction of the method necessarily used by the architects. Nevertheless, it helps to confirm what the Milanese records suggest: that the elaborate star diagrams invented by Macody Lund, Moessel and other theorists are probably without foundation. The contrast between the proportioning methods of Medieval and Renaissance architects is less profound than Wittkower implies when he writes, in *The Changing Concept of Proportion*, that

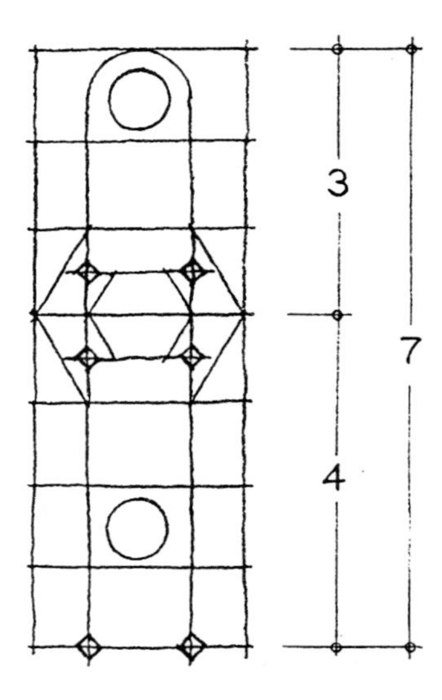

Figure 10.16 Chartres: analysis of the plan showing seven compartments.

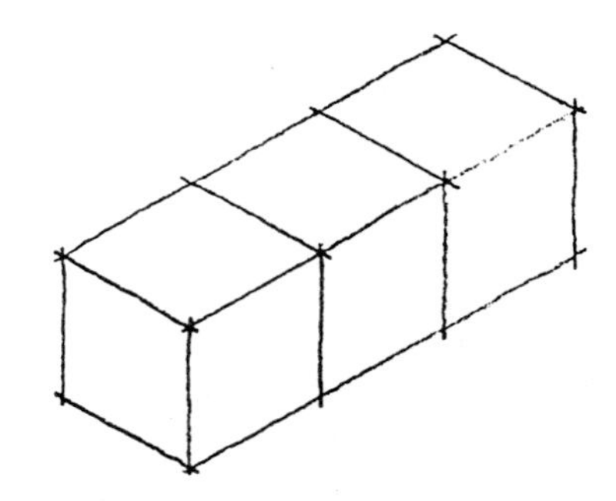

Figure 10.17 Chartres: volume of the nave and chancel contained in three cubes.

> While to the organic, metrical Renaissance view of the world rational measure was a *sine qua non*, for the logical, predominantly Aristotelian medieval approach to the world the problem of metrical measure hardly arose.[51]

10.8 THE RECOVERY OF ARISTOTLE BY THE WEST

Thus far I have discussed what can be gleaned about Gothic proportions from the examination of a particular building. The remaining sections of this chapter investigate the connections between the architecture and the philosophy of the period.

Wittkower's characterization of the Medieval world-view as 'predominantly Aristotelian' is anachronistic, if it is intended to apply to the High Gothic phase of cathedral architecture. The intense period of Gothic cathedral building in northern France was concentrated in the sixty years 1170 to 1230. The man who finally established Aristotelianism as the predominant force in Scholastic thought, St Thomas Aquinas (1224–74), was not born until the end of this period, and his most important writings belong to the decade 1263–73. On the other hand the School of Chartres was dominated by the Platonist writings of Augustine and Boethius, and by Chalcidius' translation and Macrobius' commentary on the *Timaeus*. Its mathematics was therefore more Pythagorean, Platonic and numerical than geometrical. It was a matter of counting rather than measuring.

Even in ancient times the works of Aristotle were relatively little studied before the third century AD, outside the narrow circle of his own school. They were then taken up by the Neoplatonists, who aimed to harmonize them with the teachings of Plato, and this Neoplatonic tradition was inherited by the Arabs, who conquered most of the Mediterranean lands between 632 and 732. In the works of Arabic commentators such as Avicenna and especially Averroes, Aristotle gained a prominence that he had never had before; and it was by way of Islam, and particularly from Islamic Spain, that Western Christendom was able to recover its lost contact with the sources of Greek scholarship. The newly acquired material included all the surviving works of Aristotle, together with works of mathematics and medicine.

51. R. Wittkower, 'The changing concept of proportion', p. 116.

The first translations into Latin from Arabic versions of ancient Greek texts were made before 1100, but the translation movement gained momentum in the early thirteenth century. One of the first centres of this recovered learning was the secular university of Naples founded in 1224 by the Holy Roman Emperor and prototypical Renaissance prince Frederick II (1195–1250). Frederick had himself been educated by Arab scholars at his Sicilian court, where Muslim, Greek and Italian civilizations freely intermixed. In 1228, excommunicated for failing to lead a crusade to Palestine, he won Jerusalem by peaceful negotiation without a drop of blood being spilled. This did not strike the Church as a properly Christian way of going about things.

At the time of its foundation Naples was the only university that taught not only Aristotle's logic but the whole corpus of his natural philosophy. To it in 1238 came the young Benedictine oblate Thomas Aquinas, and there he encountered not only the teachings of Aristotle, but also the recently founded mendicant teaching order of Dominicans. After six years of study at Naples he left the Benedictines to become a Dominican friar, and went to study at the University of Paris. Thus by the time Thomas was twenty he had come in contact with and been profoundly affected by all the principal forces that were radically changing Western European thought: the retrieval of Greek learning, especially the writings of Aristotle, from Islam; the mendicant teaching orders; and the universities.

Like the Dominicans, the Franciscans were actively involved in establishing the new, more critical scholarship that was emerging in the universities. The close connection between the new religious orders and the universities is illustrated by the coincidence of the foundation dates: between 1200 and 1225 the Franciscan and Dominican orders and the universities of Paris, Oxford, Padua and Cambridge were all established. Among the leading philosophers, the Franciscans included Roger Bacon, Duns Scotus and William of Ockham, while Robert Grosseteste, the first to point scholarship in a more scientific, rigorously mathematical and empirical direction, though not himself a Franciscan, was the first lecturer at the Franciscan school in Oxford. Among the Dominicans were Thomas Aquinas and his teacher in Paris, Albert the Great (*c.*1200–80).

The rediscovered works of Aristotle presented a challenge

to Western thought. Despite Boethius' translations of the logical writings in the sixth century, up to now Aristotle had been overshadowed by Plato as a result of the latter's approbation by the great Augustine. Now that his complete works became available, Aristotle appeared to present a potential threat to Christian orthodoxy. Whereas Plato's doctrine – that reality consists principally in the immaterial Forms, of which the sensible world is an inferior and untrustworthy copy – had sat comfortably with Christianity's rejection of the world and the flesh, Aristotle's principle – that reality lies in individual things, and that sight, and the senses in general, are the chief source of human knowledge – did not. The teaching of Aristotle' philosophy of nature at the university of Paris was repeatedly banned between 1210 and 1277 – the last condemnation, three years after Aquinas' death, listing 219 Aristotelian propositions, up to twenty of which can be found in Aquinas's own writings. But Aquinas had the last word. He was canonized in 1323, and his philosophy, and by implication that of Aristotle, became established as the orthodox teaching of the Catholic Church, receiving the final seal of approval by a decree of Leo XIII in 1879.

10.9 KNOWING AND MEASURING

Like Aristotle, Aquinas identifies forms with their individual manifestations – with *substances* – and rejects Plato's doctrine that true knowledge is the recollection of universal Forms already immanent in the soul. It is from the sensory experience of things that the intellect must derive its ideas, including the idea of God: 'Our minds understand material things by abstracting ideas of them from their images, and then use such knowledge to acquire knowledge of immaterial things.'[52] Knowledge is therefore a process of making or abstraction, not of belonging or empathy. So for Aquinas the mind does not receive its ideas directly, either in the form of material emanations from things (Democritus), or as spiritual impressions from the higher world of Forms (Plato), but by its own activity. Ideas of things are constructed in the mind by a special faculty, the *intellectus agens*, with the power to convert sense data into thinkable objects by abstracting universal concepts from their material conditions:

52. T. Aquinas, *Summa Theologiae*, I, 85, 1, trans. T. McDermott, Methuen, 1989, pp. 122–3.

> Sense provides the images, but they are not enough to affect the receptive mind; they provide only the material for knowledge which must be made actually understandable by the agent mind.[53]

Unlike Platonic Forms, these abstractions have no independent existence outside the mind, nor are they identical with the material thing perceived. Therefore Aquinas defines truth as an *adaequatio* – roughly translatable as a 'matching' or 'concordance' – between the thing and the intellect:

> For true knowledge consists in the concordance of thing and intellect (*ratio veri consistit in adaequatione rei et intellectus*); not the identity of one and the same thing to itself, but a conformity between different things. Hence the intellect first arrives at truth when it acquires something proper to it alone – the idea of the thing – which corresponds to the thing, but which the thing outside the mind does not have.[54]

This definition is remarkably close to later empiricism; compare it with John Locke's statement (1690) that

> The mind knows not things immediately, but only by the intervention of the ideas it has of them. Our knowledge, therefore, is real only so far as there is a *conformity* between our ideas and the reality of things.[55]

The interest of this concept, from the particular point of view of the theory of proportion, is that Aquinas sees the mind's idea of a thing as a sort of proportional mean or *tertium comparationis* between the thing and the intellect. He frequently uses the word 'measure' to describe the process of knowing: when we know something we 'measure' it, and we in turn are 'measured' by the things that we know. He posits an (erroneous) etymological connection between the words *mens* and *mensurare*:

> The name for mind (*mens*) is taken from the verb 'to measure' (*mensurare*). Now things of a kind are measured by that which is smallest and most primary of their kind.[56]

This is a reference to Aristotle's definition of the unit in the *Metaphysics*, quoted in Chapter 7: that we adopt as a unit that

53. *Ibid.*, I, 84, 6; p. 131.
54. T. Aquinas, *Quaestiones disputatae de veritate*, I, 3, S.P. Lethielleux, Paris, 1925, vol I, pp. 7–8.
55. J. Locke, *An Essay Concerning Human Understanding*, Everyman's Library, 1961, vol. I, p. xxxv.
56. T. Aquinas, *Quaestiones disputatae de veritate*, X, 1; vol, I, p. 256.

which is the first measure of its class. Aquinas continues: 'For the intellect acquires knowledge of things only by measuring them, as it were, against its own primary elements.'[57] He employs the notion of measure in drawing an analogy between the intellect of the divine creator, and that of the human artist:

> Our intellect draws knowledge from natural things, and is measured by them; but they are measured in turn by the divine intellect, which contains all created things in the same way as works of art are contained in the mind of the artist. Therefore the divine intellect measures, but is not measured; natural things both measure and are measured; and our intellect is measured, but does not measure natural things, only its artifacts.[58]

It follows that just as natural things are 'true' in so far as they are true to the divine intellect that made them, works of art are true when they are true to the human intellect:

> Things essentially relate to the mind on which they depend for existence. . . Thus man-made things are called true in relation to human minds (a house when it conforms to its architect's idea, a statement when it expresses true knowledge); whilst natural things are called true in relation to God's Idea of them. Truth then is primarily defined as a quality of mind: *truth reveals and makes clear what it is*.[59]

At least two twentieth-century architects have been inspired by these thoughts. Mies van der Rohe recalled that it was the discovery of Aquinas' definition of truth as *adaequatio rei et intellectus* that put him on the track of 'finding out what architecture really is'.[60] And the central principle of Dom Hans van der Laan's theory of art is derived from the text about the measure-relations between divine and human intellect, nature and art. In *Architectonic Space* (1977) and *The Form-play of the Liturgy* (1985) he describes the cycle of art as an imitation of the cycle of nature. In both, a spiritual intellect creates material things that, for the cycle to be complete, must return to that intellect.[61] Our intellect is fed by the information it draws from sensory experience of things – both natural things and works of art; so we must make things in such a way that they

57. *Ibid.*
58. *Ibid.*, I, 2; vol. I, p. 6.
59. T. Aquinas, *Summa Theologiae*, I, 16, 1; p. 45.
60. P. Carter, 'Mies van der Rohe, an appreciation', *Architectural Design*, March 1961, p. 97; also R. Padovan, 'Machines à méditer', in *Mies van der Rohe: Architect as Educator*, University of Chicago Press, 1986, pp. 17–26.
61. H. van der Laan, *De architectonische ruimte*, E.J. Brill, 1977, pp. 179–80, and *Het vormenspel der Liturgie*, E.J. Brill, 1985, p. 36.

contain such information. They must *reveal and make clear what they are.* Architecture does this specifically by embodying proportions that 'give measure' to natural space.[62]

10.10 GOTHIC ARCHITECTURE AND SCHOLASTICISM

The influence of Aquinas' Aristotelian philosophy on the architecture of his own time is less easy to discern. Erwin Panofsky, in his essay *Gothic Architecture and Scholasticism* (1951), makes a detailed comparison between the architecture of the classic French cathedral and the logical construction of the Scholastic *Summa.* He begins with a warning: the natural inclination to divide history into mutually distinct and internally unified 'periods' is so strong that 'Few men can resist the temptation of either ignoring or slightly deflecting such lines as refuse to run parallel.'[63] Neverthless, he argues,

> There exists between Gothic architecture and Scholasticism a palpable and hardly accidental concurrence in the purely factual domain of time and place – a concurrence so inescapable that the historians of medieval philosophy . . . have been led to periodize their material in precisely the same way as do the art historians theirs.[64]

– that is, into 'Early', 'Classic' and 'Late' phases:

> For both the new style of thinking and the new style of building. . . spread from an area comprised within a circle drawn around Paris with a radius of less than a hundred miles. And they continued to be centred in this area for a century and a half.[65]

Within this period we shall here concentrate on Panofsky's treatment of the 'Classic' phase, which corresponds, in his view, to the building of the High Gothic cathedrals and the composition of the great Scholastic treatises of Aquinas and his contemporaries. He identifies this phase with the reign of St Louis (1226–70).

The formal parallels that Panofsky brings out are certainly striking. In order to achieve the greatest possible clarity of

62. H. van der Laan, *De architectonische ruimte*, p. 50.
63. E. Panofsky, *Gothic Architecture and Scholasticism*, Meridian Books, 1957, p. 2.
64. *Ibid.*, pp. 2–3.
65. *Ibid.*, pp. 4–5.

exposition, the Scholastic *summa* – of which Aquinas' *Summa Theologiae* is the prime example

> is divided into *partes* which. . . could be divided into smaller *partes;* the *partes* into *membra, quaestiones* or *distinctiones*, and these into *articuli*. Within the *articuli*, the discussion proceeds according to a dialectical scheme involving further subdivision, and almost every concept is split up into two or more meanings. . . according to its varying relation to others.[66]

The treatise is therefore composed in a way that conforms to Vitruvius' definition of proportion in architecture: the whole is divided and subdivided into articulated parts bound together by consistent mutual relations of larger to smaller: 'Proportion,' writes Vitruvius, 'is a correspondence among the measures of the members of an entire work, and of the whole to a certain part selected as standard.[67]

In architecture, Panofsky finds the same tendency to seek clarity through lucid articulation:

> As High Scholasticism was governed by the principle of *manifestatio*, so was High Gothic architecture dominated. . . by what may be called the 'principle of transparency'. . . Like the High Scholastic *Summa*, the High Gothic cathedral aimed, first of all, at 'totality' and therefore tended to approximate, by synthesis as well as elimination, one perfect and final solution. . . Instead of the Romanesque variety of western and eastern vaulting forms. . . we have the newly developed rib vault exclusively so that the vaults of even the apse, the chapels and the ambulatory no longer differ in kind from those of nave and transept.[68]

At the same time as total unity was thus achieved by standardization of forms, the number of separate parts was multiplied:

> At the height of the development, supports were divided and subdivided into main piers, major shafts, minor shafts, and still minor shafts; the tracery of windows, triforia, and blind arcades into primary, secondary, and tertiary mullions and profiles; ribs and arches into a series of mouldings.[69]

---

66. *Ibid.*, pp. 33–4.
67. Vitruvius, *The Ten Books on Architecture*, p. 72.
68. E. Panofsky, *Gothic Architecture and Scholasticism*, pp. 43–6.
69. *Ibid.*, p. 48.

Theoretically, such fractionalization could be pursued to a point where the individual parts become so minute that their separate forms merge and are lost in an overall 'texture'. But in Gothic architecture, as in Scholastic writing, the process of subdivision was limited, according to Panofsky, by the counter-requirement of absolute distinctness:

> According to classic High Gothic standards the individual elements, while forming an indiscerptible whole, yet must proclaim their identity by remaining clearly separated from each other – the shafts from the wall or the core of the pier, the ribs from their neighbours, all vertical members from their arches; and there must be an unequivocal correlation between them.[70]

As Panofsky analyses the High Gothic pursuit of total lucidity of expression in ever greater detail – examining the

> three characteristic Gothic 'problems' – or, as we might say, *quaestiones*: the rose window in the west facade, the organization of the wall beneath the clerestory, and the conformation of the nave piers[71]

a case builds up in the reader's mind that seems almost unanswerable. There is one problem, however, and it is the one that he has hinted at in the opening pages: the historian's natural tendency to strengthen his argument by 'slightly deflecting such lines as refuse to run parallel'.[72] Panofsky's case rests on three essential premises:

(1) However self-evident a parallel may seem, we cannot be content 'if we cannot imagine how it came about'.[73]
(2) The parallel between Gothic architecture and Scholastic philosophy 'is a genuine cause-and-effect relation', and not a 'mere "parallelism" '.[74]
(3) It is backed up by a 'concurrence in the purely factual domain of time and place'.[75]

Within the range of possible cause-and-effect relations, Panofsky distinguishes between direct 'influence' – for instance, advice to an individual artist by some erudite advisor – and a more generalized 'diffusion', that is, the 'spreading. . . of a mental habit'.[76] He opts for the latter, and offers a compelling contemporary example:

70. *Ibid.*, p. 50.
71. *Ibid.*, p. 70.
72. *Ibid.*, p. 2.
73. *Ibid.*
74. *Ibid.*, p. 20.
75. *Ibid.*, p. 2.
76. *Ibid.*, p. 21.

> All of us, without a thorough knowledge of biochemistry or psychoanalysis, speak with the greatest of ease of vitamin deficiencies, allergies, mother fixations, and inferiority complexes.[77]

The diffusion of such 'habits of mind' takes several years, however, even in an age of mass communication. Presumably it was no quicker in the thirteenth century. In any case, one thing is certain: an effect cannot precede its cause. If what we are talking about is a diffusion of ideas and methods *from* philosophy *into* architecture, then we must expect the *Summa* to be written at least a few decades before the cathedral is built. The dates do not bear this out. The approximate dates of the designs of the High Gothic churches that Panofsky cites – and he always regards as significant the date the design was established, not the date of completion – are as follows: Sens, 1140; Laon, 1160; Noyon, 1170; Chalons-sur-Marne, 1185; Chartres, 1194; Bourges, 1195; Notre Dame, Paris, 1200; Reims, 1211; Amiens, 1220; St Denis (nave by Pierre de Montereau), 1231. The dates of the principal High Scholastic *Summae* that he mentions are: Alexander of Hales, *Summa Theologica* – not in fact written by him, but a later compilation[78] – *c.* 1245; St Bonaventure, *Commentary on the Sentences*, 1251; St Thomas Aquinas, *Commentary on the Sentences*, 1253; *Summa contra Gentiles*, 1264; *Summa Theologiae* (unfinished) 1266–74. In short, the churches were designed over a period of just under a hundred years, between 1140 and 1231, the treatises written within the thirty years 1245–74. The two periods do not overlap. On average, the architecture antedates the philosophy by nearly eight decades.

Thus Panofsky's thesis is founded on a similar anachronism to Wittkower's, mentioned above. A diffusion of the particular philosophical 'habits of mind' into the particular architecture he discusses is not credible. If there was indeed an interaction between Gothic architecture and Scholastic philosophy, it must have been architecture that influenced philosophy, not the reverse; the cathedral was the model for the *summa*, not the *summa* for the cathedral. In other words, ideas first worked out in stone were only later translated into abstract thought and writing in the philosopher's study. Concepts born in the world of concrete things matured later into pure abstract speculation. Our resistance to this order of events is due to a peculiarly

77. *Ibid.*
78. G. Leff, *Medieval Thought*, Penguin Books, 1958, pp. 194–5.

modern assumption: that the relation of architecture to the world of ideas is an entirely passive one, its role the reflection of a culture, not the shaping of it. Such an attitude would have been incomprehensible to an Alberti or a Christopher Wren. As we saw in Chapter 5, John Pennethorne came to a similar conclusion about the relation between the buildings on the Acropolis and the development of Greek mathematics and philosophy: that architecture led the way for science.

Chapter eleven

HUMANISM AND ARCHITECTURE

With the invention of perspective the modern notion of individualism found its artistic counterpart. Every element in a perspective representation is related to the unique point of view of the individual spectator.[1]

11.1 THE INDIVIDUAL FOCUS

It used to be assumed that the Renaissance overthrew the 'predominantly Aristotelian medieval approach to the world' (as Wittkower calls it[2]) in favour of a wholly Platonist one. The assumption embodies two over-simplifications. In the first place, the dominant philosophy in the West through most of the thousand years from 350 to 1350 was Augustinian, and therefore Platonist. And in the second, while the Renaissance brought a revived interest in Plato, it by no means rejected Aristotle. The historian of Renaissance thought Paul Oskar Kristeller writes that

> The actual facts suggest almost exactly the opposite. . . In other words, as far as Italy is concerned, Aristotelian scholasticism, just like classical humanism, is fundamentally a phenomenon of the Renaissance period whose ultimate roots can be traced in a continuous development to the very latest phase of the Middle Ages.[3]

A second over-simplification is the identification of the Renaissance with a modern conception of 'Humanism'. When Geoffrey Scott and Rudolf Wittkower entitled their respective books *The Architecture of Humanism*[4] and *Architectural Principles in the Age of Humanism*[5] they reflected this identification. It is largely the creation of nineteenth-century historians such as Jacob Burckhardt. It is expressed most famously and concisely in the chapter on 'The

1. S. Giedion, *Space, Time and Architecture*, Harvard University Press, 1941, p. 31.
2. R. Wittkower, 'The changing concept of proportion' (1960), in *Idea and Image*, Thames & Hudson, 1978, p. 116.
3. P.O. Kristeller, *Renaissance Thought*, Harper Torchbooks, 1961, pp. 35–6.
4. G. Scott, *The Architecture of Humanism* (1914), The Architectural Press, 1980.
5. R. Wittkower, *Architectural Principles in the Age of Humanism* (1949), Alec Tiranti, 1952.

development of the individual' in Burckhardt's *The Civilization of the Renaissance in Italy*, where he writes that

> In the Middle Ages both sides of human consciousness – that which was turned within as that which was turned without – lay dreaming or half awake beneath a common veil. . . In Italy this veil first melted into air; an *objective* treatment and consideration of the State and of all the things of this world became possible. The *subjective* side at the same time asserted itself with corresponding emphasis; man became a spiritual *individual*, and recognized himself as such.[6]

This conception of Humanism accords well with the much broader meaning that the word has now acquired: roughly that we alone are responsible for our fate, and that we are what we choose to make ourselves. The attribution of this viewpoint to the Humanists of the Renaissance is rejected by Kristeller as 'that widespread tendency among historians to impose the terms and labels of our modern time upon the thought of the past'.[7] In its time, he maintains, Humanism was a rather narrowly circumscribed area of scholarly disciplines, centred on the study of Greek and Latin literature.

Nevertheless, Kristeller's strictly accurate definition robs the term Humanism of much of its descriptive value. It is technically correct, but unilluminating. Because it is so narrow it fails to cover more than a small part of Renaissance thought, and he is forced to identify at least three other distinct strands. He distinguishes:

(1) Humanism proper (for example Francesco Petrarca and Lorenzo Valla),
(2) Neoplatonism (Marsilio Ficino and Pico della Mirandola),
(3) Aristotelianism (Pietro Pomponazzi), and
(4) Naturalism (Francesco Patrizi and Giordano Bruno).[8]

The argument comes down in the end to one of terminology. If the Renaissance had a distinct character, marking it off from the late Middle Ages on the one hand and the age of Galileo and Newton on the other – if it was not merely a period of transition, a confusion of heterogeneous tendencies – there must be some broad distinguishing ethos shared by such diverse Renaissance thinkers as Petrarca, Pico and

6. J. Burckhardt, *The Civilization of the Renaissance in Italy* (1860), Phaidon Press, 1944, p. 81.
7. P.O. Kristeller, *Renaissance Thought*, p. 8.
8. P.O. Kristeller, *Eight Philosophers of the Italian Renaissance*, Stanford, 1964.

Bruno. And that ethos needs a name. The modern concept of Humanism describes it rather well.

To illustrate the continuity of this broad view of the human condition from the Renaissance to the present we need only compare two discourses, one composed in the fifteenth century and the other in the twentieth: the *Oration on the Dignity of Man* (1486) by Pico della Mirandola, and the Existentialist philosopher Jean-Paul Sartre's lecture *L'Existentialisme est un humanisme* (1946). In the latter Sartre, echoing Pico's title, defends Existentialism – the theory that absolute truth 'consists in one's immediate sense of one's self' – as the only philosophy 'compatible with the dignity of man, it is the only one which does not make man an object.'[9]

In both texts the idea appears clearly that man's unique status in the world derives precisely from the fact that God has *not* defined him, nor is he determined by nature, like other animals, but solely by his own free choice. Pico pictures God speaking to Adam at the Creation:

> The nature of all other beings is limited and constrained within the bounds of laws prescribed by Us. Thou, constrained by no limits, in accordance with thy own free will, in whose hands We have placed thee, shalt ordain for thyself the limits of thy nature. . . We have made thee neither of heaven nor of earth, neither mortal nor immortal, so that with freedom of choice and with honour, as though the maker and molder of thyself, thou mayest fashion thyself in whatever shape thou shalt prefer.[10]

But Sartre's God has not merely stepped aside, leaving man free to chose his fate; his God does not exist, and man is utterly on his own:

> If God does not exist there is at least one being whose existence comes before its essence, a being that exists before it can be defined by any conception of it. . . Man is nothing else but that which he makes of himself. . . But what do we mean to say by this, but that man is of a greater dignity than a stone or a table? For we mean to say that man primarily exists – that man is, before all else, something that propels itself towards a future and is aware that he is doing so. Man is, indeed, a project which possesses a subjective life, instead of being a kind of moss, or a fungus or a cauliflower.[11]

9. J.-P. Sartre, *Existentialism and Humanism*, Eyre Methuen, 1973, pp. 44–5.
10. G. Pico della Mirandola, 'Oration on the Dignity of Man', in E. Cassirer, P.O. Kristeller and J.H. Randall, *The Renaissance Philosophy of Man*, University of Chicago Press, 1956, pp. 224–5.
11. J.-P. Sartre, *Existentialism and Humanism*, p. 28.

For both Pico and Sartre, man must define himself, impelled by his free will; but not himself alone, because his choice affects to a greater or lesser degree what humanity as a whole is to become. Each individual is reponsible for the life of mankind. In the same way, Sartre suggests, a painter who starts out on the construction of a new work cannot know how it will end up; but by producing the work he changes, however subtly, the climate in which works of art will in future be created and judged.[12]

The link between the Renaissance, Burckhardt and Sartre is Burckhardt's colleague at Basle and fellow admirer of Renaissance individualism, and a forerunner of Existentialism: Friedrich Nietzsche. *Thus Spake Zarathustra* is a late offshoot of the Renaissance ideal of man as Superman: humanity as a self-creation or a self-surpassing. Incidentally, Zarathustra (or Zoroaster) also figures prominently in the *Oration*. At one point Pico quotes him as saying 'that the soul is winged and that, when the wings drop off, she falls headlong into the body; and then, after her wings have grown again sufficiently, she flies back to heaven.'[13] The themes of soaring and of sun worship occur in both Nietzsche and Pico. Nietzsche's Zarathustra

> sprang out of his bed, girded his loins, and emerged from his cave, glowing and strong, like a morning sun emerging from behind dark mountains. 'Great star,' he said. . . 'you profound eye of happiness, what would all your happiness be if you did not have *those* for whom you shine!'. . . Zarathustra had said this to his heart when the sun rose: then he looked inquiringly aloft, for he heard above him the sharp cry of his eagle. 'Very well!' he cried up. . . 'My eagle is awake and, like me, does honour to the sun. With eagle's claws it reaches out for the new light.'[14]

This reads like an echo of Pico's interpretation of Zoroaster's teaching:

> Surely nothing else but that we should wash away the uncleanness from our eyes by moral science as by the western waves;. . . that we should then accustom them to endure in the contemplation of nature the still feeble light of truth as if it were the first rays of the rising sun, so that at last. . . we may like heavenly eagles boldly endure the most brilliant splendour of the meridian sun.[15]

---

12. ***Ibid.*, p. 49.**
13. G. Pico della Mirandola, 'Oration on the Dignity of Man', p. 236.
14. F. Nietzsche, *Thus Spake Zarathustra*, Penguin Books, 1969, pp. 333–4.
15. G. Pico della Mirandola, 'Oration on the Dignity of Man', pp. 236–7.

Kristeller himself describes Pico's *Oration* as 'the most famous expression of that humanist credo to which he gave a novel philosophical interpretation'.[16] If we are justified in regarding it, therefore, as a sufficient example and expression of the spirit of the age it throws an interesting light on the question: where to place the Renaissance in relation to the twin poles of empathy and abstraction. The most obvious course is to place it firmly on the side of empathy. Worringer certainly takes this view: for Classical man, he writes,

> The world is no longer something strange, inaccessible, and mystically great, but a living completion of his own Ego, and he sees in it, as Goethe says, the responsive counterparts of his own sensations.[17]

The conclusion that the Renaissance world view is essentially empathic is supported by Alberti's statement that 'Nothing should be attempted that lies beyond human capacity, or anything undertaken that might immediately come into conflict with Nature.'[18] But on the other hand, does not Pico have God tell Adam that he must 'himself ordain the limits of his nature'?

Again, Alberti constantly reiterates the importance of nature's *concinnitas* or harmony as the criterion of beauty in art:

> Neither in the whole body nor in its parts does *concinnitas* flourish as much as it does in Nature herself; thus I might call it the spouse of the soul and of reason. It has a vast range in which to exercise itself and bloom – it runs through man's entire life and government, it molds the whole of Nature. Everything that Nature produces is regulated by the law of *concinnitas*, and her chief concern is that whatever she produces should be absolutely perfect. . . Beauty is a form of sympathy and consonance of the parts within a body. . . as dictated by *concinnitas*, the absolute and fundamental rule of Nature. This is the main object of the art of building, and the source of her dignity, charm, authority, and worth. All that has been said our ancestors learned through observation of Nature herself. . .; not without reason they declared that Nature, as the perfect generator of forms, should be their model.[19]

Clearly, for Alberti, beauty in art comes through the

16. P.O. Kristeller, *Renaissance Thought*, p. 60.
17. W. Worringer, *Form in Gothic*, G.P. Putnam's Sons, 1927, p. 27.
18. L.B. Alberti, *On the Art of Building in Ten Books*, trans. J. Rykwert, N. Leich and R. Tavernor, MIT Press, 1988, p. 35.
19. *Ibid.*, pp. 302–3.

imitation of nature's *concinnitas*. Moreover, the inclination to do this lies deep within human nature:

> When you make judgements of beauty, you do not follow mere fancy, but the workings of a reasoning faculty that is inborn in the mind. . . For within the form and figure of a building there resides some natural excellence and perfection that excites the mind and is immediately recognized by it.[20]

But Pico tells a different story: for him, man is 'the maker and molder of himself, and may fashion himself in whatever shape he shall prefer', just as for Sartre 'Man is nothing else but that which he makes of himself.' For the Humanist, as for the Existentialist, it is a question of making, not of belonging; not of obeying or imitating nature's laws, but of shaping the laws of our own nature. Pico's *Oration* exposes with particular clarity the paradox inherent in an empathic view of the world, already noted in Chapter 2. Empathy is not the naturalization of the human but the humanization of nature. Worringer writes that Classical man's

> assumption of a worldwide and joyful pantheism, is the culmination of the world's anthropomorphizing process. . . The ideal unity of God and the world which has now been attained [by Classical man] is but another name for the unity of man and the world, that is to say, for the completely accomplished subjugation of the world by mind and sense which annihilates the original dualism.[21]

The order and harmony that Classical man perceives in the external world is his own self-projection. We must conclude, therefore, that Renaissance Humanism is indeed characterized by empathy, but that like all empathy it carries within it an unconscious undercurrent of abstraction.

Man is for Pico the centre and focus of his universe, and from this vantage point he can take an objective view of all creation. God says, 'We have set thee at the world's center that thou mayest from thence more easily observe whatever is in the world.'[22] The Renaissance focus on humanity and on the human being's central place in the world manifested itself in a new consciousness of the human body as something both potentially beautiful and immensely interesting, at once worthy of celebration and of painstaking anatomical

20. *Ibid.*, p. 302.
21. W. Worringer, *Form in Gothic*, p. 28.
22. G. Pico della Mirandola, 'Oration on the Dignity of Man', p. 225.

dissection. In architecture, this is manifested in an identification of the human body with the body of the building itself, by means of the proportions between the parts and, above all, of centralized planning and a geometry that unites the circle with the square. No other part of Vitruvius' *De architectura* held such a fascination for Renaissance artists as the short passage at the start of Book III in which he first says that a temple must be designed with the same proportions between its members as are found in the human body, and immediately follows this with a description of the body as the generator of the circle and the square. Alberti almost paraphrases Vitruvius in *De re aedificatoria (On the Art of Building)* when he writes that

> Just as the head, foot, and indeed any member must correspond to each other and to all the rest of the body of an animal, so in a building, and especially in a temple, the parts of the whole body must be so composed that they all correspond one to another, and any one, taken individually, may provide the dimensions of all the rest.[23]

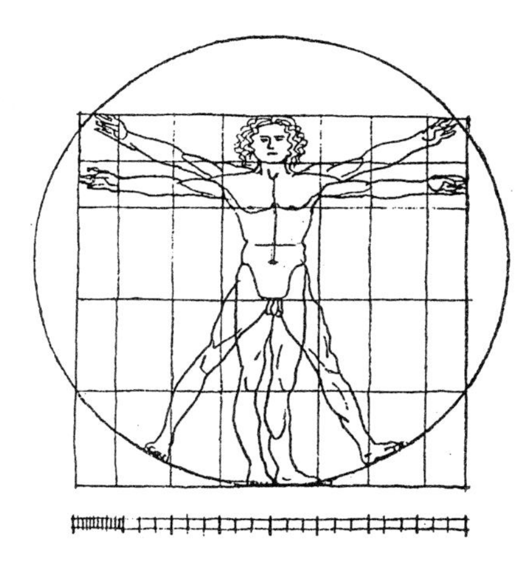

Figure 11.1 Human figure describing circle and square, after Leonardo da Vinci, 1485–90.

The human occupant of the building is united with it through the proportions between his own limbs. His relation to the architecture is that of microcosm.

And just as the human body is a microcosm of the building, the building is in turn a microcosm of the city. Thus the city itself can be conceived as a great body, as Francesco di Giorgio represents it in a famous drawing (1470–80).[24] Body, house, city, and cosmos are all representations of each other, each ordered according to the same hierarchical plan, with head, body, limbs and so on. The hierarchical articulation of space is called by Alberti *compartition*, and he says that it demands 'all the powers of invention, all the skill and experience in the art of building'. For 'If (as the philosophers maintain) the city is like some large house, and the house is in turn like some small city, cannot the various parts of the house. . . be considered miniature buildings?'[25]

A second way in which the body is represented in the Renaissance building is through circle-and-square geometry. Leonardo's famous drawing of 1485–90 is the most convincing of many attempted reconstructions of Vitruvius' description (see Figure 11.1). Above all, this concept is manifested in centralized churches such as Brunelleschi's

23. L.B. Alberti, *On the Art of Building in Ten Books*, p. 199.
24. L. Benevolo, *The Architecture of the Renaissance*, Routledge & Kegan Paul, 1978, Fig. 171, p. 182.
25. L.B. Alberti, *On the Art of Building in Ten Books*, p. 23.

S. Maria degli Angeli, Florence (1434) and Alberti's S. Sebastiano, Mantua (1460) (see Figure 11.2). In Renaissance buildings, as Geoffrey Scott writes, '*We transcribe architecture in terms of ourselves*. This is the humanism of architecture.'[26] Finally, there is a third way in which this Humanism manifests itself: through perspective. But that demands a section to itself.

11.2 PROPORTION IN PERSPECTIVE

A common objection to mathematical proportioning in architecture is that the calculated proportions cannot be perceived as one moves around a building because they are 'distorted by perspective'. But the key to the Renaissance discovery of systematic laws of perspective was that these laws are themselves ruled by proportion. The proportions that Renaissance architects applied to the measures of their buildings were the same ones that governed the way these buildings were seen in perspective. Therefore, as Rudolf Wittkower writes in his essay 'Brunelleschi and "Proportion in Perspective" ', they 'saw no contradiction between objective proportions and subjective impressions of a building.'[27]

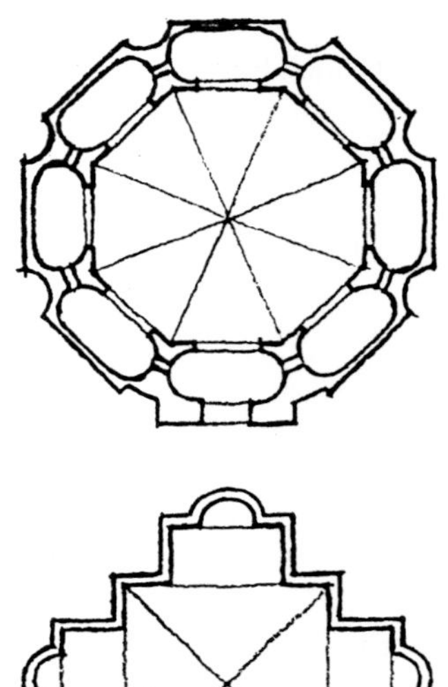

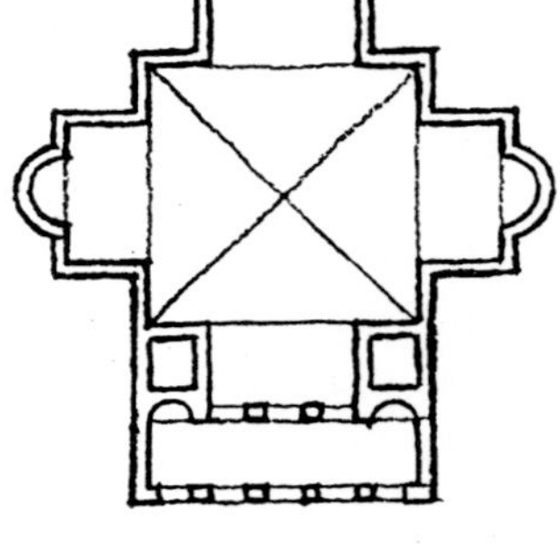

Figure 11.2 Filippo Brunelleschi, Santa Maria degli Angeli, Florence (1434), and Leone Battista Alberti, San Sebastiano, Mantua (*c.* 1460).

Filippo Brunelleschi (1377–1446) is credited with the discovery of the Renaissance theory of perspective. The fact that painters' perspective was invented by an architect is significant, for in Renaissance art the distinction between the real and the painted building virtually disappears. As Wittkower writes:

> The invention of linear perspective was a vital and necessary step in the rationalization of space, a conception on which the whole edifice of Renaissance art rests. . . The architectural setting of Masaccio's 'Trinity' [1425], the first great work of Renaissance illusionism made under the impact of Brunelleschi's ideas, obliterated. . . the borderline between real and painted architecture: the beholder looks, as it were, into a real chapel.[28]

Brunelleschi did not describe his discovery in writing. The first formal exposition of perspective theory was given by Leon Battista Alberti (*c.* 1404–72) in his treatise *Della pittura* (1435).[29] It was given greater numerical precision by

26. G. Scott, *The Architecture of Humanism*, p. 213.
27. R. Wittkower, 'Brunelleschi and "Proportion in Perspective"' (1953), in *Idea and Image*, Thames & Hudson, 1978, p. 126.
28. *Ibid.*, pp. 125, 134.
29. L.B. Alberti, *On Painting*, Yale University Press, 1966, pp. 51–9.

Piero della Francesca (*c.* 1416–92) in *De prospectiva pingendi* (*c.* 1480) and by Leonardo da Vinci (1452–1519) in his notebooks of the early 1490s. Leonardo's concise definition of the laws of perspective is that 'In the case of equal things there is the same proportion of size to size as that of distance to distance from the eye that sees them.'[30] This means that if four objects of equal size are placed at distances from the eye of, say, one, two, three and four metres, their apparent sizes, taking the nearest as unity, will be 1/1, 1/2, 1/3 and 1/4. If the nearest object is replaced by a picture plane of the same size, then the dimensions of the other three will be represented as respectively half, a third and a quarter of the dimension of the picture (see Figure 11.3). According to Wittkower, Leonardo also states that 'The same harmonies reign in music and perspective space.'[31] He illustrates this with a diagram in which the line of the picture plane is regarded as a monochord, and

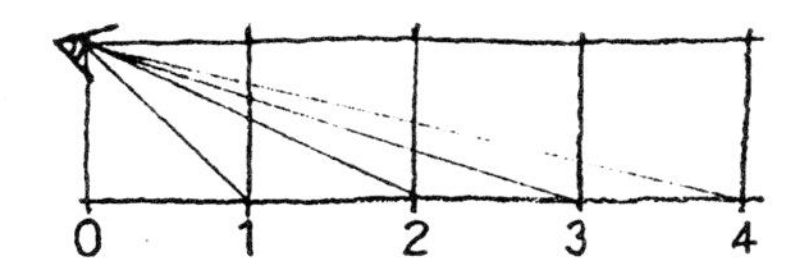

Figure 11.3 Perspective diminution, after Leonardo da Vinci.

> Equal and equidistant objects in space determine points on this line which divide it in the ratios $1 : {}^{1}/_{2}$ or $2 : 1$, $1 : {}^{2}/_{3}$ or $3 : 2$, $1 : {}^{3}/_{4}$ or $4 : 3$ which are the ratios of octave, fifth and fourth. These ratios, which may be noted as the progression of the first four integers $(1 : 2 : 3 : 4)$, form the hard core of Renaissance proportion.[32]

We have already encountered these ratios in Chapters 4 and 6, in connection with Pythagoras' discovery of the ratios of musical harmony and Plato's application of them to the composition of the World's Soul in the *Timaeus*. In this chapter we shall meet with them again in Alberti's prescriptions for architectural proportion. But so far the rule applies only to regularly spaced objects, and to strictly Pythagorean proportions arising from the ratios between the first four natural numbers, 1, 2, 3 and 4. As Wittkower concludes, when in the sixteenth century

> architects began to abandon Brunelleschi's formal principles of homogeneous wall, space and articulation, it was a signal for the break-up of the Renaissance unity between objective proportions and the subjective optical appearance of buildings.[33]

Unlike Leonardo, Piero fails to make the connection between perspective proportion and musical harmony. He

30. L. da Vinci, notebook IV.10.r, in *The Notebooks of Leonardo da Vinci*, trans. E. MacCurdy, Jonathan Cape, 1938, vol. II, p. 350.
31. R. Wittkower, 'Brunelleschi and "Proportion in Perspective"', p. 131.
32. *Ibid.*
33. *Ibid.*, p. 135.

stresses not the ratio of each objective length to the apparent length projected onto the picture plane, but the relative diminution of each object with respect to its nearest neighbour. He gives two examples: in both, the objects are respectively one, two and three spatial units beyond the picture plane, but in the first case the picture plane is four, and in the second case six, units distant from the eye. In the first case the nearest object appears 4/5 of its actual size, the second 5/6 of the first, and the third 6/7 of the second (see Figure 11.4). The total diminutions of the three objects, which Piero does not state, are therefore 4/5, 4/6 and 4/7. In the second case, the relative diminutions are 6/7, 7/8 and 8/9, and the absolute ones 6/7, 6/8 and 6/9. In each case the numerator of the absolute ratio is constant, corresponding to the distance of the picture plane from the eye, and the denominator is determined by the number of units that separate each object from the eye.

We can now state the rule more generally, as follows. The apparent sizes of a series of equal objects spaced at regular intervals from the eye form a harmonic progression: that is, a series of fractions in which the numerator is constant and the denominators constitute an arithmetical progression. The general form for all harmonic progressions is

$$A/B,\ A/(A+B),\ A/(A+2B),\ A/(A+3B),\ldots,$$

where A is any number and B is a constant increment. Thus if $A = B = 1$ we get the series 1/1, 1/2, 1/3, 1/4 etc., as in Leonardo's example. If $A = 4$ and $B = 1$, we get Piero's first example, and if $A = 6$ and $B = 1$, we get Piero's second example. The fundamental unity of all the examples is shown in Table 11.1, which includes the cases where $A = 2, 3$ or 5. In each column two figures are given: first the absolute diminutions, then the relative ones.

The reason why Piero did not recognize the connection with Pythagorean harmony is probably that ratios such as 4/5, 5/6, 6/7 and 7/8 had no place in it. Wittkower concludes that

> Leonardo's interest was focused on demonstrating the potency of Pythagorean-Platonic harmonies in optical space, while Piero seems to have wished to establish a general and infallible law of perspective ratios.[34]

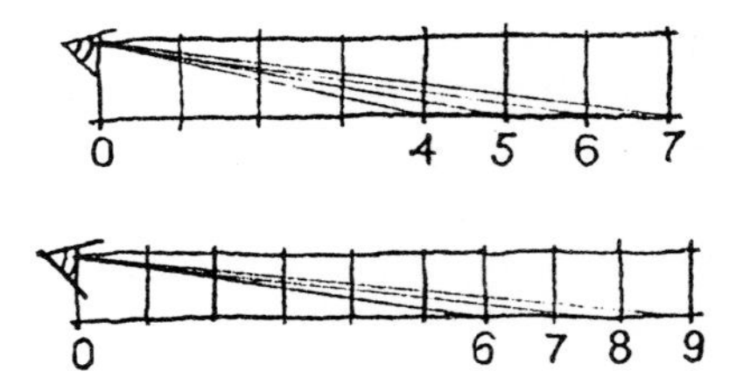

Figure 11.4 Perspective diminution, after Piero della Francesca.

TABLE 11.1

A	*B*	1ST DIM.		2ND DIM.		3RD DIM.		
1	1	1/2	1/2	1/3	2/3	1/4	3/4	Leonardo
2	1	2/3	2/3	1/2	3/4	2/5	4/5	–
3	1	3/4	3/4	3/5	4/5	1/2	5/6	–
4	1	4/5	4/5	2/3	5/6	4/7	6/7	Piero I
5	1	5/6	5/6	5/7	6/7	5/8	7/8	–
6	1	6/7	6/7	3/4	7/8	2/3	8/9	Piero II

34. *Ibid.*, p. 131.

These ratios embodying 5 and 7 do have a place in mathematical proportion *as such*, however, and they inevitably arise in perspective as soon as the total number of spatial units involved exceeds four. If the connection between perspective proportion and theoretical proportion breaks down so soon, can Wittkower's concept of 'a unity between objective proportions and the subjective optical appearance' be said to have any general validity? What happens, for instance, if either the size or the spacing of the objects increases in a progression?

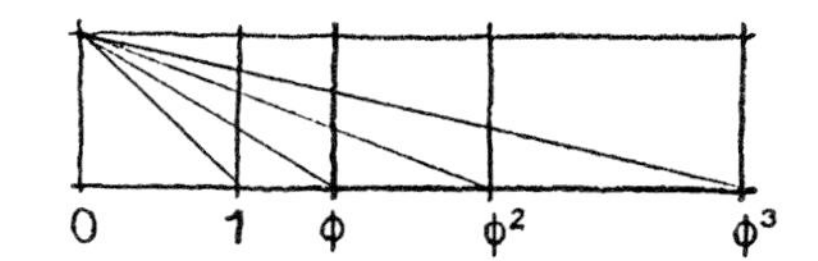

Figure 11.5 Perspective diminution of objects spaced at golden section intervals.

Suppose that instead of being equally spaced, a series of equal objects is arranged at increasing distances from the eye, and that these distances constitute a geometric progression with B as constant multiplier. The successive distances from the eye are then $A, BA, B^2A, B^3A,\ldots, B^nA$, and the successive absolute diminutions form the decreasing geometric progession $A/BA, A/B^2A, A/B^3A,\ldots, A/B^nA$. The value of B can be anything we like: for instance $\sqrt{2}$, $\sqrt{3}$, $\sqrt{4}$, $\sqrt{5}$ or ϕ. Let $B = \phi$, and let A, the distance from the eye to the picture plane $= 1$. The distance from the eye to the nearest object, BA, therefore equals ϕ, that to the second equals ϕ^2, and so on (see Figure 11.5). The absolute diminutions are now $1/\phi$, $1/\phi^2$, $1/\phi^3,\ldots, 1/\phi^n$, while the relative diminutions are constant, $1/\phi$. The progression is no longer harmonic, but geometric. The possible permutations of perspectival and actual proportions are endless, *but it is always a question of proportion*. It is not unreasonable to speculate that the perceiving brain is able to process these multiple relationships, just as it processes the far more complex relations that it encounters in the natural environment. Our innate sense of proportion arises from the biological need that we share with other organisms to survive in a complex spatial environment, and specifically the need to judge distances and shapes when they are foreshortened or distorted by perspective. Therefore it should not surprise us that, as Wittkower says, there is 'no contradiction between objective proportions and subjective impressions of a building'. His Renaissance example is merely the simplest case of a far more general phenomenon.

In the buildings of Brunelleschi and other fifteenth-century Italian architects, objects such as columns are purposefully arranged to produce this extreme simplicity of perspective organization. Thus in Brunelleschi's church of S. Lorenzo (1419), as Wittkower describes,

> The floor of the nave is laid out in squares corresponding to the size of the bays, and the dark line of the central axis invites the visitor to move along it so that both walls of the nave seem to diminish equally towards the vanishing point. The squares of the floor together with the coffers of the ceiling supply spatial coordinates, and their function as metrical guides is comparable to the function given in Renaissance pictures to the foreshortened marble floor. . . Granting that Brunelleschi wanted his buildings to be looked at as if they were projected on to an intersection, the difference between architecture and painting becomes one of artistic medium rather than of kind. . . Not only does [this manifest observation] throw light on the deep gulf separating ancient and Renaissance architecture, but also on the revolutionary development of the Renaissance stage, on the sudden flowering of the art of the *intarsiatori* and the meaning of painted illusionism.[35]

The most interesting point here is the emphasis on perspective's role in creating the 'deep gulf' that separates Renaissance architecture from the ancient Classical architecture that Brunelleschi and his successors had set out to restore. In every field, the Renaissance sought to recover antiquity, but in architecture as in other fields it did so with unintentionally revolutionary results. 'The great forward movements of the Renaissance all derive their vigour, their emotional impulse, from looking backwards.'[36] These words, the opening sentence of Frances Yates' study of the Renaissance philosopher Giordano Bruno, are relevant to almost all aspects of Renaissance activity. They apply equally to architecture, to astronomy – Copernicus did not intend to bring about the Copernican revolution – and to Humanism.

Sigfried Giedion introduces *Space, Time and Architecture* by acknowledging his debt to Burckhardt, of whom his own teacher, Heinrich Wölfflin, had been the pupil and became the successor at the University of Basle: 'He first showed how a period could be treated in its entirety.'[37] Giedion (1894–1968) is a final link in the chain that connects the Humanism of the Renaissance, by way of Pico, Burckhardt, Nietzsche and Sartre, to our own. In his interpretation of perspective as the manifestation of the new Renaissance sense of the individual, he follows closely in Burckhardt's footsteps. In a perspective composition, he writes:

35. *Ibid.*, pp. 132–4.
36. F.A. Yates, *Giordano Bruno and the Hermetic Tradition*, Routledge & Kegan Paul/University of Chicago Press, 1964, p. 1.
37. S. Giedion, *Space, Time and Architecture*, p. 3.

> The whole picture or design is calculated to be valid for one station or observation point only. To the fifteenth century the principle of perspective came as a complete revolution, involving an extreme and violent break with the medieval conception of space, and with the flat, floating arangements which were its artistic expression. With the invention of perspective the modern notion of individualism found its artistic counterpart. Every element in a perspective representation is related to the unique point of view of the individual spectator.[38]

11.3 ALBERTI ON THE ART OF BUILDING

In fifteenth-century Italy, for the first time, artists began to claim that they, just like philosophers and mathematicians, were concerned with knowledge, and that their specializations should therefore be regarded as *liberal arts*: that is, as sciences. The mathematics of perspective and proportion became central to painting and architecture. But more importantly, perspective and proportion were no longer seen as mere technical skills, pressed into the service of some material aim. The plastic arts shared the same aim as the other sciences: they were means of discovering and representing the world. If the early Greek scientists had begun by looking upon the world as a kind of house, and their arithmetic and geometry had grown out of the practical arts of keeping accounts, weighing out goods and measuring fields, now the direction was reversed. The Renaissance architect took the cosmos as his model, and applied to the church and the palace the measures and proportions that Plato had attributed to the soul and body of the universe. Philosophy became the criterion of architecture; the house became a representation of the world.

Leon Battista Alberti (1404–72) was a Humanist and a scholar before he was an architect. He was the son of an exiled member of the Florentine ruling class, and he studied classics, mathematics and canon law at the universities of Padua and Bologna. As its title and its division into ten books suggest, he modelled his treatise *On the Art of Building* (*De re aedificatoria*) on the *De architectura* of Vitruvius; but he clearly intended to surpass it, in literary elegance, in coherence of

38. *Ibid.*, p. 31.

structure, and in boldness of vision. Vitruvius had written, as Joseph Rykwert observes,

> to record a passing epoch rather than open a new one. . . The essential difference between Alberti and Vitruvius is therefore that the ancient writer tells you how the buildings that you may admire as you read him *were* built, while Alberti is prescribing how the buildings of the future *are to be* built.[39]

Moreover, Alberti's ultimate model is neither contemporary nor ancient architecture, but nature itself. Throughout, he cites nature as the yardstick by which men must measure their own creations. The ideal figure, which nature prefers above all others, is the circle, followed closely by the primary regular figures: hexagon, square, octagon, etc.

> It is obvious from all that is fashioned, produced, or created under her influence, that Nature delights primarily in the circle. Need I mention the earth, the stars, the animals, their nests, and so on, all of which she has made circular? We notice that Nature also delights in the hexagon. For bees, hornets, and insects of every kind have learned to build the cells of their hives entirely out of hexagons.[40]

In particular, Alberti presents a mathematically more coherent theory of proportion, one that owes more to the Pythagorean and Platonic theory of cosmic harmony than to Vitruvius. Introducing the subject of proportion, he writes:

> For us, the outline is a certain correspondence between the lines that define the dimensions; one dimension being length, another breadth, and the third height. . . I affirm again with Pythagoras: it is absolutely certain that Nature is wholly consistent. . . The very same numbers that cause sounds to have concinnitas, pleasing to the ears, can also fill the eyes and mind with wondrous delight. From musicians therefore. . . or from those objects in which Nature has displayed some evident and noble quality, the whole method of outlining is derived.[41]

Alberti's prescriptions for proportion, in the ninth of the

39. J. Rykwert, in L.B. Alberti, *On the Art of Building in Ten Books*, pp. ix–x.
40. L.B. Alberti, *ibid.*, p. 196.
41. *Ibid.*, p. 305.

ten books *On the Art of Building*, are the first example since Vitruvius of specific proportions being set down in writing by the architect himself. The analysis of the proportions of his buildings is therefore no longer a matter of pure speculation. He begins in fact with an exposition of the principal harmonies in music, which he then translates directly into architectural proportions: first, the proportions of horizontal spaces – *areas* – which have only two dimensions, and then those of rooms, which involve three. *Areas* can be either short, medium or long. Within these categories, however, Alberti generally lists the proportions in order of the relative complexity of the ratio rather than its absolute size. For instance, 2 : 3 comes before 3 : 4, and 9 : 16 after 1 : 2 and 4 : 9.

He composes the longer *areas* in a way that seems far from obvious to the modern reader. Thus the ratio 4 : 9 is described as a *double sesquialtera* because it is first composed as a simple *sesquialtera* – that is, 2 : 3 or 4 : 6 – and then the length is extended again in the same ratio: 6 : 9. Similarly the ratio 9 : 16, called *double sesquitertia*, starts as a simple *sesquitertia* (3 : 4 or 9 : 12), and this ratio is then repeated to give 12 : 16. The long *areas* are articulated in the same way. Thus we get the ratios shown in Table 11.2 (see Figure 11.6).

What Alberti seems to intend is to compose all more extreme or more complicated ratios out of the simple ratios 3 : 2, 4 : 3 and 2 : 1 – in musical terms, the basic Pythagorean harmonies: fifth, fourth and octave. Wittkower describes Alberti's procedure as follows:

> Now, the double proportion 1 : 2 (musically an octave) is a composite of the two ratios 2 : 3 and 3 : 4 (for 1/2 = 2/3 × 3/4) so that it is generated from 2 : 3 : 4 or 3 : 4 : 6 (musically from fifth to fourth or fourth to fifth). We can now say that, for instance, the proportion of 1 : 4 is generated from 2 : 3 : 4 : 8, or 2 : 3 : 4 : 6 : 8 (i.e. from fifth and fourth, and fifth and fourth), or 3 : 6 : 9 : 12, or 3 : 4 : 6 : 9 : 12 (i.e. from fourth and fifth, and fifth and fourth), etc. For Alberti the splitting up of compound proportions into the smallest harmonic ratios is not an academic matter, but a spatial experience. . . A wall is seen as a unit which contains certain harmonic potentialities. The lowest sub-units, into which the whole unit can be broken up, are the consonant intervals of the musical scale, the cosmic validity of which was not doubted.[42] [See Figure 11.6]

TABLE 11.2

SHORT *AREAS*	MEDIUM *AREAS*	LONG *AREAS*
1 : 1 *(square)*	1 : 2 *(double)*	1 : 3 (1 : 2 : 3)
2 : 3 *(sesquialtera)*	4 : 9 (4 : 6 : 9)	3 : 8 (3 : 6 : 8)
3 : 4 *(sesquitertia)*	9 : 16 (9 : 12 : 16)	1 : 4 (1 : 2 : 4)

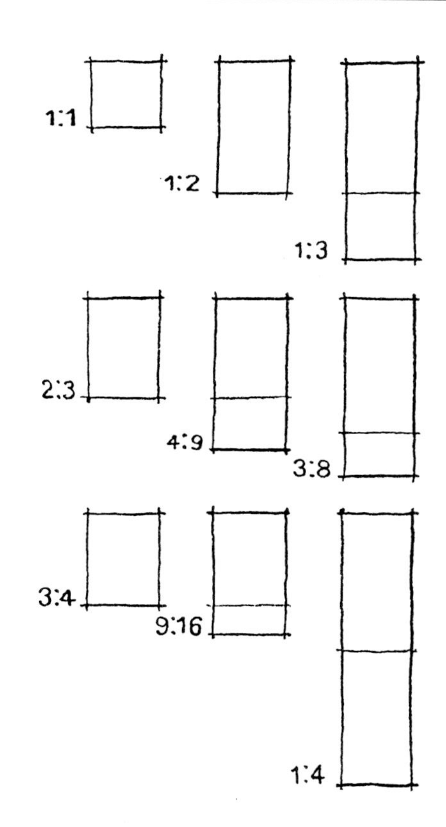

Figure 11.6 Alberti, recommended proportions for areas.

42. R. Wittkower, *Architectural Principles*, pp. 101–2.

Alberti follows the same procedure in order to compose spatial volumes. He recommends, in the case of 'short' or double square plans, that the median dimension, the height, should be either the arithmetic or the harmonic mean of the smallest and largest measures. Either the smaller dimension is first enlarged by a *sesquialtera* to produce the mean and then by a *sesquitertia* to produce the double, or vice versa. In the case of longer rooms, a second intermediate dimension may be introduced, in order to reduce the component ratios to a *sesquialtera* or a *sesquitertia*. This produces the sequences shown in Table 11.3 (see Figure 11.7).

According to Wittkower, Renaissance proportion cannot be appreciated unless this principle of decomposing ratios is grasped:

> It can even be said that, without it, it is impossible fully to understand the intentions of a Renaissance architect. We are touching here on the fundamentals of the style as a whole; for simple shapes, plain walls and clear divisions are necessary presuppositions for that 'polyphony of proportions' which the Renaissance mind understood and a Renaissance eye was able to see.[43]

The relations between Alberti's nine ratios – 1/1, 3/2, 4/3, 2/1, 9/4, 16/9, 3/1, 8/3 and 4/1 – become clearer as soon as they are set out as a grid. First, however, it must be explained that every integer can be expressed as a fraction with the number 1 as the denominator (for example, 4 = 4/1), and every rational fraction is in turn a ratio between two integers. Therefore the fraction 9/4, for instance, can be written 9/1 : 4/1. Moreover, any such ratio between two fractions remains unaffected when the denominators and numerators are transposed: for example, 9/1 : 4/1 = 9/4 : 1/1. Thus we can express all Alberti's ratios as relations to the basic fraction 1/1.

This principle is employed in Table 11.4. Each fractional number in the table is the product of its corresponding numbers in the top row and the left-hand column: for example, 8/3 = 3/2 × 16/9, and 3/1 = 9/4 × 4/3. Each move from left to right represents an enlargement by the *sesquialtera* ratio 3/2 and each vertical move downwards the *sesquitertia* ratio 4/3, while each diagonal move downwards from left to right results in a doubling, and a move upwards from left to right gives the ratio 9/8 (musically, the tone).

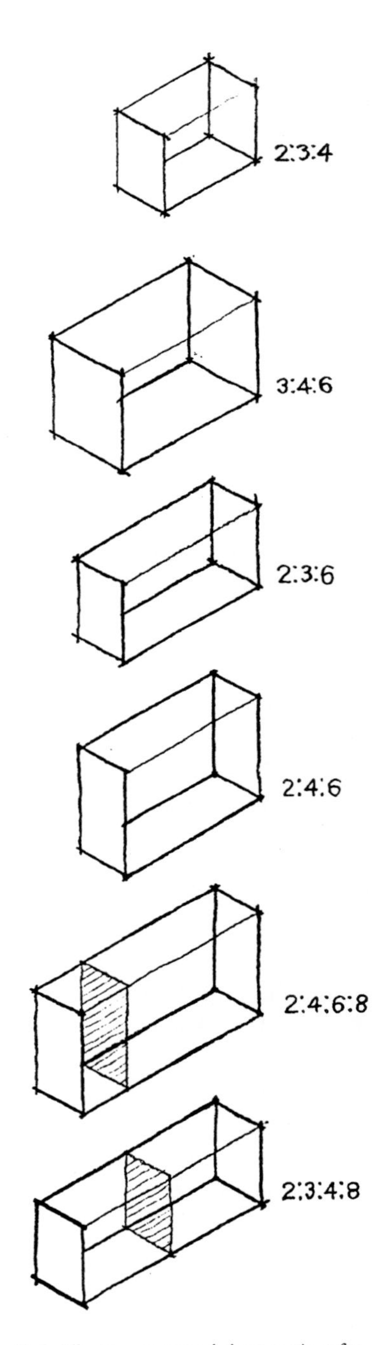

Figure 11.7 Alberti, recommended proportions for rooms.

43. *Ibid.*, pp. 102–3.

Admittedly, it can be objected that this explanation goes far beyond Alberti's own intentions; it is nevertheless a logical development from them. But his exposition of his system is mathematically neither systematic nor complete – far less complete, for example, than that given by Plato in the *Timaeus*, and expounded, a few decades after Alberti, by the Franciscan monk and Neoplatonist Francesco Giorgi in his significantly titled treatise *On the Harmony of the World.*[44] Giorgi illustrates the *lambda* with the double intervals subdivided by harmonic and arithmetic means, just as Plato describes it, and also an alternative diagram in which the numbers are multiplied throughout by 6 to eliminate fractions, and combined in a continuous series with the intervals and sub-intervals indicated by arcs (see Figure 11.8). The underlying structure of Giorgi's system is brought out still more clearly by rearranging the numbers as a grid, as in Table 11.5. Any vertical move gives the ratio 1 : 2, any horizontal move 1 : 3, while various diagonal moves give the ratios 2 : 3, 3 : 4, 8 : 9 etc. To complete the stepped triangle of the grid, the numbers 1, 2, 3, 4, 72 and 243 (printed in italics) are added to Giorgi's set. The seven numbers of the original Λ or *lambda* (now multiplied by 6) are printed bold. In the rearranged grid thus formed, the Λ is rotated through 45°, forming the letter Γ (*gamma*).

If each term of the 'Albertian' Table 11.4 is multiplied by 36, as in Table 11.6, the fractions are eliminated. The resulting set of whole numbers reveals itself as an extension of Table 11.4. The shaded lower right portion of the table shows the Albertian numbers multiplied by 36, and the upper left portion shows them unmultiplied. Table 11.6 is also essentially a rearrangement of the 'Giorgian' Table 11.5. The only difference is that in Table 11.5 vertical and horizontal moves give the ratios 1 : 2 and 1 : 3, and diagonal moves give the ratios 2 : 3, 3 : 4 etc., while conversely in Table 11.6 the latter ratios are given by horizontal and vertical moves, and the former by diagonals.

Wittkower plays down – even denies – the importance in Renaissance proportion of irrational numbers such as the square roots of two and three. He mentions in passing that Alberti, Serlio and Palladio include the ratio 1 : $\sqrt{2}$ among the otherwise entirely rational proportions recommended in their treatises, and that the first two writers, but not Palladio, point out its incommensurability. Wittkower comments that

Table 11.3

FOR SHORT ROOMS	FOR LONGER ROOMS
2 : 3 : 4	2 : 3 : 6
3 : 4 : 6	2 : 4 : 6
	2 : 4 : 8
	2 : 4 : 6 : 8
	2 : 3 : 4 : 8

Table 11.4

1/1	3/2	9/4
4/3	2/1	3/1
16/9	8/3	4/1

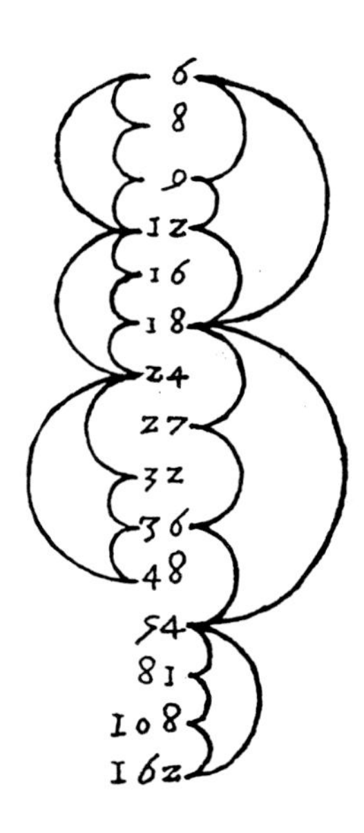

Figure 11.8 Arithmetic and harmonic divisions of double and triple intervals, after F. Giorgi, 1525.

44. F. Giorgi, *De harmonia mundi totius*, Venice, 1525.

As far as we can see, this is the only irrational number of importance involved in the Renaissance theory of architectural proportion. It came straight out of Vitruvius, where its occurrence – amidst a module system, which otherwise presupposes commensurable ratios – has been thought with good reason to be a residue of the Greek architectural theory of proportion, all but forgotten in Roman times. It is probably true to say that neither Palladio nor any Renaissance architect ever in practice used irrational proportions. . .[45]

As we shall see, however, there is strong evidence to suggest that Palladio's best-known villa, the Rotonda, may be based on the irrational proportion 1 : $\sqrt{3}$, and that similar irrational ratios, or rational approximations of them, appear elsewhere in his work. Nor can it be overlooked that Alberti immediately follows his account of the whole-number musical ratios with an exposition of what he calls 'certain natural relationships that cannot be defined by numbers, but that may be obtained through roots and powers'.[46] Contrary to Wittkower's assertion, these are the irrational numbers that arise with the diagonals of squares and cubes, and they comprise not only the square root of two but also the square root of three. That Alberti regards them as being of practical rather than merely academic interest appears from his recommendation that 'Each should be employed with the shortest line serving as the width of the *area*, the longest as the length, and the intermediate one as the height.'[47] He would not express himself in this way if he did not envisage the proportion being used.

As with his rational series, Alberti takes two as his unit rather than one, explaining that 'The primary cube, whose root is one, is consecrated to the Godhead, because the cube of one remains one.'[48] He therefore starts with a cube whose edge is two, which gives an *area* of four and a cube of eight. From these he derives the diagonal of the *area*, the square root of eight, and the diagonal of the cube, which is the square root of twelve. Lastly, he considers the diagonal of an *area* whose two sides are the square roots of four (that is, two) and twelve. This length gives the square root of sixteen (that is, four). If we reduce all these numbers by taking a single cube as starting point, we get the numbers shown in Table 11.7.

Alberti thus shows that while the diagonals of the unit square and cube are the incommensurable square roots of

TABLE 11.5

1	*3*	9	27	81	*243*
2	**6**	**18**	**54**	**162**	
4	**12**	36	108		
8	**24**	*72*			
16	**48**				
32					

TABLE 11.6

1	3/2	9/4						
4/3	2	3	9/2					
16/9	8/3	4	6	9				
		16/3	8	12	18	27		
				16	24	36	54	81
					32	48	72	108
						64	96	144

TABLE 11.7

Diagonal of unit square	$\sqrt{2}$
Diagonal of unit cube	$\sqrt{3}$
Diagonal of $\sqrt{3}$ rectangle	$\sqrt{4} = 2$

45. R. Wittkower, *Architectural Principles*, p. 95.
46. L.B. Alberti, *On the Art of Building in Ten Books*, p. 307.
47. *Ibid.*, p. 308.
48. *Ibid.*, p. 307.

two and three, the diagonal of a $\sqrt{3}$ rectangle brings us back to a rational number, two. The relations between the three square roots (to which we can add the square root of five, which Alberti does not mention) can be illustrated in a single diagram (see Figure 11.9).

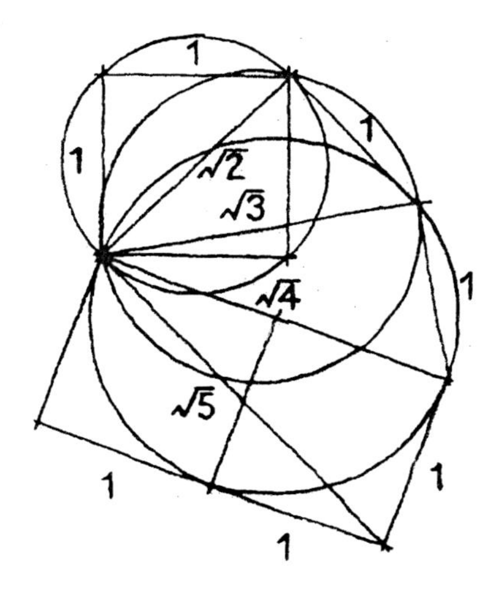

Figure 11.9 Relations between square roots of 2, 3, 4 and 5.

11.4 SAN SEBASTIANO, MANTUA

Although the ratios prescribed in *On the Art of Building* remove some of the uncertainties about the proportions of Alberti's own buildings, there remains wide room for speculation. Unlike Vitruvius, who describes in some detail the proportional scheme of his basilica at Fano, Alberti gives no account of any building that he actually designed. It is therefore important to try to find out how he applied his theory in practice. For this purpose I have chosen to investigate the proportions of the church of S. Sebastiano in Mantua, which Alberti is thought to have designed in about 1460, ten years after completing the first manuscript of his treatise on architecture. It is the first of the many centrally planned Greek cross structures of the Renaissance, the forerunner of such churches as S. Maria delle Carceri, Prato, by Giuliano da Sangallo (1485), certain projects sketched by Leonardo da Vinci (*c.* 1489), S. Biagio, Montepulciano, by Antonio da Sangallo the Elder (1518), and above all the plans for St Peter's by Bramante (1506), Peruzzi (*c.* 1520), Antonio da Sangallo the Younger (1539) and Michelangelo (1546).[49] The spatial composition of the interior is of the greatest simplicity and monumentality: a central cube surmounted by a cross vault, with smaller barrel-vaulted arms on all four sides; the central cube is thus circumscribed within a notional larger square. Three of the arms terminate in half-cylindrical apses roofed by half-domes, miniature echoes of the form of the central space (see Figure 11.2).

Since its inception, S. Sebastiano has had a chequered history. Alberti was able to give it only intermittent attention during the long years of its construction; changes were still being made to the design in 1470, when his client Lodovico Gonzaga, the ruler of Mantua, wrote to the builder Luca Fancelli concerning Alberti's 'opinion about the diminishing of the piers of the portico'.[50] Two years later Alberti died, leaving the church unfinished. Work on it was resumed in 1499 under the supervision of Pellegrino Ardizoni, and it

49. P. Murray, *The Architecture of the Italian Renaissance*, Thames & Hudson, 1969, Figs 58–60, 64–5, 85, 88–91, pp. 103, 110–11, 136, 138–9.

50. J. Rykwert and R. Tavernor, 'The Church of S. Sebastiano in Mantua', *Architectural Design*, vol. 49, nos. 5–6, 1979, p. 88.

was finally consecrated on the occasion of the Emperor Charles V's visit to Mantua in 1530. 'After that there is talk of a fire',[51] and the church became part of the Austrian barracks in 1848. It was reconsecrated and restored to its present state by Andrea Schiavi in 1925. Somehow, despite all these vicissitudes, the grandeur of the original conception still shines through. But the uncertainty about Alberti's design has made S. Sebastiano the subject of intense speculation and controversy among architectural historians.

In particular, the phrase 'diminish the piers' has led to much discussion. Wittkower, in his *Architectural Principles*, translates *minuire* as 'reduce the number of', and concludes that this explains the decidely odd facade composition that we see today, in which as he says 'An unusually heavy entablature rests on unusually thin pilasters. . . [while] the central bay is astonishingly narrow and the side bays astonishingly large'[52] (see Figure 11.10). Reasoning that 'The width of the wall in the large outer bays of the present facade corresponds exactly to twice the width of the central bay plus one pilaster,' he proposes to restore the two missing pilasters, which he presumes Alberti for some unexplained reason decided in 1470 to omit, to give 'an equally spaced distribution of six pilasters over the plane of the facade'.[53] The resulting intercolumniations are all 8/3 of the pilaster width, conforming roughly to the *diastyle* column spacing of Vitruvius (see Figure 11.11). The result (coincidentally similar to Nicholas Hawksmoor's portico of St Alphege, Greenwich, 1712[54]) is certainly more harmonious than the existing facade. Furthermore it conforms logically to the five-bay articulation of the interior, underlined by the arrangement of the columns in the crypt (see Figure 11.12). In 1979 Joseph Rykwert and Robert Tavernor pointed out, however, that *minuire* may mean reduction in either 'width, height, or number'.[55] They put forward several alternative solutions for the latter, most of which involve widening the four pilasters by a quarter to give them a height/width ratio of 8 : 1, normal for the Doric order.[56] This also reduces, though it does not altogether remove, the disproportion of the pilaster height to the very deep entablature (barely 3 : 1). For Doric this ratio tends to be 4 : 1, but for Corinthian 5 : 1. But if the pilaster width can be changed so can the depth of the entablature, and none of their tetrastyle proposals looks as satisfactory as their version of Wittkower's hexastyle one.[57]

Figure 11.10 S. Sebastiano, Mantua: existing facade.

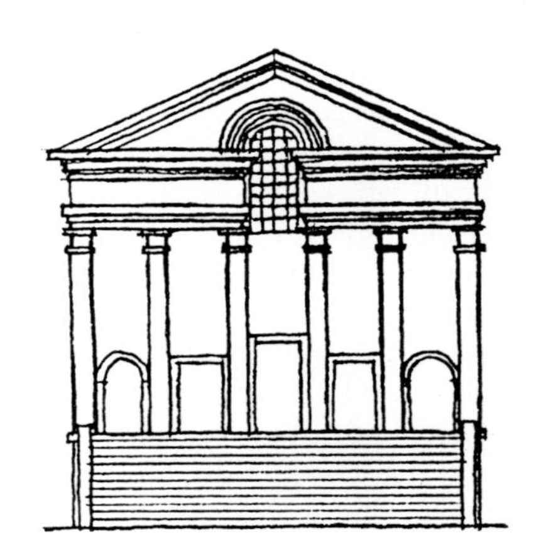

Figure 11.11 S. Sebastiano, Mantua: facade restoration proposed by R. Wittkower.

51. *Ibid.*, p. 89.
52. R. Wittkower, *Architectural Principles*, p. 42.
53. *Ibid.*, p. 43.
54. K. Downes, *Hawksmoor*, Thames & Hudson, 1969, Figs 96–8, pp. 112–3.
55. J. Rykwert and R. Tavernor, 'The Church of S. Sebastiano', p. 88.
56. *Ibid.*, pp. 80–2.
57. *Ibid.*

I shall here concentrate, however, on the proportions of the interior. Lionel March offers several ingenious alternative analyses, based on the 20-21-29 Pythagorean triangle, on rational convergents for $\sqrt{2}$, $\sqrt{3}$, $\sqrt{5}$ and, most intriguingly, on the Fibonacci series.[58] Since he is primarily interested in the ethical, theological and occult symbolism of architectural proportions – their role as cosmogony or 'world-making' and as 'rithomachy' or philosophical war-games played with numbers[59] – he is relatively unconcerned with the tangible experience of masses and spaces, and is not troubled that many of the key dimensions he relies on have no physical embodiment in the visible fabric of the building. What matters, for him, is the *eidos* or mental image, manifested in an 'eidetic mesh' of invisible lines underlying the plan, rather than measures and shapes that can actually be seen by the visitor. In contrast, the solutions proposed by Rykwert and Tavernor are relatively simple and straightforward. Every quantity they describe is plainly visible as a line, a surface or a volume, and the mathematically most important quantities are also the most important visually.

Because of the doubtful authenticity of Schiavi's restoration, and the long drawn-out and frequently interrupted history of the building's construction and completion, the most reliable evidence we have of Alberti's original intention is a dimensioned sketch made by Antonio Labacco, possibly in 1526–7, shortly before the completion and consecration of the church. The sketch is presumably taken from a drawing or model rather than the actual building,[60] since Labacco states that the plan is '*di mano di mesere battista alberti*' ('by the hand of Master Battista Alberti'). He must therefore have had some reason to believe that the original he saw was made by Alberti himself. Although the sketch is very rough, it is dimensioned. It is the starting point for March's interpretation, and for those of Rykwert and Tavernor[61] and recently Tavernor alone.[62] Labacco gives two slightly different sets of dimensions: whole number measures on the plan itself, and others, often involving fractions, in an accompanying note. Both sets are shown in Table 11.8, together with the actual dimensions in Mantuan *braccia* of 467 mm[63] (see Figure 11.13).

In their 1979 paper Rykwert and Tavernor assume, on the basis of the information then available to them, that the Mantuan *braccio* measured not 467 but 634–644 mm.[64] They therefore conclude that

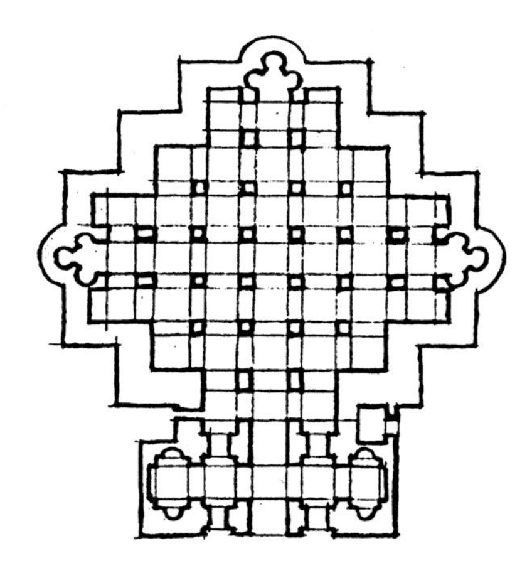

Figure 11.12 S. Sebastiano, Mantua: plan of crypt.

TABLE 11.8

	PLAN	NOTE	ACTUAL
A	58	$56^2/_3$	$56^1/_2$
B	34	34	$34^1/_2$
A/2	29	$28^1/_3$	$28^1/_4$
C	20	20	$20^1/_6$
D	12	12	11
E	8	8	$8^1/_6$
F	7	7	$7^1/_6$
G	6	6	6
E/2	4	4	$4^1/_{12}$

58. L. March, *Architectonics of Humanism*, Academy Editions, 1998, pp. 199–205.
59. *Ibid.*, pp. 49–52.
60. R. Tavernor, *On Alberti and the Art of Building*, Yale University Press, 1998, p. 127.
61. J. Rykwert and R. Tavernor, 'The Church of S. Sebastiano'.
62. R. Tavernor, *On Alberti and the Art of Building*.
63. Adapted from data in A. Calzona and L. Volpi Ghirardini, *Il San Sebastiano di Leon Battista Alberti*, Leo S. Olschi, Florence, 1994, pp. 87–8, 228–34.
64. J. Rykwert and R. Tavernor, 'The Church of S. Sebastiano', p. 89.

> The values given by L'Abacco do not fall easily into the Albertian system of a generation of ratios [that is, the Pythagorean ratios given here in section 11.3]; nor, when applied to the survey of the church, do they yield anything like a *braccio* of any Italian town.[65]

In his subsequent publications Tavernor has revised this opinion, and accordingly produced a quite different interpretation of the church's proportions involving repetitions of the ratio 6 : 10.[66] However, analyses of individual buildings have been included in the present book, not as definitive answers to the question 'What method did the architect actually follow?', but as illustrations of the way contrasting systems of proportion can be applied to the same building. Therefore, although the earlier hypothesis must now be regarded as superseded, it has an intrinsic value as an attempt to explain the composition in accordance with the Platonic ratios expounded by Alberti in Book IX of *On the Art of Building*.

Rykwert and Tavernor begin by dividing Labacco's overall measures into the then available survey measurements, obtaining a common dimension of about 480 mm, which they interpret as 3/4 of an assumed Mantuan *braccio* of 640 mm. Besides this 'lower module' they posit an 'upper module' 5/4 of the lower one – that is, 600 mm – and explain the proportions as an interplay between these two units of measure. For brevity, I shall henceforth refer to the two modules as LM and UM respectively.

The two authors first test the modules on the crypt, finding that the 16 square piers each measure 2 × 2 LM on plan and the eight oblong piers 2 LM × 2 UM, while the intercolumniations are 5 × 5 LM or 4 × 4 UM. In the upper church, the nominal dimension of the central square appears to be 27 UM, and the overall internal length, measured between the faces of the far walls of the chapels that form the arms of the cross, 54 = 2 × 27 LM. They suppose the plan of each chapel to be an exact half square, 16 × 8 UM. Finally, the radius and diameter of the apses are 4 and 8 LM. The plan of the church is thus interpreted as an overlaying of three systems of squares (see Figure 11.14):

(1) The overall outline defined by the far walls of the chapels comprises four 27 m squares.
(2) Within this outline, four 16 UM squares define the width and depth of the arms.

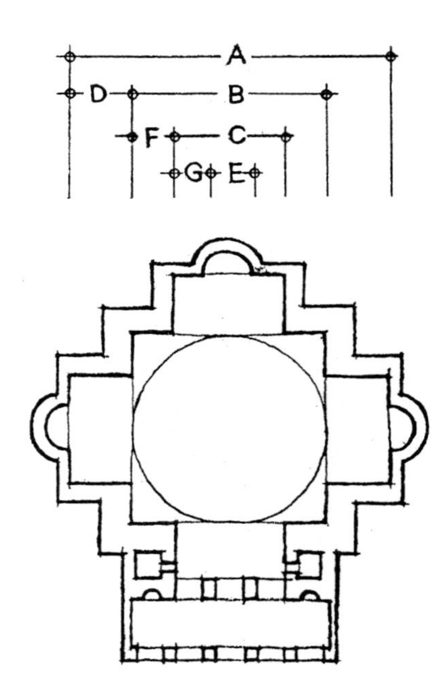

Figure 11.13 S. Sebastiano, Mantua: plan dimensions.

65. *Ibid.*
66. R. Tavernor, *On Alberti and the Art of Building*, pp. 142–3.

(3) The large square of the central space measures 27 UM.

The 27 UM dimension also equals the height to the top of the pendentives that once supported the hemispherical dome shown in Labacco's drawing, so the central volume of the church is contained within one 27 UM cube or twenty-seven 9 UM cubes. Similarly, the overall interior volume, measured from end to end of the arms and to the summit of the cupola, comprises eight 27 LM cubes (see Figure 11.15). All these numbers are squares or cubes: $4 = 2^2, 8 = 2^3, 9 = 3^2$, $16 = 4^2$ and $27 = 3^3$. The highest value was placed on such numbers, both by Alberti and, as Auguste Choisy points out, by the ancient Greeks.[67] The numbers 4, 8, 9 and 27 will also be recognized from Plato's account of the formation of the World Soul in the *Timaeus*. The Rykwert/Tavernor measures are summarized in Table 11.9.

Leaving aside the problem of the basic measure and the fact that certain key dimensions have been superseded by more recent surveys, a further objection to this interpretation is its complexity. Not only does it depend on two sets of measures, but only three of the nine key dimensions can be expressed simply as multiples of 1 UM. There are good grounds to believe that Alberti, no less than the ancient Greeks or the builders of Chartres, went out of his way to preserve integral measures. In the Tempio Malestestiano at Rimini, for instance, Alberti adopted a Roman foot of 296 mm instead of the local measure, and made the width of the facade exactly one hundred feet.[68] The same objection can be raised to the fractional measures given by Labacco in the note that accompanies his plan. If these were merely translations into Mantuan *braccia* of measurements taken from a model or from the building itself, they do not necessarily reflect Alberti's own intentions. It therefore seems worth investigating whether a solution is possible that relies on a uniform integral measure, preferably expressed in round numbers like fifty or one hundred.

Let us start from the assumption that Alberti made all key dimensions multiples of a uniform measure, and that this measure is retrievable by looking for a common factor among the measured dimensions of the building. Table 11.10 shows the result of this investigation. Most of the actual measures[69] are approximate multiples of a hypothetical unit somewhere between 320 and 330 mm. The mean average between these, 325 mm, has been assumed in the table. The

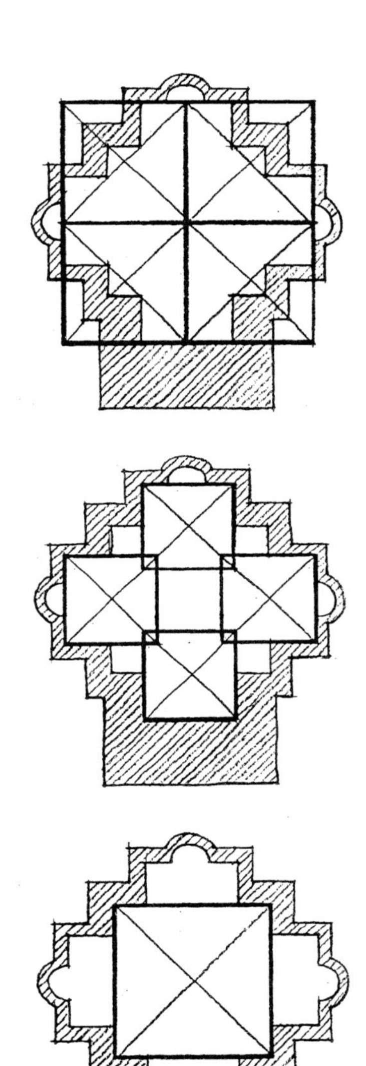

Figure 11.14 S. Sebastiano, Mantua: plan proportions, after J. Rykwert and R. Tavernor, 1979.

67. A. Choisy, *Histoire de l'architecture*, Bibliothèque de l'Image, 1996, vol. I, p. 390.
68. R. Tavernor, *On Alberti and the Art of Building*, p. 75.
69. Derived from A. Calzona and L. Volpi Ghirardini, *Il San Sebastiano*, pp. 87–8.

margin of error is sometimes rather large, but in view of the conditions under which S. Sebastiano was built, not incredible. Similar discrepancies occur between the foot measures intended by Palladio as shown in the *Four Books on Architecture*[70] and the real dimensions of Palladio's buildings published by Bertotti Scamozzi.[71] If a unit of about 325 mm was indeed the one chosen by Alberti, it is clearly a foot measure of some sort. It corresponds closely to both the 'Olympic' or 'Periclean' foot of 326–328 mm, which Rhys Carpenter puts forward as a measure for the Parthenon[72] (and which in fact appears to fit the temple rather well – see Table 5.4), and the 'Cretan' foot of 320 mm proposed in the last chapter as a measure possibly used at Chartres (see Tables 10.1 and 10.3). That the same measure happens to fit (give or take a few millimetres) all three of the buildings selected for examination in this book is a remarkable coincidence. But it is *merely* a coincidence. Whether Alberti, or for that matter the builders of the Parthenon or Chartres, actually used such a measure, I do not pretend to judge. We shall find in Chapter 15 that the 'blue' measures of Le Corbusier's *modulor*, and consequently the dimensions of the *Unité d'habitation* at Marseilles, converge to multiples of a 330 mm 'foot'; yet that was certainly not Le Corbusier's conscious intention.

The same measures recur with the vertical dimensions of S. Sebastiano. The height of the intended dome shown in Labacco's drawing is about 80 units (A), that of the arches that support it (that is, of the present cross-vault) is 50 (B), that of the vaults over the chapels 40 (A/2), that of the springing of the arches of the main space and of the vaults of the chapels both 25 (B/2), and the height of the half-domes of the apses 20 (A/4) (see Figure 11.16). The common factor of all the principal dimensions is 5 units, so the main scheme can be reinterpreted as a grid of 5 ft cubes. All the dimensions are shown in Table 11.11, first in 325 mm 'feet' and then where possible in 5 ft or 1.625 m units.

The presence of the proportion 3 : 5 : 8 or 6 : 10 : 16 recalls Vitruvius' discussion of the so-called 'perfect numbers', and relates to Robert Tavernor's recent exposition based on a recurrence of the ratio 6 : 10. Vitruvius writes in the *Ten Books* that

> As the perfect number the ancients fixed upon ten. . . Again, while ten is naturally perfect, as being made up by

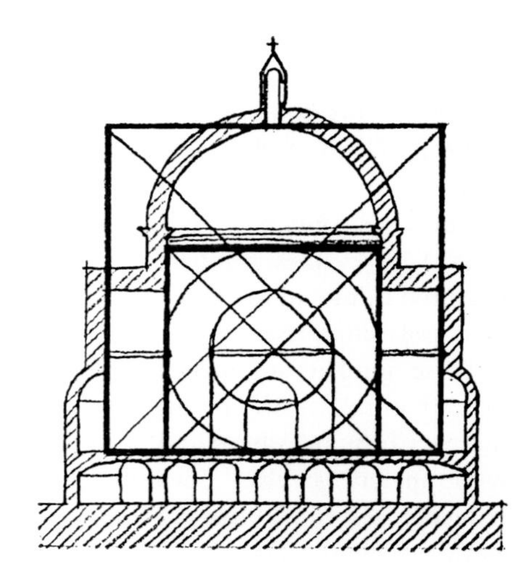

Figure 11.15 S. Sebastiano, Mantua: cross-section proportions, after J. Rykwert and R. Tavernor, 1979.

TABLE 11.9

	LM	UM
A	54	43.2
B	34	27
A/2	27	21.6
C	20	16
D	10	8
E	8	6.4
F	7	5.6
G	6	4.8
E/2	4	3.2

70. A. Palladio, *The Four Books on Architecture* (1570), trans. R. Tavernor and R. Schofield, MIT Press, 1997.
71. O. Bertotti Scamozzi, *Le fabbriche e i disegni di Andrea Palladio* (1796), Alec Tiranti, 1968.
72. R. Carpenter, *The Architects of the Parthenon*, Penguin Books, 1970, pp. 117, 175.

> the fingers of two palms, Plato also said that this number was perfect because ten is composed of the individual units, called by the Greeks *monades*. . . The mathematicians, however, maintaining a different view, have said that the perfect number is six. . . And further, as the foot is one sixth of a man's height, the height of the body as expressed in number of feet being limited to six, they held that this was the perfect number. . . But our countrymen. . . observing that six and ten were both of them perfect numbers, they combined the two, and thus made the most perfect number, sixteen.[73]

The description combines the mathematical concept of perfect numbers with the proportions of the body. Six is mathematically perfect because it is the sum of its own factors (1 + 2 + 3 = 6) and ten because it is the sum of the first four natural numbers (1 + 2 + 3 + 4 = 10), while sixteen, besides being the sum of six and ten, is the square of the first square number ($2^2 = 4, 4^2 = 16$).

In terms of the body, both Vitruvius and Alberti[74] take six to be the number of feet in a man's height. Ten is the number of fingers in both hands and sixteen the number of finger-widths, or digits in Roman measures, that make up a foot. Thus the major proportions of S. Sebastiano, 6 : 10 : 16, can be seen both as an embodiment of all three kinds of perfect number identified by Vitruvius, and as combining number theory with measures derived from the human body. Finally, the continued proportion 3 : 5 : 8 comprises the third, fourth and fifth Fibonacci numbers, so there is an approximation of the golden section.

What is remarkable about this analysis, however, is that it does not correspond to Alberti's recommendations for proportions in *The Art of Building* – either the whole-number measures shown in Tables 11.2–11.4 or the square root proportions shown in in Table 11.7. What conclusion one must draw from this is not clear. Did Alberti simply fail to practise what he preached, or are all the recent interpretations on the wrong track? One thing is certain: that despite the existence of the architect's own treatise containing prescriptions for proportion, the analysis of the proportions of his buildings leaves considerable room, after all, for speculation. When the measures shown in Table 11.11 are arranged as a grid of interwoven geometric progressions, they reveal themselves as belonging to a variant of the

TABLE 11.10

	METRES ACTUAL	METRES THEOR.	325mm FEET	% ERROR
A	26.371	26.0	80	1.4
B	16.099	16.25	50	0.9
A/2	13.186	13.0	40	1.4
C	9.416	9.75	30	3.5
D	5.136	4.875	15	5.1
E	3.809	3.9	12	2.4
F	3.341	3.25	10	2.7
G	2.803	2.925	9	4.3
E/2	1.904	1.95	6	2.4

TABLE 11.11

	325 mm FEET	1.625 m UNITS
A	80	16
B	50	10
A/2	40	8
C	30	6
B/2	25	5
A/4	20	4
D	15	3
E	12	–
F	10	2
G	9	–
E/2	6	–

73. Vitruvius, *The Ten Books on Architecture*, Dover Publications, 1960, pp. 73–4.
74. L.B. Alberti, 'On sculpture', in *On Painting and On Sculpture: The Latin Texts*, ed. and trans. C. Grayson, London, 1972.

Pythagorean system shown in Table 11.5. Interwoven with the two series formed by multiplying the unit by 2 (vertical) and 3 (horizontal), we now find two additional series based on 5 and its multiplication by 2 and 3. These series are shown in Table 11.12, with the quintuple progressions displaced diagonally with respect to the original ones (ideally the table would be three-dimensional, with the two grids shown on parallel planes). The measures of Table 11.11 are printed in bold.

Note that each quintuple number is the sum of the two original numbers diagonally upwards from left to right, and also the difference between those diagonally upwards from right to left: for example, 5 = 2 + 3, and 5 = 6 − 1. This system, which has great advantages from the point of view of flexibility, is generally thought to have been first introduced into architecture nearly a century later by Palladio. As such, it will be described in more detail in the following section. If it is indeed the basis of Alberti's design of S. Sebastiano, it indicates that the assumed chronology of the evolution of architectural proportion is in need of revision.

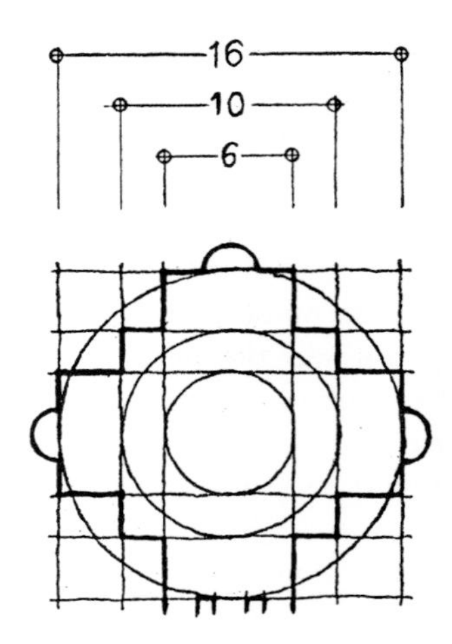

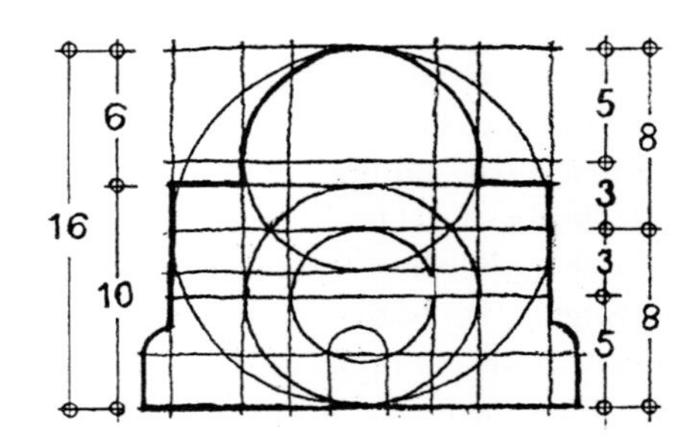

Figure 11.16 S. Sebastiano, Mantua: analysis of plan and section proportions.

TABLE 11.12

1		3		9
	5		15	
2		6		18
	10		30	
4		12		36
	20		60	
8		24		72
	40		120	
16		48		144
	80		240	

11.5 THE VILLAS OF PALLADIO

Andrea Palladio (1508–80) did not belong, like Alberti, to a wealthy family, and he did not have a university education. He was apprenticed at thirteen to a stone-carver in Padua, but broke the contract after three years and worked for a further fourteen years as apprentice and assistant to the stone-carvers Giovanni and Girolamo Pedemuro in Vicenza. His introduction to Humanist culture came only in his late twenties, when he was employed by the classical scholar, writer and amateur architect Count Giangiorgio Trissino (1478–1550) to make additions to his villa. Trissino took him under his wing, educated him, gave him the classical name Palladio, and took him to Rome to see the monuments of antiquity.[75] Later Palladio came in contact with other Humanists like Daniele Barbaro (1513–70) and the mathematician Silvio Belli, who may have been a source of his proportion theory.[76] Palladio later contributed drawings to Barbaro's edition of Vitruvius (1556), and designed the Villa Barbaro at Maser for him and his brother Marcantonio (1555–9).[77]

The Venetian villas on the *terrafirma* were part of a vast

75. R. Wittkower, *Architectural Principles*, pp. 52–5.
76. *Ibid.*, pp. 120–4, and J.S. Ackerman, *Palladio*, Penguin Books, 1966, p. 161.
77. J.S. Ackerman, *Palladio*, pp. 27, 36–40.

programme of economic consolidation by which the capitalist patrician families responded to the Republic's declining political and commercial importance by investing their fortunes in the land. On their newly reclaimed estates they needed a new sort of house, which combined the functional practicality of an agricultural building with classical elegance and grandeur: part farmstead, part palace. To design it, they needed a new sort of architect, and that, as James Ackerman writes,

> was Palladio: 'had he not existed he would have had to be invented.' In a sense, he was invented. If the quasi-country gentleman, Trissino, had not drawn him out of the stoneyard at the dawn of the agricultural revolution, he would not have been Palladio, much less an architect.[78]

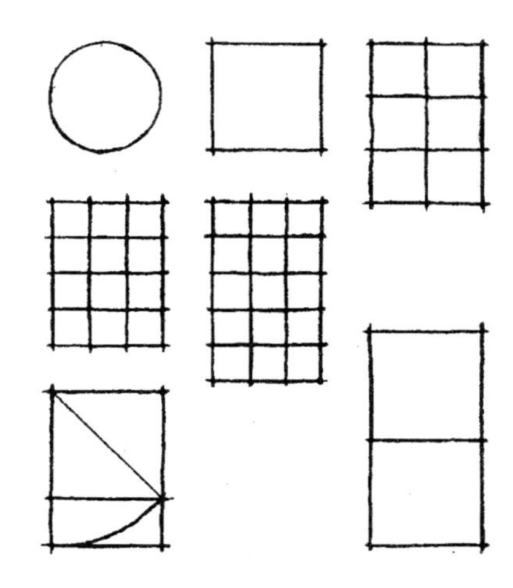

Figure 11.17 Andrea Palladio, recommended plan shapes for rooms.

Palladio's theory of proportion must be gleaned from the dimensioned plans in his *Four Books on Architecture*[79] rather than from the very brief text. The text furnishes only two relevant pieces of information. Like Alberti, Palladio recommends that the heights of rooms should be either the harmonic, geometric or arithmetic means of the lengths and breadths. For instance, for a double square plan the three dimensions can be either as 6 : 8 : 12 (harmonic) or as 6 : 9 : 12 (arithmetic). He warns, however, that a convenient numerical expression of the geometric mean is not always possible; in fact it is so only when the product of the length and breadth is a perfect square, their geometric mean being then the square root of that product: for example, 4 : 6 : 9.

He also shows seven examples of vaulted rooms, with as plan-shapes the circle, the square, the square-and-a-half, the square-and-a-third, the square-and-two-thirds, the double square, and finally a $\sqrt{2}$ rectangle with its length equal to the diagonal of the square on its shorter side (see Figure 11.17). The last-mentioned shape introduces an irrational proportion among the whole-number ratios of the other six plans, suggesting that Palladio, like Alberti, did not exclude incommensurable proportions in theory. Did he use them in practice? Wittkower asserts that 'neither Palladio nor any other Renaissance architect ever in practice used irrational proportions'.[80] If by irrational proportions is meant proportions that cannot be measured out, but only constructed geometrically with cords and pegs, this is probably quite true. But that is not quite what Wittkower implies, and

78. *Ibid.*, pp. 53–4.
79. A. Palladio, *The Four Books on Architecture*.
80. R. Wittkower, *Architectural Principles*, p. 95.

Palladio's published plans indicate that he did indeed use proportions derived from the irrational square roots of two and three, expressed as measurable lengths by means of rational convergents.

The square-and-two-thirds or three-by-five shape is also a departure from Alberti's and Giorgi's strictly Pythagorean ratios, and proportions involving ratios such as 5 : 4, 5 : 3 and 15 : 8 occur frequently in Palladio's plans. Wittkower links their introduction to the influence of contemporary developments in north Italian music theory, and specifically to the treatises of Ludovico Fogliano[81] and Gioseffo Zarlino.[82] These aimed to replace the complicated ratios that arise with the Pythagorean scale, such as the hemitone (256/243) and major third (81/64), with simpler and more harmonious ones. In Table 11.13 the octave divisions of the Pythagorean and diatonic scales are compared.

Mathematically, the argument for introducing five and its multiples is very strong. Study of Table 11.5 shows that the sums or differences of pairs of Pythagorean measures frequently equal five or multiples of five, as in Table 11.14.

The flexibility of the system is therefore greatly increased by interweaving a quintuple grid with the original one based on twos and threes, as in Table 11.15. Note that this is an extension of Table 11.12, which we derived from the measures of Alberti's S. Sebastiano. If the quintuple system was indeed anticipated by Alberti, it throws an interesting new light on Wittkower's theory. Not too much weight should be placed on this, however, since it is of course pure speculation.

A further innovation by Palladio is the use of continuous sequences of proportions between juxtaposed spaces. Alberti discusses only the proportions of individual rooms or *areas*; as we have seen, he defines the 'outline' as a correspondence between the length, breadth and height of a single volume:[83] in other words, as what Vitruvius calls 'eurhythmy' (in Van der Laan's interpretation of that term). Palladio seems to be the first Renaissance architect to apply the Vitruvian concept of 'symmetry': that is, to relate the corresponding measures of several interconnected spaces. At the Villa Malcontenta near Venice (before 1560) the lateral sequences are 1 : 2 : 1 and 3 : 2 : 3. As Wittkower points out,

> The systematic linking of one room to the other by harmonic proportions was the fundamental novelty of Palladio's architecture, and we believe that his wish to

TABLE 11.13

	C	D	E	F	G	A	B	C
Pythagorean	1/1	9/8	81/64	4/3	3/2	27/16	243/128	2/1
Diatonic	1/1	9/8	5/4	4/3	3/2	5/3	15/8	2/1

TABLE 11.14

1 + 4 = 5	2 + 3 = 5	1 + 9 = 10	6 − 1 = 5
8 − 3 = 5	9 − 4 = 5	16 − 1 = 15	32 − 27 = 5

TABLE 11.15

1		3		9		27		81		243
	5		15		45		135		405	
2		6		18		54		162		
	10		30		90		270			
4		12		36		108				
	20		60		180					
8		24		72						
	40		120							
16		48								
	80									
32										

81. L. Fogliano, *Musica theorica*, Venice, 1529.
82. G. Zarlino, *Le istitutioni harmoniche*, Venice, 1558.
83. L.B. Alberti, *On the Art of Building in Ten Books*, p. 305.

demonstrate this innovation had a bearing on the choice and character of the plates [in Palladio's *Four Books on Architecture*] and the inscription of measurements. Those proportional relationships which other architects had harnessed for the two dimensions of a facade or the three dimensions of a single room were employed by him to integrate a whole structure.[84]

We can now examine how far these measures correspond to the dimensions in Vicentine feet given in Palladio's plans. Some buildings – for instance the Villa Sarego at Miega (see Figure 11.18) – fit the scheme perfectly. In Table 11.16 the dimensional scheme is shown as a fragment of Table 11.15.

Many villas – including the Pisani at Bagnolo, the Malcontenta, the Godi at Lonedo, the Emo at Fanzolo, and the Tiene at Cicogna – are strictly Pythagorean: that is, they do not contain five or its multiples. Others again, however, and among them the most famous, conspicuously refuse to conform to either version of the whole-number scale. Mixed in with multiples of two, three and five one finds repetitions of certain typical ratios and sequences, such as 17 : 12, 7 : 4, 13 : 8, 15 : 11 and 26 : 15. The last two are the key ratios of Palladio's best-known work, the Villa Rotonda (see Figure 11.19).

How can this be explained? Lionel March argues that they are rational convergents or whole-number approximations for irrational proportions based on square roots, and that this was the normal method of expressing irrationals for the mathematicians of the time. Thus $\sqrt{2}$ was expressed by the series of continued fractions 1/1, 3/2, 7/5, 17/12, 41/29,. . ., $\sqrt{3}$ by the series 1/1, 2/1, 5/3, 7/4, 19/11, 26/15,. . ., and ϕ by the Fibonacci series 1/1, 2/1, 3/2, 5/3, 8/5, 13/8,. . . He concludes that

> The harmony expressed in 'La Rotonda' by the architect and patron is not in tune with the limited and restrictive harmonic intervals of musical theory, but is shaped by the more permissive possibilities of arithmetic and the rational measurement of geometric figures. . . Certainly, as in music, simple numbers are the grounds and generators for this harmony, be they the numbers 1, 2, 3, 4; or the threeness of the triangle, the fourness of the square, the fiveness of the pentagon. . .[85]

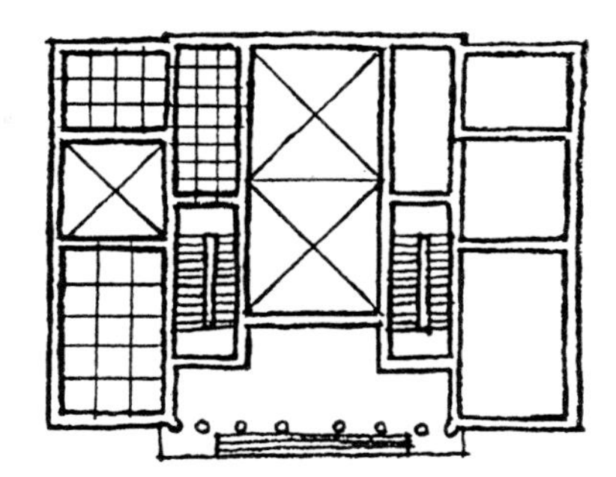

Figure 11.18 Andrea Palladio, Villa Sarego, Miega: plan.

TABLE 11.16

*		*		9		27
	*		15		*	
*		*		18		*
	10		*		*	
4		12		*		*
	20		*		*	
8		24		*		
	40		*			
16		*				

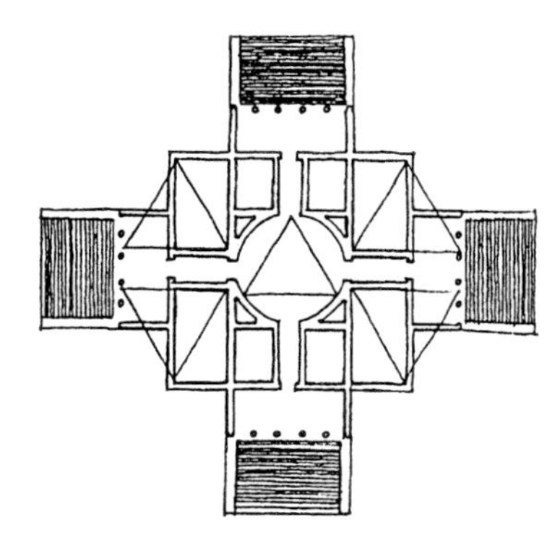

Figure 11.19 Andrea Palladio, Villa Rotonda, Vicenza: plan.

84. R. Wittkower, *Architectural Principles*, p. 113.
85. L. March, *Architectonics of Humanism*, p. 265.

Now, of the typical Palladian ratios listed above, 17 : 12 is a rational convergent for $\sqrt{2}$; 7 : 4 and 26 : 15 converge towards $\sqrt{3}$; and 13 : 8 is a Fibonacci ratio, and thus a rational convergent for ϕ. The most puzzling relation, 15 : 11, the proportion of the smaller rooms at the Villa Rotonda, turns out to be a very close approximation to $(\sqrt{3} + 1) : 2$, or 2.732 : 2. This seems more plausible when one considers that the proportion of the adjoining larger rooms is 26 : 15 or $\sqrt{3} : 1$, so there is a direct relation between the two shapes. The $\sqrt{3}$ theme is further reinforced by the central rotonda, whose diameter is thirty and its radius fifteen feet. Consequently the side of an equilateral triangle inscribed within it would measure almost exactly twenty-six feet, and the rectangle defined by the radius of the circle and the side of the inscribed triangle – that is, 26 × 15 – is identical in size and shape to the plan of the main rooms (see Figure 11.19). Conversely, the diameter of the circle, thirty feet, equals the diagonal of the room plan.

All these sequences of ratios were explored in Chapter 3, Tables 3.3–3.17. Table 11.17 shows the key dimensions of the Rotonda (printed in bold) in the context of the complete system to which they belong. Compare this with Table 3.17 in Chapter 3.

If this speculation is correct, the dimensions of many of Palladio's plans prove to be far less arbitrary than they previously appeared. Each villa may be based on a particular mathematical theme, very possibly with a symbolic significance. The Renaissance was an age that delighted in number symbolism and in mathematical games, analogies and conceits, whether in musical composition, the making of verse, or architecture. There are strong grounds for thinking that the 'conceit' of the Rotonda is based on three and the square root of three, perhaps a metaphor for the Trinity – an appropriate theme considering that the client was a retired Monsignore.

Furthermore, this theory implies that Palladio and the Humanist scholars of his circle in the Accademia Trissiniana and Accademia Olimpica[86] were interested in *both* aspects of Plato's mathematics: not only the whole-number harmonic intervals, as Wittkower supposes, but also the ratios resulting from the irrational square roots of two and three, and from the golden section – in fact all the ratios generated by the five regular polyhedra.

TABLE 11.17

1	3	4	**11**	**15**
2	5	7	19	**26**
3	9	**12**	33	45

86. J.S. Ackerman, *Palladio*, p. 31.

Chapter twelve

RENAISSANCE COSMOLOGY

The mathematical things are the cause of the physical because God from the beginning of time carried within himself in simple and divine abstraction the things as prototypes of the materially planned quantities.[1]

12.1 EMPATHIC AND ABSTRACT TENDENCIES

Two contrasting directions can be discerned in Renaissance cosmology, both of which led eventually to the scientific revolution of the seventeenth century: to Galileo, Descartes and Newton. The first direction was inspired chiefly by mathematics, and it was principally the work of Nicolas Copernicus (1473–1543) and Johannes Kepler (1571–1630). The second, represented by the thought of Nicholas Cusanus (*c.* 1400–64) and Giordano Bruno (1548–1600), was more speculative and philosophical in nature. The first, which in Kepler's words regarded 'the mathematical things as the cause of the physical', may be described as tending towards empathy; the second, towards abstraction.

Like almost every aspect of the Renaissance, both tendencies were rooted in the past. Frances Yates' remark is again relevant: 'The great forward movements of the Renaissance all derive their vigour, their emotional impulse, from looking backwards.'[2] They looked backwards, however, to a different past; and they also moved forwards in contrasting directions. The past to which Copernicus and Kepler looked back was the mathematical universe of Plato's *Timaeus* and Euclid's *Elements*. The ideas of Cusanus and Bruno were likewise influenced by Neoplatonism, but they had roots also in a more recent period. Cusanus has been described as 'the last great philosopher of the dying Middle

1. J. Kepler, quoted in M. Caspar, *John Kepler*, New York, 1960, p. 67.
2. F.A. Yates, *Giordano Bruno and the Hermetic Tradition*, Routledge & Kegan Paul/University of Chicago Press, 1964, p. 1.

Ages',[3] and his thought derived partly from that of the late Medieval mystic Meister Eckhart (1260–1328), just as Bruno's was indebted to the Hermetic magic of Marsilio Ficino and Pico della Mirandola.[4] And when one considers what the seventeenth century owed to these four men, there is again a divergence. The continuity with Copernicus and Kepler is more obvious; but the space of Copernicus, unlike Newton's, is still a finite sphere, and his celestial bodies are still carried round by crystalline spheres, while Kepler's universe is ruled by the Platonic geometry of regular polyhedra and the numbers of musical harmony. In contrast, Cusanus, 100 years earlier, already describes the world as limitless (*interminatum*), and Bruno rejoices in its infinity, and was prepared to burn for it. So paradoxically the less systematic, less 'scientific' thinkers came closer to the universal, infinite and acentric space of Newton's *Principia* (1687).

12.2 LEARNED IGNORANCE

Nicholas of Cusa (or *Cusanus*) was born in 1401 at Cues on the Moselle, and studied law and theology at Padua and Cologne. He was made Cardinal by Pope Nicholas V in 1448. The central doctrines of his treatise *De docta ignorantia* ('Of learned ignorance') are the notion of infinity and the relativity of all human knowledge. His 'negative theology' teaches that God's nature is beyond human comprehension. If we are not blasphemously to ascribe to Him human attributes – to shape Him in our own image – we can only define Him negatively, by describing what we do *not* know. True learning is the recognition of the extent of our ignorance. Cusanus' cosmology is a development, and as it were an illustration, of his theology.

Considered in terms of infinity, all opposites meet. In geometry, curves and straight lines are regarded as opposites; but the circumference of an infinitely large circle coincides with its tangent, and of an infinitely small one, with its diameter. Similarly, the opposition of motion and rest disappears at infinity: a body that moves in a circle at infinite speed is always in the same place, and at the same time also elsewhere.

The world, being by definition the totality of all physical things, can have no circumference – because that would

3. A. Koyré, *From the Closed World to the Infinite Universe*, Johns Hopkins University Press, 1957, p. 6.
4. F.A. Yates, *Giordano Bruno*.

imply that it is delimited by something existing outside itself – and consequently no centre. And

> Since, therefore, it is impossible to enclose the world between a corporeal centrum and a circumference, it is [impossible for] our reason to have a full understanding of the world, as it implies the comprehension of God who is the center and the circumference of it.[5]

Thus, a century before Copernicus, Cusanus reasons that the earth cannot be the centre of the universe. But whereas Copernicus merely displaces the earth to make way for the sun, Cusanus starts out from a more radical position: the earth cannot be at the centre because there *is* no centre. Consequently he does not place the sun at the centre either, or any other body: for 'It is impossible for the machine of the world to have any fixed and motionless center; be it this sensible earth, or the air, or fire or anything else.'[6] Many of Cusanus' statements appear to anticipate the concept of relativity; with one foot in the thirteenth century, he seems to have the other in the twentieth, even foreshadowing the Einsteinian simile of a passenger in a moving vehicle:

> For it is clear that this earth really moves, though it does not appear to us to do so, because we do not apprehend motion except by a certain comparison with something fixed. Thus if a man in a boat, in the middle of the stream, did not know that the water was flowing and did not see the bank, how would he apprehend that the boat was moving?[7]

Wherever the observer is stationed, whether on the earth, on the sun or some other celestial body, he will appear to himself to be the unmoving centre with respect to which everything else moves; but what he experiences as a state of rest will be seen as motion from another viewpoint.

In Cusanus' relativistic world, as Alexandre Koyré writes,

> The very ideal of Greek and mediaeval astronomy, that is, the reduction of celestial motions to a system of interlocking uniform circular ones which would 'save' the phenomena by revealing the permanent stability of the real behind the seeming irregularity of the apparent, is fallacious and must be abandoned. Yet Nicholas of Cusa

5. N. Cusanus, *De docta ignorantia* (1440), quoted in A. Koyré, *From the Closed World to the Infinite Universe*, p. 11.
6. *Ibid.*
7. *Ibid.*, p. 17.

> goes even further and. . . asserts that the world-image of a given observer is determined by the place he occupies in the universe; and as none of these places can claim an absolutely privileged value. . . we have to admit. . . the utter impossibility of forming an objectively valid representation of the universe.[8]

On the other hand, Koyré insists, one must beware of the temptation to

> read into him all kinds of anticipations of later discoveries, such, for instance, as the flattened form of the earth, the elliptic trajectories of the planets, the absolute relativity of space, the rotation of the heavenly bodies upon their axes.[9]

If at times he seems to assert all of these things, what separates him from the world-view of the seventeenth century as well as of the twentieth is that 'He denies the very possibility of the mathematical treatment of nature.'[10]

12.3 THE COPERNICAN REVOLUTION

In astronomy as in architecture, the Renaissance brought about a revolution. In neither case, however, was a revolution intended. It grew, in both cases, out of the Humanist drive to restore ancient Classical civilization and recover the authenticity of ancient texts. Just as Alberti's *On the Art of Building* was modelled on Vitruvius' *De Architectura*, so the *De Revolutionibus* of Copernicus arose from a careful study of, and aimed only to resolve problems inherent in, the ancient text that had dominated astronomical theory for fourteen centuries, the *Almagest* of the Alexandrian geometer and astronomer Claudius Ptolemy (*c*. AD 100–168).

The Ptolemaic system had in turn been designed to overcome various problems that arose in the earlier cosmology of Aristotle, who assumed that the earth was the fixed point at the centre of the universe, and that the celestial bodies were attached to a series of concentric crystalline spheres rotating around it. Moving outwards from the earth, the planets were the moon, Mercury, Venus, the sun, Mars, Jupiter and Saturn. Outside the sphere of Saturn was that of the fixed stars, beyond which was placed the sphere of the *primum mobile*, the motive force that kept the whole

8. *Ibid.*, p. 16.
9. *Ibid.*, p. 19.
10. *Ibid.*

mechanism revolving at the enormous speeds required.

In order to fit this conception to observed phenomena, the system had to be made increasingly elaborate. In Ptolemy's version, only the fixed stars moved in a perfect or 'deferent' circle around the earth. All the other bodies were seen to move in more complicated ways – appearing to be at different distances from the earth at various times – and also to move at varying speeds, the planets sometimes actually moving backwards against the background of the stars. To explain this, more circles were added: 'epicycles', small circles centred on the circumference of the deferent, causing the planet's orbit to make a series of loops as it circled the earth; 'eccentrics' (larger circles centred on points that themselves rotated around the earth); and 'equants' (see Figure 12.1).

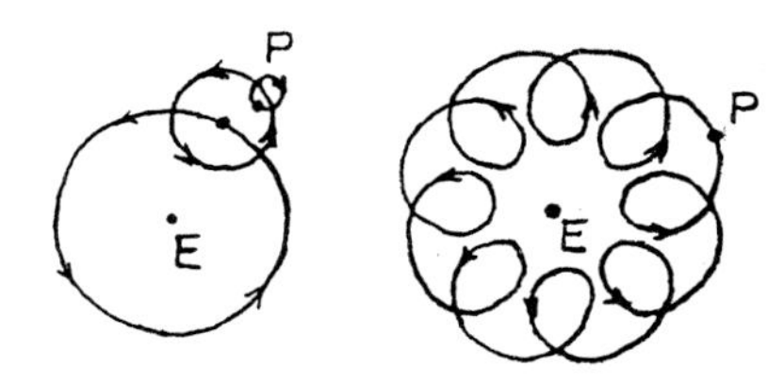

Figure 12.1 Ptolemaic system: arrangements of epicyclic and deferent circles cause planet (P) to move in a series of loops around the central earth (E), from T.S. Kuhn, *The Copernican Revolution*.

Until Galileo began to use his improved telescopes (about 1610), these complex devices adequately took account of all the movements that could be observed, so from a strictly scientific point of view there was not yet a pressing need to replace them. At the time that Copernicus wrote, no new discovery forced a reinterpretation. What drove him to seek alternative explanations was not scientific need but a conviction – the opposite of Cusanus' denial of the possibility of mathematical exactitude – that the universe must be a mathematically ordered harmony. It must have, as it were, that same *concinnitas* that Alberti demanded in architecture. The Ptolemaic system, with all its complex devices, was too contrived, too *untidy*, to satisfy this belief.

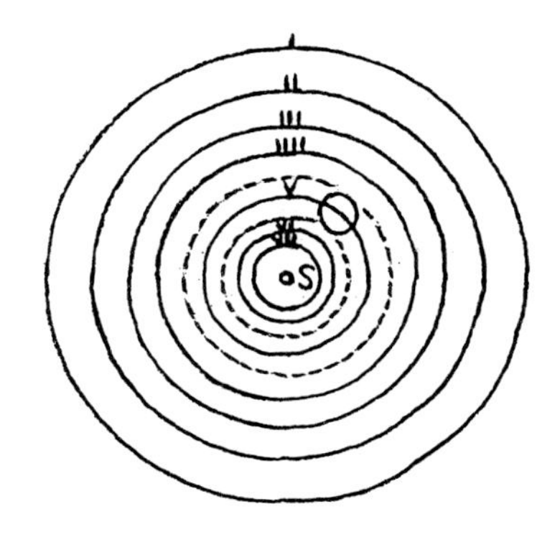

Figure 12.2 Copernican system of the world: S = Sun; I–VII = Saturn, Jupiter, Mars, Earth, Venus and Mercury; from N. Copernicus, *De revolutionibus orbium Coelestium* (1543).

In proposing to replace the geocentric system of Ptolemy with his own heliocentric one (see Figure 12.2), Copernicus had to face objections that today appear trivial, but to which his answers sounded to most contemporary ears implausible. For did not all our physical experience confirm that the earth was stationary? If it rotated, why were not its atmosphere and everything detached from its surface left behind? How was gravity to be explained, if the earth was not the centre to which everything in the universe gravitated? If the moon still revolved around the earth, was it not simpler to explain the motion of the other bodies in the same way? Above all, why did not the annual revolution of the earth about the sun result in an observable parallax or apparent mutual shifting of the stars? (Copernicus correctly responded that the sphere of fixed stars was far more distant than had formerly been assumed, and that the parallax was consequently too small to be seen; the angle of parallax was only finally determined in 1838.) Thus in many respects the Copernican universe seemed in its time to raise more questions than it answered. Its only practical advantages were the comparative simplicity and somewhat greater accuracy of its mathematics.

Copernicus' aim, however, was not to solve problems of day-to-day astronomy, nor to rid the Ptolemaic scheme of what today would be regarded as its physical implausibilities (he retained, for example, the crystalline spheres); rather, it was to construct a geometrically and conceptually more coherent picture of the world.

> The Copernican would replace the Ptolemaic system, he believed, because it was simpler, more harmonious, more ingenious and more in keeping with the underlying philosophical basis, which demanded that the motions of the heavenly bodies, being perfectly circular, be represented by mathematical curves that were as nearly perfect circles as might be. It was on this that he wished to be judged.[11]

It has been argued that by removing the earth from the centre Copernicus demoted it, and with it the home of mankind, to an inferior and less dignified place in the cosmos. The opposite is the case. As A.O. Lovejoy has pointed out, the centre of the universe was not, for the Medieval mind, a position of honour, but (in Montaigne's words) the place of 'the filth and mire of the world, the worst, lowest, most lifeless part of the universe, the bottom story of the house', and the farthest removed from the celestial region beyond the sphere of the fixed stars which was God's habitation:

> The actual centre, indeed, was Hell; in the spatial sense the medieval world was literally diabolocentric. . . [The] geocentric cosmography served rather for man's humiliation than for his exaltation, and. . . Copernicism was opposed partly on the ground that it assigned too dignified and lofty a position to his dwelling-place.[12]

The theological objection to heliocentricism was the objection to Renaissance Humanism in general: that it tended to elevate man to an almost godlike status.

Copernicus' placing of the sun at the centre of the

11. M. Boas, *The Scientific Renaissance 1450–1630*, Fontana/Collins, 1970, p. 71.
12. A.O. Lovejoy, *The Great Chain of Being*, Harper & Row, 1960, pp. 101–2.

universe (or to be exact, *near* its centre, since observation showed the orbits of the planets to be slightly eccentric) also had a classical and Humanist motivation. He believed that he was thereby returning to Pythagorean teaching, although in fact his system was more closely anticipated by Aristarchos of Samos (*c.* 270 BC). Marsilio Ficino, the Humanist scholar and translator of Plato, had composed in 1463 a rhapsody to the sun as the source of all goodness – light, warmth and generation:

> Perhaps light is itself the celestial spirit's sense of sight, or its act of seeing, operating from a distance, linking all things to heaven, yet never leaving heaven nor mixing with external things. . . Just look at the skies. . . The sun can signify God to you, and who shall say that the sun is false?[13]

The Ptolemaic system's treatment of the sun as merely another planet conflicted with this special status. But Copernicus, like Ficino, writes in *De Revolutionibus* that

> In the centre of all resides the Sun. Who, indeed, in this most magnificent temple would put the light in another, or in a better place than that one wherefrom it could at the same time illuminate the whole of it?[14]

This architectural metaphor is a last, lingering manifestation of the ancient empathic notion of the universe as a vast building – the house as model for the cosmos – which was so striking a feature of early Greek science, and indeed of still older, more primitive ideas about the world. After Copernicus and Kepler, this connection was finally broken – with profound consequences, as we shall see, for the theory of architectural proportion.

The source of this rupture was the transition from what Alexandre Koyré has called 'the closed world' to 'the infinite universe'.[15] Koyré points out that the Copernican universe, like that of Plato and Aristotle, was still finite and hierarchical: the sun was its centre, the sphere of the fixed stars its limit. He cites Copernicus' statement that

> The universe is spherical; partly because this form, being a complete whole, needing no joints, is the most perfect of all; partly because it constitutes the most spacious form

13. M. Ficino, *De sole* (1463), quoted in A.G. Debus, *Man and Nature in the Renaissance*, Cambridge University Press, 1978, p. 79.
14. N. Copernicus, *De Revolutionibus* (1543), quoted in A.G. Debus, *Man and Nature in the Renaissance*, p. 82.
15. A. Koyré, *From the Closed World to the Infinite Universe*, p. 2.

> which is thus best suited to contain and retain all things; or also because all discrete parts of the world, I mean the sun, the moon and the planets, appear as spheres.[16]

All the evidence confirms, concludes Koyré, that

> The world of Copernicus is finite. Moreover, it seems to be psychologically quite normal that the man who took the first step, that of arresting the motion of the sphere of the fixed stars, hesitated before taking the second, that of dissolving it in boundless space; it was enough for one man to move the earth and to enlarge the world so as to make it immeasurable – *immensum*; to ask him to make it infinite is obviously asking too much.[17]

12.4 THE INFINITE UNIVERSE AND THE INFINITY OF WORLDS

Although immeasurably larger than the Medieval world, the world of Copernicus is still delimited, still something that can bear some relation to and serve as a model for human creations, including architecture. Later Copernicans, like Thomas Digges (*c.* 1543–95), Giordano Bruno and William Gilbert (1540–1603), took the step that Copernicus stopped short of, proposing an infinite and thereby implicitly (and in the case of Bruno also explicitly) acentric universe.

Giordano Bruno was born at Nola near Naples in 1548. He studied at Naples university and entered the Dominican order – thus following in the footsteps that his countryman Thomas Aquinas had taken more than three hundred years earlier. His independence of mind and his disputatious nature soon got him into trouble with his superiors, and in 1576 he quitted the order. After three years roaming round Italy he became an exile, establishing himself in Geneva, Toulouse, Paris and England. Leaving England in 1585 he resumed his wanderings on the continent. In 1592 he unwisely returned to Venice, where the following year he was arrested by the Inquisition and brought to Rome. There he spent seven years in prison before being tried and burnt at the stake in 1600.

He embraced with enthusiasm the new cosmology of Copernicus, but went beyond him in asserting, like Cusanus,

16. N. Copernicus, quoted in *ibid.*, p. 31.
17. A. Koyré, *From the Closed World to the Infinite Universe*, pp. 33–4.

Already in his first book, the *Mysterium Cosmographicum*, written in 1596 before he had access to Tycho's observations, he believed he had found the solution in the five elementary solids or regular polyhedra, the basic elements of the World's Body in the *Timaeus*, the book that Kepler regarded as 'beyond all possible doubt, a commentary on the book of Genesis. . . transforming it into Pythagorean philosophy, as will be easily apparent to an attentive reader who compares it with Moses' own words'.[30]

As Euclid demonstrates in the thirteenth book of the *Elements*, there can be no more than five regular solids, so there is one for each interval between the six planets. The relative sizes of these intervals, Kepler proposes, is determined by the ratios of their circumspheres and *inspheres* (that is, the inscribed spheres that touch the centres of the faces of the polyhedra). At this stage he still assumes the planetary orbits to be circular, but eccentric with respect to the sun (elliptical orbits make their first appearance in the *Astronomia Nova*, 1609). Each orbit occupies a notional sphere (no longer the material, crystalline spheres of Ptolemy and Copernicus), which has a certain thickness to accommodate the diameter of the planet. Between the inner face of the orb of one planet and the outer face of that of the next Kepler places one of the five polyhedra. Thus the inner face of the upper orb corresponds to the circumsphere, and the outer face of the lower orb corresponds to the insphere, of the solid.

But in what order should the polyhedra be placed? Kepler is not content with an arbitrary or merely convenient order, for God made a perfect world. He therefore bases his arrangement on a hierarchy. He distinguishes three primary solids – tetrahedron, cube and dodecahedron – on the grounds that each of these has a different type of face, unique to itself, and has simple solid angles at which three faces meet, whereas the two secondary forms – octahedron and icosahedron – both have triangular faces borrowed from the tetrahedron, and four or five faces meet at each vertex. He regards the octahedron as derived from the cube, since it can be inscribed within it by joining the centres of the cube's six faces (see Figure 8.19 in Chapter 8), and the icosahedron as derived from the dodecahedron in the same way (see Figure 8.18). Other arguments he advances for the classification include: that the primary solids are best appreciated when standing on one face, the secondary ones when suspended

30. J.V. Field, *Kepler's Geometrical Cosmology*, Athlone Press, 1988, p. 1.

from a vertex, and that 3 is a perfect number, 2 imperfect. Kepler's cosmological model is illustrated by a beautiful engraving, which shows the polyhedra as armatures nestling between the solid planetary orbs. Starting from the outermost planet, Saturn, they are arranged in the following order: cube, tetrahedron, dodecahedron, icosahedron, octahedron (see Figure 12.3).

By means of this essentially Platonic classification, Kepler is able to conclude that the placing of the earth so that its sphere divides the primary and secondary solids is right and inevitable, and he draws on theological arguments as to why there should be three solids outside and two inside. He proceeds to make further distinctions within the two sets of forms, arguing that the cube is the most perfect, the tetrahedron the next, and the dodecahedron the least perfect of the primary solids, and that their derived forms have a corresponding status among the secondary ones. Thus the order of the solids, and thereby the special status of earth as the home of man, are explained. The reasoning is aesthetic rather than scientific or rational in any sense that would be understood today.

Thus the ratios that determine the proportions of Kepler's universe are the same that governed Plato's world and the geometry of Euclid, and have traditionally been the basis of proportion in architecture: $1 : \sqrt{2}$, $1 : \sqrt{3}$, $1 : \sqrt{5}$, $1 : 2$, $1 : 3$ and $1 : \phi$, in various combinations. Table 12.1 repeats Table 8.3 from Chapter 8, but this time also includes the values of the inspheres.

Table 12.2 translates the same values into decimal approximations. The edges are omitted as irrelevant to the present argument, but the midspheres are still included because Kepler rather casually substitutes the midsphere for the insphere of the octahedron, since it happens to give a value closer to the observed distance.

Table 12.3 compares the calculated values resulting from the polyhedral ratios with Copernicus' observational data, the only ones then available to Kepler.

Kepler concludes that 'The corresponding numbers are close to one another, and those for Mars and Venus are the same.'[31] In view of the rather large divergence between the theoretical and observed value for Saturn/Jupiter, and the cavalier substitution of the midsphere for the insphere of the octahedron to make it fit the interval between Venus and Mercury, one might disagree. The fact is that Kepler's three

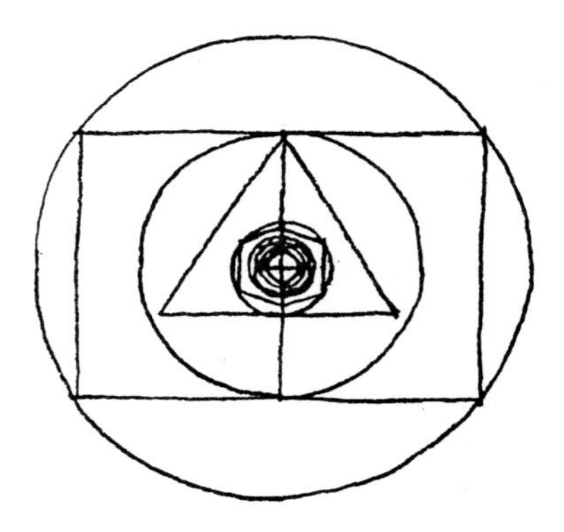

Figure 12.3 Kepler's system of the world based on mutually inscribed regular polyhedra: cube, tetrahedron, dodecahedron, icosahedron, octahedron; from J. Kepler, *Mysterium Cosmographicum* (1596).

TABLE 12.1

FORM	EDGE	IS	M/S	C/S
Tetrahedron	$\sqrt{2}/\sqrt{3}$	$1/3$	$1/\sqrt{3}$	1
Cube	$1/\sqrt{3}$	$1/\sqrt{3}$	$\sqrt{2}/\sqrt{3}$	1
Octahedron	$1/\sqrt{2}$	$1/\sqrt{3}$	$1/\sqrt{2}$	1
Icosahedron	$1/\sqrt{\phi\sqrt{5}}$	$1/\sqrt{15-6\sqrt{5}}$	$\phi/\sqrt{\phi\sqrt{5}}$	1
Dodecahedron	$1/\phi\sqrt{3}$	$1/\sqrt{15-6\sqrt{5}}$	$\phi/\sqrt{3}$	1

TABLE 12.2

FORM	I/S	M/S	C/S
Tetrahedron	0.3333	0.5773	1
Cube	0.5773	0.8165	1
Octahedron	0.5773	0.7071	1
Icosahedron	0.7947	0.8506	1
Dodecahedron	0.7947	0.9342	1

31. *Ibid.*, p. 48.

laws were the happy result of mistaken preconceptions. As we shall see in Chapter 15, there is a certain parallel in this respect, in the field of architectural proportion, with Le Corbusier's *modulor*. Neither author makes any attempt to conceal his blind alleys, but on the contrary devotes the major part of his text to the exposition of them. Both are glorious exceptions to the law of 'didactic inversion', according to which writers generally present their discoveries not in the order in which they actually made them, but in that which they would logically have followed if they had known where they were going when they started out. But Kepler, as Marie Boas says, 'never spared the reader any step of his own painful progress'.[32]

TABLE 12.3

PLANET	CIRCUMSCRIBED SOLID	CALCULATED OUTER RADIUS OF LOWER ORB IF INNER RADIUS OF UPPER ORB = 1	OBSERVED DITTO	DIFFERENCE AS % OF OBSERVED DATA
Saturn	–	–	–	–
Jupiter	Cube	0.5773	0.635	–9
Mars	Tetrahedron	0.3333	0.333	0
Earth	Dodecahedron	0.7947	0.757	+5
Venus	Icosahedron	0.7947	0.794	0
Mercury	Octahedron	0.7071 (M/S)	0.723	–2

12.7 THE MUSIC OF THE SPHERES

Nor did he himself regard the polyhedral scheme as a blind alley. He republished the *Mysterium Cosmographicum*, with extensive comments, in 1621, and it forms a major part of his mature theory, published as *Harmonices Mundi Libri V*, in 1619. There he makes another vain attempt to determine the relations of the planetary orbits on the basis of a Platonic mathematics, but this time in a still more complex way, by combining the geometry of regular polygons with the arithmetical intervals of the musical scale. Although this scheme, like the earlier one, fits the observed distances only approximately and coincidentally it is important for the connection between proportion in architecture (and art in general) and ideas about the harmony of nature. Karl Popper draws a parallel with music:

> Indeed, a great work of music (like a scientific theory) is a cosmos imposed upon chaos – in its tensions and harmonies inexhaustible even for its creator. This was described with marvellous insight by Kepler in a passage devoted to the music of the heavens.[33]

Here is the passage cited by Popper:

> Thus the heavenly motions are nothing but a kind of heavenly concert, rational rather than audible or vocal. They move through the tension of dissonances which are like syncopations or suspensions with their resolutions

32. M. Boas, *The Scientific Renaissance*, p. 283.
33. K.R. Popper, *Unending Quest*, Fontana Paperbacks, 1976, p. 59.

(by which men imitate the corresponding dissonances of nature), reaching secure and predetermined closures, each containing six terms like a chord consisting of six voices. And by these marks they distinguish and articulate the immensity of time. Thus there is no marvel greater or more sublime than the rules of singing in harmony together in several parts, unknown to the ancients but at last discovered by man, the ape of his Creator; so that, through the skilful symphony of many voices, he should actually conjure up in a short part of an hour the vision of the world's total perpetuity in time; and that, in the sweetest sense of bliss enjoyed through Music, the echo of God, he should almost reach the contentment which God the Maker has in His Own works.[34]

To appreciate this direct relation between the works of God and of man, one has to try to see it through Kepler's eyes, the eyes of a Renaissance man, standing with one foot, as it were, upon the *Timaeus* and the other on the Bible. He describes his theory of the heavens as physical 'or, if you prefer, metaphysical',[35] as if the two words were for him virtual synonyms. Clearly, he did not mean what today would be meant by the word 'physical'. The polyhedral armatures are not conceived as physical, material structures, nor are the planetary orbs any longer the solid crystalline spheres of Copernicus. 'Physical' is used here in the same sense as in the title of Aristotle's *Physics*, that is in the original meaning of the Greek word *physis*: Nature. And 'the mathematical things are the cause of the physical'. Nature is the product of its mathematical laws.

34. J. Kepler, *Gesammelte Werke*, vol. VI, p. 328.
35. J.V. Field, *Kepler's Geometrical Cosmology*, p. 52.

Chapter thirteen

THE WORLD AS A MACHINE

Mathematical Demonstrations being built upon the impregnable foundations of Geometry and Arithmetick, are the only Truths, that can sink into the mind of man, void of all uncertainty; and all other Discourses participate more or less of Truth, according as Their Subjects are more or less capable of Mathematical Demonstration.[1]

13.1 RUDOLF WITTKOWER AND THE COLLAPSE OF UNIVERSAL VALUES

In Chapter 1 I discussed briefly Rudolf Wittkower's opinion that the emergence of modern science in the seventeenth century brought about a collapse of 'universal values' – that is, of values based on systems of religious, magical or cosmological belief – and with them, of the main foundation of systems of proportion in art. Both *Architectural Principles in the Age of Humanism* (1949) and *The Changing Concept* (1953) end on this rather defeatist note, with 'the break-away from the laws of harmonic proportion in architecture'[2] about three centuries ago, and the improbability of a widespread return to them in the foreseeable future. In the later essay in particular, Wittkower argues that the new 'universe of mechanical laws' established by Isaac Newton and others in the seventeenth century – a world 'of iron necessity with no ulterior plan' – led, by the eighteenth, to a breakdown of the Pythagorean-Platonic tradition according to which, up to then, the necessity of objective, universally validated standards of proportion had been an unquestioned assumption.[3] Consequently the world of value, in which such concepts as 'harmony', 'beauty' and 'the good' had been objectively valid, was reduced to an excusively human, almost arbitrary affair, a question of 'taste', divorced from

1. C. Wren, Inaugural Lecture, Gresham College, 1657; quoted in M. Whinney, *Wren*, Thames & Hudson, 1971, p. 9.
2. R. Wittkower, *Architectural Principles in the Age of Humanism*, Alec Tiranti, 1952, pp. 124–35.
3. R. Wittkower, 'The changing concept of proportion', in *Idea and Image*, Thames & Hudson, 1978, p. 117.

the world of facts whose laws are purely 'mechanical' and devoid of human significance. The attitude of a man like Le Corbusier, for whom works of art proceed from and express the same mathematical laws by which nature is ruled,[4] must be seen as then no more than a relic from a credulous past. The universe is not, after all, ordered and harmonious, and order in art cannot be justified as a continuation of the natural order.

Wittkower's view is supported by the historian of science Alexandre Koyré. In *From the Closed World to the Infinite Universe* Koyré writes that

> The scientific and philosophical revolution. . . can be described roughly as bringing forth the destruction of the Cosmos, that is, the disappearance from philosophically and scientifically valid concepts, of the conception of the world as a finite, closed, and hierarchically ordered whole. . . and its replacement by an indefinite and even infinite universe which is bound together by the identity of its fundamental components and laws, and in which all these components are placed on the same level of being. This, in turn, implies the discarding by scientific thought of all considerations based upon value-concepts, such as perfection, harmony, meaning and aim, and finally the utter devalorization of being, the divorce of the world of value from the world of facts.[5]

The validity of this judgement must now be examined more closely, in the context of the philosophical and cosmological basis of systems of proportion in art and architecture. There is no doubt that since about the eighteenth century the question of mathematical systems of order in art has become problematical; the ancient certainty, which ruled up to and including the Renaissance, has been damaged if not destroyed. However, the historical connection between this and the scientific revolution can be quesioned. The decline of Renaissance canons of proportion in Mannerist and Baroque art and architecture *preceded*, by as much as a century, any possible influence from Baroque science. Conversely, in the eighteenth century, when that science did finally come to dominate educated thought, it coincided not with a final abandonment of the Renaissance canons, but a marked revival of them. The chronology does not bear out Wittkower's thesis.

4. Le Corbusier, *The Modulor*, Faber & Faber, 1961, pp. 29–30.
5. A. Koyré, *From the Closed World to the Infinite Universe*, Johns Hopkins University Press, 1957, p. 2.

Second, although the new cosmology involved an infinite universe obeying 'mechanical laws', the scientists themselves did not regard their universe as being without an 'ulterior plan'. The world described by Newton (1642–1727) in his *Philosophiae naturalis principia mathematica* or *Mathematical Principles of Natural Philosophy* (1687) is a world entirely governed, like the world of the *Timaeus*, by mathematical harmony. And Galileo Galilei (1564–1642) writes in *The Assayer* (1623) that

> Philosophy is written in this grand book, the universe, which stands continually open to our gaze. But the book cannot be understood unless one first learns to comprehend the language and read the letters in which it is composed. It is written in the language of mathematics, and its characters are triangles, circles, and other geometric figures without which it is humanly impossible to understand a single word of it. . .[6]

Had Plato – who forbade anyone ignorant of geometry to enter the Academy – been alive in the seventeenth century, he would have embraced with enthusiasm this new mathematical pattern, which brought the phenomena of motion within the scope of the ideal forms of mathematics.

Nor did the new scientific thought dispense with the need for a divine creator or, as Le Corbusier puts it, 'a single will'[7] underlying the order of the universe. Perfect laws demanded a perfect lawgiver, and the perfection of nature's architecture proved it to be the work of a faultless architect. If there were disagreements, they were about such questions as whether God was still an active force in the world, sustaining and occasionally adjusting its mechanism (as Newton believed) or whether this would imply (as Leibniz objected) that His work was imperfect, and He an unskilful workman, 'often obliged to mend his Work and to set it Right'.[8] Either way, it was agreed that 'This most beautiful system of the sun, planets, and comets could only proceed,' in Newton's words, 'from the counsel and dominion of an intelligent and powerful Being.'[9]

The universe revealed by seventeenth-century science was certainly mechanical, but it was a mathematically ordered, perfectly functioning machine, and moreover conceived as the creation of a divine intelligence. There could be no clearer model for the buildings and other works of art

6. Galileo, *The Assayer* (1623), in S. Drake, *Discoveries and Opinions of Galileo*, Doubleday, 1957, pp. 237–8.
7. Le Corbusier, *Towards a New Architecture*, Architectural Press, 1946, p. 193.
8. Leibniz, letter to Dr Clarke, November 1715, quoted in A. Koyré, *From the Closed World to the Infinite Universe*, p. 236.
9. I. Newton, *Mathematical Principles of Natural Philosophy*, trans. A. Motte, University of California Press, 1960, p. 544.

placed within that machine. At first sight there is no obvious reason why the scientific revolution should have undermined belief in the application of mathematical laws to art. But before dismissing Wittkower altogether, we must look a little more closely at the nature of the world that the scientific revolution revealed.

13.2 THE ATOMIST UNIVERSE

That world had been mapped out in its essentials more than two thousand years before, by Leucippus, Democritus and Epicurus, whose teaching was now revived by Pierre Gassendi (1592–1655) and others, mainly by way of Lucretius' poem *De rerum natura*. The ancient theory of atomism anticipated the corpuscular-kinetic world-picture of Galileo and Newton, and even the mechanistic determinism of nineteenth-century physicists like Pierre Laplace. Milic Capek writes:

> The only difference between Greek atomism and nineteenth-century physics was that the latter had incomparably more efficient and conceptual tools at its disposal than Democritus and Leucippus. . . Fundamentally, however, the basic conceptions were the same. This was the deep historical reason why the birth of modern science occurred simultaneously with the revival of atomism by Bruno, Bacon, Gassendi, and others.[10]

The ancient roots and main characteristics of the new world-picture are concisely summarized by Robert Boyle (1627–92) in his treatise *The Origin of Forms and Qualities*:

> I agree with our Epicureans in thinking the world is made up of an innumerable multitude of singly insensible corpuscles endowed with their own sizes, shapes and motions. . . If we should conceive that the rest of the universe were annihilated, except any of these entire and undivided corpuscles, it is hard to say what could be attributed to it, besides matter, motion (or rest), bulk and shape.[11]

The atomist universe is composed of four distinct entities:

---

10. M. Capek, *The Philosophical Impact of Contemporary Physics*, D. Van Nostrand Company, 1961, p. 123.

11. R. Boyle, *The Origin of Forms and Qualities* (1666), quoted in J.R. Urmson, *Berkeley*, Oxford University Press, 1982, p. 6.

(1) absolute space,
(2) absolute time,
(3) matter and
(4) motion or change.

These comprise two basic kinds of things: space and time, which are both empty, neutral containers; and matter and motion, which are their respective contents. Absolute space, in this world-view, conforms exactly to the requirements of Euclidian geometry. It is homogeneous (no point in space differs in any way from another) and therefore continuous: that is, both infinitely extended and infinitely divisible. It is also 'causally inert': that is, it does not imply, nor can it affect or be affected by, the matter contained in it. As Newton writes:

> Absolute space, in its own nature, without regard to anything external, remains always similar and immovable. Relative space is some movable dimension or measure of the absolute space; which our senses determine by its position to bodies. . .[12]

Absolute time shares these characteristics of space: it is homogeneous, infinite, continuous, uniform and inert with respect to its contents. It neither causes nor implies change:

> Absolute, true and mathematical time, of itself and by its own nature, flows uniformly, without regard to anything external, and by another name is called duration: relative, apparent, and common time, is some sensible and external. . . measure of duration by the means of motion. . .[13]

Thus both relative space and relative time are measured in relation to their contents: relative space by material bodies, relative time by motions. On the other hand, neither absolute space nor absolute time can have any beginning or end: the concept of a first moment that thereby differs from all others is as unthinkable as that of an ultimate point beyond which space ceases to exist. Therefore the creation must have taken place *in* time, and not have been, as theology demanded, the beginning *of* time.

Matter, in contrast to space and time, is discontinuous, comprising innumerable, perfectly rigid (that is, impenetrable), indivisible and indestructible atoms or 'corpuscles'.

12. I. Newton, *Mathematical Principles*, p. 6.
13. *Ibid.*

Their only properties are solidity, spatial extension, and inertia, as defined by Newton's first law of motion: that '*Every body continues in its state of rest, or of uniform motion in a right line, unless it is compelled to change that state by forces impressed upon it.*'[14] And just as matter fills portions of space, motions fill portions of time. In the words of Newton's tutor Isaac Barrow: 'Time is in some sort the Space of Motion.'[15] Since space and time are both causally inert, and atoms can act upon each other only mechanically – that is, by physical impact – nothing but motion can be either the cause, or the effect, of motion. On the other hand, motion is the only one of the four entities whose existence requires all the other three: it takes place *in* time and space, and its vehicle is a material body. In David Hume's words: 'The idea of motion necessarily supposes that of a body moving.'[16]

13.3 THE CHANGED NATURE OF MATHEMATICAL PROPORTION

The relations governing the motion of bodies in space and time in the Newtonian mechanical universe are determined, no less than in the world of the *Timaeus*, by precise mathematical *proportions*. The acceleration of a body is measured as a proportion of velocity to time, or of distance to time squared, and the force required to cause that acceleration is proportional to the acceleration and to the body's mass. As Newton states it in his second law of motion, '*The change of motion is proportional to the motive force impressed. . .*'[17] The centrifugal force resulting from the tendency of a planet orbiting about the sun to fly off tangentially in a straight line is exactly balanced by the centripetal or gravitational force that holds it in its orbit, and both are directly proportional to the product of the masses of the two bodies and inversely proportional to the square of the distance between their centres. If this balance were upset the planets would move off into space or crash into the sun. It is no coincidence that the universe was compared to a great clock, and its Creator to a clockmaker, or that these discoveries coincided with the development of the first reliable chronometers.

Why, then, did this new world-picture undermine the necessary and fundamental connection between natural philosophy and architectural proportion? Was not the 'great

14. ***Ibid.*, p. 13.**
15. I. Barrow, *On Space and Impenetrability*, quoted in M. Capek, *The Philosophical Impact of Contemporary Physics*, p. 38.
16. D. Hume, *A Treatise of Human Nature*, Everyman's Library, 1911, vol. I, p. 218.
17. I. Newton, *Mathematical Principles*, p. 13.

book of the universe' (as Galileo called it) more than ever written in the language of geometry and proportion? Was it not a still more perfect and conclusive realization of the ideal mathematical cosmology than could ever have been dreamed of by Pythagoras, Plato or Alberti? The universe was now shown, more clearly than ever before, to be governed by simple mathematical laws that the human mind was uniquely adapted to discover and understand. Rather than an abandonment of mathematical systems by artists, one might expect an unprecedented upsurge of enthusiasm; for this was surely the final victory of empathy over abstraction.

The problem is that the universe now revealed by science was in fact so completely *abstract* and mathematical that it ceased to have any apparent relation to the world of the senses, such as even the cosmology of the *Timaeus* had retained. Plato's four elements are composed of atomic geometrical forms, but they are still tangible. The element of fire is tetrahedral, because that form is the 'lightest', 'most mobile', and the 'sharpest and most penetrating' of the four chosen regular solids; earth, conversely, is cubic, because for Plato the cube is the most stable form. But the atomic matter of seventeenth-century science has lost this tangibility. And qualitative impressions like colour or warmth are not properties of matter as such, but superficial effects caused by the motion of atoms, combined with subjective additions supplied by the perceiving mind. As Galileo writes:

> To excite in us tastes, odors, and sounds I believe that nothing is required in external bodies except shapes, numbers, and slow or rapid movements. I think that if ears, tongues and noses were removed, shapes and numbers would remain, but not odors or tastes or sounds. . . Having shown that many sensations which are supposed to be qualities residing in external objects have no real existence save in us. . . I now say that I am inclined to believe heat to be of this character.[18]

Furthermore, while the new equations *saved the appearances* – that is, there was, or rather seemed to be, a perfect fit between the mathematical formulae and phenomena – they did not explain the causes of the phenomena as such. The fall of an apple, or the motions of the heavenly bodies, appeared to conform exactly to Newton's equation for gravity, but the equation did not explain *how* these masses could act upon

18. Galileo, *The Assayer*, pp. 276–7.

each other at a distance. In the *General Scholium* that concludes Newton's *Principia* he points out that although he has explained the phenomena of the solar system by the power of gravity, he has so far

> not been able to discover the cause of those properties of gravity from phenomena, and I frame no hypotheses; for whatever is not deduced from the phenomena is an hypothesis; and hypotheses, whether metaphysical or physical, whether of occult qualities or mechanical, have no place in experimental philosophy.[19]

There remained also the unresolved dispute about the nature of light: did it consist of particles or corpuscles *emitted* by the sources and able to travel through empty space, as Newton believed, or of waves *transmitted* through the space-filling ether, as held by Christian Huygens (1629–95)? The theory of the ether, which survived from Aristotle into the nineteenth and even the twentieth century, became less a description of something physically existing in the world than a description of the kind of mathematics necessary to quantify certain observed phenomena.

Alberto Pérez-Gómez concludes that

> In Galilean thought, visible reality loses importance in order to come to terms with a world of abstractions, relations and equations. In this world, truth becomes transparent, but only to the degree to which it avoids the irregularities of lived experience. . . Galilean science. . . was the beginning of the dissolution of the traditional cosmos.[20]

A century after Galileo's death, Hume would describe as the fundamental principle of the modern philosophy

> the opinion concerning colours, sounds, tastes, smells, heat, and cold; which it asserts to be nothing but impressions in the mind, derived from the operation of external objects, and without any resemblance to the qualities of the objects.[21]

In short, the analogy, underlined in my first chapters, between the house and the universe, which was essential to the traditional philosophical basis of architectural propor-

19. I. Newton, *Mathematical Principles*, p. 547.
20. A. Pérez-Gómez, *Architecture and the Crisis of Modern Science*, MIT Press, 1983, p. 19.
21. D. Hume, *A Treatise of Human Nature*, vol. I, p. 216.

tion, was no longer tenable. The abstract, infinite universe described by Galileo and Newton had no resemblance to a house, a palace, or a building of any kind.

13.4 SCIENCE AND ART

An intimate connection has often been argued between the revolutionary cosmology revealed by the new physics, and the Baroque art and architecture that more or less coincided with its development. It is one of the central themes of Sigfried Giedion's classic history of the Modern Movement, *Space, Time and Architecture*. He writes:

> In the late seventeenth century we find the baroque universality working with the infinite in the field of mathematics as a basis for practical calculations. In painting and architecture the impression of infinity – the infinite in a linear sense, as an indefinitely extended perspective – is being used as a means for artistic effect. Thus, early in the century, the Dutch landscape painters introduce an 'atmospheric infinity' into their works; somewhat later the Roman architects succeed in realizing the same mystical feeling of endlessness – often in astonishingly small churches – through a simultaneous exploitation of all the resources of painting, sculpture, architecture, and optical theory. With the French landscape architects of the late seventeenth century there appears the artistic employment of the infinity of nature. . . For the first time in history their gardens incorporated great highways as essential parts of an architectonic expression, and were placed by this means in direct and obvious relation with the unending extension of space. . . These gardens, in their total effect, stood as models of the baroque universe, and retained its aspect of infinity.[22]

In *Four Stages of Renaissance Style* the literary historian Wylie Sypher writes:

> The concepts of dynamic force, of inertia, of weight, mass, and motion, entered physics with Galileo. . . Newton gave these baroque laws of force their threefold definition, distinguishing between mass and weight, and formulating the dynamics of action and reaction, direction, and

22. S. Giedion, *Space, Time and Architecture*, Oxford University Press, 1941, p. 43.

> momentum. The rhythmical movement – the momentum, so to speak – in baroque style is analogous to the play of forces in baroque physics, matter having 'mass' as well as 'weight', and obviously a principle of 'motion compounded'. In baroque architecture the heaviest walls 'move' and 'swing' as they do in San Carlo alle Quattro Fontane, Rome (1638–68). . . with [its] facade activated throughout its two stories of half-engaged columns. . . The interior, a complicated ellipse, gives a similar impression of great masses in motion. . . Borromini has succeeded in endowing insignificant space with the aspect of containing massive forces in full play.[23]

How much truth is there in this analogy? It is tempting, for instance, to link the elliptical plan of Borromini's church[24] – and of others like Rainaldi's Santa Maria di Monte Santo (1662)[25] or Bernini's Sant'Andrea al Quirinale (1658),[26] not to mention the latter's elliptical Piazza San Pietro (1659)[27] – with the introduction by Kepler and Newton of elliptical orbits, replacing the circular ones of Ptolemy and Copernicus. But unless art and architecture led the way for, instead of following, developments in science and philosophy, the chronological facts are hard to reconcile. The abandonment of proportional rules by artists is more obvious in the Baroque age, which coincided with, and to some extent even preceded, the development of the new cosmology, than in the post-Newtonian eighteenth century that followed it. In the later period there was if anything a return to them, as we shall see, among the English neo-Palladians, and in France in the writings of Jacques-François Blondel (1705–74) and Charles-Etienne Briseux.

So if there is a connection, it cannot be a causal one. For example, the first appearance of oval plans in architecture and town planning far pre-dates even Kepler, let alone Newton. Sebastiano Serlio includes an oval temple in his *Fifth Book on Architecture*, published in 1547,[28] and the oval paving of Michelangelo's Capitol is thought to have been designed still earlier, by 1538.[29] Vignola built the oval church of Santa Anna dei Palafrenieri in 1572,[30] and Francesco Volterrano's San Giacomo degli Incurabili is dated 1592.[31] But Kepler's *Astronomia nova*, containing his first explanation of the elliptical orbits, was not published until 1609; his laws were not generally accepted by other astronomers, more-

23. W. Sypher, *Four Stages of Renaissance Style*, Doubleday/Anchor, 1955, pp. 201–2.
24. R. Wittkower, *Studies in the Italian Baroque*, Thames & Hudson, 1974, Fig. 224, p. 162.
25. *Ibid.*, Figs 5–6, p. 12.
26. *Ibid.*, Figs 31–3, p. 28.
27. *Ibid.*, Fig. 79, p. 56.
28. V. Hart and P. Hicks (trans), *Sebastiano Serlio on Architecture*, Yale University Press, 1996, p. 402.
29. J.S. Ackerman, *The Architecture of Michelangelo*, Penguin Books, 1970, pp. 153–6, and Figs 65–6, pp.148–9.
30. R. Wittkower, *Studies in the Italian Baroque*, Figs 23–4, p. 24.
31. *Ibid.*, Figs 25–7, p. 25.

over, until a decade or so before Newton built them into the system he published in 1687.

Unless we conclude that art and architecture led the way for science, instead of the reverse as is commonly assumed, the parallel between the two spheres is therefore significant only on one condition. It must be understood as evidence of a more vaguely defined 'concurrence of sensibilities', a new appreciation of and attraction towards more dynamic forms in general, which enables art, projective geometry and the new astronomy to escape from the ancient preconception that the circle, as the most perfect of all figures, reigns supreme in all things, including God's construction of the universe. At the same time, it leads to a far less obvious proportionality. Whether the proportions of elliptical plans are mathematically determined or not, it is virtually impossible to grasp them exactly, and one of the effects of the adoption of elliptical geometry is to make the use of precise ratios an irrelevance.

Another example, mentioned by both Giedion and Sypher, is Baroque architecture's emphasis on infinite space and movement, most clearly seen in town planning and garden design. In *The Culture of Cities* Lewis Mumford vividly describes the connection between movement and axial planning:

> The avenue is the most important symbol and the main fact about the baroque city. . . In the linear evolution of the city plan, the movement of wheeled vehicles played a critical part; and the general geometrizing of space, so characteristic of the period, would have been altogether functionless had it not facilitated the movement of traffic and transport, at the same time as it served as an expression of the dominant sense of life. . . Movement in a straight line along an avenue was not merely an economy but a special pleasure: it brought into the city the stimulus and exhilaration of swift motion. . . It was possible to increase this pleasure esthetically by the regular setting of buildings, with regular facades and even cornices, whose horizontal lines tended toward the same vanishing point as that toward which the carriage itself was rolling.[32]

That vanishing point lay at infinity. The prime examples of what Giedion calls the 'indefinitely extended perspective' – the shaft of space disappearing over the horizon – were

32. L. Mumford, *The Culture of Cities*, Secker & Warburg, 1938, pp. 94–5.

André Le Nôtre's designs for the gardens of the Tuileries, the first stage of the Champs Elysées (1649–78), Vaux-le-Vicomte (1656) and Versailles (1662).[33] Absolute space, being infinite, could not be represented by any measurable dimension in architecture; the nearest one could get to it was to create the illusion of infinity by *concealing* measure, thereby eliminating any perceptible proportion. The unprecedented scale of Baroque gardens and cities made possible the creation of dimensions that appeared literally measureless. The illusion of infinity could be achieved only at the cost of abandoning proportion. More generally, one can look for the Baroque sensibility in the awareness of *continuity*, whether in painting, sculpture and architecture or in scientific concepts of space, time and motion. This continuity might be represented, even within the limited dimensions of a painting or a small building, by blurring the articulation of parts within the whole so that they appeared to melt into each other. The effect could be enhanced if one also concealed the limits of the whole, by softening or breaking up its contours.

The most thorough analysis of this continuity, and its contrast with the Renaissance pursuit of discrete forms, is formulated by Heinrich Wölfflin in his *Principles of Art History* (1915). Wölfflin identifies five characteristic features of the transition from 'classic' (that is, Renaissance) to Baroque:

> (1) The development from the linear to the painterly. . . In the former case the stress is laid on the limits of things; in the other the work tends to look limitless. . .
> (2) The development from plane to recession. Classic art reduces the parts of a total form to a sequence of planes, the baroque emphasizes depth. . .
> (3) The development from closed to open form. . .
> (4) The development from multiplicity to unity. In the system of a classic composition, the single parts, however firmly they may be rooted in the whole, maintain a certain independence. . . For the spectator, that presupposes an articulation, a progress from part to part, which is a very different operation from perception as a whole, such as the seventeenth century applies and demands. In both styles unity is the chief aim. . . , but in the one case unity is achieved by a harmony of free parts, in the other, by a union of parts in a single theme, or by

33. B. Jeannel, *Le Nôtre*, Fernand Hazan, Paris, 1985, pp. 20–1, 30–1, 47.

the subordination, to one unconditioned dominant, of all other elements.

(5) The absolute and the relative clarity of the subject.[34]

Here again, the beginnings of the drive towards Baroque unity and fluidity can already be discerned by the mid-sixteenth century, in the work of artists like Michelangelo (1475–1564) and Tintoretto (1518–94), half a century before Galileo and more than a century before Newton. Michelangelo's remarks on the proportions of the human body are relevant here. Approaching architecture as a sculptor, he was more than normally conscious of the analogy between the body and architecture, conceiving the masses of buildings as torsos and limbs in motion, moulded and articulated by bones and muscles. He writes in a letter that 'Surely, the architectural members derive from human members. Whoever has not been or is not a good master of the figure and likewise of anatomy cannot understand [anything] of it.'[35] His attitude to the body as a dynamic structure contrasts sharply with that of other Renaissance artists fascinated by Vitruvian bodily proportions, like Leonardo da Vinci and Albrecht Dürer (1471–1528). Michelangelo's biographer Ascanio Condivi records that

> He has often had it in mind to write a treatise. . . on all manner of human movements and appearances and on the bone structure, with a brilliant theory which he arrived at through long experience. . . I know that, when he reads Albrecht Dürer, he finds his work very weak. . . And, to tell the truth, Albrecht discusses the proportions and varieties of human bodies, for which no fixed rule can be given, and he forms his figures straight upright like poles; as to what is more important, the movements and gestures of human beings, he says not a word.[36]

Moreover, the body's proportions are changed not only by movement, but also by the eye of the observer. 'All geometry,' Michelangelo asserts, 'all arithmetic, and all rules of perspective are useless without the observing eye.'[37]

Wölfflin's five developments inevitably involved the destruction of the Renaissance concept of proportion. Writing of the Baroque system of proportionality in his earlier work, *Renaissance and Baroque* (1888), he concludes that

34. H. Wölfflin, *Principles of Art History*, Dover Publications, 1915, pp. 14–15.
35. Michelangelo, letter, in G. Milanesi, *Le lettere di Michelangelo Buonarotti*, Florence, 1875, p. 554.
36. A. Condivi, *The Life of Michelangelo*, Phaidon, 1976, pp. 98–9.
37. Michelangelo, reported by P. Lomazzo in *Trattato dell'arte della Pittura*, book IV, chapter 7; quoted in C. de Tolnay, *The Art and Thought of Michelangelo*, Random House, 1964, p. 90.

> Quite early in the Renaissance the theory was formulated that the sign of perfection in a work of art was that it could not be changed, not even in the smallest detail, without destroying the beauty and the meaning of the whole. . . These terms are quite alien to the baroque, and it is inevitable that they should be; the aim of this style is not to represent a perfected state, but to suggest an incomplete process and a movement towards its completion. This is why the formal relationships become looser, for the baroque is bold enough to turn the harmony into a dissonance by using imperfect proportions.[38]

In conclusion, it seems that the sixteenth and seventeenth centuries experienced a general shift of emphasis, from the static to the dynamic space, from the delimited and discrete to the infinite and continuous. This pervaded every aspect of culture, and affected art no less, and apparently somewhat earlier, than science. It was not a question, as Wittkower implies, of developments in science forcing artists to fall back on their own resources of intuition and personal taste, but rather of a culture-wide crisis of sensibility: literally a 'parting of the ways'. In science, this made possible, and demanded, an increasing abstraction, and in art it led to a corresponding reliance on subjective feeling, emotionalism and rhetorical gesture, with the result that the two domains became increasingly insulated from each other.

13.5 BREAKING THE BOND BETWEEN SCIENCE AND ART

The ancient connection between the application of mathematics in art and in science was disrupted. To this extent Wittkower's analysis is correct. As we have just seen, however, it was not science but art that first broke the connection. And in so far as the nature of the new science affected the outcome, the reason was not that the new scientific cosmos was 'a universe of mechanical laws, of iron necessity with no ulterior plan', but rather that it had become purely abstract, a fully intelligible but intangible world of absolute time and space and invisible atoms, known only through mathematical equations and divorced from sensory experience. The men of science, as Leonardo Benevolo argues, began to use mathematics

38. H. Wölfflin, *Renaissance and Baroque*, Fontana, 1964, pp. 65–7.

> in a way completely different to that spoken of so far by philosophers and artists from Leonardo to Scamozzi and Zuccaro. . .; their work no longer had anything in common with the work of artists, but threatened architecture's claim to a scientific or objective nature. . .[39]

Nevertheless, the completeness of this crisis should not be exaggerated, nor its finality taken for granted. At the end of the seventeenth century Sir Christopher Wren (1632–1723) could still be both an eminent mathematician – Professor of Astronomy at Gresham College and Oxford University, a founder member and President of the Royal Society – and his country's leading architect. And even in the twentieth century there are still rare individuals able to move with assurance between the fields of science and the arts, and to recognize a unity between them.

Although he lays the blame for the gulf between science and art on the allegedly 'mechanical' and 'purposeless' character of the universe revealed by the scientists, the witnesses whom Wittkower cites in *Architectural Principles* to support his case are, with the sole exception of David Hume (1711–76), neither scientists nor philosophers but artists and writers on art. Even when he quotes Hume it is from his essay on taste rather than a strictly philosophical work.

His evidence is not entirely one-sided, moreover. He allows that, alongside the obvious critics and opponents of mathematical rules of proportion,

> The doctrine of a mathematical universe which, with all its emanations, was subject to harmonic ratios, was triumphantly reasserted by a number of great thinkers of the seventeenth and eighteenth centuries.

Wittkower cites Kepler, Galileo and especially Lord Shaftesbury (1671–1713) 'for whom, truly Platonic, the laws of musical harmony are effective also in human nature'.[40] He discusses numerous publications, from Sir Henry Wotton's *Elements of Architecture* (1624) and François Blondel's *Cours d'architecture* (1675–83) to Charles-Etienne Briseux's *Traité du beau essentiel* (1728),[41] Robert Morris' *Lectures on Architecture* (1734) and Bernardo Vittone's *Istruzioni* (1760–66),[42] all of which argue that proportion must be based on something more profound than mere taste or convention – on musical harmony, or some equivalent natural system of order.

39. L. Benevolo, *The Architecture of the Renaissance*, Routledge & Kegan Paul, 1978, vol. II, pp. 585–6.
40. R. Wittkower, *Architectural Principles*, p. 124.
41. C.-E. Briseux, *Traité du beau essentiel*, Paris, 1752.
42. B.A. Vittone, *Istruzioni elementari per indirizzo*, Lugano, 1760.

Thus laws of proportion were not suddenly abandoned by artists in the eighteenth century. In England, for instance – which owing to the work of Isaac Newton, Robert Hooke and Robert Boyle had become the epicentre of the scientific revolution – there was if anything a *resurgence* of their use, associated with the Palladian revival that began between 1715 and 1720, about 30 years after the publication of Newton's *Principia mathematica*. The most notable example of this resurgence was the work of Robert Morris (fl. 1728–61), the major theorist of the Palladian movement.[43] In his *Lectures* Morris puts forward a more systematic revision of Palladian proportions, comprising seven ideal rectangular forms with the commensurable ratios 1:1:1, 1:1:2, 1:2:3, 2:2:3, 2:3:4, 3:4:5 and 3:4:6 (see Figure 13.1).

Figure 13.1 Robert Morris, seven recommended proportions, from his *Lectures on Architecture* (1734); after D. Cruickshank, *An English Reason*.

The English movement was paralleled on the continent, as Wittkower points out, by a renewed interest in harmonic proportion in France and Italy, exemplified by the work of C.-E. Briseux, J.-F. Blondel,[44] Bernardo Vittone, Pierre Patte,[45] Ottavio Bertotti Scamozzi[46] and others. If the science of Galileo and Newton was indeed responsible for the loss of faith in architectural proportion in the eighteenth century, it was remarkably slow to show its effect. Briseux and Vittone are particularly interesting because they not only look back to Alberti and Palladio but cite Newton's laws as evidence of the universal validity of mathematical harmony. In the view of Pérez-Gómez, the influence of the mechanical philosophy on eighteenth-century proportion theory was far from negative. 'After 1750 numerical proportions recovered their traditional role in architectural theory,'[47] he writes, and this was due to the overwhelming stature of Newton, who was seen throughout Europe as 'a hero of superhuman dimensions, having solved once and for all the enigma of the universe'.[48] As a consequence,

> Architectural theory, sharing the basic premises, intentions, and ideals of Newtonian philosophy, adopted an implicit metaphysical dimension. The results appeared as a passionate defense of traditional positions, strengthened by a consciousness of the power of reason to control practical operations.[49]

Something had changed, however. Pérez-Gómez describes this recovery of traditional proportion doctrine as

43. A. Placzec, Foreword to R. Morris, *Select Architecture*, Da Capo Press, 1973.
44. J.-F. Blondel, *Cours d'architecture*, Paris, 1771–9.
45. P. Patte, *Mémoires sur les objets les plus importants de l'architecture*, Paris, 1769.
46. O. Bertotti Scamozzi, *Le fabbriche e i disegni di Andrea Palladio*, Vicenza 1796.
47. A. Pérez-Gómez, *Architecture and the Crisis of Modern Science*, p. 83.
48. *Ibid.*, p. 77.
49. *Ibid.*, p. 82.

'reactionary'.[50] This is a curious word to use of a tendency inspired by something as 'progressive' as Newtonian physics, but perhaps an appropriate one. The finite arithmetic and geometry of Renaissance proportion did not conflict, but had no vital connection, with the Newtonian system of the world, and could draw no strength from it. In Alberti's and Palladio's architecture the Pythagorean and Platonic ratios had been alive and vigorous. In the revived Palladianism of the eighteenth century they were a spent force, a polite convention, a device for avoiding unpleasing discords rather than for evoking profound natural harmonies. The architects failed to develop a fresh and vital system of proportions with a vigour matching that of Newtonian physics, and instead fell back on the old rules of harmony. The creativity of the style showed itself elsewhere – for instance in a new relation between buildings and the natural landscape.

If there was anything more than a coincidental connection between Baroque science and architecture, it must be looked for in the indefinite proportions and measureless dimensions of Francesco Borromini (1599–1667), André Le Nôtre (1613–1700), and Balthasar Neumann (1687–1753). The more interesting seventeenth- and eighteenth-century theorists of proportion are to be found among the witnesses for the prosecution. The architect-scientist Claude Perrault (1613–88) rejects the Renaissance doctrine of the equivalence between musical harmony and visual proportion, arguing that whereas the ear is sensitive to the smallest departure from exact tone, the eye is undisturbed by quite wide variations. By telling us only this, Wittkower and Scholfield convey the impression that Perrault sets out to attack mathematical principles of proportion as such. In fact he does nothing of the sort. What he does oppose is an unthinking application of formulae based on dogma, pedantry or lazy convention. In their place he tries to construct a system of proportions founded on knowledge and reason. His purpose, he writes in the preface to his *Ordonnance* (1683, four years before Newton's *Principia*), is 'to see if I might cause the rules for the orders of architecture to be given the precision, perfection, and ease of retention they lack. . .'[51]

He argues that

> Although no single proportion is indispensable to the beauty of a face, there still remains a standard from which

50. *Ibid.*, p. 76.
51. C. Perrault, *Ordonnance for the Five Kinds of Columns after the Method of the Ancients*, ed. A. Pérez-Gómez, Getty Centre, 1993, p. 62.

> its proportion cannot stray too far without destroying its perfection. Similarly, in architecture, there are not only general rules of proportion, such as those that. . . distinguish one order from another, but also detailed rules from which we cannot deviate without robbing an edifice of much of its grace and elegance.[52]

He points out that the wide variations of proportion found among actual examples of Classical architecture show that proportions in architecture are not so fixed and narrowly defined as musical harmonies. The eye's appraisal of visual proportion is quite different from, and more conscious and deliberate than, the ear's perception of sound.

Perrault distinguishes two kinds of beauty, including beauty of proportion. There is the beauty based on 'convincing reasons', which is universal, and the 'arbitrary' beauty that 'depends on prejudice'.[53] So far as proportion is concerned, the former beauty comprises 'symmetry', described as 'the relationship the parts have collectively as a result of the balanced correspondence of their size, number, disposition, and order'.[54] The arbitrary beauty of proportion is

> determined by our wish to give a definite proportion, shape, or form to things that might have a different form without being misshapen and that appear agreeable. . . merely by custom. . .[55]

Note that the 'universal' proportions seem to correspond to Vitruvian 'symmetry', being concerned with 'the collective relations of parts', while 'arbitrary' proportions correspond to 'eurhythmy', being a matter of the shapes and forms of separate elements.

Perrault does not deny the usefulness of mathematical norms, and in fact proposes new and simpler ones based on whole-number multiples of a special 'small' module corresponding to one third of a column diameter instead of the usual whole or half diameter.[56] Basing his norms for the proportions of columns on averages calculated from up to a dozen ancient or Renaissance examples of each, he fixes the heights of the Tuscan, Doric, Ionic, Corinthian and Composite orders at respectively 28, 30, 32, 34 and 36 modules. Of these totals the entablature always occupies two diameters or six modules, leaving column heights of 22, 24, 26, 28 and 30 modules. When pedestal heights of respectively 6, 7, 8, 9 and

52. *Ibid.*, pp. 47–8.
53. *Ibid.*, p. 50.
54. *Ibid.*
55. *Ibid.*, p. 51.
56. *Ibid.*, pp. 68–9.

10 modules are added, the totals become 34, 37, 40, 43 and 46 modules. The value of the system does not lie in any metaphysical principle but in the fact that it enables the observer to recognize and judge by eye the proportions, and thus the distinctive character, of each order. Perrault's arithmetical progressions do not, however, constitute a true system of proportions: that is, one that combines the additive and multiplicative principles, as defined in Chapter 3.

Like Perrault, the Baroque architect Guarino Guarini (1624–83)[57] and the Neoclassicist Francesco Milizia[58] consider the only basis of proportion to be the eye of the perceiver, allied to experience. As Wittkower comments: 'The modern approach of the architect to proportion is taking shape.'[59] In other words, proportion, if it is to survive, must be refounded on the basis of explicable psychological phenomena instead of unfounded metaphysical dogma. Wittkower assumes that the 'modern approach' is exclusively subjective and aesthetic. He concludes that

> With the rise of the new science the synthesis which had held microcosm and macrocosm together, that all-pervading order and harmony in which thinkers had believed from Pythagoras' days to the 16th and 17th centuries, began to disintegrate. This process of 'atomization' led, of course, to a re-orientation in the field of aesthetics and, implicitly, of proportion.[60]

I shall argue, however, that it is still possible to construct a new objective foundation for proportion upon the ruins of the old cosmology left by the empiricist and phenomenalist world-view. The relevance of this empiricist approach to proportion to developments in eighteenth-century philosophy is the subject of the following chapter.

It was in Britain that the new empiricist philosophy evolved, and it was there, as Wittkower says, 'that the whole structure of classical aesthetics was overthrown from the bottom'.[61] Thus Perrault's rejection of the musical theory is echoed by the painter William Hogarth and the architect Sir John Soane, the latter dismissing as 'fanciful opinion' the idea 'that no building could be beautiful if all its parts were not in Arithmetical and Geometrical Proportion'.[62] Similarly, David Hume argues that to reduce beauty to 'geometrical truth and exactness' would produce work that is 'insipid and disagreeable',[63] and Edmund Burke (1729–97) that 'Method

57. G. Guarini, *Architettura civile*, Turin, 1737.
58. F. Milizia, *Memorie degli architetti antichi e moderni*, Parma, 1781.
59. R. Wittkower, *Architectural Principles*, p. 131.
60. *Ibid.*, p. 125.
61. *Ibid.*, p. 131.
62. J. Soane, *Lectures on Architecture* (1809), Sir John Soane's Museum, 1929, p. 100.
63. D. Hume, 'Of the standard of taste', in *Essays, Moral, Political and Literary*, Oxford University Press, 1963, p. 236.

and exactness, the soul of proportion, are found rather prejudicial than serviceable to the cause of beauty.'[64]

The reduction of artistic decisions to matters of taste had deeper causes, however, than the severing of the link between music and the visual arts. Wittkower's witnesses, and others like Archibald Alison, represent the start of what would become a growing tendency in the nineteenth and twentieth centuries: the replacement of objective or universal standards in the judgement of art by subjective and personal ones. As the objective grounds of judgement slipped away, it was natural to turn inwards: to study the mental processes of the individual artist or the individual viewer. Beauty came to lie firmly in the eye of the beholder. Hume, in the essay quoted above, describes this opinion as follows:

> Beauty is no quality in things themselves; it exists merely in the mind which contemplates them; and each mind perceives a different beauty. One person may even perceive deformity, where another is sensible of beauty; and every individual ought to acquiesce in his own sentiment, without pretending to regulate those of others.[65]

True, he himself qualifies this view, allowing that

> Though it be certain that beauty and deformity. . . are not qualities in objects, but belong entirely to the sentiment, internal or external, it must be allowed, that there are certain qualities in objects which are fitted by nature to produce those particular feelings.[66]

But this is a long way from saying that these 'qualities' are due to universal laws pervading or sustaining the natural world.

The tendency to subjectivity had its roots in philosophy, which now turned its attention from the interpretation of the physical world to the study of our mental processes, and particularly of the grounds of human knowledge. This shift from the physical to the psychological sphere, from the outer to the inner world, had important consequences for the theory of proportion in art.

64. E. Burke, *A Philosophical Enquiry into the Origin of our Ideas of the Sublime and Beautiful* (1756), Oxford University Press, 1990, p. 86.
65. D. Hume, 'Of the standard of taste', pp. 124–5.
66. *Ibid.*, p. 240.

Chapter fourteen

FROM THE OUTER TO THE INNER WORLD

And I am the more fully convinced, that the patrons of proportion have transferred their artificial ideas to nature, and not borrowed from thence the proportions they use in works of art; because in any discussion of this subject, they always quit as soon as possible the open field of natural beauties, the animal and vegetable kingdoms, and fortify themselves within the artificial lines and angles of architecture.[1]

14.1 CLEARING THE GROUND OF THE OBSTACLES TO KNOWLEDGE

The publication of Newton's *Principia* in 1687 marks a turning point. The corpuscular-kinetic explanation of the external world, initiated by Galileo and Gassendi at the beginning of the century, was now essentially complete. For the next two hundred years it would stand up against all opposition, until finally overthrown by Einstein in 1915. For Immanuel Kant, according to Karl Popper, 'Newton's theory was simply true, and the belief remained unshaken for a century after Kant's death.'[2] It was not merely a provisional hypothesis, but a final truth, an absolute knowledge at which the human intellect must inevitably arrive: 'Thus the problem is no longer how Newton could make his discovery but how everybody else could have failed to make it.'[3]

After 1687, therefore, the burning question is no longer 'What is the nature of the external world?' but 'How does the human understanding acquire its knowledge of that world?' The titles alone of the new philosophical treatises reflect this: John Locke's *Essay Concerning the Human Understanding* (1690); George Berkeley's *The Principles of Human Knowledge* (1710); David Hume's *Treatise on Human Nature* (1739–40) and his *Enquiry Concerning Human Understanding*

1. E. Burke, *A Philosophical Enquiry into the Origin of our Ideas of the Sublime and Beautiful* (1756), Oxford University Press, 1998, p. 91.
2. K.R. Popper, *Conjectures and Refutations*, Routledge & Kegan Paul, 1965, p. 94.
3. *Ibid.*, p. 95.

(1748). The conclusion of Newton's *Principia* itself shows the urgency of these investigations. His mathematical laws 'saved' the appearances, but they did not explain them; they did not help us to understand the underlying causes. Newton admits that he has so far 'not been able to discover the cause of those properties of gravity from phenomena, and I frame no hypotheses'.[4]

To frame no hypotheses, and to reject all answers that cannot be deduced from phenomena, is all very well; but what is the precise nature of phenomena? The more the grounds of human knowledge were investigated, the less solid and knowable the 'real' world, as distinct from the world of appearances that could be experienced, began to appear. Plato's distinction between the products of pure thought and the products of sensation was as relevant as ever, but the empiricist philosophers drew the opposite conclusion: that only that which could be experienced by the senses was a proper object of knowledge. This had a profound impact on the cosmological foundations of order in art.

In the introduction to his *Treatise*, David Hume (1711–76) begins by arguing that since 'the science of man is the only solid foundation for the other sciences',[5] it makes sense for philosophy,

> instead of taking now and then a castle or a village on the frontier, to march up directly to the capital or centre of these sciences, to human nature itself; which being once masters of, we may everywhere else hope for an easy victory.[6]

He compares the shift of focus from the physical to the psychological world taking place in his own time to the similar shift that occurred in Greek thought at the time of Socrates. The same shift is highlighted by Francis Cornford in *Before and After Socrates*:

> It was not only the man Socrates, but philosophy itself that turned, in his person, from the outer to the inner world. Up to that moment, the eyes of philosophy had been turned outwards to seek a reasonable explanation of the shifting spectacle of surrounding Nature. Now their vision is directed to another field – the order and purposes of human life – and, at the centre of that field, to the nature of the individual soul.[7]

4. I. Newton, *Mathematical Principles of Natural Philosophy*, trans. A. Motte, University of California Press, 1960, p. 547.
5. D. Hume, *A Treatise of Human Nature*, Everyman's Library, 1911, vol. I, p. 5.
6. *Ibid.*
7. F.M. Cornford, *Before and after Socrates*, Cambridge University Press, 1968, p. 4.

Hume writes:

> It is no astonishing reflection to consider, that the application of experimental philosophy to moral subjects should come after that to natural, at the distance of above a whole century; since we find in fact, that there was about the same interval betwixt the origins of these sciences; and that, reckoning from Thales to Socrates, the space of time is nearly equal to that betwixt my Lord Bacon and some late philosophers in England, who have begun to put the science of man on a new footing. . .[8]

Hume's parallel is not exact, however. Socrates, having concluded that the natural sciences based on observation led to a blind alley, decided that

> I must have recourse to theories, and use them in trying to discover the truth about things. . . and in every case I first lay down the theory which I judge to be the soundest; and then whatever seems to agree with it. . . I assume to be true. . .[9]

The aim of the new school of British empirical philosophers was exactly the opposite: to compound no theories, but apply the experimental methods of physical science to the processes of the mind.

In the *Epistle to the Reader* that introduces his *Essay Concerning Human Understanding*, published only three years after Newton's *Principia*, John Locke (1632–1704), the first of these philosophers, claims to do no more than try to clear away some of the debris surrounding the new cosmological construction erected by the seventeenth-century scientists. Interestingly he uses, like so many philosophers before him, an architectural metaphor. He likens the new world-order being put together by science to a great complex of buildings rising up on a vast construction site:

> The commonwealth of learning is not at this time without its master-builders, whose mighty designs, in advancing the sciences, will leave lasting monuments to the admiration of posterity.. . .; and in an age that produces such masters as the great *Huygenius* and the incomparable Mr *Newton*, with some others of that strain, it is ambition enough to be employed as an under-labourer in clearing

8. D. Hume, *A Treatise of Human Nature*, pp. 5–6.
9. Plato, *Phaedo*, in H. Tredennick (trans/ed.), *The Last Days of Socrates*, Penguin Books, 1959, p. 158.

> the ground a little, and removing some of the rubbish that lies in the way to knowledge. . .[10]

As this modest introduction suggests, the *Essay* sticks faithfully to the mechanical picture of the world already expounded by Galileo, Boyle, Huygens, Hooke and Newton. Where Locke breaks new ground is in turning his attention from the external world to the internal world of the human mind. This he interprets in a manner that precisely imitates the structure of the external world worked out by the physical scientists. He posits a mind that closely resembles Newtonian space: an empty receptacle, causally inert, that is to say incapable by itself of generating ideas, just as Newtonian space is incapable of generating matter: 'a white paper void of all characters, without any *ideas*'.[11] All the contents of the mind originate in experience:

> In that all our knowledge is founded, and from that it ultimately derives itself. Our observation, employed either about *external objects, or about the internal operations of our minds perceived and reflected upon by ourselves, is that which supplies our understandings with all the materials of thinking.*[12]

So just as space is conceived as a vacuum in which innumerable separate particles or atoms move and collide with each other, so the mind, as pictured by Locke, is initially an empty receptacle ready to receive the succession of atomic perceptions or *sensations* that enter it through the senses. The sensations themselves are mechanically caused, either by direct contact (touch) or by the impact on the sense organs of minute particles given off by the external objects. From these the mind itself develops a second class of ideas called *reflections*.

14.2 THE DUPLICATION OF WORLDS

It follows from Locke's premiss that it is these mental sensations and reflections, and not the external things which initially prompt them, that are the objects of our awareness and knowledge. Every object is duplicated: in so far as it is perceived, it exists as an idea in the mind; and this perception is presumed to be caused by, but not identical with, a material object 'out there' in the external world. For

10. J. Locke, *An Essay Concerning Human Understanding*, Everyman's Library, 1961, vol. I, p. xxxv.
11. *Ibid.*, p. 77.
12. *Ibid.*

> The mind knows not things immediately, but only by the intervention of the ideas it has of them. Our knowledge, therefore, is real only so far as there is a *conformity* between our ideas and the reality of things. But what shall be the criterion? How shall the mind, when it perceives nothing but its own ideas, know that they agree with things themselves?[13]

Or, one might go on to ask, that the things exist at all, outside the mind?

Locke concludes rather lamely that

> Sensation convinces us that there are solid, extended substances; and reflection, that there are thinking ones. . . and that one hath a power to move body by impulse, the other by thought. . . But beyond these *ideas*. . . our faculties will not reach.[14]

Seizing on this, George Berkeley (1685–1753) argues that if the mind has no direct awareness of external objects as such, there is no need for the material objects to exist at all; for

> If there were external bodies, it is impossible we should ever come to know it; and if there were not, we might have the very same reasons to think there were that we have now.[15]

The hypothesis of an external reality, which somehow provokes sensations but of which we can have no direct knowledge, is nothing but a superfluous and unnecessary complication.

The impossibility, for Locke, of proving the existence of external objects, is compounded by the distinction he makes, following Democritus, Galileo[16] and others, between the *primary* qualities that are inseparable from the bodies themselves – 'solidity, extension, figure, motion or rest, and number'[17] – and the *secondary* qualities, such as colours, sounds and tastes, which are partly subjective, since they appear differently under different conditions of the observer. Thus fire produces, at a distance, sensations of light and colour; when closer, of warmth; and still closer, of pain. These secondary qualities, unlike the primary, depend entirely on being perceived:

13. *Ibid.*, vol. II, p. 167.
14. *Ibid.*, vol. I, p. 260.
15. G. Berkeley, *The Principles of Human Knowledge*, Collins/Fontana, 1962, p. 74.
16. Galileo, *The Assayer*, in S. Drake, *Discoveries and Opinions of Galileo*, Doubleday, New York, 1957, pp. 276–7.
17. J. Locke, *An Essay Concerning Human Understanding*, vol. I, p. 104.

> Take away the sensation of them. . . and all colours, tastes, odours, and sounds. . . vanish and cease, and are reduced to their causes, i.e. bulk, figure, and motion of parts.[18]

This distinction lays the way open for Berkeley to point out that

> These arguments which are thought manifestly to prove that colours and tastes exist *only* in the mind. . . may with equal force be brought to prove the same thing of extension, figure, and motion.[19]

He concludes that it is impossible that either primary or secondary qualities exist 'in an unthinking subject without the mind, or in truth, that there should be any such thing as an outward object'.[20] Later, Hume will likewise reject Locke's distinction between primary and secondary qualities, writing that

> If colours, sounds, tastes, and smells be merely perceptions, nothing, we can conceive, is possessed of a real, continued, and independent existence; not even motion, extension, and solidity, which are the primary qualities chiefly insisted on.[21]

Berkeley therefore simply denies the existence of matter, or of external objects that exist when we are not perceiving them. One 'need only open his eyes to see' the obvious truth that

> All those bodies which compose the mighty frame of the world, have not any subsistence without a mind – that their *being* is *to be perceived or known;* that consequently so long as they are not actually perceived by me, or do not exist in my mind or that of any created spirit, they must either have no existence at all, or else subsist in the mind of some Eternal Spirit.[22]

The 'Works of Nature' – that is to say, the whole contents of the mind apart from those 'ideas of imagination' that the mind itself produces – are spiritual ideas directly projected into the mind by God. Although spiritual, they are no illusions, but *real things*, acting consistently with nature's laws. Berkeley's system has an elegance and simplicity that Locke's

18. *Ibid.*, p. 107.
19. G. Berkeley, *The Principles of Human Knowledge*, pp. 69–71.
20. *Ibid.*, p. 72.
21. D. Hume, *A Treatise of Human Nature*, vol. I, p. 218.
22. G. Berkeley, *The Principles of Human Knowledge*, pp. 67–8.

entirely lacks. In order to explain the existence of ideas, Locke finds it necessary to posit no less than seven different kinds of entity: (1) God, to make (2) matter, which impinges on (3) the senses, giving rise to 'ideas of sensation', which can be either (4) primary or (5) secondary, by reflecting upon which the mind (6) finally gives rise to (7) 'ideas of reflection'. Berkeley cuts down Locke's inventory from seven items to four. These are (1) God, the source of (2) our 'ideas of sense', from which (3) the mind elaborates (4) 'ideas of imagination'.

Thus Berkeley uses Locke's theory to subvert the very mechanistic world-view that Locke has written to defend. A future Anglican divine and eventually bishop, he sees in Newtonian science a threat to religion, since it reduces the world to a vast piece of smoothly functioning clockwork, and God to a merely hypothetical clockmaker, superfluous once the mechanism has been set in motion (or only required, as Newton supposes, to tinker with it from time to time to keep it going). And just as Berkeley demolishes the material foundation of Locke's epistemology, Hume, with ruthless logic, will sweep away the spiritual foundation of Berkeley's.

By arguing that the mind has no innate or *a priori* concepts, and that all our thinking is based on impressions and images derived from experience, thinkers like Locke, Berkeley and Hume expose the great difficulties that lie in the way of explaining how human beings can acquire knowledge of the very external world that science claims to have so triumphantly revealed. Science gives men the illusion of an almost god-like power to know all things; the empirical philosophy designed to explicate it ends by questioning their ability to know almost anything at all. Bertrand Russell states the paradox succinctly:

> Scientific scripture, in its most canonical form, is embodied in physics. . . Physics assures us that the occurrences which we call 'perceiving objects' are at the end of a long causal chain which starts from the objects, and are not likely to resemble the objects except, at best, in certain very abstract ways. We all start from 'naive realism', i.e., the doctrine that things are what they seem. . . But physics assures us that the greenness of grass, the hardness of stones, and the coldness of snow, are not the greenness, hardness, and coldness that we know in our own experience, but

> something very different. The observer, when he seems to himself to be observing a stone, is really, if physics is to be believed, observing the effects of the stone upon himself. Thus science seems to be at war with itself: when it most means to be objective, it finds itself plunged into subjectivity against its will. Naive realism leads to physics, and physics, if true, shows that naive realism is false. Therefore naive realism, if true, is false; therefore it is false.[23]

Thus Locke, in his attempt to clear the philosophical ground upon which physics stands, unintentionally reveals the shakiness of its foundations. Not only does he expose the tenuous relation between our empirical sense-data and the material objects that they are supposed to reflect, but he fails to show how a passive mind, without innate ideas, might transform these data into 'reflections' or concepts, and so 'furnish the understanding with another set of *ideas*, which could not be had from things without'.[24]

14.3 THE DISSOLUTION OF MIND

Hume, one of the few contemporary thinkers who appreciated the importance of Berkeley's critique,[25] observes perceptively that (contrary to the latter's intention) his writings 'form the best lessons of scepticism'.[26] Locke still retains the Cartesian notion of two distinct kinds of substance, matter and spirit: 'solid, extended substances; and. . . thinking ones'. Berkeley sweeps away the first; Hume gets rid of both. He questions the rational grounds for believing in the existence, not only of material bodies, but also of minds, as distinct from their contents. 'As the Bishop undid the whole material world,' commented his contemporary interpreter Thomas Reid, Hume, 'upon the same grounds, undoes the world of the spirits, and leaves nothing in nature but ideas and impressions, without any subject on which they can be impressed.'[27]

Philosophers, Hume writes,

> begin to be reconciled to the principle, *that we have no idea of external substance, distinct from the ideas of particular qualities*. This must pave the way for a like principle with regard to the mind, *that we have no notion of it, distinct from the particular perception*.[28]

23. B. Russell, *An Inquiry into Meaning and Truth*, Penguin Books, 1962, p. 13.
24. J. Locke, *An Essay Concerning Human Understanding*, vol. I, p. 78.
25. D. Hume, *A Treatise of Human Nature*, p. 25.
26. D. Hume, *Enquiries Concerning Human Understanding and Concerning the Principles of Morals*, Oxford University Press, 1975, p. 155, note.
27. T. Reid, *An Inquiry into the Human Mind on the Principles of Common Sense* (1764), quoted in A. Ballantyne, *Architecture, Landscape and Liberty*, Cambridge University Press, 1997, p. 77.
28. D. Hume, *A Treatise of Human Nature*, vol. II, p. 318.

He observes that

> For my part, when I enter most intimately into what I call *myself*, I always stumble on some particular perception or other, of heat or cold, light or shade, love or hatred, pain or pleasure. I never can catch *myself* at any time without a perception, and never can observe anything but the perception. When my perceptions are removed for any time, as by sound sleep, so long am I insensible of *myself*, and may truly be said not to exist. And were all my perceptions removed by death. . . I should be entirely annihilated, nor do I conceive what is further requisite to make me a perfect nonentity.[29]

He concludes that, leaving aside any 'metaphysicians' who may lay claim to a different experience, and with whom he is unable to reason further,

> I may venture to affirm of the rest of mankind, that they are nothing but a bundle or collection of different perceptions, which succeed each other with an inconceivable rapidity, and are in a perpetual flux and movement.[30]

Thus of the four entities to which Berkeley had reduced Locke's original seven, now only two are left: *impressions* and *ideas*. Rather confusingly, Hume employs a different terminology from either of his predecessors: 'impressions' (that is, sensations, passions and emotions) and 'ideas' (that is, the copies of impressions as thoughts, memories and imaginings) together make up the totality of our 'perceptions' (that is, the total contents of the mind).

Hume is the most elusive of writers, and it is not always easy to be certain where he stands on any issue. The more radical or subversive his argument, the more he pretends to distance himself from it, presenting it as the opinion of 'a friend who loves sceptical paradoxes',[31] or of 'the free-thinker',[32] or as 'the sceptical philosophy'.[33] Unlike Berkeley, he neither denies nor affirms the existence of matter, God or the soul; since these questions cannot be settled empirically one way or the other, they lie beyond the scope of his philosophy. Thus at one moment he asserts that outside our perceptions 'Nothing, we can conceive, is possessed of a real, continued, and independent existence; not even motion, extension, and solidity, which are the primary qualities

29. *Ibid.*, vol. I, p. 239.
30. *Ibid.*
31. D. Hume, *Enquiries Concerning Human Understanding*, p. 132.
32. D. Hume, *A Treatise of Human Nature*, vol. I, p. 228.
33. *Ibid.*, p. 149.

chiefly insisted on.'[34] At another, he states that 'It is vain to ask, *Whether there be body or not?* That is an opinion which we must take for granted in all our reasonings.'[35] And: 'If my philosophy therefore makes no addition to the arguments for religion, I have at least the satisfaction to think it takes nothing from them, but that everything remains precisely as before.'[36]

It is not just a matter of timidity or prudence, however. If Hume avoids putting forward a self-consistent metaphysical system of the world or of man, as previous philosophers, including even Locke and Berkeley, have done, it is because he does not aim to arrive at a final conclusion about the way things are, but rather to criticize the dogmatic assumptions of earlier thinkers, to observe how he and other human beings in fact typically arrive at their conclusions about the world, and to analyse the motives that might influence their actions. He refuses to sweep uncomfortable inconsistencies under the carpet, but brings them out into the daylight. Rather than force the facts to fit a neatly packaged system, he prefers to accept that 'There is a direct and total opposition betwixt our reason and our senses.'[37] Faced with this dilemma, he resolves not so much to philosophize, in the traditional sense, as to *psychologize*, or simply to observe. As readers, we expect philosophers to present us with answers to the great questions; it is because Hume frustrates this expectation that we find him so difficult to read, that he so often appears to contradict himself, and that he is liable to such varied interpretations.

Speaking for once unambiguously in his own voice, he compares the mind to 'a kind of theatre, where several perceptions successively make their appearance; pass, repass, glide away, and mingle in an infinite variety of postures and situations'.[38] But he points out that the analogy with the theatre is inexact:

> They are the successive perceptions only, that constitute the mind; nor have we the most distant notion of the place where these scenes are represented, or of the materials of which it is composed.[39]

He concludes that with respect to personal identity the same argument applies as with

> the identity of plants, and animals, and ships, and houses, and all the complicated and changeable productions

34. *Ibid.*, p. 218.
35. *Ibid.*, p. 183.
36. *Ibid.*, p. 238.
37. *Ibid.*, p. 221.
38. *Ibid.*, pp. 239–40.
39. *Ibid.*, p. 240.

whether of art or nature. The identity which we ascribe to the mind of man is only a fictitious one, and of a like kind with that which we ascribe to vegetable and animal bodies.[40]

14.4 PASSION REPLACES REASON

Although Hume's reduction of nature to a single entity – 'perceptions' – is at one level a drastic simplification, figuratively throwing away the container and retaining only the contents, his analysis of the contents themselves is complex, involving no less than eight distinct sub-categories. Only the primary division that he makes in the opening words of the *Treatise* need concern us, however:

> All the perceptions of the human mind resolve themselves into two distinct kinds, which I shall call *impressions* and *ideas*. . . Those perceptions which enter with most force and violence, we may name *impressions*, and under this name, I comprehend all our sensations, passions and emotions. . . By *ideas*, I mean the faint images of these in thinking and reasoning. . .[41]

Thought and reasoning, being only 'faint images of impressions', are powerless to direct the much stronger, more vivid and more compelling innate passions and emotions, which are as real and inescapable as our sensory perceptions. In an often quoted passage in the *Treatise* Hume writes that

> Abstract or demonstrative reasoning. . . never influences any of our actions. . . We speak not strictly and philosophically, when we talk of the combat of passion and of reason. Reason is, and ought only to be, the slave of passions, and can never pretend to any other office than to serve and obey them.[42]

He has in mind here moral judgements and actions, but the same principle applies to our understanding of the natural world, or our artistic choices and decisions.

The implication, for artistic judgements, of Hume's assertion that 'Reason is, and ought only to be, the slave of passions' is obvious. Rationality, in the form of mathematical principles of composition such as rules of proportion,

40. *Ibid.*, p. 245.
41. *Ibid.*, p. 11.
42. *Ibid.*, vol. II, pp. 126–7.

cannot, and should not, determine the form of a work of art. Passion, in this case the artist's instinctive judgement, must always take the lead in creative decisions, and the role of reason is only to serve it in the practical sphere, by choosing technical means appropriate to the ends desired, and ensuring that these ends are attainable; but provided a passion (or by inference, the will of the artist)

> is neither founded on false suppositions, nor chooses means insufficient for the end, the understanding can neither justify nor condemn it. It is not contrary to reason to prefer the destruction of the whole world to the scratching of my finger.[43]

In *The Condition of Man* Lewis Mumford rather unfairly quotes this passage out of context, to support his contention that 'Though the eighteenth century is often called the Age of Reason, that epithet belongs more to the century that preceded it.'[44] Mumford, whose book came out in 1944, in the last insane stages of a suicidal war, continues:

> Indeed, many of the best minds of the eighteenth century ceased to look upon reason as an influence on human conduct or as a shaper of institutions. . . Reason – by which I mean the attempt to include all the facts of life within a comprehensible and intelligible order – was never more in contempt than in the Age of Reason. . . It was not in the bloody operations of the guillotine in 1793. . . [but] in the apparently innocent lucubrations of David Hume that the real Reign of Terror began: the beginnings of a nihilism that has reached its full development only in our own times.[45]

But Hume is not saying that it is *right* to prefer the destruction of the world to the scratching of one's finger, merely that reason could not *show* it to be wrong, and consequently affords no sound basis for morality. Morality is 'more properly felt than judged of'. If we choose to behave altruistically, it is because we find 'the impression arising from virtue to be agreeable, and that proceeding from vice to be uneasy'.[46] Moral decisions are made in the same way as an artist decides to put a spot of red on his canvas next to a spot of blue, because it 'feels right'.

But does the painter really work only in this way? The

43. *Ibid.*, vol. II, p. 128.
44. L. Mumford, *The Condition of Man*, Secker & Warburg, 1944, p. 267.
45. *Ibid.*, pp. 267–9.
46. D. Hume, *A Treatise of Human Nature*, vol, II, p. 178.

analogy between art and morality is valid; but does it follow that reason has no part to play in either? Reason without feeling may be impotent, but the contrary objection can equally be laid against emotion: that without reason it is incoherent. The painter's calculated judgement of the interrelations in the whole composition, and not just the feeling of the moment, determines where the red spot shall go. Mumford has a point, therefore, when he argues that

> So far from having the purely supernumerary role that reason has in Hume's analysis, impotent to affect sensation or impulse, reason performs a constant, active function in the human economy. . . Order, continuity, intelligibility, symbolic expression, in a word, design – all these are basic in human behaviour: no less basic than sensation, impulse, irrational desire.[47]

These same qualities – order, continuity, intelligibility, symbolic expression and design – apply with equal force to the making of buildings and other works of art, and specifically to the use of mathematical systems of proportion.

14.5 BERKELEY AND HUME ON PROPORTION

As the study of mental processes made the bond between the mind and its external objects seem less secure, the individual mind itself became increasingly isolated, not only from the physical world, but even from other minds. The existence of other human beings was reduced, no less than the existence of material objects, to a hypothesis. Consequently, in the making of works of art, what counted was the artist's individual choice, no longer guided either by mathematical laws, by the laws of nature, or even, in the end, by social convention. This is what Wittkower means when he writes that 'Beauty and proportion. . . were turned into psychological phenomena operating and existing in the mind of the artist.' But it was a response, not so much, as he suggests, to Newton's 'universe of mechanical laws', as to the consequences of the empiricist philosophy that flowed from it.

Berkeley's reflections on proportion in art are contained in a digression on beauty in his late dialogue *Alciphron*, the general theme of which, stated in the subtitle, is 'An Apology

47. L. Mumford, *The Condition of Man*, p. 271.

for the Christian Religion against those who are called Free-thinkers'. The main protagonists are Alciphron, a free-thinker, and Euphranor, an intelligent farmer, who more or less represents the author's own views. Alciphron begins by arguing that 'Beauty is, properly speaking, perceived only by the eye', and that it consists 'in a certain symmetry or proportion pleasing to the eye'.[48] Euphranor soon persuades him, however, that beauty of proportion depends on the function of the object concerned: for

> Is not a thing said to be perfect in its kind when it answers the end for which it was made?. . . The parts, therefore, in true proportions must be so related, and adjusted to one another, as that they may best conspire to the use and operation of the whole.

Alciphron finds himself unable to deny this. Having gained the point, Euphranor uses it to demolish Alciphron's argument that proportion is a purely visual matter:

> Proportions, therefore, are not, strictly speaking, perceived by the sense of sight, but only by reason through the means of sight. . . Consequently beauty, in your sense of it, is an object, not of the eye, but of the mind.[49]

When Alciphron still resists this conclusion, Euphranor adds a series of clinching arguments. The proportions of a chair cannot be considered beautiful if they do not make for comfort; but the eye alone cannot judge this. Again,

> The architects judge a door to be of a beautiful proportion when its height is double of the breadth. But if you should invert a well-proportioned door, making its breadth become its height, and its height the breadth, the figure would still be the same, but without that beauty in one situation which it had in another. What can be the cause of this, but that. . . the door would not yield a convenient entrance to creatures of a human figure? But if in any other part of the universe there should be supposed rational animals of an inverted stature, they must be supposed to invert the rule for proportion of doors; and to them that would appear beautiful which to us was disagreeable.[50]

48. G. Berkeley, *Alciphron, or the Minute Philosopher*, in A.A. Luce and T.E. Jessop (eds), *The Works of George Berkeley Bishop of Cloyne*, Thomas Nelson, 1950, vol. III, p. 123.
49. *Ibid.*, p. 124.
50. *Ibid.*, p. 125.

Similarly, the beautiful proportions of the classical orders were 'taken originally from nature, which in her creatures. . . referreth them to some end, use, or design'.[51] And the lasting beauty of the draped costume of the ancients, compared with the absurdity and transitoriness of modern fashions, is due to its greater functionality: 'The ancients, considering the use and end of dress, made it subservient to the freedom, ease, and convenience of the body. . .'[52]

Hume, too, argues that judgements of proportion must be subject to considerations of utility. In the chapter on *Why Utility Pleases*, in the *Enquiry Concerning the Principles of Morals* (1751) he writes:

> What praise, even of an inanimate form, if the regularity and elegance of its parts destroy not its fitness for any useful purpose! And how satisfactory an apology for any disproportion or seeming deformity, if we can show the necessity of that particular construction for the use intended! A ship appears more beautiful to an artist, or one moderately skilled in navigation, where its prow is wide and swelling beyond its poop, than if it were framed with a precise geometrical regularity, in contradiction to all the laws of mechanics. A building, whose doors and windows were exact squares, would hurt the eye by that very proportion; as ill adapted to the figure of a human creature, for whose service the fabric was intended.[53]

Both these examples, the ship and the house, are based, of course, on a mistaken identification of mathematical proportioning in art with uniformity, but as I argued in Chapter 3, an equally important objective is the exact opposite of uniformity: significant variety, or complexity. There is nothing inherently unfunctional about rectangular ships or square-windowed houses, but a real objection could be raised against them purely on grounds of proportion. Identity of dimension is, strictly speaking, no proportion at all: proportion enters in only when a number of different dimensions or shapes are brought together and interrelated in the same object. Nevertheless, Hume's intention is clear: it is to show that aesthetic judgements, like moral ones, are determined by fitness to circumstances, rather than by calculation. He therefore lays the way open for a later writer like Archibald Alison (1757–1839) to ascribe 'beauty of proportion in forms' to the fact that

51. *Ibid.*, p. 126.
52. *Ibid.*
53. D. Hume, *Enquiries Concerning Human Understanding*, pp. 212–3.

> Certain proportions affect us with the emotion of beauty, not from any original capacity in such qualities to excite this emotion, but from their being expressive to us of the fitness of the parts to the end designed.[54]

Hume draws different conclusions from Berkeley, however, regarding the role of reason in the perception of proportion. Whereas Berkeley argues that since the judgement of good proportion involves 'the comparing parts one with another, the considering them as belonging to one whole, and the referring this whole to its use or end', this judgement must be made by the reason 'through the means of sight', and not by the eye alone,[55] Hume rejects the view that proportion depends on reason, holding instead that beauty lies in the eye of the beholder. It is psychological in nature, and depends on individual character and disposition.

In the four essays *The Epicurean, The Stoic, The Platonist* and *The Sceptic* he confronts with each other, as he says, not four movements in ancient philosophy, but four characters, four types of opinion about human life and happiness, which he says naturally and perennially form themselves among men. The Platonist, carried away by his mystical vision of divine perfection, declaims:

> Consider all the works of men's hands, all the inventions of human wit, in which thou affectest so nice a discernment. Thou wilt find, that the most perfect production still proceeds from the most perfect thought, and that it is MIND alone which we admire, while we bestow our applause on the graces of a well-proportioned statue, or the symmetry of a noble pile. The statuary, the architect, come still in view. . . But why stoppest thou short?. . . Compare the works of art with those of nature. The one are but imitations of the other!. . . Art copies only the minute productions of nature, despairing to reach that grandeur and magnificence which are so astonishing in the masterly works of her original. Can we then be so blind as not to discover an intelligence and a design in the exquisite and most stupendous contrivance of the universe?[56]

Clearly, Hume's Platonist offers us a perfect example of empathy.

Against this, the sceptic (or abstractionist) declares that impressions of beauty and ugliness depend on 'the particular

54. A. Alison, *Essays on the Nature and Principles of Taste* (1790), quoted in P. Scholfield, *The Theory of Proportion in Architecture*, Cambridge University Press, 1958, p. 77.
55. G. Berkeley, *Alciphron*, p. 124.
56. D. Hume, 'The Platonist', in *Essays Moral, Political and Literary*, Oxford University Press, 1963, pp. 159–60.

fabric or structure' of the perceiving mind, and that as that structure varies, so must the sentiment:

> The sentiment being different from the object, and arising from its operation on the organs of the mind, any alteration upon the latter must vary the effect; nor can the same object, presented to a mind totally different, produce the same sentiment.[57]

Consequently, even though the geometrical form of an object may provoke the sensation of beauty in a particular individual, that beauty does not lie in the geometry, but in the particular disposition of the observer:

> Euclid has fully explained every quality of the circle, but has not, in any proposition, said a word of its beauty. The reason is evident. Beauty is not a quality of the circle. It lies not in any part of the line, *whose* parts are all equidistant from a common centre. It is only the effect, which that figure produces upon a mind, whose particular fabric or structure renders it susceptible of such sentiments.[58]

Hume's reduction of the individual mind to a succession of discrete perceptions, and his subjection to these perceptions even of the principles of geometry, leads logically to the conclusion that mathematical rules have no place in artistic composition, and that (to repeat Wittkower's characterization of post-seventeenth-century attitudes) 'beauty and proportion [are] psychological phenomena operating and existing in the mind of the artist.' However, Hume does not reject the possibility of rules in art so absolutely as Wittkower implies. The tenor of the argument is quite different, when seen in context, from that implied by Wittkower's selective quotation (here in italics):

> It is evident that none of the rules of composition are fixed by reasonings *a priori*, or can be esteemed abstract conclusions of the understanding, from comparing those habitudes and relations of ideas, which are eternal and immutable. Their foundation is the same with that of all the practical sciences, experience; nor are they any thing but general observations, concerning what has been universally found to please in all countries and in all

57. D. Hume, 'The Sceptic', in *ibid.*, p. 167.
58. *Ibid.*, pp. 167–8.

> ages. . . *To check the sallies of the imagination, and to reduce every expression to geometrical truth and exactness, would be the most contrary to the laws of criticism; because it would produce a work, which, by universal experience, has been found the most insipid and disagreeable.* But though poetry can never submit to exact truth, it must be confined by rules of art, discovered to the author either by genius or observation.[59]

Art must submit to rules, therefore. Nevertheless, these rules are not absolute truths, nor ascertainable by abstract reasoning. They must be discovered either by 'genius' – the intuition of the individual artist – or by 'observation' of that which has generally been found pleasing at all times and places. This empirical approach to beauty leads directly to the statistical and experimental aesthetics of Gustav Fechner and others in the nineteenth century, to be discussed in the next chapter. But first I want to explore a different avenue: to enquire whether some kind of objective cosmological basis for proportion cannot still be discovered, paradoxically, in Hume's destructive criticism itself, and in the general breakdown of belief in the possibility of deriving laws of proportion for art from the mathematical design of nature.

14.6 EDMUND BURKE'S ATTACK ON THE THEORY OF PROPORTION

The Irish statesman and philosopher Edmund Burke (1729–97) published his *Philosophical Enquiry into the Origin of Our Ideas of the Sublime and the Beautiful* in 1756. In it, he associates the sublime, which he regards as 'productive of the strongest emotion which the mind is capable of feeling', with terror,[60] and beauty with those qualities in things which arouse a disinterested kind of love (as distinct from desire).[61] He sums up these qualities as follows:

> First, to be comparatively small. Secondly, to be smooth. Thirdly, to have a variety in the direction of the parts; but fourthly, to have those parts not angular, but melted as it were into each other. Fifthly, to have a delicate frame, without any remarkable appearance of strength. Sixthly, to have its colours clear and bright; but not very strong and glaring. Seventhly, or if it should have any glaring colour, to have it diversified with others.[62]

59. D. Hume, *Of the Standard of Taste*, pp. 235–6.
60. E. Burke, *A Philosophical Enquiry*, p. 36.
61. *Ibid.*, p. 83.
62. *Ibid.*, p. 107.

This definition of beauty corresponds exactly to the prevailing taste of the mid-eighteenth century, as reflected for example in the influence of the French Rococo style in English interiors (like Chesterfield House by Isaac Ware, 1749). On the other hand, Burke's definition of the sublime looks forward to the overpowering scale, appearance of vast strength, ruggedness and sombre colours about to be introduced by Neoclassicism. The year before, 1755, the *abbé* Marc-Antoine Laugier (1713–69) had published the first signed edition of his *Essai sur l'architecture*: the first manifesto, as it were, of Neoclassical architecture. And between 1743 and 1751 the Italian architect and engraver Giambattista Piranesi (1720–78) published his architectural views and fantastic prison scenes, the quintessence of the sublime as *terribilità*.

In connection with beauty, Burke attacks in particular the doctrine that beauty is connected with mathematical rules of proportion, or that it matters whether one part is a half, a quarter, a fifth or a sixth of the whole. 'Beauty,' he begins,

> hath usually been said to consist in certain proportions of parts. . . Proportion is the measure of relative quantity. Since all quantity is divisible, it is evident that every distinct part into which any quantity is divided, must bear some relation to the other parts and to the whole. These relations give an origin to the idea of proportion. They are discovered by mensuration, and they are the objects of mathematical enquiry. . . But surely beauty is no idea belonging to mensuration; nor has it anything to do with calculation or geometry.[63]

Having dismissed the idea that mathematical proportions are a cause of beauty in plants and animals, on the grounds that they exhibit an infinite variety of proportions yet we consider them equally beautiful, he turns his attention to the Vitruvian notion that proportion in architecture is derived from the proportions of the human body, and particularly from the circumscribed square and circle that it generates:

> I know that it has been said long since, and echoed backward and forward from one writer to another a thousand times, that the proportions of building have been taken from those of the human body. To make this forced analogy complete, they represent a man with his

63. *Ibid.*, pp. 84–5.

arms raised and extended at full length, and then describe a sort of square, as it is formed by passing lines along the extremities of this strange figure. But it appears very clearly to me, that the human figure never supplied the architect with any of his ideas.[64]

The reasons for this are that, first, this extended posture is strained, unnatural and unbecoming; second, that it gives rise, not to a square, but to a cross; and third, that only a few buildings are actually square. Burke concludes that

> These analogies were devised to give a credit to the works of art, by shewing a conformity between them and the noblest works in nature, not that the latter served at all to supply hints for the perfection of the former. And I am the more fully convinced, that the patrons of proportion have *transferred their artificial ideas to nature, and not borrowed from thence the proportions they use in works of art*; because in any discussion of this subject, they always quit as soon as possible the open field of natural beauties. . . and fortify themselves within the artificial lines and angles of architecture.[65]

I have chosen to set this statement at the head of the present chapter, because in it Burke unintentionally provides, in the phrases here emphasized by italics, the answer to the question 'How can systems of proportion continue to be relevant if we no longer believe that they are derived from nature's harmony?' His argument against proportion turns out to be a still more powerful argument *for* it. It shows a way around the impasse apparently presented by Hume's severing of the connection between human reason and our knowledge of nature. From the point of view of empathy, the necessity of proportion in art was a self-evident consequence of the pervading mathematical order of nature; but now, seen from the point of view of abstraction, it arises precisely *because* we cannot find such an order, or at least cannot fully grasp it, in our natural environment. Just as Burke says, we no longer 'borrow' our proportions from nature, but 'transfer' them to, or impose them upon, nature. From this new viewpoint, nature appears, one could almost say, as something that inspires terror – as Worringer says it inspires terror in the primitive. The aesthetic experience of nature is closer to Burke's concept of the 'sublime' (by far the

64. *Ibid.*, p. 91.
65. *Ibid.* (author's italics).

most original aspect of the *Philosophical Enquiry*) than it is to his rather tame notion of beauty.

14.7 THE RATIONAL IMPERATIVE

All reasoning, Hume says, can be divided into two kinds: '*Relations of Ideas*, and *Matters of Fact*. Of the first kind are the sciences of Geometry, Algebra and Arithmetic. . .'[66] Such propositions as '*That three times five equals the half of thirty*' are certain, because they depend only on pure operations of thought, without reference to anything outside the mind. But '*That the sun will not rise tomorrow* is no less intelligible a proposition, and implies no more contradiction, than the affirmation, *that it will rise.*'[67]

Reason is thus absolute master in the realm of pure thought, and above all in the *deductive* fields of mathematics and logic. But in physical science, the domain of 'matters of fact', where our awareness is based only on *induction* from experience, and the nearest certainty no more than a probability, it produces only a descending spiral of doubt: an infinite regress. Reason cannot prove that the sun will rise tomorrow; it merely seems probable, on the basis of repeated experience; and reason does not deal in probabilities. Hume accepts that when two objects constantly appear in conjunction with each other, we are apt to infer a causal relation between them. But not only is the reason incapable of discovering the '*ultimate connection*' of causes and effects; it is moreover 'impossible for us to satisfy ourselves by our reason, why we should extend that experience beyond those particular instances which have fallen under our observation'.[68] No amount of repetition of an experience can enable the reason to prove that it will recur, or to penetrate to the mechanism of causation, or give us any sure knowledge of the way in which one event actually gives rise to another.

All inferences from experience are based, therefore, on habit, not reasoning. When, after a thousand repeated conjunctions of the same two objects or events, we infer that the first causes the second, our conclusion is 'at least intelligible', if not 'true'. This, and only this, explains, for Hume, why from the thousandth identical incident we can draw an inference which we could not draw from the first:

66. D. Hume, *Enquiries Concerning Human Understanding*, p. 25.
67. *Ibid.*, pp. 25–6.
68. D. Hume, *A Treatise of Human Nature*, vol. I, p. 94.

> Reason is incapable of any such variation. The conclusions which it draws from considering one circle are the same which it would form upon surveying all the circles in the universe... Custom, then, is the great guide of human life. It is that principle alone that renders our experience useful to us, and makes us expect, for the future, a similar train of events with those which have appeared in the past. Without the influence of custom, we should be entirely ignorant of every matter of fact beyond what is immediately present to the memory and senses.[69]

Since Hume, philosophers have been forced to take a position with respect to his work, for or against; to ignore it is an option only for those who are prepared to take leave of the world of scientific observation and everyday experience. Like Plato, he has become a benchmark by which philosophers are judged. But his conclusion that no certain knowledge is possible also creates an apparent *impasse*. A way through or round this must be found, if one is not to revert to some form of rationalism or idealism. Bertrand Russell writes that Hume

> represents, in a certain sense, a dead-end: in his direction, it is impossible to go further. To refute him has been, ever since he wrote, a favourite pastime among metaphysicians. For my part, I find none of their refutations convincing; nevertheless, I cannot but hope that something less sceptical than Hume's system may be discoverable.[70]

For Russell, Hume's philosophy

> represents the bankruptcy of eighteenth-century reasonableness. He starts out, like Locke, with the intention of... taking nothing on trust, but seeking whatever instruction is to be obtained from experience and observation. But... he arrives at the disastrous conclusion that from experience and observation nothing is to be learnt... It is therefore important to discover whether there is any answer to Hume within the framework of a philosophy that is wholly or mainly empirical. If not, there is no intellectual difference between sanity and insanity.[71]

Such a philosophy would start out from the principle that

69. D. Hume, *Enquiries Concerning Human Understanding*, pp. 43–5.
70. B. Russell, *History of Western Philosophy*, George Allen & Unwin, 1961, p. 634.
71. *Ibid.*, pp. 645–6.

'no intellectual knowledge is possible, unless it has first passed through the senses,'[72] but it would go beyond Hume, perhaps, in recognizing the active part played by the intellect in every sensory perception or scientific discovery.

Albert Einstein, in a critique of Russell's *Inquiry into Meaning and Truth*, objects that by demanding a framework that is wholly or mainly empirical Russell betrays what he calls his 'bad intellectual conscience' – that is, the fear, which is Hume's legacy, that all rational speculation about matters of fact (as opposed to pure logic or mathematics) is a form of metaphysics, and therefore to be rejected. 'As soon as one is at home in Hume's critique,' writes Einstein,

> one is easily led to believe that all those concepts and propositions which cannot be deduced from the sensory raw material are, on account of their 'metaphysical' character, to be removed from thinking.

However, he concludes,

> In order that thinking may not degenerate into 'metaphysics', or into empty talk, it is only necessary that enough propositions be firmly enough connected with sensory experiences and that the conceptual system, in view of its task of ordering and surveying sense experience, should show as much unity and parsimony as possible.

By denying the essential role of reason in the advancing of knowledge, the doctrinaire empiricists make the same mistake as the doctrinaire rationalists whom Locke and Hume opposed: that of thinking that a man can walk better on one leg than on two. Hume, continues Einstein,

> did not only advance philosophy in a decisive way but also – through no fault of his own – created a danger for philosophy in that. . . a fateful 'fear of metaphysics' arose which has come to be a malady of contemporary empiricistic philosophizing: this malady is the counterpart of that earlier philosophizing in the clouds, which thought it could neglect and dispense with what was given by the senses.[73]

Contrary to Hume's assumption that custom, not reason,

72. H. van der Laan, lecture, Breda, 11 June 1946, p. 3.
73. A. Einstein, 'Remarks on Bertrand Russell's Theory of Knowledge', in *Ideas and Opinions*, Dell Publishing Co., 1954, pp. 33–4.

leads us to believe that the sun will rise tomorrow, scientific discoveries generally start with reasoned speculation, and only later (sometimes much later) the resulting hypotheses are tested empirically. The history of astronomy provides numerous illustrations of the priority of conjecture over observation or experience in scientific advance, of which the following are among the most outstanding.

(1) Copernicus' replacement of the geocentric universe by a heliocentric one was not necessitated by any new empirical evidence; the observations that made the Ptolemaic system untenable followed much later. At the time, the heliocentric theory merely posed new problems, notably the impossibility of observing the stellar parallax that must result from the earth's motion; this was not confirmed empirically for almost three centuries, in 1838.
(2) One of the triumphs of Newton's system of the heavens was that it led to the discovery of Neptune in 1846. This 'discovery made with the mind's eye, in regions where sight itself was unable to penetrate',[74] was arrived at purely mathematically, and independently of each other, by J.C. Adams and U.J.J. Leverrier, a year before it was confirmed by observation.
(3) Newton might assert that 'Hypotheses. . . have no place in experimental philosophy,'[75] but his whole system was nothing but a brilliant hypothesis. Although it resisted all attempts at falsification for over 200 years, in 1915 its provisional nature was finally revealed by Einstein's General Theory of Relativity, which showed it to be merely a special case within a more comprehensive system.
(4) A crucial test of Einstein's theory was his prediction that the bending of light rays in the proximity of large masses such as the sun would be observed during a solar eclipse. The phenomenon was confirmed in 1919, six years after Einstein's original prediction. Karl Popper has commented that despite the great effectiveness of Newton's theory in accounting for empirical evidence – culminating in the discovery of Neptune –

> Einstein had managed to produce a real alternative and, it appeared, a better theory, without waiting for new experiences. Like Newton himself, he predicted new effects within (and also without) our solar system. And some of these predictions, when tested, had now proved successful. . .

74. J.H. von Mädler, *Populäre Astronomie*, Berlin, 1841, p. 345.
75. I. Newton, *Mathematical Principles*, p. 547.

> But what impressed me most was Einstein's own clear statement that he would regard his theory as untenable if it should fail in certain tests.[76]

According to the theory of knowledge advanced by Popper in *The Logic of Scientific Discovery* (1934) and in his later books,[77] testability, or 'falsifiability', is the criterion of scientific validity. No theory is ever finally verified, no matter how many tests it survives. It is by risking hypotheses that lay themselves open to refutation, and testing them to destruction, that progress is made. While agreeing that Hume 'was perfectly right in pointing out that induction cannot be logically justified,'[78] he finds that he 'never accepted the full force of his own logical analysis.'[79] Instead of concluding that some sort of non-inductive – that is, more or less rational – process was necessary, Hume 'struck a bargain with common sense, meekly allowing the re-entry of induction by repetition, in the guise of a psychological theory.'[80] Popper responds by turning Hume's theory upside down:

> Instead of explaining our propensity to expect regularities as the result of repetition, I proposed to explain repetition-for-us as the result of our propensity to expect regularities and to search for them.[81]

In support of this, he cites numerous examples that show that our ideas of causal connection are not reinforced, as Hume claims, by a thousand recurrences, but that, on the contrary, we make such connections immediately or after only very few repetitions. Like other animals, we are *programmed to look for regularities in our environment*. This, Popper says, is not an 'innate idea' as such, but certainly an innate predisposition:

> The theory of inborn *ideas* is absurd, I think; but every organism has inborn *reactions* or *responses*; and among them responses adapted to impending events. . . Thus we are born with expectations; with 'knowledge' which, although not *valid a priori*, is *psychologically or genetically a priori*, i.e. prior to all observational experience.[82]

This innate propensity enables us to build up our knowledge of our world, and to survive in it, by a process of

76. K.R. Popper, *Unended Quest*, Flamingo, 1986, pp. 37–8.
77. K.R. Popper, *The Logic of Scientific Discovery*, Hutchinson, 1959, and *Objective Knowledge*, Oxford University Press, 1979.
78. K.R. Popper, *Conjectures and Refutations*, p. 42.
79. *Ibid.*, p. 45.
80. *Ibid.*, p. 46.
81. *Ibid.*
82. *Ibid.*, p. 47.

'conjecture and refutation' that Popper condenses into a statement that incidentally could serve as a description of the rationale underlying systematic proportioning in art. This is why I have chosen it as the motto and *leitmotiv* of the present book:

> *Without waiting, passively, for repetitions to impress or impose regularities upon us, we actively try to impose regularities upon the world.* We try to discover similarities in it, and to interpret it in terms of laws invented by us. . . These may have to be discarded later, should observation show that they are wrong. . . The method of trial and error is applied not only by Einstein but, in a more dogmatic fashion, by the amoeba also.[83]

From the standpoint of what Bertrand Russell has called 'naive realism'[84] there is only one world. The world that we experience through our senses is the same as the world of reason (or common sense), and both are identical with the world that really exists 'out there'. For the ancient Greek philosophers that one world is already divided into two; Plato, for instance, distinguishes the 'real' world that is eternal and apprehensible by reason from the constantly changing world of sensation. By implication, Hume's analysis increases this to three: the world of pure relations of ideas, the world of the senses, and the external world, about which nothing definite can be known. Popper makes the interdependence of this trinity of worlds the foundation of his philosophy: 'world 1', the physical world; 'world 2', that of our conscious experiences; and 'world 3', the sum of linguistically formulated theories, accumulated throughout history, without which we could not make sense of worlds 1 and 2.

14.8 KANT: THE UNDERSTANDING AS THE ARCHITECT OF NATURE

'Man,' writes Einstein,

> has an intense desire for assured knowledge. That is why Hume's clear message seemed crushing: the sensory raw material, the only source of our knowledge, through habit may lead us to belief and expectation but not to the knowledge and still less to the understanding of lawful

83. *Ibid.*, pp. 46, 52 (author's italics).
84. B. Russell, *An Enquiry into Meaning and Truth*, p. 13.

> relations. Then Kant took the stage with an idea which, though certainly untenable in the form in which he put it, signified a step towards the solution of Hume's dilemma: whatever in knowledge is of empirical origin is never certain (Hume). If, therefore, we have definitely assured knowledge, it must be grounded in reason itself.[85]

Hume complained that his *Treatise* (1739–40) 'fell *dead-born from the press*'; and that the *Enquiry Concerning the Principles of Morals* (1752), which of all his writings he considered 'incomparably the best', came 'unnoticed and unobserved into the world'.[86] But by 1763, when he arrived in Paris attached to the embassy of Lord Hertford, he was hailed as a celebrity. France and England had just ended a long series of wars; Paris was gripped by anglomania; Hume was, as Horace Walpole remarked, 'fashion itself, although his French is almost as unintelligible as his English';[87] he was feted by Denis Diderot and the French *Encyclopédistes*. He had become one of the brightest stars of the Enlightenment.

Immanuel Kant (1724–1804), the last great philosopher of the Enlightenment, in his *Prolegomena to any Future Metaphysics* (1783), acknowledges Hume's work as 'the very thing, which many years ago first interrupted my dogmatic slumber, and gave my investigations in the field of speculative philosophy quite a new direction'.[88] By 'dogmatic slumber' he is generally taken to mean the Leibnizian rationalism in which he was educated,[89] but according to Popper, it was his unquestioning acceptance that Newton's physics and Euclid's geometry represented absolute and final truths about the world:

> Hume had taught. . . that all we know was obtained with the help of observation which could be only of singular (or particular) instances, so that all theoretical knowledge was uncertain. . . Thus arose the central problem of the *Critique:* 'How is pure natural science possible?' By 'pure natural science' Kant simply meant Newton's theory.[90]

In order to reconcile Newton with Hume, Kant had to show how we can acquire, through observation, not just a succession of provisional pictures of the world, but a final and absolutely true picture. Since Einstein, Newton's theory has no longer been regarded as a final truth; but Kant, like everyone at that time and for long after, was convinced that

85. A. Einstein, 'Remarks on Bertrand Russell's Theory of Knowledge', p. 32.
86. D. Hume, 'My own life', in *Essays Moral, Political and Literary*, pp. 608–11.
87. H. Walpole, letter to the Countess of Suffolk, 20 September 1765, quoted in P.N. Furbank, *Diderot*, Minerva, 1993, p. 265.
88. I. Kant, *Prolegomena*, Open Court Publishing Co., 1902, p. 7.
89. B. Russell, *History of Western Philosophy*, pp. 677–8.
90. K.R. Popper, *Conjectures and Refutations*, p. 94.

it was. Consequently he set out to prove more than was necessary, or possible.

This was the problem Kant set himself to overcome by his 'Copernican revolution':

> It has hitherto been assumed that our cognition must conform to the objects; but all attempts to ascertain anything about these objects *a priori*, by means of conceptions, and thus to extend the range of our knowledge, have been rendered abortive by this assumption. Let us then make the experiment whether we may not be more successful in metaphysics, if we assume that the objects must conform to our cognition. . . We propose to do just what Copernicus did in attempting to explain the celestial movements. When he found that he could no longer make progress by assuming that all the heavenly bodies revolved round the spectator, he reversed the process, and tried the experiment of assuming that the spectator revolved, while the stars remained at rest.[91]

In this way Kant arrives at the conclusion that contains in a nutshell the essence of the *Critique of Pure Reason* (1781): that

> Experience itself is a mode of cognition which requires understanding. Before objects are given to me, that is, *a priori*, I must presuppose in myself laws of the understanding which are expressed in conceptions *a priori*. To these conceptions, then, all the objects of experience must necessarily conform.[92]

Thus nature, or reality, is that which we can know. It is determined, not by laws external to us, but by laws built into our own cognitive apparatus. These comprise various innate 'categories' or concepts such as causality, and, most crucially, space and time, which are no longer conceived as properties of external things but as *Anschauungen* or 'modes of viewing'. These fundamental components of the Newtonian system of nature are thus transplanted from the external to the internal world.

The proposition 'that universal laws of nature can be distinctly cognized *a priori*' leads inevitably to the proposition

91. I. Kant, *Critique of Pure Reason*, Everyman's Library, 1934, p. 12.
92. *Ibid*.

> that the highest legislation of nature must lie in ourselves, i.e. in our understanding, and that we must not seek the universal laws of nature in nature by means of experience, but conversely must seek nature, as to its universal conformity to law, in the conditions of the possibility of experience, which lie in our sensibility and our understanding. . . *The understanding does not derive its laws (a priori) from, but prescribes them to, nature.*[93]

In other words, we can discover the absolute truth about the world because the absolute truth about the world is that which, given the nature of our sensory and mental equipment, we must inevitably discover. The only puzzle is why, in that case, the human race had to wait for Newton to discover it.[94]

All phenomena are therefore a human construction, distinct from the external world proper, the 'thing-in itself' or *noumenon*, about which we can know nothing, but only infer that it must exist as the source of our impressions. For

> As. . . the senses never and in no manner enable us to know things in themselves, but only their appearances. . . we conclude that 'all bodies, together with the space in which they are, must be considered nothing but representations in us, and exist nowhere but in our thoughts'.[95]

This, of course, is the victory of abstraction. In Kant's theory of knowledge, nature is equated with what we can know, and what we can know is what we make. We do not know nature, conceived in this way, because we are part of the natural creation; nature is knowable because it is a human construction.

In the search for a cosmological (or epistemological) ground for proportion, the great value of Kant is that he indicates a way in which the concept of 'nature's laws', and of order and regularity in the world we see around us, might survive the destructive criticism of Hume and the empiricists, and still provide a foundation for developing a philosophy of proportion, no less solid than the one that Plato's cosmology provided for Alberti. But with this difference: that Kant brings out into the full daylight what had previously been hidden, even from the empiricists: that nature's laws are not 'out there', waiting to be discovered; we are ourselves the architects of nature, or at least cannot avoid

93. I. Kant, *Prolegomena*, pp. 80–2.
94. K.R. Popper, *Conjectures and Refutations*, p. 95.
95. I. Kant, *Prolegomena*, pp. 42–3.

shaping its architecture. We cannot sit back, like passive receptors, waiting for nature to reveal herself to us, but must actively interrogate her. In Popper's vivid metaphor, our minds must be like searchlights, not buckets.[96] Kant describes how the great physicists like Galileo

> learned that reason only perceives that which it produces after its own design; that it must not be content to follow, as it were, in the leading-strings of nature, but must proceed in advance with principles of judgement according to unvarying laws, and compel nature to reply to its questions.[97]

If Kant is right, we must seek a foundation for architectural proportion, not in 'things-in-themselves', but in the structure of the mind. This is not to say that we do not still look for it in phenomena; but that we recognize that these phenomena are themselves shaped by our mental structure. As Sir Arthur Eddington, who conducted the tests of Einstein's predictions during the solar eclipse of 1919, has written:

> The mind has by its selective power fitted the processes of Nature into a frame of law or a pattern largely of its own choosing; and in the discovery of this system of law the mind may be regarded as regaining from Nature that which the mind has put into Nature.[98]

Nor does this conclusion imply that we should expect to discover quite different proportions from those that were formerly attributed to nature alone, such as the Pythagorean-Platonic ratios of Alberti and Palladio, or the golden section and the Fibonacci numbers of Le Corbusier and other modern theorists. It is just that we now recognize that these proportions are, and always have been, creations of the human mind.

Finally, Popper regards Kant's insight, that 'It is only the principles of reason which can give to concordant phenomena the validity of law',[99] as an indispensable condition, both for modern science, and for the arts:

> We must give up the idea that we are passive observers, waiting for nature to impress its regularity upon us. Instead we must adopt the view that in digesting our sense-data

96. K.R. Popper, *Objective Knowledge*, Oxford University Press, 1979, pp. 341–61.
97. I. Kant, *Critique of Pure Reason*, p. 10.
98. A.S. Eddington, *The Nature of the Physical World*, J.M. Dent & Sons, 1935, p. 238.
99. I. Kant, *Critique of Pure Reason*, p. 10.

we actively impress the order and the laws of our intellect upon them. Our cosmos bears the imprint of our minds. By emphasizing the role played by the observer, the investigator, the theorist, Kant made an indelible impression not only upon philosophy but also upon physics and cosmology. There is a Kantian climate of thought without which Einstein's theories or Bohr's are hardly conceivable; and Eddington might be said to be more of a Kantian, in some respects, than Kant himself. . . Here, I believe, is a wonderful philosophical find. It makes it possible to look upon science, whether theoretical or experimental, as a human creation, and to look upon its history as part of the history of ideas, on a level with the history of art or literature.[100]

100. K.R. Popper, *Conjectures and Refutations*, pp. 180–1.

Chapter fifteen

THE GOLDEN SECTION AND THE GOLDEN MODULE

All this work on proportioning and measures is the outcome of a passion, disinterested and detached, an exercise, a game, a preoccupation and an occupation, a need and a duty, a ceaseless facing up to life, a seeking after proof, a right to march forward, a duty to be straight and loyal, dealing in honest-to-goodness, clean merchandise.[1]

15.1 THE REDISCOVERY OF THE GOLDEN SECTION

As we saw in Chapter 8, the golden section, or division in extreme and mean ratio, figures largely in the *Elements* of Euclid, but despite the many modern attempts to show that it was also the basis of proportions of the Parthenon and other Greek temples,[2] there is no positive evidence for this. Later, the golden section was an object of interest to Medieval Arabic mathematicians. Influenced by them, Leonardo of Pisa, called Fibonacci (*c.* 1170–1240), investigated the geometry of the regular pentagon, icosahedron and dodecahedron, all of which involve the golden section,[3] but he is associated in particular with the number series that bears his name, and which converges towards ϕ as limit. The mathematical revival during the Renaissance brought renewed interest in the golden section, seen in the mathematical works of, among others, Piero della Francesca, Luca Pacioli and Johannes Kepler. However, there is no firm evidence that Piero applied the golden section in his paintings, and although Leonardo da Vinci was the illustrator of Pacioli's *De divina proportione* (1498–1509), there too the golden section is approached from a strictly mathematical

1. Le Corbusier, *The Modulor*, Faber & Faber, 1961, p. 80.
2. See for example J. Hambidge, *The Parthenon and other Greek Temples: Their Dynamic Symmetry*, Yale University Press, 1924.
3. R. Herz-Fischler, *A Mathematical History of Division in Extreme and Mean Ratio*, Wilfrid Laurier Press, 1987, pp. 121–44.

viewpoint. P.H. Scholfield even concludes that it is

> not very clear how far it is correct to speak of the *rediscovery* of the principle of the golden section in the nineteenth century. . . A fairly good case could be made out for the view that the nineteenth century actually *discovered* the golden section as an instrument of architectural proportion, however close other periods may have come to this discovery.[4]

The earliest use of the name 'golden section' or '*goldene Schnitt*' appears to have been in 1835, in Ohm's treatise *Die reine Elementar-Mathematik*,[5] and it was first put forward unambiguously as the underlying secret of all natural and artistic form by Adolf Zeising in his *New Theory of the Proportions of the Human Body* (1854). Even so, as late as 1914 Sir Theodore Cook was writing of the ϕ progression as 'a new mathematical conception'.[6] Only eight years later we find him attacking the rapid growth of the cult of the golden section, being promoted at that time by writers like Jay Hambidge, as 'a new disease in architecture'.[7] It is significant that this resurgence of the golden section in art, and in the relatively new sciences of biology, psychology and aesthetics, occurred at a time when pure mathematics and 'hard' sciences like physics and astronomy were becoming increasingly abstract and remote from normal human experience. Nature's laws ceased to be seen as evidence of a universal *concinnitas*, so that, as Wittkower says, 'Beauty and proportion were no longer regarded as being universal, but were turned into psychological phenomena originating and existing in the mind of the artist.'[8] A way out of this total subjectivism seemed to be offered by the discovery of logarithmic spirals based on the golden section, and of the Fibonacci series, in the organic growth of plants and animals, and also by the scientific investigation of the psychology of perception and aesthetic choice.

15.2 ADOLF ZEISING

Adolf Zeising's main interests were mathematics and philosophy, but he was also known as a poet, novelist and playwright. In the field of botany he discovered the golden section in the arrangement of branches along the stems of

4. P.H. Scholfield, *The Theory of Proportion in Architecture*, Cambridge University Press, 1958, p. 98 (author's italics).
5. R. Herz-Fischler, *A Mathematical History*, p. 168.
6. T.A. Cook, *The Curves of Life*, Constable, 1914, and Dover Publications, 1979, p. 427.
7. T.A. Cook, 'A new disease in architecture', in *The Nineteenth Century*, 91, 1922, p. 521 ff.
8. R. Wittkower, 'The changing concept of proportion', in *Idea and Image*, Thames & Hudson, 1978, p. 117.

plants, and of veins in leaves. From this starting point he extended his researches to the skeletons of animals and the branchings of their veins and nerves, to the proportions of chemical compounds and the geometry of crystals, to the physics of light, sound and magnetism, and to the distances, sizes and revolution times of heavenly bodies, and finally to human and artistic proportion. In all of these phenomena he saw the operation of a universal law,

> in which is contained the ground-principle of all formative striving for beauty and completeness in the realms of both nature and art, and which permeates, as a paramount spiritual ideal, all structures, forms and proportions, whether cosmic or individual, organic or inorganic, acoustic or optical; which finds its fullest realization, however, in the human form.[9]

That universal law was, in effect, the golden section.

Turning to this 'fullest realization of the spiritual ideal of beauty', Zeising divides the total height of a man's body into four principal zones: top of head to shoulder, shoulder to navel, navel to knee, and knee to base of foot. The first three form an ascending golden section progression, but the fourth is equal to the second. Each zone is further subdivided into five segments, making twenty in all. The segments are arranged symmetrically within each zone: either ABBBA or BABAB, i.e. always 2A + 3B, the ratio A : B being 1 : ϕ (see Figure 15.1). Thus the dimensions of the zones are made up as follows, taking the Fibonacci number 21 to represent the smallest segment:

$(3 \times 34) + (2 \times 21) = 144$
$(3 \times 55) + (2 \times 34) = 233$
$(3 \times 89) + (2 \times 55) = 377$
$(3 \times 55) + (2 \times 34) = 233$

Zeising erroneously substitutes 90 for the Fibonacci number 89; this has here been corrected. The proportion of the first two zones (head to navel) to the second two (navel to feet), and of the latter to the whole height, is again 1 : ϕ, since

$144 + 233 = 377$
$377 + 233 = 610$
$377 + 610 = 987$

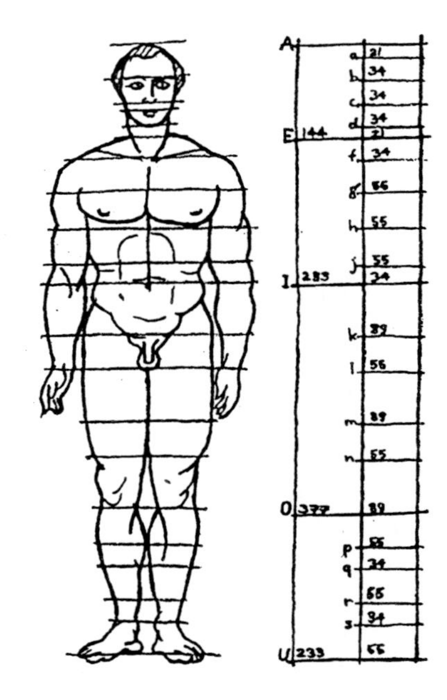

Figure 15.1 Adolf Zeising, human proportions based on the golden section; after A. Zeising, *Neue Lehre von den Proportionen des menschlichen Körpers* (1854).

9. A. Zeising, *Neue Lehre von den Proportionen des meschlischen Körpers*, Leipzig, 1854, preface.

and all these are consecutive terms of the Fibonacci series. In fact all the measures of the parts, sub-parts and the whole form a consecutive sequence: 21, 34, 55, 89, 144, 233, 377, 610, 987.

In his *Aesthetic Investigations* of the following year,[10] Zeising has a convincing answer to the obvious objection to all theories concerning the 'ideal' proportions of the body: that the different parts grow at unequal rates, so the proportions of the body are not constant. He gives ratios of the total height to the height of the navel, and of the height to the navel to the distance from the navel to the top of the head, during a particular individual's growth from birth to twenty-one, showing that the two ratios start at birth as 2 : 1 and 1 : 1 and reach parity at thirteen as ϕ : 1, and that this ideal proportion is slightly overshot at seventeen and recovered at twenty-one. In other words the golden section is so to speak a 'goal' to which the body 'aspires', and which it achieves at maturity.[11]

15.3 GUSTAV FECHNER

Twenty years after Zeising first proclaimed the golden section as the key to proportion in nature and in art, another German, Gustav Theodore Fechner (1834–87) founded the science of experimental aesthetics. His *Zur experimentalen Aesthetik* (1871) and *Vorschule der Aesthetik* (1876) grew almost by accident out of a desire to combat what he saw as the materialism of the age. Fechner was by inclination 'a humanist, a satirist, a poet',[12] and the aesthetic studies that made him famous occupied only a decade of his life. His philosophical works are closer in spirit to Spinoza, Plato, or the pre-Socratics than to nineteenth-century materialism and positivism. In his treatise *Zend-Avesta* (1851) he argues that everything in the universe, including the earth, the planets and the stars, possesses a soul. The sphere is the perfect form, exhibited in the eye itself, and the spherical form of the heavenly bodies proves their superior spiritual status: the stars and planets are in fact great eyes, creatures of pure vision, pure contemplation. The totality of the surfaces of all existing things is the retina of God.[13]

The irony is that he was so successful in developing scientific methods, derived from physics, for measuring subjective sensations, that as George A. Miller observes,

10. A. Zeising, *Aesthetische Forschungen*, 1855.
11. M. Ghyka, *The Geometry of Art and Life*, Dover Publications, 1977, pp. 107–8.
12. E.G. Boring, *A History of Experimental Psychology*, Appleton-Century-Crofts, New York, 1950, pp. 275–6; quoted in G.A. Miller, *Psychology*, Penguin Books, 1966, p. 110.
13. R. Arnheim, 'The other Gustav Fechner', in *New Essays on the Psychology of Art*, University of California Press, 1986, pp. 39–49.

> What he was most interested in – sensation, mind, the subjective view of reality – became excess baggage. Instead of proving by empirical evidence that sensations were real because they could be measured by physical units, he provided a way to talk about them that was completely materialistic.[14]

And Rudolf Arnheim comments that

> There are indications that Fechner, once he had decided to embark on a substantial work on aesthetics, felt obliged to deal with the topics that dominated other major treatises in the field. . . There is little in the *Vorschule* to compare, for instance, to the inspiration Fechner drew from seeing a waterlily spread its leaves on a pond and offer its open flower to the light. He cites this experience in his book on the soul of the planets to suggest that the lily is enabled by its shape to enjoy the pleasures of the bath and the warmth of the light to the fullest.[15]

In a way, the whole exercise was a great missed opportunity. Had he followed his own insights, and explored the mathematical and aesthetic consequences of his pantheistic geometry of nature, Fechner might have re-established the study of proportion on the ancient empathic vision of cosmic unity. But the world, writes E.G. Boring, 'chose for him; it seized upon the psychological experiments, which Fechner meant merely as contributory to his philosophy, and made them into an experimental psychology'.[16]

15.4 THE STATISTICAL APPROACH TO THE GOLDEN SECTION

The experimental approach to beauty that Fechner felt constrained to follow was a logical development of the recent trend of aesthetic speculation in Germany, away from philosophy and towards psychology. Typical of this was the view of Johann Friedrich Herbart (1776–1841) that beauty could not be explained in terms of the harmonious order of the universe, and had no significance beyond itself. It had therefore to be examined as a purely psychological phenomenon; it was necessary to investigate objectively which conditions produced certain positive or negative responses.[17]

14. G.A. Miller, *Psychology*, p. 111.
15. R. Arnheim, 'The other Gustav Fechner', p. 43.
16. E.G. Boring, *A History of Experimental Psychology*.
17. J.F. Herbart, *Lehrbuch zur Einleiting in die Philosophie*, 1813–37; K.E. Gilbert and H. Kuhn, *A History of Esthetics*, The Macmillan Co., New York, 1939, pp. 513–15.

Fechner, contrary perhaps to his own inclination, followed Herbart's rejection of metaphysical speculation. He defined beauty simply as a term applying to 'everything with the property of arousing pleasure directly and immediately, and not only on reflection or because of consequences'.[18]

He used three different kinds of experimental approach: those of *choice*, in which subjects were asked to select or reject certain proportions; of *construction*, in which they were required to complete a figure (for example, to place the dot on a letter 'i'); and of *use*, which involved the measuring of everyday objects such as cards, books and pictures. In the most famous of the experiments of choice, he asked his subjects (selected as being educated but without artistic training) to indicate, from a range of ten rectangular cards of equal area but varying in proportion from a square to two and a half squares, those they found most and least pleasant.

The ratios of the cards were 1:1, 6:5, 5:4, 4:3, 10:7, 29:20, 34:21, 23:13, 2:1 and 5:2 (see Figure 15.2A). Over 74% of subjects preferred one or other of the three ratios between 3:2 and 23:13; the most popular shape, with 35% of the total vote, was the 34:21 shape, which is very close to the golden rectangle. It is significant, however, that 65% did *not* choose this shape. The fact that there was also a small but significant peak of preference (about 3% of subjects) for the square was explained by Fechner on the grounds that some subjects might have felt obliged to recognize the authority of such a clear geometrical shape. But does not this explanation undermine the whole result? For the general preference for figures between a square and a half and a square and three quarters could equally be due simply to the subjects' familiarity with similar shapes in such everyday things as playing cards, window panes, books and paintings. In other words, it may have been based on habituation and convention (as Hume might have argued) rather than any deep-seated law of human nature.

Another objection is that Fechner's ratios are very unevenly distributed. The ratio 34 : 21, in fact very close to the geometric mean of the two extremes 1 : 1 and 5 : 2, appears seventh in the range of ten proportions. This can be corrected by a substitute series (see Figure 15.2B). There is a natural inclination to choose the middle within any range of choice unless there is a positive reason to do otherwise. May not the subjects have simply gravitated towards the mean or 'norm'?

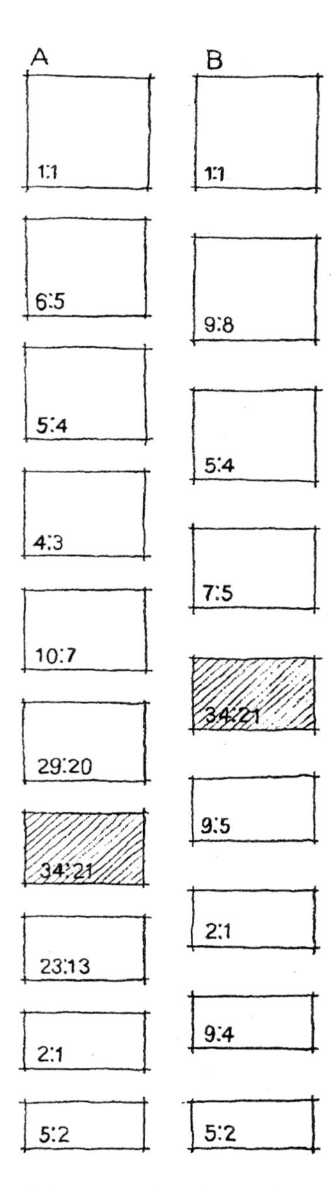

Figure 15.2 Gustav Fechner, shape preference experiment using a set of ten cards. The hatched shape, approximately a ϕ rectangle, was chosen by the greatest number of subjects. Fechner's series (A) is compared with an alternative series (B) in which the ϕ rectangle is shown to be roughly the geometric mean between the extremes.

18. G. Fechner, *Vorschule der Aesthetik*, 1876, I, p.15.

15.5 ATTEMPTS TO EXPLAIN THE PHENOMENON

Despite these objections, the experiment aroused worldwide interest and seemed to provide convincing evidence of the aesthetic supremacy of the golden section. After Fechner's publication of his findings, related experiments were carried out, and his conclusions revised, and sometimes repudiated, by numerous other investigators.[19] Various explanations were put forward to account for the apparent statistical preference.

The most common was that the repetition, in the ratio between the two parts of a line, of that between the whole line and its larger part – that is, $A/B = B/(A - B)$ – provided an ideal balance of unity and variety that was unconsciously perceived and gave aesthetic pleasure. The fact that the golden rectangle contains a square plus its own reciprocal (that is, a similar but smaller and oppositely oriented figure) has been seen by some researchers as precisely the key to its perceived beauty (see Figure 15.3). One is supposed to grasp intuitively the presence of the two component figures concealed within the whole. Matila Ghyka, for instance, speculates that 'Even without actually drawing the square, this operation and the continuous proportions characteristic of the series of correlated segments and surfaces are subconsciously suggested to the eye.'[20]

P.H. Scholfield denies this: 'The explanation is. . . applicable only to divisions of lines, and not to the golden section rectangle.'[21] M. Borissavlievitch even rejects the notion that the eye can perceive the two ratios simultaneously, whether in the subdivision of a line or in a rectangle. In the first case, he argues, only the ratio of the two juxtaposed parts is perceptible; in the second, only that of its two perpendicular sides, not that between the implied square and the reciprocal. The ratio $A/B = B/(A - B)$ is a purely mathematical phenomenon, and its agreement with our aesthetic feeling 'due to pure chance'.[22] He offers two alternative kinds of explanation, one optical and the other psychological, and neither very convincing:

(1) 'The visual field for both eyes represents an oval shape exactly inscribed in a Golden Rectangle. Therefore the latter (specially in an oval frame) is a shape fitted to our binocular vision.'[23] But this argument, like two other optical justifications that he puts forward, applies exclusively to *horizontal*

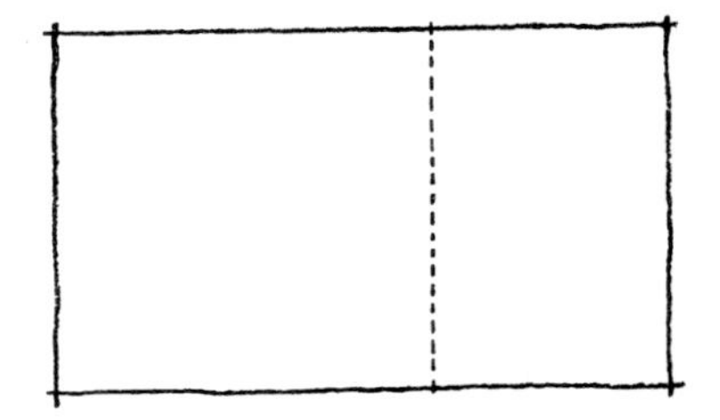

Figure 15.3 The ϕ rectangle and its reciprocal.

19. See for example O. Kuelpe, *Grundriss der Psychologie auf experimenteller Grundlage*, 1893; L. Witmer and E. Pierce, 'Aesthetic of simple forms', *The Psychological Review*, 1894 and 1896; R.P. Angier, 'The aesthetics of equal division', *The Psychological Review*, 1903; C. Lalo, *L'esthétique expérimentale contemporaine*, 1908; M. Borissavlievitch, *The Golden Number*, Tiranti, 1958; I.C. McManus, 'The aesthetics of simple figures', *British Journal of Psychology*, 71, 1980.
20. M. Ghyka, *The Geometry of Art and Life*, Dover, 1977, p. 10.
21. P.H. Scholfield, *The Theory of Proportion in Architecture*, p. 100.
22. M. Borissavlievitch, *The Golden Number*, p. 32.
23. *Ibid.*, pp. 37–8.

golden rectangles – an objection that he airily brushes aside by saying that the vertical rectangle must be considered 'equally beautiful' despite the fact that 'we could not explain its beauty'.[24]
(2) The golden section 'represents the balance between two unequal asymmetrical parts, which means that the dominant is neither too big nor too small, so that this ratio appears at once clear and "of just measure"'. This vague statement might be applied, however, to a wide range of proportions.

Borissavlievitch's second explanation is similar to that offered earlier by Theodor Lipps, who likewise concludes that the golden section, as such, was 'entirely without aesthetic significance. . . The rectangles in question are just those in which the smaller dimension is decisively subordinated to the greater. . .'[25] Rectangles so short as to be close to a square are ambiguous, while those whose dimensions differ too much appear 'insufficient, thin, attenuated'. According to this view, if approximate golden rectangles are pleasant, as experimental evidence seems to confirm, it is because they lie at an ideal point between these extremes.

This is very close to the conclusion reached recently by two British psychologists, I.C. McManus and P. Weatherby, applying the theory of 'fuzzy sets' or broad perceptual categories:

> In effect only five different categories will be generally available: 'square', 'vertical line', 'horizontal line', 'vertical rectangle' and 'horizontal rectangle'. The position of the function delineating the two 'rectangles' will be a matter for individual variation, but in general it must occur somewhere near the Golden Section. . . The particular predominance of the Golden Section does not therefore arise because of its intrinsic mathematical properties, but rather because our minds necessarily classify phenomena, and that classification requires us to have a category called 'rectangle', which in general is particularly well satisfied by the actual figure whose ratio is 1 : 1.6180. But a rectangle of ratio 1 : 1.58 or 1 : 1.65 would almost certainly do as well.[26]

Fechner's experiment does not, therefore, prove a clear-cut preference for the golden rectangle, but at best one

24. *Ibid.*, p.39.
25. T. Lipps, *Aesthetik: Psychologie des Schoenen und der Kunst*, 1903, I, pp. 66–7, quoted by G.D. Birkhoff in *Aesthetic Measure*, 1933, pp. 29–30.
26. I.C. McManus and P. Weatherby, undated paper, Dept of Psychology, University College, London, pp. 14–16.

for a rather broad range of shapes, extending between about one and a half and two squares. But a more damning argument against such experiments is Rudolf Arnheim's, that the very nature of the experimental method unfits it for the exploration of all but the most superficial levels of aesthetic experience. In order to make such experience measurable under experimental conditions, it has to be reduced to a single simply quantifiable variable, like the length/width ratio of a card. In just the same way, a recipe for baked beans might be tested by varying only the proportion of sugar. As Arnheim points out in an essay on Fechner,

> Practically the entire body of experimental aesthetics. . . was cast in the convenient format of a hedonistic psychophysics, with the consequence that the more strictly investigators adhered to the criterion of preference, the more completely their results neglected everything that distinguishes the pleasure generated by a work of art from the pleasure generated by a dish of ice cream.[27]

In other words, the method not only overlooks the infinite complexity of actual artistic experience, it also reduces it to its most banal manifestation: mass appeal. Aesthetic judgement is reduced to market research. No gastronome would accept that the most popular brand of baked beans or ice cream was necessarily the best, and it is equally ridiculous to set up popularity as the index of artistic value. The very conception of art as a source of pleasure is, in Arnheim's words, 'insipid and unfruitful'.[28] Or as Ludwig Wittgenstein remarked: 'You might think Aesthetics is a science telling us what's beautiful – almost too ridiculous for words. I suppose it ought to include also what sort of coffee tastes well.'[29]

Even Jay Hambidge, great champion though he was of the golden rectangle, concludes that all attempts to prove by experiment the visual superiority of a single ratio or figure are doomed to failure: 'There is little ground', he writes, 'for the assumption that any shape, *per se,* is more beautiful than any other. Beauty, perhaps, may be a matter of functional co-ordination.'[30] Nevertheless, the beautiful simplicity of the golden section, and its occurrence in so many and so varied phenomena, from geometry to organic growth, acquired, once recognized, an unstoppable momentum. By the early years of this century the notions of 'beauty of proportion' and 'the golden section' seemed to have become virtually synonymous.

27. R. Arnheim, 'The other Gustav Fechner', p. 45.
28. *Ibid.*
29. L. Wittgenstein, *Lectures and Conversations on Aesthetics, Psychology and Religious Belief*, ed. C. Barrett, Blackwell, 1978; quoted in R. Monk, *Ludwig Wittgenstein*, Jonathan Cape, 1990, p. 405.
30. J. Hambidge, *Dynamic Symmetry: The Greek Vase*, Yale University Press, 1920, p. 59.

15.6 THE CURVES OF LIFE

One of the foremost expositions of the golden section in the early years of the twentieth century is *The Curves of Life* by Theodore Cook (1914). In the preface he says that his interest in spirals in nature started out from an investigation of their importance in art, and he soon discovered that 'In shells, in plants, in the bodily structure of men and animals, the spiral formation is certainly a common factor in a multitude of phenomena apparently widely different.'[31] He criticizes the positivist school of nineteenth-century thinkers and scientists, from Auguste Comte (1798–1857) to Ernst Mach (1838–1916), who, following the scepticism of British empiricist philosophers like David Hume, would limit the role of science to the description of observations, without speculation about first causes and ultimate ends. For, Cook writes,

> We do not want mere catalogues. If every generation of great thinkers had not thirsted for explanations also, we should never have evolved the complexity and beauty of modern science at all. . . Newton arrived at his theory of the movements of the celestial bodies in our own solar system by postulating *perfect movement* and by calculating from that the apparently erratic orbits of the planets. In just the same way may it not be possible to postulate *perfect growth* and from that to calculate and define the apparently erratic growth and forms of living things?[32]

Nevertheless, like Hume and Kant, Cook does not try to conceal, but exposes, the paradoxical character of the mind's encounter with the external world:

> I do not ask you to believe that the occurrence of similar curvilinear formations in various organic and inorganic phenomena is a proof of 'conscious design'. I only suggest that it indicates a community of process imposed by the operation of universal laws. I am, in fact, not so much concerned with origins or reasons as with relations or resemblances. It is still more important not to see in any given natural object that spiral formation which may merely be a useful convention of the mind.[33]

Further on he warns that

31. T.A. Cook, *The Curves of Life*, p. vii.
32. *Ibid.*, pp. vii–viii.
33. *Ibid.*, p. 4.

> Mathematics is an abstract science; the spiral is an abstract idea in our minds which we can put on paper for the sake of greater clearness; and we evoke that idea in order to help us to understand a concrete natural object, and even to examine that object's life and growth by means of conclusions originally drawn from mathematics. It is only by such means that the human mind, which hungers for finality and definite conceptions, can ever intelligibly deal with the constantly changing and bewilderingly varied phenomena of organic life.[34]

Precisely because the world revealed by science is inevitably shaped by the investigating human mind, it is analogous, Cook argues, to the world revealed by art, and it is reasonable to conclude that the same ratios and shapes are valid for both. The golden section or ϕ spiral, which he discovered in plants, shells, horns and numerous other natural phenomena, may also be connected with

> those workings of the artist's brain which result in the spectator observing certain pleasing qualities of space and proportion in the picture. . . His picture, therefore, (or his statue, his building, or his music), may be fairly compared with the living things in the world of which he is at once a part and an interpreter. These organisms have reached certain forms through the essential processes of life. The creations of his art are, I suggest, equally essential (if more subtle) manifestations of those same processes.[35]

Cook's great innovation is to have introduced (building on the work of William Schooling) the concept of the ϕ progression as an infinite series, instead of just the golden section as the division of a given length into two parts. He also shows the intimate connection between the ϕ progression and the Fibonacci series. Each successive power of ϕ is composed of various sums of the unit and ϕ, the proportion between the two being a ratio between consecutive Fibonacci numbers. Thus:

$\phi^2 = 1 + \phi$
$\phi^3 = 1 + 2\phi$
$\phi^4 = 2 + 3\phi$
$\phi^5 = 3 + 5\phi$

34. *Ibid.*, p. 24.
35. *Ibid.*, p. 424.

$\phi^6 = 5 + 8\phi$
$\phi^7 = 8 + 13\phi$

and so on.

Cook claims that this 'new mathematical conception' is

> the best formula for the hypothesis of Perfect Growth, and a better instrument than has yet been published for kindred forms of scientific research; but also that it suggests an underlying reason for artistic proportions, and provides an exquisitely delicate standard by which to appreciate divergences and variations of different kinds.[36]

For the point is not that life or beauty are 'strictly mathematical':

> If a nautilus shell were put before me which exactly reproduced a logarithmic spiral, I should remain unmoved, because a machine can make me such a shape if I desire it. . . What I want to see, after comparing a given nautilus with a given logarithmic spiral, is a statement of the difference between the two; for in that difference lies something which I cannot make. . . the mystery of life. . .[37]

The more highly developed an organism, the more sensitive the genius of an artist, the harder it will be to explain the forms they produce in purely mathematical terms, and the more they will challenge us to invent still more complex mathematical instruments. Cook quotes the observation of Charles Darwin (1809–82) that 'I mean by Nature, only the aggregate action and product of many natural laws; and by laws the sequence of events as ascertained by us.'[38] He comments:

> In reality nothing is abnormal. We must always be ready, in every scientific investigation, for occurrences which might, in a narrow view, be called 'exceptions', but which in reality provide an indication of the presence of some other principles conditioning the whole of our original hypothesis.[39]

Applying the newly discovered ϕ progression to the proportions of the human body, Cook anticipates the principle of the *modulor* by thirty years. He not only proposes a system of ϕ proportions similar to Le Corbusier's (but more

36. *Ibid.*, p. 427.
37. *Ibid.*
38. C. Darwin, *The Origin of Species*, Everyman's Library, 1928, p. 81.
39. T.A. Cook, *The Curves of Life*, p. 428.

flexible, since it embodies a sliding scale, which allows any measure at all to be chosen as a basic unit (see Figure 15.4)); he also applies it to the human body in much the same way. The main difference is that he takes as a standard height 68 inches (that is, twice the Fibonacci number 34) instead of Le Corbusier's 72 inches (half the Fibonacci number 144). He writes:

> Take a well-proportioned man 68 inches in height, or ϕ^4 if we take 10 inches as our unit of measurement. From the ground to his navel is 42 inches, or ϕ^3; from his navel to the crown of his head is 26 inches, or ϕ^2; from the crown of his head to the line of his breasts is 16 inches, ϕ; and from his breasts to his navel is 10 inches, or the unit of measurement, or 1, which is ϕ^0.[40]

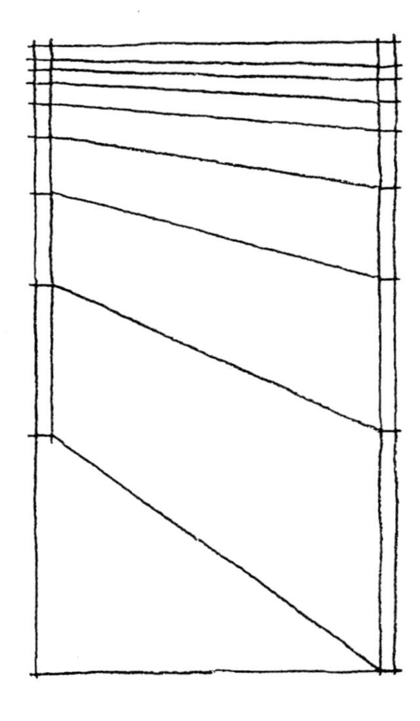

Figure 15.4 Theodore Cook, sliding scale of ϕ proportions.

Unlike Le Corbusier, however, he does not go so far as to conclude that 'Nature is ruled by mathematics.'[41] He constantly warns that the mathematical principles we apply to the scientific interpretation of natural forms, and also in artistic creation, are not inherent in nature itself, but are an essentially human construct:

> Because we can draw a spiral line through a series of developing members, it does not follow that a plant or a shell is attempting to make a spiral, or that a spiral series would be of any advantage to it. All spiral appearances should properly be considered as subjective... Geometrical constructions do not, in fact, give any clue to the causes which produce them, but only *express* what is seen, and the subjective connection of the leaves of a plant by a spiral curve does not at all imply any *inherent* tendency of the plant to such a construction...[42]

15.7 THE GOLDEN SECTION IN LE CORBUSIER'S EARLY WORK

I know of no evidence that Le Corbusier (1887–1965) read any of the books so far mentioned, but the climate of thought he absorbed as a student of Charles L'Eplattenier at the School of Art in La Chaux-de-Fonds was permeated by such ideas. Near the beginning of his book *The Modulor* he says that

40. *Ibid.*, p. 420.
41. Le Corbusier, *The Modulor*, p. 29.
42. T.A. Cook, *The Curves of Life*, p. 23.

> From 1900 until 1907, he studied nature under an excellent master; he observed natural phenomena in a place far from the city, in the mountains of the High Jura. The call was for the renewal of the decorative elements by the direct study of plants, animals, the changing sky. Nature is order and law, unity and diversity without end, subtlety, harmony and strength: that is the lesson he learned between fifteen and twenty.[43]

Of the leaders of Modernism, Le Corbusier was the only one who put systems of harmony and proportion at the centre of his design philosophy. His faith in the mathematical order of the universe was closely bound up with the golden section and Fibonacci series, which he described as

> rhythms apparent to the eye and clear in their relations with one another. And these rhythms are at the very root of human activities. They resound in man by an organic inevitability, the same fine inevitability which causes the *tracing out of the Golden Section* by children, old men, savages and the learned.[44]

At the time he wrote this, just after the First World War, Hambidge was writing and publishing his books on dynamic symmetry (1919–24). It seems unlikely that Le Corbusier became acquainted with the golden section much before about 1910, when he was working in the office of Peter Behrens (1868–1940). The student sketch of the branchings of a tree with which Le Corbusier illustrates the recollection just quoted is obviously out of proportion. At that time he seems to have been unaware of the golden section's connection with plant growth, and he made the gaps between branches get smaller towards the bottom, as he frankly admits, because of 'the smallness of my sheet of paper'.[45]

In the early paintings and buildings (say, after about 1916–18), and in *Towards a New Architecture* (1923), he based his compositions on *tracés régulateurs*. These 'regulating lines' were the diagonals of significant rectangular parts of facades (only facades at this stage, not plans), which, by their parallelism or perpendicular intersections, revealed the recurrence of one or a few shapes throughout the whole composition. The composition was thus determined by a geometry of similar rectangles, the preferred figure being that which has

43. Le Corbusier, *The Modulor*, p. 25.
44. *Ibid.*, p. 68.
45. *Ibid.*

its sides in the golden section ratio. In *The Modulor* Le Corbusier claims to have discovered this method by accident:

> One day, under the oil lamp in his little room in Paris, some picture postcards were spread out on his table. His eye lingered on a picture of Michelangelo's Capitol in Rome. He turned over another card, face down, and intuitively projected one of its angles (a right angle) on to the facade of the Capitol. Suddenly he was struck afresh by a familiar truth: the places of the right angle command the entire composition[46] (see Figure 15.5).

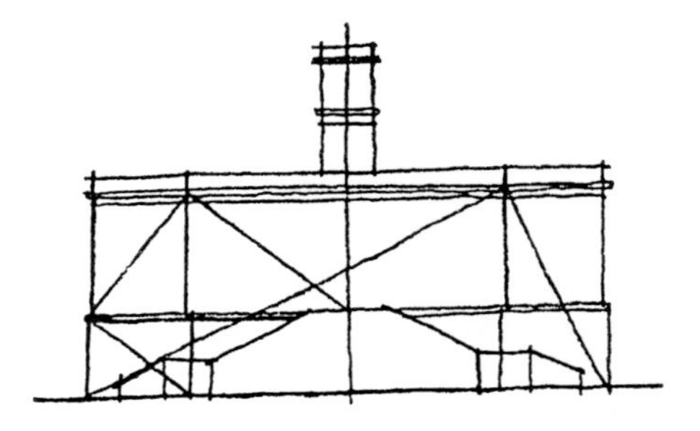

Figure 15.5 Le Corbusier, proportional analysis of Michelangelo's Capitol, Rome.

This is unlikely to have happened during his first stay in Paris while working for Auguste Perret, in 1908–9; at that time he had not yet been to Rome – his Italian journey of the previous year took him no further than Florence – and had no interest in Classical architecture.[47] It is more likely to have occurred during his second Paris visit in 1912. His story is that his eyes were opened to Classicism by his 'Journey to the East', which included Athens and Rome (1911); but before that he spent a year in Germany, working in Peter Behrens' office. Le Corbusier is perpetually laying false trails, designed (quite unnecessarily) to make him appear even more innovative and original than he really was. In particular, he plays down his debt to Behrens and to his German experience in general.[48] The concept of proportion based on similar figures revealed by diagonal regulating lines seems to have been invented by August Thiersch in the 1870s, inspired by Fechner's recently published researches and by the philosophical ideas of his grandfather the philosopher Friedrich von Thiersch, friend and associate of the Munich Neoclassicist architect Leo von Klenze (see Figure 15.6). The method is described by August Thiersch as follows:

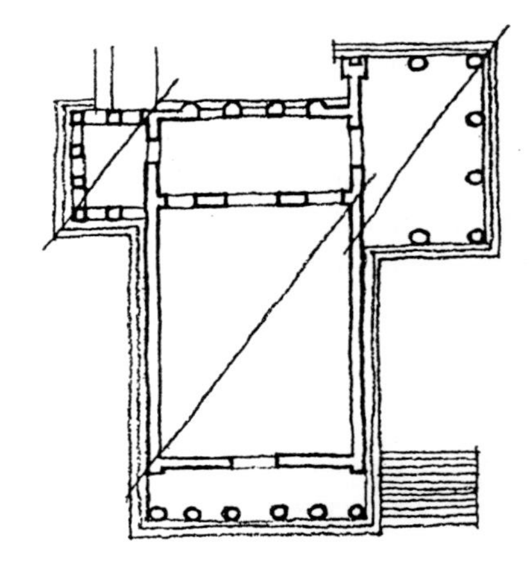

Figure 15.6 August Thiersch, proportional analysis of the Erechtheum; from *Handbuch der Architektur* (1883).

> We have found, in observing the most succcessful products of art in all important periods, that in each of them a fundamental shape is repeated, and that the parts form, by their composition and disposition, similar figures. Harmony results from the repetition of the fundamental form of the plan throughout its subdivisions.[49]

The theory was taken up by Heinrich Wölfflin (1864–1945), who published analyses of Greek and Renaissance facades

---

46. *Ibid.*, p. 26.
47. H.A. Brooks, *Le Corbusier's Formative Years*, University of Chicago Press, 1997, p. 96.
48. *Ibid.*, pp. 245–7.
49. A. Thiersch, in *Handbuch der Architektur*, Darmstadt, 1883, vol. IV, p. 39; quoted by M. Ghyka, 'The Modulor', *Architectural Review*, Feb 1948, and by P.H. Scholfield, *The Theory of Proportion in Architecture*, p. 102.

using Thiersch's method in 1889.[50] Early in 1910 Le Corbusier tried unsuccessfully to get work with the Munich architect Theodor Fischer, a convert to Thiersch's theory.[51] He probably encountered the theory a few months later, however, in Behrens' office, in the Dusseldorf branch of which Thiersch's son, the architect Paul Thiersch, worked from 1906 to 1907.[52]

In the years immediately following the First World War, when Le Corbusier was directing the review *L'Esprit Nouveau* with the painter Amedée Ozenfant, between 1920 and 1925, there was a widespread drive towards the standardization and mechanization of building, as there would be again in the 1940s at the time of the creation of the *modulor*. Le Corbusier at once saw the connection between standardization and systems of proportion. Hence his many experiments with mass-production housing around 1920. In 1917, soon after his definitive return to Paris, he set up, unsuccessfully, his own company to manufacture lightweight concrete blocks.[53] Hence also his later attempts to patent the *modulor*, and to sell the idea to manufacturers such as Kaiser.[54] If economic and technological forces require the house to be mass-produced like a motor car, has not the car been perfected by its standardization, and was not the Greek temple perfected in the same way? In *Towards a New Architecture* Le Corbusier writes:

> The Parthenon is a product of selection applied to an established standard. Already for a century the Greek temple had been standardized in all its parts. . . Standardization is imposed by the law of selection and is an economic and social necessity. Harmony is a state of agreement with the norms of our universe. Beauty governs all; she is of purely human creation; she is the overplus necessary only to men of the highest type. But we must first of all aim at the setting up of standards in order to face the problem of perfection.[55]

Thus if standardization is imposed by economics, it is still possible to distil out of this necessity that 'overplus', that aesthetic harmony, that is required by a higher civilization.

The principle of *tracés régulateurs* was applied in the early houses, notably at the La Roche-Jeanneret houses in Paris, 1923 (see Figure 15.7). But of all Le Corbusier's 'ideal mathematical villas' of the 1920s, the one that most clearly

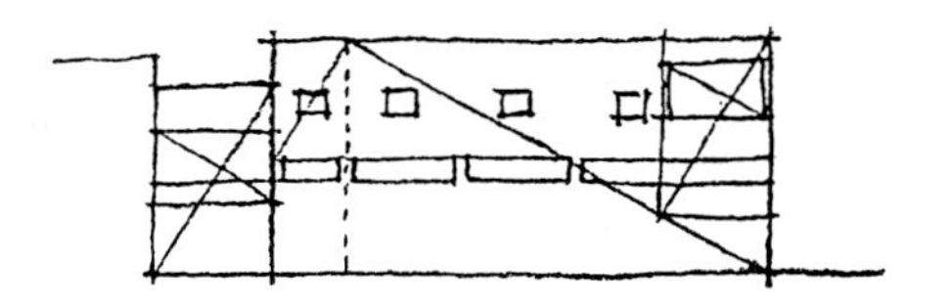

Figure 15.7 Le Corbusier, proportional analysis of the La Roche-Jeanneret houses, Paris (1924); from *Le Corbusier et Pierre Jeanneret: Oeuvre complète de 1910–1929*.

50. H. Wölfflin, *Zur Lehre von den Proportionen*, 1889, reprinted in *Kleine Schriften*, Basle, 1946; see also P.H. Scholfield, *The Theory of Proportion in Architecture*, pp. 103–4.
51. H.A. Brooks, *Le Corbusier's Formative Years*, pp. 213–14.
52. J. Paul, 'German neo-Classicism and the Modern Movement', *Architectural Review*, Sept 1978, pp. 176–80; and H.A. Brooks, *Le Corbusier's Formative Years*, p. 447.
53. J. Lowman, 'Corb as structural rationalist', *Architectural Review*, Oct. 1978, pp. 232–3.
54. Le Corbusier, *The Modulor*, pp. 52–3.
55. Le Corbusier, *Towards a New Architecture*, pp. 123, 138.

embodies what he calls 'the place of the right angle', and which also leads on most directly to his final solution, the *modulor*, is the Villa Stein at Garches, 1927. This is one of five examples of his earlier works that he illustrates in his book *Le Modulor* to demonstrate his use of regulating lines and the golden section: 'Both the paintings and the architectural designs make use of the golden section, the "place of the right angle". . .'[56] Of the five works, the villa is the only building; three of the other four are paintings and one a town plan.

The two main facades of the house are approximate golden rectangles; in fact the basic diagram of the facade is identical with one of the classic methods of constructing a golden section (see Figure 15.8A). The only difference is that here a reciprocal golden rectangle (that is, one of the same shape but opposite orientation, equal in length to the breadth of the original one) is inscribed at *both* ends (see Figure 15.8B). The inscribing of the reciprocal is unusual for Le Corbusier, who at the La Roche-Jeanneret and other earlier houses constructed it *outside* the main rectangle, as with his analysis of the postcard of the Capitol, and not, as in this case, inside.

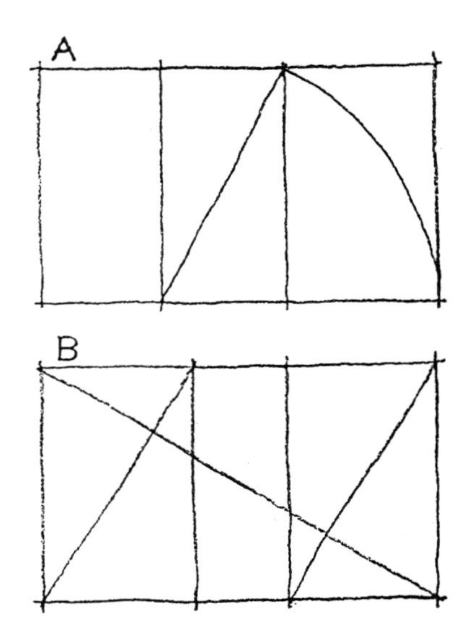

Figure 15.8 (A) Method of constructing a golden rectangle. (B) Reciprocal rectangle applied at both ends.

His commentary on the house when it was published in his *Complete Work* reads:

> The impression of luxury is not provided by expensive materials, but simply by the arrangement of the interior and by proportioning. The design of the entire house was governed by rigorous regulating lines that had the effect of modifying the dimensions of various parts – sometimes by one centimetre. Here mathematics brings reassuring verities: one does not stop working until one is certain to have achieved exactitude.[57]

The golden section geometry is in fact less rigorous than Le Corbusier suggests: the dimensions are 4.96, 7.87, 12.83 and 20.7 m. These diverge, not by 1 but by between 4 and 7 cm from the 'exact' ϕ measures, and result in ratios varying between 1 : 1.63 and 1 : 1.59 instead of 1 : 1.618. But to the eye even these variations are negligible: what counts is the apparently consistent repetition of similar proportions throughout the design. The golden rectangle is echoed, not only in the whole facade and its main divisions, but also in the smaller features. Above all, the external stair that leads

56. Le Corbusier, *The Modulor*, p. 35.
57. Le Corbusier, *Oeuvre Complète de 1910–1929*, Editions Girsberger, 1956, p. 144.

down from the covered terrace on the garden side is made parallel with the main diagonal (see Figure 15.9).

The fairly consistent application of golden sections throughout the villa seems to justify Le Corbusier's choice of this, from all his pre-war buildings, to illustrate the long development that finally led him to the *modulor.* For the *modulor* gave him what he must have unconsciously wished for in those years: a complete system of measures that automatically generated golden sections and related ratios in whatever he designed.

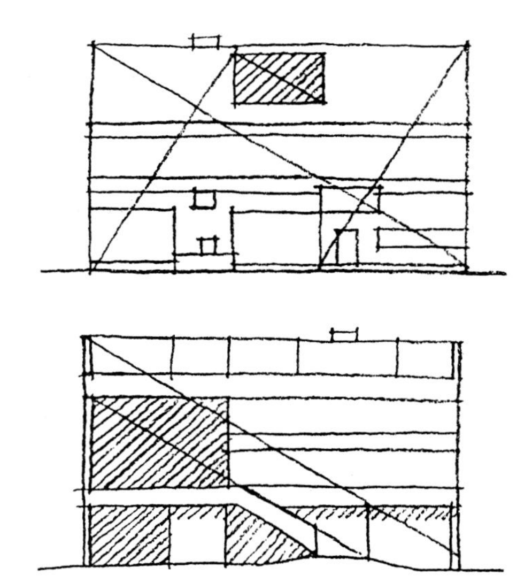

Figure 15.9 Le Corbusier, proportional analysis of the Villa Stein, Garches (1927); from *Oeuvre complète.*

15.8 ORIGINS AND AIMS OF THE *MODULOR*

During the German occupation of Paris, between 1943 and 1944, Le Corbusier and his team of helpers, having abandoned the geometrical method of composition based on *tracés régulateurs*, developed a more flexible system: the *modulor*, a scale of dimensions fixed by the height of a six-foot man and constituting two interwoven ϕ progressions. The name is a condensation of *module d'or*, 'golden module': hence the title of this chapter.

The book on the *modulor* is largely autobiographical; clearly, Le Corbusier wanted to tell the story as an exciting voyage of discovery. His stated aim was to make a measuring instrument that was more subtle, more organic and better attuned to human dimensions than either the metric system or the system of feet and inches, and which at the same time would overcome the discrepancies between these systems, converting one 'automatically' into the other.[58] Whereas AFNOR (the official group set up by the Vichy régime to study post-war standardization) proposed to employ an 'arbitrary and poor' method based on simple arithmetic and the rationalization of existing practice, Le Corbusier and his group, ASCORAL, turned back to an ancient principle: the origin of measures in the dimensions and proportions of the human body. An inchoate system of proportions is already contained in the system of inches, feet and yards, which, according to Vitruvius, grew out of the way builders would naturally use their own bodies as measures on the building-site: 'It was from the members of the body that they [our forefathers] derived the fundamental idea of the measures which are obviously necessary in all works, as the finger, palm, foot, and cubit.'[59]

58. Le Corbusier, *The Modulor*, pp. 57–8.
59. Vitruvius, *The Ten Books on Architecture*, Dover Publications, 1960, p. 73.

Building on the golden section's supposed foundation in the human form and thereby in nature's harmony, Le Corbusier dreamed of setting up

> on the building sites which will spring up all over our country one day, a 'grid of proportions', drawn on the wall or made of a strip of iron, which will serve as a rule for the whole project, a norm offering an endless series of different combinations and proportions; the mason, the carpenter, the joiner will consult it whenever they have to choose the measures for their work; and all the things they make, different and varied as they are, will be united in harmony.[60]

If his aim was really, as he claimed, to devise an efficient method of rationalizing construction and rebuilding after the war, he chose to reach it by such a roundabout route that it is tempting to conclude that his real motivation was psychological rather than practical. Le Corbusier's instruction to his assistant Hanning in 1943 contains an elementary geometrical error:

> Take a man-with-arm-upraised, 2.20 m in height; put him inside two squares. . .; put a third square astride these first two squares. . . The *place of the right angle* should help you to decide where to put this third square.[61]

The instruction combines two quite plausible intuitions: the idea (derived ultimately from Vitruvius) that the proportions of the human body were the key to architectural proportion, and a guess that these proportions might be integrated with the classic method of constructing a golden rectangle by means of a double square. Combining these two ideas, Le Corbusier assumes that (1) the golden section holds the definitive key to the proportions of the human body, and (2) it can be constructed geometrically by finding 'the place of the right angle' slightly off-centre within a double square. I believe the first assumption is mistaken; the second is certainly so. Le Corbusier's earlier obsession with regulating lines put him on the wrong track.

The fact that the *modulor* was erected on these rather shaky foundations does not necessarily rule it out as a valid system of proportion. It would not be the first time that a great discovery grew out of a misconception (Columbus,

60. Le Corbusier, *The Modulor*, pp. 36–7.
61. *Ibid.*, p. 37.

after all, set out to reach the Indies, not to discover America.) It illustrates once more, however, the principle that the connection between nature, mathematics and art is a matter of faith and intuition rather than reason or empirical knowledge.

15.9 THE GEOMETRY OF THE *MODULOR*

The construction Le Corbusier proposes is similar to the method of constructing a golden section by starting from the bisection of a square as in Figure 15.8A.

(1) Draw a square ABCD, bisected by EF.
(2) Draw the diagonal ED and with this as radius and E as centre, draw an arc to cut BA extended at G. Then AB : BG = 1 : ϕ. Complete the rectangle BCHG (see Figure 15.10).

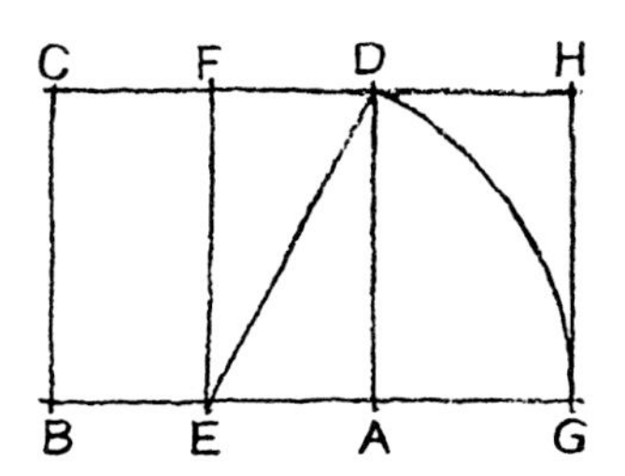

Figure 15.10 Le Corbusier, construction of golden rectangle; from *Le Modulor* (1950).

So far, the diagram exactly corresponds to that of the Villa Stein. At this point, however, in order to give the whole figure the double square shape that he intuitively feels to be necessary, Le Corbusier makes three further steps (see Figure 15.11).

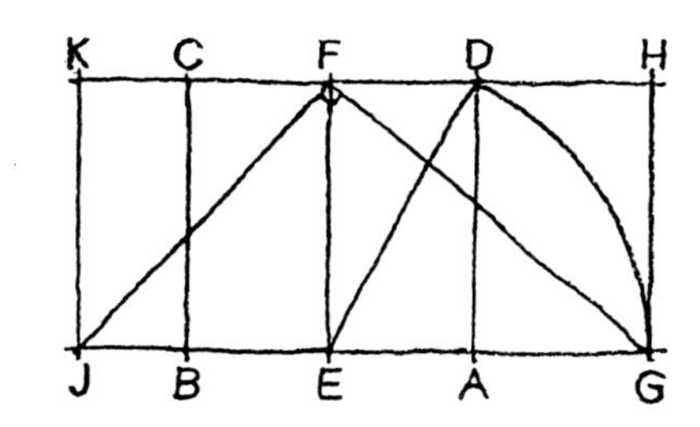

Figure 15.11 Le Corbusier, 'double square' formed by constructing a right angle on the centre line of the original square; from *Le Modulor*.

(3) Join FG. Construct FJ perpendicular to FG, cutting GB extended at J.
(4) Complete the rectangle GHKJ.

This, Le Corbusier claims, comprises 'two contiguous squares, each equal to the initial square'.[62] But point F does not in fact coincide with Le Corbusier's 'place of the right angle', and cannot possibly do so. If GHJK is indeed a double square, the angle GFH must be slightly less than 90°; conversely, if GFH is a right angle as he insists, then GHJK is slightly longer than two squares.

Early in 1944, having discovered this, Hanning writes to tell Le Corbusier: 'Only one right-angle is possible, namely that formed by the diagonals of the two squares.'[63] Unwilling, however, to accept that 'the first principle' of the *modulor* could be thus flawed, yet still uneasy about it, late in 1948 Le Corbusier consults the mathematician M. Taton, who confirms that the two apparent 'squares' are only approximately so, being in fact longer by 0.006 : 1. Faced with this setback, Le Corbusier typically presents it as a victory:

62. *Ibid.*, p. 38.
63. *Ibid.*, p. 42.

> In everyday practice, six thousandths of a value are what is called a negligible quantity.. . . But in philosophy (and I have no key to that austere science), I suspect that these six thousandths of a value have an infinitely precious importance: the thing is not open and shut, it is not sealed; there is a chink to let in the air; life is there. . . And that is what creates movement.[64]

Underlying this statement is a certain truth: an intuition that in art as in nature the vitality, the 'sense of life' that we recognize as beauty owes as much to small departures from exact mathematical regularity as it does to the mathematical scheme itself. As Theodore Cook points out, natural forms

> almost invariably exhibit those subtle variations from mechanical accuracy (those inexplicable factors, 'isolated'. . . from the simpler mathematical processes) which are essential to life, and, as I think, to beauty.[65]

Often, too, these variations themselves require only a more complex or more subtle mathematical explanation, but that would reveal yet further, more minute variations demanding yet more complex subtleties:

> It would be possible to imagine life or beauty as being 'strictly mathematical' if we ourselves were such infinitely capable mathematicians as to be able to formulate their characteristics in mathematics so extremely complex that we have never yet invented them.[66]

But this is something quite different from Le Corbusier's arbitrary ratio of 0.006 : 1, which has no connection with life or nature but is simply due to his misunderstanding of an elementary geometrical principle.

Moreover, the right angle is quite unnecessary; the 'place of the right angle' has nothing whatever to do with the way the double square is divided by the *modulor*. Let us return to Le Corbusier's process, and repeat its first two stages (see Figure 15.10). Instead of drawing, as Le Corbusier demands, the diagonal FG, we need only draw (3) the diagonal BD of the original square, and construct DM perpendicular to BD, cutting BG extended at M. Then complete the double square BCLM (see Figure 15.12). The three segments BA, AG and GM are three consecutive terms of a descending ϕ

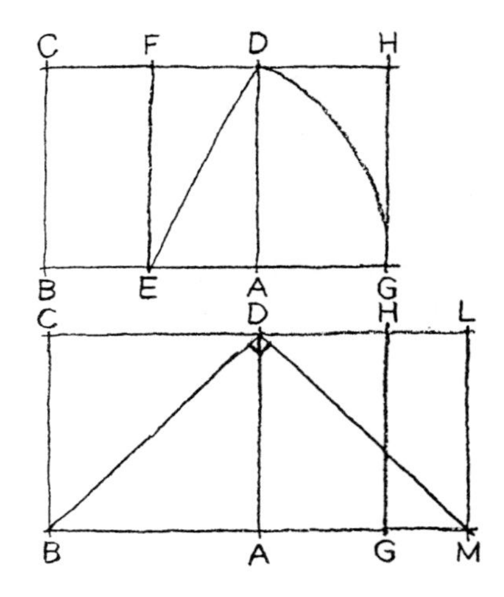

Figure 15.12 Correct method of constructing a double square by constructing a perpendicular to the *diagonal* of the original square.

64. *Ibid.*, pp. 234–5.
65. T.A. Cook, *The Curves of Life*, pp. 220–1.
66. *Ibid.*, pp. 427–8.

progression: that is, 1, ϕ^{-1}, ϕ^{-2}, or approximately 1.0, 0.618, 0.382. This follows from the fact that the sum of three consecutive terms of a ϕ progression is twice the largest term. The three figures ABCD, ADHG and GHLM comprise respectively a square, a golden rectangle and a golden rectangle elongated by a square. This is the diagram within which, when set vertically, Le Corbusier inscribes his human figure (see Figure 15.13). The *modulor* man has his feet planted on the base of the square, BC; his navel is placed on the opposite side of the square, AD; GH grazes the top of his head; and the fingertips of his raised hand touch LM. The diagram simply illustrates the fact that, given any three consecutive terms of a ϕ progression, the largest is the sum of the two smallest.

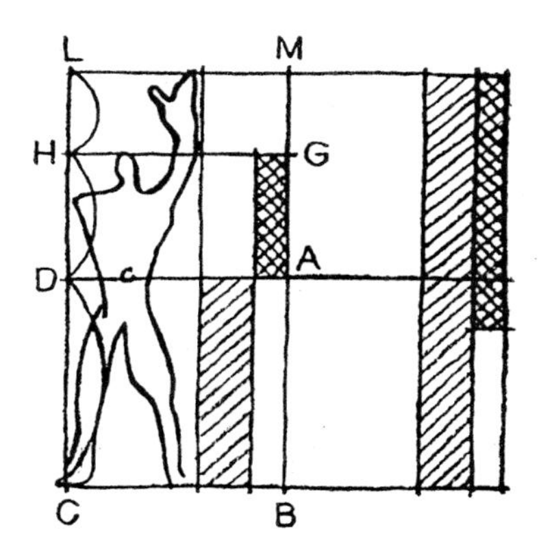

Figure 15.13 Le Corbusier, red (hatched) and blue (cross-hatched) series of the *modulor* derived from the human body; from *Le Modulor*.

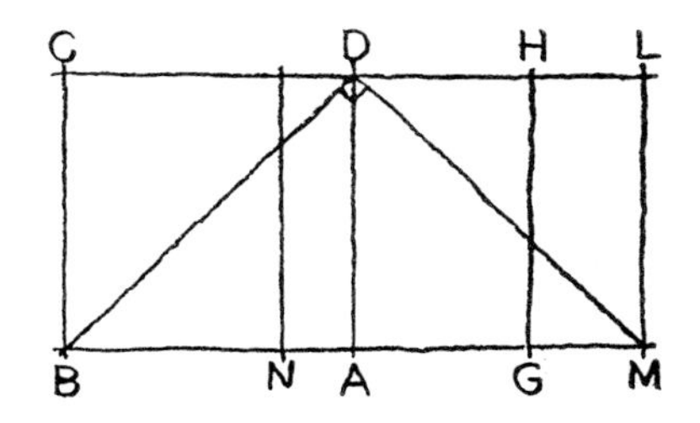

Figure 15.14 The point N divides BM by the golden section, generating the blue series.

Such simplicity appears not to have suited Le Corbusier, who in his two books on the *modulor* wraps it in mystery, in the manner of a detective story writer laying false trails. But what matters is not that Le Corbusier's geometry is muddled, or that he lays false trails, but that what inspired him was an intuition, not a deduction. He was led to the discovery of the *modulor*, not by scientific or mathematical knowledge, but by an overriding faith in the harmony of nature and of art. Without that intuition – without that *mistake* – he might not have hit on a genuinely original idea, which distinguishes the *modulor* from all previous systems of proportion based on the golden section, and adds greatly to its value as an instrument of design: that of interweaving a double or 'blue' series with the original 'red' ϕ progression. With the double square as his starting point, the idea of a double series was almost inevitable, for if the short side of the double square is a single measure, its long side is automatically a double one. This double measure is the sum of three consecutive single measures, as we have just seen with the three segments of the line BM. But this line also divides into its two component double or blue measures, BN and MN (see Figure 15.14).

15.10 THE *MODULOR*'S ARITHMETIC

The *modulor* measures cannot simply be the incommensurable ones that would be generated by the geometry just described. Unless one sets out a building using cords and pegs exclusively, as some theorists suggest was done by the

Medieval master masons, all dimensions used in building must by definition be capable of being measured out, and therefore commensurable. Le Corbusier is well aware of this. The solution is to replace the incommensurable values by an additive whole-number series such as the golden section's close relatives the Fibonacci and Lucas series. Whether by chance or by judgement – he does not say – Le Corbusier arrives at this answer straight away. Later, however, he veers away from it.

He starts out from an old idea of his, that in order to have a human scale normal living spaces should be no higher than a man can reach with his raised hand, a dimension that he first sets at 2.20 m.[67] Measured in centimetres this happens to be four times the Fibonacci number 55. Le Corbusier assumes the height of the navel to be exactly midway between the sole of the foot and the tip of the raised hand, so it is 1.10 m, or 55 × 2 cm. The two measures are members of a double (blue) and a single (red) series respectively. The navel is assumed to divide a man's height by the golden section, so the height must be 89 × 2 cm = 1.78 m. In Table 15.1 the Fibonacci numbers 8–89 are shown in the top row, with below them the corresponding red and blue measures. The three key body dimensions are printed in bold.

Unfortunately for the clarity of his system, Le Corbusier then decides for no apparent reason to reduce the man's height from 1.78 to 1.75 m. This small reduction has the effect of throwing out all the dimensions so that they become very complicated, involving millimetres, and lose all connection with the Fibonacci series.[68] Table 15.2 illustrates this. Note that here as in all the following tables the blue measures have been shifted one column to the right, in order to relate them to their corresponding (that is, nearest) red measures.

This is not the end of the story, however, because Le Corbusier envisages the *modulor* as a means of resolving the conflict between the metric system and English feet and inches. For this purpose he needs dimensions that fit both systems. But

> Ill luck had it that almost all these metric values were practically untranslatable into feet and inches. Yet the 'Modulor' would, one day, claim to be the means of unification for manufactured articles in all countries. . . One day when we were working together, absorbed in

TABLE 15.1

Fibonacci	8	13	21	34	55	89
Red	0.16	0.26	0.42	0.68	**1.10**	**1.78**
Blue	0.32	0.52	0.84	1.36	**2.20**	3.56

TABLE 15.2

Red	0.160	0.254	0.414	0.668	**1.082**	**1.750**
Blue	0.188	0.320	0.508	0.828	1.336	**2.164**

67. Le Corbusier, *The Modulor*, p. 37.
68. *Ibid.*, p. 43.

> the search for a solution, one of us – Py – said: 'The values of the "Modulor" in its present form are determined by the body of a man 1.75 m in height. But isn't that rather a *French* height? Have you never noticed that in English detective novels, the good-looking men, such as the policemen, are always six feet tall?' We tried to apply this standard: six feet = 6 × 30.48 = 182.88 cm. To our delight, the graduations of a new 'Modulor'. . . translated themselves before our eyes into round numbers in feet and inches![69]

In fact, they could not do otherwise, because 6 feet equals 72 inches: that is, half the Fibonacci number 144. Therefore the single series, which Le Corbusier dubbed the 'red' series, comprises a Fibonacci series measured in half-inches, and the double or 'blue' series consists of the same numbers in inches. The resulting foot–inch system is shown in Table 15.3.

The equivalent metric measures do not work out so well, being merely decimal approximations of the foot–inch values. They are shown in metres, rounded off to the nearest centimetre, in Table 15.4. The lower measures are exact multiples of the Fibonacci ones, but the higher ones gradually increase to approximate the English dimensions. Consequently the sum of two consecutive measures does not always equal the next, as it must do if measurements are to fit together exactly in a building: for example, 0.26 + 0.43 = 0.69, not 0.70.

It is a curious coincidence that just as the proportions of the Parthenon, Chartres Cathedral and S. Sebastiano in Mantua all lend themselves to analyses based on a foot measure between 320 and 330 mm, so does the *modulor*. The measures of the blue series approach Lucas multiples of 330 mm. However, in the case of the *modulor*, as of all additive convergent series, this is no accident. What determines such series is the additive rule, not the numbers (see section 3.4 in Chapter 3). For instance, the same blue measures also approach *Fibonacci* multiples of 282 mm, while the corresponding red measures approach *double* Fibonacci multiples of 298 mm. The possibilities are endless (see Table 15.5).

Le Corbusier's attempt to reconcile the metric and imperial systems now seems rather academic, since the latter have been abandoned even in Britain; and in any case the reconciliation was never more than approximate. The *modulor* can be made a mathematically more viable system by

TABLE 15.3

Red	4	$6^1/_2$	$10^1/_2$	17	$27^1/_2$	**$44^1/_2$**	**72**
Blue	5	8	13	21	34	55	**89**

TABLE 15.4

Red	0.10	0.16	0.26	0.43	0.70	**1.13**	**1.83**
Blue	0.12	0.20	0.33	0.53	0.86	1.40	**2.26**

TABLE 15.5

Blue measures (m)	**2.26**	**3.66**	**5.92**	**9.57**	**15.49**	**25.07**	**40.56**
330 mm units	6.85	11.09	17.94	29.0	46.94	75.97	122.91
	(7)	(11)	(18)	(29)	(47)	(76)	(123)
282 mm units	8.01	12.98	20.99	33.94	54.93	88.90	143.83
	(8)	(13)	(21)	(34)	(55)	(89)	(144)
Red measures (m)	**1.83**	**2.96**	**4.79**	**7.74**	**12.53**	**20.28**	**32.81**
298 mm units	6.14	9.93	16.07	25.97	42.05	68.05	110.10
	(6)	(10)	(16)	(26)	(42)	(68)	(110)

69. *Ibid.*, p. 56.

slightly increasing Le Corbusier's metric measures to restore them to numerical consistency. This can be achieved most simply by substituting the Lucas for the Fibonacci series. The height of a man is raised to 1.88 m: that is, the Lucas number 47 multiplied by 4 cm. At the same time I propose to increase the system's flexibility by augmenting it with a third, 'yellow' series comprising the contraharmonic means of pairs of red measures. These yellow measures are the sums of alternate red measures: for example, 0.28 + 0.72 = 1.00. They form a Fibonacci series based on a unit of 20 cm (Table 15.6). The new series doubles the number of ratios in which a given length can be subdivided, from two to four (see Figure 15.15).

TABLE 15.6

Red	0.12	0.16	0.28	0.44	0.72	**1.16**	**1.88**
Blue	0.08	0.24	0.32	0.56	0.88	1.44	**2.32**
Yellow	0.20	0.20	0.40	0.60	1.00	1.60	2.60

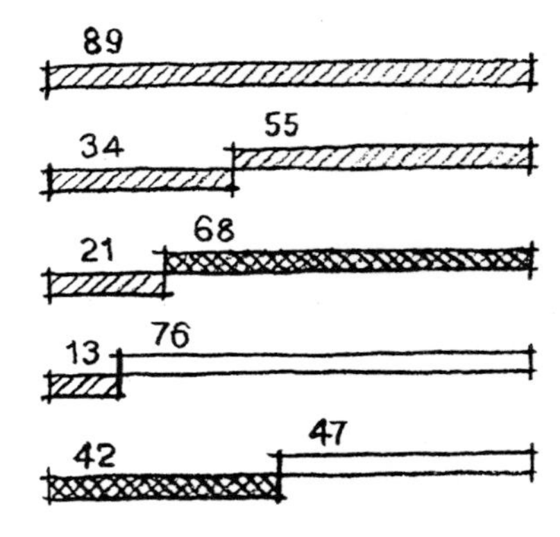

Figure 15.15 Blue (cross-hatched) and yellow (blank) measures increase the possible ways of dividing the red measure 89 from one to four.

In a penetrating critique of the *modulor* Rudolf Arnheim argues that for a proportion system to be effective as a means of knitting together a whole composition, the eye of the observer must be led by a series of steps from the smaller to the larger units. Le Corbusier's system lacks such gradations, since the measures follow each other in two unbroken series, which in theory have no lower or upper limits. Consequently the system's proportions dissolve in an endless and aesthetically meaningless profusion. Only the neighbouring measures of each series have a simple relationship to each other, and between measures of the two series only the ratio 2 : 1 is at all simple: 'The harmony of the whole is pieced together by a creeping sequence of concords between neighbor and neighbor, thus neglecting the cross-connections of distant elements.'[70] Arnheim points out that the musical scale exemplifies the kind of stepped system he has in mind. Within each octave, any two notes are connected by simple auditory and arithmetical relations, such as 3 : 4 or 4 : 5. But in addition each note of one octave is directly connected by the ratio 1 : 2 with its corresponding note – and a little less directly to every other note – in the octave above or below it.

In order to overcome this problem I propose to break down Le Corbusier's continuous scale into consecutive 'orders of size', roughly equivalent to octaves in music, but with a ratio of about 1 : 11 or 1 : ϕ^5 between corresponding measures. The red, blue and yellow series are shown in Table 15.8 (p. 333), comprising three successive orders. In each series, the largest measure of a lower order becomes the smallest measure or unit for the next. The aim of the revised system is to bring a certain coherence to Le Corbusier's

70. R. Arnheim, 'A review of proportion', in *Towards a Psychology of Art*, Faber & Faber, 1967, p. 110.

modulor dimensions, allowing sums of consecutive measures to form new measures consistently so that the larger dimensions in a building are exact sums of smaller ones. Furthermore, by containing limited groups of measures within orders of size, it ensures that they retain a certain proportion to each other. That is, each measure has a more or less simple relation to its close neighbours in the same order, not exceeding about 1 : 15. Each measure also has a constant relation of 1 : 11 to its corresponding measure in the next order.

15.11 THE ANTHROPOMETRICS OF THE *MODULOR*

The same lack of clarity that characterizes Le Corbusier's treatment of geometry and number recurs in the other principal aspect of the *modulor* – its derivation from the human body. Le Corbusier defines the system, straightforwardly enough, as

> a measuring tool based on the human body and on mathematics. A man-with-arm-upraised provides, at the determining points of his occupation of space – foot, solar plexus, head, tips of fingers of the upraised arm – three intervals which give rise to a series of golden sections, called the Fibonacci series.[71]

But this is too down-to-earth for him. The *modulor* must be shown to be rooted in the whole of nature:

> The Golden Mean governs a part of things which constitute the spectacle open to our eyes – the ramifications of a leaf, the structure of a giant tree or a shrub, the bone structure of a giraffe or a man – things which have been our daily bread, or our exceptional visual experience, for millions of years. Things which constitute our environment. . . Man occupies it by means of his members: his legs, his trunk, his arms, outstretched or raised. He bends at the solar plexus, linch-pin of his movements. Strangely simple mechanism! And yet it is the only setting for our behaviour, our taking possession of space.[72]

In reality, however, the body does not bend at the solar plexus or at the navel, where Le Corbusier shows it cut by

71. Le Corbusier, *The Modulor*, p. 55.
72. Le Corbusier, *Modulor 2*, Faber & Faber, 1958, pp. 19, 49.

the golden section, but at the hip joint. If he wanted to base his system on the 'linch-pin of our movements. . . of our taking possession of space', the golden section was the wrong proportion. More generally, the whole idea that the *modulor* or any modular system of proportions can be derived from the human body depends on the assumption that its proportions are constant at all ages and among all individuals.

We have seen that Zeising already had an answer to this objection. However, in a critique of the *modulor*, the biologist C.H. Waddington denies that the golden section can be 'an idea of a biological type', because growing organisms change their proportions continuously.[73] He cites a diagram from P.B. Medawar's book *Essays on Growth and Form*[74] (see Figure 15.16), showing how the proportions of the average human body change radically from before birth to maturity, the head becoming proportionately smaller, and the limbs longer, as growth proceeds. It is not only the proportions of the mature individual that are significant, but those attained at each stage of growth. While biological forms cannot be reduced to any all-pervading principle of proportion, Waddington argues that there nevertheless exists a kind of order peculiar to life and growth:

> The growth constants of neighbouring segments, whether of the main body or the legs, are nearly always closely related to each other.. . . For instance, a child's leg is not only shorter than an adult's in proportion to the body, but also has a different internal system of proportions between the thigh, knee, calf, ankle, etc. But both in the child and the adult the lengths of the segments form a *system* of proportions, and the legs do not give the impression of a mere assemblage of unrelated segments.[75]

What is wrong with the *modulor*, in his view, is that it sets up a single rigid series of proportions as a universal formula, instead of recognizing that in nature all sorts of proportions are possible, and that what is constant is not a single ratio or system of ratios, but *proportionality as such*.

Le Corbusier repeatedly claims in the book that the measures of the *modulor*, being based on the human scale, 'pin down the human body at the decisive points of its occupation of space: they are therefore *anthropocentric*'.[76] The implication is that, being derived *from* the body, the system will

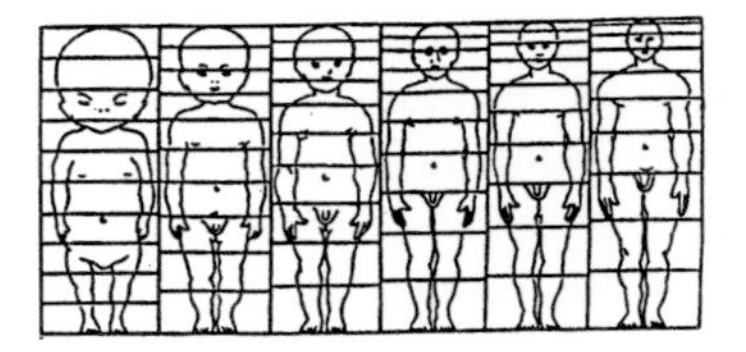

Figure 15.16 Changing proportions of the human body from birth to maturity; from P.B. Medawar, *Essays on Growth and Form*.

73. C.H. Waddington, 'The modular principle and biological form', in G. Kepes, *Module, Symmetry, Proportion*, Studio Vista, 1966, p. 37.
74. P.B. Medawar, *Essays on Growth and Form*, Oxford University Press, 1945.
75. C.H. Waddington, 'The modular principle', p. 35.
76. Le Corbusier, *The Modulor*, p. 50.

inevitably produce measures that are comfortable and convenient *for* the body (see Figure 15.17). But because its measures are *identical* with those of the body (or meant to be), the system lacks some of the most necessary functional dimensions, such as the height of a normal door or the length of a bed, which must exceed the normal height of a man by a comfortable margin.

Figure 15.17 Le Corbusier, characteristic relations of *modulor* measures to the human body; from *Le Modulor*.

The 'anthropocentricity' of Le Corbusier's 'decisive point', the navel, is symbolic rather than biological. It has less to do with human physiology than with mythology – the ancient idea of the *umbilicus mundi*, and the concept of the human body as an image of the world.[77] Thus Le Corbusier's choice of the human body as the proving-ground of his proportion system is the consequence, not so much of practical considerations of providing an anthropometrically convenient system of measures, as of his deep affinity with the Classical vision of man as microcosm. In Chapter 9 I compared Le Corbusier's treatment of the body with Vitruvius' description of the body as generator of the square and circle, and in particular with Leonardo da Vinci's illustration of that idea (see Figure 11.1 in Chapter 11). Vitruvius takes the navel as the centre of a circle circumscribing the outstretched hands and feet (in effect, the *modulor* man with arm upraised).[78] No mention is made of the golden section, however; in the preceding passage Vitruvius divides the length of the body into aliquot parts: 1/3, 1/4, 1/6, 1/8 and 1/10. In Leonardo's drawing the ratio of the diameter of the circle to the side of the square is 1.2174 : 1, very close to Le Corbusier's relation between the heights to the tip of the raised hand and to the top of the head, 89 : 72 or 1.236 : 1.

I conclude that neither Le Corbusier nor Vitruvius, nor even Leonardo with his expertise in anatomy, is really deriving a system of proportions *from* the human body. How could they, given the wide variations of proportion between individuals? Rather, each of them imposes a rational mathematical schema *upon* a generalized image of the body. Provided the schema is rich enough in measures, and one is free to choose which features of the body are significant, it cannot fail to fit the average body reasonably well. In fairness it must be pointed out that elsewhere Le Corbusier more exactly describes the *modulor* as 'a measuring tool based on the human body *and* on mathematics' (my italics). The mathematical schema cannot be an entirely arbitrary one,

77. J. Rykwert, *The Dancing Column*, MIT Press, 1996, pp. 68–95.
78. Vitruvius, *The Ten Books on Architecture*, p. 72.

nor can it be entirely derived from nature. It is a fitting together of two mutually complementary but not identical sets of data: the experience of nature's endless variation, and our human, intellectual desire for order and unity.

15.12 THE *MODULOR* IN PRACTICE: THE *UNITÉ D'HABITATION*

It is significant that in designing the *Unité d'habitation* at Marseilles (1947–52), the major example of Le Corbusier's use of the *modulor*, he applied its measures, as he makes clear in his book, only within a restricted range: to the dimensions of the individual apartments, of the separate elements of the facades and of the various small superstructures on the roof.[79] He implies that the overall dimensions of the building, 140 × 56 × 24 m, play no part in the proportional composition, and in fact none of them is an exact *modulor* measure. However, 140 m differs only imperceptibly (by less than 1%) from the red *modulor* measure 139.01 m, and is therefore near enough from the point of view of perception to be taken, even without adjustment, as the same. Le Corbusier does not mention this. Perhaps he recognized the problem that Arnheim points out, and concluded that relations between measures so remote from each other in the scale as (for instance) the width of each cell (3.66 m) and the total length of the building (139.01 m) – a ratio of 1 : 38 or approximately 2 : ϕ^9 – could not be appreciated and were not worth taking into consideration.

If, however, we consider the two elevations and the plan as *shapes*, they turn out to be quite close to exact and relatively simple ϕ ratios. The three shapes composing the overall building form are roughly as follows:

(1) *long elevations*: very nearly a ϕ^2 rectangle (that is, an upright golden rectangle between two squares, a ratio of 2.618 : 1);
(2) *end elevations*: a $\sqrt{5}$ rectangle (that is, a square between two transverse golden rectangles, a ratio of 2.236 : 1);
(3) *plan*: a $\phi^2\sqrt{5}$ rectangle (that is, three transverse golden rectangles alternating with four squares, a ratio of 5.854 : 1; see Figure 15.18).

If my proposed revision of the *modulor* is applied to the

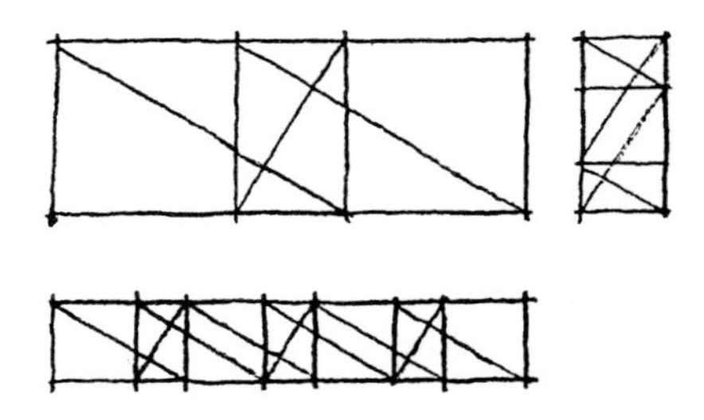

Figure 15.18 Le Corbusier, *Unité d'habitation*, Marseilles (1947–52): proportional analysis of elevations and plan, showing recurrence of squares and ϕ rectangles.

TABLE 15.7

LC	RP	SERIES	OCCURRENCE
0.43	0.44	R	Height, balcony grille
			Depth, balcony ledge
0.53	0.56	B	Floor and wall thicknesses
0.86	0.88	B	Stairwell width
			Partition panels and doors
1.13	1.16	R	Balustrade height
			Balcony depth to ledge
1.56	1.60	Y	Total balcony depth
1.83	1.88	R	Width of child's room
2.26	2.32	B	Ceiling height
2.96	3.04	R	Width of *rue intérieure*
3.66	3.76	B	Internal apartment width
4.19	4.20	Y	Centre to centre, party walls
–	12.88	R	Width of circulation tower
			Length of blank end walls of south-facing apartments
–	20.84	R	Internal apartment depth
24.0*	25.76	B	Total depth of building
–	41.68	B	9 bays of apartments
56.0*	54.56	R	Height of building, excl. pilotis
			9 bays + blank walls
–	75.40	Y	17 bays of apartments
–	88.28	R	17 bays + circulation tower
140.0*	142.84	R	Length of building

79. Le Corbusier, *The Modulor*, pp. 132–51.

Unité, not only the smaller dimensions of the individual cells but also the three major dimensions – the height, length and breadth of the whole building – find their place in it with relatively minor proportional adjustments. The key dimensions in metres are listed in Table 15.7: first, Le Corbusier's measures (where available), followed by my adjusted measures. Asterisks indicate dimensions not intended by Le Corbusier as *modulor* measures.

The revised measures used in the building are printed in bold in Table 15.8. The fact that the measures tend to form clusters within each order indicates a correspondingly simple relation between them, and a simplicity of the resulting geometry. In other words, all these relations could be made easily 'readable' by the observer, in the sense that Arnheim demands, provided that they were brought out in the detailed articulation of the elevations. In fact, the east and west elevations of the *Unité d'habitation* are divided vertically into four clearly defined zones: two groups of apartments (one 17 bays wide, the other nine) and two roughly equal strips: the circulation tower and the blank end walls of the south-facing apartments. The widths of these four zones can be set at 75.40, 41.68, 12.88 and 12.88 m respectively (see Figure 15.19). The repeated 12.88 dimension embodied in the two strips is particularly important as the geometric mean of the measures 1.16 and 142.84. As Table 15.8 shows, these three measures mark the limits of the consecutive orders of size, forming a bridge between the small dimensions of each individual apartment, which Le Corbusier recognizes, and those of the building as a whole, which he ignores. A constant ratio of about 1 : 11 or 1 : ϕ^5 binds together three major features of the facade: the balustrade height, the width of the two solid vertical strips, and the total length of the building. Furthermore, if the height of the block is taken as 54.56 m, the whole facade comprises a 54.56 m square plus a 54.56 × 88.28 m golden rectangle, each incorporating one of the vertical strips.

These relations may be purely coincidental, or perhaps Le Corbusier incorporated them instinctively, for in his writings he seems unconscious of the crucial importance of such articulation for the aesthetic effectiveness of his system. Seeing the *modulor* as comprising merely an infinite series of potential measures, without significant intervals other than those between consecutive measures, he seems to have been content to select measures from the scale more or less

TABLE 15.8

Red	0.12	0.16	0.28	**0.44**	0.72	**1.16**
Blue	0.08	0.24	0.32	**0.56**	**0.88**	1.44
Yellow	0.20	0.20	0.40	0.60	1.00	**1.60**
Red	**1.16**	**1.88**	**3.04**	4.92	7.96	**12.88**
Blue	1.44	**2.32**	**3.76**	6.08	9.84	15.92
Yellow	**1.60**	2.60	**4.20**	6.80	11.00	17.80
Red	**12.88**	**20.84**	33.72	**54.56**	**88.28**	**142.84**
Blue	15.92	**25.76**	**41.68**	67.44	109.12	176.56
Yellow	17.80	28.80	46.60	**75.40**	122.00	197.40

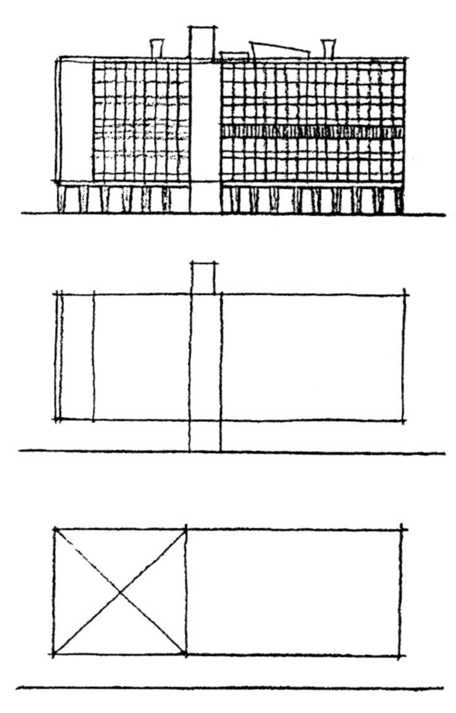

Figure 15.19 Le Corbusier, *Unité d'habitation*: proportional analysis of main facade, showing square and ϕ rectangle defined by edge of circulation tower.

arbitrarily, purely on the basis of whether or not the chosen measure is close enough to the functionally required dimension. The overall dimensions of the building are left outside the system. But if the use of a proportion system is to mean anything, it must be more than an arbitrary trimming of dimensions to fit a list of required measures. An architectural composition, like a musical one, must express its measure-system determinately and unambiguously. Only if all its proportions are designed to be as clear as possible, and are extended to encompass the scheme as a whole, can one speak, with Le Corbusier, of architecture as 'the first manifestation of man creating his own universe, submitting to the laws of nature, the laws which govern our own nature, our universe'.[80]

Le Corbusier believed, in his more euphoric moments, that he had found the final answer to the problem of proportion, and that the system he had established would in due course revolutionize architecture and production throughout the world, supplanting both the metric and the foot-inch systems, and affecting every aspect of economic and social organization. The offspring of 'higher mathematics', it would have repercussions 'on the bare bones of life, on useful objects and consumer goods: from kitchen equipment to the future cathedrals of a world searching for its unity'.[81] This did not happen. Despite the enormous interest sparked off by the publication of *Le Modulor* in 1950, the system was eventually applied in very few buildings, apart from Le Corbusier's own. Did the *modulor* fail because its philosophical premiss, the mathematical foundation of nature's harmony, was flawed? Or because its supposed derivation from the human body was arbitrary? Or simply because it was not applied with sufficient mathematical and aesthetic rigour?

Nature, writes Le Corbusier in *The Modulor*, is ruled by mathematics, and so too is art, which must conform to nature's laws.[82] But a few pages further on he describes mathematics itself as 'the majestic structure conceived by man to grant him comprehension of the universe'.[83] Which is it to be? Is mathematics the law of nature, or an artificial framework constructed by man in order to make nature comprehensible? The first statement is a pure expression of what I have called empathy; the second, of abstraction. The shortcomings of the *modulor* originate, I suspect, at the most fundamental level, from Le Corbusier's failure to resolve the

80. Le Corbusier, *Towards a New Architecture*, pp. 69–70.
81. Le Corbusier, *The Modulor*, p. 239.
82. *Ibid.*, pp. 29–30.
83. *Ibid.*, p. 71.

conflict in his own thinking between the two viewpoints. His constructions of the 1950s in France and India were the last great works of architecture inspired and determined by a system of proportion. In the past forty years such systems have virtually been forgotten by architects. If they are to have a role in the future it will depend on the resolution of that conflict.

Chapter sixteen

THE HOUSE AS A FRAME FOR LIVING AND A DISCIPLINE FOR THOUGHT

There is something which charms me utterly about this house. It is whitewashed and square & has four rooms, each of the same size. It is a house reduced to its very elements, with empty holes for windows and doors, so that one looks from one room into the next – & through that to the outside, the surrounding shacks, the clustered peaks of the huts or the bald, enigmatic rocks. The house is a kind of frame for living or discipline for thought. . .[1]

16.1 ARCHITECTURE: A PRACTICAL OR A SPECULATIVE ART?

Before we can begin to ponder the future role of mathematical systems of proportion in architecture, we must first attempt to define what architecture *as such* means, for us, today. Much of what follows coincides with the recurrent theme of Colin St John Wilson's *Architectural Reflections* – that the most urgent task facing us is to repair the division brought about by the eighteenth century's application to architecture of the concept of 'aesthetics':

> Even Kant himself finally saw that his definition of the aesthetic object as 'disinterested' and 'purposeful without purpose' was inapplicable to architecture. But the damage was done and a wedge driven between the concept of Form and the concept of Use. This led to a class distinction between 'Architecture' (monumental and 'purposeless') and 'building' (day-to-day and 'utilitarian').[2]

1. A. Hollinghurst, *The Swimming Pool Library*, Penguin Books, 1988, pp. 206–7.
2. C. St John Wilson, *Architectural Reflections*, Butterworth Architecture, 1992, p. viii.

This separation of architecture from building is also my starting point, and I shall refer again to *Architectural Reflections* from time to time in the course of this chapter.

Wilson's reunification of architecture and building is achieved at a cost. The price he pays is to separate architecture, as a 'practical' art, from the 'fine' or 'speculative' arts. 'It is of the essence of architecture,' he writes, 'that it belongs to the practical order, always serving an end other than itself.'[3] What defines the nature of a work of art is

> the way it is called into being in the first instance. For a work of architecture this differs radically from that process in the other Arts. . . A work of architecture is called into being to serve the cause of innumerable and unpredictable patterns of operation in day-to-day life.[4]

Form in architecture, for Wilson, must always follow function. He approves Adolf Loos' statement that

> We do not sit in a particular way because a carpenter has made a chair in such and such a manner. A carpenter makes a chair in a particular manner because that is how we wish to sit.[5]

But we *also* sit in a certain way because chairs form part of our culture: they form the way we live. People in cultures that do not include the chair (for instance the Japanese) sit in a completely different way. Therefore, I shall argue, the distinction between architecture and painting or sculpture is accidental rather than substantial. Wilson argues that 'Architecture can never be "pure" but will always serve the double allegiance of the Practical Arts'.[6] And it is true that buildings are generally designed to serve a particular occasion, whereas painting and sculpture are no longer 'occasional': they are no longer expected, as in the past, to carry a religious or secular message. Asked in an interview whether there was a content expressed in his work, the sculptor Carl Andre replied:

> I think art is expressive but it is expressive of that which can be expressed in no other way. Hence, to say that art has meaning is mistaken because then you believe that there is some message that the art is carrying like the telegraph, as Noel Coward said.[7]

---

3. *Ibid.*, p. ix.
4. *Ibid.*, p. 31.
5. A. Loos, 'Kulturenartung (Cultural Degeneracy)' (1908), in T. and C. Benton and D. Sharp (eds), *Form and Function*, Granada Publishing/Open University Press, 1975, p. 40.
6. C. St John Wilson, *Architectural Reflections*, p. ix.
7. C. Andre, interviewed by P. Tuchman, *Artforum*, 8(6), June 1970, pp. 55–61.

But I believe that the same revolution that at the beginning of this century freed the other arts from their traditional obligation to represent also made possible, in principle, an abstract architecture – an architecture of pure proportion – however exceptional that may be in practice. Thus I go along with Le Corbusier's formulation:

> To provoke elevated sensations is the prerogative of proportion, which is a sensed mathematic; it is afforded most particularly by architecture, painting and sculpture – works of no immediate utility, disinterested, exceptional, works that are plastic creations invested with passion.[8]

16.2 PHYSICAL VERSUS INTELLECTUAL FUNCTIONS

'By means of the house,' writes Van der Laan in *Architectonic Space*, 'we make the space of nature at one and the same time both habitable and intelligible.'[9] John Ruskin (1819–1900) opens the first chapter of *The Seven Lamps of Architecture* with the aphorism: '*All architecture proposes an effect on the human mind, not merely a service to the human frame*.'[10] The two statements seem almost identical, but there is a profound difference of context. Ruskin reflects the post-Enlightenment separation of form and use, architecture and construction. For him, it is architecture's effect on the mind that distinguishes it from the great mass of ordinary building which 'merely' serves the body. He goes on to say that

> It is very necessary, in the outset of all inquiry, to distinguish carefully between Architecture and Building. . . Let us, therefore, confine the name [architecture] to that art which, taking up and admitting, as conditions of its working, the necessity and common uses of the building, impresses on its form certain characters venerable or beautiful, but otherwise unnecessary.[11]

For Van der Laan, on the other hand, 'architecture' and 'the house' are synonymous. The creation of habitable space is not just a *condition* of making architecture, it *defines* architecture, at the same time as it is defined by the intelligibility of that space. In other words, architecture is not something added to building, it *is* building.

8. Le Corbusier, *The Decorative Art of Today*, Architectural Press, 1987, p. 86.
9. H. van der Laan, *Architectonic Space*, E.J. Brill, 1983, p. 184.
10. J. Ruskin, *The Seven Lamps of Architecture* (1849), George Allen, 1889, p. 8.
11. *Ibid.*, p. 9.

Is this not simply a restatement of Functionalism, widely regarded as the constituent principle of the early Modern Movement? Odd as it may seem, it is hard to find, among the statements of the leaders of Modernism, any that equate architecture with building, intelligibility with habitability, in the way that Van der Laan does. One of the rare exceptions turns out to be Hannes Meyer's famous declaration at the Bauhaus in 1928 that

> building is a biological process. building is not an aesthetic process. in its basic design the new dwelling house becomes not only a piece of machinery for living but also a biological apparatus serving the needs of body and mind.[12]

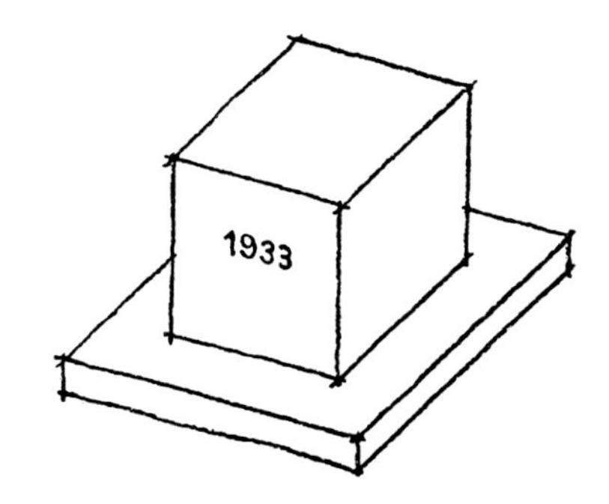

Figure 16.1 Adolf Loos, design for his own tomb, based on a sketch made in hospital (1931).

In St John Wilson's view Meyer's address typifies what he calls 'naive' Functionalism; but significantly, in quoting it, he fundamentally alters its message by omitting the last sentence, with the important little words 'and mind'.[13]

In general, however, the founders of modern architecture maintain the same dualistic separation of the two domains that we have seen in Ruskin. The most uncompromising is Adolf Loos (1870–1933): 'Only a very small part of architecture belongs to art: the tomb and the monument. Everything else, everything which serves a purpose should be excluded from the realms of art'[14] (see Figure 16.1). Loos preaches a Manichaean separation of matter and spirit; to try to make one thing serve both ends is to him a profanation:

> Whoever realizes that the purpose of art is to guide man ever onwards and upwards, making him ever more God-like, senses that the fusion of art with functional ends is a profanation of the highest degree.[15]

(We must take care not to be confused by the slight shift in terminology: Loos' *architecture-as-art* clearly corresponds to what Ruskin, and as we shall see in a moment Le Corbusier, call 'architecture' *tout court*.) Loos' objection to the profanation of sacred things by misappropriating them for material use, or more usually by borrowing their forms to give a spurious dignity to utilitarian objects, is stated even more succinctly by his friend the social critic and satirist Karl Kraus (1874–1936):

12. H. Meyer, 'bauen', in *Hannes Meyer, Bauten, Projecte und Schriften*, Alec Tiranti, 1965, p. 95.
13. C. St John Wilson, *Architectural Reflections*, p. 21.
14. A. Loos, 'Architecture' (1910), in T. and C. Benton and D. Sharp (eds), *Form and Function*, p. 45.
15. *Ibid.*

> Adolf Loos and I. . . have done nothing more than show that there is a difference between an urn and a chamberpot. . . The others, who fail to make this distinction, are divided between those who use the urn as a chamberpot and those who use the chamberpot as an urn.[16]

Kraus and Loos erect as it were a clear *vertical* division among the things we make. Objects belong on one side of the fence or the other; a thing is either 'art' through and through, or not art at all; it is either entirely spiritual or wholly material; it cannot be both at the same time. Outside the sacred precinct of art lie the great mass of useful artefacts; within it, only a few consecrated objects, the tomb, the monument, the urn. This is quite different from Ruskin, for whom architecture is an additional layer that we are free to apply, if we wish, to adorn 'the edifices raised by man, *for whatsoever uses*'.[17] For

> There are few buildings which have not some pretence or colour of being architectural; neither can there be any architecture which is not based on building. . .; but it is perfectly easy. . . to keep the ideas distinct, and to understand fully that Architecture concerns itself only with those characters of an edifice which are above and beyond its common use.[18]

Ruskin makes, so to speak, a *horizontal* division: not one that separates one building from another, according to type, but one that potentially cuts across every building. Below the line, one finds the basic construction that serves a 'common use'; above it, the architectural features that are 'above and beyond' that use. So in total contrast to Loos, for Ruskin *every* building has the potential for architecture, but *no* building is architecture through and through. Architecture is literally skin-deep, superficial and superfluous. It is not the whole structure that must not be profaned by usefulness if it is to remain art, but only this added layer. Architecture does not enter, for instance, into the necessary construction of a fortress, but if to this 'be added an unnecessary feature, as a cable moulding, *that* is Architecture'.[19]

The very same element – decoration – that for Ruskin *constitutes* architecture, for Loos *excludes* – no less than the service of a function – any object from the realm of art. If he allows ornament into his own houses it is precisely because

16. K. Kraus, *Die Fackel*, No. 389-90, Dec 1913, p. 37.
17. J. Ruskin, *The Seven Lamps of Architecture*, p. 8 (author's italics).
18. *Ibid.*, p. 9.
19. *Ibid.*

the house has 'nothing to do with art'.[20] The purpose of the house is to serve one's comfort, and that means also that it must be home-like: 'The room must look comfortable, the house cosy.'[21] Hence the classical columns, rustic inglenooks and fake wood-beamed ceilings. Functional use and ornamentation are alike *concessions* that Loos makes to society, just as he submits to wearing shoes decorated with scallops and holes because they give pleasure to the shoemaker:

> I am preaching to the aristocrat. . . I tolerate the ornaments of the Kaffir, the Persian, the Slovak peasant woman, my shoemaker's ornaments, for they all have no other way of attaining the high points of their existence. We have art, which has taken the place of ornament. After the toils of the day, we go to Beethoven or Tristan.[22]

Next to Loos, the most eloquent writer among modern architects is Le Corbusier. By far the greatest influence on him in his early years was Ruskin;[23] later, he came strongly under the influence of Loos. It is not surprising, therefore, to find echoes of both writers in Le Corbusier's view of architecture. In *The Decorative Art of Today* he almost paraphrases Loos:

> Decoration is of a sensorial and elementary order, as is colour, and is suited to simple races, peasants and savages. Harmony and proportion incite the intellectual faculties and arrest the man of culture. The peasant loves ornament and decorates his walls. The civilized man wears a well-cut suit and is the owner of easel pictures and books. Decoration is the essential overplus, the quantum of the peasant; and proportion is the essential overplus, the quantum of the cultivated man.[24]

He also tries to adopt Loos' strict vertical classification of things into two self-contained categories: works of art, and objects of use. Architecture, however, architecture *as such*, is placed in the former category, with the other fine arts – 'works of no immediate utility, disinterested, exceptional' – since its purpose, for Le Corbusier, is not to be useful but to embody mathematical proportions; and by embodying proportions, to provoke 'elevated sensations'. He tries to draw a clear distinction between two aspects of our life: work and thought.

20. A. Loos, 'Kulturenartung', p. 45.
21. *Ibid.*
22. A. Loos, 'Ornament and crime', in U. Conrads, *Programmes and Manifestoes on 20th-Century Architecture*, Lund Humphries, 1970, p. 24.
23. H.A. Brooks, *Le Corbusier's Formative Years*, University of Chicago Press, 1997, pp. 68–9.
24. Le Corbusier, *Towards a New Architecture* (1923), Architectural Press, 1946, p. 133.

> Now and always there is a hierarchy. There is a time for work, when one uses oneself up, and also a time for meditation, when one recovers one's bearing and rediscovers harmony. There should be no confusion between them. . . Everything has its classification; work and meditation.[25]

And the same classification that orders our lives applies equally to the things we make. With Calvinist zeal he condemns those who (like William Morris and Ruskin) seek to raise the objects of use that surround us to the status of works of art, 'to give them souls':

> *We protest. The objects of utility in our lives have freed the slaves of a former age. They are in fact themselves slaves, menials, servants. Do you want them as your soul-mates? We sit on them, work on them, make use of them, use them up; when used up, we replace them.*[26]

But with Le Corbusier things are never as straightforward as he would have them appear. Where, for instance, does the house come in this hierarchy? Does it belong to architecture or is it merely a tool? In *Towards a New Architecture* he defines the house as a machine for living in: 'Baths, sun, hot-water, cold-water, warmth at will, conservation of food, hygiene, beauty in the sense of good proportion. An armchair is a machine for sitting in, and so on.'[27] Chairs, we have just seen, are undoubtedly tools: *We sit on them. . . use them up; when used up, we replace them.* The same applies, presumably, to the dwelling, which must therefore be excluded from the realm of 'architecture, painting and sculpture – works of no immediate utility'. Later in the same book, however, two houses are contrasted. The first is practical: 'I thank you [but] you have not touched my heart.'[28] The second is a work of art: 'By the use of inert materials and *starting from* conditions more or less utilitarian, you have established certain relationships which have aroused my emotions. This is Architecture.'[29] The house is not, as with Loos, inartistic *in itself*, but only if it fails to realize its potential.

The ambiguity comes about because whereas in theory Le Corbusier adopts Loos' standpoint, in practice he remains closer to Ruskin's. The house, for Loos, has 'nothing to do with art',[30] but Le Corbusier defines architecture, much as Ruskin does, as 'a thing of art. . . lying outside questions of

25. Le Corbusier, *The Decorative Art of Today*, Architectural Press, 1987, p. 86.
26. *Ibid.*, p. xxi.
27. Le Corbusier, *Towards a New Architecture*, p. 89.
28. *Ibid.*, p. 187.
29. *Ibid.*
30. A. Loos, 'Architecture', p. 45.

construction and beyond them. The purpose of construction is to make things hold together; of architecture to move us.'[31] For both Ruskin and Le Corbusier, architecture is something added to the inert construction of the building. They both divide buildings 'horizontally', into a functional/constructional substructure common to all, and a visible upper layer restricted to those that it is proper to call works of architecture.

There is a difference, however. The functionally unnecessary surface treatment that Le Corbusier demands is not, like Ruskin's, a decorative elaboration of construction – a sort of tattooing or make-up applied to the face of the building – but a mask covering it up. Reviewing the *De Stijl* projects exhibited in Paris by Theo van Doesburg in 1923, he looks forward to a time

> when it is realized that light is much more generous with a simple prism. Then this complexity, this abusive richness and these exuberant forms will be disciplined under the shield of pure form. . . This tendency towards a pure whole, covering abundance with a mask of simplicity, can be the only outcome.[32]

In *Towards a New Architecture* he unites both ideas – the masking of construction and the non-utilitarian nature of architecture – in a single sentence: 'Architecture has another meaning and other ends to pursue than showing construction and responding to needs (and by "needs" I mean utility, comfort and practical arrangement).'[33] Paradoxically, both Ruskin and Le Corbusier preach what is essentially Robert Venturi's doctrine of the decorated shed, where 'systems of space and structure are directly at the service of program, and ornament is applied independently of them'.[34] The difference lies in the style of the ornament: for Ruskin, polychromy; for Le Corbusier, 'the Law of Ripolin: a coat of whitewash'.[35]

16.3 THE ABSTRACT REVOLUTION

Ruskin wrote *The Seven Lamps* in 1849; Loos, *Architecture* in 1910; Le Corbusier, *The Decorative Art of Today* in 1925; and Venturi, *Learning from Las Vegas* in 1972. Whatever validity the separation of architecture from construction may have

31. Le Corbusier, *Towards a New Architecture*, p. 23.
32. Le Corbusier, *L'Esprit Nouveau*, May 1924.
33. Le Corbusier, *Towards a New Architecture*, p. 102.
34. R. Venturi, D. Scott-Brown and S. Izenour, *Learning from Las Vegas*, MIT Press, 1977, p. 89.
35. Le Corbusier, *The Decorative Art of Today*, p. 188.

had in the mid-nineteenth century it has certainly lost by the late twentieth. Venturi's revived Ruskinianism can be dismissed as an irrelevance. Le Corbusier himself changed direction soon after he wrote; the Villa Savoye (1929–31) is his last *maison Ripolin*. The Errazuris project, the Villa De Mandrot, the *Clarté* building in Geneva (all designed in 1930) already mark a new principle, which he would hold to, despite changes, throughout his career: a principle in which materials are used 'as found' and the construction is exposed. The separation of architecture and building began to disappear: not because architecture was subordinated to utility, but because construction was recognized as intrinsic to architecture, indeed as the core of architecture. It was now realized – by Le Corbusier and others – that architecture can only be defined by what unites all building, not by what divides one building from another. It is not a special quality that only some buildings possess, but the essential property of building *as such*: what St John Wilson calls the thread that runs from the shed to the cathedral.[36]

The immediate source of that realization was the abstract revolution that took place in the plastic arts at the beginning of this century, and which I have linked to the writings of Worringer and Kandinsky. But its roots lie further back, in the philosophical abstraction of Berkeley, Hume and Kant, which severed the link between what Hume calls '*Relations of Ideas*' and '*Matters of Fact*',[37] and therefore the connection between human pictures of reality and things *as such*. In our century the spectral nature of reality has been heightened by the theory of relativity and the uncertainty principle. Werner Heisenberg writes that in science 'The object of research is no longer nature itself but man's investigation of nature. Here, again, man confronts himself alone.'[38] Man confronts himself alone, not only in science but in art.

With respect to architecture this revolution was first manifested in the writings of the *abbé* Marc-Antoine Laugier (1713–69); its most recent exponent, I argue, has been Dom Hans van der Laan. The affinity between Laugier and Van der Laan, which struck me when I reviewed their books together in 1979,[39] has remained for me a compelling one ever since. They seem to stand like terminal figures, containing between them the history of modern architecture.

Laugier initially published his *Essai sur l'architecture* anonymously in 1753, five years after after Hume's *Enquiry Concerning Human Understanding*. The path to Laugier's

36. C. St John Wilson, *Architectural Reflections*, p. 62.
37. D. Hume, *An Enquiry Concerning Human Understanding*, Oxford University Press, 1975, p. 25.
38. W. Heisenberg, *The Physicist's Conception of Nature*, The Scientific Book Guild, 1962, p. 24.
39. R. Padovan, 'Laugier to Van der Laan', in *Architectural Design*, 49(12), 1979, pp. 324–6; *Dom Hans van der Laan: Modern Primitive*, Architectura & Natura Press, 1994.

primeval hut (see Figure 16.2), built by 'man in his earliest origin, without other help or other guide than the natural instinct of his needs',[40] is now well trodden, but it is worth revisiting. According to him, it is 'by coming as close as possible in one's work to the simplicity of this first model that one avoids fundamental defects and achieves true perfection'.[41] By taking this little cabin as a yardstick,

> It is now easy to distinguish those parts which are *essential* components of an order of architecture from those which are introduced out of *necessity*, or added by caprice. The beauty consists in the essential parts; the concessions, in those that are introduced only out of necessity; the defects, in those added by caprice. . . Never let us lose sight of our little rustic hut.[42]

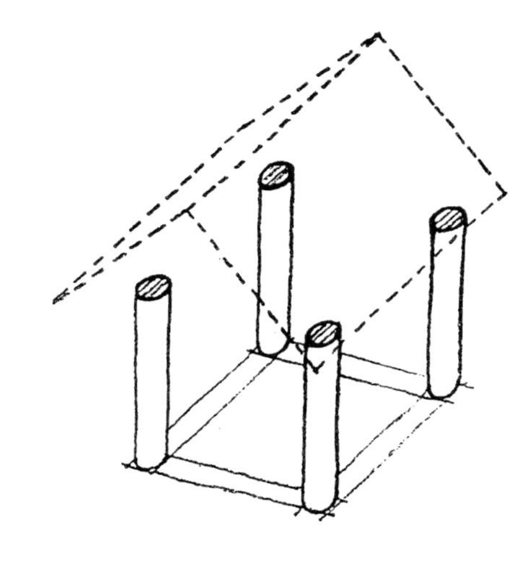

Figure 16.2 Primitive hut, based on M.-A. Laugier's description of the first dwelling in the *Essai sur l'architecture* (1753).

16.4 THE NECESSARY AND THE ESSENTIAL

To distinguish the essential from the necessary: that, rather than his fanciful anthropology, is Laugier's crucial discovery. Architecture can never be defined by the necessities, because these vary from building to building. For example, the things that Le Corbusier lists in his definition of the house-machine are necessities: baths, hot water, central heating, a kitchen, and so on. But there are also necessities of the mind: the communication of an idea or an emotion. Architecture can exist, however, without any of these particular things, either physical or mental. This is where I part company with St John Wilson, who seems (though not always) to identify the essence of architecture precisely with the service of particular necessities.

> The essential characteristics of a work of practical art are significantly shaped by the way it is called into being in the first instance. . . A work of architecture is called into being to serve the cause of innumerable and unpredictable patterns of operation in day-to-day life. Its conception can therefore never be immaculate.[43]

If this is true, architecture cannot be defined in general terms but only by the way each building serves its unique purpose. 'Architecture' is then simply a certain loose relationship that

40. M.-A. Laugier, *Essai sur l'architecture*, Pierre Mardaga, 1979, p. 8.
41. *Ibid.*, p. 10.
42. *Ibid.* (author's italics).
43. C. St John Wilson, *Architectural Reflections*, p. 31.

we recognize as connecting innumerable individual 'architectures'. To underline this point Wilson quotes a passage from Ludwig Wittgenstein's *Philosophical Investigations*, substituting the word 'architecture' for 'language':

> Instead of producing something common to all that we call 'architecture' I am saying that these phenomena have no one thing in common which makes us use the same word for all – but they are *related* to one another in many different ways. And it is because of these relationships that we call them all 'architecture'.[44]

But I believe that there *is* nevertheless something common to all architecture, besides a loose and more or less accidental series of interrelations: something that, even if it nearly always, in the normal course of events, 'serves ends other than itself', still remains after those particular ends have been pared away. According to Wilson 'The notion of pure architecture is meaningless',[45] and 'A folly is not architecture.'[46] Pure architecture exists, however, not just as a theoretical possibility, but in reality. For an example, one has to look no further than Mies van der Rohe's Barcelona Pavilion (1929): an exhibition pavilion in name only, since there were no exhibits. It was a pure spatial construction, architecture for architecture's sake. Abstraction has abolished the boundary between architecture and sculpture, so that any work of abstract sculpture that encloses a space large enough to enter and move about in is *de facto* a work of architecture. Many of the works of Carl Andre, Richard Serra and Donald Judd fall into this category.

The *essentials* of architecture, then, for Laugier, are neither more nor less than what the hut comprises: four cylindrical uprights supporting a roof, which terminates in a gable at either end. The *necessities* are whatever is needed to make it comfortable or convenient, such as walls, windows and a door. The *defects* are pretty well all the conventions of the academic architecture of Laugier's time: engaged columns and pilasters; entablatures not carried on columns, or recessed between them; pediments that are not true gables, or cornices that are not true eaves. In short, the only classical decoration he allows is that which is inherent in the peristyle itself, used as a real structure, standing directly on the ground without a pedestal. The very decoration that in Ruskin's opinion constitutes the whole of architecture is for Laugier

44. *Ibid.*, p. 37.
45. *Ibid.*, p. 61.
46. *Ibid.*, p. 63.

merely a defect. Architecture is not a kind of bonus added *after* the necessities have been satisfied, but the essential precondition of satisfying those necessities.

The little hut is not yet an adequate model, however, since architecture includes unroofed spaces such as city squares. What is essential in it is not, after all, the roof and columns, but the fact that it delimits a space that a human being might occupy and move about in. So finally, we can define architecture as *the demarcation of habitable space.* Note that this is precisely how Nikolaus Pevsner, at the start of his *Outline of European Architecture*, defines what is *not* architecture, merely building. He writes: 'Nearly everything that encloses space on a scale sufficient for a human being to move in is a building; the term architecture applies only to buildings designed with a view to aesthetic appeal.'[47] I turn Pevsner's definition on its head: what he regards as common to all building, for me defines architecture; 'aesthetic appeal', which for him defines architecture, I regard as a mere 'necessity'. Of Pevsner's two examples, the one that he excludes from architecture – the bicycle shed – is by my definition no less architecture than the other, Lincoln Cathedral. In fact it is a purer example of architecture, being more elementary, less encumbered by necessities such as liturgical requirements and religious symbolism. Laugier's hut would make an excellent bicycle shed; one might bring up to date his plea in the *Essai*: 'Never let us lose sight of our little bicycle shed.'

The confusion, of which Pevsner's definition is so magnificent an example, arises because the essentials, too, concern both the body and the mind; indeed, they must do so, if they are to serve as a foundation for the necessities. The specific utilitarian needs of this or that building can be served only because every building, as building, is already a physical enclosure of space. Likewise the symbolic message or meaning that we may wish a particular building to carry can be borne only because every building, by its nature, is potentially a metaphor.

This is easier to understand if one considers an example. The symbolism and emotive power of the tomb – for Loos almost the whole of architecture – relies on the intrinsic expressiveness of the house as an elementary shelter, which it embodies in a condensed, rudimentary and archetypal form (see Figure 16.1). The complex interrelations of the ideas of house (*domus*), dome and tomb are fascinatingly explored by

47. N. Pevsner, *An Outline of European Architecture* (1943), Penguin Books, 1963, p. 15.

E. Baldwin Smith in *The Dome: a Study in the History of Ideas*.[48] Conversely, a fully developed house, with specialized rooms serving different physical functions, is an elaboration of the essential space-cell, Laugier's primal hut (see Figure 16.2). Thus the necessities depend on the essentials, and not vice versa. The distinction between the necessary and the essential lies not in the contrast between bodily and mental functions – uses and meanings – but in that between the particular and the universal. Uses and meanings are like specialized attributes or accessories that we append to the common supporting core of architecture: the marked-out space. Ruskin and Loos, Le Corbusier and Pevsner, see the contrast between physical and mental necessities as the division separating building from architecture or art. The central core, common to all building and all architecture, upon which the particular uses and specific metaphors depend, they leave out of account.

16.5 THE SEARCH FOR A STARTING POINT

The problem we now face is that if the common core of building is to act as the bearer of all possible kinds of physical functions and symbolic or emotional content that we may wish to attach to it, it must itself embody a form. If this initial form is not generated by specific physical needs, social patterns or symbolic meanings, we must look for some other determinant that will serve as a generator or catalyst at the start of the design process.

For Laugier the solution is simple: that determinant is nature itself. The first chapter of the *Essai* begins with the words: 'In architecture it is the same as in all the other arts: its principles are founded on nature itself, and in nature's processes are to be found clearly written the laws of architecture.'[49] This is a survival from the Renaissance tradition of empathy: Laugier's statement is not a far cry from Alberti's *concinnitas*. By his time that tradition was no more than a convention, however. Hume had already hinted, and Kant was about to confirm, that instead of our works (that is, works of scientific interpretation as well as art) proceeding from nature's laws, we ourselves, through our works, must write those laws. We must then look for a purely architectonic generator for the form of our elementary piece of space.

48. E.B. Smith, *The Dome: A Study in the History of Ideas*, Princeton University Press, 1950.
49. M.-A. Laugier, *Essai sur l'architecture*, p. 8.

John Summerson began to address this problem in a paper entitled 'The case for a theory of modern architecture', given at the RIBA in May 1957, just a month before the debate on proportion mentioned at the start of Chapter 1. In it he states that 'The programme as the source of unity is, so far as I can see, the one new principle involved in modern architecture.'[50] Wilson interprets this as the whole message,[51] but Summerson's point is really the opposite: that the functional programme is an *insufficient* basis for design. He argues that

> The forms of classical antiquity or (in the 19th century) mediaeval antiquity, provided something essential to the creative designer – a bulwark of certainty, of unarguable authority on which his understanding leans while his conception of the building as a whole, as a *unity*, takes shape. The most interesting, indeed the dominating question, in a search for the modern *principia*, is: where, if not in antique forms, or some equivalent substitute, is the source of unity?[52]

The programme, of course, is precisely what Laugier calls the 'necessities': the specific needs of a particular building; but the satisfaction of these, I argue, depends on the existence of the very generic form that we are trying to determine. What is required, as Summerson points out, quoting Walter Gropius, is 'an objective common denominator of design', something that will serve 'as the controlling agent within the creative act'.[53] But that is

> a precise description of the functions served by antiquity in the classical centuries! The dilemma is really an enlargement of the flaw already apparent in mid-18th century theory – the flaw that while antiquity was eliminated as an absolute, nothing was introduced which took its place as a universally accredited language of architectural form.[54]

The flaw lay, as with most revolutions, not in the revolution as such but in its incompleteness: the failure to grasp that art does not imitate nature, but nature, art. Nature had always been looked upon as the starting point of architecture. But it was a nature already embodied in an architectonic form: the human body 'embodied' in the classical

50. J. Summerson, 'The case for a theory of modern architecture', *RIBA Journal*, June 1957, p. 309.
51. C. St John Wilson, *Architectural Reflections*, p. 26.
52. J. Summerson, 'The case for a theory of modern architecture', p. 308.
53. W. Gropius, *The Scope of Total Architecture* (1954), quoted in J. Summerson, *ibid.*, p. 310.
54. J. Summerson, *ibid.*, p. 310.

orders. 'A body is like a building,' writes Joseph Rykwert, 'and the building in turn is like the world.'[55] The body–world metaphor was fundamental to architecture (as I shall soon argue, it still is). The central theme of Rykwert's book *The Dancing Column* is the mimetic role of architecture as a metaphor of the body and thereby of the world – itself understood as a kind of body. This metaphor, he argues,

> is an essential part of the business of building, as of all human activity. . . I have come to think it may direct the way all men and women relate themselves to what they build.[56]

The problem with this, which becomes apparent when in the concluding chapter he confronts the state of modern architecture, is that in architecture *mimesis* was bound up with the conventions of Classicism. The Classical column, composed of capital, shaft and base, is like a body; the unarticulated concrete post or steel stanchion is not.

The functional programme, which Summerson rightly identifies as the 'one new principle' contained in Modernist theory, is really just 'nature' in a new dress: a force outside architecture, which determines what architecture shall be. At all costs, it seems, architects want to shrug off responsibility for what they design. The shortcomings of the programme as a substitute for intrinsically architectonic determinants was highlighted thirty-five years before Summerson, at the birth of the Modern Movement, by Adolf Behne in *Der moderne Zweckbau* (*The Modern Functional Building*). Behne contrasts 'rationalism' (exemplified by Le Corbusier) with 'functionalism' (Scharoun):

> Nothing is more self-evident than that a rationalist should stress form. Form is nothing more than the consequence of establishing a relationship between human beings. For the isolated and unique figure in nature there is no problem of form. . . Form is an eminently social matter. Anyone who recognizes the right of society recognizes the right of form. If humanity were just the sum of individuals, it would probably be possible to see the house as a pure tool, as purely functional. . . [But] if every building is part of a built whole, then it recognizes from its aesthetic and formal requirements certain universally valid rules, rules that do not arise from its individual functional character [*Zweckcharakter*] but from the

55. J. Rykwert, *The Dancing Column*, MIT Press, 1996, p. 373.
56. *Ibid.*, p. 117.

> requirements of this whole. . .The functionalist prefers to exaggerate the purpose to the point of making it unique and momentary (a house for each function!) but the rationalist takes the purpose broadly and generally as readiness for many cases, simply because he gives thought to the enduring qualities of buildings, which perhaps see many generations with changing requirements and therefore cannot live without leeway.[57]

Seeking an intrinsically architectonic starting-point to replace the functional programme Summerson turns, hesitantly,

> to the ancient axiom that architecture is fundamentally concerned with the regular solids and simple ratios. . . On this principle of geometrical absolutes it is possible to erect systems of disciplines to guide the architect towards that final ordering of form which he must achieve. Of these systems the most celebrated is Le Corbusier's *Modulor*.[58]

Curiously enough, much the same tentative conclusion is reached, forty years later, by Joseph Rykwert. The ancient techniques of *mimesis*, 'embodied' in the conventional forms and proportions of the Classical orders,

> have been so neglected that they will need to be reinvented for our own times if we are to master them again. . . One example of what can be done seems to be provided by Le Corbusier's *Modulor*. It was perhaps the most convincing attempt to set out a mimetic teaching.[59]

The *modulor*, however, is too literal a transcription of the body's measures, and too deeply rooted in Le Corbusier's essentially empathic vision, to satisfy the need for an intrinsically architectonic generator of form. For a less literal, more abstract and deeper analysis of architecture's relation to the body, we must turn to Van der Laan.

16.6 THE INTRINSIC MEANING OF ARCHITECTURE

The body–world metaphor is fundamental to Van der Laan's architectural theory. For him the house is built in the first

57. A. Behne, *The Modern Functional Building* (1923), The Getty Research Institute, 1996, pp. 137–8.
58. J. Summerson, 'The case for a theory of modern architecture', p. 310.
59. *Ibid.*, p. 390.

place to shield the body from wind and weather. It takes the place of the body in confronting the environment; *it represents the body to the world*. But conversely, the sheltered interior of the house is like a smaller world: it *represents the world to the body*. Or as Van der Laan puts it in *The Plastic Number*:

> With respect to our body the space within the house takes the place of the natural environment, but in a tempered and adapted form. And with respect to the environment the wall of the house takes the place of the body, which it represents in a strengthened form, confronting on its behalf the forces of nature.[60]

But Van der Laan's concept of the body–house relation is a wholly abstract one. It is not a question of the house looking like a body, being a symbol for the body, or even, as with Le Corbusier, deriving its proportions from the measures of the body. Rather, it is a matter of establishing an abstract proportional relation between three elements: body : house : world. Van der Laan transposes the qualitative analogy into a quantitative one, literally a proportional relation: 'The wall is to the body, as the interior space is to the natural environment.'[61] One can write this as a proportion between two ratios, $W/B : A/N$, where W, B, A and N stand respectively for 'wall', 'body', 'architectonic space' and 'natural space'. Now, in such cases, the proportion remains unaffected when the terms of the two ratios are interchanged: for example, $1/2 : 3/4 = 1/3 : 2/4$. Thus the proportion can be rewritten as $W/A : B/N$. 'So one can say that the wall relates to the interior space as the body relates to the environment.'[62] Almost the same phrase, first stated near the beginning of the book, reappears at the end like a *leitmotiv*: 'In the relation between wall and walled-off space we can see an objective image of our own relation to surrounding nature.'[63]

The mathematical equation must not be taken too literally, of course. In Van der Laan's architecture the wall thickness has a precise mathematical proportion to the space between the walls, in fact 1 : 7. Obviously the body has no such determinate quantitative relation to the limitless natural space around it. Therefore the phrase 'objective image' is exact: the mathematically precise ratio is the objective representation of the subjective body–world relationship. In other

60. H. van der Laan, *Het plastische getal*, E.J. Brill, 1967, p. 5.
61. *Ibid.*, p. 7.
62. *Ibid.*, p. 8.
63. *Ibid.*, p. 116.

words, architecture as such can express only a single idea: the elementary principle of human habitation, the demarcation by walls of a measured habitable space within the measureless space of nature. Architecture, as essential building, is not a medium of particular communications.

At one point, apparently without realizing it, St John Wilson comes very close to such a definition of architecture in terms of its core function: as pure spatial delimitation in relation to the body. Referring to the psychoanalytical theory of art propounded by Adrian Stokes, he writes that

> It is a marked property of the art most loved by Stokes that architecture and the human figure were linked as the supreme metaphors in a code through which all that is most urgent in human conflict and its resolution could be represented – the 'body-figure', Michelangelo's sole metaphor not only in sculpture and painting but also in architecture. . . Architecture offers a whole typology of counterforms to the 'positions' experienced in this body language. . . The simplest forms are ranged at each end of the spectrum that stretches between envelopment and exposure.'[64]

As examples of envelopment he cites the room and the roof, and as an example of exposure the experience of approaching a monumental facade across a vast open space. Later, he quotes Kant's statement in the *Critique of Pure Reason* that 'All our awareness is grounded in spatial experience', and develops from it the argument that

> If we spell out that experience in terms of envelopment and exposure (of being inside or outside or on the threshold between) then it is not a far cry to call all such experience, even if it is in the forest or on the cliff edge, at one with the essential medium of architecture – the purposeful inhabitation of space.[65]

Note the use of the word 'essential'. It is hard to see what separates this notion of 'the essential medium of architecture' from the definition of architecture that I am putting forward; on the other hand, it seems a long way from Wilson's later formulation: 'Architecture only comes into being by answering to a call from outside its own discipline to serve a set of needs in society.'[66] However, the resolution

64. C. St John Wilson, *Architectural Reflections*, pp. 12–14.
65. *Ibid.*, p. 24.
66. *Ibid.*, p. 62.

of this conflict, and an indication that my quarrel with Wilson may be more apparent that real, is perhaps contained in what immediately follows that formulation:

> By this we mean two things. First, to set up a spatial order that makes possible the fulfilment of manifold operations in an *effective* way. This is the base of common use. Second, to bring to life an order of representation that embodies those occasions so that they can be recognized in an *intelligible* way. This is the part of gesture, the use of play.[67]

I find myself in total agreement with the last statement. What I call the common core of building is nothing else than a 'playful' (that is, abstract) spatial order that makes possible the effective fulfilment of 'manifold operations': that is, particular physical and mental necessities. The house can become 'a frame for living and a discipline for thought'. But these metaphors have nothing to do with the work of art *as such*, or with its proportions. The numerical ordering of the building must derive from intrinsically architectonic considerations, and not from those of number symbolism or 'sacred geometry'. This, at any rate, is Van der Laan's view. In the lecture *On Measure and Number in Architecture* (1949) he says that

> It is quite wrong to establish a causal relation between symbolism and architectural design: they are independent spheres. For example, we may place twelve columns in a church because of the advantage this number has from an architectonic viewpoint. But to say that we make twelve columns because there are twelve apostles is a poetic licence that has nothing to do with architecture.[68]

16.7 THE FIRST BUILDING

If number symbolism has nothing to with architecture, if we cannot derive architectural proportions directly from the body as with the *modulor*, and if the relation of the body to natural space is not a fixed mathematical ratio that can be translated directly into the proportions of the building, there seems to be no solid ground on which to base a system of measures. To resolve this dilemma we must think again about what it is that architecture can express. It is not enough to

67. *Ibid.*
68. H. van der Laan, 'Over maat en getal in de architectuur', lecture, 's Hertogenbosch, 23–24 April 1949, p. 3.

say, as I have already done, that it expresses the building's 'essential relation to the world', because it is that very relation that we need to determine. What is the essential nature of the architectonic act, the act of building? I agree with Van der Laan that it is the placing of solid elements on the ground in such a way that they mark out a space between them. In his view these elements are primarily walls; for Laugier, they are columns and a roof. Van der Laan's conception is more general, because architecture must include unroofed urban space, but the difference is not fundamental. What is common to both writers is a 'thought-experiment' by which they try to define architecture by tracing it back to its origin, the first structure built by the first man. Just as Laugier imagines 'man in his earliest origin, without other help or other guide than the natural instinct of his needs',[69] so Van der Laan, as Egbert Koster writes, 'begins his exposition as if nothing had ever been built since man's arrival on the earth, as if absolutely no architectural history existed'.[70]

The following is a resumé of Van der Laan's description of the first architectonic act. First, space can only be defined by its opposite, solid masses taken from the earth: 'Similarly we can only interrupt silence by noise, or rest by movement.'[71] A single block or column, however, is like a dot on a blank sheet of paper: it marks a position, but it does not yet mark out a space. Even if a row of columns is built to form a wall (like a straight line on paper), no separate space is yet formed within the whole of space: 'To cut off a piece of space within the major space a second wall is needed that relates to the first in such a way that a new space is generated between the two.'[72] The relation of the space to the walls is not a question of form, however, but of proportion. The form of a *solid* is defined by its surfaces. If the space were defined in the same way it would as it were 'steal the surface from the wall', usurping its form; for 'A form can exist only against a formless ground, which means that a surface can only belong to one form.'[73] A two-dimensional equivalent of this phenomenon is the diagram that can be read either as a chalice or as two heads, but not both together, because the same lines are needed to define both images (see Figure 16.3). Therefore, Van der Laan concludes, the space must be defined, not by the wall surface, but by the complete *form* of the walls. The third 'dimension' of the space is not a linear measure, like the third dimension of a solid form, but a

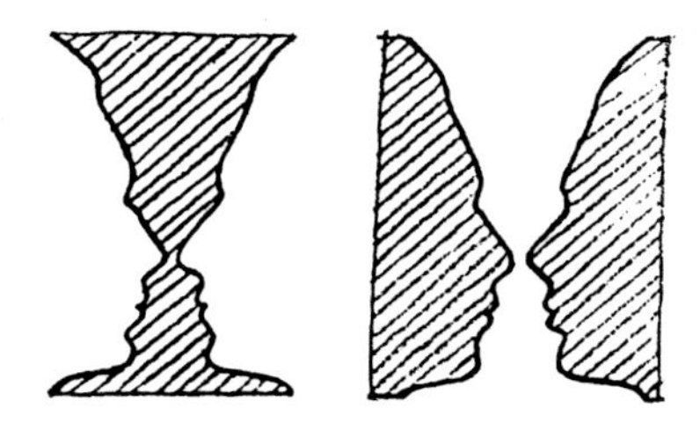

Figure 16.3 Figure–ground experiment: a figure can be seen only against a shapeless ground. We can recognize the image as chalice or two heads, but not both together.

69. M.-A. Laugier, *Essai sur l'architecture*, p. 8.
70. E. Koster, 'Dom Van der Laan's Arcadian architecture', *Architectura & Natura Quarterly*, no. 1, 1992, p. 36.
71. H. van der Laan, *Architectonic Space*, p. 7.
72. *Ibid.*, p. 10.
73. *Ibid.*, p. 35.

proportion between the thickness and distance apart of the walls, which Van der Laan calls the *mutual neighbourhood* of the walls.

What this proportion must be is not yet clear. It is determined, in fact, by the need to maintain the formal integrity of the wall masses. If the walls are too thick in relation to the size of the space, the space appears as a hollowed-out cavity within the mass, usurping its form. If they are too thin (as happens in Van der Laan's opinion in much modern architecture) it appears as a space bubble enclosed by surfaces whose thickness is negligible with respect to the space. To avoid both extremes, wall thickness and space should lie at the limits of an order of size, so that the wall thickness acts as a unit for the width of the space. The two dimensions are then just close enough to count for each other, but not close enough to appear as measures of the same kind: that is, as parts of a larger whole.

This, then, is the 'first building': just two parallel walls set a determined distance apart (see Figure 16.4). The relation of the walls to the space is the primary architectonic proportion that affords us 'an objective image of our own relation to surrounding nature'.[74] But since the relation of the body to natural space is not mathematically definable, it still gives us no indication as to what that primary architectonic proportion should be.

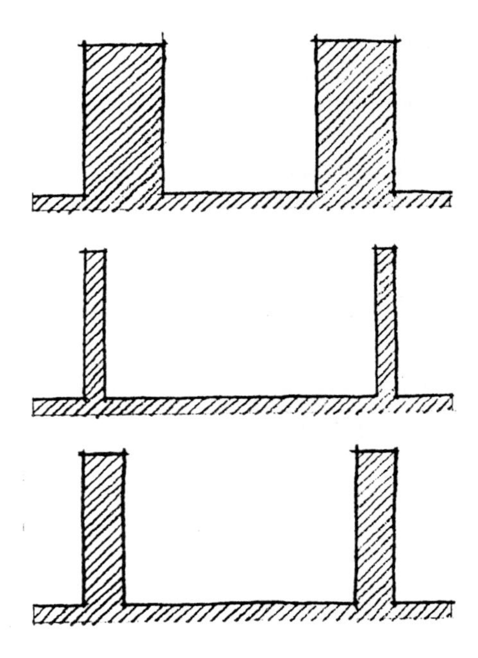

Figure 16.4 Dom Hans van der Laan, architectonic space construction. Walls that are too thick (top) give rise to a hollowed-out void within the total mass; walls that are too thin (centre) produce a 'space-bubble'; only walls that have just the right proportion of thickness to distance apart bring the true architectonic space into being (bottom).

16.8 ARTICULATE BUILDING

The Plastic Number contains another pregnant sentence that takes us a little further towards the definition of a proportion suited to architecture. It is: 'Homogeneous, unarticulated building-forms can never lay claim to architectonic expressiveness; there must always be a whole and parts.'[75]

The adjective 'articulate' has two distinct but connected meanings, applicable to artefacts or to verbal communication. The *Concise Oxford Dictionary* gives: 'jointed; distinctly jointed; with clearly distinguishable parts (*articulate speech*); able to express oneself fluently and coherently.' In architecture, a single, undivided mass remains literally 'inarticulate', unable to express itself. The core of architecture is *con-struction*, the putting together of separate parts to make an articulate whole. Van der Laan extends this principle to all making, to all the fundamental arts of life: the provision of

74. H. van der Laan, *Het plastische getal*, p. 116.
75. *Ibid.*, p. 136.

food, clothes, and shelter.[76] Every work of art must be *articulated* in order to become *articulate*: that is, expressive of its function. In *The Form-play of the Liturgy* he writes that

> If the intellect is to be informed, through the senses, about the function of a thing, there must be a relation that can be read within the form itself. So the form of the work must comprise terms between which relationships exist that give expression, through a certain likeness, to the terms of the original function. . . At the level of function it is a matter of the relation of the whole work to the natural given, but at the level of expression, of the relation between parts of the whole.[77]

Thus a building that has as yet no specific function, but only the general function of marking off a habitable 'inside' within the limitless natural 'outside', acquires through its articulation an expressive form, capable of expressing that elementary function (the complex spatial articulation of the Barcelona Pavilion is an example of this). The building then not only serves the body but also speaks of that service to the mind. Subsequently, this *essential* function and this *essential* expression become in turn the foundation for whatever particular, *necessary* functions and meanings we may attach to them. Thus the concept of a generic architectural form leads to the idea of articulating that form in order to make it expressive of its essential function. This articulation involves relations between parts, and therefore an embryonic notion of scale or proportion.

Human thought has always depended on our ability to divide the continua of our world into discrete segments, to name them and order them in relation to each other. Systems of proportion play a part in this process. Their role in architecture is to ensure that each part and sub-part of the articulate architectonic object – be it a house or a city – becomes a reflection of the whole: that each house is like a little city, each city like a great house. The ancient house–city analogy mentioned by Alberti[78] is revived today by, among others, Aldo van Eyck[79] and Joseph Rykwert.[80] This self-reflection of architecture at various scales enables it to function in turn as a metaphor for other things: for the world, or for the human body. Van der Laan makes the same observation:

76. H. van der Laan, *Het vormenspel der liturgie*, E.J. Brill, 1985, p. 15, and *Architectonic Space*, p. 1.
77. H. van der Laan, *Het vormenspel der liturgie*, pp. 28–9.
78. L.B. Alberti, *On the Art of Building*, trans. J. Rykwert, N. Leach and R. Tavernor, MIT Press, 1988, p. 23.
79. A. van Eyck, Team 10, Royaumont, Sept. 1962, in F. Strauven, *Aldo van Eyck*, Architectura & Natura, 1998, p. 398.
80. J. Rykert, *The Dancing Column*, pp. 65–6.

> This. . . was something that has fascinated me ever since my childhood: to find in the subdivisions of a thing the aspect of the whole. Thus I remember my discovery, as a schoolboy with a passion for nature, that the profile of the tree is reflected in the form of its leaves. . . That rediscovery of the whole in its parts, and the analogous relationships that arise from it, became the *leitmotiv* of all my studies in the liturgical, architectonic and philosophical fields.[81]

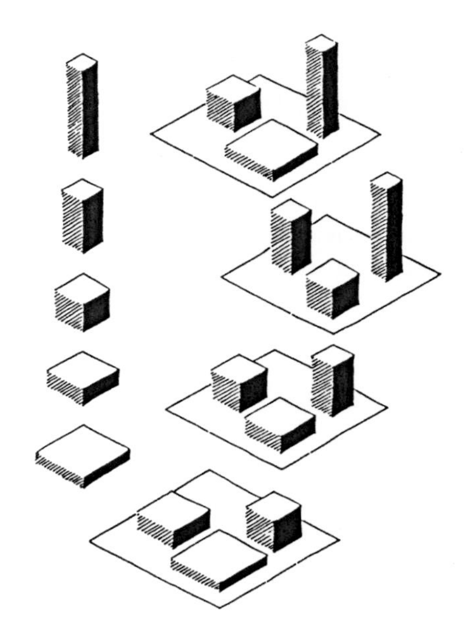

Figure 16.5 Dom Hans van der Laan, compositions of standing, sitting and lying forms; from *Een architectuur op basis van het ruimtelijk gegeven van de natuur* (1989).

So we are concerned with two kinds of relations. The first is the relation within each thing (room, house or city) between its separate parts, and between these and the whole: for instance, the relation of rooms to the house, or of the house to the city. The second is the relation of the artefact to other domains – for instance to the natural world or the world of abstract ideas. Only the first kind of relation is precisely quantifiable; for 'the measure is always akin to the thing measured'.[82] The second relation, between things of fundamentally different kinds, is based on analogy. It is not itself quantifiable, but it is given concrete expression by the quantitative relations embodied in art. Thus the same process of dividing, ordering and relating that enables us to think *about* architecture is extended, *through* architecture, to all other fields. In the first instance the things we make must express themselves – their own essential function. But that essential expression then becomes the bearer of other meanings: 'Once the house has been fully developed, it can serve all possible further analogies.'[83]

In the final phase of Van der Laan's theory he devised a new 'first building', a new example of pure architecture. He replaced his earlier introverted wall-and-court conception with a more open one, in which a space was defined by free-standing forms of various heights. To illustrate this conception, he devised a typology of twenty-five arrangements of three forms – blocks, bars and slabs. The arrangements correspond to the fundamental human 'positions' – standing, sitting and lying. They suggest what Wilson calls a 'typology of counterforms to the 'positions' experienced in. . . body language.[84] Instead of a unitary form, or a unitary space between two wall masses, an articulated form now gives rise to a more complex, articulated space (see Figure 16.5). The number of solid and spatial elements is increased, but the number of measures, and still more the number of *relations*

81. H. van der Laan, unpublished letter to the author, 24 August 1987, p. 2.
82. Aristotle, *Metaphysics*, Everyman's Library, 1956, p. 307.
83. H. van der Laan, unpublished letter to the author, 29 June 1984, p. 2.
84. C. St John Wilson, *Architectural Reflections*, p. 14.

between these measures, increase disproportionately. With two walls and a space between, four measures are involved (the length, height and thickness of the walls, and the width of the space), generating six relations. With three contrasting forms, these increase to twelve measures (the three dimensions of each form, and the three distances between them) and sixty-six relations. The number of relations constitutes the series of triangular numbers, as shown in Table 16.1.

TABLE 16.1

Measures	2	3	**4**	5	6	7	8	9	10	11	**12**
Relations	1	3	**6**	10	15	21	28	36	45	55	**66**

The key to these relations is the system of proportion. If what I have called the 'common core of all building' is the foundation upon which all particular functions and meanings rest, the very essence of that core is something still more fundamental, still more abstract and rarefied, than masses and spaces: pure proportion. It is proportion that sets the process of articulation going.

16.9 WHAT SYSTEM OF PROPORTION DO WE NEED?

Of the few writers quoted by Van der Laan, by far the most influential for him was Vitruvius. In Chapter 9 we saw that Vitruvius defines ordonnance, symmetry and proportion in strikingly similar ways:

> *Ordonnance* is the balanced agreement of the measures of the building's members. . .This is achieved through quantity. Quantity is determined by taking units of measure, derived from the building itself in the form of elementary parts of its members, and brought into relation to the building as a whole.[85]

> *Symmetry* is the proper mutual agreement between the members of the building, and the relation, in accordance with a certain part selected as standard, of the separate parts to the figure of the building as a whole.[86]

> *Proportion* is a correspondence among the measures of the members of an entire work, and of the whole to a certain part selected as standard.[87]

I concluded that all three definitions make the same three demands:

85. Vitruvius, *The Ten Books on Architecture*, Book I, Chap. 2, author's translation.
86. *Ibid.*
87. *Ibid.*, Book III, Chap. 1, M.H. Morgan translation, Dover Publications, 1960, p. 72.

(1) The measures of all the parts and of the whole must agree or correspond with each other. I take this to mean that they must constitute a chain of related measures, perhaps connected by a constant ratio between one measure and the next. In that case, they would form a geometric progression.
(2) There must be a direct relation between the whole or largest measure and an elementary unit or standard module, derived from the smallest part: for example, in Classical architecture, the column diameter.
(3) It follows from (1) and (2) that the measures of all intermediate parts must relate both to the whole and to the unit.

TABLE 16.2

1	3	9	27	81	243
2	6	18	54	162	
4	12	36	108		
8	24	72			
16	48				
32					

These three demands are directly relevant to the choice of a proportion system, since the 'generic architectonic form' derives its expressiveness from its articulation – that is, from being a *whole* composed of related *parts*. At first sight the Pythagorean-Platonic or Renaissance system seems to offer the best answer to Vitruvius' three demands. Table 16.2 shows the system as a filled-in *lambda* or triangular grid of measures. It is not of course possible for every measure to be at once a simple multiple of all smaller measures and an integral factor of all larger ones, but every measure does have a more or less simple arithmetical relation to all others. It can be regarded either as a whole, of which all smaller measures are parts, or as a unit, of which all larger measures are multiples. For instance, 24 can be considered a 'part' of 36, or as a 'multiple' of 18. The system therefore satisfies requirements (2) and (3) fairly well.

Its drawback is that the measures do not constitute a uniform progression with a constant ratio between consecutive terms. Starting with 1, the successive ratios are 1 : 2, 2 : 3, 3 : 4, 2 : 3, 3 : 4, 8 : 9, 3 : 4, 3 : 4, 8 : 9, 3 : 4, 8 : 9, 27 : 32, and so on. Because of this, each measure has a different set of multiple and fractional relations to all others. One must construct a separate 'system' for every measure. In other words, the Pythagorean system does not satisfy the first Vitruvian demand: the measures cannot be said to 'agree or correspond with each other'. That sort of consistency is provided only by systems like the *modulor* and the plastic number, which are based on a single geometric progression, or at most an interweaving of two or more identical progressions.

The *modulor* raises another problem, however. The

products of Fibonacci numbers are not higher terms of the series (for example, 5 × 8 = 40, not 34 or 55). Thus the system satisfies requirement (1) but not (2) or (3). This can be overcome by replacing the Fibonacci with the Lucas series (as I have proposed with my modified version of the system, Tables 15.6 and 15.8). The products of consecutive Lucas numbers *are* higher terms of the same series, plus or minus a small tolerance. For example:

$3 \times 4 = 11 + 1$ $4 \times 7 = 29 - 1$ $7 \times 11 = 76 + 1$ $11 \times 18 = 199 - 1$

The difference alternates between +1 and −1, so as the numbers increase it becomes vanishingly small. Note also that the products of neighbouring Lucas and Fibonacci numbers converge towards Fibonacci numbers:

$4 \times 3 = 13 - 1$ $7 \times 5 = 34 + 1$ $11 \times 8 = 89 - 1$ $18 \times 13 = 233 + 1$

The plastic number has much the same property as the Lucas series, but with the advantage that even the products of remote measures always equal higher measures, less a tolerance that instead of vanishing settles down, after initial fluctuation, at about 1/50 of the measure concerned:

$4 \times 4 = 16$	$4 \times 9 = 37 - 1$	$4 \times 21 = 86 - 2$	$4 \times 49 = 200 - 4$
$4 \times 5 = 21 - 1$	$4 \times 12 = 49 - 1$	$4 \times 28 = 114 - 2$	$4 \times 65 = 265 - 5$
$4 \times 7 = 28$	$4 \times 16 = 65 - 1$	$4 \times 37 = 151 - 3$	$4 \times 86 = 351 - 7$

The system combines the (nearly) constant intervals between consecutive measures, characteristic of systems like the *modulor*, with the mutual commensurability of the whole-number Renaissance measures. With some justice Van der Laan claimed that 'the plastic number throws a bridge. . . between the two mutually exclusive kinds of quantity, the discrete and the continuous (the how-many and the how-much)'.[88] In fact, the plastic number has the remarkable property of 'shadowing' the Renaissance system despite being based on a single geometric progression which converges towards an irrational limit. When expressed as simplified fractions the plastic number ratios are either identical with the Pythagorean ratios, or differ by at most 28 : 27, i.e. by 3.6%. Table 16.3 compares the two systems. Asterisks indicate ratios recommended by Alberti.

TABLE 16.3

PLASTIC RATIOS		PYTHAGOREAN RATIOS	
6 : 7	(24 : 28)	8 : 9*	(24 : 27)
3 : 4		3 : 4*	
2 : 3		2 : 3*	
4 : 7	(36 : 63)	9 : 16*	(36 : 64)
1 : 2		1 : 2*	
3 : 7	(12 : 28)	4 : 9*	(12 : 27)
3 : 8		3 : 8*	
1 : 3		1 : 3*	
2 : 7	(8 : 28)	8 : 27	
1 : 4		1 : 4*	
3 : 14	(6 : 28)	2 : 9	(6 : 27)
3 : 16		3 : 16	
1 : 6		1 : 6	
1 : 7	(4 : 28)	4 : 27	

88. H. van der Laan, 7th lecture on the plastic number, 's Hertogenbosch, 29 May 1954, p. 9.

Thus the plastic number has a strong claim – though not in my opinion an exclusive one – to be considered the system that best satisfies the three demands that Vitruvius makes of symmetry and proportion, if one interprets them as meaning that architectonic expression is founded on articulation, and on proportional relations between the whole and its parts. The following two sections explore some of the fundamental ideas underlying the plastic number.

16.10 KNOWING BY NOT KNOWING

Dom Hans van der Laan was a philosopher of architecture, or rather he philosophized *through* architecture. He did not merely use philosophy in order to construct a theory of architecture, but used architecture in order to construct a philosophy. This philosophy has its roots in a problem analogous to David Hume's. Hume concluded that the apparent lawfulness and regularity of nature is founded on nothing more certain than repeated experience: we expect the sun to rise tomorrow for no better reason than that it rose today and yesterday. Therefore certain knowledge is an impossibility for human beings, and since science is founded on the metaphysical principle that nature is inherently intelligible, Hume's philosophy seems to undermine the very foundation of science. Kant's *Critique of Pure Reason* meets this challenge head-on by declaring that nature is intelligible because the understanding is itself the lawgiver of nature. Van der Laan treats the problem of architectural measure in a similar way.

Each thing that we make is at the same time a little world within the world. In the midst of the great unknowable reality there now exists a little piece of reality that we do know, because we have made it. By making things, we make our world, and to the extent that we have made it, we can know it. This is, of course, the definition of what I have called the *abstract* standpoint towards the world. Now, the measures embodied in that little piece of reality permeate, as it were, the greater reality around it. We measure out our house, and the house in turn *gives measure* to the surrounding space. The system of proportions is like a frame of reference projected onto, or *imposed* upon, the natural world, and the purpose of architecture is to *manifest* that framework.

But how do we determine these measures in the first place? In the script for a television broadcast made in 1988 Van der Laan sums up the basis of the system as follows. The fundamental difficulty we face in deciding how big to make something is that measuring, unlike counting, deals with a continuum. Space embodies no inherent unit. 'We ourselves can only count things, taking as our measure the individual unity of the things that we count; but the size of a thing, being infinitely divisible, embodies no unit.'[89] The way to overcome this is to use – like Kant – the very impossibility of certain knowledge to *construct* a kind of certainty:

> We have tried to solve the problem by means of a paradox. . . We have discovered that it is possible to know sizes precisely because we do not know them. I cannot give a name to a concrete size, in the way that I can give a name to a number: *one, two, three,* and so on. But I can indeed give a name to things that are of roughly the same size: I call them 'of the same size'. Now it is no longer a question of the size of a given thing, but of a thing of a given size: a size of which I can form a mental concept.[90]

The plastic number is not, therefore, just a system of fixed measures and ratios to be imposed on the objects we make, but primarily a means of *looking at* and *understanding* the world around us, with its infinite continuum of sizes and shapes. In contrast to most previous theorists of proportion, Van der Laan does not regard his measures as mathematically fixed, but rather as typical representatives of a certain cluster of possible sizes of things in the real world: sizes that the intellect recognizes as belonging to the same 'type'. Since the sizes of these things (pebbles on a beach, leaves on a tree, etc.) form a continuum it makes no sense to try to distinguish them individually, so they cannot strictly speaking be said to have a 'proportion' to each other. However, when the leaves or pebbles are sorted into groups – large, medium, small, and so on – then a proportion does arise between the limits of these groups. Proportion is a matter of *classification* and of *relative scale.* Once we appreciate this intimate connection between proportion and scale, the central importance of proportion in design becomes apparent. It can no longer be regarded as a problem of fine tuning, to be considered, if at all, only at a late stage of the design process. It is now crucial to the very way we build.

89. H. van der Laan, TV script, 30.6.1988, p. 21.
90. *Ibid.*, pp. 21–2.

Van der Laan's whole theory of proportion, and indeed of architecture, might be reduced to this: that there are limits within which sizes can be related to each other, and other limits beyond which this relation breaks down. Taking these limits as a basis, it is possible to establish a chain of relationships by which the whole architectonic environment, from a brick to a whole town, can be connected together and made intelligible and humane. From being part of a measureless continuum, a certain part of the space of nature has become a delimited territory, marked off in clearly recognizable graded intervals. A piece of the unknown has become known: and precisely by exploiting the fact that we cannot know it.

16.11 TYPES AND ORDERS OF SIZE

What matters for Van der Laan is thus not our ability to discern proportions but our *inability* to do so. The very basis of his scale of measures is the observation that we deal with small differences of size by simply disregarding them, calling all sizes within a certain range 'of the same type'. This range is not to be confused with the much lower limit of *visual* discernment, plus or minus about 2%:

> For the eye the just noticeable difference is about 1/50 of the size concerned, but the *formal* difference, enough for us to make an intellectual distinction between sizes and so to speak give them a name, is much larger.[91]

Nevertheless, he takes that visual limit as his starting point. He imagines a collection of objects – pebbles, for example – the linear dimensions of which increase by increments of 4%, so that the difference between one object and its nearest neighbours is barely perceptible. The series of pebbles thus represents, so far as the eye can tell, a virtual continuum. Van der Laan uses thirty-six pebbles (see Figure 16.6), but here, for reasons that will be apparent later, it will be convenient to take fifty. Suppose the length of the smallest pebble is 16 mm, and that of the largest 114 mm. To simplify the arithmetic we can regard the increment as increasing in stages, instead of maintaining a perfectly constant relation to each pebble. Let the pebbles increase in size as in Table 16.4.

The experiment consists in asking volunteers to sort the

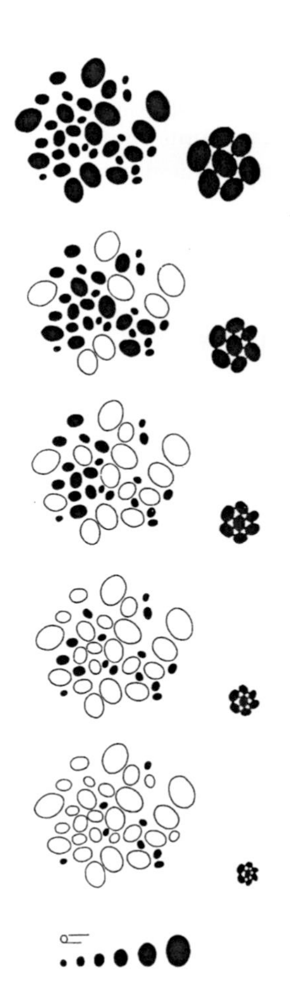

Figure 16.6 Dom Hans van der Laan, derivation of the plastic number by distinguishing types of size among 36 pebbles; from Dom H. van der Laan *Een architectur op basis van het ruimtelijk gegeven van de natuur* (1989).

TABLE 16.4

SIZE OF PEBBLE	INCREMENT
16–18 mm	0.5 mm
18–31 mm	1.0 mm
31–43 mm	1.5 mm
43–59 mm	2.0 mm
59–86 mm	3.0 mm
86–114 mm	4.0 mm

91. H. van der Laan, *Het plastische getal*, p. 26.

pebbles into types of size, starting by setting aside all those that belong to a largest type, until a pebble appears that unmistakably no longer belongs to that group. This becomes the first of a second group, and so on, until none is left. According to Van der Laan, the normal response is to arrange the pebbles in groups of seven, leaving one over, the first representative of a last, still smaller type of size: that is, $(5 \times 7) + 1 = 36$ (see Figure 16.6). With fifty pebbles we get $(7 \times 7) + 1 = 50$. Thus eight pebbles are picked out, representing the 'thresholds' or defining measures of seven consecutive types of size (see Figure 16.7). These delimiting measures are:

Figure 16.7 The same experiment extended to 50 pebbles.

16 mm	21 mm	28 mm	37 mm
49 mm	65 mm	86 mm	114 mm

The ratio between consecutive measures is nearly constant at just under 3 : 4, or more exactly 1 : 1.325, the basic ratio of the plastic number. The experiment with pebbles does not of course 'prove', nor does Van der Laan claim that it proves, that the plastic number is the only possible system (he does in fact claim that, but bases his argument on Aristotle's definition of the unit and the sequences of lines, planes and volumes discussed in Chapter 7, section 7.6).[92] All the pebble experiment does is illustrate the phenomenon of continuity, and show how a system of proportions might arise out of it. A volunteer prepared to tolerate a wider range – say 12 pebbles in each group – might instead arrive at the following thresholds:

Figure 16.8 The Fibonacci series derived from the pebble experiment.

16 mm	26 mm	42 mm	68 mm	110 mm

These are easily recognizable as Fibonacci numbers doubled, and consequently the constant ratio tends towards $1 : \phi$ (see Figure 16.8).

The plastic number is defined, however, not by one limit but by two. We regard any two sizes within the first or narrower limit as too similar to be clearly distinguishable from each other: we say that they belong to a same *type* of size. For instance, all pebbles between 16 and 21 mm are considered to be of the same size. But there is also a wider limit beyond which they differ too much to count for each other: they then belong to different *orders* of size. As Van der Laan expresses it:

92. H. van der Laan, *Architectonic Space*, pp. 55–8, 72–7, 96–7.

(a) Within the limits of a type of size we call all concrete measures identical; there is as yet no question of proportion.
(b) Within the limits of an order of size the types of size can be compared with each other; here it is a question of proportion.
(c) Beyond the limits of an order of size no relation is any more possible between types of size; there can no longer be any question of proportion.[93]

The extent of the order of size is determined as follows. If the eight threshold measures chosen – that is, from 16 to 114 mm – are regarded as the *central representatives* rather than the limits of their respective types of size, then each measure appears surrounded by a band of smaller and larger concrete sizes belonging to the same type: sizes that we identify with that measure. The relation of each measure to the extent of its band of attached sizes must be constant, since any measure will be equally affected by the addition or subtraction of the same portion of itself. Therefore the point at which the sizes belonging to one measure shade off into those of the next divides the difference between the two measures in the same ratio that exists between the measures themselves – in this case, about 3 : 4.

The number that divides the difference between two others in the same ratio that they have to each other is their harmonic mean (see Chapter 6, section 6.3). In our example, since the difference between the two largest measures, 86 and 114 mm, is 28 mm, it follows that their harmonic mean lies $28 \times 3/7 = 12$ mm above the lower measure and $28 \times 4/7 = 16$ mm below the higher one. It is therefore 98 mm.[94] This measure, 98 mm, marks the lower limit of the type of size of which 114 mm is the central or typical measure, and the upper limit of the type whose central measure is 86 mm. Note that it is also twice 49 mm, the fifth measure in the series; for in any series in which the sum of two consecutive terms equals a higher term, the harmonic mean between two consecutive terms is always the double of a lower term. The harmonic or double measures form in Van der Laan's system a second series, interwoven with the first; he calls this the 'derived' series, and the original single series 'authentic'. The two series correspond to the red and blue series of the *modulor*, but for Van der Laan, unlike Le Corbusier, they have distinct roles to play. Each authentic measure marks the centre of a type of size, of which the derived measures above and below it mark the upper and lower thresholds.

93. H. van der Laan, *Het plastische getal*, p. 30.
94. Note that all plastic number ratios are round-number approximations. An exact expression of the harmonic mean of 86 and 114 would be $(2 \times 86 \times 114)/(86 + 114) = 98.04$.

The smallest measure, 16 mm, represents the amount of addition or subtraction that just begins to affect the largest measure – or just fails to affect it, which comes to the same thing since we are speaking of limits. In other words, 16 is the smallest measure that still counts with respect to 114 mm. The measures 16 and 114 comprise *the lower and upper limits of an order of size*, and the extreme ratio of this order is 16 : 114 or about 1 : 7 (see Figure 16.9). The order of size is therefore composed of seven consecutive types, defined by eight measures. That is why it was convenient to begin with fifty pebbles. The two ratios, 3 : 4 and 1 : 7, determine each other, because as soon as one decides how much two sizes can differ without ceasing to count for each other, one also fixes the point at which they differ just enough to be distinct, and vice versa.

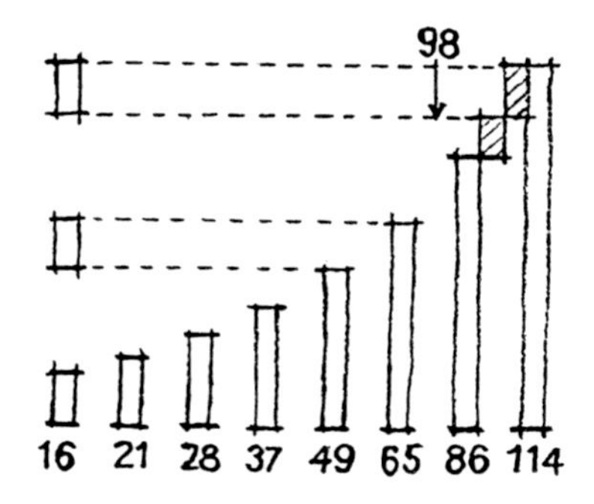

Figure 16.9 The smallest measure (16) represents the addition or subtraction that just begins to affect the largest measure of the same order of size (114).

The relations between plastic number measures can be expressed in three ways:

(1) as simple fractions (for example 3/4);
(2) as ratios between terms of an additive number series (for example 86 : 114);
(3) still more accurately, using algebra (for example 1 : ψ, where ψ represents the irrational limit towards which the series converges).

TABLE 16.5

3/4	4/7	3/7	1/3	1/4	3/16	1/7
86 : 114	65 : 114	49 : 114	37 : 114	28 : 114	21 : 114	16 : 114
1 : ψ	1 : ψ^2	1 : ψ^3	1 : ψ^4	1 : ψ^5	1 : ψ^6	1 : ψ^7

Van der Laan himself rejects algebraic expression, on the grounds that the architectonic reality of buildings and spaces consists of measurable quantities, and even of tangible units like bricks. The irrational numbers that arise from algebra have no place in it.[95] Nevertheless, algebra can be useful as a shorthand means of expressing the general laws underlying the slightly varying relations between particular measures. Table 16.5 expresses the seven relations that exist between the eight measures of an order of size in all three ways.

The two basic additive rules of the plastic number are:

(1) The largest of any four consecutive measures always equals the sum of the two smallest (expressed algebraically, $\psi^3 = \psi + 1$).
(2) The difference between the two largest of any *six* consecutive measures always equals the smallest (i.e. $\psi^5 - \psi^4 = 1$).

Compared with the golden section, the plastic number

95. H. van der Laan, *Architectonic Space*, p. 99.

produces a larger number of different but interrelated ratios. This is partly because the basic ratio is smaller (3 : 4 instead of about 3 : 5), so there are more measures within a given range. A more significant reason, however, is that the measures combine in more ways to produce higher measures. With the golden section, each measure equals the sum of two consecutive smaller measures ($\phi^2 = 1 + \phi$), but with the plastic number it is also the sum of three or of five consecutive measures. Also, by subtracting two consecutive, or three *alternate* measures, we get a smaller measure. Taking ψ to represent the basic ratio, then:

$$\psi^3 = 1 + \psi$$

$$\psi^5 = 1 + \psi + \psi^2 \qquad 1 = \psi^5 - \psi^4$$

$$\psi^8 = 1 + \psi + \psi^2 + \psi^3 + \psi^4 \qquad 1 = \psi^8 - \psi^6 - \psi^4$$

Table 16.6 shows the authentic and derived measures resulting from our consideration of the series of pebbles. By subtracting the derived measure in the second row from the authentic measure in the top row, we obtain, in the third row, a new series of authentic measures, comprising a second, lower order of size. Note that the highest measure of the lower order is also the lowest measure of the higher order.

In fact, the authentic and derived series can be formed using any convenient numbers, according to the job in hand. In this respect the plastic number differs sharply from the *modulor* with its fixed measures based on a six-foot man. All that matters is that the series obeys the additive rule by which the largest of any four consecutive measures always equals the sum of the two smallest. For instance, in the pebble experiment we can substitute any size of smallest pebble between 16 and 21 mm, each size generating a different number series, as in Table 16.7. Row I is the original or 'authentic' series, row VI the same series enlarged by one type of size. Row III is a 'derived' series comprising the harmonic means of the measures of rows I or VI, while row IV comprises their contraharmonic means, which will be recognized from Table 3.19, Chapter 3. This series corresponds to the yellow or $\sqrt{5}$ series that in the last chapter I added to the red and blue series of the *modulor*, and if introduced, it would further enhance the versatility of the system.

The great merit of Van der Laan's system lies, however, not in the details of its mathematics, but rather in the broad concepts of types and orders of size. The order determines

TABLE 16.6

16	21	28	37	49	65	86	114
14	18	24	32	42	56	74	98
2	3	4	5	7	9	12	16

TABLE 16.7

I	16	21	28	37	49	65	86	114
II	17	23	31	40	54	71	94	125
III	18	24	32	42	56	74	98	130
IV	19	25	33	44	58	77	102	135
V	20	27	35	47	62	82	109	144
VI	21	28	37	49	65	86	114	151

the extreme range beyond which sizes cease to have value for each other, and thus prevents proportions from dissolving in an endless proliferation like those of Le Corbusier's indefinitely extended *modulor*. The type, on the other hand, liberates proportion from the usual obsession with exactness. Each measure is conceived as 'about so large'. It is not a rigid, mathematically calculated quantity but the representative of a type, and the range of smaller and larger sizes of the same type forms a margin or halo around it. Within this margin, any divergence between an actual size and the nominal measure is regarded as a 'shading' of that measure. Van der Laan often introduced such nuances in his work. He would shorten a proportion slightly to make it look sturdier, or stretch it to make it more elegant.[96] The system is by no means a straitjacket or a restriction of the designer's intuitive judgement, but rather a frame of reference which assists that judgement to be made: a sort of genetic code or 'law of growth' that determines from its inception the broad lines along which the design will evolve. Lastly, by introducing the concept of types of size based on our normal ability to recognize typical sizes, Van der Laan opens up the theory of proportion to the description of objects in general, in nature and in art, and not only to those that are known to embody mathematically precise ratios.

16.12 CONCLUSION

The mathematics of architectural proportion are necessarily very simple. There are only a handful of known systems, of which three – the 'Renaissance' system, the family of systems derived from $\sqrt{5}$ and the golden section, and the plastic number – offer by far the richest possibilities. Of these, the first two were already known, in principle, to the ancient Greeks, while the last, although probably a modern discovery, is closer in spirit to Greek mathematics than to twentieth-century science. Must we agree, then, with Robin Evans' remark that architects prefer a 'dead geometry', precisely because they use geometry as a foundation, and the job of a foundation is to be inert: 'as firm as a rock'?[97] If there is no correlation between architectural proportion and contemporary advances in mathematical theory, has our long odyssey through nearly three thousand years of history in search of the relation between them been in vain?

96. *Ibid.*, p. 107.
97. R. Evans, *The Projective Cast*, MIT Press, 1995, p. xxvii.

A relation is not necessarily a correlation. What I have discovered through the writing of this book is that whereas science and architecture may have common roots – the universe being at first conceived as a kind of house, and its geometry borrowed from the arts of weaving, pottery or basket-making – in historical times they have run alongside each other on parallel but largely independent tracks. Even when a cross-connection occurs – as for instance, between Pythagorean mathematics and Renaissance proportion theory – it is rarely simultaneous. A discovery made in one field can take centuries if not millennia to make its influence felt in another. Nor are such influences always one-way, from science to architecture, as is generally assumed. John Pennethorne may well have been right that discoveries first made in the design of Greek temples led to developments in ancient mathematics, and not vice versa. And we have seen that the Gothic cathedral may have foreshadowed the Scholastic *summa*, and that Mannerist art prefigured certain aspects of seventeenth-century science.

The sort of relation I have in mind is not based on mutual influences, however. What is common to science and art is that they are both essentially ways of *constructing the world*. Our world does not reveal itself to us like an open book. In order to understand it we have first to make it. But that is as far as the relation goes. The kinds of world constructed by science and art are generally quite distinct. In the case of science this construction is disciplined by the need to 'save the phenomena'. In the case of architecture it is constrained by the limited ways in which solid elements can be joined together to make walls, walls to make houses, and houses to make cities. Consequently proportion systems in architecture were never dependent on developments in science, and did not become obsolete as a result of either the scientific revolution of the seventeenth century or the empiricist philosophy of the eighteenth. On the contrary: it is precisely *because* the ancient empathy with the natural world, conceived as a finite and mathematically ordered *cosmos*, has been undermined by those developments, precisely *because* nature has become an abstract human construction, that it is more than ever necessary to embody a mathematical order in our works of art, just as it is increasingly embodied in the methodology of science.

To demand more than this – to require architecture to keep pace with the latest developments in physics or pure mathematics – is to succumb to the Romantic nineteenth-century delusion of the *Zeitgeist:* the belief in the inevitability – indeed, the moral imperative – of progress. It is to suppose that any advance made in one field at a given time must quickly be reflected in all others, and that to fail to 'keep up with the march of progress' is to be guilty of a form of backsliding or recidivism. A prime example of such naive historicism is Sigfried Giedion's *Space, Time and Architecture* (1941), in which he argues that it is the duty of the historian to separate out within the flow of history those tendencies that are 'constituent' – that is, progressive – from those that are merely 'transitory' or retrogressive.[98] He sees modern art and architecture as a direct consequence of developments in geometry and physics:

> The three-dimensional space of the Renaissance is the space of Euclidian geometry. But about 1830 a new sort of geometry was created, one which differed from that of Euclid in employing more than three dimensions. Such geometries have continued to be developed, until now a stage has been reached where mathematicians deal with figures and dimensions that cannot be grasped by the imagination. . . Space in modern physics is conceived of as relative to a moving point of reference, not as the absolute and static entity of the baroque system of Newton. And in modern art, for the first time since the Renaissance, a new conception of space leads to a self-conscious enlargement of our ways of perceiving space. . . Cubism. . . views objects relatively: that is, from several points of view. . . The poet Guillaume Apollinaire was the first to recognize and express this change, around 1911. . . It is a temporal coincidence that Einstein should have begun his famous work, *Elektrodynamik bewegter Körper*, in 1905 with a careful definition of simultaneity.[99]

Giedion's use of the phrase 'temporal coincidence' is disingenuous; it is clear from the context that he means much more than this. Unable to claim that Apollinaire – still less Picasso or Braque, who abhorred pseudo-scientific explanations of Cubism in terms of non-Euclidian geometry and the fourth dimension[100] – had read or were even aware of Einstein's paper, Giedion's whole argument nevertheless relies on a quasi-mystical causative connection: the spirit of the age is at work behind the scenes.

98. S. Giedion, *Space, Time and Architecture*, Harvard University Press, 1941, pp. 17–19.
99. *Ibid.*, pp. 356–7.
100. J. Richardson, *A Life of Picasso*, Jonathan Cape, 1996, vol. II, pp. 214–15.

Today, as in the past, architecture simply 'gives measure' to our spatial environment. It deals with the world as we experience it, with all the limitations that that implies. It is as little concerned with the curvature of space, or even the curvature of the earth, as music, which gives measure to time, is concerned with the speed of sound or the time it takes light to reach us from a distant galaxy. As Le Corbusier writes in *The Modulor*,

> Man becomes an abstraction when he shuts his eyes and becomes absorbed in all the possibilities. If he builds, he does so with his eyes open; he looks with his eyes. . . Architecture is judged by eyes that see, by the head that turns, and the legs that walk.[101]

Much the same attitude appears in Van der Laan's recollection of his first experience of mathematical abstractions:

> For the first arithmetic lesson the teacher put an apple on his desk, then two, then three and finally five. After that they were divided into two groups: one of two and one of three apples, and we were supposed to conclude that these together made five apples. But in order then to teach us that 2 + 3 = 5, even without any apples, the apples were sliced up and divided among the boys. . . But all my life I have been unwilling to forget those apples, and that is why I became an architect and not a mathematician.[102]

101. Le Corbusier, *The Modulor*, pp. 72–3.
102. H. van der Laan, unpublished letter to J.S. Folkers, 30 September 1987.

REFERENCES

Achilles, R., Harington, K. and Myhrum, C. (eds) *Mies van der Rohe: Architect as Educator*, University of Chicago Press, Chicago, 1986.

Ackerman, J.S. *The Architecture of Michelangelo*, A. Zwemmer, London, 1961; Penguin Books, Harmondsworth, 1970.

——— *Palladio*, Penguin Books, Harmondsworth, 1966.

——— *Distance Points*, MIT Press, Cambridge, MA., 1991.

Alberti, L.B. *On Painting*, ed. and trans. J.R. Spencer, Yale University Press, New Haven, 1956.

——— *On Painting and On Sculpture: The Latin Texts*, ed and trans. C. Grayson, Phaidon, London, 1972.

——— *On the Art of Building in Ten Books*, MIT Press, Cambridge, MA., 1988.

Alexander, C. 'Perception and modular co-ordination', *RIBA Journal*, October 1959.

Alison, A. *Essays on the Nature and Principles of Taste*, Edinburgh, 1790.

Anderson, W.J., Phené Spiers, R. and Ashby, T. *The Architecture of Ancient Rome*, B.T. Batsford, London, 1927.

Andre, C. Interview by P. Tuchman in *Artforum*, **8**(6), June 1970; reprinted in *Carl Andre Sculptor 1996*, Oktagon, Stuttgart, 1996.

Aquinas, T. *Quaestiones disputatae*, S.P. Lethielleux, Paris, 1925.

——— *Summa Theologica*, Burns Oates & Wasbourne, London, 1922; (*Summa Theologiae*) Methuen, London, 1989.

——— *Selected Writings*, Everyman's Library, London, 1939; revised edn 1964.

Aristotle *Metaphysics*, Everyman's Library, London, 1956.

——— *Physics*, Oxford University Press, Oxford, 1996.

——— 'Categories'; 'On the Heavens'; 'On the Parts of Animals'; 'On the Soul': in *The Works of Aristotle*, Encyclopaedia Brittannica, Chicago, 1952.

Arnheim, R. *Towards a Psychology of Art*, Faber & Faber, London, 1967.

——— *New Essays on the Psychology of Art*, University of California Press, Berkeley, 1986.

Augustine *The City of God*, Penguin Books, Harmondsworth, 1972.

Ballantyne, A. *Architecture, Landscape and Liberty: Richard Payne Knight and the Picturesque*, Cambridge University Press, Cambridge, 1997.

Behne, A. *Der moderne Zweckbau*, 1923; *The Modern Functional Building*, The Getty Research Institute, Santa Monica, 1996.

Benevolo, L. *The Architecture of the Renaissance*, Routledge & Kegan Paul, London, 1978.

Bergson, H. *Creative Evolution* (*Evolution Créatrice*), Macmillan & Co., London, 1st edition 1911.

Berkeley, G. *The Principles of Human Knowledge* (1710); in *A New Theory of Vision and Other Writings*, Everyman's Library, London, 1910; and *The Principles of Human and Knowledge with Other Writings*, Collins/Fontana, Glasgow, 1962.

——— *Alciphron, or the Minute Philosopher*, in A.A. Luce and T.E. Jessop (eds), *The Works of George Berkeley Bishop of Cloyne*, vol. III, Thomas Nelson, Edinburgh, 1950.

Bertotti Scamozzi, O. *Le fabbriche e i disegni di Andrea Palladio* (1796), Alec Tiranti, London, 1968.

Birkhoff, G.D. *Aesthetic Measure*, Harvard University Press, Cambridge, MA., 1933.

Blake, W. *Complete Writings*, Nonsuch Press, 1957; Oxford University Press, Oxford, 1966.

Blondel, J.-F. *Cours d'architecture*, Paris, 1771–9.

Boas, M. *The Scientific Renaissance 1450–1630*, William Collins & Sons, Glasgow, 1962; Fontana edition 1970.

Boesiger, W. and Stonorov, O. (eds) *Le Corbusier et Pierre Jeanneret: Oeuvre complète de 1910–1929*, 6th edn, Editions Girsberger, Zurich, 1956.

Boëthius, A. and Ward-Perkins, J.B. *Etruscan and Roman Architecture*, Penguin Books, Harmondsworth, 1970.

Boring, E.G. *A History of Experimental Psychology*, Appleton-Century-Crofts, New York, 1950.

Borissavlievitch, M. *The Golden Number*, Alec Tiranti, London, 1958.

Briseux, C.E. *Traité du beau essential*, Paris, 1752.

Brooks, H.A. *Le Corbusier's Formative Years*, University of Chicago Press, Chicago, 1997.

Bruno, G. *La cena de le ceneri*, London, 1584; *The Ash Wednesday Supper*, Mouton & Co., The Hague, 1975.

——— *De l'infinito universo e mondi*, Venice, 1584.

Burke, E. *A Philosophical Enquiry into the Origin of our Ideas of the Sublime and the Beautiful* (1756), Oxford University Press, Oxford, 1990.

Burnet, J. *Early Greek Philosophy*, A & C Black, London, 1st edn 1892, 4th edn 1930.

——— *Greek Philosophy: Thales to Plato*, Macmillan & Co., 1914.

Calzona, A. and Volpi Ghirardini, L. *Il San Sebastiano di Leon Battista Alberti*, Leo S. Olschi, Florence, 1994.

Capek, M. *The Philosophical Impact of Contemporary Physics*, D. Van Nostrand Co., New York, 1961.

Carpenter, R. *The Architects of the Parthenon*, Penguin Books, Harmondsworth, 1970.

Carritt, E.F. *The Theory of Beauty*, Methuen & Co., London, 1914.

Carter, P. 'Mies van der Rohe, an appreciation', *Architectural Design*, March 1961.

Caspar, M. *John Kepler* (original German edn 1938); New York, 1960.

Cassirer, E., Kristeller, P.O. and Randall, J.H. (eds) *The Renaissance Philosophy of Man*, University of Chicago Press, Chicago, 1956.

Choisy, A. *Histoire de l'architecture* (1899); Bibliothèque de l'Image, Paris, 1996.

Conant, K.J. 'The after-life of Vitruvius in the Middle Ages', *Journal of the Society of Architectural Historians*, **XXVII**(1), March 1968.

Condivi, A. *Vita di Michelangelo Buonarotti*, Rome, 1553; *The Life of Michelangelo*, Phaidon, Oxford, 1976.

Cook, T.A. *The Curves of Life*, 1st edn Constable & Co., London, 1914; facsimile edn Dover Publications, New York, 1979.

Le Corbusier 'La maison suisse', in *Etrennes Helvétiques*, 1914.

——— *Towards a New Architecture* (*Vers un architecture*), Editions Crès, Paris, 1923; Architectural Press, London, 1946.
——— *L'Esprit Nouveau*, May 1924.
——— *The City of Tomorrow* (*Urbanisme*), Editions Crès, Paris, 1925; Architectural Press, London, 1971.
——— *The Decorative Art of Today* (*L'Art décoratif d'aujourd'hui*), Editions Crès, Paris, 1925; Architectural Press, London, 1987.
——— *Le Modulor*, Editions de l'Architecture d'aujourd'hui, Boulogne sur Seine, 1950; *The Modulor*, Faber & Faber, London, 1961.
——— *Le Modulor 2*, Editions de l'Architecture d'aujourd'hui, Boulogne sur Seine, 1950; *Modulor 2*, Faber & Faber, London, 1958.
Cornford, F.M. *Before and After Socrates*, Cambridge University Press, Cambridge, 1st edn 1932; paperback edn 1960.
——— *Plato's Theory of Knowledge*, Routledge & Kegan Paul, London, 1935.
——— *Plato's Cosmology*, Routledge & Kegan Paul, London, 1937.
——— *Plato and Parmenides*, Kegan Paul, Trench, Trubner, London, 1939.
Coulton, J.J. *Ancient Greek Architects at Work*, Cornell University Press, Ithaca, NY, 1977.
Critchlow, K. *Order in Space*, Thames & Hudson, London, 1969.
Crombie, A.C. *Augustine to Galileo*, William Heinemann, London, 1952; Mercury Books, London, 1961.
Dantzig, T. *Number*, George Allen & Unwin, London, 1930; 4th edn 1962.
Darwin, C. *The Origin of Species* (1859); Everyman Library, London, 1928.
Debus, A.G. *Man and Nature in the Renaissance*, Cambridge University Press, Cambridge, 1978.
Doczi, G. *The Power of Limits*, Shambhala Publications, Boston, MA., 1981.
Drake, S. *Discoveries and Opinions of Galileo*, Doubleday, New York, 1957.
Eco, U. *La struttura assente: Introduzione alla ricerca semiologica*, Bompiani, Milan, 1968; 'Function and Sign: The Semiotics of Architecture', in Broadbent, G., Bunt, R. and Jencks, C. (eds), *Signs, Symbols and Architecture*, John Wiley & Sons, Chichester, 1980.
——— 'Sviluppo dell'estetica medievale', in *Momenti e problemi di storia dell'estetica*, vol. I, Marzorati Editore, Milan, 1959; *Art and Beauty in the Middle Ages*, Yale University Press, New Haven, 1986.
Eddington, A.S. *The Nature of the Physical World*, Everyman's Library, London, 1935.
Elgar, F. *Mondrian*, Thames & Hudson, London, 1968.
Einstein, A. *Relativity: the Special and the General Theory* (1916), Methuen & Co., London, 1920; University Paperback 1960.
——— (with L. Infeld) *The Evolution of Physics*, Simon & Schuster, New York, 1938.
——— *Ideas and Opinions*, Dell Publishing Co., New York, 1954.
Euclid *The Thirteen Books of the Elements*, Dover Publications, New York, 1956; abridged edn, Everyman's Library, London, 1933.
Evans, R. *The Projective Cast*, MIT Press, Cambridge, MA., 1995.

Eysenck, H.J. *Sense and Nonsense in Psychology*, Penguin Books, Harmondsworth, 1957, 1958.
Farrington, B. *Greek Science*, Penguin Books, Harmondsworth, 1944; 2nd edn 1949.
Feather, N. *Mass, Length and Time*, Edinburgh University Press, 1959; Penguin Books, Harmondsworth, 1961.
Fechner, G. *Vorschule der Aesthetik* (1870), Georg Holms, Hildesheim, 1978.
Field, J.V. *Kepler's Geometrical Cosmology*, Athlone Press, London, 1988.
Firpo, L. *Il processo di Giordano Bruno*, Edizioni Scientifiche Italiane, Naples, 1949.
Fogliano, L. *Musica theorica*,Venice, 1529.
Furbank, P.N. *Diderot*, Minerva, London, 1993.
Ghyka, M. *Esthétique des proportions dans la nature et dans les arts*, Paris, 1927.
——— *The Geometry of Art and Life*, Sheed & Ward, New York, 1946; Dover Publications, New York, 1977.
——— 'The Modulor', *Architectural Review*, February 1948.
Giedion, S. *Space, Time and Architecture*, Harvard University Press, Cambridge MA., 1941.
——— *The Beginnings of Architecture*, Princeton University Press, Princeton, NJ, 1964.
Gilbert, K.E. and Kuhn, H. *A History of Esthetics*, The Macmillan Co., New York, 1939.
Giorgi, F. *De harmonia mundi totius*,Venice, 1525; Paris, 1545.
Gombrich, E.H. *Art and Illusion* (1959), Phaidon Press, Oxford, 1960; 5th edn 1977.
——— *The Sense of Order*, Phaidon Press, Oxford, 1979; 2nd edn 1984.
Guarini, G. *Architettura Civile*,Turin, 1737.
Haan, H. de and Haagsma, I. 'Dom H van der Laan: speuren naar de grondbeginselen van architectuur', interview in *intermediair*, 13 February 1981.
Hambidge, J. *The Elements of Dynamic Symmetry*,Yale University Press, 1920; Dover Publications, New York, 1967.
——— *Dynamic Symmetry: The Greek Vase*,Yale University Press, New Haven, 1920.
——— *The Parthenon and other Greek Temples*,Yale University Press, New Haven, 1924.
Hay, D.R. *The Science of Beauty as Developed in Nature and Applied to Art*, Edinburgh, 1856.
Heath, T.H. *A History of Greek Mathematics*, Oxford University Press, 1921.
Heisenberg, W. *Das Naturbild der Heutigen Physik*, Rowolt, Hamburg, 1955; *The Physicist's Conception of Nature*, Hutchinson & Co., London, 1958;The Scientific Book Guild, London, 1962.
Herbart, J.F. *Lehrbuch zur Einleitung in die Philosophie*, 1813–37.
Herz-Fischler, R. *A Mathematical History of Division in Extreme and Mean Ratio*,Wilfred Laurier University Press,Waterloo, Ontario, 1987.
Hollinghurst, A. *The Swimming Pool Library*, Chatto & Windus, London, 1988.
Hume, D. *A Treatise of Human Nature* (1739–40), Everyman's Library, 1911.

——— *Essays Moral, Political and Literary* (1742), Oxford University Press, 1963.

——— *Enquiries Concerning Human Understanding and Concerning the Principles of Morals* (1748–51), Oxford University Press, Oxford, 1975.

Ivins, W.M. *Art and Geometry: A Study in Space Intuitions*, Dover Publications, New York, 1964.

James, J. *The Contractors of Chartres*, Mandorla Publications, Wyong, NSW, 1981.

Jeannel, B. *Le Nôtre*, Fernand Hazan, Paris, 1985.

Jencks, C. and Baird, G. (eds) *Meaning in Architecture*, Barrie & Rockliff; The Cresset Press, London, 1969.

Jung, C.G. *Psychological Types* (*Psychologische Typen*, Rascher, Zurich, 1921); Kegan Paul, Trench, Trubner & Co., London, 1946.

Kandinsky, W. *Concerning the Spiritual Art* (*Über das Geistige in der Kunst*, 1911); Dover Publications, New York, 1977.

Kant, I. *Critique of Pure Reason* (*Kritik der reinen Vernunft*, 1781), Everyman's Library, London, 1934.

——— *Prologomena* (*Prologomena zu einer jeden künftigen Metaphysik, die als Wissenschaft wird auftreten können*, 1783), Open Court Publishing Co., La Salle, IL, 1902.

Kepes, G. *Module, Symmetry, Proportion*, Studio Vista, London, 1966.

Kepler, J. *Gesammelte Werke*, ed. M. Caspar, Munich, 1938.

Kline, M. *Mathematics: The Loss of Certainty*, Oxford University Press, Oxford, 1980.

Koster, E. 'Dom Van der Laan's Arcadian architecture', *Architectura & Natura Quarterly*, Amsterdam, no. 1, 1992.

Koyré, A. *From the Closed World to the Infinite Universe*, Johns Hopkins University Press, Baltimore, MD, 1957.

Kraus, K. *Die Fackel*, no. 389-90, December 1913.

Kristeller, P.O. *Renaissance Thought*, Harper & Row, New York, 1961; vol. II, 1965.

——— *Eight Philosophers of the Italian Renaissance*, Stanford University Press, 1964.

Külpe, O. *Grundriss der Psychologie auf experimenteller Grundlage*, 1893.

Laan, H. van der *Le Nombre plastique*, E.J. Brill, Leiden, 1960; *Het plastische getal*, E.J. Brill, Leiden, 1967.

——— 'Beschouwingen over het huis', *Plan*, June 1972.

——— *De architectonische ruimte*, E.J. Brill, Leiden, 1977; 2nd edn 1992; *Architectonic Space*, E.J. Brill, Leiden, 1983.

——— 'Het menselijk verblijf: grootte, vorm, ruimte', *Plan*, April 1977.

——— *Het vormenspel der liturgie*, E.J. Brill, Leiden, 1985.

——— (with N. van der Laan) 'Kapel te Helmond', *Bouwkundig Weekblad* 35/36, 1951.

Lalo, C. *L'Esthétique expérimentale contemporaine*, 1908.

Lasserre, F. *The Birth of Mathematics in the Age of Plato*, Hutchinson, London, 1964.

Laugier, M.-A. *Essai sur l'architecture*, Paris, 1755; Pierre Mardaga, Brussels, 1979.

Lawlor, R. *Sacred Geometry*, Thames & Hudson, London, 1982.

Lawrence, A.W. *Greek Architecture*, Penguin Books, Harmondsworth, 1957; revised edn by R.A. Tomlinson, 1983.

Leff, G. *Medieval Thought*, Penguin Books, Harmondsworth, 1958.

Lesser, G. *Gothic Cathedrals and Sacred Geometry*, Alec Tiranti, London, 1957.
Lethaby, W.R. *Architecture, Mysticism and Myth* (1891), Architectural Press, 1974.
——— *Architecture, Nature and Magic* (1928), Gerald Duckworth & Co., 1956.
Lindberg, D.C. *The Beginnings of Western Science*, University of Chicago Press, Chicago, 1992.
Lipps, T. *Aesthetik: Psychologie des Schönen und der Kunst*, 1903.
Lloyd, W.W. *Memoir of the Systems of Proportion Employed in the Design of the Doric Temples at Phigaleia and Aegina*, London, 1860.
Locke, J. *An Essay Concerning Human Understanding* (1690), Everyman's Library, London, abridged edn 1947, complete edition 1961.
Loos, A. *Ornament und Verbrechen* (*Ornament and Crime*) 1908, *Kulturenartung* (*Cultural Degeneracy*) 1908, and *Architektur* (*Architecture*) 1910; all reprinted in Adolf Loos, *Trotzdem (1900–1930)*, Innsbruck, 1931 and *Adolf Loos, Sämtliche Schriften*, Verlag Herold, Vienna, 1962; the first also in U. Conrads (ed.), *Programmes and Manifestoes on 20th-century Architecture*, Lund Humphries, London, 1970, the others in T. and C. Benton and D. Sharp, *Form & Function*, Granada Publishing/Open University Press, London, 1975.
Lowman, J. 'Corb as structural rationalist', *Architectural Review*, October 1978.
Lovejoy, A.O. *The Great Chain of Being*, Harper & Row, New York, 1960.
Lund, F.M. *Ad Quadratum: A Study of the Geometrical Bases of Classic and Medieval Religious Architecture*, B.T. Batsford, London, 1921.
Luning Prak, N. 'Measurements of Amiens Cathedral', *Journal of the Society of Architectural Historians*, **XXV**(3), October 1966.
MacCurdy, E. (ed.) *The Notebooks of Leonardo da Vinci*, Johathan Cape, London, 1938.
Macmanus, I. 'The aesthetics of simple figures', *British Journal of Psychology*, no. 71, 1980.
Maëdler, J.H. von *Populäre Astronomie*, Berlin, 1841.
March, L. *Architectonics of Humanism*, Academy Editions, Chichester, 1998.
Medawar, P. *Essays on Growth and Form*, Oxford University Press, Oxford, 1945.
Meyer, H. 'bauen' (1928), in C. Schnaidt, *Hannes Meyer, Bauten, Projekte und Schriften*, Alec Tiranti, London, 1965.
Michell, J. *The Dimensions of Paradise*, Thames & Hudson, London, 1988.
Milanesi, G. *Le lettere di Michelangelo Buonarotti*, Florence, 1875.
Milizia, F. *Memorie degli architetti antichi e moderni*, Parma, 1781.
Miller, G.A. *Psychology*, Penguin Books, Harmondsworth, 1966.
Moessel, E. *Die Proportionen in Antike und Mittelalter*, Munich, 1926.
Mondrian, P. 'Natuurlijke en abstracte realiteit', *De Stijl*, **III**(5), 1920.
Monk, R. *Ludwig Wittgenstein*, Jonathan Cape, London, 1990.
Mumford, L. *The Culture of Cities*, Secker & Warburg, London, 1938.
——— *The Condition of Man*, Secker & Warburg, London, 1944.
Murray, P. *The Architecture of the Italian Renaissance*, Thames & Hudson, London, 1969.

Newton, I. *Mathematical Principles of Natural Philosophy*, trans A. Motte, University of California Press, Berkeley, 1960.
Nietzsche, F. *Thus Spake Zarathustra*, Penguin Books, Harmondsworth, 1969.
Onians, J. *Bearers of Meaning*, Princeton University Press, Princeton, NJ, 1988.
Palladio, A. *I Quattro libri dell'architettura*, Venice, 1570; *The Four Books on Architecture*, trans. R. Tavernor and R. Schofield, MIT Press, Cambridge, MA, 1997.
Panofsky, E. *Idea: a Concept in Art Theory* (1924); University of South Carolina Press, Columbia, 1968.
——— *Gothic Architecture and Scholasticism* (1951); Meridian Books/Thames & Hudson, London, 1957.
——— *Meaning in the Visual Arts*, Doubleday, New York, 1955; Penguin Books, 1970.
——— *Renaissance and Renascences in Western Art*, Almqvist & Wiksell, 1960; Granada Publishing, London, 1970.
Padovan, R. 'Laugier to Van der Laan', *Architectural Design*, **49**(12), 1979.
——— *Dom Hans van der Laan: Modern Primitive*, Architectura & Natura Press, Amsterdam, 1994.
Pascal, B. *Pensées* (1657–60), Penguin Books, Harmondsworth, 1961.
Patte, P. *Mémoires sur les objets les plus importants de l'architecture*, Paris, 1769.
Paul, J. 'German neo-Classicism and the Modern Movement', *Architectural Review*, September 1978.
Pennethorne, J. *The Elements and Mathematical Principles of the Greek Architects and Artists*, William Clowes & Sons, London, 1844.
Pennick, N. *Sacred Geometry: Symbolism and Purpose in Religious Structures*, Turnstone Press, Wellingborough, Northants, 1980.
Penrose, F.C. *An Investigation of the Principles of Athenian Architecture*, London, 1851.
Pérez-Gómez, A. *Architecture and the Crisis of Modern Science*, MIT Press, Cambridge, MA., 1983.
——— (with L. Pelletier) *Architectural Representation and the Perspective Hinge*, MIT Press, Cambridge, MA., 1997.
Perrault, C. *Ordonnance for the Five Kinds of Columns after the Method of the Ancients*, ed. A. Pérez-Gómez, Getty Research Institute, Santa Monica, 1993.
Pevsner, N. *An Outline of European Architecture*, Penguin Books, Harmondsworth, 1943; 7th edn 1963.
Placzek, A. (ed.) *Robert Morris: Select Architecture*, Da Capo Press, New York, 1973.
Plato 'Meno', in *Five Dialogues of Plato on Poetic Inspiration*, Everyman's Library, London, 1910.
——— 'Phaedo', in *Five Dialogues of Plato on Poetic Inspiration*, Everyman's Library, London, 1910; and in *The Last Days of Socrates*, Penguin Books, Harmondsworth, 1959.
——— 'Theaetetus' and 'The Sophist', in F.M. Cornford, *Plato's Theory of Knowledge*, Routledge & Kegan Paul, London, 1935; and in *Parmenides and Other Dialogues*, Everyman's Library, London, 1961.
——— 'Timaeus', in F.M. Cornford, *Plato's Cosmology*, Routledge & Kegan Paul, London, 1937; Everyman's Library, London,

1965; *Timaeus and Critias*, Penguin Books, Harmondsworth, 1971.
——— *The Republic*, trans. F.M. Cornford, Oxford University Press, Oxford, 1941.
——— *Philebus*, Penguin Books, Harmondsworth, 1982.
Plomer, H. *Ancient and Classical Architecture*, Longmans, London, 1956.
Plotinus *The Enneads*, Faber & Faber, London, 1956.
Poincaré, H. *La Science et l'hypothèse*, Paris 1902; Flammarion, Paris, 1968.
——— *Dernières Pensées*, Paris, 1913.
Popper, K.R. *The Logic of Scientific Discovery* (*Logik der Forschung*), Springer Verlag, Vienna, 1934; Hutchinson & Co., London, 1959.
——— *The Open Society and its Enemies*, Routledge & Kegan Paul, London, 1945; 5th edn, 1966.
——— *Conjectures and Refutations*, Routledge & Kegan Paul, London, 1963, 2nd edn, 1965.
——— *Objective Knowledge*, Oxford University Press, Oxford, 1972.
——— *An Autobiography of Karl Popper*, Open Court Publishing Co., La Salle, IL., 1974; revised edn *The Unended Quest*, Collins/Fontana, Glasgow, 1976; Flamingo edition 1986.
RIBA Debate on the motion 'That systems of proportion make good design easier and bad design more difficult', *RIBA Journal*, September 1957.
Richardson, J. *A Life of Picasso*, Jonathan Cape, London, 1996.
Robertson, D.S. *A Handbook of Greek and Roman Architecture*, 1945.
Rowe, C. *The Mathematics of the Ideal Villa*, first published in *Architectural Review*, 1947; MIT Press, Cambridge, MA., 1976.
Ruskin, J. *The Seven Lamps of Architecture* (1849); 6th edn George Allen, Orpington, Kent, 1889.
——— *The Stones of Venice* (1851–53), Everyman's Library, London, 1907.
Russell, B. *An Inquiry into Meaning and Truth*, George Allen & Unwin, London, 1940; Penguin Books, Harmondsworth, 1962.
——— *History of Western Philosophy*, George Allen & Unwin, London, 1st edn, 1946; 2nd edn 1961.
Rykwert, J. and Tavernor, R. 'Church of S Sebastiano in Mantua', *Architectural Design*, **49**(5–6), 1978.
Rykwert, J. *The Dancing Column*, MIT Press, Cambridge, MA., 1996.
Saccheri, G. *Euclides ab omni naevo vindicatus*, Milan, 1733.
Sartre, J.-P. *L'Existentialisme est un humanisme*, Les Editions Nagel, Paris, 1946; *Existentialism and Humanism*, Eyre Methuen, London, 1973.
Scholfield, P.H. *The Theory of Proportion in Architecture*, Cambridge University Press, Cambridge, 1958.
Schlemmer, O. *Oskar Schlemmer: Briefe und Tagebücher*, Albert Langen/Georg Müller Verlag, Munich, 1958; *The Letters and Diaries of Oskar Schlemmer*, Northwestern University Press, Evanston, IL., 1990.
Schulze, F. *Mies van der Rohe*, University of Chicago Press, Chicago, 1985.
Scott, G. *The Architecture of Humanism*, Constable & Co. London, 1914; Architectural Press, London, 1980.

Serlio, S. *On Architecture*, trans. V. Hart and P. Hicks, Yale University Press, New Haven, 1996.
Shelby, L.R. *Gothic Design Techniques*, Southern Illinois University Press, Carbondale & Edwardsville, 1977.
Simson, O. von *The Gothic Cathedral*, Bollingen Foundation, New York, 1956; Harper & Row, New York, 2nd edn, 1962.
Smith, E.B. *The Dome: A Study in the History of Ideas*, Princeton University Press, Princeton, NJ, 1950.
Soane, J. *Lectures on Architecture* (1809), Sir John Soane's Museum, London, 1929.
Strauven, F. *Aldo van Eyck*, Architectura & Natura Press, Amsterdam, 1998.
Summerson, J. 'The case for a theory of modern architecture', *RIBA Journal*, June 1957; reprinted in J. Summerson, *The Unromantic Castle*, Thames & Hudson, London, 1990.
Sypher, W. *Four Stages of Renaissance Style*, Doubleday/Anchor, Garden City, NY, 1955.
Szabó, A. *The Beginnings of Greek Mathematics*, D. Reidel, Dordrecht, 1978.
Tavernor, R. *On Alberti and the Art of Building*, Yale University Press, New Haven, 1998.
Teague, W.D. *Design this Day*, Studio Publications, London, 1946.
Thompson, D'A.W. *On Growth and Form*, Cambridge University Press, 1917; abridged edn 1961.
Tolnay, C. de *The Art and Thought of Michelangelo*, Random House, New York, 1964.
Tomkins, P. *Secrets of the Great Pyramid*, Penguin Books, Harmondsworth, 1978.
Turnbull, H.W. *The Great Mathematicians*, Methuen & Co., London, 1929; University Paperback edn 1962.
Urmson, J.R. *Berkeley*, Oxford University Press, Oxford, 1982.
Vasari, G. *The Lives of the Artists*, Penguin Books, Harmondsworth, 1965.
Venturi, R., Scott-Brown, D. and Izenour, S. *Learning from Las Vegas*, MIT Press, Cambridge, MA., 1977.
Viollet-le-Duc, E.E. *Discourses on Architecture* (*Entretiens sur l'architecture*, 1860); George Allen & Unwin, London, 1959.
Vitruvius *The Ten Books on Architecture*, trans. W. Newton, London, 1791; trans. M.H. Morgan, Dover Publications, New York, 1960.
Vittone, B.A. *Istruzioni elementari per indirizzo*, Lugano, 1760.
Waele, J. van de 'Vitruvius en de klassieke dorische tempel', in R. Rolf (ed.), *Vitruviuscongres 1995*, Vitruvianum Publicaties, Heerlen, 1997.
Waerden, B.L. van *Science Awakening*, Noordhoff, Groningen, 1954.
——— *Geometry and Algebra in Ancient Civilizations*, Springer Verlag, Berlin, 1983.
Weyl, H. *Symmetry*, Princeton University Press, Princeton, NJ, 1952.
Whinney, M. *Wren*, Thames & Hudson, London, 1971.
Whitehead, A.N. *The Concept of Nature*, Cambridge University Press, Cambridge, 1950.
Wiegand, C. von 'The meaning of Mondrian', *Journal of Aesthetics*, **II**(8), 1943.
Wilson, C. St John *Architectural Reflections*, Butterworth Architecture, Oxford, 1992.

Wingert, P.S. *Primitive Art*, New American Library, New York, 1962.
Wittaker, E. *From Euclid to Eddington*, Cambridge University Press, London, 1949.
Wittgenstein, L. *Tractatus Logico-Philosophicus*, Routledge & Kegan Paul, London, 1922.
——— *Lectures and Conversations on Aesthetics, Psychology and Religious Belief*, ed. C. Barrett, Blackwell, Oxford, 1978.
Wittkower, R. *Architectural Principles in the Age of Humanism*, Vol. 19, *Studies of the Warburg Institute*, 1949; Alec Tiranti, London, 1952.
——— 'The changing concept of proportion', *Architects' Year Book V*, 1953; in *Idea and Image*, Thames & Hudson, London, 1978.
——— 'Brunelleschi and "Proportion in Perspective"', *Journal of the Warburg and Courtauld Institutes*, **XVI**, 1953; in *Idea and Image*, Thames & Hudson, London, 1978.
——— *Gothic versus Classic*, Thames & Hudson, London, 1974.
——— *Studies in the Italian Baroque*, Thames & Hudson, London, 1974.
Wölfflin, H. *Renaissance and Baroque* (1888), Benno Schwabe & Co., Basel, 1961; Collins/Fontana, Glasgow, 1964.
——— *Zur Lehre von den Proportionen* (1889), reprinted in Gantner, J. (ed.), *Kleine Schriften*, Basel, 1946.
——— *Kunstgeschichtliche Grundbegriffe*, Munich, 1915; *Principles of Art History*, trans. M. Hottinger, London, 1932; paperback edn Dover Publications, New York.
Worringer, W. *Abstraction and Empathy* (*Abstraktion und Einfühlung*, 1907), Routledge & Kegan Paul, London, 1963.
——— *Form in Gothic* (*Formprobleme der Gotik*, 1912); G.P. Putnam's Sons, London, 1927.
Yates, F. *Giordano Bruno and the Hermetic Tradition*, Routledge & Kegan Paul, London, 1964.
Zarlino, G. *Le istitutioni harmoniche*, Venice, 1558.
Zeising, A. *Neue Lehre von den Proportionen des menschlichen körpers*, Leipzig, 1854.
——— Aesthetische Forschungen, 1855.
Zevi, B. *Architecture as Space*, Horizon Press, New York, 1974.

INDEX